www.wadsworth.com

wadsworth.com is the World Wide Web site for
Wadsworth Publishing Company and is your direct
source to dozens of online resources.

At *wadsworth.com* you can find out about
supplements, demonstration software, and
student resources. You can also send e-mail to
many of our authors and preview new publications
and exciting new technologies.

wadsworth.com
Changing the way the world learns®

LIFE AND DEATH

A Reader in Moral Problems

SECOND EDITION

Louis P. Pojman
West Point Military Academy

Wadsworth Publishing Company

I⟨T⟩P® An International Thomson Publishing Company

Belmont, CA • Albany, NY • Boston • Cincinnati • Johannesburg • London • Madrid • Melbourne
Mexico City • New York • Pacific Grove, CA • Scottsdale, AZ • Singapore • Tokyo • Toronto

Philosophy Editor: Peter Adams
Assistant Editor: Kerri Abdinoor
Editorial Assistant: Mindy Newfarmer
Marketing Manager: Dave Garrison
Print Buyer: Stacey Weinberger
Permissions Editor: Bob Kauser
Production: Matrix Productions

Copy Editor: Betty Duncan
Cover Design: Cassandra Chu
Cover Image: The Voyage of Life: Childhood,
    Thomas Cole; National Gallery of Art,
    Washington; Ailsa Mellon Bruce Fund
Compositor: Scratchgravel Publishing Services
Printer: Webcom

For permission to use material from this text, contact us:
    web   www.thomsonrights.com
    fax   1-800-730-2215
    phone   1-800-730-2214

Printed in Canada
1 2 3 4 5 6 7 8 9 10

Wadsworth Publishing Company
10 Davis Drive
Belmont, CA 94002

International Thomson Publishing Europe
Berkshire House
168-173 High Holborn
London, WC1V 7AA, United Kingdom

Nelson ITP, Australia
102 Dodds Street
South Melbourne
Victoria 3205 Australia

Nelson Canada
1120 Birchmount Road
Scarborough, Ontario
Canada M1K 5G4

International Thomson Editores
Seneca, 53
Colonia Polanco
11560 México D.F. México

International Thomson Publishing Asia
60 Albert Street #15-01
Albert Complex
Singapore 189969

International Thomson Publishing Japan
Hirakawa-cho Kyowa Building, 3F
2-2-1 Hirakawa-cho, Chiyoda-ku
Tokyo 102, Japan

International Thomson Publishing Southern Africa
Building 18, Constantia Square
138 Sixteenth Road, P.O. Box 2459
Halfway House, 1685 South Africa

Library of Congress Cataloging-in-Publication Data
Life and death : a reader in moral problems / [edited by] Louis P.
  Pojman. — 2nd ed.
    p. cm.
  ISBN 0-534-50825-1
  1. Ethics. 2. Social ethics. 3. Life. 4. Death. I. Pojman,
  Louis P.
  BJ1012.L52 1999
  179.7—dc21   98-55383

To my students
whose probing questions and insights
have enriched my life and made teaching philosophy
a most enjoyable vocation

Contents

Preface

This is an anthology of contemporary moral dilemmas having to do with issues relating to life and death. It was written as a companion to my textbook *Life and Death: Grappling with the Moral Dilemmas of Our Time,* but it can be used on its own.

At the present time society is deeply divided on the matters of life and death discussed in this work: the sanctity of life, the meaning of death and dying, suicide, euthanasia, abortion, human cloning, the death penalty, animal rights, war, and world hunger. I have put together for you an anthology in a dialectical form, representing the best readings (from the point of view of accessibility, clarity, and cogency of argument) from opposite points of view.

I have written a short introduction to each section of the book as well as individual introductions to each reading in order to aid you in locating the problem and position of the author. I have not tried to analyze the argument in these brief introductions—that is your job as a student—only to prepare you for the reading.

The accompanying textbook, *Life and Death: Grappling with the Moral Dilemmas of Our Time,* provides an analysis of all of the issues discussed and many of the articles used in this book. It will help you locate the wider philosophical context of these readings, grapple directly with the arguments, and point to wider implications. However, the selections in this work are rich. They are the best representatives of opposing viewpoints on each issue. If the two books are used together, I recommend that you read the selections before you consult the textbook. Of course, this reader can be used independently of the textbook.

You will need to read many readings two or even three times. I suggest that you use the SQ2R approach: survey, question, read, reflect. That is, read the article lightly, without being too concerned whether you fully grasped all the major points, then go over the study questions, and then read the article more carefully with them in mind. Finally, reflect on the questions again after you have finished your reading.

Nothing is more important for our age, nothing is more inspiring for the thoughtful person, nothing is more challenging for our society than to think clearly, comprehensively, and imaginatively about the moral life. Little guidance is given to ordinary people to enable them to evaluate and construct good moral reasoning. It is with this hope of shedding light on the moral life and helping equip ordinary men and women to reflect critically on the moral dilemmas of our time that I have put together these twin books for you.

For this second edition I have added a section on cloning and new articles on abortion and suicide and have revised others.

Finally, a number of people have helped me put together this reader. My students over a twenty-year period have made me aware of the nuances of the issues and the priority of some readings over others. To them this work is dedicated as a token of my debt. The reviewers Ronald Cox, San Antonio College; Dan Crawford, University of Nebraska; Christopher Morris, Bowling Green State University; and Mark Schersten, Siena Heights University gave me good suggestions in improving this book. Robert Ginsberg, the philosophy editor of Jones and Bartlett, was an invaluable critic and guide. Arthur Bartlett encouraged me in editing the first edition, and Peter Adams and Jake Warde were enormously helpful in putting together this second edition. Matrix Productions and Betty Duncan did an excellent job putting this book into its final form. Most of all, I'm grateful for the support of my wife, Trudy, without whose grace and love I would accomplish very little in life.

Louis P. Pojman

Part I

Ethical Theory

Introduction

Ethics is about right and wrong behavior, about the way we ought to live. It offers a set of rules as guides to action. It has many functions, including the promotion of happiness, the amelioration of suffering, the resolution of conflicts of interest by impartial criteria, and the assignment of praise and blame. Whether the rules are universally valid or simply dependent on specific cultures, every society has at its heart a set of moral rules that it seeks to inculcate in the young. Without some set of action-guiding rules, human life tends to degenerate.

This book contains readings about the application of ethical principles to life and death issues: the value of life, abortion, suicide, euthanasia, the death penalty, animal rights, war, and other topics. But first we need to have an understanding of the basic theoretical options, without which our attempt at application will lack structure. To paraphrase Kant: Practical ethics without theory is blind, and ethical theory without practice is sterile.

Our first three readings have to do with three classical ethical theories: deontological, utilitarian, and contractual. Deontological (from the Greek *deon* for "duty") theories place the emphasis on the kind of act in question. Value inheres in *right* kinds of acts, such as truth telling, promise keeping, fidelity, and the like. Utilitarian theories place the emphasis not on the kind of act but on the likely consequences to be achieved by the act. That act is right that will produce the most *good*. The motto of utilitarianism is "the greatest happiness for the greatest number." Simple slogans will help you to remember the difference: For deontologists, the end never justifies the means; for utilitarians, the end always justifies the means. In our readings, Immanuel Kant represents the deontological position, and John Stuart Mill represents the utilitarian position.

The third position that we discuss is the contractual theory of ethics, first mentioned by Glaucon in Plato's *Republic*.

> By nature, they say, to commit injustice is good and to suffer it is an evil, but that the excess of evil in being wronged is greater than the excess of good in doing wrong, so that

when men do wrong and are wronged by one another and taste of both, those who lack the power to avoid the one and take the other determine that it is for their profit to make a compact with one another neither to commit nor to suffer injustice, and that this is the beginning of legislation and of covenants between men, and that they name the commandment of the law the lawful and the just, and that this is the genesis and essential nature of justice—a compromise between the best, which is to do wrong with impunity, and the worst, which is to be wronged and be impotent to get one's revenge. Justice . . . being midway between the two, is accepted and approved, not as a real good, but as a thing honored in the lack of vigor to do injustice, since anyone who had the power to do it and was in reality "a man" would never make a compact with anybody neither to wrong nor to be wronged, for he would be mad.

(Book II, trans. Benjamin Jowett)

Morality (or "justice" in Plato's discussion) is a necessary evil invented because of our need for protection in a world of limited resources and unlimited desires. It represents a compromise: I'll restrain myself so long as you do, too.

The classic expression of contractualism is the *Leviathan* (1651) written by Thomas Hobbes, a selection of which appears as our third reading. Hobbes, following Glaucon's statement, posits that without agreed-on rules that resolve conflicts of interest, life becomes chaotic, a war of everyone against everyone, "solitary, poor, nasty, brutish, and short." To prevent this "state of nature," we devise rules for resolving our differences peacefully and contract to abide by these rules. This commits us to a compromise. We surrender some of our freedom for greater security, but it is in our self-interest to make such an agreement.

Whereas for the deontologists and utilitarians moral rules are objective principles to be *discovered* by rational agents, for the contractualist they are *invented* by society. For example, suppose you and I are strangers and afraid of each other. Our fear is consuming a lot of time and energy. We would be better off if we could agree on a nonaggression pact between us, perhaps hiring a third party to monitor the agreement or finding a project in which to cooperate, so that it would be in our self-interest to refrain from violence.

Whereas deontological ethics emphasizes disinterested devotion to duty and utilitarianism emphasizes the disinterested devotion to maximizing happiness, contractual ethics is egoistic. Its motivation derives from our self-interest.

The second set of readings in this introductory section have to do with the question of whether ethical rules are universally valid or simply relative to culture. Let me describe this difference more fully.

Ethical relativism is the notion that no universally valid moral principles exist but that all moral principles are valid relative to cultural or individual choice. It is to be distinguished from *moral skepticism,* the view that there are no valid moral principles at all (or none about which we can be confident). There are two forms of ethical relativism: (1) *subjectivism,* which views morality as a personal decision ("Morality is in the eyes of the beholder"), and (2) *conventionalism,* which views moral validity in terms of social acceptance. Opposed to ethical relativism are various theories of *ethical objectivism.* All forms of objectivism affirm the universal validity of some moral principles. The strongest form, *moral absolutism,* holds that there is exactly one right answer to every question, "What should I do in situation *x*?" (whatever that situation might be), and that a moral principle can never be overridden—even by another moral principle. A weaker form of objectivism sees moral principles as universally valid but not always applicable. That is, moral principle A could be overridden by moral principle B in a given situation, and in other situations, no right answer might exist. In our fourth reading, Herodotus offers an example of cultural difference that has moral force. In our fifth reading Ruth Benedict argues for moral relativism; in the last reading I offer a critique of relativism and defense of objectivism.

Let us now turn to our first reading, Kant's *Deontological Ethics.*

CHAPTER 1

Deontological Ethics

Duty

IMMANUEL KANT

Immanuel Kant (1724–1804), who was born to a deeply pietistic Lutheran family in Königsberg, Germany (now a part of Russia), lived in that town his entire life and taught at the University of Königsberg. He lived a duty-bound, methodical life, so regular that citizens were said to have set their clocks by his walks. Kant is one of the premier philosophers in the Western tradition. In his monumental work *The Critique of Pure Reason* (1781), he inaugurated a Copernican revolution in the theory of knowledge by reversing the way we understood the relationship between the mind and the world. Before Kant, most philosophers thought that such categories as causality, time, and space were in the world itself. Kant cogently argued that these categories were in our mind and determined the way we saw the world.

Our reading is from his classic work, *The Foundations of the Metaphysic of Morals,* written in 1785, in which he outlines his ethical system. Kant is concerned to reject those ethical theories, such as the Theory of Moral Sentiments set forth by the Scottish moralists Francis Hutcheson (1694–1746) and David Hume (1711–1776), in which morality is *contingent* and *hypothetical.* The Moral Sentiment theory views ethics as contingent rather than necessary. That is, if we had been created differently, we would now have a different kind of nature and so have different needs and desires and feelings. If we were created without a need for ownership in a world with unlimited resources, for example, we would not have (or at least not need) the concept of property, and so not need a rule against stealing. Furthermore, the Moral Sentiment school asserted that moral duties or imperatives are hypothetical in that they depend on our desires for their realization. The hypothetical takes the form, "If you want *x,* then you should do *y.*" For example, if you want to be happy, find someone to love; if you want to live in peace, mutually refrain from harming each other, obey the laws of the state, and so forth. There is nothing absolute about these rules. They could be overridden by other considerations. For example, if you don't want to live in peace, there's no reason to refrain from harming another.

Kant rejects this naturalistic (i.e., based on human nature) account of ethics. Ethics is not contingent but absolute, and its duties or imperatives are not hypothetical but categorical (nonconditional, without qualification). Ethics is based not on feeling but on reason. It is because we are rational beings that we are valuable and capable of discovering moral laws binding on all persons at all times. As such, our moral duties are not dependent on our human nature or on feelings but on reason.

Reprinted from The Foundations of the Metaphysic of Morals *(1873), translated by T. K. Abbott.*

Moral.
duties

They are <u>unconditional</u>, <u>universally valid</u>, and <u>necessary</u>, regardless of the possible utilitarian consequences or opposition to our <u>inclinations</u>.

Kant's first formulation of his *categorical imperative* is "<u>Act only on that maxim</u> whereby thou <u>canst at the same time will that it would become a universal law.</u>" This imperative is given as the criterion by which to judge all other principles. Test every maxim (a suggested rule of action; *e.g.,* "Let me break a promise when it serves my purpose to do so") by the ideal of universal law. If you can consistently will that everyone would do some type of action, then there is an application of the categorical imperative enjoining that type of action. If you cannot consistently will that everyone would do some type of action, then that type of action is morally wrong. Kant argues, for example, that we cannot universalize the maxim "Let me break my promise whenever it serves my purpose to do so," since the very institution of promising entails or depends on general adherence to promise keeping or an intention to do so.

Kant offers a second formulation of his <u>dominant moral criterion</u>: "<u>So act as to</u> <u>treat humanity, whether in your own person or in that of any other, in every case as</u> <u>an end and never as merely a means only.</u>" Each person by virtue of his or her reason has dignity and profound worth, which entails that he or she must never be exploited or manipulated or merely used as a means to our idea of what is for the general good. Although Kant is unclear on the matter, many scholars believe that we must combine the two formulations to obtain a full deontological system: (1) The categorical imperative gives us the formal structure of ethics: universalizing of moral principles; (2) the equal-respect principle gives content to our principles, "Do what enhances respect for persons." We turn to our reading.

Preface

AS MY CONCERN HERE is with moral philosophy, I limit the question suggested to this: Whether it is not of the utmost necessity to construct a pure moral philosophy, perfectly cleared of everything which is only empirical, and which belongs to anthropology? for that such a philosophy must be possible is evident from the common idea of duty and of the moral laws. Everyone must admit that <u>if a law is to have moral</u> force, *i.e.,* to be the basis of an obligation, <u>it</u> <u>must carry with it absolute necessity</u>; that, for example, the precept, "Thou shall not lie," is not valid for men alone, as if other rational beings had no need to observe it; and so with all the other moral laws properly so called; that, therefore, the basis of obligation must not be sought in the nature of man, or in the circumstances in the world in which he is placed, but *a priori* simply in the conception of pure reason;

and although any other precept which is founded on principles of mere experience may be in certain respects universal, yet in as far as it rests even in the least degree on an empirical basis, perhaps only as to a motive, such a precept, while it may be a practical rule, can never be called a moral law. . . .

The Good Will

<u>Nothing can possibly be conceived in the world,</u> <u>or even out of it, which can be called good, with-</u> <u>out qualification, except a Good Will.</u> Intelligence, wit, judgment, and the other *talents* of the mind, however they may be named, or courage, resolution, perseverance, as qualities of temperament, are undoubtedly good and desirable in many respects; but these gifts of nature may also become extremely bad and mischievous if

the will which is to make use of them, and which, therefore, constitutes what is called *character,* is not good. It is the same with the *gifts of fortune.* Power, riches, honour, even health, and the general well-being and contentment with one's conditions which is called *happiness,* inspire pride, and often presumption, if there is not a good will to correct the influence of these on the mind, and with this also to rectify the whole principle of acting, and adapt it to its end. The sight of a being who is not adorned with a single feature of a pure and good will, enjoying unbroken prosperity, can never give pleasure to an impartial rational spectator. Thus a good will appears to constitute the indispensable condition even of being worthy of happiness.

There are even some qualities which are of service to this good will itself, and may facilitate its action, yet which have no intrinsic unconditional value, but always presuppose a good will, and this qualifies the esteem that we justly have for them, and does not permit us to regard them as absolutely good. Moderation in the affections and passions, self-control, and calm deliberation are not only good in many respects, but even seem to constitute part of the intrinsic worth of the person; but they are far from deserving to be called good without qualification, although they have been so unconditionally praised by the ancients. For without the principles of a good will, they may become extremely bad; and the coolness of a villain not only makes him far more dangerous, but also directly makes him more abominable in our eyes than he would have been without it.

A good will is good not because of what it performs or effects, not by its aptness for the attainment of some proposed end, but simply by virtue of the volition, that is, it is good in itself, and considered by itself to be esteemed much higher than all that can be brought about by it in favour of any inclination, nay, even of the sum-total of all inclinations. Even if it should happen that, owing to special disfavour of fortune, or the

niggardly provision of a step-motherly nature, this will should wholly lack power to accomplish its purpose, if with its greatest efforts it should yet achieve nothing, and there should remain only the good will (not, to be sure, a mere wish, but the summoning of all means in our power), then, like a jewel, it would still shine by its own light, as a thing which has its whole value in itself. Its usefulness or fruitlessness can neither add to nor take away anything from this value. It would be, as it were, only the setting to enable us to handle it the more conveniently in common commerce, or to attract to it the attention of those who are not yet connoisseurs, but not to recommend it to true connoisseurs, or to determine its value.

Why Reason Was Made to Guide the Will

There is, however, something so strange in this idea of the absolute value of the mere will, in which no account is taken of its utility, that notwithstanding the thorough assent of even common reason to the idea, yet a suspicion must arise that it may perhaps really be the product of mere high-blown fancy, and that we may have misunderstood the purpose of nature in assigning reason as the governor of the will. Therefore we will examine this idea from this point of view.

In the physical constitution of an organized being, that is, a being adapted suitably to the purposes of life, we assume it as a fundamental principle that no organ for any purpose will be found but what is also the fittest and best adapted for that purpose. Now in a being which has reason and a will, if the proper object of nature were its *conservatism,* its *welfare,* in a word, its *happiness,* then nature would have hit upon a very bad arrangement in selecting the reason of the creature to carry out this purpose. For all the actions which the creature has to perform with a view to this purpose, and the whole rule of its conduct, would be far more surely prescribed to it by instinct, and that end would have been attained thereby much more certainly than it ever can be by reason. Should reason have been communicated to this favoured creature over and above, it must only have served it to contemplate the happy constitution of its nature, to admire it, to congratulate itself thereon, and to feel thankful for it to the beneficent cause, but not that it should subject its desires to that weak and delusive guidance, and meddle bunglingly with the purpose of nature. In a word, nature would have taken care that reason should not break forth into *practical exercise,* nor have the presumption, with its weak insight, to think out for itself the plan of happiness, and of the means of attaining it. Nature would not only have taken on herself the choice of the ends, but also of the means, and with wise foresight would have entrusted both to instinct.

And, in fact, we find that the more a cultivated reason applies itself with deliberate purpose to the enjoyment of life and happiness, so much the more does the man fail of true satisfaction. And from this circumstance there arises in many, if they are candid enough to confess it, a certain degree of *misology,* that is, hatred of reason, especially in the case of those who are most experienced in the use of it, because after calculating all the advantages they derive, I do not say from the invention of all the arts of common luxury, but even from the sciences (which seem to them to be after all only a luxury of the understanding), they find that they have, in fact, only brought more trouble on their shoulders, rather than gained in happiness; and they end by envying, rather than despising, the more common stamp of men who keep closer to the guidance of mere instinct, and do not allow their reason much influence on their conduct. And this we must admit, that the judgment of those who would very much lower the lofty eulogies of the advantages which reason gives us in regard to the happiness and satisfaction of life, or who would even reduce them below zero, is by no means morose or ungrateful to the goodness with which the world is governed, but that there lies at the root of these judgments the idea that our existence has a different and far nobler end, for which, and not for happiness, reason is properly intended, and which must, therefore, be regarded as the supreme condition to which the private ends of man must, for the most part, be postponed.

For as reason is not competent to guide the will with certainty in regard to its objects and the satisfaction of all our wants (which it to some extent even multiplies), this being an end to which an implanted instinct would have led with much greater certainty; and since, nevertheless, reason is imparted to us as a practical faculty *i.e.,* as one which is to have influence on the *will,* therefore, admitting that nature generally in the distribution of her capacities has adapted the means to the end, its true destination must be to produce a *will,* not merely good as a *means* to something else, but *good in itself,* for which reason was absolutely necessary. This will then, though not indeed the sole and complete good, must be the supreme good and the condition of every other, even of the desire of happiness. Under these circumstances, there is nothing inconsistent with the wisdom of nature in the fact that the cultivation of the reason, which is requisite for the first and unconditional purpose, does in many ways interfere, at least in this life, with the attainment of the second, which is always conditional, namely, happiness. Nay, it may even reduce it to nothing, without nature thereby failing in her purpose. For reason recognizes the establishment of a good will as its highest practical destination, and in attaining this purpose is capable only of a satisfaction of its own proper kind, namely, that from the attainment of an end, which end again is determined by reason only, notwithstanding that this may involve many a disappointment to the ends of inclination.

The First Proposition of Morality [An Action Must Be Done from a Sense of Duty, If It Is to Have Moral Worth]

We have then to develop the notion of a will which deserves to be highly esteemed for itself, and is good without a view to anything further, a notion which exists already in the sound natural understanding, requiring rather to be cleared up than to be taught, and which in estimating the value of our actions always takes the first place, and constitutes the condition of all the rest. In order to do this, we will take the notion of duty, which includes that of a good will, although implying certain subjective restrictions and hindrances. These, however, far from concealing it, or rendering it unrecognizable, rather bring it out by contrast, and make it shine forth so much the brighter.

 I omit here all actions which are already recognized as inconsistent with duty although they may be useful for this or that purpose, for with these the question whether they are done *from duty* cannot arise at all, since they even conflict with it. I also set aside those actions which really conform to duty, but to which men have *no* direct *inclination,* performing them because they are impelled thereto by some other inclination. For in this case we can readily distinguish whether the action which agrees with duty is done *from duty,* or from a selfish view. It is much harder to make this distinction when the action accords with duty, and the subject has besides a *direct* inclination to it. For example, it is always a matter of duty that a dealer should not overcharge an inexperienced purchaser; and wherever there is much commerce the prudent tradesman does not overcharge, but keeps a fixed price for everyone, so that a child buys of him as well as any other. Men are thus *honestly* served; but this is not enough to make us believe that the tradesman has so acted from duty and from principles of honesty: his own advantage required it; it is out of the question in this case to suppose that he might besides have a direct inclination in favour of the buyers, so that, as it were, from love he should give no advantage to one over another. Accordingly the action was done neither from duty nor from direct inclination, but merely with a selfish view.

On the other hand, it is a duty to maintain one's life; and, in addition, everyone has also a direct inclination to do so. But on this account the often anxious care which most men take for it has no intrinsic worth, and their maxim has no moral import. They preserve their life *as duty requires,* no doubt, but not *because duty requires.* On the other hand, if adversity and hopeless sorrow have completely taken away the relish for life; if the unfortunate one, strong in mind, indignant at his fate rather than desponding or dejected, wishes for death, and yet preserves his life without loving it—not from inclination or fear, but from duty—then his maxim has a moral worth.

To be beneficent when we can is a duty; and besides this, there are many minds so sympathetically constituted that, without any other motive of vanity or self-interest, they find a pleasure in spreading joy around them, and can take delight in the satisfaction of others so far as it is their own work. But I maintain that in such a case an action of this kind, however proper, however amiable it may be, has nevertheless no true moral worth, but is on a level with other inclinations, *e.g.,* the inclination to honour, which, if it is happily directed to that which is in fact of public utility and accordant with duty, and consequently honourable, deserves praise and encouragement, but not esteem. For the maxim lacks the moral import, namely, that such actions be done *from duty,* not from inclination. Put the case that the mind of that philanthropist was clouded by sorrow of his own, extinguishing all sympathy with the lot of others, and that while he still has the power to benefit others in distress, he is not touched by their trouble because he is absorbed with his own; and now sup-

maxim - rule or principle by which we act.

pose that he tears himself out of this dead insensibility, and performs the action without any inclination to it, but simply from duty, then first has his action its genuine moral worth. Further still; if nature has put little sympathy in the heart of this or that man; if he, supposed to be an upright man, is by temperament cold and indifferent to the sufferings of others, perhaps because in respect of his own he is provided with the special gift of patience and fortitude, and supposes, or even requires, that others should have the same—and such a man would certainly not be the meanest product of nature—but if nature had not specially framed him for a philanthropist, would he not still find in himself a source from whence to give himself a far higher worth than that of a good-natured temperament? Unquestionably. It is just in this that the moral worth of the character is brought out which is incomparably the highest of all, namely that he is beneficent, not from inclination, but from duty.

To secure one's own happiness is a duty, at least indirectly; for discontent with one's condition, under a pressure of many anxieties and amidst unsatisfied wants, might easily become a great *temptation to transgression of duty*. But here again, without looking to duty, all men have already the strongest and most intimate inclination to happiness, because it is just in this idea that all inclinations are combined in one total. But the precept of happiness is often of such a sort that it greatly interferes with some inclinations, and yet a man cannot form any definite and certain conception of the sum of satisfaction of all of them which is called happiness. It is not then to be wondered at that a single inclination, definite both as to what it promises and as to the time within which it can be gratified, is often able to overcome such a fluctuating idea, and that a gouty patient, for instance, can choose to enjoy what he likes, and to suffer what he may, since, according to his calculation, on this occasion at least, he has [only] not sacrificed the enjoyment of the present moment to a possibly

mistaken expectation of a happiness which is supposed to be found in health. But even in this case, if the general desire for happiness did not influence his will, and supposing that in his particular case health was not a necessary element in this calculation, there yet remains in this, as in all other cases, this law, namely, that he should promote his happiness not from inclination but from duty, and by this would his conduct first acquire true moral worth.

It is in this manner, undoubtedly, that we are to understand those passages of Scripture also in which we are commanded to love our neighbour, even our enemy. For love, as an affection, cannot be commanded, but beneficence for duty's sake may; even though we are not impelled to it by any inclination—nay, are even repelled by a natural and unconquerable aversion. This is *practical* love, and not *pathological* [passional or emotional—ED.]—a love which is seated in the will, and not in the propensions of sense—in principles of action and not of tender sympathy; and it is this love alone which can be commanded.

The Second Proposition of Morality

The second proposition is: That an action done from duty derives its moral worth, *not from the purpose* which is to be attained by it, but from the maxim by which it is determined, and therefore does not depend on the realization of the object of the action, but merely on the *principle of volition* by which the action has taken place, without regard to any object of desire. It is clear from what precedes that the purposes which we may have in view in our actions, or their effects regarded as ends and springs of the will, cannot give to actions any unconditional or moral worth. In what, then, can their worth lie, if it is not to consist in the will and in reference to its expected effect? It cannot lie anywhere but in the *principle of the will* without regard to the ends which can be attained by the action. For the will stands between its *a priori principle*, which is formal, and its *a posteriori* spring, which is material, as between two roads, and as it must be determined by something, it follows that it must be determined by the formal principle of volition when an action is done from duty, in which case every material principle has been withdrawn from it.

[handwritten margin note: act of making a choice or decision]

The Third Proposition of Morality

The third proposition, which is a consequence of the two preceding, I would express thus: *Duty is the necessity of acting from respect for the law.* I may have *inclination* for an object as the effect of my proposed action, but I cannot have *respect* for it, just for this reason, that it is an effect and not an energy of will. Similarly, I cannot have respect for inclination, whether my own or another's; I can at most, if my own, approve it; if another's, sometimes even love it; *i.e.,* look on it as favourable to my own interest. It is only what is connected with my will as a principle, by no means as an effect—what does not subserve my inclination, but overpowers it, or at least in case of choice excludes it from its calculation—in other words, simply the law of itself, which can be an object of respect, and hence a command. Now an action done from duty must wholly exclude the influence of inclination, and with it every object of the will, so that nothing remains which can determine the will except objectively the *law,* and subjectively *pure respect* for this practical law, and consequently the maxim that I should follow this law even to the thwarting of all my inclinations.

Thus the moral worth of an action does not lie in the effect expected from it, nor in any principle of action which requires to borrow its motive from this expected effect. For all these effects—agreeableness of one's condition, and even the promotion of the happiness of others—

could have been also brought about by other causes, so that for this there would have been no need of the will of a rational being; whereas it is in this alone that the supreme and unconditional good can be found. The pre-eminent good which we call moral can therefore consist in nothing else than *the conception of law* in itself, *which certainly is only possible in a rational being,* in so far as this conception, and not the expected effect, determines the will. This is a good which is already present in the person who acts accordingly, and we have not to wait for it to appear first in the result.

The Supreme Principle of Morality: The Categorical Imperative

But what sort of law can that be, the conception of which must determine the will, even without paying any regard to the effect expected from it, in order that this will may be called good absolutely and without qualification? As I have deprived the will of every impulse which could arise to it from obedience to any law, there remains nothing but the universal conformity of its actions to law in general, which alone is to serve the will as a principle, *i.e.,* I am never to act otherwise than so *that I could also will that my maxim should become a universal law.* Here, now, it is the simple conformity to law in general, without assuming any particular law applicable to certain actions, that serves the will as its principle, and must so serve it, if duty is not to be a vain delusion and a chimerical notion. The common reason of men in its practical judgments perfectly coincides with this, and always has in view the principle here suggested. Let the question be, for example: May I when in distress make a promise with the intention not to keep it? I readily distinguish here between the two significations which the question may have: Whether it is prudent, or whether it is right, to make a false promise? The former may undoubtedly often be the case. I see clearly indeed that it is not enough to extricate myself from a present difficulty by means of this subterfuge, but it must be well considered whether there may not hereafter spring from this lie much greater inconvenience than that from which I now free myself, and as, with all my supposed *cunning*, the consequences cannot be so easily foreseen but that credit once lost may be much more injurious to me than any mischief which I seek to avoid at present, it should be considered whether it would not be more *prudent* to act herein according to a universal maxim, and to make it a habit to promise nothing except with the intention of keeping it. But it is soon clear to me that such a maxim will still only be based on the fear of consequences. Now it is a wholly different thing to be truthful from duty, and to be so from apprehension of injurious consequences. In the first case, the very notion of the action already implies a law for me; in the second case, I must first look about elsewhere to see what results may be combined with it which would affect myself. For to deviate from the principle of duty is beyond all doubt wicked; but to be unfaithful to my maxim of prudence may often be very advantageous to me, although to abide by it is certainly safer. The shortest way, however, and an unerring one, to discover the answer to this question whether a lying promise is consistent with duty, is to ask myself, Should I be content that my maxim (to extricate myself from difficulty by a false promise) should hold good as a universal law, for myself as well as for others? and should I be able to say to myself, "Every one may make a deceitful promise when he finds himself in a difficulty from which he cannot otherwise extricate himself"? Then I presently become aware that while I can will the lie, I can by no means will that lying should be a universal law. For with such a law there would be no promises at all, since it would be in vain to allege my intention in regard to my future actions to those who would not believe this allegation, or if they over-hastily did so, would pay me

back in my own coin. Hence my maxim, as soon as it should be made a universal law, would necessarily destroy itself.

I do not, therefore, need any far-reaching penetration to discern what I have to do in order that my will may be morally good. Inexperienced in the course of the world, incapable of being prepared for all its contingencies, I only ask myself: Canst thou also will that thy maxim should be a universal law? If not, then it must be rejected, and that not because of a disadvantage accruing from myself or even to others, but because it cannot enter as a principle into a possible universal legislation, and reason extorts from me immediate respect for such legislation. I do not indeed as yet *discern* on what this respect is based (this the philosopher may inquire), but at least I understand this, that it is an estimation of the worth which far outweighs all worth of what is recommended by inclination, and that the necessity of acting from *pure* respect for the practical law is what constitutes duty, to which every other motive must give place, because it is the condition of a will being good *in itself*, and the worth of such a will is above everything.

Thus, then, without quitting the moral knowledge of common human reason, we have arrived at its principle. And although, no doubt, common men do not conceive it in such an abstract and universal form, yet they always have it really before their eyes, and use it as the standard of their decision. . . .

Nor could anything be more fatal to morality than that we should wish to derive it from examples. For every example of it that is set before me must be first itself tested by principles of morality, whether it is worthy to serve as an original example, *i.e.,* as a pattern, but by no means can it authoritatively furnish the conception of morality. Even the Holy One of the Gospels must first be compared with our ideal of moral perfection before we can recognize Him as such; and so He says of Himself, "Why call ye Me [whom you see] good; none is good [the model of

good] but God only [whom ye do not see]."
But whence have we the conception of God as
the supreme good? Simply from the *idea* of
moral perfection, which reason frames *a priori*,
and connects inseparably with the notion of a
free will. Imitation finds no place at all in morality, and examples serve only for encouragement,
i.e., they put beyond doubt the feasibility of
what the law commands, they make visible that
which the practical rule expresses more generally, but they can never authorize us to set aside
the true original which lies in reason, and to
guide ourselves by examples.

From what has been said, it is clear that all
moral conceptions have their seat and origin
completely *a priori* in the reason, and that,
moreover, in the commonest reason just as truly
as in that which is in the highest degree speculative; that they cannot be obtained by abstraction
from any empirical, and therefore merely contingent knowledge; that it is just this purity of
their origin that makes them worthy to serve as
our supreme practical principle, and that just in
proportion as we add anything empirical, we de-
tract from their genuine influence, and from the
absolute value of actions; that it is not only of
the greatest necessity, in a purely speculative
point of view, but is also of the greatest practical
importance, to derive these notions and laws
from pure reason, to present them pure and unmixed, and even to determine the compass of
this practical or pure rational knowledge, *i.e.*, to
determine the whole faculty of pure practical
reason; and, in doing so, we must not make its
principles dependent on the particular nature of
human reason, though in speculative philosophy
this may be permitted, or may even at times be
necessary; but since moral laws ought to hold
good for every rational creature, we must derive
them from the general concept of a rational being. In this way, although for its *application* to
man morality has need of anthropology, yet, in
the first instance, we must treat it independently
as pure philosophy, *i.e.*, as metaphysic, complete
in itself (a thing which in such distinct branches

of science is easily done); knowing well that unless we are in possession of this, it would not
only be vain to determine the moral element of
duty in right actions for purposes of speculative
criticism, but it would be impossible to base
morals on their genuine principles, even for
common practical purposes, especially of moral
instruction, so as to produce pure moral dispositions, and to engraft them on men's minds to
the promotion of the greatest possible good in
the world. . . .

The Rational Ground of the Categorical Imperative

. . . the question, how the imperative of *morality*
is possible, is undoubtedly one, the only one,
demanding a solution, as this is not at all hypothetical, and the objective necessity which it presents cannot rest on any hypothesis, as is the
case with the hypothetical imperatives. Only
here we must never leave out of consideration
that we *cannot* make out *by any example*, in
other words empirically, whether there is such
an imperative at all; but it is rather to be feared
that all those which seem to be categorical may
yet be at bottom hypothetical. For instance,
when the precept is: Thou shalt not promise de-
ceitfully; and it is assumed that the necessity of
this is not a mere counsel to avoid some other
evil, so that it should mean: Thou shalt not
make a lying promise, lest if it become known
thou shouldst destroy thy credit, but that an action of this kind must be regarded as evil in itself, so that the imperative of the prohibition is
categorical; then we cannot show with certainty
in any example that the will was determined
merely by the law, without any other spring of
action, although it may appear to be so. For it is
always possible that fear of disgrace, perhaps also
obscure dread of other dangers, may have a secret influence on the will. Who can prove by experience the nonexistence of a cause when all

that experience tells us is that we do not perceive it? But in such a case the so-called moral imperative, which as such appears to be categorical and unconditional, would in reality be only a pragmatic precept, drawing our attention to our own interests, and merely teaching us to take these into consideration.

We shall therefore have to investigate *a priori* the possibility of a categorical imperative, as we have not in this case the advantage of its reality being given in experience, so that [the elucidation of] its possibility should be requisite only for its explanation, not for its establishment. In the meantime it may be discerned beforehand that the categorical imperative alone has the purport of a practical law: all the rest may indeed be called *principles* of the will but not laws, since whatever is only necessary for the attainment of some arbitrary purpose may be considered as in itself contingent, and we can at any time be free from the precept if we give up the purpose: on the contrary, the unconditional command leaves the will no liberty to choose the opposite; consequently it alone carries with it that necessity which we require in a law.

Secondly, in the case of this categorical imperative or law of morality, the difficulty (of discerning its possibility) is a very profound one. It is an *a priori* synthetical practical proposition; and as there is so much difficulty in discerning the possibility of speculative propositions of this kind, it may readily be supposed that the difficulty will be no less with the practical.

First Formulation of the Categorical Imperative: Universal Law

In this problem we will first inquire whether the mere conception of a categorical imperative may not perhaps supply us also with the formula of it, containing the proposition which alone can be a categorical imperative; for even if we know the tenor of such an absolute command, yet

how it is possible will require further special and laborious study, which we postpone to the last section.

When I conceive a hypothetical imperative, in general I do not know beforehand what it will contain until I am given the condition. But when I conceive a categorical imperative, I know at once what it contains. For as the imperative contains besides the law only the necessity that the maxims shall conform to this law, while the law contains no conditions restricting it, there remains nothing but the general statement that the maxim of the action should conform to a universal law, and it is this conformity alone that the imperative properly represents as necessary.

There is therefore but one categorical imperative, namely, this: *Act only on that maxim whereby thou canst at the same time will that it should become a universal law.*

Now if all imperatives of duty can be deduced from this one imperative as from their principle, then, although it should remain undecided whether what is called duty is not merely a vain notion, yet at least we shall be able to show what we understand by it and what this notion means.

Since the universality of the law according to which effects are produced constitutes what is properly called *nature* in the most general sense (as to form), that is the existence of things so far as it is determined by general laws, the imperative of duty may be expressed thus: *Act as if the maxim of thy action were to become by thy will a universal law of nature.*

Four Illustrations

We will now enumerate a few duties, adopting the usual division of them into duties to ourselves and to others, and into perfect and imperfect duties.

1. A man reduced to despair by a series of misfortunes feels wearied of life, but is still so far in possession of his reason that he can ask himself

whether it would not be contrary to his duty to himself to take his own life. Now he inquires whether the maxim of his action could become a universal law of nature. His maxim is: From self-love I adopt it as a principle to shorten my life when its longer duration is likely to bring more evil than satisfaction. It is asked then simply whether this principle founded on self-love can become a universal law of nature. Now we see at once that a system of nature of which it should be a law to destroy life by means of the very feeling whose special nature it is to impel to the improvement of life would contradict itself, and therefore could not exist as a system of nature; hence the maxim cannot possibly exist as a universal law of nature, and consequently would be wholly inconsistent with the supreme principle of all duty.

2. Another finds himself forced by necessity to borrow money. He knows that he will not be able to repay it, but sees also that nothing will be lent to him, unless he promises stoutly to repay it in a definite time. He desires to make this promise, but he has still so much conscience as to ask himself: Is it not unlawful and inconsistent with duty to get out of a difficulty in this way? Suppose, however, that he resolves to do so, then the maxim of his action would be expressed thus: When I think myself in want of money, I will borrow money and promise to repay it, although I know that I never can do so. Now this principle of self-love or of one's own advantage may perhaps be consistent with my whole future welfare; but the question is, Is it right? I change then the suggestion of self-love into a universal law, and state the question thus: How would it be if my maxim were a universal law? Then I see at once that it could never hold as a universal law of nature, but would necessarily contradict itself. For supposing it to be a universal law that everyone when he thinks himself in a difficulty should be able to promise whatever he pleases, with the purpose of not keeping his promise, the promise itself would become impossible, as well as the end that one

might have in view in it, since no one would consider that anything was promised to him, but would ridicule all such statements as vain pretenses.

3. A third finds in himself a talent which with the help of some culture might make him a useful man in many respects. But he finds himself in comfortable circumstances, and prefers to indulge in pleasure rather than to take pains in enlarging and improving his happy natural capacities. He asks, however, whether his maxim of neglect of his natural gifts, besides agreeing with his inclination to indulgence, agrees also with what is called duty. He sees then that a system of nature could indeed subsist with such a universal law although men (like the South Sea islanders) should let their talents rest, and resolve to devote their lives merely to idleness, amusement, and propagation of their species—in a word, to enjoyment; but he cannot possibly *will* that this should be a universal law of nature, or be implanted in us as such by a natural instinct. For, as a rational being, he necessarily wills that his faculties be developed, since they serve him, and have been given him, for all sorts of possible purposes.

4. A fourth, who is in prosperity, while he sees that others have to contend with great wretchedness and that he could help them, thinks: What concern is it of mine? Let everyone be as happy as Heaven pleases, or as he can make himself; I will take nothing from him nor even envy him, only I do not wish to contribute anything to his welfare or to his assistance in distress! Now no doubt if such a mode of thinking were a universal law, the human race might very well subsist, and doubtless even better than in a state in which everyone talks of sympathy and good-will, or even takes care occasionally to put it into practice, but, on the other side, also cheats when he can, betrays the rights of men, or otherwise violates them. But although it is possible that a universal law of nature might exist in accordance with that maxim, it is impossible to *will* that such a principle should have the universal validity of a

law of nature. For a will which resolved this would contradict itself, inasmuch as many cases might occur in which one would have need of the love and sympathy of others, and in which, by such a law of nature, sprung from his own will, he would deprive himself of all hope of the aid he desires.

These are a few of the many actual duties, or at least what we regard as such, which obviously fall into two classes on the one principle that we have laid down. We must be *able to will* that a maxim of our action should be a universal law. This is the canon of the moral appreciation of the action generally. Some actions are of such a character that their maxim cannot without contradiction be even *conceived* as a universal law of nature, far from it being possible that we should *will* that it *should* be so. In others this intrinsic impossibility is not found, but still it is impossible to *will* that their maxim should be raised to the universality of a law of nature, since such a will would contradict itself. It is easily seen that the former violate strict or rigorous (inflexible) duty; the latter only laxer (meritorious) duty. Thus it has been completely shown by these examples how all duties depend as regards the nature of the obligation (not the object of the action) on the same principle. . . .

Second Formulation of the Categorical Imperative: Humanity as an End in Itself

Now I say: man and generally any rational being *exists* as an end in himself, *not merely as a means* to be arbitrarily used by this or that will, but in all his actions, whether they concern himself or other rational beings, must be always regarded at the same time as an end. All objects of the inclinations have only a conditional worth; for if the inclinations and the wants founded on them did not exist, then their ob-

ject would be without value. But the inclinations themselves being sources of want are so far from having an absolute worth for which they should be desired, that, on the contrary, it must be the universal wish of every rational being to be wholly free from them. Thus the worth of any object which is *to be acquired* by our action is always conditional. Beings whose existence depends not on our will but on nature's, have nevertheless, if they are non-rational beings, only a relative value as means, and are therefore called *things;* rational beings, on the contrary, are called *persons,* because their very nature points them out as ends in themselves, that is as something which must not be used merely as means, and so far therefore restricts freedom of action (and is an object of respect). These, therefore, are not merely subjective ends whose existence has a worth *for us* as an effect of our action, but *objective ends,* that is things whose existence is an end in itself: an end moreover for which no other can be substituted, which they should subserve *merely* as means, for otherwise nothing whatever would possess *absolute worth;* but if all worth were conditioned and therefore contingent, then there would be no supreme practical principle of reason whatever.

If then there is a supreme practical principle or, in respect of the human will, a categorical imperative, it must be one which, being drawn from the conception of that which is necessarily an end for everyone because it is *an end in itself,* constitutes an *objective* principle of will, and can therefore serve as a universal practical law. The foundation of this principle is: *rational nature exists as an end in itself.* Man necessarily conceives his own existence as being so: so far then this is a *subjective* principle of human actions. But every other rational being regards its existence similarly, just on the same rational principle that holds for me: so that it is at the same time an objective principle, from which as a supreme practical law all laws of the will must be capable of being deduced. Accordingly the practical imperative will be as follows: *So act as to treat humanity, whether in thine own person or in that of any other, in every case as an end withal, never as means only. .* .

. . . Looking back now on all previous attempts to discover the principle of morality, we need not wonder why they all failed. It was seen that man was bound to laws by duty, but it was not observed that the laws to which he is subject are *only those of his own giving*, though at the same time they are *universal*, and that he is only bound to act in conformity with his own will; a will, however, which is designed by nature to give universal laws. For when one has conceived man only as subject to a law (no matter what), then this law required some interest, either by way of attraction or constraint, since it did not originate as a law from *his own* will, but this will was according to a law obliged by *something else* to act in a certain manner. Now by this necessary consequence all the labour spent in finding a supreme principle of *duty* was irrevocably lost. For men never elicited duty, but only a necessity of acting from a certain interest. Whether this interest was private or otherwise, in any case the imperative must be conditional, and could not by any means be capable of being a moral command. I will therefore call this the principle of *Autonomy* of the will, in contrast with every other which I accordingly reckon as *Heteronomy*.

The Kingdom of Ends

The conception of every rational being as one which must consider itself as giving in all the maxims of its will universal laws, so as to judge itself and its actions from this point of view—this conception leads to another which depends on it and is very fruitful, namely, that of a *kingdom of ends*.

By a *kingdom* I understand the union of different rational beings in a system by common laws. Now since it is by laws that ends are determined as regards their universal validity, hence, if we abstract from the personal differences of rational beings, and likewise from all the content of their private ends, we shall be able to conceive all ends combined in a systematic whole (including both rational beings as ends in themselves, and also the special ends which each may propose to himself), that is to say, we can conceive a kingdom of ends, which on the preceding principles is possible.

For all rational beings come under the *law* that each of them must treat itself and all others *never merely as means*, but in every case *at the same time as ends in themselves*. Hence results a systematic union of rational beings by common objective laws, *i.e.,* a kingdom which may be called a kingdom of ends, since what these laws have in view is just the relation of these beings to one another as ends and means. . . .

Study Questions

1. Do you agree with Kant that the only good without qualification is the good will? What does Kant mean by that? Can you think of counterexamples to his claim?
2. Compare Kant's Categorical Imperative to the Golden Rule: "Do unto others what you would have them do unto you."
3. Kant's ethics are sometimes criticized for having no place for the emotions and for being too rigid. According to this criticism, Kant allows no place to the inclinations or sentiments in helping us arrive at decisions. Furthermore, all moral principles are absolutes that may not be overridden, no matter what the consequences. Do you agree with these criticisms?

4. Kant's ethics have also been criticized for being too broad. It is said that the Categorical Imperative is merely a highfalutin name for the principle of universalizability; that is, whatever you can permit everyone else to do, you may do. For example, John might love painting so much that he would like to abandon his wife and children in order to migrate to the desert where he paints until he dies. John may claim to be justified by Kantian principles in abandoning his family, since he is willing for everyone to do likewise. Is this a fair interpretation of Kant?

CHAPTER 2

Utilitarianism

JOHN STUART MILL

John Stuart Mill (1806–1873), a great philosopher of the nineteenth century, was born in London and educated by his father. He learned Greek at the age of three and Latin at the age of eight. By the time he was fourteen he had received a thorough classical education at home. He began work as a clerk for the East India Company at the age of seventeen and eventually became director of the company. He was elected to Parliament in 1865. A man of liberal ideas and a penetrating mind, he made significant contributions to logic, philosophy of science, philosophy of religion, political theory, and ethics. His principal works are *A System of Logic* (1843), *Utilitarianism* (1863), *On Liberty* (1859), and *The Subjection of Women* (1869).

Mill defends utilitarianism, a form of teleological ethics, against more rule-bound "deontological" systems, the kind we considered in the last selection, Kant's categorical imperative.

Traditionally, two major types of ethical systems have dominated the field. In deontological ethics the locus of value is the act or kind of act, whereas in teleological (from the Greek *teleos*, meaning "end" or "goal") ethics the locus of value is the outcome or consequences of the act.

The standard of right or wrong action for the teleologist is the comparative consequences of the available actions. The act that is right produces the best consequences. Whereas the deontologist is concerned only with the rightness of the act itself, the teleologist asserts that there is no such thing as an act with intrinsic worth. While there is something intrinsically bad about lying for the deontologist, the only thing wrong with lying for the teleologist is the bad consequences it produces. If you can reasonably calculate that a lie will do even slightly more good than telling the truth, you have an obligation to lie.

This selection was written by Mill against the background of a debate over Jeremy Bentham's hedonistic (from the Greek *hedon*, meaning "pleasure") version of utilitarianism, which failed to differentiate between kinds and quality of pleasure, and so received the name of "pig philosophy." Mill meets this charge by substituting a more complex theory of happiness for Bentham's undifferentiated pleasure.

What Utilitarianism Is

...THE CREED WHICH ACCEPTS as the foundation of morals, Utility, or the Greatest Happiness Principle, holds that actions are right in proportion as they tend to promote happiness, wrong as they tend to produce the reverse of happiness. By happiness is intended pleasure, and the absence of pain; by unhappiness, pain, and the privation of pleasure. To give a clear

From Utilitarianism *(1861), Chapters 2 and 4.*

view of the moral standard set up by the theory, much more requires to be said; in particular, what things it includes in the ideas of pain and pleasure; and to what extent this is left an open question. But these supplementary explanations do not affect the theory of life on which this theory of morality is grounded—namely, that pleasure, and freedom from pain, are the only things desirable as ends; and that all desirable things (which are as numerous in the utilitarian as in any other scheme) are desirable either for the pleasure inherent in themselves, or as a means to the promotion of pleasure and the prevention of pain.

Now, such a theory of life excites in many minds, and among them in some of the most estimable in feeling and purpose, inveterate dislike. To suppose that life has (as they express it) no higher end than pleasure—no better and nobler object of desire and pursuit—they designate as utterly mean and grovelling; as a doctrine worthy only of swine, to whom the followers of Epicurus were, at a very early period, contemptuously likened; and modern holders of the doctrine are occasionally made the subject of equally polite comparisons by its German, French, and English assailants.

When thus attacked, the Epicureans have always answered, that it is not they, but their accusers, who represent human nature in a degrading light; since the accusation supposes human beings to be capable of no pleasures except those of which swine are capable. If this supposition were true, the charge could not be gainsaid, but would then be no longer an imputation; for if the sources of pleasure were precisely the same to human beings and to swine, the rule of life which is good enough for the one would be good enough for the other. The comparison of the Epicurean life to that of beasts is felt as degrading, precisely because a beast's pleasures do not satisfy a human being's conception of happiness. Human beings have faculties more elevated than the animal appetites, and when once made conscious of them, do not regard anything as happiness which does not include their gratification. I do not, indeed, consider the Epicureans to have been by any means faultless in drawing out their scheme of consequences from the utilitarian principle. To do this in any sufficient manner, many Stoic, as well as Christian elements require to be included. But there is no known Epicurean theory of life which does not assign to the pleasures of the intellect, of the feelings and imagination, and of the moral sentiments, a much higher value as pleasures than to those of mere sensation. It must be admitted, however, that utilitarian writers in general have placed the superiority of mental over bodily pleasures chiefly in the greater permanency, safety, uncostliness, etc., of the former—that is, in their circumstantial advantages rather than in their intrinsic nature. And on all these points utilitarians have fully proved their case; but they might have taken the other, and, as it may be called, higher ground, with entire consistency. It is quite compatible with the principle of utility to recognise the fact, that some *kinds* of pleasure are more desirable and more valuable than others. It would be absurd that while, in estimating all other things, quality is considered as well as quantity, the estimation of pleasures should be supposed to depend on quantity alone.

If I am asked, what I mean by difference of quality in pleasures, or what makes one pleasure more valuable than another, merely as a pleasure, except its being greater in amount, there is but one possible answer. Of two pleasures, if there be one which all or almost all who have experience of both give a decided preference, irrespective of any feeling of moral obligation to prefer it, that is the more desirable pleasure. If one of the two is, by those who are competently acquainted with both, placed so far above the other that they prefer it, even though knowing it to be attended with a great amount of discontent, and would not resign it for any quantity of the other pleasure which their nature is capable of, we are justified in ascribing to the preferred enjoyment a superiority in quality, so far outweighing quantity as to render it, in comparison, of small account.

Now it is an unquestionable fact that those who are equally acquainted with, and equally capable of appreciating and enjoying, both, do give a most marked preference to the manner of existence which employs their higher faculties. Few human creatures would consent to be changed into any of the lower animals, for a promise of the fullest allowance of a beast's pleasures; no intelligent human being would consent to be a fool, no instructed person would be an ignoramus, no person of feeling and conscience would be selfish and base, even though they should be persuaded that the fool, the dunce, or the rascal is better satisfied with his lot than they are with theirs. They would not resign what they possess more than he for the most complete satisfaction of all the desires which they have in common with him. If they ever fancy they would, it is only in cases of unhappiness so extreme, that to escape from it they would exchange their lot for almost any other, however undesirable in their own eyes. A being of higher faculties requires more to make him happy, is capable probably of more acute suffering, and certainly accessible to it at more points, than one of an inferior type; but in spite of these liabilities, he can never really wish to sink into what he feels to be a lower grade of existence. We may give what explanation we please of this unwillingness; we may attribute it to pride, a name which is given indiscriminately to some of the most and to some of the least estimable feelings of which mankind are capable; we may refer it to the love of liberty and personal independence, an appeal to which was with the Stoics one of the most effective means for the inculcation of it; to the love of power, or to the love of excitement, both of which do really enter into and contribute to it: but its most appropriate appellation is a sense of dignity, which all human beings possess in one form or another, and in some, though by no means in exact, proportion to their higher faculties, and which is so essential a part of the happiness of those in whom it is strong, that nothing which conflicts with it

could be, otherwise than momentarily, an object of desire to them. Whoever supposes that this preference takes place at a sacrifice of happiness—that the superior being, in anything like equal circumstances, is not happier than the inferior—confounds the two very different ideas, of happiness, and content. It is indisputable that the being whose capacities of enjoyment are low, has the greatest chance of having them fully satisfied; and a highly endowed being will always feel that any happiness which he can look for, as the world is constituted, is imperfect. But he can learn to bear its imperfections, if they are at all bearable; and they will not make him envy the being who is indeed unconscious of the imperfections, but only because he feels not at all the good which those imperfections qualify. It is better to be a human being dissatisfied than a pig satisfied; better to be Socrates dissatisfied than a fool satisfied. And if the fool, or the pig, are of a different opinion, it is because they only know their own side of the question. The other party to the comparison knows both sides.

It may be objected, that many who are capable of the higher pleasures, occasionally, under the influence of temptation, postpone them to the lower. But this is quite compatible with a full appreciation of the intrinsic superiority of the higher. Men often, from infirmity of character, make their election for the nearer good, though they know it to be the less valuable; and this is no less when the choice is between two bodily pleasures, than when it is between bodily and mental. They pursue sensual indulgences to the injury of health, though perfectly aware that health is the greater good. It may be further objected, that many who begin with youthful enthusiasm for everything noble, as they advance in years sink into indolence and selfishness. But I do not believe that those who undergo this very common change, voluntarily choose the lower description of pleasures in preference to the higher. I believe that before they devote themselves exclusively to the one, they have already become incapable of the other. Capacity for the nobler feelings is in most natures a very tender plant, easily killed, not only by hostile influences, but by mere want of sustenance; and in the majority of young persons it speedily dies away if the occupations to which their position in life has devoted them, and the society into which it has thrown them, are not favourable to keeping that higher capacity in exercise. Men lose their high aspirations as they lose their intellectual tastes, because they have not time or opportunity for indulging them; and they addict themselves to inferior pleasures, not because they deliberately prefer them, but because they are either the only ones to which they have access, or the only ones which they are any longer capable of enjoying. It may be questioned whether any one who has remained equally susceptible to both classes of pleasures, ever knowingly and calmly preferred the lower; though many, in all ages, have broken down in an ineffectual attempt to combine both.

From this verdict of the only competent judges, I apprehend there can be no appeal. On a question which is the best worth having of two pleasures, or which of two modes of existence is the most grateful to the feelings, apart from its moral attributes and from its consequences, the judgment of those who are qualified by knowledge of both, or, if they differ, that of the majority among them, must be admitted as final. And there needs to be the less hesitation to accept this judgment respecting the quality of pleasures, since there is no other tribunal to be referred to even on the question of quantity. What means are there of determining which is the acutest of two pains, or the intensest of two pleasurable sensations, except the general suffrage of those who are familiar with both? Neither pains nor pleasures are homogeneous, and pain is always heterogeneous with pleasure. What is there to decide whether a particular pleasure is worth purchasing at the cost of a particular pain, except the feelings and judgment of the experienced? When, therefore, those feelings and judgment declare the pleasures derived from the higher fac-

ulties to be preferable *in kind,* apart from the question of intensity, to those of which the animal nature, disjoined from the higher faculties, is susceptible, they are entitled on this subject to the same regard.

I have dwelt on this point, as being a necessary part of a perfectly just conception of Utility or Happiness, considered as the directive rule of human conduct. But it is by no means an indispensable condition to the acceptance of the utilitarian standard; for that standard is not the agent's own greatest happiness, but the greatest amount of happiness altogether; and if it may possibly be doubted whether a noble character is always the happier for its nobleness, there can be no doubt that it makes other people happier, and that the world in general is immensely a gainer by it. Utilitarianism, therefore, could only attain its end by the general cultivation of nobleness of character, even if each individual were only benefited by the nobleness of others, and his own, so far as happiness is concerned, were a sheer deduction from the benefit. But the bare enunciation of such an absurdity as this last, renders refutation superfluous.

According to the Greatest Happiness Principle, as above explained, the ultimate end, with reference to and for the sake of which all other things are desirable (whether we are considering our own good or that of other people), is an existence exempt as far as possible from pain, and as rich as possible in enjoyments, both in point of quantity and quality; the test of quality, and the rule for measuring it against quantity, being the preference felt by those who in their opportunities of experience, to which must be added their habits of self-consciousness and self-observation, are best furnished with the means of comparison. This, being, according to the utilitarian opinion, the end of human action, is necessarily also the standard of morality; which may accordingly be defined, the rules and precepts for human conduct, by the observance of which an existence such as has been described might be, to the greatest extent possible, secured to all mankind; and not to them only, but, so far as the nature of things admits, to the whole sentient creation. . . .

The objectors to utilitarianism cannot always be charged with representing it in a discreditable light. On the contrary, those among them who entertain anything like a just idea of its disinterested character, sometimes find fault with its standard as being too high for humanity. They say it is exacting too much to require that people shall always act from the inducement of promoting the general interests of society. But this is to mistake the very meaning of a standard of morals, and confound the rule of action with the motive of it. It is the business of ethics to tell us what are our duties, or by what test we may know them; but no system of ethics requires that the sole motive of all we do shall be a feeling of duty; on the contrary, ninety-nine hundredths of all our actions are done from other motives, and rightly so done, if the rule of duty does not condemn them. It is the more unjust to utilitarianism than this particular misapprehension should be made a ground of objection to it, inasmuch as utilitarian moralists have gone beyond almost all others in affirming that the motive has nothing to do with the morality of the action, though much with the worth of the agent. He who saves a fellow-creature from drowning does what is morally right, whether his motive be duty, or the hope of being paid for his trouble; he who betrays the friend that trusts him, is guilty of a crime, even if his object be to serve another friend to whom he is under greater obligation. But to speak only of actions done from the motive of duty, and in direct obedience to principle: it is a misapprehension of the utilitarian mode of thought, to conceive it as implying that people should fix their minds upon so wide a generality as the world, or society at large. The great majority of good actions are intended not for the benefit of the world, but for that of individuals, of which the good of the world is made up; and the thoughts of the most virtuous man need not on these occasions travel beyond the particular persons concerned, except so far as is necessary to assure himself that in benefiting them he is not violating the rights, that is, the legitimate and authorized expectations, of anyone else. The multiplication of happiness is, according to the utilitarian ethics, the object of virtue: the occasions on which any person (except one in a thousand) has it in his power to do this on an extended scale, in other words to be a public benefactor, are but exceptional; and on these occasions alone is he called on to consider public utility; in every other case, private utility, the interest or happiness of some few persons, is all he has to attend to. Those alone the influence of whose actions extends to society in general, need concern themselves habitually about so large an object. In the case of abstinences indeed—of things which people forbear to do from moral considerations, though the consequences in the particular case might be beneficial—it would be unworthy of an intelligent agent not to be consciously aware that the action is of a class which, if practised generally, would be generally injurious, and that this is the ground of the obligation to abstain from it. The amount of regard for the public interest implied in this recognition, is no greater than is demanded by every system of morals, for they all enjoin to abstain from whatever is manifestly pernicious to society. . . .

Chapter IV
Of What Sort of Proof the Principle of Utility Is Susceptible

It has already been remarked, that questions of ultimate ends do not admit of proof, in the ordinary acceptation of the term. To be incapable of proof by reasoning is common to all first principles; to the first premises of our knowledge, as well as to those of our conduct. But the former, being matters of fact, may be the subject of a direct appeal to the faculties which judge of fact—namely, our senses, and our internal consciousness. Can an appeal be made to the same faculties on questions of practical ends? Or by what other faculty is cognisance taken of them?

Questions about ends are, in other words, questions about what things are desirable. The utilitarian doctrine is, that happiness is desirable, and the only thing desirable, as an end; all other things being desirable as means to that end. What ought to be required of this doctrine—what conditions is it requisite that the doctrine should fulfil—to make good its claim to be believed?

The only proof capable of being given that an object is visible, is that people actually see it. The only proof that a sound is audible, is that people hear it: and so of the other sources of our experience. In like manner, I apprehend, the sole evidence it is possible to produce that anything is desirable, is that people do actually desire it. If the end which the utilitarian doctrine proposes to itself were not, in theory and in practice, acknowledged to be an end, nothing could ever convince any person that it was so. No reason can be given why the general happiness is desirable, except that each person, so far as he believes it to be attainable, desires his own happiness. This, however, being a fact, we have not only all the proof which the case admits of, but all which it is possible to require, that happiness is a good: that each person's happiness is a good to that person, and the general happiness, therefore, a good to the aggregate of all persons. Happiness has made out its title as *one* of the ends of conduct, and consequently one of the criteria of morality.

But it has not, by this alone, proved itself to be the sole criterion. To do that, it would seem, by the same rule, necessary to show, not only that people desire happiness, but that they never desire anything else. . . .

We have now, then, an answer to the question, of what sort of proof the principle of utility is susceptible. If the opinion which I have now stated is psychologically true—if human nature is so constituted as to desire nothing which is not either a part of happiness or a means of happiness, we can have no other proof, and we require no other, that these are the only things desirable. If so, happiness is the sole end of human action, and the promotion of it the test by which to judge of all human conduct; from whence it necessarily follows that it must be the criterion of morality, since a part is included in the whole.

And now to decide whether this is really so; whether mankind do desire nothing for itself but that which is a pleasure to them, or of which the absence is a pain; we have evidently arrived at a question of fact and experience, dependent, like all similar questions, upon evidence. It can only be determined by practised self-consciousness and self-observation, assisted by observation of others. I believe that these sources of evidence, impartially consulted, will declare that desiring a thing and finding it pleasant, aversion to it and thinking of it as painful, are phenomena entirely inseparable, or rather two parts of the same phenomenon; in strictness of language, two different modes of naming the same psychological fact: that to think of an object as desirable (unless for the sake of its consequences), and to think of it as pleasant, are one and the same thing; and that to desire anything, except in proportion as the idea of it is pleasant, is a physical and metaphysical impossibility.

Study Questions

1. Utilitarianism has sometimes been called a "pig philosophy" because it emphasizes the quantity of pleasure as the single criterion for moral rightness. It is claimed that if pleasure is all we are after, why should we struggle for excellence and complex achievements since they usually cause suffering? How does Mill reply to such charges?

2. What, according to Mill, is a definition of happiness? Do you agree? Explain.

3. Imagine the following situation. In a small town with racial tensions, a black woman has been raped and left to die. Before she dies, she tells a group of friends that it was a middle-aged white man who raped and attacked her. Then she dies. She is the third black woman to die after being raped in the past month. A riot breaks out as a segment of the black community protests yet another violation of its rights. Soon, whites and blacks are killing each other. You are the mayor of the town and know that the rioting will cease if someone is punished for the rape and murder. You are able to frame a homeless, unemployed middle-aged man for the crime. You are pretty sure that no one will ever find out that you have framed him. Should you do it? What would a utilitarian do?

4. What are the overall merits and liabilities of deontological and utilitarian theories?

CHAPTER 3

Contractual Ethics

THOMAS HOBBES — *Amaterialist (matter + motion)* [handwritten]

Thomas Hobbes (1588–1679) is the greatest English political philosopher. He gave
classic expression to the idea that morality and politics arise out of a social contract.
Born in Gloucestershire during the approach of the Spanish Armada, he was the son
of a clergyman. Educated at Oxford University, he lived through an era of political
revolutions as a scholar and tutor (he was tutor to Charles II of England). He trav-
eled widely and was in communication with most of the intellectual luminaries of his
day, both on the Continent (Galileo, Gassendi, and Descartes) and in England
(Francis Bacon, Ben Jonson, and William Harvey), and was regarded as a brilliant, if
somewhat unorthodox and controversial, intellectual.

   Hobbes's masterpiece in political theory is the *Leviathan* (1651), a book that was
suppressed in his own day for its controversial ideas. In this book, from which our *time of civil unrest.* [handwritten]
selection is taken, he develops a moral and political theory based on psychological
egoism. Hobbes believed that we always act in our own self-interest, to obtain gratification and avoid harm. However, we cannot obtain any of the basic goods because
of the inherent fear and insecurity in an unregulated "state of nature," in which life
is "solitary, poor, nasty, brutish, and short." Because of this "war of every man
against every man," we cannot relax our guard. There is little time to build or cultivate the earth or enjoy life, since our neighbor may be plotting to undo us. In this
state of anarchy, the prudent person concludes that it really is in everyone's self-
interest to make a contract to sustain a minimal morality of respecting human life,
keeping covenants made, and obeying the laws of society. This minimal morality,
which Hobbes refers to as "the Laws of Nature" is nothing more than a set of maxims of prudence. To ensure that we all obey this covenant, Hobbes proposes a
strong sovereign state—the Leviathan—to impose severe penalties on those who
disobey the laws, for "covenants without the sword are but words."

Of the Natural Condition of Mankind as Concerning Their Felicity, and Misery

Men by Nature Are Equal

NATURE HATH MADE MEN so equal, in
the faculties of the body, and mind; so that
though there be found one man sometimes
manifestly stronger in body, or of quicker mind
than another; yet when all is reckoned together,
the difference between man, and man, is not so
considerable, as that one man can thereupon
claim to himself any benefit, to which another
may not pretend, as well as he. For as to the
strength of body, the weakest has strength
enough to kill the strongest, either by secret
machination, or by confederacy with others, that
are in the same danger with himself.

From Leviathan *(1651), edited by Louis P. Pojman.*

And as to the faculties of the mind, setting aside the arts grounded upon words, and especially that skill of proceeding upon general, and infallible rules, called science; which very few have, and but in few things; as being not a native faculty, born with us; nor attained, as prudence, while we look after somewhat else, I find yet a greater equality amongst men, than that of strength. For prudence, is but experience; which equal time, equally bestows on all men, in those things they equally apply themselves unto. That which may perhaps make such equality incredible, is but a vain conceit of one's own wisdom, which almost all men think they have in a greater degree, than the vulgar; that is, than all men but themselves, and a few others, whom by fame, or for concurring with themselves, they approve. For such is the nature of men, that howsoever they may acknowledge many others to be more witty, or more eloquent, or more learned; yet they will hardly believe there be many so wise as themselves; for they see their own wit at hand, and other men's at a distance. But this proveth rather that men are in that point equal, than unequal. For there is not ordinarily a greater sign of the equal distribution of any thing, than that every man is contented with his share.

From Equality Proceeds Fear

From this equality of ability, arises equality of hope in the attaining of our ends. And therefore if any two men desire the same thing, which nevertheless they cannot both enjoy, they become enemies; and in the way to their end, which is principally their own preservation, and sometimes their enjoyment only, endeavour to destroy, or subdue one another. And from hence it comes to pass, that where an invader hath no more to fear, than another man's single power; if one plant, sow, build, or possess a convenient seat, others may probably be expected to come prepared with forces united, to dispossess, and deprive him, not only of the fruit of his labour, but also of his life, or liberty. And the invader again is in the like danger of another.

From Fear Proceeds War

And from this fear of one another, there is no way for any man to secure himself, so reasonable, as anticipation; that is, by force, or wiles, to master the persons of all men he can, so long, till he see no other power great enough to endanger him: and this is no more than his own preservation requireth, and is generally allowed. Also because there be some, that taking pleasure in contemplating their own power in the acts of conquest, which they pursue farther than their security requires; if others, that otherwise would be glad to be at ease within modest bounds, should not by invasion increase their power, they would not be able, long time, by standing only on their defence, to subsist. And by consequence, such increase of dominion over men being necessary to a man's preservation, it ought to be allowed him.

Again, men have no pleasure, but on the contrary a great deal of grief, in keeping company, where there is no power able to over-awe them all. For every man desires that his companion should value him, at the same rate he sets upon himself: and upon all signs of contempt, or undervaluing, naturally endeavours, as far as he dares, (which amongst them that have no common power to keep them in quiet, is far enough to make them destroy each other), to extort a greater value from his contemners, by damage; and from others, by the example.

So that in the nature of man, we find three principal causes of quarrel. First, competition; secondly, fear; thirdly, glory.

The first, maketh men invade for gain; the second, for safety; and the third, for reputation. The first use violence, to make themselves masters of other men's persons, wives, children, and cattle; the second, to defend them; the third, for trifles, as a word, a smile, a different option, and any other sign of undervalue, either direct in their persons, or by reflection in their kindred, their friends, their nation, their profession, or their name.

Out of Civil States There Is Always War of Everyone Against Everyone

Hereby it is manifest, that during the time men live without a common power to keep them all in awe, they are in that condition which is called war; and such a war, as is of every man, against every man. For war consists not in battle only or the act of fighting; but in a tract of time, wherein the will to contend by battle is sufficiently known: and therefore the notion of *time,* is to be considered in the nature of war; as it is in the nature of weather. For as the nature of foul weather, lies not in the shower or two of rain; but in an inclination thereto of many days together: so the nature of war, consists not in actual fighting; but in the known disposition thereto, during all the time there is no assurance to the contrary. All other time is PEACE.

The Problems and Inconvenience of Such a War

Whatsoever therefore occurs in a time of war, where every man is enemy to every man; the same occurs in the time, wherein men live without other security, than what their own strength, and their own invention shall furnish them withal. In such condition, there is no place for industry; because the fruit thereof is uncertain: and consequently no culture of the earth; no navigation, nor use of the commodities that may be imported by sea; no commodious building; no instruments of moving, and removing, such things as require much force; no knowledge of the face of the earth; no account of time; no arts; no letters; no society; and which is worst of all, continual fear, and danger of violent death; and the life of man, solitary, poor, nasty, brutish, and short.

It may seem strange to some man, that has not well weighed these things; that nature should thus dissociate, and render men apt to invade, and destroy one another: and he may therefore, not trusting to this inference, made from the passions, desire perhaps to have the same confirmed by experience. Let him therefore consider with himself, when taking a journey, he arms himself, and seeks to go well accompanied; when going to sleep, he locks his doors; when even in his house he locks his chests; and this when he knows there be laws, and public officers, armed, to revenge all injuries shall be done him; what opinion he has of his fellow-subjects, when he rides armed; of his fellow citizens, when he locks his doors; and of his children, and servants, when he locks his chests. Does he not there as much accuse mankind by his actions, as I do by my words? But neither of us accuse man's nature in it. The desires, and other passions of man, are in themselves no sin. No more are the actions, that proceed from those passions, till they know a law that forbids them: which till laws be made they cannot know: nor can any law be made, till they have agreed upon the person that shall make it.

It may perhaps be thought, there was never such a time, nor condition of war as this; and I believe it was never generally so, over all the world: but there are many places, where they live so now. For the savage people in many places of America, except the government of small families, the concord whereof depends on natural lust, have no government at all; and live at this day in that brutish manner, as I said before. Howsoever, it may be perceived what manner of life there would be, where there were no common power to fear, by the manner of life, which men that have formerly lived under a peaceful government, use to degenerate into, in a civil war.

But though there had never been any time, wherein particular men were in a condition of war one against another; yet in all times, kings, and persons of sovereign authority, because of their independency, are in continual jealousies, and in the state and posture of gladiators; having their weapons pointing, and their eyes fixed on one another; that is, their forts, garrisons, and guns upon the frontiers of their kingdoms; and continual spies upon their neighbours; which is a posture of war. But because they uphold thereby, the industry of their subjects; there does not follow from it, that misery, which accompanies the liberty of particular men.

In This State of War Nothing Is Unjust

To this war of every man, against every man, this also is a result; that nothing can be unjust. The notions of right and wrong, justice and injustice have there no place. Where there is no common power, there is no law: where no law, no injustice. Force, and fraud, are in war the two cardinal virtues. Justice, and injustice are none of the faculties neither of the body, nor mind. If they were, they might be in a man that were alone in the world, as well as his senses, and passions. They are qualities, that relate to men in society, not in solitude. It is consequent also to the same condition, that there be no property, no ownership, no *mine* and *thine* distinct; but only that to be every man's, that he can get; and for so long, as he can keep it. And thus much for the ill condition, which man by mere nature is actually placed in; though with a possibility to come out of it, consisting partly in the passions, partly in his reason.

The Passions Which Incline Men to Peace

The passions that incline men to peace, are fear of death; desire of such things as are necessary to commodious living; and a hope by their industry to obtain them. And reason suggests convenient articles of peace, upon which men may be drawn to agreement. These articles, are they, which otherwise are called the Laws of Nature: whereof I shall speak more particularly, in the two following chapters.

Of the First and Second Natural Laws, and of Contracts

The Right of Nature

The right of nature, which writers commonly call *jus naturale*, is the liberty each man hath, to use his own power, as he will himself, for the preservation of his own nature; that is to say, of his own life; and consequently, of doing any thing, which in his own judgment, and reason, he shall conceive to be the best means thereunto.

Liberty

By LIBERTY, is understood, according to the proper signification of the word, the absence of external impediments: which impediments, may oft take away part of a man's power to do what he would; but cannot hinder him from using the power left him, according as his judgment, and reason shall dictate to him.

A Law of Nature

A LAW OF NATURE, *lex naturalis*, is a precept or general rule, found out by reason, by which a man is forbidden to do that, which is destructive of his life, or taketh away the means of preserving the same; and to omit that, by which he thinketh it may be best preserved. For though they that speak of this subject, use to confound *jus*, and *lex*, *right* and *law*; yet they ought to be distinguished; because RIGHT, consisteth in liberty to do, or to forbear; whereas law, determines, and binds to one of them: so that law, and right, differ as much, as obligation and liberty; which in one and the same matter are inconsistent.

In the State of Nature Every Man Has a Right to Everything

And because the condition of man, as has been shown in the precedent chapter, is a condition of war of every one against every one; in which case every one is governed by his own reason;

and there is nothing he can make use of, that may not be a help unto him, in preserving his life against his enemies; it followeth, that in such a condition, every man has a right to every thing; even to one another's body. And therefore, as long as this natural right of every man to every thing endures, there can be no security to any man, how strong or wise soever he be, of living out the time, which nature ordinarily alloweth men to live. And consequently it is a precept, or general rule of reason, *that every man, ought to endeavour peace, as far as he has hope of obtaining it; and when he cannot obtain it, that he may seek, and use, all helps, and advantages, of war.* The first branch of which rule, contains the first, and fundamental law of nature; which is, *to seek peace, and follow it.* The second, the sum of the right of nature; which is, *by all means we can, to defend ourselves.*

The Second Law of Nature

From this fundamental law of nature, by which men are commanded to endeavour peace, is derived this second law; *that a man be willing, when others are so too, as far-forth, as for peace, and defence of himself he shall think it necessary, to lay down this right to all things; and be contented with so much liberty against other men, as he would allow other men against himself.* For as long as every man holds this right, of doing any thing he likes, so long are all men in the condition of war. But if other men will not lay down their right, as well as he; then there is no reason for any one, to divest himself of his: for that were to expose himself to prey, which no man is bound to, rather than to dispose himself to peace. This is that law of the Gospel; *whatsoever you require that others should do to you, that do ye to them.* And that law of all men, "What you do not want done to you, do not do to others."

Giving Up a Right

To *lay down a man's right* to any thing, is to *divest* himself of the *liberty,* of hindering another of the benefit of his own right to the same. For he that renounces, or passes away his right, gives not to any other man a right which he had not before; because there is nothing to which every man had not right by nature: but only stands out of his way, that he may enjoy his own original right, without hindrance from him; not without hindrance from another. So that the effect which redounds to one man, by another man's defect of right, is but so much diminution of impediments to the use of his own right original.

Right is laid aside, either by simply renouncing it; or by transferring it to another. By *simply* RENOUNCING; when he cares not to whom the benefit thereof redounds. By TRANSFERRING; when he intends the benefit thereof to some certain person, or persons. And when a man has in either manner abandoned, or granted away his right; then is he said to be OBLIGED, or BOUND, not to hinder those, to whom such right is granted, or abandoned, from the benefit of it: and that he *ought,* and it is his DUTY, not to make void that voluntary act of his own: and that such hindrance is INJUSTICE, and INJURY, as being "without right," the right being before renounced, or transferred. So that *injury,* or *injustice,* in the controversies of the world, is somewhat like to that, which in the disputations of scholars is called *absurdity.* For as it is there called an absurdity, to contradict what one maintained in the beginning: so in the world, it is called injustice, and injury, voluntarily to undo that, which from the beginning he had voluntarily done. The way by which a man either simply renounces, or transfers his right, is a declaration, or signification, by some voluntary and sufficient sign, or signs, that he does so renounce, or transfer; or has so renounced, or transferred the same, to him that accepts it. And these signs are either words only, or actions only; or, as it happens most often, both words, and actions. And the same are the BONDS, by which men are bound, and obliged: bonds, that have their strength, not from their own nature, for nothing is more easily broken than a man's word, but from fear of some evil consequence upon the rupture.

Some Rights Are Inalienable

Whensoever a man transfers his right, or re-nounces it; it is either in consideration of some right reciprocally transferred to himself; or for some other good he hopes for thereby. For it is a voluntary act: and of the voluntary acts of every man, the object is some *good to himself.* And therefore there be some rights, which no man can be understood by any words, or other signs, to have abandoned, or transferred. At first a man cannot lay down the right of resisting them, that assault him by force, to take away his life; because he cannot be understood to aim thereby, at any good to himself. The same may be said of wounds, and chains, and imprisonment; both because no benefit proceeds from such patience; as there is to the patience of suffering another to be wounded, or imprisoned: as also because a man cannot tell, when he seeth men proceed against him by violence, whether they intend his death or not. And lastly the motive, and end for which this renouncing, and transferring of right is introduced, is nothing else but the security of a man's person, in his life, and in the means of so preserving life, as not to be weary of it. And therefore if a man by words, or other signs, seem to despoil himself of the end, for which those signs were intended; he is not to be understood as if he meant it, or that it was his will; but that he was ignorant of how such words and actions were to be interpreted.

The Contract

The mutual transferring of right, is that which men call CONTRACT.

There is a difference between transferring of right to the thing; and transferring, or tradition, that is delivery of the thing itself. For the thing may be delivered together with the translation of the right; as in buying and selling with ready money; or exchange of goods, or lands: and it may be delivered some time after.

The Covenant

Again, one of the contractors, may deliver the thing contracted for on his part, and leave the other to perform his part at some determinate time after, and in the meantime be trusted; and then the contract on his part, is called PACT, or COVENANT: or both parts may contract now, to perform hereafter: in which cases, he that is to perform in time to come, being trusted, his performance is called *keeping of promise,* or faith; and the failing of performance, if it be voluntary, *violation of faith.*

When the transferring of right, is not mutual: but one of the parties transferreth, in hope to gain thereby friendship, or service from another, or from his friends; or in hope to gain the reputation of charity, or magnanimity; or to deliver his mind from the pain of compassion; or in hope of reward in heaven, this is not contract, but GIFT, FREE-GIFT, GRACE: which words signify one and the same thing.

Signs of contract, are either *express,* or *by inference.* Express, are words spoken with understanding of what they signify: and such words are either of the time *present,* or *past;* as, *I give, I grant, I have given, I have granted, I will that this be yours:* or of the future; as, *I will give, I will grant:* which words of the future are called PROMISE.

When Covenant of Mutual Trust Become Invalid

If a covenant be made, wherein neither of the parties perform presently, but trust one another; in the condition of mere nature, which is a condition of war of every man against every man, upon any reasonable suspicion, it is void: but if there be a common power set over them both, with right and force sufficient to compel performance, it is not void. For he that performs first, has no assurance the other will perform after; because the bonds of words are too weak to bridle men's ambition, avarice, anger, and other passions, without the fear of some coercive power; which in the condition of mere nature, where all men are equal, and judges of the justness of their own fears, cannot possibly be supposed. And therefore he which performs first, does but betray himself to his enemy; contrary to the right, he can never abandon, of defending his life, and means of living.

But in a civil estate, where there is a power set up to constrain those that would otherwise violate their faith, that fear is no more reasonable: and for that cause, he which by the covenant is to perform first, is obliged so to do.

The cause of fear, which maketh such a covenant invalid, must be always something arising after the covenant made; as some new fact, or other sign of the will not to perform: else it cannot make the covenant void. For that which could not hinder a man from promising, ought not to be admitted as a hindrance of performing.

Of Other Laws of Nature

The Third Law of Nature: Justice

From that law of nature, by which we are obliged to transfer to another, such rights, as being retained, hinder the peace of mankind, there followeth a third; which is this, *that men perform their covenants made:* without which, covenants are in vain, and but empty words; and the right of all men to all things remaining, we are still in the condition of war.

And in this law of nature, consists the fountain and origin of JUSTICE. For where no covenant has preceded, there has no right been transferred, and every man has right to every thing; and consequently, no action can be unjust. But when a covenant is made, then to break it is *unjust:* and the definition of INJUSTICE, is no other than *the not performance of covenant.* And whatsoever is not unjust, is *just.*

Justice and Injustice Come into Being with the Creation of the Commonwealth

But because covenants of mutual trust, where there is a fear of not performance on either part, as hath been said in the former chapter, are invalid; though the origin of justice be the making of covenants; yet injustice actually there can be none, till the cause of such fear be taken away; which while men are in the natural condition of war, cannot be done. Therefore before the names of just, and unjust can have place, there must be some coercive power, to compel men equally to the performance of their covenants, by the terror of some punishment, greater than the benefit they expect by the breach of their covenant; and to make good that propriety, which by mutual contract men acquire, in recompense of the universal right they abandon: and such power there is none before the erection of a commonwealth. And this is also to be gathered out of the ordinary definition of justice in the Schools: for they say, that *justice is the constant will of giving to every man his own,* and therefore where there is no *own,* that is, no property, there is no injustice; and where there is no coercive power erected, that is, where there is no commonwealth, there is no property; all men having right to all things: therefore where there is no commonwealth, there nothing is unjust. So that the nature of justice, consists in keeping of valid covenants: but the validity of covenants begins not but with the constitution of a civil power, sufficient to compel men to keep them: and then it is also that property begins. . . .

On the Duty to Submit to Arbitration

And because, though men be never so willing to observe these laws, there may nevertheless arise questions concerning a man's action; first, whether it were done, or not done; secondly, if done, whether against the law, or not against the law; the former whereof, is called a question of fact; the latter a question of right, therefore unless the parties to the question, covenant mutually to stand to the sentence of another, they are as far from peace as ever. This other to whose sentence they submit is called an ARBITRATOR. And therefore it is of the law of nature, *that they that are at controversy, submit their right to the judgment of an arbitrator.*

And seeing every man is presumed to do all things in order to his own benefit, no man is a fit arbitrator in his own cause; and if he were never so fit; yet equity allowing to each party equal benefit, if one be admitted to the judge, the other is to be admitted also; and so the controversy, that is, the cause of war, remains, against the law of nature.

For the same reason no man in any cause ought to be received for arbitrator, to whom greater profit, or honour, or pleasure apparently ariseth out of the victory of one party, than of the other: for he hath taken, though an unavoidable bribe, yet a bribe; and no man can be obliged to trust him. And thus also the controversy, and the condition of war remaineth, contrary to the law of nature.

And in a controversy of *fact*, the judge being to give no more credit to one, than to the other, if there be no other arguments, must give credit to a third; or to a third and fourth; or more: for else the question is undecided, and left to force, contrary to the law of nature.

These are the laws of nature, dictating peace, for a means of the conservation of men in multitudes; and which only concern the doctrine of civil society. There be other things tending to the destruction of particular men; as drunkenness, and all other parts of intemperance; which may therefore also be reckoned amongst those things which the law of nature hath forbidden; but are not necessary to be mentioned, nor are pertinent enough to this place.

A Rule by Which the Laws of Nature May Be Examined

And though this may seem too subtle a deduction of the laws of nature, to be taken notice of

by all men; whereof the most part are too busy getting food, and the rest too negligent to understand; yet to leave all men inexcusable, they have been contracted into one easy sum, intelligible even to the meanest capacity; and that is, *Do not that to another, which thou wouldest not have done to thyself;* which shows him that he has no more to do in learning the laws of nature, but, when weighing the actions of other men with his own, they seem too heavy, to put them into the other part of the balance, and his own into their place, that his own passions, and self-love, may add nothing to the weight; and then there is none of these laws of nature that will not appear unto him very reasonable.

The Laws of Nature Oblige in Conscience Always, but in Effect Only When There Is Security

The laws of nature oblige *in foro interno*;[1] that is to say, they bind to a desire they should take place: but *in foro externo*,[2] that is, to the putting them in act, not always. For he that should be modest, and tractable, and perform all he promises, in such time, and place, where no man else should do so, should but make himself a prey to others, and procure his own certain ruin, contrary to the ground of all laws of nature, which tend to nature's preservation. And again, he that having sufficient security, that others shall observe the same laws towards him, observes them not himself, seeketh not peace, but war; and consequently the destruction of his nature by violence.

And whatsoever laws bind *in foro interno*, may be broken, not only by a fact contrary to the law, but also by a fact according to it, in case a man think it contrary. For though his action in this case, be according to the law; yet his purpose was against the law; which, where the obligation is *in foro interno*, is a breach.

The Laws of Nature Are Eternal

The laws of nature are immutable and eternal; for injustice, ingratitude, arrogance, pride, iniquity, acception of persons, and the rest, can never be made lawful. For it can never be that war shall preserve life, and peace destroy it.

The same laws, because they oblige only to a desire, and endeavour, I mean an unfeigned and constant endeavour, are easy to be observed. For in that they require nothing but endeavour, he that endeavoureth their performance, fulfilleth them; and he that fulfilleth the law, is just.

The Science of These Laws Is the True Moral Philosophy

And the science of them, is the true and only moral philosophy. For moral philosophy is nothing else but the science of what is *good*, and *evil*, in the conversation, and society of mankind. *Good*, and *evil*, are names that signify our appetites, and aversions; which in different tempers, customs, and doctrines of men, are different: and divers men, differ not only in their judgment, on the sense of what is pleasant, and unpleasant to the taste, smell, hearing, touch, and sight; but also of what is conformable, or disagreeable to reason, in the actions of common life. Nay, the same man, in divers times, differs from himself; and one time praises, that is, calls good, what another time he dispraises, and calls evil: from whence arise disputes, controversies, and at last war. And therefore so long as a man is in the condition of mere nature, which is a condition of war, as private appetite is the measure of good, and evil: and consequently all men agree on this, that peace is good, and therefore also the way, or means of peace, which, as I have showed before, are *justice, gratitude, modesty, equity, mercy,* and the rest of the laws of nature, are good; that is to say; *moral virtues;* and their contrary *vices,* evil. Now the science of virtue and vice, is moral philosophy; and therefore the true doctrine of the laws of nature, is the true moral philosophy. But the writers of moral philosophy, though they acknowledge the same virtues and vices; yet not seeing wherein consisted their goodness; nor that they come to be praised, as the means of peaceable, sociable, and

comfortable living, place them in a mediocrity of passions: as if not the cause, but the degree of daring, made fortitude; or not the cause, but the quantity of a gift, made liberality.

These dictates of reason, men used to call by the name of laws, but improperly: for they are but conclusions, of theorems concerning what conduces to the conservation and defence of themselves; whereas law, properly, is the word of him, that by right hath command over others. But yet if we consider the same theorems, as delivered in the word of God, that by right commandeth all things; then are they properly called laws.

Of the Causes, Generation, and Definition of a Commonwealth

The final cause, end, or design of men, who naturally love liberty, and dominion over others, in the introduction of that restraint upon themselves, in which we see them live in commonwealths, is the foresight of their own preservation, and of a more contented life thereby; that is to say, of getting themselves out from that miserable condition of war, which is necessarily consequent, as has been shown, to the natural passions of men, when there is no visible power to keep them in awe, and tie them by fear of punishment to the performance of their covenants, and observation of those laws of nature set down in the fourteenth and fifteenth chapters.

For the laws of nature, as *justice, equity, modesty, mercy,* and, in sum, *doing to others, as we would be done to,* of themselves, without the terror of some power, to cause them to be observed, are contrary to our natural passions, that carry us to partiality, pride, revenge, and the like. And covenants, without the sword, are but words, and of no strength to secure a man at all. Therefore notwithstanding the laws of nature, which every one hath then kept, when he has the will to keep them, when he can do it safely, if there be no power erected, or not great enough for our security; every man will, and may lawfully rely on his own strength and art, for caution against all other men. And in all places, where men have lived by small families, to rob and spoil one another, has been a trade, and so far from being reputed against the law of nature, that the greater spoils they gained, the greater was their honour; and men observed no other laws therein, but the laws of honour; that is, to abstain from cruelty, leaving to men their lives, and instruments of husbandry. And as small families did then; so now do cities and kingdoms which are but greater families, for their own security, enlarge their dominions, upon all pretences of danger, and fear of invasion, or assistance that may be given to invaders, and endeavour as much as they can, to subdue, or weaken their neighbours, by open force, and secret arts, for want of other caution, justly; and are remembered for it in after ages with honour.

Why Certain Creatures Without Reason or Speech Do Nevertheless Live in Society Without Any Coercive Power

It is true, that certain living creatures, as bees, and ants, live sociably one with another, which are therefore by Aristotle numbered amongst political creatures; and yet have no other direction, than their particular judgments and appetites; nor speech, whereby one of them can signify to another, what he thinks expedient for the common benefit: and therefore some man may perhaps desire to know, why mankind cannot do the same. To which I answer,

First, that men are continually in competition for honour and dignity, which these creatures are not; and consequently among men there arises on that ground, envy and hatred, and finally war; but amongst these are not so.

Secondly, that among these creatures, the common good differs not from the private; and being by nature inclined to their private, they procure thereby the common benefit. But man, whose joy consists in comparing himself with other men, can relish nothing but what is eminent.

Thirdly, that these creatures, having not, as man, the use of reason, do not see, nor think they see any fault, in the administration of their common business; whereas among men, there are very many, that think themselves wiser, and abler to govern the public, better than the rest; and these strive to reform and innovate, one this way, another that way; and thereby bring it into distraction and civil war.

Fourthly, that these creatures, though they have some use of voice, in making known to one another their desires, and other affections; yet they want that art of words, by which some men can represent to others, that which is good, in the likeness of evil; and evil, in the likeness of good; and augment, or diminish the apparent greatness of good and evil; discontenting men, and troubling their peace at their pleasure.

Fifthly, irrational creatures cannot distinguish between *injury*, and *damage;* and therefore as long as they be at ease, they are not offended with their fellows: whereas man is then most troublesome, when he is most at ease: for then it is that he loves to shew his wisdom, and control the actions of them that govern the commonwealth.

Lastly, the agreement of these creatures is natural; that of men, is by covenant only, which is artificial: and therefore it is no wonder if there be somewhat else required, besides covenant, to make their agreement constant and lasting; which is a common power, to keep them in awe, and to direct their actions to the common benefit.

The only way to erect such a common power, as may be able to defend them from the invasion of foreigners, and the injuries of one another, and thereby to secure them in such sort, as that by their own industry, and by the fruits of the earth, they may nourish themselves and live contentedly; is, to confer all their power and strength upon one man, or upon one assembly of men, that may reduce all their wills, by plurality of voices, unto one will: which is as much as to say, to appoint one man, or assembly of men, to bear their person; and every one to own, and acknowledge himself to be author of whatsoever he that so beareth their person, shall act, or cause to be acted, in those things which concern the common peace and safety; and therein to submit their wills, every one to his will, and their judgments, to his judgment. This is more than consent, or concord; it is a real unity of them all, in one and the same person, made by covenant of every man with every man, in such manner, as if every man should say to every man, *I authorize and give up my right of governing myself, to this man, or to this assembly of men, on this condition, that thou give up thy right to him, and authorize all his actions in like manner.* This done, the multitude so united in one person, is called a COMMONWEALTH, in Latin CIVITAS. This is the generation of that great LEVIATHAN, or rather, to speak more reverently, of that *mortal god,* to which we owe under the *immortal God,* our peace and defence. For by this authority, given

him by every particular man in the commonwealth, he hath the use of so much power and strength conferred on him, that by terror thereof, he is enabled to perform the wills of them all, to peace at home, and mutual aid against their enemies abroad. And in him consisteth the essence of the commonwealth; which, to define it, is *one person, of whose acts a great multitude, by mutual covenants one with another, have made themselves every one the author, to the end he may use the strength and means of them all, as he shall think expedient, for their peace and common defence.*

And he that carrieth this person, is called SOVEREIGN, and said to have *sovereign* power; and every one besides, his SUBJECT.

Notes

1. Literally, "in the internal forum," that is, in a person's mind or conscience.—ED. note.

2. Literally, "in the external forum," that is, in the public world of action.—ED. note.

Study Questions

1. What does Hobbes mean by a "state of nature"? Can you think of situations in real life or in novels that approximate the state of nature? Does morality exist in the state of nature?

2. Describe Hobbes's view of human nature. Are people as egoistic as he describes them? Explain.

3. What is the Leviathan? Is it a plausible solution to the needs of human beings?

4. One adaptation of contractual ethics is found in the view of reciprocal altruism, or tit-for-tat morality. This ancient theory, found in the first book of Plato's *Republic*, states that we ought to help our friends and harm our enemies. The rule of this morality might be called the Brazen Rule (versus the Golden Rule). It states, "Do unto Others as they do unto you." Contrary to Jesus' "Sermon on the Mount" (Matthew, chap. 5), we ought not love our enemies or forgive those who harm us and are unrepentant. Compare tit-for-tat morality with Kant's deontological ethics and with utilitarianism.

CHAPTER 4

Custom Is King

HERODOTUS

Herodotus (485–430 B.C.E.), the Greek historian, is known as the father of history. In this brief passage from his *Histories,* he illustrates *cultural relativism,* the notion that different cultures have different moral ideas. Cultural relativism is not to be confused with *ethical relativism,* the view that moral principles derive their validity from cultural approval; cultural relativism is only the descriptive claim that different societies have different moral principles. Cultural relativism is not a claim about the validity of principles, only about their variety. But Herodotus believes that culture is very powerful. Indeed, "Custom is the king o'er all." Does that mean that he is also an ethical relativist?

THUS IT APPEARS CERTAIN TO ME, by a great variety of proofs, that Cambyses was raving mad; he would not else have set himself to make a mock of holy rites and long-established usages. For if one were to offer men to choose out of all the customs in the world such as seemed to them the best, they would examine the whole number, and end by preferring their own; so convinced are they that their own usages far surpass those of all others. Unless, therefore, a man was mad, it is not likely that he would make sport of such matters. That people have this feeling about their laws may be seen by very many proofs: among others, by the following. Darius, after he had got the kingdom, called into his presence certain Greeks who were at hand, and asked—"What he should pay them to eat the bodies of their fathers when they died?" To which they answered, that there was no sum that would tempt them to do such a thing. He then sent for certain Indians, of the race called Callatians, men who eat their fathers, and asked them, while the Greeks stood by, and knew by the help of an interpreter all that was said— "What he should give them to burn the bodies of their fathers at their decease?" The Indians exclaimed aloud, and bade him forbear such language. Such is men's wont herein; and Pindar was right, in my judgment, when he said, "Custom is the king o'er all."

Study Question

1. Do you agree with Herodotus that "Custom is the king o'er all?" Explain.

Herodotus, The Histories of Herodotus, *translated by George Rawlinson (New York: Appleton, 1859).*

CHAPTER 5

A Defense of Ethical Relativism

RUTH BENEDICT

Ruth Benedict (1887–1948), a foremost American anthropologist, taught at Columbia University, and she is best known for her book *Patterns of Culture* (1935). Benedict views social systems as communities with common beliefs and practices that have become integrated patterns of ideas and practices. Like a work of art, a culture chooses which theme from its repertoire of basic tendencies to emphasize and then produces a grand design, favoring those tendencies. The final systems differ from one another in striking ways, but we have no reason to say that one system is better than another. Once a society has made the choice, normalcy will look different, depending on the idea–practice pattern of the culture.

Benedict views morality as dependent on the varying histories and environments of different cultures. In this essay she assembles an impressive amount of data from her anthropological research of tribal behavior on an island in northwest Melanesia from which she draws her conclusion that moral relativism is the correct view of moral principles.

comparative anthropology

MODERN SOCIAL ANTHROPOLOGY has become more and more a study of the varieties and common elements of cultural environment and the consequences of these in human behavior. For such a study of diverse social orders primitive peoples fortunately provide a laboratory not yet entirely vitiated by the spread of a standardized worldwide civilization. Dyaks and Hopis, Fijians and Yakuts are significant for psychological and sociological study because only among these simpler peoples has there been sufficient isolation to give opportunity for the development of localized social forms. In the higher cultures the standardization of custom and belief over a couple of continents has given a false sense of the inevitability of the particular forms that have gained currency, and we need to turn to a wider survey in order to check the conclusions we hastily base upon this near-universality of familiar customs. Most of the simpler cultures did not gain the wide currency of the one which, out of our experience, we identify with human nature, but this was for various historical reasons, and certainly not for any that gives us as its carriers a monopoly of social good or of social sanity. Modern civilization, from this point of view, becomes not a necessary pinnacle of human achievement but one entry in a long series of possible adjustments.

These adjustments, whether they are in mannerisms like the ways of showing anger, or joy, or grief in any society, or in major human drives like those of sex, prove to be far more variable than experience in any one culture would suggest. In

From Ruth Benedict, "Anthropology and the Abnormal," Journal of General Psychology, *10, 1934.*
Reprinted with permission of the Helen Dwight Reid Educational Foundation. Published by Heldref
Publications, 4000 Albemarle St., N.W., Washington, D.C. 20016. Copyright © 1934.

certain fields, such as that of religion or of formal marriage arrangements, these wide limits of variability are well known and can be fairly described. In others it is not yet possible to give a generalized account, but that does not absolve us of the task of indicating the significance of the work that has been done and of the problems that have arisen.

One of these problems relates to the customary modern normal-abnormal categories and our conclusions regarding them. In how far are such categories culturally determined, or in how far can we with assurance regard them as absolute? In how far can we regard inability to function socially as diagnostic of abnormality, or in how far is it necessary to regard this as a function of the culture?

As a matter of fact, one of the most striking facts that emerge from a study of widely varying cultures is the ease with which our abnormals function in other cultures. It does not matter what kind of "abnormality" we choose for illustration, those which indicate extreme instability, or those which are more in the nature of character traits like sadism or delusions of grandeur or of persecution, there are well-described cultures in which these abnormals function at ease and with honor, and apparently without danger or difficulty to the society.

The most notorious of these is trance and catalepsy. Even a very mild mystic is aberrant in our culture. But most peoples have regarded even extreme psychic manifestations not only as normal and desirable, but even as characteristic of highly valued and gifted individuals. This was true even in our own cultural background in that period when Catholicism made the ecstatic experience the mark of sainthood. It is hard for us, born and brought up in a culture that makes no use of the experience, to realize how important a role it may play and how many individuals are capable of it, once it has been given an honorable place in any society. . . .

Cataleptic and trance phenomena are, of course, only one illustration of the fact that those whom we regard as abnormals may function adequately in other cultures. Many of our culturally discarded traits are selected for elaboration in different societies. Homosexuality is an excellent example, for in this case our attention is not constantly diverted, as in the consideration of trance, to the interruption of routine activity which it implies. Homosexuality poses the problem very simply. A tendency toward this trait in our culture exposes an individual to all the conflicts to which all aberrants are always exposed, and we tend to identify the consequences of this conflict with homosexuality. But these consequences are obviously local and cultural. Homosexuals in many societies are not incompetent, but they may be such if the culture asks adjustments of them that would strain any man's vitality. Wherever homosexuality has been given an honorable place in any society, those to whom it is congenial have filled adequately the honorable roles society assigns to them. Plato's *Republic* is, of course, the most convincing statement of such a reading of homosexuality. It is presented as one of the major means to the good life, and it was generally so regarded in Greece at that time.

The cultural attitude toward homosexuals has not always been on such a high ethical plane, but it has been very varied. Among many American Indian tribes there exists the institution of the berdache, as the French called them. These men-women were men who at puberty or thereafter took the dress and the occupations of women. Sometimes they married other men and lived with them. Sometimes they were men with no inversion, persons of weak sexual endowment who chose this role to avoid the jeers of the women. The berdaches were never regarded as of first-rate supernatural power, as similar men-women were in Siberia, but rather as leaders in women's occupations, good healers in certain diseases, or, among certain tribes, as the genial organizers of social affairs. In any case, they were socially placed. They were not left exposed to the conflicts that visit the deviant who is excluded from participation in the recognized patterns of his society.

The most spectacular illustrations of the extent to which normality may be culturally defined are those cultures where an abnormality of our culture is the cornerstone of their social structure. It is not possible to do justice to these possibilities in a short discussion. A recent study of an island of northwest Melanesia by *Fortune* describes a society built upon traits which we regard as beyond the border of paranoia. In this tribe the exogamic groups look upon each other as prime manipulators of black magic, so that one marries always into an enemy group which remains for life one's deadly and unappeasable foes. They look upon a good garden crop as a confession of theft, for everyone is engaged in making magic to induce into his garden the productiveness of his neighbors'; therefore no secrecy in the island is so rigidly insisted upon as the secrecy of a man's harvesting of his yams. Their polite phrase at the acceptance of a gift is, "And if you now poison me, how shall I repay you this present?" Their preoccupation with poisoning is constant; no woman ever leaves her cooking pot for a moment unattended. Even the great affinal economic exchanges that are characteristic of this Melanesian culture area are quite altered in Dobu since they are incompatible with this fear and distrust that pervades the culture. They go farther and people the whole world outside their own quarters with such malignant spirits that all-night feasts and ceremonials simply do not occur here. They have even rigorous religiously enforced customs that forbid the sharing of seed even in one's family group. Anyone else's food is deadly poison to you, so that communality of stores is out of the question. For some months before harvest the whole society is on the verge of starvation, but if one falls to the temptation and eats up one's seed yams, one is an outcast and a beachcomber for life. There is no coming back. It involves, as a matter of course, divorce and the breaking of all social ties.

Now in this society where no one may work with another and no one may share with another, *Fortune* describes the individual who was regarded by all his fellows as crazy. He was not one of those who periodically ran amok and, beside himself and frothing at the mouth, fell with a knife upon anyone he could reach. Such behavior they did not regard as putting anyone outside the pale. They did not even put the individuals who were known to be liable to these attacks under any kind of control. They merely fled when they saw the attack coming on and kept out of the way. "He would be all right tomorrow." But there was one man of sunny, kindly disposition who liked work and liked to be helpful. The compulsion was too strong for him to repress it in favor of the opposite tendencies of his culture. Men and women never spoke of him without laughing; he was silly and simple and definitely crazy. Nevertheless, to the ethnologist used to a culture that has, in Christianity, made his type the model of all virtue, he seemed a pleasant fellow. . . .

. . . Among the Kwakiutl it did not matter whether a relative had died in bed of disease, or by the hand of an enemy, in either case death was an affront to be wiped out by the death of another person. The fact that one had been caused to mourn was proof that one had been put upon. A chief's sister and her daughter had gone up to Victoria, and either because they drank bad whiskey or because their boat capsized they never came back. The chief called together his warriors, "Now I ask you, tribes, who shall wail? Shall I do it or shall another?" The spokesman answered, of course, "Not you, Chief. Let some other of the tribes." Immediately they set up the war pole to announce their intention of wiping out the injury, and gathered a war party. They set out, and found seven men and two children asleep and killed them. "Then they felt good when they arrived at Sebaa in the evening."

The point which is of interest to us is that in our society those who on that occasion would feel good when they arrived at Sebaa that evening would be the definitely abnormal. There would be some, even in our society, but it is not a recognized and approved mood under the circumstances. On the Northwest Coast those are favored and fortunate to whom that mood under those circumstances is congenial, and those to whom it is repugnant are unlucky. This latter minority can register in their own culture only by doing violence to their congenial responses and acquiring others that are difficult for them. The person, for instance, who, like a Plains Indian whose wife has been taken from him, is too proud to fight, can deal with the Northwest Coast civilization only by ignoring its strongest bents. If he cannot achieve it, he is the deviant in that culture, their instance of abnormality.

This head-hunting that takes place on the Northwest Coast after a death is no matter of blood revenge or of organized vengeance. There is no effort to tie up the subsequent killing with any responsibility on the part of the victim for the death of the person who is being mourned. A chief whose son has died goes visiting wherever his fancy dictates, and he says to his host, "My prince has died today, and you go with him." Then he kills him. In this, according to their interpretation, he acts nobly because he has not been downed. He has thrust back in return. The whole procedure is meaningless without the fundamental paranoid reading of bereavement. Death, like all the other untoward accidents of existence, confounds man's pride and can only be handled in the category of insults.

The behavior honored upon the Northwest Coast is one which is recognized as abnormal in our civilization, and yet it is sufficiently close to the attitudes of our own culture to be intelligible to us and to have a definite vocabulary with which we may discuss it. The megalomaniac paranoid trend is a definite danger in our society. It is encouraged by some of our major preoccupations, and it confronts us with a choice of two possible attitudes. One is to brand it as abnormal and reprehensible, and is the attitude we have chosen in our civilization. The other is to make it an essential attribute of ideal man, and this is the solution in the culture of the Northwest Coast.

These illustrations, which it has been possible to indicate only in the briefest manner, force upon us the fact that normality is culturally defined. An adult shaped to the drives and standards of either of these cultures, if he were transported into our civilization, would fall into our categories of abnormality. He would be faced with the psychic dilemmas of the socially unavailable. In his own culture, however, he is the pillar of society, the end result of socially inculcated mores, and the problem of personal instability in his case simply does not arise.

No one civilization can possibly utilize in its mores the whole potential range of human behavior. Just as there are great numbers of possible phonetic articulations, and the possibility of language depends on a selection and standardization of a few of these in order that speech communication may be possible at all, so the possibility of organized behavior of every sort, from the fashions of local dress and houses to the dicta of a people's ethics and religion, depends upon a similar selection among the possible behavior traits. In the field of recognized economic obligations or sex tabus this selection is as nonrational and subconscious a process as it is in the field of phonetics. It is a process which goes on in the group for long periods of time and is historically conditioned by innumerable accidents of isolation or of contact of peoples. In any comprehensive study of psychology, the selection that different cultures have made in the course of history within the great circumference of potential behavior is of great significance.

Every society, beginning with some slight inclination in one direction or another, carries its preference farther and farther, integrating itself more and more completely upon its chosen basis, and discarding those types of behavior that are uncongenial. Most of those organizations of personality that seem to us most uncontrovertibly abnormal have been used by different civilizations in the very foundations of their institutional life. Conversely the most valued traits of our normal individuals have been looked on in differently organized cultures as aberrant. Normality, in short, within a very wide range, is culturally defined. It is primarily a term for the socially elaborated segment of human behavior in any culture; and abnormality, a term for the segment that particular civilization does not use. The very eyes with which we see the problem are conditioned by the long traditional habits of our own society.

It is a point that has been made more often in relation to ethics than in relation to psychiatry. We do not any longer make the mistake of deriving the morality of our locality and decade directly from the inevitable constitution of human nature. We do not elevate it to the dignity of a first principle. We recognize that morality differs in every society, and is a convenient term for socially approved habits. Mankind has always preferred to say, "It is a morally good," rather than "It is habitual," and the fact of this preference is matter enough for a critical science of ethics. But historically the two phrases are synonymous.

The concept of the normal is properly a variant of the concept of the good. It is that which society has approved. A normal action is one which falls well within the limits of expected behavior for a particular society. Its variability among different peoples is essentially a function of the variability of the behavior patterns that different societies have created for themselves, and can never be wholly divorced from a consideration of culturally institutionalized types of behavior.

Each culture is a more or less elaborate working-out of the potentialities of the segment it has chosen. In so far as a civilization is well integrated and consistent within itself, it will tend to carry farther and farther, according to its nature, its initial impulse toward a particular type of action, and from the point of view of any other culture those elaborations will include more and more extreme and aberrant traits.

Each of these traits, in proportion as it reinforces the chosen behavior patterns of that culture, is for that culture normal. Those individuals to whom it is congenial either congenitally, or as the result of childhood sets, are accorded prestige in that culture, and are not visited with the social contempt or disapproval which their traits would call down upon them in a society that was differently organized. On the other hand, those individuals whose characteristics are not congenial to the selected type of human behavior in that community are the deviants, no matter how valued their personality traits may be in a contrasted civilization.

The Dobuan who is not easily susceptible to fear of treachery, who enjoys work and likes to be helpful, is their neurotic and regarded as silly. On the Northwest Coast the person who finds it difficult to read life in terms of an insult contest will be the person upon whom fall all the difficulties of the culturally unprovided for. The person who does not find it easy to humiliate a neighbor, nor to see humiliation in his own experience, who is genial and loving, may, of course, find some unstandardized way of achieving satisfactions in his society, but not in the major patterned responses that his culture requires of him. If he is born to play an important role in a family with many hereditary privileges, he can succeed only by doing violence to his whole personality. If he does not succeed, he has betrayed his culture; that is, he is abnormal.

I have spoken of individuals as having sets toward certain types of behavior, and of these sets as running sometimes counter to the types of behavior which are institutionalized in the culture to which they belong. From all that we know of contrasting cultures it seems clear that differences of temperament occur in every society. The matter has never been made the subject of investigation, but from the available material it would appear that these temperament types are very likely of universal recurrence. That is, there is an ascertainable range of human behavior that is found wherever a sufficiently large series of individuals is observed. But the proportion in which behavior types stand to one another in different societies is not universal. The vast majority of individuals in any group are shaped to the fashion of that culture. In other words, most individuals are plastic to the moulding force of the society into which they are born. In a society that values trance, as in India, they will have supernormal experience. In a society that institutionalizes homosexuality, they will be homosexual. In a society that sets the gathering of possessions as the chief human objective, they will amass property. The deviants, whatever the type of behavior the culture has institutionalized, will remain few in number, and there seems no more difficulty in moulding the vast malleable majority to the "normality" of what we consider an aberrant trait, such as delusions of reference, than to the normality of such accepted behavior patterns as acquisitiveness. The small proportion of the number of the deviants in any culture is not a function of the sure instinct with which that society has built itself upon the fundamental sanities, but of the universal fact that, happily, the majority of mankind quite readily take any shape that is presented to them.

Study Questions

1. What is Benedict's view about normalcy and abnormalcy? How does it relate to ethics?
2. What is Benedict's view of morality? What is the significance of her final comments on the range of human behavioral tendencies? What does she mean by the phrase "the proportion in which behavior types stand to one another in different societies is not universal"?
3. According to Benedict's theory, how should we regard the reformer who is in the minority in a given culture; e.g., Socrates, Jesus, the abolitionist in a society that approves of slavery, the prophet who rails against an injustice that the majority approves of?

CHAPTER 6

A Defense of Ethical Objectivism

LOUIS P. POJMAN

I am a professor of philosophy at the United States Military Academy and the author of several books and articles in the areas of philosophy of religion and ethics, including *Ethics: Discovering Right and Wrong* (1999), from which this selection is taken. I am also the editor of this volume.

In the following essay I first analyze the structure of ethical relativism as constituted by two theses: the diversity thesis and the dependency thesis. I then examine two types of ethical relativism: subjectivism and conventionalism, both of which are beset by serious problems. I indicate a way of taking into account the insights of relativism while maintaining an objectivist position, and I end the essay by offering suggestions about why people have been misled by relativist arguments.

THERE IS ONE THING a professor can be absolutely certain of: almost every student entering the university believes, or says he believes, that truth is relative. If this belief is put to the test, one can count on the students' reaction: they will be uncomprehending. That anyone should regard the proposition as not self-evident astonishes them, as though he were calling into question 2 + 2 = 4. . . . The danger they have been taught to fear from absolutism is not error but intolerance. Relativism is necessary to openness; and this is the virtue, the only virtue, which all primary education for more than fifty years has dedicated itself to inculcating.

ALAN BLOOM, *The Closing of the American Mind*

IN THE NINETEENTH CENTURY, Christian missionaries sometimes used coercion to change the customs of pagan tribal people in parts of Africa and the Pacific Islands. Appalled by the customs of public nakedness, polygamy, working on the Sabbath, and infanticide, they paternalistically went about reforming the "poor pagans." They clothed the people, separated secondary wives from their polygamous husbands in order to create monogamous households, made the Sabbath a day of rest, and put an end to infanticide. In the process, they sometimes created social malaise, causing the estranged women to despair and their children to be orphaned. The

Adapted from Chapter 2 of Ethics: Discovering Right and Wrong *(Belmont, Calif.: Wadsworth, 1999). Copyright © Louis P. Pojman, 1999.*

natives often did not understand the new religion, but accepted it in deference to white power. The white people had guns and medicine.

Since the nineteenth century, we've made progress in understanding cultural diversity and realize that the social dissonance caused by do-gooders was a bad thing. In the last century or so, anthropology has exposed our penchant for ethnocentrism—the prejudicial view that interprets all reality through the eyes of our cultural beliefs and values. We have come to see enormous variety in social practices throughout the world.

Some Eskimo tribes allow their elderly to die by starvation, while we believe that this is morally wrong. The Spartans of ancient Greece and Dobu of New Guinea believe that stealing is morally right, but we believe it is wrong. Many cultures, past and present, have practiced or still practice infanticide. A tribe in East Africa once threw deformed infants to the hippopotamus, but our society condemns such acts. Sexual practices vary over time and clime. Some cultures permit, while others condemn homosexual behavior. Some cultures, including Moslem societies, practice polygamy, while Christian cultures view it as immoral. Ruth Benedict describes a tribe in Melanesia that views cooperation and kindness as vices, and Colin Turnbull has documented that the Ik in northern Uganda have no sense of duty toward their children or parents. There are societies that make it a duty for children to kill (sometimes by strangling) their aging parents.

The ancient Greek historian, Herodotus (485–430 B.C.E.) tells the story of how Darius, the king of Persia, once brought together some Callatians (Asian tribal people) and some Greeks. He asked the Callatians how they disposed of their deceased parents. They said they ate their dead parents. The Greeks, who cremated their parents, were horrified at such barbarous behavior. No amount of money could tempt them to do such an irreverent thing.

Then Darius asked the Callatians what he could give them to persuade them to burn their dead parents instead. The Callatians were utterly horrified at such barbarous behavior and begged Darius to stop talking so irreverently. Herodotus concludes that "Custom is the king o'er all."[1]

Today we condemn ethnocentrism—the uncritical belief in the inherent superiority of one's own culture—as a variety of prejudice tantamount to racism and sexism. What is right in one culture may be wrong in another, what is good east of the river may be bad west of the same river, what is a virtue in one nation may be seen as a vice in another, so it behooves us not to judge others but to be tolerant of diversity.

This rejection of Western ethnocentrism has helped shift public opinion about morality, so that for a growing number of Westerners, consciousness raising about the validity of other ways of life has gradually eroded belief in moral objectivism, the view that there are universal moral principles, valid for all people at all times and climes. For example, in polls taken in my ethics and introduction to philosophy classes (in three different universities, in three areas of the country) over the past several years students by a 2-to-1 ratio affirmed a version of *moral relativism* over *moral absolutism*. Barely 3 percent considered a stance in between these two polar opposites. Of course, I'm not suggesting that all these students clearly understand what relativism entails. Many who say they are ethical relativists also may state (on the same questionnaire) that "Abortion except to save the mother's life is always wrong," that "Capital punishment is always morally wrong," or that "Suicide is never morally permissible." The apparent contradictions signal an apparent confusion on the matter.

I want to argue that ethical relativism is a mistaken theory and that the cultural differences do not demonstrate that all ways of life are equally valid from a moral perspective. Indeed, ethical relativism, were it true, would spell the death of ethics. In spite of cultural divergences, there is a universally valid core morality. I call this core morality "moral objectivism" to distinguish it from both moral absolutism and moral relativism.

An Analysis of Relativism

Ethical relativism is the theory that there are no universally valid moral principles; that all moral principles are valid relative to *culture* or *individual choice*. There are two types of relativism: *conventionalism* holds that moral principles are relative to the culture or society, and *subjectivism* holds that individual choice determines the validity of a moral principle. We'll start with conventionalism. Philosopher John Ladd, of Brown University, defines *conventional ethical relativism* this way:

> Ethical relativism is the doctrine that the moral rightness and wrongness of actions varies from society to society and that there are no absolute universal moral standards binding on all men at all times. Accordingly, it holds that whether or not it is right for an individual to act in a certain way depends on or is relative to the society to which he belongs.[2]

According to Ladd, ethical relativism consists of two theses: (1) a *diversity thesis*, which specifies that what is considered morally right and wrong varies from society to society, so that there are no moral principles accepted by all societies, and (2) a *dependency thesis*, which specifies that all moral principles derive their validity from cultural acceptance. From these two ideas he concludes that there are no universally valid moral principles, objective standards that apply to all people everywhere and at all times.

The first thesis, the *diversity thesis*, or what may simply be called *cultural relativism*, is an anthropological thesis, registering the fact that

moral rules differ from society to society. As noted at the beginning of this essay, there is enormous variety in what may count as a moral principle in a given society. The human condition is extremely malleable, allowing any number of folkways or moral codes. As Ruth Benedict has written,

> The cultural pattern of any civilization makes use of a certain segment of the great arc of potential human purposes and motivations . . . that any culture makes use of certain selected material techniques or cultural traits. The great arc along which all the possible human behaviors are distributed is far too immense and too full of contradictions for any one culture to utilize even any considerable portion of it. Selection is the first requirement.[3]

The second thesis, the *dependency thesis,* asserts that individual acts are right or wrong depending on the nature of the society from which they emanate. What is considered morally right or wrong must be seen in a context, depending on the goals, wants, beliefs, history, and environment of the society in question. As William Graham Sumner says, "We learn the [morals] as unconsciously as we learn to walk and hear and breathe, and they never know any reason why the [morals] are what they are. The justification of them is that when we wake to consciousness of life we find them facts which already hold us in the bonds of tradition, custom, and habit."[4] Trying to see things from an independent, noncultural point of view would be like taking out our eyes in order to examine their contours and qualities. We are simply culturally determined beings.

In a sense, we all live in radically different worlds. Each person has a different set of beliefs and experiences, a particular perspective that colors all of his or her perceptions. Do the farmer, the real estate dealer, and the artist, looking at the same spatiotemporal field, see the *same* field? Not likely. Their different orientations, values, and expectations govern their perceptions, so that different aspects of the field are highlighted and some features are missed. Even as our individual values arise from personal experience, so social values are grounded in the peculiar history of the community. Morality, then, is just the set of common rules, habits, and customs that have won social approval over time, so that they seem part of the nature of things, as facts. There is nothing mysterious or transcendent about these codes of behavior. They are the outcomes of our social history.

The conclusion that there are no absolute or objective moral standards binding on all people follows from the first two propositions. Cultural relativism (the diversity thesis) plus the dependency thesis yields ethical relativism in its classic form. If there are different moral principles from culture to culture and if all morality is rooted in culture, then it follows that there are no universal moral principles, valid for all cultures and people at all times.

Subjective Ethical Relativism (Subjectivism)

Some people think that even this conclusion is too tame, and maintain that morality does not depend on the society but on the individual him or herself. As students sometimes maintain, "Morality is in the eye of the beholder." Ernest Hemingway wrote, "So far, about morals, I know only that what is moral is what you feel good after and what is immoral is what you feel bad after and judged by these moral standards, which I do not defend, the bullfight is very moral to me because I feel very fine while it is going on and have a feeling of life and death and mortality and immortality, and after it is over I feel very sad but very fine."[5]

This form of moral subjectivism has the sorry consequence that it makes morality a useless concept, for on its premises little or no interpersonal criticism or judgment is logically possible. Hemingway may feel good about killing bulls in a bullfight, while Albert Schweitzer or Mother Teresa may feel the opposite. No argument about the matter is possible. The only basis for judging Hemingway or anyone else wrong would be if he failed to live up to his own principles, but, of course, one of Hemingway's principles could be that hypocrisy is morally permissible (he feels good about it), so that it would be impossible for him to do wrong. For Hemingway, both hypocrisy and non-hypocrisy are morally permissible. On the basis of subjectivism, Adolf Hitler is as moral as Gandhi, so long as each believes he is living by his chosen principles. Notions of moral good and bad, right or wrong, cease to have interpersonal evaluative meaning.

Columbia University professor Sidney Morgenbesser once taught a class of philosophy students who argued vehemently for subjectivism. When a test was taken, Morgenbesser returned all the tests marked "F"—even though his comments showed that most of the tests were of a very high quality. When the students expressed outrage at this injustice, Morgenbesser answered that he had accepted the notion of subjectivism for purposes of marking the exams, in which case the principle of justice had no objective validity.

Absurd consequences follow from subjective ethical relativism. If it is correct, then morality reduces to esthetic tastes over which there can be no argument nor interpersonal judgment. Although many people say that they hold this position, it seems to conflict with other of their moral views (for example, that Hitler is really morally bad, or capital punishment is always wrong). There seems to be a contradiction between subjectivism and the very concept of morality it is supposed to characterize, for morality concerns "proper" resolution of interpersonal conflict and the amelioration of the human predicament. Whatever else it does, morality has a minimal aim of preventing a state of chaos where life is "solitary, poor, nasty, brutish, and short." But subjectivism is no help at all in doing this, for it doesn't rest on social *agreement* of principle (as the conventionalist maintains) or on an objectively independent set of norms that bind all people for the common good.

Subjectivism treats individuals as billiard balls on a societal pool table where they meet only in radical collisions, each aiming for its own goal and striving to do in the other fellow first. This atomistic view of personality contrasts with the fact that we develop in families and mutually dependent communities, in which we share a common language, common institutions, and habits, and that we often share each other's joys and sorrows. As John Donne said, "No man is an island, entire of itself; every man is a piece of the continent."

Radical individualistic relativism seems incoherent. So the only plausible form of ethical relativism must be one that grounds morality in the group or culture. This form of relativism is called *conventionalism*, at which we looked earlier and to which we now return.

Conventional Ethical Relativism (Conventionalism)

Conventional ethical relativism—the view that there are no objective moral principles but that all valid moral principles are justified by virtue of their cultural acceptance—recognizes the social nature of morality. That is precisely its power and virtue. It does not have the same absurd consequences that plague subjectivism. Recognizing the importance of our social environment in generating customs and beliefs, many people suppose that ethical relativism is the correct ethical theory. Furthermore, they are drawn to it for its liberal philosophical stance. It seems an enlightened response to the "sin of ethnocentricity," and seems to entail or strongly imply an attitude of tolerance toward other cultures. As Benedict says, in recognizing ethical relativity "we shall arrive at a more realistic social faith, accepting as grounds of hope and as new bases for tolerance the coexisting and equally valid patterns of life which mankind has created for itself from the raw materials of existence."[6] The most famous person holding this position is anthropologist Melville Herskovits, who argues even more explicitly than Benedict that ethical relativism entails intercultural tolerance.[7]

The view contains a contradiction. If no moral principles are universally valid, how can tolerance be universally valid? Whence comes its validity? If morality is simply relative to each culture and if the culture does not have a principle of tolerance, then its members have no obligation to be tolerant. Herskovits seems to be treating the *principle of tolerance* as the one exception to his relativism—as an absolute moral principle. But from a relativistic point of view there is no more reason to be tolerant than to be intolerant, and neither stance is objectively morally better than the other.

Not only do relativists fail to offer a basis for criticizing those who are intolerant, but they cannot rationally *criticize* anyone who espouses what they might regard as an evil principle. If (as seems to be the case) valid criticism supposes an objective or impartial standard, then relativists cannot morally criticize anyone outside their own culture. Adolf Hitler's genocidal actions, as long as they are culturally accepted, are thus as morally legitimate as Mother Teresa's works of mercy. If conventional relativism is accepted, then racism, genocide of unpopular minorities, oppression of the poor, slavery, and even the advocacy of war for its own sake are as equally moral as their opposites. And if a subculture decided that starting a nuclear war was somehow morally acceptable, we could not morally criticize these people. Any actual morality, whatever its content, is as valid as every other, and more valid than ideal moralities—because the latter aren't adhered to by any culture.

There are other disturbing consequences of ethical relativism. It seems to entail that reformers are always (morally) wrong, because they go against the cultural tide. Thus William Wilberforce was wrong in the eighteenth century to oppose slavery, and the British were immoral in opposing suttee in India (the burning of widows, now illegal in India). The early Christians were wrong in refusing to serve in the Roman army or bow down to Caesar because most people in the Roman Empire believed these two acts were moral duties. In fact, Jesus himself was immoral: he broke the law by healing on the Sabbath day and by advocating the principles expressed in the Sermon on the Mount, because few people in his time (or in ours) accepted these principles.

Yet we normally feel just the opposite: that the reformer is the courageous innovator who is right, who has the truth, against the mindless majority. Sometimes the individual must stand alone with the truth, risking social censure and persecution. Dr. Stockman says in Ibsen's *Enemy of the People*, after he loses the battle to declare his town's profitable polluted tourist spa unsanitary, "The most dangerous enemy of the truth and freedom among us—is the compact majority. Yes, the damned, compact and liberal majority. The majority has *might*—unfortunately—but *right* it is not. Right—are I and a few others." Yet if relativism is correct, the opposite is necessarily the case. Truth is with the crowd, and error with the individual.

There is an even more basic problem with the idea that morality depends on cultural acceptance for validity. The problem is that "culture" or "society" is notoriously difficult to define. This is especially so in a pluralistic society like our own, which seems to be vague, with unclear boundary lines. One person may belong to several societies (subcultures) with different value emphases and arrangements of principles. A person may belong to the nation as a single society with certain values of patriotism, honor, courage, and laws (including some

that are controversial but have majority acceptance, such as the law on abortion). But a person may also belong to a church that opposes some of the laws of the state. He or she may also be an integral member of a socially mixed community where different principles hold sway, and may belong to clubs and a family where still other rules are adhered to. Relativism would seem to tell us that where people are members of societies with conflicting moralities they must be judged both wrong and not wrong, whatever they do. For example, if Mary is a U.S. citizen and a member of the Roman Catholic Church, she is wrong (as a Catholic) if she chooses to have an abortion and not wrong (as a U.S. citizen) if she acts against the teaching of the Church on abortion. As a member of a racist organization, the Ku Klux Klan or KKK, John has no obligation to treat his fellow black citizen as an equal, but as a member of the university community itself (where the principle of equal rights is accepted) he does have that obligation; but as a member of the surrounding community (which may reject the principle of equal rights) he again has no such obligation; and again, as a member of the nation at large (which accepts the principle), he is obligated to treat his fellow with respect. What is the morally right thing for John to do? The question no longer makes much sense in this moral Babel. It has lost its action-guiding function.

Perhaps the relativist would adhere to a principle that says that in such cases the individual may choose which group to belong to as primary. If Mary chooses to have an abortion, she is choosing to belong to the general society, relative to that principle. And John must likewise choose between groups. The trouble with this option is that it seems to lead back to counterintuitive results. If Gangland Gus of Murder, Incorporated, feels like killing Bank President Ortcutt and wants to feel good about it, he identifies with the Murder, Incorporated, society rather than the general public morality. Does this justify the killing? In fact, couldn't one justify anything simply by forming a small sub-culture that approved of it? Charles Manson would be morally pure in killing innocents simply by virtue of forming a little coterie. How large must the group be in order to be a legitimate subculture or society? Does it need ten or fifteen people? How about just three? Come to think about it, why can't my burglary partner and I found our own society with a morality of its own. Of course, if my partner died, I could still claim that I was acting from an originally social set of norms. But why can't I dispense with the interpersonal agreements altogether and invent my own morality—since morality, on this view, is only an invention anyway? Conventionalist relativism seems to reduce to subjectivism. And subjectivism leads, as we have seen, to the demise of morality altogether.

Where does the relativist go wrong? I think the relativist makes an unwarranted slide from (1) the observation that different cultures have different rules, to (2) the conclusion that no culture's set of rules are better than any other culture's set of rules or even any ideal set of rules. But some sets of rules *are* better than other sets relative to the purposes of morality. If we suppose that morality answers to a set of social purposes, and that the purposes of morality are the survival of society, alleviation of suffering, encouragement of human flourishing, and the just resolution of conflicts of interest, these purposes will yield a set of common principles that may actually underlie some of the cultural differences reported by anthropologists. E. O. Wilson has identified over a score of common features, and before him Clyde Kluckhohn has noted some significant common ground:

> Every culture has a concept of murder, distinguishing this from execution, killing in war, and other "justifiable homicides." The notions of incest and other regulations upon sexual behavior, the prohibitions upon untruth under defined circumstances, of restitution and reciprocity, of mutual obligations between parents and chil-

dren—these and many other moral concepts are altogether universal.[8]

And Colin Turnbull, whose description of the sadistic, semidisplaced Ik in northern Uganda was seen as evidence of a people without principles of kindness and cooperation, has produced evidence that underneath the surface of this dying society, there is a deeper moral code from a time when the tribe flourished. Occasionally this deeper code surfaces and shows its nobler face.

The nonrelativist can accept a certain relativity in the way moral principles are *applied* in various cultures, depending on beliefs, history, and environment. For example, a raw environment with scarce natural resources may justify the Eskimos' brand of euthanasia to the objectivist, who in another environment would consistently reject that practice. The Greeks and Callatians disposed of their parents differently, but that does not prove that conventionalism is correct. Actually, both groups seem to adhere to a common principle of showing respect to one's elders. There can be latitude in how that respect is shown.

The members of a tribe in the Sudan throw their deformed children into the river because of their belief that such infants *belong* to the hippopotamus, the god of the river. We believe that they have a false belief about this, but the point is that the same principles of respect for property and respect for human life is operative in these contrary practices. They differ with us only in belief, not in substantive moral principle. This is an illustration of how nonmoral beliefs (for example, deformed children belong to the hippopotamus) when applied to common moral principles (such as give to each his or her due) generate different actions in different cultures.

In our own culture, differences in nonmoral belief about the status of a fetus generate opposite moral prescriptions. Both the prochoice movement and the antiabortionists agree that it is wrong to kill innocent people, but they disagree as to a fact (not the principle) of whether a fetus is a *person* (someone having a right to life). Roman Catholics believe that the fetus is a person because it has a soul, whereas most liberal Protestants and secularists deny this. Abortion is a serious moral issue, but what divides many of us is not a moral principle but how that principle should be applied. Antiabortionists believe the principle of not killing innocent people applies to fetuses, whereas prochoicers do not—but they do not disagree on the fundamental principle.

The relativist may respond to this point and argue that even if we do often share deep principles, we don't always share them. Some people may not value life at all. How can we prove them wrong? Who's to say which culture is right and which is wrong? This response seems dubious. We can reason and perform thought experiments in order to make a case for one system over another. We may not be able to *know* with certainty that our moral beliefs are closer to the truth than those of another culture or those of others within our own culture, but we may be *justified* in believing that they are. If we can be closer to the truth regarding factual or scientific matters, why can't we be closer to the truth on moral matters? Why can't a culture simply be confused or wrong about its moral perceptions? Why can't we say that the society like the Ik, which sees nothing wrong with enjoying watching its own children fall into fires, is less moral in that regard than the culture that cherishes children and grants them protection and equal rights? To take such a stand is not to commit the fallacy of ethnocentrism, for we are seeking to derive principles through critical reason, not simply uncritical acceptance of one's own mores.

The Case for Moral Objectivism

The discussion heretofore has been largely negative, against relativism. Now I want to make a positive case for a core set of moral principles

that are necessary to the good society and the good life.

First, I must make it clear that I am distinguishing moral *absolutism* from moral *objectivism*. The absolutist believes that there are nonoverridable moral principles that ought never to be violated. Kant's system is a good example: one ought *never* break a promise or tell a lie, no matter what. An objectivist, however, need not posit any nonoverridable principles, at least not in unqualified general form, and so need not be an absolutist. As Renford Bambrough put it,

> To suggest that there is a *right* answer to a moral problem is at once to be accused of or credited with a belief in moral absolutes. But it is no more necessary to believe in moral absolutes in order to believe in moral objectivity than it is to believe in the existence of absolute space or absolute time in order to believe in the objectivity of temporal and spatial relations and of judgments about them.[9]

In the objectivist's account, moral principles are what Oxford University philosopher William Ross (1877–1971) refers to as *prima facie* principles, valid rules of action that should generally be adhered to, but that may be overridden by another moral principle in cases of moral conflict.[10] For example, while a principle of justice generally outweighs a principle of benevolence, at times enormous good could be done by sacrificing a small amount of justice, so that an objectivist would be inclined to act according to the principle of benevolence. There may be some absolute or nonoverridable principles (indeed, the next principle I mention is probably one), but there need not be any or many for objectivism to be true.

If I can establish or show that it is reasonable to believe that at least one objective moral principle is binding on all people everywhere in some ideal sense, I shall have shown that relativism is probably false and that a limited objectivism is true. Actually, I believe that many qualified general ethical principles are binding on all rational beings, but one will suffice to re-

There must be some standard or basis for where these come from.

fute relativism. The principle I've chosen is the following:

1. It is morally wrong to torture people for the fun of it.

I claim that this principle is binding on all rational agents. If some agent, S, rejects Principle 1, we should not let that affect our intuition that Principle 1 is a true principle but rather try to explain S's behavior as perverse, ignorant, or irrational instead. For example, suppose Adolf Hitler doesn't accept Principle 1. Should that affect our confidence in its truth? Isn't it more reasonable to infer that Hitler is morally deficient, morally blind, ignorant, or irrational than to suppose that his noncompliance is evidence against the truth of Principle 1?

Suppose, further, that a tribe of Hitlerites enjoys torturing people. The whole culture accepts torturing others for the fun of it. Suppose that Mother Teresa and Gandhi try unsuccessfully to convince them that they should stop torturing people altogether, and they respond by torturing Teresa and Gandhi. Should this affect our confidence in Principle 1? Would it not be more reasonable to look for some explanation of Hitlerite behavior? For example, we might hypothesize that this tribe lacked a developed sense of sympathetic imagination that is necessary for the moral life. Or we might theorize that this tribe was on a lower evolutionary level than most *Homo sapiens*. Or we might simply conclude that the tribe was closer to a Hobbesian state of nature than most societies, and as such probably would not survive. But we need not know the correct answer as to why the tribe was in such bad shape, in order to maintain our confidence in Principle 1 as a moral principle. If Principle 1 is a basic or core belief for us, we will be more likely to doubt the Hitlerites' sanity or ability to think morally than to doubt the validity of Principle 1.

We can perhaps produce other candidates for membership in our minimally basic objective moral set. For example,

2. Do not kill innocent people.
3. Do not cause pain or suffering except when a higher duty prescribes it.
4. Do not commit rape.
5. Keep your promises and contracts.
6. Do not deprive another person of his or her freedom.
7. Do justice, treating equals equally and unequals unequally.
8. Tell the truth.
9. Help other people.
10. Obey just laws.

Principles 1 through 10 are examples of the core morality, principles necessary for the good life. Fortunately, it isn't as though 1 to 10 were arbitrary principles, for we can give reasons why we believe that these rules will be necessary to any satisfactory social order. Principles such as the Golden Rule, not killing innocent people, treating equals equally, truth telling, promise keeping, and the like are central to the fluid progression of social interaction and the resolution of conflicts of which ethics are about (at least minimal morality is, even though there may be more to morality than simply these kinds of concerns). For example, language itself depends on a general and implicit commitment to the principle of truth telling. Accuracy of expression is a primitive form of truthfulness. Hence, every time we use words correctly we are telling the truth. Without this behavior, language wouldn't be possible. Likewise, without the recognition of a rule of promise keeping, contracts are of no avail and cooperation is less likely to occur. And without the protection of life and liberty, we could not secure our other goals.

A morality would be adequate if it contained the principles of the core morality, but there could be more than one adequate morality that *applied* these principles differently. That is, there may be a certain relativity to secondary principles (whether to opt for monogamy rather than polygamy, whether to include high altruism in the set of moral duties, whether to allocate more resources to medical care than to environmental concerns, whether to require driving on the left side of the road or on the right side, and so forth). But in every morality a certain core will remain, applied somewhat differently because of differences in environment, belief, tradition, and the like.

The core moral rules are analogous to the core vitamins necessary for a healthy diet. We need an adequate amount of each vitamin—some humans need more of one than another—but in prescribing a nutritious diet we don't have to set forth recipes, specific foods, place settings, or culinary habits. Gourmets, ascetics, and vegetarians may meet the requirements differently, but the basic nutrients may be had by all without rigid regimentation or an absolute set of recipes.

Imagine that you have been miraculously transported to the dark kingdom of hell, and there you get a glimpse of the sufferings of the damned. What is their punishment? Well, they have eternal back itches that ebb and flow constantly. But they cannot scratch their backs, for their arms are paralyzed in a frontal position. And so they writhe with itchiness through eternity. But just as you are beginning to feel the itch in your own back, you are suddenly transported to heaven. What do you see in the kingdom of the blessed? Well, you see people with eternal back itches, who cannot scratch their own backs. But they are all smiling instead of writhing. Why? Because everyone has his or her arms stretched out to scratch someone else's back, and, so arranged in one big circle, a hell is turned into a heaven of ecstasy.

If we can imagine some states of affairs or cultures that are better than others in a way that depends on human action, we can ask what character traits make them so. In our story, people in heaven, but not those in hell, cooperate to ameliorate suffering and produce pleasure. These goods are very primitive, not sufficient for a full-blown morality, but they give us a hint as to the objectivity of morality. Moral goodness has

something to do with the amelioration of suffering, the resolution of conflict, and the promotion of human flourishing. If our heaven is really better than the eternal itchiness of hell, then whatever makes it so is constitutively related to moral rightness.

An Explanation of the Attraction of Ethical Relativism

Why, then, is there such a strong inclination toward ethical relativism? I think that there are three reasons, which haven't been emphasized. One is the fact that the options are usually presented as though absolutism and relativism were the only alternatives, so conventionalism wins out against an implausible competitor. The questionnaire I give my students reads as follows: "Are there any ethical absolutes, moral duties binding on all persons at all times, or are moral duties relative to culture? Is there any alternative to these two positions?" Only 3 percent of students suggest a third position, and very few of them identify objectivism. Granted, it takes a little philosophical sophistication to make the crucial distinctions (and it is precisely for lack of this sophistication or reflection that relativism has procured its enormous prestige). But, as Ross and others have shown, and as I have argued in this essay, one can have an objective morality without being absolutist.

The second reason is that our recent sensitivity to cultural relativism and the evils of ethnocentricism, which have plagued European and American relations with other cultures, has made us conscious of how frail many aspects of our moral repertoire are, so that we tend to wonder "Who's to judge what's really right or wrong?" However, the move from a reasonable cultural relativism, which rightly causes us to rethink our moral systems, to an ethical relativism, which causes us to give up the heart of morality altogether, is an instance of the fallacy of confusing factual or descriptive statements with normative ones. Cultural relativism doesn't entail ethical relativism. The very reason why we are against ethnocentricism is the same reason why we are for an objective moral system: impartial reason draws us to it.

We may well agree that cultures differ and that we ought to be cautious in condemning what we don't understand. But this agreement in no way needs to imply that there are not better and worse ways of living. We can understand and excuse, to some degree at least, people who differ from our best notions of morality, without abdicating the notion that cultures without principles of justice, promise keeping, or protection of the innocent are morally poorer for these omissions.

A third factor which has driven some to moral nihilism and others to relativism, is the decline of religion in Western society. As one of Dostoevsky's characters said, "If God is dead, all things are permitted." The person who has lost religious faith feels a deep vacuum and understandably confuses it with a moral vacuum, or may finally resign him- or herself to a form of secular conventionalism. Such people reason that if there is no God to guarantee the validity of the moral order, there must not be a universal moral order. There is just radical cultural diversity and death at the end.

But even if there turns out to be no God and no immortality, we still will want to live happy, meaningful lives during our four-score years on earth. If this is true, then it matters by which principles we live and those which win out in the test of time will be objectively valid principles.

To sum up: there are moral truths, principles belonging to the core morality, without which society will not long survive and individuals will not flourish. Reason can discover these principles, and it is in our interest to promote them.

So "Who's to judge what's right or wrong?" We are. We are to do so on the basis of the best reasoning we can bring forth, and with sympathy and understanding.

Notes

1. *Histories of Herodotus,* trans. George Rawlinson (New York: Appleton, 1859), bk 3, chap. 38.

2. *Ethical Relativism* (Belmont, Calif: Wadsworth, 1973), p. 1.

3. *Patterns of Culture* (New York: Houghton Mifflin, 1935), p. 219.

4. *Folkways* (New York: 1906), Section 80. Ruth Benedict indicates the depth of our cultural conditioning this way: "The very eyes with which we see the problem are conditioned by the long traditional habits of our own society" ("Anthropology and the Abnormal," *Journal of General Psychology,* 1934), pp. 59–82.

5. *Death in the Afternoon* (New York: Scribner, 1932), p. 4.

6. *Patterns of Culture,* p. 257.

7. *Cultural Relativism* (New York: Random House, 1972).

8. Kluckhohn, "Ethical Relativity: Sic et Non," *Journal of Philosophy* 52, 1955.

9. *Moral Skepticism and Moral Knowledge* (London: Routledge & Kegan Paul, 1979), p. 33.

10. *The Right and the Good* (Oxford: Oxford University Press, 1931).

Study Questions

1. What is the difference between cultural relativism and ethical relativism?

2. What is wrong with the relativist's contention that "being an ethical relativist promotes tolerance since we see that there is nothing superior in any moral system"?

3. What is the main argument for ethical objectivism? Are some moralities better than others? Explain.

4. What is the difference between ethical objectivism and ethical absolutism?

For Further Reading

Code: D = deontological; U = utilitarian; C = contractualist or egoist; O = objectivist; R = relativist; I = intuitionist

Baier, Kurt. *The Moral Point of View.* Ithaca, N.Y.: Cornell University Press, 1958. This influential work sees morality primarily in terms of social control. (C)(O)

Dawkins, Richard. *The Selfish Gene,* 2d ed. Oxford: Oxford University Press, 1989. A brilliant and fascinating study on the subject, defending limited altruism from the perspective of self-interest. (a type of C)

Frankena, William K. *Ethics,* 2d ed. Englewood Cliffs, N.J.: Prentice Hall, 1973. A succinct, reliable guide. (D)(O)(I)

Gert, Bernard. *Morality: A New Justification of the Moral Rules,* 2d ed. Oxford: Oxford University Press, 1988. A clear and comprehensive discussion of the nature of morality. (C)

Hobbes, Thomas, *Leviathan* (1651) Indianapolis: Bobbs-Merrill, 1958; Parts 1 and 2. Classic work in contractarian ethics. (C)

Kant, Immanuel. *Foundations of the Metaphysics of Morals,* trans. Lewis White Beck. Indianapolis: Bobbs-Merrill, 1959. Classic work in deontological ethics. (D)

MacIntyre, Alasdair. *A Short History of Ethics.* London: Macmillan, 1966. A lucid, if uneven, survey of the history of Western ethics.

Mackie, J. L. *Ethics: Inventing Right and Wrong.* London: Penguin Books, 1976. A modern classic defense of relativism. (R)

Mill, John Stuart. *Utilitarianism.* Indianapolis: Bobbs-Merrill, 1957. A classic work in utilitarianism.(U)

Nielsen, Kai. *Ethics Without God.* Buffalo, N.Y.: Prometheus Books, 1973. A very accessible defense of secular morality. (U)

Pojman, Louis. *Ethical Theory: Classical and Contemporary Readings.* Belmont, Calif.: Wadsworth, 1999. An anthology containing readings on all the major positions.

———. *Ethics: Discovering Right and Wrong.* Belmont, Calif.: Wadsworth, 1999. An objectivist perspective. (O)

Quinton, Anthony. *Utilitarian Ethics.* London: Macmillan, 1973. A clear exposition of classical utilitarianism. (O)(U)

Rachels, James. *The Elements of Moral Philosophy.* New York: Random House, 1986. One of the clearest introductions to moral philosophy. (O)

Singer, Peter. *The Expanding Circle: Ethics and Sociobiology.* Oxford: Oxford University Press, 1983. A fascinating attempt to relate ethics to sociobiology. (U)(O)

Taylor, Richard. *Good and Evil.* Buffalo, N.Y.: Prometheus Books, 1970. A lively, easy-to-read work that sees the main role of morality to be the resolution of conflicts of interest. (C)(R)

Van Wyk, Robert. *Introduction to Ethics.* New York: St. Martin's Press, 1990. A clearly written recent introduction to the subject. (O)(attacks some versions of C)

Part II

The Sanctity of Life and the Quality of Life

[handwritten: 10-24-2021]

Introduction

In the Book of Genesis, the first book of the Bible, God says to his worshipers, the ancient Israelites, "You shall be holy, for I am holy." Holiness in the Hebrew Bible (Old Testament) is a quality inhering in God. It includes intrinsic goodness, the source of all other values. It is transcendent, beyond our understanding, and yet we can become holy and godlike through following God's commands and participating in worship of him. Human beings are valuable and have goodness because they have been created in the image and likeness of God. Their goodness is a derived goodness. Because they have this quality, it is wrong to kill humans. "Whoever sheds the blood of man, by man shall his blood be shed; for God made man in his own image" (Gen. 9:6). Of none of the other creatures is this true. Humans beings are to be stewards of the earth, caretakers of the environment, but they are permitted to use animals for their own purposes—for labor, for food—and to be their lords.

[handwritten margin note: eating crickets noted. I only eat dead chickens or dead cows, rabbits lives + die - 10-24-2021]

Human beings alone have the essential property of being created in God's image. Not all of life is intrinsically valuable. Only human life has this feature, which enables human beings to act morally and to achieve fellowship with God.

So for Jews and Christians it is not the quantity of life that is important but the quality. What is sacred is not biological life but the image of God within each man and woman. That feature separates us from mere brutes and makes us supremely worthy. As such, human life is sacred. The quality of life is important to determine our eternal destiny, but it is the quality *in* humans that bestows on us our worth and dignity. Leonard Weber puts it this way:

[handwritten margin note: Not 7 ≤ But Do.]

> The quality-of-life ethics puts the emphasis on the type of life being lived, not upon the fact of life. . . . What the life means to someone is what is important. Keeping this in mind, it is not inappropriate to say that some lives are of *greater value than others,* that the condi-

tion or meaning of life does have much to do with the justification for terminating that life. The sanctity of life ethics defends two propositions: 1. That human life is sacred by the very fact of its existence; its value does not depend upon a certain condition or perfection of that life. 2. That, therefore, all human lives are of *equal value;* all have the same right to life. The quality of life ethic finds neither of these two propositions acceptable.[1]

Other traditions, animist and Hindu, extend the idea of holiness or value to include all of life. All sentient beings are possessed of God, are part of the Great Ocean of Divine Being. All life is sacred and worthy of reverence. We are all connected in a symbiotic, sacred web. The bear and the buffalo are our sister and brother. All nature is a holy family. This view is sometimes referred to as *vitalism,* which says that life itself is powerful and sacred and cannot be reduced to the categories of chemistry or physics.

In our readings Albert Schweitzer reflects on the sanctity-of-life view within the Christian tradition.

Most secular philosophers do not include a transcendent dimension or a sense of the holy in their theories. For them, life itself is not valuable, but the kind of life one leads is. Secularists divide into two camps on the question of what is valuable. Objectivists assert that such qualities as reason, health, knowledge, freedom, happiness, and friendship are valuable in their own right whether or not anyone recognizes them as such. These characteristics have objective value. Subjectivists assert, on the contrary, nothing has objective value, but things obtain value simply by being desired, so what is valuable will differ from person to person and from animal to animal. If someone likes cocaine more than being healthy, then cocaine is more valuable to him, regardless of what it may do to his health. For the subjectivist, value—like beauty—lies in the mind of the beholder.

From the objectivist secular view, some lives will be worth more than others, according to how much the objective values are present in them. From the subjective secular account, no life has intrinsic value, but lives obtain value by being desired either by the person in question or by others.

In our readings Jonathan Glover and H. Tristram Engelhardt, Jr., represent these two versions of the secular view that emphasize the quality of life rather than the sanctity of life. Glover argues that, though something is intuitively appealing about the notion of the sanctity of life, it cannot stand up to rigorous scrutiny. Not the value of mere living but the value of a worthwhile life should cause us to respect our own and other people's lives. Since we cannot know what makes life worthwhile to others, we should respect their choices. Engelhardt reinterprets the idea of the sanctity of life as an ambiguous notion with different underlying meanings. Two central notions are (1) the Kantian idea of *personhood*—persons have dignity by virtue of being self-conscious, self-determining agents; and (2) the utilitarian idea of the *social role* of human beings—infants and severely retarded children may be valued not for their intrinsic personhood qualities but for the roles they play in families and society. Engelhardt applies his distinction to the issue of abortion.

Daniel Callahan brings these matters together in a final, comprehensive discussion. After assessing the merits of religious and secular views of the sanctity of life, he locates a common core in both traditions that results in a set of rules that preserves the species, the family, and the individual. Seen in this way, Callahan argues, the sanctity of life can function as the new moral consensus for a pluralistic world order.

Note

1. Leonard Weber, *Who Shall Live?* (New York: Paulist Press, 1976), pp. 41–42.

CHAPTER 7

The Divine Creation of Humanity

THE BIBLE: GENESIS AND PSALM 8

We begin our readings with the classic passage from the Bible. Tradition says that the Book of Genesis was written by Moses over 3,000 years ago. It is the first book in the Old Testament (Hebrew Bible). In this opening passage from Chapter 1 the Hebrew version of creation is recorded. Human beings are shown to have value because they have been created in the image of God. The second passage is from Psalm 8, a song of praise to God, in which humanity is seen as the high point of God's creation.

The Book of Genesis

IN THE BEGINNING God created the heavens and the earth. The earth was without form and void, and darkness was upon the face of the deep; and the Spirit of God was moving over the face of the waters. And God said, "Let there be Light;" and there was light. And God separated the light from the darkness. God called the light Day, and the darkness he called Night. And there was evening and there was morning, one day. . . . And God said, "Let the waters bring forth swarms of living creatures, and let birds fly above the earth across the firmament of the heavens." So God created the great sea monsters and every living creature that moves, with which the waters swarm, according to their kind. And God saw that it was good. And God blessed them, saying, "Be fruitful and multiply and fill the waters in the seas, and let birds multiply on the earth." And there was evening and there was morning, a fifth day. And God said, "Let the earth bring forth living creatures according to their kinds: cattle and creeping things and beasts of the earth according to their kind." And it was

so. And God made the beasts of the earth according to their kind and the cattle according to their kinds, and everything that creeps upon the ground according to its kind. And God saw that it was good. Then God said, "Let us make man in our image, after our likeness; and let them have dominion over the fish of the sea, and over the birds of the air, and over the cattle, and over all the earth, and over every creeping thing that creeps upon the earth." So God created man in his own image, in the image of God he created him; male and female he created them. And God blessed them, and God said to them, "Be fruitful and multiply, and fill the earth and subdue it; and have dominion over the fish of the sea and over the birds of the air and over every living thing that moves upon the earth." And God said, "Behold, I have given you every plant yielding seed which is upon the face of all the earth, and every tree with seed in its fruit; You shall have them; for food. And to every beast of the earth, and to every bird of the air, and to every thing that creeps on the earth, everything that has the breath of life, I have given every green plant for food." And it was so. And God

From the Revised Standard Version of the Bible.

saw everything that he had made, and behold, it was very good. And there was evening and there was morning, a sixth day. 6Th day

Thus the heavens and the earth were finished, and all the host of them. And on the seventh day God finished his work which he had done, and he rested on the seventh day from all his work which he had done.(Genesis 1 and 2)

Heirarchy of life

Psalm 8

O Lord, our Lord, how majestic is thy name in all
    the earth!
Thou whose glory above the heavens is chanted
by the babes and infants,
thou has founded a bulwark because of thy foes,

to still the enemy and the avenger.
When I look at thy heavens, the work of thy
    fingers,
the moon and the stars which thou hast
    established;
what is man that thou art mindful of him,
and the son of man that thou dost care for him?
Yet thou hast made him little less than God,
and dost crown him with glory and honor.
Thou hast given him dominion over the works of
    thy hands;
thou hast put all things under his feet,
all sheep and oxen,
and also the beasts of the field,
the birds of the air, and the fish of the sea,
whatever passes along the path of the sea.
O Lord, our Lord,
how majestic is thy name in all the earth.

Study Questions

1. Go over the two biblical selections and identify the statements about the value of human beings. Why are humans valuable? Do these passages show or suggest that all humans are equally valuable?
2. Contrast these accounts of the creation of humanity with Darwin's evolutionary account. If human beings were not created by God in the image of God but simply evolved from lower forms of life, can we impute the same value to them?
3. Why do you think human beings are valuable?

CHAPTER 8

Reverence for Life

ALBERT SCHWEITZER

Albert Schweitzer (1875–1965) was born in Kaiserberg, Germany, and educated at Strasbourg. He was an extraordinarily versatile genius: a concert organist, a musicologist, a New Testament scholar, a theologian, a missionary, a philosopher, and a physician who dedicated his life to the amelioration of suffering and the promotion of life. He built and served in a hospital in Lambarene in French Equatorial Africa (now Gabon). His most famous writings are *The Quest for the Historical Jesus* (1906), *Out of My Life and Thought* (1933), and *Civilization and Ethics* (1923), from which the present selection is taken.

Schweitzer describes his theory of Reverence for Life—the idea that all of life is sacred and that we must live accordingly, treating each living being as an inherently valuable "will-to-live."

Schweitzer relates how the phrase "Reverence for Life" came to him one day in 1915 while on a river journey to assist a missionary's sick wife.

At sunset of the third day, near the village of Igendja, we moved along an island in the middle of the wide river. On a sandbank to our left, four hippopotamuses and their young plodded along in our same direction. Just then, in my great tiredness and discouragement, the phrase "Reverence for Life" struck me like a flash. As far as I knew, it was a phrase I had never heard nor ever read. I realized at once that it carried within itself the solution to the problem that had been torturing me. Now I knew a system of values which concerns itself only with our relationship to other people is incomplete and therefore lacking in power for good. Only by means of reverence for life can we establish a spiritual and humane relationship with both people and all living creatures within our reach. Only in this fashion can we avoid harming others, and, within the limits of our capacity, go to their aid whenever they need us.

The following passage is a fuller description of his views. He begins by citing the French philosopher, René Descartes (1596–1650), and contrasting that theory of knowledge which begins with an abstract, isolated self, with the deeper self-awareness that comes from our understanding that all living things ("will-to-lives") are sacred and interdependent.

DESCARTES TELLS US that philosophizing is based on the judgment: "I think, therefore I am." From this meagre and arbitrarily selected beginning it is inevitable that it should wander into the path of the abstract. It does not find the entrance to the ethical realm, and remains held

Reprinted from Civilization and Ethics, *translated by A. Naish (London: Black, 1923).*

If a child has a father + Mother Does he not have a great respect for Life + Self?

No father, with matriarctial or mother only background learn art for one. No self respect for Men or others.

fast in a dead view of the world and of life. True philosophy must commence with the most immediate and comprehensive facts of consciousness. And this may be formulated as follows: "I am life which wills to live, and I exist in the midst of life which wills to live." This is no mere excogitated subtlety. Day after day and hour after hour I proceed on my way invested in it. In every moment of reflection it forces itself on me anew. A living world- and life-view, informing all the facts of life, gushes forth from it continually, as from an eternal spring. A mystically ethical oneness with existence grows forth from it unceasingly.

Just as in my own will-to-live there is a yearning for more life, and for that mysterious exaltation of the will-to-live which is called pleasure, and terror in face of annihilation and that injury to the will-to-live which is called pain; so the same obtains in all the will-to-live around me, equally whether it can express itself to my comprehension or whether it remains unvoiced.

Ethics thus consists in this, that I experience the necessity of practising the same reverence for life toward all will-to-live, as toward my own. Therein I have already the needed fundamental principle of morality. It is *good* to maintain and cherish life; it is *evil* to destroy and to check life.

As a matter of fact, everything which in the usual ethical valuation of inter-human relations is looked upon as good can be traced back to the material and spiritual maintenance or enhancement of human life and to the effort to raise it to its highest level of value. And contrariwise everything in human relations which is considered as evil, is in the final analysis found to be material or spiritual destruction or checking of human life and slackening of the effort to raise it to its highest value. Individual concepts of good and evil which are widely divergent and apparently unconnected fit into one another like pieces which belong together, the moment they are comprehended and their essential nature is grasped in this general notion.

The fundamental principle of morality which we seek as a necessity for thought is not, however, a matter only of arranging and deepening current views of good and evil, but also of expanding and extending these. A man is really ethical only when he obeys the constraint laid on him to help all life which he is able to succour, and when he goes out of his way to avoid injuring anything living. He does not ask how far this or that life deserves sympathy as valuable in itself, nor how far it is capable of feeling. To him life as such is sacred. He shatters no ice crystal that sparkles in the sun, tears no leaf from its tree, breaks off no flower, and is careful not to crush any insect as he walks. If he works by lamplight on a summer evening, he prefers to keep the window shut and to breathe stifling air, rather than to see insect after insect fall on his table with singed and sinking wings.

If he goes out into the street after a rainstorm and sees a worm which has strayed there, he reflects that it will certainly dry up in the sunshine, if it does not quickly regain the damp soil into which it can creep, and so he helps it back from the deadly paving stones into the lush grass. Should he pass by an insect which has fallen into a pool, he spares the time to reach it a leaf or stalk on which it may clamber and save itself.

He is not afraid of being laughed at as sentimental. It is indeed the fate of every truth to be an object of ridicule when it is first acclaimed. It was once considered foolish to suppose that coloured men were really human beings and ought to be treated as such. What was once foolishness has now become a recognized truth. To-day it is considered as exaggeration to proclaim constant respect for every form of life as being the serious demand of a rational ethic. But the time is coming when people will be amazed that the human race was so long before it recognized that thoughtless injury to life is incompatible with real ethics. Ethics is in its unqualified form extended responsibility with regard to everything that has life.

The general idea of ethics as a partaking of the mental atmosphere of reverence for life is not perhaps attractive. But it is the only complete notion possible. Mere sympathy is too narrow a

Do. If you are not a recognized husband by family matters with out husband society looks Ashard respect for life in others So they turn to gangry or authority is no will out respect for life? whole but This idea does't it help respect of person for others with love which shows by both mother + father in their creation Do, There may be exceptions when? Improve

Men, in a matriarctial home (only) become a mockery the Lord's Church and loss respect for elders. Do.

What is motivated for "reverence for life"? Sermon Topic —

Oct 28, 2021

a smile

concept to serve as the intellectual expression of the ethical element. It denotes, indeed, only a sharing of the suffering of the will-to-live. But to be ethical is to share the whole experience of all the circumstances and aspirations of the will-to-live, to live with it in its pleasures, in its yearnings, in its struggles toward perfection.

Love is a more inclusive term, since it signifies fellowship in suffering, in joy, and in effort. But it describes the ethical element only as it were by a simile, however natural and profound that simile may be. It places the solidarity created by ethics in analogy to that which nature has caused to come into being in a more or less superficial physical manner, and with a view to the fulfillment of their destiny, between two sexually attracted existences, or between these and their offspring.

Thought must strive to find a formula for the essential nature of the ethical. In so doing it is led to characterize ethics as self-devotion for the sake of life, motived by reverence for life. Although the phrase "reverence for life" may perhaps sound a trifle unreal, yet that which it denotes is something which never lets go its hold of the man in whose thought it has once found a place. Sympathy, love, and, in general, all enthusiastic feeling of real value are summed up in it. It works with restless vitality on the mental nature in which it has found a footing and flings this into the restless activity of a responsibility which never ceases and stops nowhere. Reverence for life drives a man on as the whirling thrashing screw forces a ship through the water.

Not Screw

Screw

"crew"

The ethic of reverence for life, arising as it does out of an inward necessity, is not dependent on the question as to how far or how little it is capable of development into a satisfactory view of life. It does not need to prove that the action of ethical men, as directed to maintaining, enhancing and exalting life, has any significance for the total course of the world-process. Nor is it disturbed by the consideration that the preservation and enhancement of life which it practises are of almost no account at all beside the mighty destruction of life which takes place every moment as the result of natural forces. Determined as it is to act, it is yet able to ignore all the problems raised as to the result of its action. The fact that in the man who has become ethical a will informed by reverence for life and self-sacrifice for the sake of life exists in the world, is itself significant for the world.

The universal will-to-live experiences itself in my personal will-to-live otherwise than it does in other phenomena. For here it enters on an individualization, which, so far as I am able to gather in trying to view it from the outside, struggles only to live itself out, and not at all to become one with will-to-live external to itself. The world is indeed the grisly drama of will-to-live at variance with itself. One existence survives at the expense of another of which it yet knows nothing. But in me the will-to-live has become cognizant of the existence of other will-to-live. There is in it a yearning for unity with itself, a longing to become universal.

Why is it that the will-to-live has this experience only in myself? Is it a result of my having become capable of reflection about the totality of existence? Whither will the evolution lead which has thus begun in me?

There is no answer to these questions. It remains a painful enigma how I am to live by the rule of reverence for life in a world ruled by creative will which is at the same time destructive will, and by destructive will which is also creative.

I can do no other than hold on to the fact that the will-to-live appears in me as will-to-live which aims at becoming one with other will-to-live. This fact is the light which shines for me in the darkness. My ignorance regarding the real nature of the objective world no longer troubles me. I am set free from the world. I have been cast by my reverence for life into a state of unrest foreign to the world. By this, too, I am placed in a state of beatitude which the world cannot give. If in the happiness induced by our independence of the world I and another afford each other mutual help in understanding and in forgiveness, when otherwise will would harass other will, then the will-to-live is no longer at variance with itself. If I rescue an insect from a pool of water, then life has given itself for life, and again the self-contradiction of the will-to-live has been removed. Whenever my life has given itself out in any way for other life, my eternal will-to-live experiences union with the eternal, since all life is one. I possess a cordial which secures me from dying of thirst in the desert of life.

Therefore I recognize it as the destiny of my existence to be obedient to the higher revelation of the will-to-live which I find in myself. I choose as my activity the removal of the self-contradiction of the will-to-live, as far as the influence of my own existence extends. Knowing as I do the one thing needful, I am content to offer no opinion about the enigma of the objective world and my own being.

Thought becomes religious when it thinks itself out to the end. The ethic of reverence for life is the ethic of Jesus brought to philosophical expression, extended into cosmical form, and conceived as intellectually necessary.

The surmising and longing of all deeply religious personalities is comprehended and contained in the ethic of reverence for life. This, however, does not build up a world-view as a completed system, but resigns itself to leave the cathedral perforce incomplete. It is only able to finish the choir. Yet in this true piety celebrates a living and continuous divine service. . . .

The ethic of reverence for life also proves its own truth by the way in which it comprehends and includes the most various forms of the ethical impulse. No ethical system has yet proved capable of presenting the effort to attain self-perfection, in which man works on his own being without any action directed externally, on the one hand, and the activist ethic on the other hand, in connection and interrelation. The ethic of reverence for life accomplishes this, and in such a way that it does not merely solve an aca-demic problem, but brings with it a real deepening of ethical insight.

Ethics is in fact reverence for the will-to-live both within and without my own personality. The immediate product of reverence for the will-to-live which I find in myself is the profound life-affirmation of resignation. I comprehend my will-to-live not only as something which lives itself out in fortunate moments of success, but also as something which is conscious of itself and its own experiences. If I do not allow this experiencing of myself to be dissipated by heedless lack of reflection, but, on the contrary, deliberately pause in it as one who feels its real value, I am rewarded by a disclosure of the secret of spiritual independence. I become a partaker in an unguessed-at freedom amid the destinies of life. At moments when I should otherwise have thought myself to be overwhelmed and crushed, I feel myself uplifted in a state of inexpressible joy, astounding to myself, in which I am conscious of freedom from the world and experience a clarifying of my whole view of life. Resignation is the vestibule through which we pass in entering the palace of ethics. Only he who experiences inner freedom from external events in profound surrender to his own will-to-live is capable of the profound and permanent surrender of himself for the sake of other life.

As I struggle for freedom from the external occurrences of life in reverence for my own will-to-live, so also do I wrestle for freedom from myself. I practise the higher independence not only with regard to that which happens to me personally, but also in respect to the way in which I behave towards the world.

As the result of reverence for my own existence I force myself to be sincere with myself. Anything that I acquire by acting contrary to my convictions is bought too dearly. I am afraid of wounding my will-to-live with poisoned spears by disloyalty to my own personality.

That Kant places sincerity toward oneself in the very centre of his ethical system is a witness to the profundity of his own ethical perception.

We started Many Churches for others in many places, But never started a congregation for ourselves

Why? Our congregation was started by John & Mary Henson, Jones, ... & Earl Brooks & Van Eaton

But he is unable to grasp the connection between self-sincerity and activist ethics because in his search for the essential nature of the ethical he never gets as far as the idea of reverence for life. *what is life for a congregation — ?*

In actual practice the ethic of self-sincerity passes over unconsciously into that of self-sacrifice for others. Sincerity toward myself forces me to acts which appear so much like self-sacrifice that the current ethic derives them from this latter impulse.

Why do I forgive my fellow-man? The current ethic says that it is because I sympathize with him. It presents men as impossibly good when they forgive, and allows them to practise a kind of forgiveness which is really humiliating to the person forgiven. Thus it turns forgiveness into a sort of sweetened triumph of self-sacrifice.

The ethic of reverence for life clears away these obscure and misty notions. All forbearance and forgiveness is for it an act to which it is compelled by sincerity towards itself. I am obliged to exercise unlimited forgiveness because, if I did not forgive, I should be untrue to myself, in that I should thus act as if I were not guilty in the same way as the other has been guilty with regard to me. I must forgive the lies directed against myself, because my own life has been so many times blotted by lies; I must forgive the lovelessness, the hatred, the slander, the fraud, the arrogance which I encounter, since I myself have so often lacked love, hated, slandered, defrauded, and been arrogant. I must forgive without noise or fuss. In general I do not forgive, I do not even get as far as being merely just. And this also is no exaggeration, but a necessary extension and refinement of our usual ethic.

We have to conduct the fight against the evil element which exists in man, not by judging others, but only by judging ourselves. The conflict with our own nature, and sincerity towards ourselves, are the instruments with which we work on others. We move silently into the midst of the struggle for that profound spiritual independence which grows from reverence for our own life. True power makes no noise. It is there, and it produces its effect. True ethic begins where the use of words stops.

The most essential element of activist ethics, even if it does appear as surrender, is thus a product of the impulse to sincerity towards oneself, and in that is contained its real value. The whole ethic of independence from the world only runs as a clear stream when it issues from this source. I am not gentle, peaceable, patient and friendly from a kindly disposition towards others, but because I thus secure the most profound independence. There is an indissoluble connection between the reverence for life with which I face my own existence, and that in which I relate myself to others in acts of self-sacrifice.

what then is mission work?

It is because the current ethic possesses no fundamental principle of morality that it plunges immediately into the discussion of various conflicting opinions in the ethical realm. The ethic of reverence for life is in no hurry to do this. It takes its own time to think out its fundamental moral principle on all sides. Then, complete in itself, it takes up its own position with regard to these conflicts. *What is spiritual life?*

Ethics has to come to an understanding with three opponents; with lack of thought, with egoistic independence, and with the community.

Of the first of these, ethics has not usually taken sufficient account, because it never comes to any open conflict between the two. But, unnoticed, this opponent is constantly on the offensive. *What is the role of Good News Spiritual*

Ethics can take possession of an extensive tract without encountering the troops of egoism. A man can do a great deal of good without being obliged to sacrifice his own interests or desires. Even if he does lose a little bit of his own life in so doing, it is such an insignificant fragment that he misses it no more than he would a single hair or a tiny scale of skin.

To a very large extent the attainment of inner freedom from the world, loyalty to one's own being, existence in distinction from the world, even self-sacrifice for the sake of other life, is only a matter of concentrating attention on this relation. We miss so much of it because we do not keep steadfastly to the point. We do not place ourselves directly under the pressure of the inner impulse to ethical existence. Steam spurts out in all directions from a leaky boiler. The losses of energy on every side are so great in the current ethic because it has at its command no single fundamental moral principle which can act on its thought. It cannot make its boiler steam-tight, nay, it does not even thoroughly inspect it. But reverence for life, which is always present to thought, informs and penetrates, continually and in every direction, a man's observation, reflection and decisions. He can as little resist this process as water can hinder the dyestuff dropped into it from tinting it. The struggle with lack of thought is a conscious process and is always going on.

How does the ethic of reverence for life stand in the conflicts which arise between the inner impulse to self-sacrifice and necessary self-maintenance?

I also am subject to the variance with itself of the will-to-live. My existence is in conflict at a thousand points with that of others. The necessity is laid upon me of destroying and injuring life. If I walk along a lonely road my foot brings annihilation and pain on the tiny beings which people it. In order to maintain my own existence I am obliged to protect it from the existences which would harm it. I become a persecutor of the little mouse which inhabits my dwelling, a destroyer of the insect which desires to breed there, no less than a wholesale murderer of the bacteria which may endanger my life. I can only secure nourishment for myself by destroying animals and plants. My own good fortune is built on the injuries and hardships of my fellow-men.

How is ethics to exist at all amid the gruesome necessities to which I am a slave because the will-to-live is at variance with itself?

The current ethic seeks for a compromise. It tries to lay down rules as to how much of my own existence and of my own happiness I must give up, and how much I may continue to hold at the expense of the existence and happiness of other life. In so deciding it creates an experimental and relative ethic. That which is actually not ethical at all, but is a hotch-potch of non-ethical necessity and of real ethics, gives itself out as genuinely ethical and normative. Thus a monstrous confusion arises, and thereby a constantly increasing obscuration of the notion of the ethical element.

The ethic of reverence for life recognizes no such thing as a relative ethic. The maintenance and enhancement of life are the only things it counts as being good in themselves. All destruction of and injury to life, from whatever circumstances they may result, are reckoned by it as evil. It does not give place to ready-made accommodations of ethics and necessity which are too eager to occupy the ground. The absolute ethic of reverence makes its own agreements with the individual from moment to moment, agreements always fresh and always original and basic. It does not relieve him of the conflict, but rather forces him to decide for himself in each case how far he can remain ethical and how far he must submit himself to the necessity of destroying and harming life and thus become guilty. Man does not make ethical progress by assimilating instruction with regard to accommodations between the ethical and the necessary, but only by hearing ever more clearly the voice of the ethical element, by being ever more under the control of his own yearning to maintain and to enhance life, and by becoming ever more obstinate in his opposition to the necessity of destroying and injuring life.

In ethical conflicts it is only subjective decisions that a man has to face. No one else can determine for him where lies the utmost limit of the possibility of continuing to maintain and cherish life. He alone has to judge by allowing himself to be led by a sense of responsibility for other lives raised to the highest degree possible. We must never let this sense become dulled and blunted. In effect, however, we are doing so, if we are content to find the conflicts becoming continually more insoluble. The good conscience is an invention of the devil.

What does reverence for life teach us about the relations of man and the non-human animals?

Whenever I injure life of any kind I must be quite clear as to whether this is necessary or not. I ought never to pass the limits of the unavoidable, even in apparently insignificant cases. The countryman who has mowed down a thousand blossoms in his meadow as fodder for his cows should take care that on the way home he does not, in wanton pastime, switch off the head of a single flower growing on the edge of the road, for in so doing he injures life without being forced to do so by necessity.

Those who test operations or drugs on animals, or who inoculate them with diseases so that they may be able to help human beings by means of the results thus obtained, ought never to rest satisfied with the general idea that their dreadful doings are performed in pursuit of a worthy aim. It is their duty to ponder in every separate case whether it is really and truly necessary thus to sacrifice an animal for humanity. They ought to be filled with anxious care to alleviate as much as possible the pain which they cause. How many outrages are committed in this way in scientific institutions where narcotics are often omitted to save time and trouble! How many also when animals are made to suffer agonizing tortures, only in order to demonstrate to students scientific truths which are perfectly well known. The very fact that the animal, as a victim of research, has in his pain rendered such services to suffering men, has itself created a new and unique relation of solidarity between him and ourselves. The result is that a fresh obligation is laid on each of us to do as much good as we possibly can to all creatures in all sorts of circumstances. When I help an insect out of his troubles all that I do is to attempt to remove

some of the guilt contracted through these crimes against animals.

Wherever any animal is forced into the service of man, the sufferings which it has to bear on that account are the concern of every one of us. No one ought to permit, in so far as he can prevent it, pain or suffering for which he will not take the responsibility. No one ought to rest at ease in the thought that in so doing he would mix himself up in affairs which are not his business. Let no one shirk the burden of his responsibility. When there is so much maltreatment of animals, when the cries of thirsting creatures go up unnoticed from the railway trucks, when there is so much roughness in our slaughterhouses, when in our kitchens so many animals suffer horrible deaths from unskilful hands, when animals endure unheard-of agonies from heartless men, or are delivered to the dreadful play of children, then we are all guilty and must bear the blame.

We are afraid of shocking or offending by showing too plainly how deeply we are moved by the sufferings which man causes to the non-human creatures. We tend to reflect that others are more "rational" than we are, and would consider that which so disturbs us as customary and as a matter of course. And then, suddenly, they let fall some expression which shows us that they, too, are not really satisfied with the situation. Strangers to us hitherto, they are now quite near our own position. The masks, in which we had each concealed ourselves from the other, fall off. We now know that neither of us can cut ourselves free from the horrible necessity which plays ceaselessly around us. What a wonderful thing it is thus to get to know each other!

The ethic of reverence for life forbids any of us to deduce from the silence of our contemporaries that they, or in their case we, have ceased to feel what as thinking men we all cannot but feel. It prompts us to keep a mutual watch in this atmosphere of suffering and endurance, and to speak and act without panic according to the responsibility which we feel. It inspires us to join in a search for opportunities to afford help of some kind or other to the animals, to make up for the great amount of misery which they endure at our hands, and thus to escape for a moment from the inconceivable horrors of existence.

But the ethic of reverence for life also places us in a position of fearful responsibility with regard to our relations to other men.

We find, again, that it offers us no teaching about the bounds of legitimate self-maintenance; it calls us again to come to a separate understanding with the ethic of self-sacrifice in each individual case. According to the sense of responsibility which is my personal experience so I must decide what part of my life, my possessions, my rights, my happiness, my time or my rest, I ought to give up, and what part I ought to keep back.

Regarding the question of property, the ethic of reverence for life is outspokenly individualist in the sense that goods earned or inherited are to be placed at the disposition of the community, not according to any standards whatever laid down by society, but according to the absolutely free decision of the individual. It places all its hopes on the enhancement of the feeling of responsibility in men. It defines possessions as the property of the community, of which the individual is sovereign steward. One serves society by conducting a business from which a certain number of employees draw their means of sustenance; another, by giving away his property in order to help his fellow-men. Each one will decide on his own course somewhere between these two extreme cases according to the sense of responsibility which is determined for him by the particular circumstances of his own life. No one is to judge others. It is a question of individual responsibility; each is to value his possessions as instruments with which he is to work. It makes no difference whether the work is done by keeping and increasing, or by giving up, the property. Possessions must belong to the community in the most various ways, if they are to be used to the best advantage in its service.

Those who have very little that they can call their own are in most danger of becoming purely egoistic. A deep truth lies in the parable of Jesus, which makes the servant who had received the least the least faithful of all.

The ethic of reverence for life does not even allow me to possess my own rights absolutely. It does not allow me to rest in the thought that I, as the more capable, advance at the expense of the less capable. It presents to me as a problem what human law and opinion allow as a matter of course. It prompts me to think of others and to ponder whether I can really allow myself the intrinsic right of plucking all the fruits which my hand is physically able to reach. And then it may occur that, following my regard for the existence of others, I do what appears as foolishness to the generality of men. It may, indeed, prove itself to have been actually foolishness in so far as my renunciation for the sake of others has really no useful effect. Yet all the same I was right in doing as I did. Reverence for life is the supreme motive. That which it commands has its own meaning, even if it seem foolish or useless. Indeed, we all really seek in one another for that sort of foolishness which shows that we are impelled by the higher responsibility. It is only as we become less rational in the ordinary sense of the word that the ethical disposition works out in us and solves problems previously insoluble.

Study Questions

1. What is Schweitzer's theory of Reverence for Life? Explain.
2. Do you agree with Schweitzer that all life is equally valuable, equally sacred? Explain.

CHAPTER 9

Against the Sanctity of Life Doctrine

JONATHAN GLOVER

Jonathan Glover is a tutor at New College, Oxford University, and the author of several books on ethics, among them *What Sort of People Should There Be?* (1984) and *Causing Death and Saving Lives* (1977), from which the following selection is taken.

Glover begins with the question "Why is killing wrong?" and argues that we do not need the doctrine of the sanctity of human life to justify this judgment. The idea of the sanctity of life is too vague and inappropriate for moral judgment. Instead, we should base our morality on the idea of quality of life, the notion of a life worth living. Since no one can decide for another just what kind of life is worth living, we should respect other people's assessment of whether their lives are worthwhile and refrain from taking life.

I cannot but have reverence for all that is called life. I cannot avoid compassion for all that is called life. That is the beginning and foundation of morality.

ALBERT SCHWEITZER, *Reverence for Life*

To persons who are not murderers, concentration camp administrators, or dreamers of sadistic fantasies, the inviolability of human life seems to be so self-evident that it might appear pointless to inquire into it. To inquire into it is embarrassing as well because, once raised, the question seems to commit us to beliefs we do not wish to espouse and to confront us with contradictions which seem to deny what is self-evident.

EDWARD SHILS, "The Sanctity of Life," in D. H. Labby, *Life or Death: Ethics and Options,* 1968

MOST OF US THINK IT IS WRONG to kill people. Some think it is wrong in all circumstances, while others think that in special circumstances (say, in a just war or in self-defence) some killing may be justified. But even those who do not think killing is always wrong nor-

Reprinted from Causing Death and Saving Lives *(Hammondsworth, U.K.: Penguin Books, 1977) by permission.*

mally think that a special justification is needed. The assumption is that killing can at best only be justified to avoid a greater evil.

It is not obvious to many people what the answer is to the question *'Why is killing wrong?'* It is not clear whether the wrongness of killing should be treated as a kind of moral axiom, or whether it can be explained by appealing to some more fundamental principle or set of principles. One very common view is that some principle of the sanctity of life has to be included among the ultimate principles of any acceptable moral system.

In order to evaluate the view that life is sacred, it is necessary to distinguish between two different kinds of objection to killing: direct objections and those based on side-effects.

Direct Objections and Side-Effects

Direct objections to killing are those that relate solely to the person killed. Side-effects of killings are effects on people other than the one killed. Many of the possible reasons for not killing someone appeal to side-effects. (To call them 'side-effects' is not to imply that they must be less important than the direct objections.) When a man dies or is killed, his parents, wife, children or friends may be made sad. His family may always have a less happy atmosphere and very likely less money to spend. The fatherless children may grow up to be less secure and confident than they would have been. The community loses whatever good contribution the man might otherwise have made to it. Also, an act of killing may help weaken the general reluctance to take life or else be thought to do so. Either way, it may do a bit to undermine everyone's sense of security.

Most people would probably give some weight to these side-effects in explaining the wrongness of killing, but would say that they are not the whole story, or even the main part of it.

People who say this hold that there are direct objections to killing, independent of effects on others. This view can be brought out by an imaginary case in which an act of killing would have no harmful side-effects.

Suppose I am in prison, and have an incurable disease from which I shall very soon die. The man who shares my cell is bound to stay in prison for the rest of his life, as society thinks he is too dangerous to let out. He has no friends, and all his relations are dead. I have a poison that I could put in his food without him knowing it and that would kill him without being detectable. Everyone else would think he died from natural causes.

In this case, the objections to killing that are based on side-effects collapse. No one will be sad or deprived. The community will not miss his contribution. People will not feel insecure, as no one will know a murder has been committed. And even the possible argument based on one murder possibly weakening my own reluctance to take life in future carries no weight here, since I shall die before having opportunity for further killing. It might even be argued that consideration of side-effects tips the balance positively in favour of killing this man, since the cost of his food and shelter is a net loss to the community.

Those of us who feel that in this case we cannot accept that killing the man would be either morally right or morally neutral must hold that killing is at least sometimes wrong for reasons independent of side-effects. One version of this view that killing is directly wrong is the doctrine of the sanctity of life. To state this doctrine in an acceptable way is harder than it might at first seem.

Stating the Principle of the Sanctity of Life

The first difficulty is a minor one. We do not want to state the principle in such a way that it must have overriding authority over other

[margin note: utilitarianist justifications]

considerations. To say 'taking life is always wrong' commits us to absolute pacifism. But clearly a pacifist and a non-pacifist can share the view that killing is in itself an evil. They need only differ over when, if ever, killing is permissible to avoid other evils. A better approximation is 'taking life is directly wrong', where the word 'directly' simply indicates that the wrongness is independent of effects on other people. But even this will not quite do. For, while someone who believes in the sanctity of life must hold that killing is directly wrong, not everyone who thinks that killing is sometimes or always directly wrong has to hold that life is sacred. (It is possible to believe that killing is directly wrong only where the person does not want to die or where the years of which he is deprived would have been happy ones. These objections to killing have nothing to do with side-effects and yet do not place value on life merely for its own sake.) The best formulation seems to be *'taking life is intrinsically wrong'*.

There is another problem about what counts as 'life'. Does this include animals? When we think of higher animals, we may want to say 'yes', even if we want to give animal life less weight than human life. But do we want to count it wrong to tread on an ant or kill a mosquito? And, even if we are prepared to treat all animal life as sacred, there are problems about plant life. Plants are living things. Is weeding the garden wrong? Let us avoid these difficulties for the moment by stating the principle in terms of human life. When we have become clearer about the reasons for thinking it wrong to kill people, we will be better placed to see whether the same reasons should make us respect animal or plant life as well. So, to start with, we have the principle: 'taking human life is intrinsically wrong'.

Can any explanation be given of the belief that taking human life is intrinsically wrong? Someone who simply says that this principle is an axiom of his moral system, and refuses to give any further explanation, cannot be 'refuted' unless his system is made inconsistent by the inclu-

sion of this principle. And, even then, he might choose to give up other beliefs rather than this one. The strategy of this chapter will be to try to cast doubt on the acceptability of this principle by looking at the sort of explanation that might be given by a supporter who was prepared to enter into some discussion of it. My aim will be to suggest that the doctrine of the sanctity of life is not acceptable, but that there is embedded in it a moral view we should retain. We should reject the view that taking human life is *intrinsically* wrong, but retain the view that it is normally *directly* wrong: that most acts of killing people would be wrong in the absence of harmful side-effects.

The concept of human life itself raises notorious boundary problems. When does it begin? Is an eight-month foetus already a living human being? How about a newly fertilized egg? These questions need discussing, but it seems preferable to decide first on the central problem of why we value human life, and on that basis to draw its exact boundaries, rather than to stipulate the boundaries arbitrarily in advance. But there is another boundary problem that can be discussed first, as it leads us straight into the central issue about the sanctity of life. This boundary problem is about someone fallen irreversibly into a coma: does he still count as a living human being?

'Being Alive Is Intrinsically Valuable'

Someone who thinks that taking life is intrinsically wrong may explain this by saying that the state of being alive is itself intrinsically valuable. This claim barely rises to the level of an argument for the sanctity of life, for it simply asserts that there is value in what the taking of life takes away.

Against such a view, cases are sometimes cited of people who are either very miserable or in great pain, without any hope of cure. Might such people not be better off dead? But this could be admitted without giving up the view that life is intrinsically valuable. We could say that life has value, but that not being desperately miserable can have even more value.

I have no way of refuting someone who holds that being alive, even though unconscious, is intrinsically valuable. But it is a view that will seem unattractive to those of us who, in our own case, see a life of permanent coma as in no way preferable to death. From the subjective point of view, there is nothing to choose between the two. Schopenhauer saw this clearly when he said of the destruction of the body:

> But actually we feel this destruction only in the evils of illness or of old age; on the other hand, for the *subject*, death itself consists merely in the moment when consciousness vanishes, since the activity of the brain ceases. The extension of the stoppage to all the other parts of the organism which follows this is really already an event after death. Therefore, in a subjective respect, death concerns only consciousness.[1]

Those of us who think that the direct objections to killing have to do with death considered, from the standpoint of the person killed will find it natural to regard life as being of value only as a necessary condition of consciousness. For permanently comatose existence is subjectively indistinguishable from death, and unlikely often to be thought intrinsically preferable to it by people thinking of their own future.

'Being Conscious Is Intrinsically Valuable'

The believer in the sanctity of life may accept that being *alive* is only of *instrumental* value and say that it is *consciousness* that *is intrinsically valuable*. In making this claim, he still differs from someone who only values consciousness because

it is necessary for *happiness*. Before we can assess this belief in the intrinsic value of being conscious, it is necessary to distinguish between two different ways in which we may talk about consciousness. Sometimes we talk about *'mere'* consciousness and sometimes we talk about what might be called 'a high level of consciousness'.

'Mere' consciousness consists simply in awareness or the having of experiences. When I am awake, I am aware of my environment. I have a stream of consciousness that comes abruptly to a halt if I faint or fades out when I go to sleep (until I have dreams). There are large philosophical problems about the meaning of claims of this kind, which need not be discussed here. I shall assume that we all at some level understand what it is to have experiences, or a stream of consciousness.

But this use of 'consciousness' should be distinguished from another, perhaps metaphorical, use of the word. We sometimes say that men are at a higher level of consciousness than animals, or else that few, if any, peasants are likely to have as highly developed a consciousness as Proust. It is not clear exactly what these claims come to, nor that the comparison between men and animals is of the same sort as the comparison between peasants and Proust. But perhaps what underlies such comparisons is an attempt to talk about a person's experiences in terms of the extent to which they are rich, varied, complex or subtle, or the extent to which they involve emotional responses, as well as various kind of awareness. Again, it is not necessary to discuss here the analysis of the meaning of these claims. It is enough if it is clear that to place value on 'mere' consciousness is different from valuing it for its richness and variety. I shall assume that the claim that being conscious is intrinsically good is a claim about 'mere' consciousness, rather than about a high level of consciousness.

If one is sceptical about the intrinsic value of 'mere' consciousness, as against that of a high level of consciousness, it is hard to see what consideration can be mentioned in its favour. The advocate of this view might ask us to perform a thought experiment of a kind that G. E. Moore would perhaps have liked. We might be asked to imagine two universes, identical except that one contained a being aware of its environment and the other did not. It may be suggested that the universe containing the conscious being would be intrinsically better.

But such a thought experiment seems unconvincing. There is the familiar difficulty that, confronted with a choice so abstract and remote, it may be hard to feel any preference at all. And, since we are dealing with 'mere' consciousness rather than with a high level of consciousness, it is necessary to postulate that the conscious being has no emotional responses. It cannot be pleased or sorry or in pain; it cannot be interested or bored; it is merely aware of its environment. Views may well differ here, but, if I could be brought to take part in this thought experiment at all, I should probably express indifference between the two universes. The only grounds I might have for preferring the universe with the conscious being would be some hope that it might evolve into some more interesting level of consciousness. But to choose on these grounds is not to assign any intrinsic value to 'mere' consciousness.

The belief that the sole reason why it is directly wrong to take human life is the intrinsic value of 'mere' consciousness runs into a problem concerning animals. Many of us place a special value on human life as against animal life. Yet animals, or at least the higher ones, seem no less aware of their surroundings than we are. Suppose there is a flood and I am faced with the choice of either saving a man's life or else saving the life of a cow. Even if all side-effects were left out of account, failure to save the man seems worse than failure to save the cow. The person who believes that the sanctity of life rests solely on the value of 'mere' consciousness is faced with a dilemma. Either he must accept that the life of the cow and the life of the man are in themselves of equal value, or he must give reasons for thinking that cows are less conscious than men or else not conscious at all.

It is hard to defend the view that, while I have good grounds for thinking that other people are conscious, I do not have adequate reasons for thinking that animals are conscious. Humans and animals in many ways respond similarly to their surroundings. Humans have abilities that other animals do not, such as the ability to speak or to do highly abstract reasoning, but it is not only in virtue of these abilities that we say people are conscious. And there is no neurophysiological evidence that suggests that humans alone can have experiences.

The alternative claim is that *animals are less conscious* than we are. The view that 'mere' consciousness is a matter of degree is attractive when considered in relation to animals. The philosophical literature about our knowledge of other minds is strikingly silent and unhelpful about the animal boundaries of consciousness. How far back down the evolutionary scale does consciousness extend? What kind and degree of complexity must a nervous system exhibit to be the vehicle of experiences? What kind and degree of complexity of behaviour counts as the manifestation of consciousness? At least with our present ignorance of the physiological basis of human consciousness, any clear-cut boundaries of consciousness, drawn between one kind of animal and another, have an air of arbitrariness. For this reason it is attractive to suggest that consciousness is a matter of degree, not stopping abruptly, but fading away slowly as one descends the evolutionary scale.

But the belief that 'mere' consciousness is a matter of degree is obscure as well as attractive. Is it even an intelligible view?

There are two ways in which talk of degrees of consciousness can be made clearer. One is by explaining it in terms of the presence or absence of whole 'dimensions' of consciousness. This is the way in which a blind man is less conscious of his environment than a normal man. (Though, if his other senses have developed unusual acuity, he will in other respects be more conscious than a normal man.) But if a lower degree of consciousness consists either in the absence of a whole dimension such as sight, or in senses with lower acuity than those of men, it is not plausible to say that animals are all less conscious than we are. Dogs seem to have all the dimensions of consciousness that we do. It is true that they often see less well, but on the other hand their sense of smell is better than ours. If the sanctity of life were solely dependent on degree of consciousness interpreted this way, we often could not justify giving human life priority over animal life. We might also be committed to giving the life of a normal dog priority over the life of a blind man.

The other way in which we talk of degrees of 'mere' consciousness comes up in such contexts as waking up and falling sleep. There is a *sleepy state* in which we can be unaware of words that are softly spoken, but aware of any noise that is loud or sharp. But this again fails to separate men from animals. For animals are often alert in a way that is quite unlike the drowsiness of a man not fully awake.

Whether or not 'mere' consciousness fades away lower down on the evolutionary scale (and the idea of a sharp boundary *does* seem implausible), there seems at least no reason to regard the 'higher' animals as less aware of the environment than ourselves. (It is not being suggested that animals are only at the level of 'mere' consciousness, though no doubt they are less far above it than most of us.) If the whole basis of the ban on killing were the intrinsic value of mere consciousness, killing higher animals would be as bad as killing humans.

It would be possible to continue to hold mere consciousness to be of intrinsic value, and either to supplement this principle with others or else to abandon the priority given to human life. But when the principle is distinguished from different ones that would place a value on higher levels of consciousness, it has so little intuitive appeal that we may suspect its attractive-

ness to depend on the distinction not being made. If, in your own case, you would opt for a state never rising above mere consciousness, in preference to death, have you purged the illegitimate assumption that you would take an interest in what you would be aware of?

'Being Human Is Intrinsically Valuable'

It is worth mentioning that the objection to taking human life should not rest on what is sometimes called 'speciesism': human life being treated as having a special priority over animal life *simply* because it is human. The analogy is with racism, in its purest form, according to which people of a certain race ought to be treated differently *simply* because of their membership of that race, without any argument referring to special features of that race being given. This is objectionable partly because of its moral arbitrariness: unless some relevant empirical characteristics can be cited, there can be no argument for such discrimination. Those concerned to reform our treatment of animals point out that speciesism exhibits the same arbitrariness. It is not in itself sufficient argument for treating a creature less well to say simply that it is not a member of our species. An adequate justification must cite relevant differences between the species. We still have the question of what features of a life are of intrinsic value.

The Concept of a 'Life Worth Living'

I have suggested that, in destroying life or mere consciousness, we are not destroying anything intrinsically valuable. These states only matter because they are necessary for other things that matter in themselves. If a list could be made of all the things that are valuable for their own sake, these things would be the ingredients of a 'life worth living'.

One objection to the idea of judging that a life is worth living is that this seems to imply the possibility of comparing being alive and being dead. And, as Wittgenstein said, 'Death is not an event in life: we do not live to experience death.'

But we can have a preference for being alive over being dead, or for being conscious over being unconscious, without needing to make any 'comparisons' between these states. We prefer to be anaesthetized for a painful operation; queuing for a bus in the rain at midnight, we wish we were at home asleep; but for the most part we prefer to be awake and experience our life as it goes by. These preferences do not depend on any view about 'what it is like' being unconscious, and our preference for life does not depend on beliefs about 'what it is like' being dead. It is rather that we treat being dead or unconscious as nothing, and then decide whether a stretch of experience is better or worse than nothing. And this claim, that life of a certain sort is better than nothing, is an expression of our preference.

Any list of the ingredients of a worth-while life would obviously be disputable. Most people might agree on many items, but many others could be endlessly argued over. It might be agreed that a happy life is worth living, but people do not agree on what happiness is. And some things that make life worth living may only debatably have to do with happiness. (Aristotle:[2] 'And so they tell us that Anaxagoras answered a man who was raising problems of this sort and asking why one should choose rather to be born than not—"for the sake of viewing the heavens and the whole order of the universe".')

A life worth living should not be confused with a morally virtuous life. Moral virtues such as honesty or a sense of fairness can belong to someone whose life is relatively bleak and empty.

Music may enrich someone's life, or the death of a friend impoverish it, without him growing more or less virtuous.

I shall not try to say what sorts of things do make life worth living. (Temporary loss of a sense of the absurd led me to try to do so. But, apart from the disputability of any such list, I found that the ideal life suggested always sounded ridiculous.) I shall assume that a life worth living has more to it than mere consciousness. It should be possible to explain the wrongness of killing partly in terms of the destruction of a life worth living, without presupposing more than minimal agreement as to exactly what makes life worth-while.

I shall assume that, where someone's life is worth living, this is a good reason for holding that it would be directly wrong to kill him. This is what can be extracted from the doctrine of the sanctity of life by someone who accepts the criticisms made here of that view. If life is worth preserving only because it is the vehicle for consciousness, and consciousness is of value only because it is necessary for something else, then that 'something else' is the heart of this particular objection to killing. It is what is meant by a 'life worth living' or a 'worth-while life'.

The idea of dividing people's lives into ones that are worth living and ones that are not is likely to seem both presumptuous and dangerous. As well as seeming to indicate an arrogant willingness to pass godlike judgements on other people's lives, it may remind people of the Nazi policy of killing patients in mental hospitals. But there is really nothing godlike in such a judgement. It is not a moral judgement we are making, if we think that someone's life is so empty and unhappy as to be not worth living. It results from an attempt (obviously an extremely fallible one) to see his life from his own point of view and to see what he gets out of it. It must also be stressed that no suggestion is being made that it automatically becomes right to kill people whose lives we think are not worth living. It is only being argued that, if someone's life is worth living, this is *one* reason why it is directly wrong to kill him.

Is the Desire to Live the Criterion of a Worth-While Life?

It might be thought that a conclusive test of whether or not someone's life is worth living is whether or not he wants to go on living. The attractiveness of this idea comes partly from the fact that the question whether someone has a worth-while life involves thinking from his point of view, rather than thinking of his contribution to the lives of other people.

This proposal would commit us to believing that a person cannot want to end his life if it is worth living, and that he cannot want to prolong his life where it is not worth living. But these beliefs are both doubtful. In a passing mood of depression, someone who normally gets a lot out of life may want to kill himself. And someone who thinks he will go to hell may wish to prolong his present life, however miserable he is. The frying pan may be worse than nothing but better than the fire. And some people, while not believing in hell, simply fear death. They may wish they had never been born, but still not want to die.

For these reasons, someone's own desire to live or die is not a conclusive indication of whether or not he has a life worth living. And, equally obviously, with people who clearly do have lives worth living, the relative strength of their desires to live is not a reliable indicator of how worth-while they find their lives. Someone whose hopes are often disappointed may cling to life as tenaciously as the happiest person in the world.

If we are to make these judgements, we cannot escape appealing to our own independent beliefs about what sorts of things enrich or impoverish people's lives. But, when this has been said, it should be emphasized that, when the question arises whether someone's life is worth living at all, his own views will normally be evidence of an overwhelmingly powerful kind. Our assessments of what other people get out of their lives are so fallible that only a monster of self-confidence would feel no qualms about correcting the judgement of the person whose life is in question.

Length of Life

The upshot of this discussion is that one reason why it is wrong to kill is that it is wrong to destroy a life which is worth living.

This can be seen in a slightly different perspective when we remember that we must all die one day, so that killing and lifesaving are interventions that alter length of life by bringing forward or postponing the date of death. . . .

The objection to killing made here is that it is wrong to shorten a worth-while life. Why is a longer-lasting worth-while life a better thing than an equally worth-while but briefer life? Some people, thinking about their own lives, consider length of life very desirable, while others consider the number of years they have is of no importance at all, the quality of their lives being all that matters.

There is an argument used by Marcus Aurelius in support of the view that length of life is unimportant:

> If a god were to tell you 'Tomorrow, or at least the day after, you will be dead', you would not, unless the most abject of men, be greatly solicitous whether it was to be the later day rather than the morrow, for what is the difference between them? In the same way, do not reckon it of great moment whether it will come years and years hence, or tomorrow.

This argument is unconvincing. From the fact that some small differences are below the threshold of mattering to us, it does not follow that all differences are insignificant. If someone steals all your money except either a penny or twopence, you will not mind much which he has left you with. It does not follow that the difference between riches and poverty is trivial.

There are at least two good reasons why a longer life can be thought better than a short one. One is that the quality of life is not altogether independent of its length: many plans and projects would not be worth undertaking without a good chance of time for their fulfillment. The other reason is that, other things being equal, more of a good thing is always better than less of it. This does not entail such absurd consequences as that an enjoyable play gets better as it gets longer, without limit. The point of the phrase 'other things being equal' is to allow for waning of interest and for the claims of other activities. So, unless life begins to pall, it is not in any way unreasonable to want more of it and to place a value on the prolonging of other people's worth-while lives.

Notes

1. A. Schopenhauer: *The World as Will and Representation,* translated by E. J. F. Payne, New York, 1969, bk 4, sect. 54.

2. *Eudemian Ethics* 1216 a 11.

Study Questions

1. What is Glover's view on the sanctity of life?
2. Go through Glover's arguments for the quality of life. Do you see any weaknesses? What are his basic assumptions?
3. What are his criteria for a worthwhile life? Analyze his view.

CHAPTER 10

The Sanctity of Life and the Concept of a Person

H. TRISTRAM ENGELHARDT, JR.

H. Tristram Engelhardt, Jr., is professor of medicine and community medicine, Baylor College of Medicine, and editor of the *Journal of Medicine and Philosophy.* He has written numerous articles and books in the area of medical ethics of which the most prominent is *The Foundation of Bioethics* (1986).

In this essay he seeks to clarify the idea of the sanctity of life, separating the biological life of humans from their dignity as persons. He goes on to distinguish the inherent dignity of persons as self-conscious and self-determining agents from the social sense of persons based on their instrumental value in society. The distinction has implications for medical ethics, specifically for abortion and for euthanasia of defective neonates. Engelhardt has provided us with an afterword to this reprinted material.

RECENT ADVANCES IN MEDICINE and the biomedical sciences have raised a number of ethical issues that medical ethics or, more broadly, bioethics have treated. Ingredient in such considerations, however, are fundamentally conceptual and ontological issues. To talk of the sanctity of life, for example, presupposes that one knows (1) what life is, and (2) what makes for its sanctity. More importantly, to talk of the rights of persons presupposes that one knows what counts as a person. In this paper I will provide an examination of the concept of person and will argue that the terms "human life" and even "human person" are complex and heterogeneous terms. I will hold that human life has more than one meaning and that there is more than one sense of human person. I will then indicate how the recognition of these multiple meanings has important implications for medicine.

I. Kinds of Life and Sanctity of Life

Whatever is meant by life's being sacred, it is rarely held that all life is equally sacred. Most people would find the life of bacteria, for example, to be less valuable or sacred than the life of fellow humans. In fact, there appears to be a spectrum of increasing value to life (I will presume that the term sanctity of life signifies that life has either special values or rights). All else being equal, plants seem to be valued less than lower animals, lower animals less than higher animals (such as primates other than humans), and humans are usually held to have the highest value. Moreover, distinctions are made with respect to humans. Not all human life has the same sanctity. The issue of brain-death, for example, turns on such a distinction. Brain-dead, but otherwise alive, human beings do not have the sanctity of normal adult human beings. That

---

Reprinted from Tom L. Beauchamp and Seymour Perlin, eds., Ethical Issues in Death and Dying *(Prentice-Hall, 1978) Copyright © H. Tristram Engelhardt, Jr.; by permission of the author.*

is, the indices of brain-death have been selected in order to measure the death of a person. As a legal issue, it is a question of when a human being ceases to be a person before the law. In a sense, the older definition of death measured the point at which organismic death occurred, when there was a complete cessation of vital functions. The life of the human organism was taken as a necessary condition for being a person, and, therefore, such a definition allowed one to identify cases in which humans ceased to be persons.

The brain-oriented concept of death is more directly concerned with human *personal* life. It makes three presuppositions: (1) that being a person involves more than mere vegetative life, (2) that merely vegetative life may have value but it has no rights, (3) that a sensory-motor organ such as the brain is a necessary condition for the possibility of experience and action in the world, that is, for being a person living in the world. Thus in the absence of the possibility of brain-function, one has the absence of the possibility of personal life—that is, the person is dead. Of course, the presence of some brain activity (or more than vegetative function) does not imply the presence of a person—a necessary condition for the life of a person is not a sufficient condition for the life of a person. The brain-oriented concept of death is of philosophical significance, for, among other things, it implies a distinction between human biological life and human personal life, between the life of a human organism and the life of a human person. That human biological life continues after brain death is fairly clear: the body continues to circulate blood, the kidneys function; in fact, there is no reason why the organism would not continue to be cross-fertile (e.g., produce viable sperm) and, thus, satisfy yet one more criterion for biological life. Such a body can be a biologically integrated reproductive unit even if the level of integration is very low. And, if such a body is an instance of human biological but not human personal life, then it is open to use merely as a subject of ex-

perimentation without the constraints of a second status as a person. Thus Dr. Willard Gaylin has argued that living but brain-dead bodies could provide an excellent source of subjects for medical experimentation and education and recommends "sustaining life in the brain-dead."[1] To avoid what would otherwise be an oxymoronic position, he is legitimately pressed to distinguish, as he does in fact, between "aliveness" and "personhood," or, to use more precise terminology, between human biological and human personal life. In short, a distinction between the status of human biological and personal life is presupposed.

We are brought then to a set of distinctions: first, human life must be distinguished as human personal and human biological life. Not all instances of human biological life are instances of human personal life. Brain-dead (but otherwise alive) human beings, human gametes, cells in human cell cultures, all count as instances of human biological life. Further, not only are some humans not persons, there is no reason to hold that all persons are humans, as the possibility of extraterrestrial self-conscious life suggests.

Second, the concept of the sanctity of life comes to refer in different ways to the value of biological life and the dignity of persons. Probably much that is associated with arguments concerning the sanctity of life really refers to the dignity of the life of persons. In any event, there is no unambiguous sense of being simply "pro-life" or a defender of the sanctity of life—one must decide what sort of life one wishes to defend and on what grounds. To begin with, the morally significant difference between biological and personal life lies in the fact, to use Kant's idiom, that persons are ends in themselves. Rational, self-conscious agents can make claims to treatment as ends in themselves because they can experience themselves, can know that they experience themselves, and can determine and control the circumstances of such experience. Self-conscious agents are self-determining and can claim respect as such. That is, they can claim the right to be respected as free agents. Such a claim is to the effect that self-respect and mutual respect turn on self-determination, on the fact that self-conscious beings are necessary for the existence of a moral order—a kingdom of ends, a community based on mutual self-respect, not force. Only self-conscious agents can be held accountable for their actions and thus be bound together solely in terms of mutual respect of each other's autonomy.

What I intend here is no more than an exegesis of what we could mean by "respecting persons." Kant, for example, argued that rational beings are "persons, because their very nature [as rational beings] points them out as ends in themselves." In this fashion, Kant developed a distinction between things that have only "a worth *for us*" and persons "whose existence is an end in itself." As a result, Kant drew a stark and clear distinction between persons and nonpersons. "A person is [a] subject whose actions are capable of being imputed [that is, one who can act responsibly]. Accordingly, moral personality is nothing but the freedom of a rational being under moral laws (whereas psychological personality is merely the capacity to be conscious of the identity of one's self in the various conditions of one's existence). . . . [In contrast], a thing is that which is not capable of any imputation [that is, of acting responsibly]." To be respected as a moral agent is precisely to be respected as a free self-conscious being capable of being blamed and praised, of being held responsible for its actions. The language of respect in the sense of recognizing others as free to determine themselves (i.e., as ends in themselves) rather than as beings to be determined by others (i.e., to be used as means, instruments to goods and values) turns upon acknowledging others as free, as moral agents.

This somewhat obvious exegesis (or tautological point) is an account of the nature of the language of obligation. Talk of obligation functions (1) to remind us that certain actions cannot be reconciled with the notion of a moral community, and (2) to enjoin others to pursue particular values or goods. The only actions that strictly contradict the notion of a moral community are those that are incompatible with the notion of such a community—actions that treat moral agents as if they were objects. Morality as mutual respect of autonomy (i.e., more than conjoint pursuit of particular goods or goals) can be consistently pursued only if persons in the strict sense (i.e., self-conscious agents, entities able to be self-legislative) are treated with respect for their autonomy. Though we may treat other entities with a form of respect, that respect is never central to the notion of a community of moral agents. Insofar as we identify persons with moral agents, we exclude from the range of the concept person those entities which are not self-conscious. Which is to say, only those beings are unqualified bearers of rights and duties who can both claim to be acknowledged as having a dignity beyond a value (i.e., as being ends in themselves) and can be responsible for their actions. Of course, this strict sense of person is not unlike that often used in the law. And, as Kant suggests in the passage above, it requires as well an experience of self-identity through time.

It is only respect for persons in this strict sense that cannot be violated without contradicting the idea of a moral order in the sense of the living with others on the basis of a mutual respect of autonomy. The point to be emphasized is a distinction between value and dignity, between biological life and personal life. These distinctions provide a basis for the differentiation between biological or merely animal life, and personal life, and turn on the rather commonsense criterion of respect being given that which can be respected—that is, blamed or praised. Moral treatment comes to depend, not implausibly, on moral agency. The importance of such distinctions for medicine is that they can be employed in treating medical ethical issues. As arguments, they are attempts to sort out everyday distinctions between moral agents, other animals, and just plain things. They provide a conceptual apparatus based on the meaning of obligations as respect due that which can have obligations.

The distinctions between human biological life and human personal life, and between the value of human biological life and the dignity of human personal life, involve a basic conceptual distinction that modern medical science presses as an issue of practical importance. Medicine after all is not merely the enterprise of preserving human life—if that were the case, medicine would confuse human cell cultures with patients who are persons. In fact, a maxim "to treat patients as persons" presupposes that we do or can indeed know who the persons are. These distinctions focus not only on the newly problematic issue of the definition of death, but on the question of abortion as well: issues that turn on when persons end and when they begin. In the case of the definition of death, one is saying that even though genetic continuity, organic function, and reproductive capability may extend beyond brain death, personal life does not. Sentience in an appropriate embodiment is a necessary condition for being a person. One, thus, finds that persons die when this embodiment is undermined.

With regard to abortion, many have argued similarly that the fetus is not a person, though it is surely an instance of human biological life. Even if the fetus is a human organism that will probably be genetically and organically continuous with a human person, it is not yet such a person. Simply put, fetuses are not rational, self-conscious beings—that is, given a strict definition of persons, fetuses do not qualify as persons. One sees this when comparing talk about dead men with talk about fetuses. When speaking of a dead man, one knows of whom one speaks, the one who died, the person whom one knew before his death. But in speaking of the fetus, one has no such person to whom one can refer. There is not yet a person, a "who," to whom one can refer in the case of the fetus (compare: one can keep promises to dead men

but not to men yet unborn). In short, the fetus in no way singles itself out as, or shows itself to be, a person. This conclusion has theoretical advantages, since many zygotes never implant and some divide into two. It offers as well a moral clarification of the practice of using intrauterine contraceptive devices and abortion. Whatever these practices involve, they do not involve the taking of the life of a person. This position in short involves recurring to a distinction forged by both Aristotle and St. Thomas—between biological life and personal life, between life that has value and life that has dignity.

But this distinction does too much, as the arguments by Michael Tooley on behalf of infanticide show.[2] By the terms of the argument, infants, as well as fetuses, are not persons—thus, one finds infants as much open to infanticide as fetuses are left open to abortion. The question then is whether one can recoup something for infants or perhaps even for fetuses. One might think that a counterargument, or at least a mitigating argument, could be made on the basis of potentiality—the potentiality of infants or the potentiality of fetuses. That argument, though, fails because one must distinguish the potentialities of a person from the potentiality to become a person. If, for example, one holds that a fetus has the potentiality of a person, one begs the very question at issue—whether fetuses are persons. But, on the other hand, if one succeeds in arguing that a fetus or infant has the potentiality to become a person, one has conceded the point that the fetus or infant is not a person. One may value a dozen eggs or a handful of acorns because they can become chickens or oak trees. But a dozen eggs is not a flock of chickens, a handful of acorns is not a stand of oaks. In short, the potentiality of X's to become Y's may cause us to value X's very highly because Y's are valued very highly, but until X's are Y's they do not have the value of Y's.

Which is to say, given our judgments concerning brain-dead humans and concerning zygotes, embryos, and fetuses, we are left in a quandary with regard to infants. How, if at all, are we to understand them to be persons, beings to whom we might have obligations? One should remember that these questions arise against the backdrop of issues concerning the disposition of deformed neonates—whether they should all be given maximal treatment, or whether some should be allowed to die, or even have their deaths expedited.

In short, though we have sorted out a distinction between the value of human biological life and the dignity of human personal life, this distinction does not do all we want, or rather it may do too much. That is, it goes against an intuitive appreciation of children, even neonates, as not being open to destruction on request. We may not in the end be able to support that intuition, for it may simply be a cultural prejudice; but I will now try to give a reasonable exegesis of its significance.

II. Two Concepts of Person

I shall argue in this section that a confusion arises out of a false presupposition that we have only one concept of person: we have at least two concepts (probably many more) of person. I will restrict myself to examining the two that are most relevant here. First, there is the sense of person that we use in identifying moral agents: individual, living bearers of rights and duties. That sense singles out entities who can participate in the language of morals, who can make claims and have those claims respected: the strict sense we have examined above. We would, for example, understand "person" in this sense to be used properly if we found another group of self-conscious agents in the universe and called them persons even if they were not human, though it is a term that usually applies to normal adult humans. This sense of person I shall term the strict sense, one which is used in reference to self-conscious, rational agents. But what of the respect accorded to infants and other examples of non-self-conscious

or not-yet-self-conscious human life? How are such entities to be understood?

A plausible analysis can, I believe, be given in terms of a second concept or use of person—a social concept or social role of person that is invoked when certain instances of human biological life are treated as if they were persons strictly, even though they are not. A good example is the mother-child or parent-child relationship in which the infant is treated as a person even though it is not one strictly. That is, the infant is treated as if it had the wants and desires of a person—its cries are treated as a call for food, attention, care, etc., and the infant is socialized, placed within a social structure, the family, and becomes a child. The shift is from merely biological to social significance. The shift is made on the basis that the infant is a human and is able to engage in a minimum of social interaction. With regard to the latter point, severely anencephalic infants may not qualify for the role *person* just as brain-dead adults would fail to qualify; both lack the ability to engage in minimal social interaction. This use of person is, after all, one employed with instances of human biological life that are enmeshed in social roles as if they were persons. Further, one finds a difference between the biological mother-fetus relation and the social mother-child relation. The first relation can continue whether or not there is social recognition of the fetus, the second cannot. The mother-child relation is essentially a social practice.

This practice can be justified as a means of preserving trust in families, of nurturing important virtues of care and solicitude towards the weak, and of assuring the healthy development of children. Further, it has a special value because it is difficult to determine specifically when in human ontogeny persons strictly emerge. Socializing infants into the role *person* draws the line conservatively. Humans do not become persons strictly until sometime after birth. Moreover, there is a considerable value in protecting anything that looks and acts in a reasonably human fashion, especially when it falls within an established human social role as infants do within the role *child*. This ascription of the role *person* constitutes a social practice that allows the rights of a person to be imputed to forms of human life that can engage in at least a minimum of social interaction. The interest is in guarding anything that could reasonably play the role *person* and thus to strengthen the social position of persons generally.

The social sense of person appears as well to structure the treatment of the senile, the mentally retarded, and the otherwise severely mentally infirm. Though they are not moral agents, persons strictly, they are treated as if they were persons. The social sense of person identifies their place in a social relationship with persons strictly. It is, in short, a practice that gives to instances of human biological life the status of persons. Unlike persons strictly, who are bearers of both rights and duties, persons in the social sense have rights but no duties. That is, they are not morally responsible agents, but are treated with respect (i.e., rights are imputed to them) in order to establish a practice of considerable utility to moral agents: a society where kind treatment of the infirm and weak is an established practice. The central element of the utility of this practice lies in the fact that it is often difficult to tell when an individual is a person strictly (i.e., how senile need one be in order no longer to be able to be a person strictly), and persons strictly might need to fear concerning their treatment (as well as the inadvertent mistreatment of other persons strictly) were such a practice not established. The social sense of person is a way of treating certain instances of human life in order to secure the life of persons strictly.

To recapitulate, we value children and our feelings of care for them, and we seek ways to make these commitments perdure. That is, social roles are ways in which we give an enduring fabric to our often inconstant passions. This is not to say that the social role person is merely a convention. To the contrary, it represents a fabric of ways of nurturing the high value we place on human life, especially the life that will come to be persons such as we. That fabric constitutes a practice of giving great value to instances of human biological life that can in some measure act as if they were persons, so that (1) the dignity of persons strictly is guarded against erosion during the various vicissitudes of health and disease, (2) virtues of care and attention to the dependent are nurtured, and (3) important social goals such as the successful rearing of children (and care of the aged) succeed. In the case of infants, one can add in passing a special consideration (4) that with luck they will become persons strictly, and that actions taken against infants could injure the persons they will eventually become.

It should be stressed that the social sense of person is primarily a utilitarian construct. A person in this sense is not a person strictly, and hence not an unqualified object of respect. Rather, one treats certain instances of human life as person for the good of those individuals who are persons strictly. As a consequence, exactly where one draws the line between persons in the social sense and merely human biological life is not crucial as long as the integrity of persons strictly is preserved. Thus there is a somewhat arbitrary quality about the distinction between fetuses and infants. One draws a line where the practice of treating human life as human personal life is practical and useful. Birth, including the production of a viable fetus through an abortion procedure, provides a somewhat natural line at which to begin to treat human biological life as human personal life. One might retort, Why not include fetuses as persons in a social sense? The answer is, Only if there are good reasons to do so in terms of utility. One would have to measure the utility of abortions for the convenience of women and families, for the prevention of the birth of infants with serious genetic diseases, and for the control of population growth against whatever increased goods would come from treating fetuses as persons. In addition, there would have to be consideration of the woman's right to choose freely concerning her body, and this would weigh

heavily against any purely utilitarian considerations for restricting abortions. Early abortions
would probably have to be allowed in any case
in order to give respect due to the woman as a
moral agent. But if these considerations are met,
the exact point at which the line is drawn between a fetus and an infant is arbitrary in that
utility considerations rarely produce absolute
lines of demarcation. The best that one can say
is that treating infants as persons in a social sense
supports many central human values that abortion does not undermine, and that allowing at
least early abortions acknowledges a woman's
freedom to determine whether or not she wishes
to be a mother.

One is thus left with at least two concepts of
person. On the one hand, persons strictly can
and usually do identify themselves as such—they
are self-conscious, rational agents, respect for
whom is part of valuing freedom, assigning
blame and praise, and understanding obligation.
That is, one's duty to respect persons strictly is
the core of morality itself. The social concept of
person is, on the other hand, more mediate, it
turns on central values but is not the same as respect for the dignity of persons strictly. It allows
us to value highly certain but not all instances of
human biological life, without confusing that
value with the dignity of persons strictly. That is,
we can maintain the distinction between human
biological and human personal life. We must
recognize, though, that some human biological
life is treated as human personal life even though
it does not involve the existence of a person in
the strict sense.

Afterword

When one returns to an article a decade and a
half after it was written, it is clear that there is
much more that one should say to clarify issues
than there is space to say it. This article was written as an exegesis of the moral assumptions that
frame the language that binds moral strangers.
It points out the centrality of the concept of persons when they meet uninformed by a common
sense of God's wishes or a particular reading of
moral reasoning. It does not deny that there is a
correct understanding of God's will or of moral
reasoning, only that it cannot be rationally demonstrated in any direct fashion to moral strangers and therefore cannot serve as the basis for
the morality that binds such individuals in
peaceable, limited democracies. The author, for
example, is an Orthodox Christian who holds
that abortion is sinful. The article is a part of a
postmodern philosophical undertaking aimed at
showing that all of the hopes of modern philosophy are not dead. For more on this point,
see *Bioethics and Secular Humanism: The Search
for a Common Morality* (Philadelphia/London:
Trinity Press International/SCM, 1991).

Notes

1. Willard Gaylin, "Harvesting the Dead,"
Harper's Magazine, 249 (September 1974), 23–30.
2. Michael Tooley, "A Defense of Abortion and
Infanticide," in *The Problem of Abortion*, ed. Joel
Feinberg (Belmont, Calif.: Wadsworth Publishing
Company, 1973), pp. 51–91.

Study Questions

1. Why does Engelhardt separate the idea of the sanctity of life from the idea of
biological life?
2. What is Engelhardt's position on the conflict between the sanctity of life and the
quality of life?
3. What are the implications of Engelhardt's views for euthanasia and abortion? Is
there a discrepancy between the views stated in the article and the position expressed in the "Afterword"? Explain.

CHAPTER 11

The Sanctity of Life Principle: A New Consensus

DANIEL CALLAHAN

Daniel Callahan is the former director of the Hastings Center, a research and educational center on ethics in medicine, the life sciences, and the professions. He is the author of several works on medical ethics, including *Setting Limits: Medical Goals in an Aging Society* (1988).

In this essay Callahan seeks a minimal moral consensus in a pluralistic society on the idea of the sanctity of life. First, Callahan critically examines two views of the sanctity of life: the Christian and the experiential. Then, having shown that these views have serious problems, he reinterprets the principle to preserve a valid core of meaning common to both the religious and secular. That core of meaning implies five rules having to do with the survival and integrity of the human species, the family lineage, and the individual.

He begins the essay by pointing out that progress in medical technology, while enhancing the quality and length of our lives, created new problems and forced us to make difficult decisions. In the light of these new problems and a growing pluralism in society's values, the sanctity-of-life principle may play a significant role.

ONE PRICE OF PROGRESS is the substitution of new problems for old. That mankind seems willing enough to pay it does not make the new problems any the less real, or fearsome. The advances of medicine, technology and the life sciences have meant, among other things, a lowering of infant mortality rates, the gradual conquest of disease and disabilities, a longer life expectancy and the possibility of family limitation and population control. One can legitimately call that "progress"; mankind has indeed won for itself the possibility of greater physical security. Yet in many instances these same advances have put before man new moral dilemmas or altered the character of some old ones.

If one were seeking the most characteristic mark of these dilemmas, it might well be located in the rapid expansion of the range of human alternatives. Yet the greater the number of alternatives, the greater the number of difficult choices which must be made; the greater the number of choices, the greater the possibility of confusion, disagreement, and poor judgment. On minor issues, this concatenation of possibilities may be a source of delight and the chance of poor judgment inconsequential. On major issues, however, one may—and should—tremble. The choices will make a difference, to ourselves and to others; any delight that choices *can* be made should be tempered by the sobering thought that they increasingly *must* be made.

The issue of human control over life and death is crucial. What are the responsibilities of those doctors charged with selecting critically ill

Reprinted from The Religious Situation, *edited by Donald R. Cutler. Copyright © 1968 by Beacon Press. Reprinted by permission of Beacon Press and Daniel Callahan.*

patients for treatment with *artificial kidney ma-chines?* There are *very few of these* machines and very few specialists capable of using them, but there are many people who will surely die if de-nied such treatment. (The National Kidney Foundation estimates that 5,000–10,000 people die from kidney conditions each year, many of whom could be saved.) Who should be chosen to live and who, unselected, allowed to die? The possibility of a heart transplant is thrilling, but even with better techniques, there are unlikely to be enough heart surgeons in the foreseeable future to take care of all those whose lives could be thus saved. And how are these expensive op-erations to be paid for (so far, they have cost from $25,000 to $50,000)? Where, in any event, are the hearts to come from—from the "dying" or "dead"? But how can we be sure that someone is "dying" or "dead"? What do we mean by those words? If a person's respiration, circulation, and heart activity are kept going by artificial means, but his brain has ceased func-tioning, is he "dead"? This question will be of interest not only to the doctor looking for a sound heart for transplant purposes, but even more frequently by those doctors and families who, in other circumstances, must decide whether to cease artificial support of incurably ill, unconscious patients. What are the obliga-tions of the doctor, of the family, of the hospital, of society? It may soon be possible to engineer genetically the future of human families and, be-yond that, the future of the human species. Should this be done? If so, by whom and under what conditions? Experiments with animals and humans have shown the possibility of chemically and electrically altering human emotions and consciousness. How far can we go with such treatment? Medical science depends upon ex-perimentation with human subjects. What are the moral conditions and limits of such work?

These are only some of the pressing ques-tions. . . .

[Callahan then argues that simply leaving each person to make up that person's mind on these issues leads to chaos.]

If, then, some minimal degree of moral con-sensus is necessary on matters of life and death, what is it and on what can it be based? Without some fundamental points of moral agreement, laws cannot be framed, codes enacted, or trust engendered. To a certain degree, sensible men can enact statutes which reflect only a pragmatic agreement to abide by certain rules. But even an apparently pragmatic agreement on sheerly pro-cedural questions will almost always reflect some latent value commitment, viz., that it is good that procedures for settling disputes among men exist. Fortunately, in the principle of "the sanc-tity of life" western culture (and much of eastern culture as well) possesses one fundamental basis for an approach to moral consensus; that is, we are not forced to begin from within a sheer vacuum. On the basis of this principle, moral rules have been framed, human rights claimed and defended, and cultural, political, and social priorities established.

To be sure, the principle is vague in its word-ing, erratically affirmed in practice, and open to innumerable differences in interpretation. . . . The word "sanctity," for example, carries a reli-gious connotation not always congenial to the non-religious. "Life" does not clearly specify whether all life (as in the Hindu version) or only human life is meant. Nonetheless, the frequency of the use of the principle in ethical discussions, even by the non-religious, testifies to its con-tinuing utility, at least as a point of departure. In any case, there seems to be no other widely af-firmed principle which presently serves as well. Perhaps a better formulation for the thrust of this principle could be found—for instance, "the dignity of human life." But if one's aim is moral consensus, then it is wise to seek not originality of formulation, however brilliant, but as com-mon and widely understood a principle as pos-sible, one which still lives, is still affirmed, and still has deep cultural resonance.

If "the sanctity of life" is, preeminently, our basic western principle, what does it mean, where has it come from, and how can it effec-tively be utilized in moral decisions and the formation of moral consensus? The overall purpose of this paper is to uncover possible grounds for just such a moral consensus, and, though I will concern myself with some substantive matters, the paper is primarily structural in aim. The first task is to clarify the meaning of "the sanctity of life"; this can usefully be done by analyzing some current explanations of it.

The Christian Understanding of "The Sanctity of Life"

Paul Ramsey has effectively detailed a major Christian tradition on the origin of the principle of "the sanctity of life." In a discussion of abortion, he observes that "one grasps the religious outlook upon the sanctity of human life only if he sees that this life is asserted to be *surrounded* by sanctity that need not be in a man; that the most dignity a man ever possesses is a dignity that is alien to him. . . . A man's dignity is an overflow from God's dealing with him, and not primarily an anticipation of anything he will ever be by himself alone." Prof. Ramsey goes on to say that "The value of a human life is ultimately grounded in the value God is placing on it," and his point here is twofold. First, it is to make clear that in the religious view, the sanctity of human life is not a function of the worth any human being may attribute to it; this therefore precludes discussion of any "degrees of relative worth" a human being may have or acquire. "Life's primary value," stemming from God, transcends such distinctions. Second, Ramsey wants to make clear that a man's life "is entirely an ordination, a loan, and a stewardship. His essence is his existence before God and to God, and it is from Him." In this formulation, man must respect his own life and the life of others not only because it is grounded in God, but, equally important, because God has given man life as a value to be held in trust and used according to God's will. "Respect for life,"

Ramsey writes, "does not mean that a man must live and let live from some iron law of necessity, or even that there is a rational compulsion to do this, or a rational ground for doing so. It is rather that because God has said 'Yes' to life, man's 'yes' should echo His." Ramsey adds that it is not terribly important which specific Christian doctrine one emphasizes to reach this conclusion; any number point in the same direction, whether it be the doctrine of creation, of man's creation in the image of God, of God's covenantal relationship with His people, or the doctrine of Redemption.

Like other Protestant theologians, Ramsey makes prominent use of Karl Barth's theology of creation. In emphasizing the "respect" due human life, Barth wants to give the word "respect" a deep resonance, indicating that we should stand in awe of that human life which God has granted man: "Respect is man's astonishment, humility and awe at a fact in which he meets something superior—majesty, dignity, holiness, a mystery which compels him to withdraw and keep his distance, to handle it modestly, circumspectly and carefully. . . . In human life he meets something superior." Martin J. Buss and Helmut Thielicke have argued similarly to Ramsey and Barth. Thielicke, in particular, stresses that a theory of "alien dignity" protects human life from being subjected to utilitarian treatment at the hands of other human beings; the measure of human value is not man's "functional proficiency" or "pragmatic utility," but rather "the sacrificial love which God has invested in him." In Buss' words, "Theologically . . . the worth of man lies in his being addressed by a deity."

On the whole, the traditional Catholic analyses of the origin of life closely parallel the Protestant, emphasizing God as the source and ultimate guarantor of the sanctity of human life. Thus Josef Fuchs, S. J., asserts that "man as such belongs *directly and exclusively to God.*" Norman St. John-Stevas, who has written more extensively on "the sanctity of life" than any other recent Roman Catholic, has said that "Respect for the *lives* of others because of their eternal destiny is the essence of the Christian teaching. Its other aspect is the emphasis on the creatureliness of man. Man is not absolutely master of his own life and body. He has no *dominium* over it, but holds it in trust for God's purposes." This emphasis on God's purposes, man's creatureliness and man's holding of life in trust brings the Catholic and Protestant arguments together at a critical point. Catholic theories, however, have been much more likely than Protestant ones to stress, through man's discernment of the natural law apart from revelation, the ability of reason to ascertain the source of the sanctity of life. Quite apart from an acceptance of Christian revelation, man, according to Catholic natural law arguments, should be able to recognize man's dignity. As G. Kelly has put it, "only God has the right to take the life of the innocent; hence the direct killing of the innocent, without the authority of God, is always wrong. This truth we know through human nature (natural law) and through divine revelation (the divine positive law). . . ." But even Father Kelly, having asserted that we can understand the sanctity of life and the right to life through the natural law, concedes that it is not altogether easy to prove the point through reason alone: "The reason for this difficulty seems to be that to those who really believe in creation and the supreme dominion of God, the principle is too obvious to need proof; whereas for those who do not believe in creation there is no basis on which to build a proof."

In any event, Catholic thought as much as Protestant has pushed the sanctity of life back to a divine origin and preservation, to an "alien dignity" (though most Catholic theologians would not find that phrase very congenial because of its suggestion that man's rights are not inherent). Within this basic perspective, however, some nuances are frequently added, mainly of a pragmatic nature. St. John-Stevas adds to his argument that the sanctity of life stems from God the further contentions (a) that it is a fundamental principle which has sustained western society, the rejection or dilution of which would endanger the whole of human life and (b) that in any case, there is no other principle available which would provide a "criterion of the right to life, save that of personal taste." His fully rounded argument for the sanctity of life draws, finally, on many sources: western law and history, human experience, the Christian doctrine of man, and the continuing cultural necessity that such a principle be accepted.

Central to both Catholic and Protestant theology is the principle that God is the Lord of life and death. This is another way of proclaiming that man holds his own life in trust, another way of asserting that man's ultimate value stems from God, and another way of saying that no man can take it upon himself to place himself in total mastery over the life of another. To confess that God is lord of life and death is to affirm that man is a creature, owing his existence, his value, and his ultimate destiny to God. But like the related principle of the sanctity of life, it is a principle which conceals some difficulties. One of these is the relationship of God to the moral and physical evils of the world. Christian theodicy has long wrestled with the apparently contradictory belief that God is lord and yet that his lordship is not responsible for evil. Another difficulty is that both in principle and practice Christian theology has allowed many occasions when it is permissible for one man to take the life of another, or for the state to take the life, or imprison the body, of those it considers dangerous to the common good. Such exceptions clearly seem to presuppose that in some sense God has granted man some degree of control over human life and death, a presupposition shared by Catholic and Protestant theologians.

As the history of Christian ethics shows, it has never been possible to take decisions out of human hands for long. Even before the advent of modern technology choices had to be made among human lives and human rights. Unjust aggression, for example, raised the question whether God's sanctification of human life was consistent with laws which, in effect, granted aggressors the right to take innocent lives. The historical answer was no; hence were born laws which granted individuals and communities the right to take the lives of aggressors or deprive them of other rights. In other words, it turned out that here, as in many other instances, human decisions had to be made; they could not be left to God. The inherent stability supposedly built into a divine sanctity of life principle turned out to be something less than perfect. The present turmoil of Christian ethics is due precisely to a growing awareness that rigid, formalistic ethical codes too often break down in practice, all the more so because of the expanded range of possible choices.

While it may be perfectly reasonable to suppose that man has been given some proximate control over human life, it is a supposition which also places upon human shoulders the problem of deciding under what conditions man has the right to such control. But once these decisions have to be made, there is the danger that the principle of God's lordship may be emptied of any meaningful content. If it is man who must decide what it means to implement this lordship, of what real good is the abstract principle? This is a question to which I will return.

The advantages of the Christian approach to "the sanctity of life" are evident, just as are some of the disadvantages. The main advantage is that the foundation is laid for a theory of human life which locates man's dignity outside the evaluation of other human beings; our ultimate worth is conferred by God, not by human judgment. Thus, in principle, human life is guaranteed beyond the protection that an erratic human evaluation might accord it, whether in the form of human laws or mores. Another advantage is that the sanctity of human life is given an ultimate grounding: in God, the creator and preserver of everything which exists. Man is not forced to create his own worth; God has, from the outset, given him value.

The disadvantages, however, are no less prominent. One is that a considerable portion of humanity is not Christian and does not accept this foundation for the sanctity of human life. Hence, it does not readily provide a consensual norm to which all men can have recourse. Another disadvantage is that it leaves unclear the extent of man's intrinsic dignity. It seems to presuppose that, apart from God's conferral of dignity, man in his own right would be worthless. In the theological problematic of course, which is all-encompassing in its scope, it makes no sense to talk of man apart from his creator and redeemer; the "natural man" does not exist, but only the created and redeemed man. In part, this helps to solve the problem of an "alien dignity" which would denigrate man's intrinsic worth, but, at the same time, it requires that one accept the full theological framework; that is just what many cannot do. In his *Ethics*, Dietrich Bonhoeffer speaks of a "natural right" to bodily life, thus more consciously than most Protestant theologians trying to establish a continuum between a secular mode of describing human rights and a strictly Christian mode. But even Bonhoeffer, who uses a term such as "innate right," sees the guarantee and source of these rights wholly in God.

The Experiential Understanding of "The Sanctity of Life"

Very different from the Christian position are the arguments put forward by Edward Shils to justify the sanctity of life. Pointing to what seems an almost instinctive human revulsion at many forms of contrived intervention in human life, Shils believes that it is not possible to trace this revulsion solely to the religious belief that man is a creature of God. On the contrary, he contends that the Christian belief in the sanctity of life has been sustained by a "deeper, protoreligious 'natural metaphysic,'" which also accounts for the respect given human life by those who are neither Christian nor religious. "The chief feature of the protoreligious 'natural metaphysic' is the affirmation that life *is* sacred. It is believed to be sacred not because it is a manifestation of a transcendent creator from whom life comes: it is believed to be sacred because it is life. The idea of sacredness is generated by the primordial experience of being alive, of experiencing the elemental sensation of vitality and the elemental fear of its extinction." In another place he writes that "If life were not viewed as sacred, then nothing else would be sacred," thus echoing from within his own framework the same kind of pragmatic point made by Norman St. John-Stevas from within a very different kind of framework. Finally, Shils says: "The question still remains: is human life really sacred? I answer that it is self-evidently. Its sacredness is the most primordial of experiences."

Like the Christian formulation of the principle, Shils' way of putting the matter has both strengths and weaknesses. Its obvious strength is that the sanctity of human life does not require a justification outside of human life (i.e., in a God), thus providing a basis upon which the non-religious can affirm the sanctity of life, something which the Christian formulation does not. It also has the advantage of drawing directly upon human experience, and very root human experience at that; no divine revelation is required. Its chief weakness is that it falls afoul of some obvious philosophical rejoinders. The first would be that the mere experiencing of something as valuable is no guarantee that it *is* valuable. People frequently experience something as valuable which later reflection shows to be lacking in value, and it is common for different groups of people to experience different things as valuable. The second rejoinder would be that Shils' case could not be fully established unless we had evidence that all human beings have at all times experienced human life as valuable; it is

not easy to see how this could be done. The third rejoinder would be that "the sanctity of human life" is a human concept, one which has been considered appropriate to ascribe to certain elemental human experiences. But this ascription already presupposes the existence of a conceptual and linguistic system which may be utilized in describing experience; such a utilization, though, requires making judgments about experience, particularly judging that certain experiences are valuable. But what we decide to call a "value" will be a function of prior ethical decisions. On all three of these points, Shils' phrase "self-evidently" quoted above opens the way to a host of objections.

An Impasse

Now if both the Christian understanding of "the sanctity of life" and the experiential, non-religious interpretation put forward by Shils are open to internal objections, each also provides the grounds for a critique of the other. One important intent of the Christian understanding is to remove the ultimate source of the sanctity of life from any dependence upon human experience and judgment; this is accomplished by locating the source of the sanctity outside man. Extending Shils' argument, though, could not one say that the precise weakness of this kind of extrinsic grounding is that it requires one to affirm not only human sanctity but the source of that sanctity as well? Two affirmations are necessary, making it doubly difficult to make *any* affirmation. Moreover, it could be said that an acceptance of the sanctity of life which required that one accept a religious view of man's origin would provide a weak base upon which to build a consensus; one then would seem to be saying that there would be nothing upon which to base the sanctity of life save that of religious belief (which would logically leave the non-believer free to reject the sanctity of life). One untoward consequence, then, of the religious believer's position would be to open the way to placing his own right to life in jeopardy, by making the sanctity of his own life dependent only upon his own religious beliefs. Beyond his own beliefs, he would have nothing to appeal to in the face of aggressive action by a person denying these beliefs. An intrinsic norm for the sanctity of life, such as that proposed by Shils, would seem to avoid such untoward consequences. For it would, in principle, provide a norm to which all men could have recourse (or could have pointed out to them); one would need only to refer to a (purportedly) universal human experience and not be dependent upon any special belief about the nature of man and the source of his dignity.

At this point, however, the religious believer could point out *how precarious such an intrinsic norm is.* To be an effective norm, it would first have to be shown that all men are in fact, or potentially, aware of such an elemental experience of the sanctity of life. It would further have to be shown that human beings have a moral obligation to heed this experience, that the experience carries with it a manifest set of moral obligations. The fact that I might respect the sanctity of my own life, my own vitality, does not logically entail that I am required to respect the sanctity of anyone else's life. What would be the source of any obligation to respect the life of another? The mere existence of a common human experience would, on the face of it, entail no moral obligations or duties at all. Only the experience of an ethical framework superimposed upon the experience could supply these entailments. The strength of the believer's *extrinsic norm* is that it bypasses these difficulties; it is not dependent upon any particular human experience, it does not have to work through the hazardous business of proving that moral duties are inherent in human experience, and it provides an ethical framework binding upon all in principle. At this point, though, all the difficulties inherent in the believer's position recur. We are at an impasse.

Now it is surely conceivable that some ingenious person could find a way out of this impasse—conceivable, but not likely—at least not likely in the sense that his way out would commend itself to all sides in the debate. The very nature of the debate, which in the end opposes two fundamentally different world-views, precludes the likelihood of a common theoretical solution, short of the conversion of one side or the other. In one sense, then, we seem to be in the presence of an ill-fated debate, one which appears doomed to go on forever, perennially resistant to the formation of a socially useful moral consensus, perennially prone to leave the principle of the sanctity of life in a dangerous position. I don't think it is necessary to draw this kind of pessimistic conclusion. For one thing, it is always difficult to metaphysically ground first, or ultimate, principles but this difficulty does not necessarily stand in the way of their acceptance and use. In social, political, cultural, and medical situations, what counts most in the debate on the sanctity of life is that both sides affirm the principle, on whatever grounds, and that both sides are willing to make it their first and fundamental principle. Moreover, it is clear from a variety of human disciplines that their practitioners can often effectively talk and work together without metaphysical agreement on fundamental principles, or even when the fundamental principles themselves carry no evident intrinsic justification. The problem of induction in the philosophy of science provides a classic instance. Scientific method presupposes that the future will be like the past, that hypotheses confirmed by observed data provide a warrant for making predictions about similar, but unobserved, data, that it is legitimate to base expectations about the future behavior of material objects on our present experience with such objects. Yet it has proved exceedingly difficult to demonstrate the philosophical validity of these presuppositions. Nonetheless, the enterprise of science has been able to proceed and progress in the absence of such demonstrations and in the absence of a full philosophical consensus on the ultimate validity of scientific method.

When Shils and St. John-Stevas say that no human rights and no valuation of human life can be established without presupposing "the sanctity of life" they are saying no less than what Kant said.

Put more concretely, it is possible to see the function of the principle of the sanctity of life. If one asks, for example, "Is it a good general rule that abortions ought not to be performed?"—to take a rule which has until recently been a part of the western moral rule system—one needs a principle which operates at a higher level than the particular rule in order to judge the validity of the rule. "The sanctity of life" provides such a principle. Does that particular rule about abortion serve or enhance or exemplify "the sanctity of life"? That is the kind of question we will want to ask about the rule. That is the kind of question the principle is meant to help us answer; it provides a way of testing the rule, giving us a "frame" within which to validate it anew or to invalidate or amend it.

One might object that the principle could not serve as a measure or test of a particular rule if it was, quite literally and totally, empty. Instead of saying that these principles are "empty," it might be preferable to say that they are "indeterminate"—they convey a broad range of meaning, but not specific, determinate meanings. We know what the principle is trying to express—roughly. We know what the principle would seem to preclude—vaguely. We know, consequently, how to use the principle as a measure of rules—more or less. If asked to specify what the phrase "the sanctity of life" *means,* we could substitute phrases like "the dignity," "the ultimate value," "the worth," "the significance," "the importance" of human life for the phrase "the sanctity"—trying, all the while, to

hit upon that phrase or combination of phrases which would make clear what we had in mind when we spoke of the principle or what we take to be the principle, as commonly used, to mean. Naturally, someone could point out that defining the words of the principle in terms of a list of synonyms or near-synonyms is not altogether illuminating, having about it the odor of tautologies and circularities. About the only thing one could reply, if faced with this kind of resistance, is that one reaches a point, with any word or any phrase or any ultimate principle, where one simply cannot say anything more. The point about the phrase "the sanctity of life" is that it is trying to say the *most* that can be said about the value of life. It signifies a whole cluster of final meanings, each of which is related to and dependent upon the other to give it sense and significance. In a very real way, then, the principle of the sanctity of life *is* indeterminate and vague, but not meaningless for all that. It says life is to be affirmed, cherished, and respected, and as a principle, it can be defined in terms of a large range of words which themselves have meaning, yet without this process of definition over-defining the principle (which would make it too determinate to be useful as an ethical principle). When used in its primary function of judging lower level rules, the principle is employed to interrogate the rules: do the rules foster the respect due human life? Do the rules lead people to protect human life? Do the rules exemplify the awe we ought to feel in the presence of human life? If the answer is "no," then we would be justified in rejecting, modifying or changing the rules.

Yet further specificity is required here. If it is the general function of moral rules to guide our conduct in particular situations calling for moral decisions—"What ought I to do?"—there is also a multiplicity of rules and a multiplicity of ways in which rules are expressed. The reason for a multiplicity of rules is not hard to locate: there are many different kinds of human acts, human relationships, and human moral dilemmas. Sometimes we are concerned with human property, at other times with human lives, at other times with human political rights, at other times with human sexual duties, at other times with human economic relationships. Different general contexts call for and ordinarily exhibit different sets of rules, even though there may be and usually is a considerable overlap. The reason for a multiplicity of ways in which to express rules can be readily seen also. Sometimes rules are expressed in the form of prohibitions— "Thou shalt not. . . ." This form of rule statement is meant to draw a line beyond which one may not go; prohibitions set limits. Sometimes rules are expressed in a positive way—"One ought to do 'x,'" "One must do 'y'" —and the aim here is to specify a duty or a responsibility; a goal is established. In brief, rules are variously expressed in the language of rights, duties, prohibitions, goals, and so on, and these different expressions have different purposes: to command, to enjoin, to goad, and so on. And it is usually possible to translate one mode of expressing a rule into another mode: the prohibition "Thou shalt not steal" can be re-expressed into the command "You ought to respect the property of others," though the psychological impact of the re-expression may be somewhat different from the original expression, and the implications for behavior rather different.

The important point is to understand the possible ways that the ethical principle of "the sanctity of life" can be used to test those moral rules bearing on human life. We have already seen that the *meaning* of "the sanctity of life" is that of signifying the ultimate respect we are willing to accord human life. It expresses a willingness to treat human life with consideration, to give it dignity, to commit ourselves to its furtherance. The function of specific rules is to implement and give concreteness to these commitments; in turn these commitments, as summed up in the principle, will serve to judge the adequacy of the rules. Thus the relationship between particular

moral rules and general ethical principles is reciprocal: the rules give content, on a lower level, to the principle; the principle, on a higher level, is used to judge the rules. The social importance of the acceptance of the principle of "the sanctity of life" is not that it guarantees agreement on what the rules should be, or that recourse to it automatically resolves disputes about rules, but that a common standard exists which people can have recourse to; debate about rules has a framework of meaning, vague though it may be.

Another point is important here. When, as will be shown, we break the different rule systems down into relevant categories, it is helpful to see the way in which the different categories are related to each other. The greater the degree of relationship we can see among the categories, the more we are illuminated about, and in a position to give meaning to, "the sanctity of life." This is another way the principle provides a framework for discussing rules and rule systems. It leads us to see, it can even force us to see, that when dealing with the complexity of human life our rules should have a coherent relationship to each other. It leads us to see, to express the point another way, that *our rules should form a coherent system, each rule consistent with and supporting the other,* and all, in turn, serving and supporting the ultimate principle of "the sanctity of life." Rules dealing with medical experimentation should be congruent with rules dealing with the preservation of an individual's bodily life, which should be congruent with rules dealing with the preservation of the species, and so on. This is simply to say that just as moral rules should not be *ad hoc,* unrelated to an overarching ethical principle, neither should they be *ad hoc* in the sense of being unrelated to other rules bearing on the same overarching ethical principle. To use an image: if the ethical principle is the father of the family, then all the children (the concrete rules) should bear a family resemblance to each other.

When we look more closely at those rules and rule systems bearing on the sanctity of life their variety is manifest. There are rules dealing with (a) the survival and integrity of the human species, (b) the integrity of family lineages, (c) the integrity of bodily life, (d) the integrity of personal, mental, and emotional individuality, and (e) the integrity of personal bodily individuality. Not one of these areas has escaped the impact of recent medical, scientific, and technological change. It is this change, together with the concomitantly increasing scope of moral decisions, which has brought traditional rules into question and, beyond that, is forcing us to see whether these old rules still serve "the sanctity of life." If not, then new rules will be needed.

A further complication, moreover, is that we will not be in a position to judge the rules in relationship to the guiding principle until we have first determined their relationship to the empirical data to which they are applied. Rules are meant (either explicitly or implicitly) to exemplify principles; but their application must be in the context of data. When the data to which the rules have traditionally been applied change, this can mean either of two things: we will have to judge whether existing rules can handle the new data or whether entirely new rules are needed. Recent debates about the continuing relevance of "just war" theories provide an example of this problem. On one side are those who contend that the advent of nuclear weapons renders the traditional rules of just warfare altogether irrelevant; they were not designed to cope with weapons capable of such vast and indiscriminate destruction. On another side are those who believe that the old rules are sufficiently flexible to handle nuclear warfare. A considerable part of this debate, not surprisingly, turns on an analysis of the known data concerning the destructiveness of nuclear weapons. Short of such an analysis there is no way of knowing whether the traditional rules of just warfare are still valid; and short of knowing that there is no way of judging whether these rules still serve a commitment to the sanctity of life.

The Leading Rule Systems

I now want to survey briefly the leading rule systems subsumed under "the sanctity of life." My aim will be threefold, in line with the major issues I have discussed: to bring out the latent general content of the principle itself, to indicate what appear to be the extant western moral rules, and to point out the kinds of technical data bearing on the individual rule systems, noting in the process the implications of different kinds of data. Since the overall purpose of this paper is to uncover possible grounds for a moral consensus, rather than to propose new rules, I have to risk that my reading of the extant cultural rules is wrong. Obviously different sub-communities within the culture have different rule systems; that is why they argue with each other. And even when they agree on rule systems, they often disagree on the implications of technical data for an application of the rules. Still, I believe it is possible to discern considerable agreement among the different western moral sub-communities, at least if one remains at a fairly high level of abstraction and generality. One test is whether there are any important groups which flatly oppose the cultural rules. In any event, it is open to the reader to supply his own reading of the extant rules in place of mine. The important thing here is to uncover the logical structure of the relationship between rules and the principle of "the sanctity of life," thus laying the basis for fruitful discussion among contending sub-communities.

(a) *The survival and integrity of the human species.* The most important rule here is that the human species ought to work toward its own survival; it is good that human beings exist on earth. Encompassed within this broad rule are a number of other more specific rules: present human beings ought to behave in such a way as to insure as much as possible a viable life for future human beings; nations ought not to behave in such a way as to endanger the present and future life of the human species; human beings are responsible for a moral use of natural resources, and so forth. The rules are myriad and they are invoked, either explicitly or implicitly, when human beings discuss nuclear warfare, radiation exposure, air pollution, ecology, overpopulation, urbanization, the uses of technology, and genetic engineering. The working presumption is that "the sanctity of life" entails the need for moral rules designed to aid the survival of collective human life. Existing rules which can be shown to hinder the possibility of continuing human life would then stand under the judgment of the principle and be subject to rejection or modification.

The problem of genetic engineering, ever expanding in its possibilities, illustrates the complexities of judging old rules and forming new ones. On the one hand, there are questions of technical feasibility. To what extent, and by what means, is it possible to alter the genetic characteristics of human populations? And what are the likely consequences of choosing different means? "Positive eugenics," involving the engineered breeding of a chosen type or types of human being, poses the technical problem of accurately predicting the genetic consequences of different, artificially induced, genetic mixes. "Negative eugenics," generally understood to mean either the discouragement or forbiddance of reproduction by carriers of harmful genes, requires (as does positive eugenics) an ability to predict the long range consequences for human evolution of non-random mating patterns. "Euthenics," the alteration of environment to permit genetically abnormal people to live normal lives, poses the scientific question whether in the long run mankind might become so overburdened with genetic abnormalities as to overwhelm the possibilities of a supporting environmental change. Each of these different possible eugenic techniques, then, requires a knowledge of the different likely genetic outcomes. And any judgment of rules relating to genetic engineering will have to weigh and compare these outcomes.

On the other hand, there are questions concerning the kind of human beings we want now and in the future. Even if one can predict the outcome of different methods of genetic engineering, there still remains the further problem of deciding what characteristics are humanly desirable; and this problem requires some further scientific calculations about the conditions of human life in the future. The rules we judge desirable should, therefore, reflect a scientifically valid use of data combined with a conscious reflection upon the kinds of human beings felt desirable. And of course there is the basic question whether we have the right to do this at all. As a principle, "the sanctity of life" provides no detailed map for wending our way through this maze of problems. But it does tell us this: whatever our evolving moral rules will be, they must be designed to promote the survival of the human species; negatively, the principle tells us that any rule which is oblivious to, or harmful to, the survival of the human species is to be rejected.

(b) *The survival and integrity of family lineages.* The central rule in this instance is that individuals and families should be left free to propagate their own children and to perpetuate their family lineage. Related rules are that neither the state nor other individuals have the right to interfere with private procreative practices; neither the state nor other individuals have the right to impose or deny individual parenthood or to tamper with the process of individual procreation. The intent behind these rules would seem to be that "the sanctity of life" requires respect for family lines and for voluntary procreative choice. Artificial insemination and artificial inovulation, sterilization and contraception, as well as genetic engineering all raise technological options bearing on this rule. Beyond these options are problems concerning the common good of societies and humanity as a whole, the procreative rights of individuals in different circumstances (e.g., in times of overpopulation, or in cases where known and dangerous genetic characteristics would be perpetuated within families or transmitted to a population as a whole). Once again, rules have to be formulated in cognizance of technical knowledge; once again, choices must be made about the kind and number of human beings which families and societies judge desirable. *(amputation?)*

(c) *The integrity of bodily life.* The general rule in this case is that the individual human being has a basic right to life; neither the state nor individuals have the right to (unjustly) deprive human beings of their lives. This rule encompasses a great range of subsidiary rules, among them rules relating to abortion, euthanasia, the prolongation of moribund life, war, capital punishment, and the like. The presumption behind these rules is that "the sanctity of life" implies not only the preservation of human life as a whole but also the preservation and protection of individual human lives.

As one moves through the different detailed rule systems subsumed under the general rule, a wide range of definitional, technical, and social problems presents itself. Abortion poses the question "When does 'human life' begin?" and that question contains within it the need for a definition of "human life," for criteria which would help us decide what is meant by "begin," and for standards to govern behavior toward potential or incipient human life. Biological data are relevant to the definition difficulty, the common use of language to the establishment of criteria for "begin," and broad social goals to the forming of standards about potential human life (and these are not the only relevant considerations, just some of them). The prolongation of moribund human life also touches on the definition problem—what do we mean by "death," at what point do we say that, for all practical purposes, a human body ceases being a "human life"? An important technical context of these problems is the possibility of artificially prolonging many bodily functions indefinitely. Euthanasia forces us to ask whether there is a "right to die," and whether, in cases of excruciating pain or a hopeless prognosis we could speak of a

"right to kill" even manifestly innocent life. Whatever the continuing or developed rules, however, they would be judged in the light of an accepted implication of "the sanctity of life": human beings have a right to bodily life; any rule which threatens that right is nullified by the principle of the sanctity of life.

(d) *The integrity of personal, mental, and emotional individuality.* The key rule here is that a person has the right to be himself; phrased differently, a human being has the right to be a unique person with his own complement of voluntarily chosen mental and emotional traits (as far as is possible biologically and psychologically). Related rules are that neither the state nor other individuals have the right to tamper with or impair individual human minds or to manipulate, coerce, or alter human emotions. These rules are called into question by the possibility of electrical and chemical alterations of consciousness and affectivity which could well be judged beneficial, either to the individual or society or both. The technical problem here is that of measuring the short and long term effects of such alterations, both on the individual and on a society made up of such individuals. The impact of the use of hallucinogenics is a case in point, as is the existence of brain operations, tranquilizers, drugs, and electrical treatments which can affect thought and emotions. Whatever the rules here, worked out in relationship to scientific knowledge of the effects of different mind- and emotion-altering techniques, they are meant to embody the general rule that a person has the right to be himself. This rule is an implication of the affirmation that "the sanctity of life" entails the value of personal identity.

(e) *The integrity of personal bodily individuality.* The guiding rule in this instance is that the individual has an exclusive right to the use of his own body and all the organs therein; one should respect the integrity of human bodies. This rule comes into question when the need for medical experimentation arises, when organ transplants are required, and when (as in wartime) society may feel it necessary to place the body or bodily life of its citizens in physical jeopardy. The "need for medical experimentation" involves such technical questions as the likely scientific results which could accrue from such experimentations, the relative degree of danger involved in different kinds of experimentation, the scientific value of informing or failing to inform experimental subjects of the purpose of the experimentation (e.g., when a new pain-killing drug is being tested, necessitating an experimental and a control group of subjects). Organ transplantation from a healthy to a sick person requires knowledge of the likely effects on both individuals and an attempt to measure the relative physiological gains and losses to both. The principle of "the sanctity of life" will be violated if the moral rules governing the attitude toward human bodies involuntarily threaten the integrity of those bodies as controlled by those to whom they belong. . . .

The direction of my own decision and, I trust, of most human beings, is to affirm the value of the principle of "the sanctity of life." James Gustafson, though operating from within a Christian framework, has written what I would hope to be acceptable outside of that framework: "Life is to be preserved, the weak and the helpless are to be cared for especially, the moral requisites of trust, hope, love, freedom, justice, and others are to be met so that human life can be meaningful. This bias gives a direction. . . ."

References

Barth, Karl. *Church Dogmatics.* Vol. III/4, pt. 55. Edinburgh: T and T Clark, 1961.

Berger, Peter L. *The Sacred Canopy.* Garden City, N.Y.: Doubleday & Co, Inc., 1967.

Bonhoeffer, Dietrich. *Ethics,* trans. Neville Horton Smith. London: SCM Press, 1955.

Buss, Martin J. "The Beginning of Life as an Ethical Problem." *The Journal of Religion* (July 1967).

Cairns, David. *God Up There?* Philadelphia: Westminster Press, 1967.

Curran, Charles E. "Absolute Norms and Medical Ethics." In *Absolutes in Moral Theology,* ed. Charles E. Curran. Washington, D.C.: Corpus Books, 1968.

Fletcher, Joseph. "The Right to Die." *Atlantic Monthly,* April 1968.

Fuchs, Josef,. *Natural Law,* trans. Helmut Reckter and John A. Dowling. New York: Sheed & Ward, 1965.

Gustafson, James F. "A Christian Approach to the Ethics of Abortion." Paper delivered at Kennedy Foundation Symposium on Abortion, Harvard Divinity School, Washington, D.C., August 1967.

Guttmacher, Alan F. "The United States Medical Profession and Family Planning." In *Family Planning and Population Programs,* ed. Bernard Berelson. Chicago: University of Chicago Press, 1966.

Häring, Bernard. *The Law of Christ.* Vol. III. Westminster, Md.: Newman Press, 1965.

Hick, John. *Evil and the Love of God.* New York: Harper and Row, 1966. The best recent book on the problem of evil.

Kelly, Gerald. *Medico-Moral Problems.* Dublin: Clonmore and Reynolds, 1955.

Ramsey, Paul. "The Morality of Abortion." In *Life or Death: Ethics and Options,* ed. Daniel H. Labby. Seattle: University of Washington Press, 1968.

St. John-Stevas, Norman. "Law and the Moral Consensus." In *Life or Death: Ethics and Options,* ed. Daniel H. Labby. Seattle: University of Washington Press, 1968.

St. John-Stevas, Norman. *The Right to Life.* New York: Holt, Rinehart and Winston, 1964.

Shils, Edward. "The Sanctity of Life." In *Life or Death: Ethics and Options,* ed. Daniel H. Labby. Seattle: University of Washington Press, 1968.

Study Questions

1. What is the aim of Callahan's essay? What is he trying to do with regard to the concept of the sanctity of life? What prompts his analysis?
2. What are his criticisms with the Christian view and with Shils's view? Do you agree with his assessment?

3. Is Callahan successful in setting forth a coherent defense of the sanctity of life?
4. Compare and contrast Callahan's views with those of the other writers in this section. Which view do you accept?

For Further Reading

Glover, Jonathan. *Causing Death and Saving Lives.* London: Penguin Books, 1977.

Harris, John. *The Value of Life.* London: Routledge & Kegan Paul, 1985.

Keyserlingk, Edwin. *Sanctity of Life or Quality of Life.* Montreal: Ministry of Supply and Services, 1979.

Ladd, John, ed. *Ethical Issues Relating to Life and Death.* Oxford: Oxford University Press, 1979. Contains nine important articles, see especially Peter Singer's article.

Schweitzer, Albert. *Civilization and Ethics.* London: Black, 1923.

Weir, Robert, ed. *Essays in Death and Dying.* New York, 1980.

Part III

Death and the Meaning of Life

Introduction

Leo Tolstoy retells the Zen story of a traveler fleeing a ferocious animal. Endeavoring to save himself from the beast, the man runs toward a well and begins to climb down, when to his horror he spies a dragon with open jaws pointed directly at him waiting at the bottom of the well. The traveler dares not drop into the well for fear of the dragon, but he dare not climb out of the well for fear of the beast. Seeing a bush growing out of the wall of the well, he grasps its thickest branch and hangs onto it. Hanging there between the mouth of the well and the frightful creature below, his hands soon grow weary and he feels that he can hang on no longer, yet he manages it. As he clings to the branch for his salvation, he notices that two mice, one white and one black, are nibbling away at the main trunk of the branch onto which he is clinging. They will soon dislodge his part of the branch.

The traveler is you and I, and his plight is your plight and mine, the danger of our death on every hand. The white mouse represents our days and the black one our nights. Together they are nibbling away at the three-score years and ten, which biblically make up our branch of life. Inevitably, all will be over, and what have we to show for it? Is this all there is? Can this tiny moment in the history of the universe have significance?

The fact of death heightens the question of the meaning of life. Like a prisoner sentenced to death or a terminally ill patient, we know that, in a sense, we are all sentenced to death and are terminally ill, but we flee the thought in a thousand ways. In the Hindu Epic *Mahabharata*, Dharma, the personification of Moral Duty, asks young prince Yudhistira, "Of all the world's wonders, which is the most wonderful?" Yudhistira replies to the satisfaction of Dharma, "That no man, though he sees others dying all around him, believes that he himself will die."

In the light of death, what is the meaning of life? What is the meaning of death itself?

Different responses to the question of the meaning of life and death are presented in the following selections. Plato (427–347 B.C.E.) in our first reading has Socrates argue that death as the cessation of consciousness never occurs but that our souls survive to another existence. This is similar to the Hindu view in our last reading by Prasannatma Das.

In our second reading, Epicurus argues that since death is permanent loss of consciousness, it is not something we ever encounter. Neither Death nor I ever meet, for when I am, Death is not, and when Death is, I am not. There is no reason to fear what we never meet. So we ought not fear Death. Instead, we should enjoy the truly pleasurable things of life.

In our third reading Richard Taylor reflects on the myth of Sisyphus, arguing that there is a way to find meaning in our finite existence even if we give up the hope of life after death.

Next, Lois Hope Walker argues that religion, specifically theism, with the notion of a benevolent God, can greatly enhance the meaning of life.

In our fifth reading Jeffrie Murphy argues, following Spinoza, that to fear death is irrational and that we can make strides to rid ourselves of this unnecessary emotional strain.

Finally, Prasannatma Das presents a Hindu view of the meaning of life and death as a quest for spiritual perfection and union with God.

CHAPTER 12

Death and Immortality

PLATO

Plato (427–347 B.C.E.)—an Athenian; advisor to monarchs; Socrates' disciple and Aristotle's teacher; founder of the first school of philosophy, The Academy; and first philosopher to write systematic philosophical treatises—is almost without peer in the history of Western thought. Alfred North Whitehead calls the whole history of philosophy "a series of footnotes to Plato."

In this dialogue between Socrates and his disciples Simmias and Cebes (from the *Phaedo*), Plato describes Socrates' reflections on death. Socrates had been condemned to die by an Athenian court for blasphemy and corrupting youth. He argues that the soul, our essential self, is separate from the body and will live again in another form after death. Philosophy is the practice of death.

SOCRATES: What again shall we say of the actual acquirement of knowledge?—is the body, if invited to share in the inquiry, a hinderer or a helper? I mean to say, have sight and hearing any truth in them? Are they not, as the poets are always telling us, inaccurate witnesses? and yet, if even they are inaccurate and indistinct, what is to be said of the other senses?—for you will allow that they are the best of them?

SIMMIAS: Certainly.

SOC.: Then when does the soul attain truth?—for in attempting to consider anything in company with the body she is obviously deceived.

SIM.: Yes, that is true.

SOC.: Then must not existence be revealed to her in thought, if at all?

SIM.: Yes.

SOC.: And thought is best when the mind is gathered into herself and none of these things trouble her—neither sounds nor sights nor pain nor any pleasure,—when she has as little as possible to do with the body, and has no bodily sense of feeling, but is aspiring after being?

SIM.: That is true.

SOC.: And in this the philosopher dishonors the body; his soul runs away from the body and desires to be alone and by herself?

SIM.: That is true.

SOC.: Well, but there is another thing, Simmias: Is there or is there not an absolute justice?

SIM.: Assuredly there is.

SOC.: And an absolute beauty and absolute good?

SIM.: Of course.

SOC.: But did you ever behold any of them with your eyes?

SIM.: Certainly not.

SOC.: Or did you ever reach them with any other bodily sense? (and I speak not of these alone, but of absolute greatness, and health, and strength, and of the essence of true nature of everything). Has the reality of them ever been perceived by you through the bodily organs? or rather, is not the nearest approach to the knowledge of their several natures made by him who so orders his intellectual vision as to have the most exact

Reprinted from Phaedo, *translated by Benjamin Jowett (New York: Scribner, 1889).*

conception of the essence of that which he considers?

SIM.:   Certainly.

SOC.:   And he attains to the knowledge of them in their highest purity who goes to each of them with the mind alone, not allowing when in the act of thought the intrusion or introduction of sight or any other sense in the company of reason, but with the very light of the mind in her clearness penetrates into the very light of truth in each; he has got rid, as far as he can, of eyes and ears and of the whole body, which he conceives of only as a disturbing element, hindering the soul from the acquisition of knowledge when in company with her—is not this the sort of man who, if ever man did, is likely to attain the knowledge of existence?

SIM.:   There is admirable truth in that, Socrates.

SOC.:   And when they consider all this, must not true philosophers make a reflection, of which they will speak to one another in such words as these: We have found, they will say, a path of speculation which seems to bring us and the argument to the conclusion, that while we are in the body, and while the soul is mingled with this mass of evil, our desire will not be satisfied, and our desire is of the truth. For the body is a source of endless trouble to us by reason of the mere requirement of food; and also is liable to diseases which overtake and impede us in the search after truth: and by filling us so full of loves, and lusts, and fears, and fancies, and idols, and every sort of folly, prevents our ever having, as people say, so much as a thought. From whence come wars, and fightings, and factions? Whence but from the body and the lusts of the body? For wars are occasioned by the love of money, and money has to be acquired for the sake and in the service of the body; and in consequence of all these things the time which ought to be given to philosophy is lost. Moreover, if there is time and an inclination toward philosophy, yet the body introduces a turmoil and confusion and fear into the course of speculation, and hinders us from seeing the truth, and all experience shows that if we would have pure knowledge of anything we must be quit of the

body, and the soul in herself must behold all things in themselves: then I suppose that we shall attain that which we desire, and of which we say that we are lovers, and that is wisdom; not while we live, but after death, as the argument shows; for if while in company with the body, the soul cannot have pure knowledge, one of two things seems to follow—either knowledge is not to be attained at all, or, if at all, after death. For then, and not till then, the soul will be in herself alone and without the body. In this present life, I reckon that we make the nearest approach to knowledge when we have the least possible concern or interest in the body, and are not saturated with the bodily nature, but remain pure until the hour when God himself is pleased to release us. And then the foolishness of the body will be cleared away and we shall be pure and hold converse with other pure souls, and know of ourselves the clear light everywhere; and this is surely the light of truth. For no impure thing is allowed to approach the pure. These are the sort of words, Simmias, which the true lovers of wisdom cannot help saying to one another, and thinking. You will agree with me in that?

SIM.:   Certainly, Socrates.

SOC.:   But if this is true, O my friend, then there is great hope that, going whither I go, I shall there be satisfied with that which has been the chief concern of you and me in our past lives. And now that the hour of departure is appointed to me, this is the hope with which I depart, and not I only, but every man who believes that he has his mind purified.

SIM.:   Certainly.

SOC.:   And what is purification but the separation of the soul from the body, as I was saying before; the habit of the soul gathering and collecting herself into herself, out of all the courses of the body; the dwelling in her own place alone, as in another life, so also in this, as far as she can; the release of the soul from the chains of the body?

SIM.:   Very true.

SOC.:   And what is that which is termed death, but this very separation and release of the soul from the body?

SIM.:   To be sure.

SOC.:   And the true philosophers, and they only, study and are eager to release the soul. Is not the separation and release of the soul from the body their especial study?

SIM.:   That is true.

SOC.:   And as I was saying at first, there would be a ridiculous contradiction in men studying to live as nearly as they can in a state of death, and yet repining when death comes.

SIM.:   Certainly.

SOC.:   Then Simmias, as the true philosophers are ever studying death, to them, of all men, death is the least terrible. Look at the matter in this way: how inconsistent of them to have been always enemies of the body, and wanting to have the soul alone, and when this is granted to them, to be trembling and repining; instead of rejoicing at their departing to that place where, when they arrive, they hope to gain that which in life they loved (and this was wisdom), and at the same time to be rid of the company of their enemy. Many a man has been willing to go to the world below in the hope of seeing there an earthly love, or wife, or son, and conversing with them. And will he who is a true lover of wisdom, and is persuaded in like manner that only in the world below he can worthily enjoy her, still repine at death? Will he not depart with joy? Surely, he will, my friend, if he be a true philosopher. For he will have a firm conviction that there only, and nowhere else, he can find wisdom in her purity. And if this be true, he would be very absurd, as I was saying, if he were to fear death. . . .

And were we not saying long ago that the soul when using the body as an instrument of perception, that is to say, when using the sense of sight or hearing or some other sense (for the meaning of perceiving through the body is perceiving through the senses),—were we not saying that the soul too is then dragged by the body into the region of the changeable, and wanders and is confused; the world spins round her, and she is like a drunkard when under their influence?

CEBES: Very true.

SOC.:   But when returning into herself she reflects; then she passes into the realm of purity, and eternity, and immortality, and unchangeableness, which are her kindred, and with them she ever lives, when she is by herself and is not let or hindered; then she ceases from her erring ways, and being in communion with the unchanging is unchanging. And this state of the soul is called wisdom?

CEBES: That is well and truly said, Socrates.

SOC.:   And to which class is the soul more nearly alike and akin, as far as may be inferred from this argument, as well as from the preceding one?

CEBES: I think, Socrates, that, in the opinion of every one who follows the argument, the soul will be infinitely more like the unchangeable,—even the most stupid person will not deny that.

SOC.:   And the body is more like the changing?

CEBES: Yes.

SOC.:   Yet once more consider the matter in this light: When the soul and the body are united, then nature orders the soul to rule and govern, and the body to obey and serve. Now which of these two functions is akin to the divine? and which to the mortal? Does not the divine appear to you to be that which naturally orders and rules, and the mortal that which is subject and servant?

CEBES: True.

SOC.:   And which does the soul resemble?

CEBES: The soul resembles the divine, and the body the mortal—there can be no doubt of that, Socrates.

SOC.:   Then reflect, Cebes: is not the conclusion of the whole matter this,—that the soul is in the very likeness of the divine, and immortal, and intelligible, and uniform, and indissoluble, and unchangeable; and the body is in the very likeness of the human, and mortal, and unintelligible, and multiform, and dissoluble, and changeable. Can this, my dear Cebes, be denied?

CEBES: No indeed.

SOC.:   But if this is true, then is not the body liable to speedy dissolution? and is not the soul almost or altogether indissoluble?

CEBES: Certainly.

SOC.: And do you further observe, that after a man is dead, the body, which is the visible part of man, and has a visible framework, which is called a corpse, and which would naturally be dissolved and decomposed and dissipated, is not dissolved or decomposed at once, but may remain for a good while, if the constitution be sound at the time of death, and the season of the year favorable? For the body when shrunk and embalmed, as is the custom in Egypt, may remain almost entire through infinite ages; and even in decay, still there are some portions, such as the bones and ligaments, which are, practically indestructible. You allow that?

CEBES: Yes.

SOC.: And are we to suppose that the soul, which is invisible, in passing to the true Hades, which like her is invisible, and pure, and noble, and on their way to the good and wise God, whither, if God will, my soul is also soon to go,—that the soul, I repeat, if this be her nature and origin, is blown away and perishes immediately on quitting the body, as the many say? That can never be, my dear Simmias and Cebes. The truth rather is, that the soul which is pure at departing draws after her no bodily taint, having never voluntarily had connection with the body, which she is ever avoiding, herself gathered into herself (for such abstraction has been the study of her life). And what does this mean but that she has been a true disciple of philosophy, and has practiced how to die easily? And is not philosophy the practice of death?

CEBES: Certainly.

SOC.: That soul, I say, herself invisible, departs to the invisible world,—to the divine and immortal and rational: thither arriving, she lives in bliss and is released from the error and folly of men, their fears and wild passions and all other human ills, and forever dwells, as they say of the initiated, in company with the gods? Is not this true, Cebes?

CEBES: Yes, beyond a doubt.

Study Questions

1. What is Plato's view of human nature? What constitutes our true self?
2. According to Plato how should we view death? In this regard what is the purpose of philosophy?
3. What are Plato's arguments for life after death? Are they sound?

CHAPTER 13

Death Is Nothing to Us

EPICURUS

Epicurus (341–271 B.C.E.) was a Greek philosopher who lived in Athens where he founded the Epicurean School of Philosophy. Influenced by the materialist Democritus (460–370 B.C.E.), the first philosopher known to assert that the world was made up of atoms, Epicurus develops a philosophy based on the love of pleasure and disdain for pain, called *hedonism* (from the Greek word for "pleasure"). But for Epicurus, hedonism was not what has come to be known as "Epicureanism," a sensuous or profligate life, or one given to eating gourmet foods and drinking vintage wines. Rather, true pleasure consisted in an attitude of imperturbable emotional tranquility that needed only simple joys, a good diet, health, good friends, and good conversation. Since only good and bad sensations (pleasures and pains) should concern us and death is neither of these, we should not fear death.

Letter to Menoeceus

LET NO ONE WHEN YOUNG delay to study philosophy, nor when he is old grow weary of his study. For no one can come too early or too late to secure the health of his soul. And the man who says that the age for philosophy has either not yet come or has gone by is like the man who says that the age for happiness is not yet come to him, or has passed away. Wherefore both when young and old a man must study philosophy, that as he grows old he may be young in blessings through the grateful recollection of what has been, and that in youth he may be old as well, since he will know no fear of what is to come. We must then meditate on the things that make our happiness, seeing that when that is with us we have all, but when it is absent we do all to win it.

The things which I used unceasingly to commend to you, these do and practise, considering them to be the first principles of the good life.

First of all believe that god is a being immortal and blessed, even as the common idea of a god is engraved on men's minds, and do not assign to him anything alien to his immortality or ill suited to his blessedness: but believe about him everything that can uphold his blessedness and immortality. For gods there are, since the knowledge of them is by clear vision. But they are not such as the many believe them to be: for indeed they do not consistently represent them as they believe them to be. And the impious man is not he who denies the gods of the many, but he who attaches to the gods the beliefs of the many. For the statements of the many about the gods are not conceptions derived from sensation, but false suppositions, according to which the greatest misfortunes befall the wicked and the greatest blessings the good by the gift of the gods. For men being accustomed always to their own virtues welcome those like themselves, but regard all that is not of their nature as alien.

Reprinted from Epicurus, The Extant Remains, *translated by Cyril Bailey (1926) by permission of Oxford University Press.*

Become accustomed to the belief that death is nothing to us. For all good and evil consists in sensation, but death is deprivation of sensation. And therefore a right understanding that death is nothing to us makes the mortality of life enjoyable, not because it adds to it an infinite span of time, but because it takes away the craving for immortality. For there is nothing terrible in life for the man who has truly comprehended that there is nothing terrible in not living. So that the man speaks but idly who says that he fears death not because it will be painful when it comes, but because it is painful in anticipation. For that which gives no trouble when it comes, is but an empty pain in anticipation. So death, the most terrifying of ills, is nothing to us, since so long as we exist, death is not with us; but when death comes, then we do not exist. It does not then concern either the living or the dead, since for the former it is not, and the latter are no more.

But the many at one moment shun death as the greatest of evils, at another yearn for it as a respite from the evils in life. But the wise man neither seeks to escape life nor fears the cessation of life, for neither does life offend him nor does the absence of life seem to be any evil. And just as with food he does not seek simply the larger share and nothing else, but rather the most pleasant, so he seeks to enjoy not the longest period of time, but the most pleasant.

And he who counsels the young man to live well, but the old man to make a good end, is foolish, not merely because of the desirability of life, but also because it is the same training which teaches to live well and to die well. Yet much worse still is the man who says it is good not to be born, but "once born make haste to pass the gates of Death." For if he says this from conviction why does he not pass away out of life? For it is open to him to do so, if he had firmly made up his mind to this. But if he speaks in jest, his words are idle among men who cannot receive them.

We must then bear in mind that the future is neither ours, nor yet wholly not ours, so that we may not altogether expect it as sure to come, nor abandon hope of it, as if it will certainly not come.

We must consider that of desires some are natural, others vain, and of the natural some are necessary and others merely natural; and of the necessary some are necessary for happiness, others for the repose of the body, and others for very life. The right understanding of these facts enables us to refer all choice and avoidance to the health of the body and the soul's freedom from disturbance, since this the aim of the life of blessedness. For it is to obtain this end that we always act, namely, to avoid pain and fear. And when this is once secured for us, all the tempest of the soul is dispersed, since the living creature has not to wander as though in search of something that is missing, and to look for some other thing by which he can fulfil the good of the soul and the good of the body. For it is then that we have need of pleasure, when we feel pain owing to the absence of pleasure; but when we do not feel pain, we no longer need pleasure. And for this cause we call pleasure the beginning and end of the blessed life. For we recognize pleasure as the first good innate in us, and from pleasure we begin every act of choice and avoidance, and to pleasure we return again, using the feeling as the standard by which we judge every good.

And since pleasure is the first good and natural to us, for this very reason we do not choose every pleasure, but sometimes we pass over many pleasures, when greater discomfort accrues to us as the result of them: and similarly we think many pains better than pleasures, since a greater pleasure comes to us when we have endured pains for a long time. Every pleasure then because of its natural kinship to us is good, yet not every pleasure is to be chosen: even as every pain also is an evil, yet not all are always of a nature to be avoided. Yet by a scale of comparison and by the consideration of advantages and disadvantages we must form our judgement on all these matters. For the good on certain occasions we treat as bad, and conversely the bad as good.

And again independence of desire we think a great good—not that we may at all times enjoy but a few things, but that, if we do not possess many, we may enjoy the few in the genuine persuasion that those have the sweetest pleasure in luxury who least need it, and that all that is natural is easy to be obtained, but that which is superfluous is hard. And so plain savours bring us pleasure equal to a luxurious diet, when all the pain due to want is removed; and bread and water produce the highest pleasure, when one who needs them puts them to his lips. To grow accustomed therefore to simple and not luxurious diet gives us health to the full, and makes a man alert for the needful employments of life, and when after long intervals we approach luxuries, disposes us better towards them, and fits us to be fearless of fortune.

When, therefore, we maintain that pleasure is the end, we do not mean the pleasures of profligates and those that consist in sensuality, as is supposed by some who are either ignorant or disagree with us or do not understand, but freedom from pain in the body and from trouble in the mind. For it is not continuous drinkings and revellings, nor the satisfaction of lusts, nor the enjoyment of fish and other luxuries of the wealthy table, which produce a pleasant life, but sober reasoning, searching out the motives for all choice and avoidance, and banishing mere opinions, to which are due the greatest disturbance of the spirit.

Of all this the beginning and the greatest good is prudence. Wherefore prudence is a more precious thing even than philosophy: for from prudence are sprung all the other virtues, and it teaches us that it is not possible to live pleasantly without living prudently and honorably and justly, nor, again, to live a life of prudence, honour, and justice without living pleasantly. For the virtues are by nature bound up with the pleasant life, and the pleasant life is inseparable from them. For indeed who, think you, is a better man than he who holds reverent opinions concerning the gods, and is at all times free from

fear of death, and has reasoned out the end ordained by nature? He understands that the limit of good things is easy to fulfil and easy to attain, whereas the course of ills is either short in time or slight in pain; he laughs at destiny, whom some have introduced as the mistress of all things. He thinks that with us lies the chief power in determining events, some of which happen by necessity and some by chance, and some are within our control; for while necessity cannot be called to account, he sees that chance is inconstant, but that which is in our control is subject to no master, and to it are naturally attached praise and blame. For, indeed, it were better to follow the myths about the gods than to become a slave to the destiny of the natural philosophers: for the former suggests a hope of placating the gods by worship, whereas the latter involves a necessity which knows no placation. As to chance, he does not regard it as a god as most men do (for in a god's acts there is no disorder), nor as an uncertain cause of all things: for he does not believe that good and evil are given by chance to man for the framing of a blessed life, but that opportunities for great good and great evil are afforded by it. He therefore thinks it better to be unfortunate in reasonable action than to prosper in unreason. For it is better in a man's actions that what is well chosen should fail, rather than that what is ill chosen should be successful owing to chance.

Meditate therefore on these things and things akin to them night and day by yourself, and with a companion like to yourself, and never shall you be disturbed waking or asleep, but you shall live like a god among men. For a man who lives among immortal blessings is not like to a mortal being.

Principal Doctrines

I. The blessed and immortal nature knows no trouble itself nor causes trouble to any other, so that it is never constrained by anger or favour.

For all such things exist only in the weak.

II. Death is nothing to us: for that which is dissolved is without sensation; and that which lacks sensation is nothing to us.

III. The limit of quantity in pleasures is the removal of all that is painful. Wherever pleasure is present, as long as it is there, there is neither pain of body nor of mind, nor of both at once.

IV. Pain does not last continuously in the flesh, but the acutest pain is there for a very short time, and even that which just exceeds the pleasure in the flesh does not continue for many days at once. But chronic illnesses permit a predominance of pleasure over pain in the flesh.

V. It is not possible to live pleasantly without living prudently and honourably and justly, nor again to live a life of prudence, honour, and justice without living pleasantly. And the man who does not possess the pleasant life, is not living prudently and honourably and justly, and the man who does not possess the virtuous life, cannot possibly live pleasantly.

VI. To secure protection from men anything is a natural good, by which you may be able to attain this end.

VII. Some men wished to become famous and conspicuous, thinking that they would thus win for themselves safety from other men. Wherefore if the life of such men is safe, they have obtained the good which nature craves; but if it is not safe, they do not possess that for which they strove at first by the instinct of nature.

VIII. No pleasure is a bad thing in itself: but the means which produce some pleasures bring with them disturbances many times greater than the pleasures.

IX. If every pleasure could be intensified so that it lasted and influenced the whole organism or the most essential parts of our nature, pleasures would never differ from one another.

X. If the things that produce the pleasures of profligates could dispel the fears of the mind about the phenomena of the sky and death and its pains, and also teach the limits of desires and of pains, we should never have cause to blame

them: for they would be filling themselves full with pleasures from every source and never have pain of body or mind, which is the evil of life.

XI. If we were not troubled by our suspicions of the phenomena of the sky and about death, fearing that it concerns us, and also by our failure to grasp the limits of pains and desires, we should have no need of natural science.

XII. A man cannot dispel his fear about the most important matters if he does not know what is the nature of the universe but suspects the truth of some mythical story. So that without natural science it is not possible to attain our pleasures unalloyed.

XIII. There is no profit in securing protection in relation to men, if things above and things beneath the earth and indeed all in the boundless universe remain matters of suspicion.

XIV. The most unalloyed source of protection from men, which is secured to some extent by a certain force of expulsion, is in fact the immunity which results from a quiet life and the retirement from the world.

XV. The wealth demanded by nature is both limited and easily procured; that demanded by idle imaginings stretches on to infinity.

XVI. In but few things chance hinders a wise man, but the greatest and most important matters reason has ordained and throughout the whole period of life does and will ordain.

XVII. The just man is most free from trouble, the unjust most full of trouble.

XVIII. The pleasure in the flesh is not increased, when once the pain due to want is removed, but is only varied: and the limit as regards pleasure in the mind is begotten by the reasoned understanding of these very pleasures and of the emotions akin to them, which used to cause the greatest fear to the mind.

XIX. Infinite time contains no greater pleasure than limited time, if one measures by reason the limits of pleasure.

XX. The flesh perceives the limits of pleasure as unlimited and unlimited time is required to supply it. But the mind, having attained a reasoned understanding of the ultimate good of the flesh and its limits and having dissipated the fears concerning the time to come, supplies us with the complete life, and we have no further need of infinite time: but neither does the mind shun pleasure, nor, when circumstances begin to bring about the departure from life, does it approach its end as though it fell short in any way of the best life.

XXI. He who has learned the limits of life knows that that which removes the pain due to want and makes the whole of life complete is easy to obtain; so that there is no need of actions which involve competition.

XXII. We must consider both the real purpose and all the evidence of direct perception, to which we always refer the conclusions of opinion; otherwise, all will be full of doubt and confusion.

XXIII. If you fight against all sensations, you will have no standard by which to judge even those of them which you say are false.

XXIV. If you reject any single sensation and fail to distinguish between the conclusion of opinion as to the appearance awaiting confirmation and that which is actually given by the sensation or feeling, or each intuitive apprehension of the mind, you will confound all other sensations as well with the same groundless opinion, so that you will reject every standard of judgement. And if among the mental images created by your opinion you affirm both that which awaits confirmation and that which does not, you will not escape error, since you will have preserved the whole cause of doubt in every judgement between what is right and what is wrong.

XXV. If on each occasion instead of referring your actions to the end of nature, you turn to some other nearer standard when you are making a choice or an avoidance, your actions will not be consistent with your principles.

XXVI. Of desires, all that do not lead to a sense of pain, if they are not satisfied, are not necessary, but involve a craving which is easily

dispelled, when the object is hard to procure or they seem likely to produce harm.

XXVII. Of all the things which wisdom acquires to produce the blessedness of the complete life, by far the greatest is the possession of friendship.

XXVIII. The same conviction which has given us confidence that there is nothing terrible that lasts forever or even for long, has also seen the protection of friendship most fully completed in the limited evils of this life.

XXIX. Among desires some are natural and necessary, some natural but not necessary, and others neither natural nor necessary, but due to idle imagination.

XXX. Wherever in the case of desires which are physical, but do not lead to a sense of pain, if they are not fulfilled, the effort is intense, such pleasures are due to idle imagination, and it is not owing to their own nature that they fail to be dispelled, but owing to the empty imaginings of the man.

XXXI. The justice which arises from nature is a pledge of mutual advantage to restrain men from harming one another and save them from being harmed.

XXXII. For all living things which have not been able to make compacts not to harm one another or be harmed, nothing ever is either just or unjust; and likewise too for all tribes of men which have been unable or unwilling to make compacts not to harm or be harmed.

XXXIII. Justice never is anything in itself, but in the dealings of men with one another in any place whatever and at any time it is a kind of compact not to harm or be harmed.

XXXIV. Injustice is not an evil in itself, but only in consequence of the fear which attaches to the apprehension of being unable to escape those appointed to punish such actions.

XXXV. It is not possible for one who acts in secret contravention of the terms of the compact not to harm or be harmed, too confident that he will escape detection, even if at present he escapes a thousand times. For up to the time of death it cannot be certain that he will indeed escape.

XXXVI. In its general aspect justice is the same for all, for it is a kind of mutual advantage in the dealings of men with one another; but with reference to the individual peculiarities of a country or any other circumstances the same thing does not turn out to be just for all.

XXXVII. Among actions which are sanctioned as just by law, that which is proved on examination to be of advantage in the requirements of men's dealings with one another, has the guarantee of justice, whether it is the same for all or not. But if a man makes a law and it does not turn out to lead to advantage in men's dealings with each other, then it no longer has the essential nature of justice. And even if the advantage in the matter of justice shifts from one side to the other, but for a while accords with the general concept, it is none the less just for that period in the eyes of those who do not confound themselves with empty sounds but look to the actual facts.

XXXVIII. Where, provided the circumstances have not been altered, actions which were considered just, have been shown not to accord with the general concept in actual practice, then they are not just. But where, when circumstances have changed, the same actions which were sanctioned as just no longer lead to advantage, there they were just at the time when they were of advantage for the dealings of fellow-citizens with one another; but subsequently they are no longer just, when no longer of advantage.

XXXIX. The man who has best ordered the element of disquiet arising from external circumstances has made those things that he could akin to himself and the rest at least not alien: but with all to which he could not do even this, he has refrained from mixing, and has expelled from his life all which it was of advantage to treat thus.

XL. As many as possess the power to procure complete immunity from their neighbours, these also live most pleasantly with one another, since they have the most certain pledge of security, and after they have enjoyed the fullest intimacy, they do not lament the previous departure of a dead friend, as though he were to be pitied.

Study Questions

1. What is Epicurus's view of the meaning of life? How should we live? Describe his philosophy.
2. What is Epicurus's view of the meaning of death? What should be our attitude toward death?
3. Evaluate Epicurus's philosophy of life and death. What are the strengths and weaknesses?

CHAPTER 14

Does Life Have a Meaning?

RICHARD TAYLOR

Before retirement, Richard Taylor was professor of philosophy at the University of Rochester. One of America's most prolific philosophers, he has written important works on almost every major topic. His principal works are *Ethics, Faith, and Reason* (1985) and *Good and Evil,* from which this selection is taken.

Drawing on the ancient Greek myth of Sisyphus—the creature who was condemned by the gods to an endless repetition of rolling a boulder to the top of a mountain in Hades, retrieving it once it rolled down, and doing it again throughout eternity—Taylor sets forth alternative ways of imputing significance to Sisyphus's weary task. His task would have had meaning if he could have constructed a beautiful temple at the top of the mountain or it could have had a perverse meaning if the gods had programmed him with an obsession for stone rolling. From this option Taylor gives his solution to the problem of the meaning of life.

THE QUESTION WHETHER LIFE has any meaning is difficult to interpret, and the more one concentrates his critical faculty on it the more it seems to elude him, or to evaporate as an intelligible question. One wants to turn it aside, as a source of embarrassment, as something that, if it cannot be abolished, should at least be decently covered. And yet I think any reflective person recognizes that the question it raises is important, and that it ought to have a significant answer.

If the idea of meaningfulness is difficult to grasp in this context, so that we are unsure what sort of thing would amount to answering the question, the idea of meaninglessness is perhaps less so. If, then, we can bring before our minds a clear image of meaningless existence, then perhaps we can take a step toward coping with our original question by seeing to what extent our lives, as we actually find them, resemble that image, and draw such lessons as we are able to from the comparison.

Meaningless Existence

A perfect image of meaninglessness, of the kind we are seeking, is found in the ancient myth of Sisyphus. Sisyphus, it will be remembered, betrayed divine secrets to mortals, and for this he was condemned by the gods to roll a stone to the top of a hill, the stone then immediately to roll back down, again to be pushed to the top by Sisyphus, to roll down once more, and so on again and again, *forever*. Now in this we have the picture of meaningless, pointless toil, of a meaningless existence that is absolutely *never* redeemed. It is not even redeemed by a death that, if it were to accomplish nothing more, would at least bring this idiotic cycle to a close. If we were invited to imagine Sisyphus struggling for awhile and accomplishing nothing, perhaps eventually falling from exhaustion, so that we might suppose him then eventually turning to something having some sort of promise, then the meaninglessness of the chapter of his life would not be so stark. It would be a dark and dreadful dream, from which he eventually awakens to sunlight and reality. But he does not awaken, for there is nothing for him to awaken to. His repetitive toil is his life and reality, and it goes on forever, and it is without any meaning whatever. Nothing ever comes of what he is doing, except simply, more of the same. Not by one step, nor by a thousand, nor by ten thousand does he even expiate by the smallest token the sin against the gods that led him into this fate. Nothing comes of it, nothing at all.

This ancient myth has always enchanted men, for countless meanings can be read into it. Some of the ancients apparently thought it symbolized the perpetual rising and setting of the sun, and others the repetitious crashing of the waves upon the shore. Probably the commonest interpretation is that it symbolizes man's eternal struggle and unquenchable spirit, his determination always to try once more in the face of overwhelming discouragement. This interpretation is further supported by that version of the myth according to which Sisyphus was commanded to roll the stone *over* the hill, so that it would finally roll down the other side, but was never quite able to make it.

I am not concerned with rendering or defending any interpretation of this myth, however. I have cited it only for the one element it does unmistakably contain, namely, that of a repetitious, cyclic activity that never comes to anything. We could contrive other images of this that would serve just as well, and no mythmakers are needed to supply the materials of it.

Thus, we can imagine two persons transporting a stone—or even a precious gem, it does not matter—back and forth, relay style. One carries it to a near or distant point where it is received by the other; it is returned to its starting point, there to be recovered by the first, and the process is repeated over and over. Except in this relay nothing counts as winning, and nothing brings the contest to any close, each step only leads to a repetition of itself. Or we can imagine two groups of prisoners, one of them engaged in digging a prodigious hole in the ground that is no sooner finished than it is filled in again by the other group, the latter then digging a new hole that is at once filled in by the first group, and so on and on endlessly.

Now what stands out in all such pictures as oppressive and dejecting is not that the beings who enact these roles suffer any torture or pain, for it need not be assumed that they do. Nor is it that their labors are great, for they are no greater than the labors commonly undertaken by most men most of the time. According to the original myth, the stone is so large that Sisyphus never quite gets it to the top and must groan under every step, so that his enormous labor is all for nought. But this is not what appalls. It is not that his great struggle comes to nothing, but that his existence itself is without meaning. Even if we suppose, for example, that the stone is but a pebble that can be carried effortlessly, or that the holes dug by the prisoners are but small ones, not the slightest meaning is introduced into their lives. The stone that Sisyphus moves to the top of the hill, whether we think of it as large or small, still rolls back every time, and the process is repeated forever. Nothing comes of it, and the work is simply pointless. That is the element of the myth that I wish to capture.

Again, it is not the fact that the labors of Sisyphus continue forever that deprives them of meaning. It is, rather, the implication of this: that they come to nothing. The image would not be changed by our supposing him to push a different stone up every time, each to roll down again. But if we supposed that these stones, instead of rolling back to their places as if they had never been moved, were assembled at the top of the hill and there incorporated, say, in a beautiful and enduring temple, then the aspect of meaninglessness would disappear. His labors would then have a point, something would come of them all, and although one could perhaps still say it was not worth it, one could not say that the life of Sisyphus was devoid of meaning altogether. Meaningfulness would at least have made an appearance, and we could see what it was.

That point will need remembering. But in the meantime, let us note another way in which the image of meaninglessness can be altered by making only a very slight change. Let us suppose that the gods, while condemning Sisyphus to the fate just described, at the same time, as an afterthought, waxed perversely merciful by implanting in him a strange and irrational impulse; namely, a compulsive impulse to roll stones. We may if we like, to make this more graphic, suppose they accomplish this by implanting in him some substance that has this effect on his character and drives. I call this perverse, because from our point of view there is clearly no reason why anyone should have a persistent and insatiable desire to do something so pointless as that. Nevertheless, suppose that is Sisyphus' condition. He has but one obsession, which is to roll stones, and it is an obsession that is only for the moment appeased by his rolling them—he no sooner gets a stone rolled to the top of the hill than he is restless to roll up another.

Now it can be seen why this little afterthought of the gods, which I called perverse, was also in fact merciful. For they have by this device managed to give Sisyphus precisely what he wants—by making him want precisely what they inflict on him. However it may appear to us, Sisyphus' fate now does not appear to him as a condemnation, but the very reverse. His one desire in life is to roll stones, and he is absolutely guaranteed its endless fulfillment. Where otherwise he might profoundly have wished surcease,

and even welcomed the quiet of death to release him from endless boredom and meaninglessness, his life is now filled with mission and meaning, and he seems to himself to have been given an entry to heaven. Nor need he even fear death, for the gods have promised him an endless opportunity to indulge his single purpose, without concern or frustration. He will be able to roll stones *forever*.

What we need to mark most carefully at this point is that the picture with which we began has not really been changed in the least by adding this supposition. Exactly the same things happen as before. The only change is in Sisyphus' view of them. The picture before was the image of meaningless activity and existence. It was created precisely to be an image of that. It has not lost that meaninglessness, it has now gained not the least shred of meaningfulness. The stones still roll back as before, each phase of Sisyphus' life still exactly resembles all the others, the task is never completed, nothing comes of it, no temple ever begins to rise, and all this cycle of the same pointless thing over and over goes on forever in this picture as in the other. The *only* thing that has happened is this: Sisyphus has been reconciled to it, and indeed more, he has been led to embrace it. Not, however, by reason or persuasion, but by nothing more rational than the potency of a new substance in his veins.

The Meaninglessness of Life

I believe the foregoing provides a fairly clear content to the idea of meaninglessness and, through it, some hint of what meaningfulness, in this sense, might be. Meaninglessness is essentially endless pointlessness, and meaningfulness is therefore the opposite. Activity, and even long, drawn-out and repetitive activity, has a meaning if it has some significant culmination, some more or less lasting end that can be considered to have been the direction and purpose of the activity. But the descriptions so far also provide something else; namely, the suggestion of how an existence that is objectively meaningless, in this sense, can nevertheless acquire a meaning for him whose existence it is.

Now let us ask: Which of these pictures does life in fact resemble? And let us not begin with our own lives, for here both our prejudices and wishes are great, but with the life in general that we share with the rest of creation. We shall find, I think, that it all has a certain pattern, and that this pattern is by now easily recognized.

We can begin anywhere, only saving human existence for our last consideration. We can, for example, begin with any animal. It does not matter where we begin, because the result is going to be exactly the same.

Thus, for example, there are caves in New Zealand, deep and dark, whose floors are quiet pools and whose walls and ceilings are covered with soft light. As one gazes in wonder in the stillness of these caves it seems that the Creator has reproduced there in microcosm the heavens themselves, until one scarcely remembers the enclosing presence of the walls. As one looks more closely, however, the scene is explained. Each dot of light identifies an ugly worm, whose luminous tail is meant to attract insects from the surrounding darkness. As from time to time one of these insects draws near it becomes entangled in a sticky thread lowered by the worm, and is eaten. This goes on month after month, the blind worm lying there in the barren stillness waiting to entrap an occasional bit of nourishment that will only sustain it to another bit of nourishment until. . . . Until what? What great thing awaits all this long and repetitious effort and makes it worthwhile? Really nothing. The larva just transforms itself finally to a tiny winged adult that lacks even mouth parts to feed and lives only a day or two. These adults, as soon as they have mated and laid eggs, are themselves caught in the threads and are devoured by the cannibalist worms, often without having ventured into the day, the only point to

their existence having now been fulfilled. This has been going on for millions of years, and to no end other than that the same meaningless cycle may continue for another millions of years.

All living things present essentially the same spectacle. The larva of a certain cicada burrows in the darkness of the earth for seventeen years, through season after season, to emerge finally into the daylight for a brief flight, lay its eggs, and die—this all to repeat itself during the next seventeen years, and so on to eternity. We have already noted, in another connection, the struggles of fish, made only that others may do the same after them and that this cycle, having no other point than itself, may never cease. Some birds span an entire side of the globe each year and then return, only to insure that others may follow the same incredibly long path again and again. One is led to wonder what the point of it all is, with what great triumph this ceaseless effort, repeating itself through millions of years, might finally culminate, and why it should go on and on for so long, accomplishing nothing, getting nowhere. But then one realizes that there is no point to it at all, that it really culminates in nothing, that each of these cycles, so filled with toil, is to be followed only by more of the same. The point of any living thing's life is, evidently, nothing but life itself.

This life of the world thus presents itself to our eyes as a vast machine, feeding on itself, running on and on forever to nothing. And we are part of that life. To be sure, we are not just the same, but the differences are not so great as we like to think; many are merely invented, and none really cancels the kind of meaninglessness that we found in Sisyphus and that we find all around, wherever anything lives. We are conscious of our activity. Our goals, whether in any significant sense we choose them or not, are things of which we are at least partly aware and can therefore in some sense appraise. More significantly, perhaps men have a history, as other animals do not, such that each generation does not precisely resemble all those before. Still, if we can in imagination disengage our wills from our lives and disregard the deep interest each man has in his own existence, we shall find that they do not so little resemble the existence of Sisyphus. We toil after goals, most of them—indeed every single one of them—of transitory significance and, having gained one of them, we immediately set forth for the next, as if that one had never been, with this next one being essentially more of the same. Look at a busy street any day, and observe the throng going hither and thither. To what? Some office or shop, where the same things will be done today as were done yesterday, and are done now so they may be repeated tomorrow. And if we think that, unlike Sisyphus, these labors do have a point, that they culminate in something lasting and, independently of our own deep interests in them, very worthwhile, then we simply have not considered the thing closely enough. Most such effort is directed only to the establishment and perpetuation of home and family; that is, to the begetting of others who will follow in our steps to do more of the same. Each man's life thus resembles one of Sisyphus' climbs to the summit of his hill, and each day of it one of his steps; the difference is that whereas Sisyphus himself returns to push the stone up again, we leave this to our children. We at one point imagined that the labors of Sisyphus finally culminated in the creation of a temple, but for this to make any difference it had to be a temple that would at least endure, adding beauty to the world for the remainder of time. Our achievements, even though they are often beautiful, are mostly bubbles; and those that do last, like the sand-swept pyramids, soon become mere curiosities while around them the rest of mankind continues its perpetual toting of rocks, only to see them roll down. Nations are built upon the bones of their founders and pioneers, but only to decay and crumble before long, their rubble then becoming the foundation for others directed to exactly the same fate. The picture of Sisyphus is the picture of existence of the individual man, great or unknown, of nations, of the race of men, and of the very life of the world.

On a country road one sometimes comes upon the ruined hulks of a house and once extensive buildings, all in collapse and spread over with weeds. A curious eye can in imagination reconstruct from what is left a once warm and thriving life, filled with purpose. There was the hearth, where a family once talked, sang, and made plans; there were the rooms, where people loved and babes were born to a rejoicing mother; there are the musty remains of a sofa, infested with bugs, once bought at a dear price to enhance an ever-growing comfort, beauty, and warmth. Every small piece of junk fills the mind with what once, not long ago, was utterly real, with children's voices, plans made, and enterprises embarked upon. That is how these stones of Sisyphus were rolled up, and that is how they became incorporated into a beautiful temple, and that temple is what now lies before you. Meanwhile other buildings, institutions, nations, and civilizations spring up all around, only to share the same fate before long. And if the question "What for?" is now asked, the answer is clear: so that just this may go on forever.

The two pictures—of Sisyphus and of our own lives, if we look at them from a distance—are in outline the same and convey to the mind the same image. It is not surprising, then, that men invent ways of denying it, their religions proclaiming a heaven that does not crumble, their hymnals and prayer books declaring a significance to life of which our eyes provide no hint whatever.[1] Even our philosophies portray some permanent and lasting good at which all may aim, from the changeless forms invented by Plato to the beatific vision of St. Thomas and the ideals of permanence contrived by the moderns. When these fail to convince, then earthly ideals such as universal justice and brotherhood are conjured up to take their places and give meaning to man's seemingly endless pilgrimage, some final state that will be ushered in when the last obstacle is removed and the last stone pushed to the hilltop. No one believes, of course, that any such state will be final, or even wants it to be in case it means that human existence would then cease to be a struggle; but in the meaning such ideas serve a very real need.

The Meaning of Life

We noted that Sisyphus' existence would have meaning if there were some point to his labors, if his efforts ever culminated in something that was not just an occasion for fresh labors of the same kind. But that is precisely the meaning it lacks. And human existence resembles his in that respect. Men do achieve things—they scale their towers and raise their stones to their hilltops—but every such accomplishment fades, providing only an occasion for renewed labors of the same kind.

But here we need to note something else that has been mentioned, but its significance not explored, and that is the state of mind and feeling with which such labors are undertaken. We noted that if Sisyphus had a keen and unappeasable desire to be doing just what he found himself doing, then, although his life would in no way be changed, it would nevertheless have a meaning for him. It would be an irrational one, no doubt, because the desire itself would be only the product of the substance in his veins, and not any that reason could discover, but a meaning nevertheless.

And would it not, in fact, be a meaning incomparably better than the other? For let us examine again the first kind of meaning it could have. Let us suppose that, without having any interest in rolling stones, as such, and finding this, in fact, a galling toil, Sisyphus did nevertheless have a deep interest in raising a temple, one that would be beautiful and lasting. And let us suppose he succeeded in this, that after ages of dreadful toil, all directed at this final result, he did at last complete his temple, such that now

he could say his work was done and he could rest and forever enjoy the result. Now what? What picture now presents itself to our minds? It is precisely the picture of infinite boredom! Of Sisyphus doing nothing ever again, but contemplating what he has already wrought and can no longer add anything to, and contemplating it for an eternity! Now in this picture we have a meaning for Sisyphus' existence, a point for his prodigious labor, because we have put it there; yet, at the same time, that which is really worthwhile seems to have slipped away entirely. Where before we were presented with the nightmare of eternal and pointless activity, we are now confronted with the hell of its eternal absence.

Our second picture, then, wherein we imagined Sisyphus to have had inflicted on him the irrational desire to be doing just what he found himself doing, should not have been dismissed so abruptly. The meaning that picture lacked was no meaning that he or anyone could crave, and the strange meaning it had was perhaps just what we were seeking.

At this point, then, we can reintroduce what has been until now, it is hoped, resolutely pushed aside in an effort to view our lives and human existence with objectivity; namely, our own wills, our deep interest in what we find ourselves doing. If we do this we find that our lives do indeed still resemble that of Sisyphus, but that the meaningfulness they thus lack is precisely the meaningfulness of infinite boredom. At the same time, the strange meaningfulness they possess is that of the inner compulsion to be doing just what we were put here to do, and to go on doing it forever. This is the nearest we may hope to get to heaven, but the redeeming side of that fact is that we do thereby avoid a genuine hell.

If the builders of a great and flourishing ancient civilization could somehow return now to see archaeologists unearthing the trivial remnants of what they had once accomplished with such effort—see the fragments of pots and vases, a few broken statues, and such tokens of another age and greatness—they could indeed ask themselves what the point of it all was, if this is all it finally came to. Yet, it did not seem so to them then, for it was just the building, and not what was finally built, that gave their life meaning. Similarly, if the builders of the ruined home and farm that I described a short while ago could be brought back to see what is left, they would have the same feelings. What we construct in our imaginations as we look over these decayed and rusting pieces would reconstruct itself in their very memories, and certainly with unspeakable sadness. The piece of a sled at our feet would revive in them a warm Christmas. And what rich memories would there be in the broken crib? And the weed-covered remains of a fence would reproduce the scene of a great herd of livestock, so laboriously built up over so many years. What was it all worth, if this is the final result? Yet, again, it did not seem so to them through those many years of struggle and toil, and they did not imagine they were building a Gibraltar. The things to which they bent their backs day after day, realizing one by one their ephemeral plans, were precisely the things in which their wills were deeply involved, precisely the things in which their interests lay, and there was no need then to ask questions. There is no more need of them now—the day was sufficient to itself, and so was the life.

This is surely the way to look at all of life—at one's own life, and each day and moment it contains; of the life of a nation; of the species; of the life of the world; and of everything that breathes. Even the glow worms I described, whose cycles of existence over the millions of years seem so pointless when looked at by us, will seem entirely different to us if we can somehow try to view their existence from within. Their endless activity, which gets nowhere, is just what it is their will to pursue. This is its whole justification and meaning. Nor would it be any salvation to the birds who span the globe every year, back and forth, to have a home made for them in a cage with plenty of food and protection, so that they would not have to migrate any more. It would be their condemnation, for it is the doing that counts for them, and not what they hope to win by it. Flying these prodigious distances, never ending, is what it is in their veins to do, exactly as it was in Sisyphus' veins to roll stones, without end, after the gods had waxed merciful and implanted this in him.

A human being no sooner draws his first breath than he responds to the will that is in him to live. He no more asks whether it will be worthwhile, or whether anything of significance will come of it, than the worms and the birds. The point of his living is simply to be living, in the manner that it is his nature to be living. He goes through his life building his castles, each of these beginning to fade into time as the next is begun; yet, it would be no salvation to rest from all this. It would be a condemnation, and one that would in no way be redeemed were he able to gaze upon the things he has done, even if these were beautiful and absolutely permanent, as they never are. What counts is that one should be able to begin a new task, a new castle, a new bubble. It counts only because it is there to be done and he has the will to do it. The same will be the life of his children and of theirs; and if the philosopher is apt to see in this a pattern similar to the unending cycles of the existence of Sisyphus, and to despair, then it is indeed because the meaning and point he is seeking is not there—but mercifully so. The meaning of life is from within us, it is not bestowed from without, and it far exceeds in both its beauty and permanence any heaven of which men have ever dreamed or yearned for.

Note

1. A popular Christian hymn, sung often at funerals and typical of many hymns, expresses this thought:

> Swift to its close ebbs out life's little day;

Earth's joys grow dim, its glories pass away;
Change and decay in all around I see:
O thou who changest not, abide with me.

Study Questions

1. Retell the myth of Sisyphus. How does Taylor use it to discuss the meaning of life?
2. According to Taylor, what is the meaning of life? Do you agree with him?

CHAPTER 15

Religion and the Meaning of Life and Death

LOIS HOPE WALKER

> Lois Hope Walker is the pen name of a contemporary author who desires to remain anonymous. In this essay Walker argues that religion, specifically theistic religion, gives special meaning to life, unavailable in secular worldviews. Furthermore, the autonomy that secularists prize is not significantly diminished by religious faith.

SEVERAL YEARS AGO during a class break, I was discussing the significance of religion in our society with a few students in the college lounge. I, at that time an agnostic, was conceding to a devout Christian that it would be nice if theism were true, for then the world would not be simply a matter of chance and necessity, a sad tale with a sadder ending. Instead, "the world would be personal, a gift from our heavenly Father, who provides a basis for meaning and purpose." A mature woman from another class, whom I knew to be an atheist, overheard my remarks, charged through a group of coffee drinkers and angrily snapped at me, "That is the most disgusting thing I've ever heard!" I inquired why she thought this, and she replied, "Religion keeps humans from growing up. We don't need a big Daddy in the sky. We need to grow up and become our own parents."

I recalled Nietzsche's dictum that now that "God is dead," now that we have killed the Holy One, we must ourselves become gods to seem worthy of the deed. The atheist woman was prizing autonomy over meaning and claiming that religion did just the opposite.

In other words, she held two theses:

1. It is more important to be free or autonomous than to have a grand meaning or purpose to life.
2. Religion provides a grand meaning or purpose to life, but it does not allow humans to be free or autonomous.

I've thought a lot about that woman's response over the years. I think that she is wrong on both counts. In this essay I will defend religion against her two theses and try to show that meaning and autonomy are both necessary or important ingredients for an ideal existence and that they are compatible within a religious framework.

Let me begin with the first thesis, that it is more important to be free than that there be meaning in life. First let us define our terms. By "autonomy" I mean self-governing, the ability to make choices on the basis of good reasons rather than being coerced by threats or forces from without.

By "meaning" in life I mean that life has a purpose. There is some intrinsic rationale or plan to it. Now this purpose can be good, bad, or indifferent. An example of something with a

Reprinted from Philosophy: The Quest for Truth, *edited by Louis Pojman (Belmont, Calif.: Wadsworth Publishing Company, 1989), by permission.*

bad purpose is the activity of poisoning a reservoir on which a community depends for its sustenance. An example of something with an indifferent purpose might be pacing back and forth to pass the time of day (it is arguable that this is bad or good depending on the options and context, and if you think that then either choose your own example or dismiss the category of indifferent purpose). An example of a good purpose is digging a well in order to provide water to a community in need of water.

Now it seems to be the case that, as a value, autonomy is superior to indifferent and bad purposes, since it has positive value but these other two categories do not. Autonomy may be more valuable to us than some good purposes, but it does not seem to be superior to *all* good purposes. While it may be more valuable to be free than to have this or that incidental purpose in life, freedom cannot really be understood apart from the notion of purposiveness. To be free is to be able to do some act *A,* when you want to, in order to reach some goal *G.* So the two ideas are related.

But the atheist woman meant more than this. She meant that if she had to choose whether to have free will or to live in a world that had a governing providential hand, she would choose the former. But this seems to make two mistakes. (1) It makes autonomy into an unjustified absolute and (2) it creates a false dilemma.

Consider two situations: In situation A you are as free as you are now (say you have 100 units of autonomy—call these units "autonotoms") but are deeply miserable because you are locked in a large and interesting room which is being slowly filled with poisonous gas. You can do what ever you want for five more minutes but then you will be dead. In situation B, however, you have only 95 autonotoms (that is, there are a few things that you are unable to do in this world—say commit adultery or kill your neighbor) but the room is being filled with sunshine and fresh air. Which world would you choose? I would choose situation B, for au-

tonomy, it seems to me, is not the only value in the universe, nor is it always the overriding value. I think most of us would be willing to give up a few autonotoms for an enormous increase in happiness. And I think that a world with a good purpose would be one in which we would be willing to give up a few bits of freedom. If we were told that we could eliminate poverty, crime, and great suffering in the world by each sacrificing one autonotom, wouldn't we do this? If so, then autonomy is not an absolute which always overrides every other value. It is one important value among others.

I turn to the atheist's second thesis, that religion always holds purpose as superior to autonomy. I think that this is a misunderstanding of what the best types of religion try to do. As Jesus said in John 8:32, "Ye shall know the truth and the truth shall set you free." Rather than seeing freedom and meaning as opposites, theism sees them as inextricably bound together. Since it claims to offer us the truth about the world, and since having true beliefs is important in reaching one's goals, it follows that our autonomy is actually heightened in having the truth about the purpose of life. If we know why we are here and what the options in our destiny really are, we will be able to choose more intelligently than the blind who lead the blind in ignorance.

Indeed theistic religion (I have in mind Judaism, Christianity, and Islam, but this could apply to many forms of Hinduism and African religions as well) claims to place before us options of the greatest importance, so that if it is true the world is far better (infinitely better?) than if it is not.

Let me elaborate on this point. If theism is true and there is a benevolent supreme being governing the universe, the following eight theses are true:

1. We have a satisfying explanation of the origin and sustenance of the universe. We are the product not of chance and necessity or an impersonal Big Bang, but of a Heavenly Being who cares about us. As William James says, if

religion is true, "the universe is no longer a mere *It* to us, but a *Thou* . . . and any relation that may be possible from person to person might be possible here." We can take comfort in knowing that the visible world is part of a more spiritual universe from which it draws its meaning and that there is, in spite of evil, an essential harmonious relation between our world and the transcedent reality.

2. Good will win out over evil—we're not fighting alone, but God is on our side in the battle. So, you and I are not fighting in vain—we'll win eventually. This thought of the ultimate victory of Goodness gives us confidence to go on in the fight against injustice and cruelty when others calculate that the odds against righteousness are too great to fight against.

3. God loves and cares for us—His love compels us (II Corinthians 5:7), so that we have a deeper motive for morally good actions, including high altruism. We live deeply moral lives because of deep gratitude to One who loves us and whom we love. Secularism lacks this sense of cosmic love, and it is, therefore, no accident that it fails to produce moral saints like Jesus, St. Francis, Gandhi, Martin Luther King, and Mother Theresa. You need special love to leave a world of comfort in order to go to a desolate island to minister to lepers, as Father Damian did.

4. We have an answer to the problem why be moral—it's clearly in your interest. Secular ethics has a severe problem with the question, Why be moral when it is not in your best interest, when you can profitably advance yourself by an egoistic act? But such a dilemma does not arise in religious ethics, for Evil really is bad for you and the Good good for you.

5. Cosmic Justice reigns in the universe. The scales are perfectly balanced so that everyone will get what he or she deserves, according to their moral merit. There is no moral luck (unless you interpret the grace which will finally prevail as a type of "luck"), but each will be judged according to how one has used one's talents (Matthew, chapter 25).

6. All persons are of equal worth. Since we have all been created in the image of God and are His children, we are all brothers and sisters. We are family and ought to treat each other benevolently as we would family members of equal worth. Indeed, modern secular moral and political systems often assume this equal worth of the individual without justifying it. But without the Parenthood of God it makes no sense to say that all persons are innately of equal value. From a perspective of intelligence and utility, Aristotle and Nietzsche are right, there are enormous inequalities, and why shouldn't the superior persons use the baser types to their advantage? In this regard, secularism, in rejecting inegalitarianism, seems to be living off of the interest of a religious capital which it has relinquished.

7. Grace and forgiveness—a happy ending for all. All's well that ends well (the divine comedy). The moral guilt which we experience, even for the most heinous acts, can be removed, and we can be redeemed and given a new start. This is true moral liberation.

8. There is life after death. Death is not the end of the matter, but we shall live on, recognizing each other in a better world. We have eternity in our souls and are destined for a higher existence. (Of course, hell is a problem here—which vitiates the whole idea somewhat, but many variations of theism [e.g., varieties of theistic Hinduism and the Christian theologians Origen (in the second century), F. Maurice, and Karl Barth] hold to universal salvation in the end. Hell is only a temporary school in moral education—I think that this is a plausible view). So if Hebraic-Christian theism is true, the world is a friendly home in which we are all related as siblings in one family, destined to live forever in cosmic bliss in a reality in which good defeats evil.

If theism is false and secularism is true, then there is no obvious basis for human equality, no reason to treat all people with equal respect, no simple and clear answer to the question, Why be moral even when it is not in my best interest? no sense of harmony and purpose in the universe, but "Whirl has replaced Zeus and is king" (Sophocles).

Add to this the fact that theism doesn't deprive us of any autonomy that we have in non-theistic systems. We are equally free to choose the good or the evil whether or not God exists (assuming that the notions of good and evil make sense in a non-theistic universe)—then it seems clear that the world of the theist is far better and more satisfying to us than one in which God does not exist.

Of course, the problem is that we probably do not know if theism, let alone our particular religious version of it, is true. Here I must use a Pascalean argument to press my third point that we may have an obligation or, at least, it may be a good thing, to live *as if* theism is true. That is,

unless you think that theism is so improbable that we should not even consider it as a candidate for truth, we should live in such a way as to allow the virtues of theism to inspire our lives and our culture. The theistic world view is so far superior to the secular that—even though we might be agnostics or weak atheists—it is in our interest to live as though it were true, to consider each person as a child of God, of high value, to work as though God is working with us in the battle of Good over evil, and to build a society based on these ideas. It is good then to gamble on God. Religion gives us a purpose to life and a basis for morality that is too valuable to dismiss lightly. It is a heritage that we may use to build a better civilization and one which we neglect at our own peril.

Study Questions

1. What does Walker mean by "autonomy"? How does she differ with the atheist on whether religion robs us of our autonomy?
2. Examine each of Walker's eight claims on the value of religion for the meaning of life. Do you agree with her assessment? Explain.
3. Karl Marx said that religion was the opium of the people, for it deludes them into thinking that their lot, however miserable, is the will of God with which they should be content. Religious people sanction rather than fight against social injustice. How would Walker respond to Marx? Who is right?

CHAPTER 16

Rationality and the Fear of Death

JEFFRIE MURPHY

Jeffrie Murphy is professor of philosophy at Arizona State University and the author of several books and articles in ethics and political philosophy, including *Kant: The Philosophy of Right* (1970).

In this article Murphy argues that fearing death is irrational. He sets forth four conditions for rational fear and then contends that fearing death is incompatible with them. Murphy believes that death is an evil and characterizes it as the end of our projects. Although it is rational to have a prudential fear of death, a fear that will enable you to fulfil your projects, it is irrational to fear death itself, since there is nothing we can do about it.

Cowards die many times before their deaths;
The valiant never taste of death but once.
Of all the wonders that I yet have heard,
It seems to me most strange that men should fear;
Seeing that death, a necessary end,
Will come when it will come.

SHAKESPEARE, *Julius Caesar*

I

"TO PHILOSOPHIZE" writes Montaigne, *"is to learn to die."*[1] This remark forms part of a long-standing tradition in philosophy which teaches that a truly wise or rational man will not fear death; and this tradition has found its way into our ordinary language—e.g. it is common to describe a person who accepts a terminal illness with patience as "philosophical" about his death. And most people would, I think, so describe the attitude expressed in the quoted remark given to Caesar—a remark particularly interesting because, in addition to telling us a great deal about the kind of person Shakespeare conceived Caesar to be, it appears to contain what has often been offered as an *argument* that one is irrational in fearing death. The argument is that *death is necessary or inevitable in the natural order of things and that, once one sees this, one will also see that fearing death is irrational.* Such an idea is found in the Stoics and the Epicureans among others and is, in many respects, interestingly different from the way of thinking about death that Christianity introduced into our civilization. The most illustrious and systematic

defender of the pagan conception, of course, is
Spinoza:

> A free man, that is to say, a man who lives accord-
> ing to the dictates of reason alone, is not led by
> fear of death, but directly desires the good, that is
> to say, desires to act, to live, and to preserve his
> being in accordance with the principle of seeking
> his own profit. He thinks, therefore, of nothing
> less than death, and his wisdom is a meditation
> upon life (*Ethics,* Four, LXVII).[2]

I shall now proceed by arguing in the following stages. First, I shall develop a general account of the concepts "rational fearing" and
"irrational fearing." Second, I shall attempt to
analyze the concept of *death*—what is it and why
do people tend to regard it as a terrible and thus
fearful thing? Finally, I shall apply the general
account of rational fearing to the topic of death.

II

I should like to develop a general account of the
*distinction between rational fearing and irratio-
nal fearing* in the hope that this account may ultimately be used to illuminate the fear of death.
The account that I shall offer purports to capture and distinguish between some intuitively
acceptable cases of fearings that are clearly rational and fearings that are clearly irrational. If the
account looks correct for the clear cases, then
we may have some confidence that it will help us
come to terms with the rational status of the fear
of death—a case where pretheoretical convictions no doubt are in conflict.

Now at the outset, it is important to realize
that the expression "Jones is irrational in fearing" is crucially ambiguous. On the one hand,
we can mean that *the fear itself is irrational*—i.e.
inappropriate or not fitting to its object. On the
other hand, we can mean that the *person is irrational in the role that he allows his fears* (however
rational in the first sense) to have in his life.

Spinoza, remember, does not say that the fear of
death is itself irrational. What he says is that a rational man will not let himself be *led* by the fear
of death. There is a sense in which fear of death
is obviously rational—i.e. obviously fitting or
appropriate. Indeed, as I shall later suggest,
one's own death and suffering in part define the
concept of the fearful. However, just because
fear is rational in this sense, it does not follow
that a person is rational in being led by this fear.
This sense of "rational," characterizing persons,
involves more than fittingness or appropriateness and requires a consideration of *utility*.
(Again we have a parallel with the moral feeling
of guilt. Are Dostoevskiian characters—e.g.
Stavrogin—who live a life dominated by guilt
for their wrongdoings to be judged rational or
irrational? In one sense, I should argue, they are
rational; for guilt is the appropriate or fitting
feeling for moral wrongdoing toward others.
They are not like persons who feel guilt when
they have really done nothing wrong, and thus
they are not irrational in *that* sense. However,
though their guilt feelings may not themselves
be irrational, the *characters* seem irrational because they allow themselves to be dominated
and destroyed by those feelings.) In this paper, I
am interested primarily in the question "When is
a *person* rational in fearing?" and am interested
in the rationality of feelings themselves only insofar as this issue is relevant to the rationality of
persons.

My controlling assumption throughout is
that Spinoza is fundamentally correct, at least in
this context, in his attempt to analyze the concept of rationality (for persons) in such a way as
to give a central place to concepts of self-interest
or self-realization—what he calls "profit." The
basic idea in some ways anticipates Darwin and
Freud in claiming that man is basically an animal
whose *reason functions,* as instincts function in
other animals, *primarily for self-preservation and
self-enrichment.* A similar concept of rationality
is found in Hobbes, who argues that no rational
man could knowingly frustrate his own long-

range self-interest. And Philippa Foot has recently reiterated this view: "Irrational actions are those in which a man in some way *defeats his own purposes,* doing what is calculated to be disadvantageous or to frustrate his ends." This "egoistic" analysis of rationality might be challenged by philosophers of Kantian sympathies who believe (as I am inclined to) that *moral rationality involves something different.* However, since I do not see the problem of the rationality of fearing death as a moral problem, I do not think that Kantian scruples need detain us on this particular issue. Fear, after all, is not a likely candidate for a moral feeling. Its primary significance, unlike that of such genuine moral feelings as guilt and shame, lies simply in the avoidance of danger.

Having laid my controlling assumption on the table, I shall now offer the following as an account of the distinction between rational and irrational fearing:

It is rational for a person *P* to fear some state of affairs *S* if and only if:

(1) *P* holds the reasonable belief that *S* obtains or is likely to obtain,

(2) *P* holds the reasonable belief that *S* (a) is not easily avoided and (b) is very undesirable, bad, or evil for *P,*

(3) the fear of *S* could be instrumental in bringing about some behavior or action that would allow *P* to *avoid S,* and

(4) the fear of *S* is compatible, at least in the long run, with the satisfaction of the other important desires of *P.*

If conditions (1) and (2) obtain, the fear is rational in the sense of being fitting or appropriate to its object. Conditions (3) and (4) have to obtain, however, in order for the person to be rational in his fearing.

Since this general account is probably not intuitively obvious, I shall comment upon each of the four conditions separately.

(1) *P holds the reasonable belief that S obtains or is likely to obtain.* This, I take it, is the least controversial of the conditions I have put forth. Perhaps paradigm examples of people who suffer fears we regard as irrational are those who suffer from psychotic delusions. Paranoids, or alcoholics experiencing delirium tremens, for example, may fear the demons in the water faucets, the Martians in the closet, or the pink spiders on the wall. The best reason we have for thinking that these fears are irrational is the absence of any grounds or evidence that there might be demons in the water faucets, Martians in the closet, or pink spiders on the wall.

(2) *P holds the reasonable belief that S (a) is not easily avoided and (b) is very undesirable, bad, or evil for P.* Except for one problem to be noted shortly, this condition also seems fairly noncontroversial. Phobias, I take it, are acceptable examples of irrational fears. We should tend to characterize as irrational persons who are "scared to death" of (nonpoisonous) snakes or of high places. This is not because, as was the case in (1) above, there are no snakes or high places, but is rather because snakes and high places are normally harmless. Typically we pass these fears off as "silly" and would not regard a person experiencing them as seriously irrational unless they had other harmful effects—a point to be explored when I discuss (4) below.

Now what may appear to some as a problem with the condition is the claim that *S* must be bad *for P.* This may strike some as too egoistic; and they might argue that it is perfectly rational to fear that something bad will happen to another. On this point I am inclined to argue as follows: One can certainly care deeply (perhaps on moral grounds) that others not die; but this caring typically is not, in my judgment, to be explicated as a kind of *fearing.* Wanting others in general not to die is, I suppose, simply part of what it means to be a morally sensitive person placing a high value on human life. One's own fear of dying, however, is hardly to be understood in this way. Fear is a very personal (self-regarding) feeling, and thus it seems to be tautological that one can literally fear only that which deeply involves oneself. The following conversation, for example, would be extremely odd: "I am terribly afraid." "Why?" "Because people are continuing to die in Bangladesh." One's own suffering and death, it could be said, *define* the concept of the fearful.

Thus I am inclined to think that one can literally *fear* evil happening to another only if that other is so close to one (a wife or child perhaps) that what happens to that other in a sense happens to oneself. As Freud says about the death of a child: *"Our* hopes, *our* pride, *our* happiness, lie in the grave with him, we will not be consoled, we will not fill the loved one's place." For reasons that will become apparent when I later analyze the nature of death, I think there is a sense in which it is true (at least for some parents) that a part of them would die in the death of their child.

It is perhaps morally regrettable that most of us do not identify a very wide range of persons (perhaps the whole human race) with ourselves to such an extent that we could fear their deaths. It is surely not psychologically regrettable, of course, since if we did make such an identification we could probably not stand the emotional damage that would result. However, regrettable or not, it is false that very many people would sincerely agree with John Donne's observation that each man's death diminishes me. We may not be islands, but neither are we continents or worlds.

(3) *The fear of S could be instrumental in bringing about some behaviour or action that would allow P to avoid S.* This condition is at the heart of Spinoza's concept of rationality as involving self-preservation, as securing a "profit" in one's life. One way to characterize an activity as rational is to see that it has a point or purpose—that it at least appears to accomplish something. And surely it is avoidance behavior that gives fearing its significance. Suppose we imagined ourselves to be in a position of a Cre-

ator giving man the instinct of fear. What could this be except giving man the general capacity to make self-protective responses to danger? Fear's primary biological function is found in self-defensive behavior—what physiologists call the "fight or flight" reflex. And surely such fear, in addition to being biologically functional, is a part of what we understand by a rational approach to danger. If one discovers a hungry and aggressive tiger in the room, a state of affairs which surely satisfies conditions (1) and (2), who would doubt that the resulting fear is appropriate and that a person is rational in being "led" by the fear to the extent that he attempts to get out of the room as quickly as possible?

Since this condition will (not surprisingly) play a role in my later argument that it is irrational to fear death, I shall defer further discussion of it until later.

(4) *The fear of S is compatible, at least in the long run, with the satisfaction of the other important desires of P.* If the first three conditions are unsatisfied, we can perhaps, some may argue, conclude nothing more than that in such fearing the person is *non*rational. The present condition, however, surely gives us a test for genuine *ir*rationality with respect to fearing; and indeed its nonsatisfaction is a mark of fearings which we should call *neurotic*. A phobia, for example, becomes clearly a neurotic symptom, and not just something silly or eccentric, when it so pervades the life of the person who experiences it that he is rendered incapable of leading a successful and satisfying life. A person who merely shudders when he sees a spider, for example, is perhaps just a little silly. A person who is so afraid that he might see a spider that he never leaves his home and has that home visited by a pest exterminator several times a week is something more than silly. He is pathetic and is in need of help.

Even fearings which would normally be quite rational become irrational when this condition is unsatisfied. A certain fear of germs, for example, is certainly rational. There are germs, many germs are very harmful, and a fear of them can prompt a person to take reasonable precautions against disease. However, a person who is so afraid of germs that he washes twenty times a day, sprays all items in his house with germicide, refuses to leave his sanitized bedroom, etc., has crossed the boundary between reasonable prudence and irrational fearing.

As with condition (3), this condition will play an important role in my later discussion of the fear of death.

III

The conditions I have outlined above provide a very rough way of distinguishing two very different ways of attempting to come to terms with death—what I shall call the "other-worldly" and the "naturalistic." Other-worldly Christians, for example, who counsel that at least certain persons (the saved) should not fear death, tend to argue that the fear of death fails to satisfy conditions (1) or (2)—i.e. they argue either that there is no such thing as death or that death is a good thing. In practice, of course, these two claims—insofar as they are intelligible at all—tend to be collapsed together. Naturalistic writers, such as Spinoza, tend to argue that a rational person will not be led by the fear of death because such fearing fails to satisfy conditions (3) or (4)—i.e. they argue that the fear of death is pointless (since it cannot help us to avoid death) or harmful (because it interferes with the satisfactions that life offers).

Though my primary purpose is to develop the pagan *naturalistic tradition* represented by *Spinoza*, it might be worth pausing a few moments over the obvious weakness in the other-worldly tradition. First, and most obvious, the set of beliefs that underlie that tradition (distinction between soul and body, immortality of the soul, etc.) are not very likely candidates for reasonable beliefs. Indeed, if they are held in a literal or "fundamentalist" sense, they might bet-

ter be offered as candidates for obscurantist superstition. Second, and more important for our present purposes however, is the following: Even if these beliefs are accepted, there is an important sense in which they really do not provide answers to the question "How are we to come to terms with death?" For they are, after all, *denials* that there is such a thing as genuine death. Socrates (at least according to Plato) seemed to have this kind of other-worldly outlook—e.g. he says in *Apology* that, after his body passes away, it is not unlikely that his soul (his true person) will pass to a kind of heaven where he will converse with such departed luminaries as Hesiod and Homer. This seems to me to be a way of *not* facing death and certainly does not deserve to be characterized, as many people have characterized it, as facing death with *courage*. For what is courageous about accepting the fact that one will move to a place where one will be better off than ever before? And what is intellectually commendable about believing such things in the absence of any shred of evidence?

There is one other argument that condition (2) is not satisfied which, though also found in naturalistic writers (e.g. Lucretius and Hobbes), shares a common feebleness with the arguments noted above. It is, very generally, the argument that the death of P is not bad for P because it cannot *hurt* P. Hobbes puts the argument in the following way:

> There be few lingeringe diseases or sudden paynes that be not more sensible and paynefull then death, and therefore I see little reason why a man that lives well should feare death more then sicknesse.
>
> "Of Death"

Even more comforting thoughts are expressed by the Christian poet John Donne:

> From rest and sleep, which but thy picture be,
> Much pleasure; then from thee much more must flow.
>
> "Death, Be Not Proud"

These arguments are so far beside the point that they at most demonstrate only one thing—namely, that the fear of death must be very terrible indeed for some people if they are willing to grab at such small straws and take comfort in such inanity. Though it is natural that some people might confuse a fear of death with a fear of pain (or, in our own day, with a fear of winding up one's days being treated as a nonperson in one of our contemporary hospitals), it is quite obvious on reflection that the fear of death and the fear of pain are quite distinct. It should also be clear on reflection that all things bad for us (e.g. loss of reputation) do not necessarily have to "hurt" in any literal sense. If the fear of death just was the fear of pain, then there would indeed be little reason why anyone should fear death. For death is not always a painful affair; and, in most of those cases where it might be, we have drugs or (if it comes to it) suicide. Thus Hobbes and Donne have perhaps provided us with reasons why we should not fear a *painful* death, but these are not reasons why we should not fear death *simpliciter.* They have not given us reasons why death itself, independent of suffering, is not a very undesirable, bad, or evil thing for a person.

IV

What, then, is death such that it is a very undesirable, bad, or evil thing for a person? *That* it is bad is, I take it, obvious; for death, along with suffering, in part define the very concept of what is a bad thing for a person and (as I suggested earlier) the very concept of the fearful. Thus, I should argue, explaining what is bad or fearful about death is part of explaining what death itself is.

The death of a *person,* unlike the death of a beast, represents not merely the extinction of an organism. It also represents the end of a conscious history which transcends itself in thought.

All I mean by this high-sounding phrase is that, to use the language of Sartre, persons define themselves in large measure in terms of their future-oriented *projects.* What I am is in large measure what I want to accomplish. This is perhaps a very "bourgeois" conception of personality, for it is a definition in terms of individual agency. In more collectivist societies the conception of a person might well (for better or worse) be different and the fear of death correspondingly different. However, the analysis I am offering does seem to me true of at least a great many persons in society as we now find it. Our self-identifying projects may be bound up with persons very close to us; and this explains why we sometimes, as I noted earlier, see the deaths of our children or wives as a partial death of our own persons. But it is rare (and perhaps regrettable) that the range of such persons included in self-identification is anything but quite narrow.

If I am correct that a person is self-defined largely in terms of certain *projects*—e.g. the desire to accomplish something in one's profession, to provide for one's family, to achieve certain satisfactions, to redress moral injuries done, etc.—then we can see wherein much of the badness of death lies: *Death represents lost opportunity.* My death might prevent me from finishing a book, from getting my children through school, from rendering aid to those who have a claim on my benevolence, from making amends for moral wrongs against others. It is this idea that death means *no more chances* which tormented Ivan Ilych—a man who had already thrown away the chances he had to live the right sort of life.

His mental sufferings were due to the fact that that night, as he looked at Gerasim's sleepy, good-natured face with its prominent cheekbones, the question suddenly occurred to him: "What if my whole life has been wrong?" It occurred to him that what had appeared perfectly impossible before, namely that he had not spent his life as he should have done, might after all be true. It occurred to him that his scarcely perceptible attempts to struggle against what was considered good by the most highly placed people, those scarcely noticeable impulses which he had immediately suppressed, might have been the real thing, and all the rest false. . . . "But if that is so," he said to himself, "and I am leaving this life with the consciousness that I have lost all that was given me and it is impossible to rectify it—what then?"

Mary Mothersill has put the point in the following way:

> *Death is the deadline for all my assignments.* . . . To know what it is like to hope that one will not be interrupted is to know something about (one sort) of fear of death. We may think of death (rather grandiosely) as the person from Porlock but for whose untimely visit, Kubla Khan, or so Coleridge claimed, would have been much, much longer than it is.

At this point, I should like to raise the following query: Would one fear death more than (or in a way different from) the fear of permanent coma resulting from massive brain damage? If, as I suspect, most people would answer *no,* then this is support for the account I have been offering.

Now one thing we can learn from this account is in keeping with the Christian message that we should (within reason of course) live each day as though it may be our last. Knowing that death will come, we can make an effort to accomplish what we feel we need to accomplish—realizing that there will not always be chances to "do it later." There are, of course, those unfortunate and generally neurotic individuals who have no sense of self-worth, who feel that they never can accomplish anything that matters, who feel that their very existence is an injury to others. These persons, unless they are helped by therapy, really lack self-defining projects and thus really lack a strong sense of themselves as persons. Not surprisingly, such in-

dividuals tend to fear death with the greatest intensity of all. For they fear, not simply that they will not finish, but that they will never even get started.

Even if we are fortunate and are not plagued by neurotic self-doubts, and even if we make a prudent effort to accomplish what we think important with some sense of urgency in order to "beat death," we shall never be completely successful. Not only will we always fail to get something done which we think we ought to have done, but we shall also (as long as we remain persons) continue to generate new self-defining projects as we grow older. Thus, though with diligence we can perhaps prevent death from being as bad as it might be, for most of us it will, when it comes, be bad enough.

V

What does all of this tell us about the rationality of fearing death? Applying conditions (3) and (4) of the previously developed analysis, conditions which I regard as perhaps doing little more than formalizing Spinoza's general account of the fear of death, I should conclude that a *prudent fear of death is perfectly rational.* By a prudent fear of death I mean simply (a) *one which provokes people into maintaining a reasonable* (though not neurotic compulsive) *diligence with respect to living the kind of life they regard as proper or meaningful* (e.g. maintaining their health, not making the mistake of Ivan Ilych, etc.) and (b) *one which is kept in its proper place*—i.e. does not sour all the good things in one's life. If the fear of death, even if initially inspired by the desire to accomplish important things in time, becomes a neurotic compulsion, then the saying "In the midst of life we are in death" is exemplified.

Fear of death is irrational and properly extinguished, then, when it can serve no legitimate purpose in our lives—i.e. when it cannot aid us in avoiding bad things (e.g. failed assignments) in a way which is consistent with the successful and satisfying integration and functioning of our person. As Spinoza would put it, the fear of death is irrational when it redounds, not to our profit, but to our loss. For, other things (especially moral things) being equal, the pursuit of loss rather than profit could not be the goal of any rational man.

To call the fear of death irrational is not, of course, moralistically to *condemn* those who feel it. A man is fairly to be blamed only for that which is in his control, and typically feelings are not in our control—at least not in our direct control. The irrational fear of death, if it pervades the life of a person, becomes a kind of neurosis; and normally the proper response to a fearful neurotic is not blame but is rather a suggestion that he seek therapeutic help in extinguishing his fears.

If a person can extinguish or have extinguished such irrational fears of death he will move toward being, in Spinoza's sense, liberated or free. To fear irrationally is to be a kind of prisoner to one's pointless passions, in bondage to feelings that preclude the enjoyment of what is now valued and the pursuit of what is wanted for the future. The meaningfulness of the present and the future are destroyed, and one is put in the pitiful position, described by Socrates, of caring so much about simply living that one loses whatever it is that makes life *worth* living. To quote Montaigne again:

> The thing I fear most is fear. . . . He who has learned how to die has unlearned how to be a slave. . . . For as it is impossible for the soul to be at rest when she fears death, so, if she can gain assurance against it, she can boast of a thing as it were beyond man's estate: that it is impossible for worry, torment, fear, or even the slightest displeasure to dwell in her. . . . She is made mistress of her passions and lusts, mistress over indigence, shame, poverty, and all other wounds of fortune. Let us gain this advantage, those of us who can;

this is the true and sovereign liberty, which enables us to thumb our noses at force and injustice and to laugh at prisons and chains.

VI

I am not sure how much comfort or solace, if any, can be derived from the way of thinking about death that I have outlined. One small comfort, at least to me, is that this way of thinking about death under some circumstances *renders suicide a reasonable option, not merely for coming to terms with such misfortunes as pain, but also as a way of fulfilling* (or at least not compromising) *one's conception of oneself as a person.* For if what one really values is the preservation of oneself as a certain *kind* of person (e.g. one who does not become a vegetable as a result of a debilitating illness, one who does not dishonor oneself and betray one's friends under torture, etc.) one can see, in voluntary death, at least this comfort—that one will end as the person one is and perhaps admires, not as another person that one perhaps would despise. What this shows is that the general reasons we have for not wanting to die may, in a particular case, constitute reasons for wanting to die. An American journalist, Charles Wertenbaker, wrote the following before his own suicide:

> Problem with death is to recognize the point at which you can die with all your faculties, take a healthy look at the world and people as you go out of it. Let them get you in bed, drug you or cut you, and you become sick and afraid and disgusting, and everybody will be glad to get rid of you. It shouldn't be such a problem if you can remember how it was when you were young. You wouldn't give up something for instance to add ten years to your life. All right, don't ask for them now. You wouldn't give up drinking and love-making and eating—and why should you have given them up? Nothing is ever lost that has been

experienced and it can all be there at the moment of death—if you don't wait too long.

In a case like this, it is possible to see suicide, not merely as reasonable, but even as noble. This way of thinking, found in Greek, Roman and some Oriental civilizations, and eloquently defended by David Hume (*Of Suicide*), provides the man who accepts it with an ultimate "out." And having an out is having a certain kind of limited freedom. For at least one's bondage is not total.

In closing, I must admit that even the above provides precious little in the way of comfort. The universe is impersonal, and is thus not kind. And it is just false that there is to be found, even by the exercise of our reason, a comfort for every sorrow. Even a man who clearly recognizes the irrationality of fearing death will sometimes, I am sure, be tormented by that fear anyway; and I make no pretense that I am any different. However, I am confident of one thing: that any occasional comfort, however little, that may be derived from rational understanding, unlike that which may flow from various forms of superstitious obscurantism, is at least consistent with human dignity and intellectual integrity. And that, I think, is something.

Notes

1. *Montaigne's Essays*, trans. Donald Frame (Stanford: Stanford University Press, 1958), p. 56. Montaigne is here paraphrasing a remark made by Cicero. The thought, of course, goes back much further—at least to Socrates.

2. Spinoza agrees with the Stoics and Epicureans that the fear of death is irrational. He disagrees with them, however, on the question of how the fear is to be extinguished. The Stoics and Epicureans counsel that we should desensitize ourselves to death by thinking of it constantly (a thought shared by Montaigne). Spinoza, on the other hand, suggests that we should try to avoid thinking of death entirely, to forget about death in the pursuit of the values of life. As Woody Allen has remarked, *"It is impossible to experience one's own death objectively and still carry a tune"* (*Getting Even* [New York: Random House, 1972], p. 31).

Study Questions

1. According to Murphy, is the fear of death rational? Why or why not?
2. What is his argument for his thesis? Do you agree with it?
3. Is death an evil for Murphy?
4. Compare Murphy's views with Lois Hope Walker's. How do they differ?

CHAPTER 17

A Hindu Theory of Life and Death

PRASANNATMA DAS

Prasannatma Das is a young Hindu philosopher who studied at the Krishna Temple in Vrindavan, India. In this essay he describes the basic Hindu view of karma, the doctrine that says how we live in this life will determine our initial state in the next life, and reincarnation, the notion that the same person lives in a different body in future lives based on the idea of karma. Prasannatma Das appeals to the *Bhagavad Gita,* the most sacred of Hindu scriptures, for his exposition. Lord Krishna, the main speaker in that work, is viewed by Hindus as an avatar (manifestation) of God.

You should be aware that, as with most major religions, there are many versions of Hinduism. This is one important Hindu version of the meaning of life and death, but not the only one.

The term *cosmogonal* in the quotation from Thoreau refers to the origin of the world.

A Hindu View of Life and Death

IN A PREVIOUS AGE, there lived a wise king named Yudhisthira. Having been banished by an evil cousin, he and his four brothers were wandering in a forest. One day the youngest brother went to get water from a nearby lake. When, after a time, he did not come back, the next brother went. He did not come back either. Twice more this happened until finally Yudhisthira himself went. He came to the lake and was about to drink from it when suddenly a voice boomed forth, "Do not drink this water. I am the owner of this lake, and if you drink this water, you shall die like your brothers have before you!" Yudhisthira then saw the lifeless bodies of his brothers lying nearby. The voice continued. "You may drink of this water only on the condition that you answer my questions. If

you answer them correctly, you and your brothers shall live. If you fail, then you too shall die."

The voice then presented a series of questions to the king, all of which he answered perfectly. One of these questions was, "Of all the amazing things in this world, what is the most amazing?" The king replied, "The most amazing thing is that although everyone sees his parents dying, and everything around him dying, still we live as though we will live forever. This is truly amazing."

It is indeed amazing that even in the face of inevitable death, few perceive the urgency of our predicament; however, in every culture and tradition there have been those thoughtful souls who have done so. Within the Hindu tradition many such seekers have found the teachings of Lord Krishna as presented in the *Bhagavad Gita* to be a source of knowledge and inspiration. Ap-

---

This article was commissioned for the first edition of this anthology. All references are to the Bhagavad Gita, *translated by A. C. Bhaktivedanta Swami Prabhupada (Los Angeles: Bhaktivedanta Book Trust, 1983).*

pearing as an episode in the great epic of ancient India, the *Mahabharata*, the *Bhagavad Gita* is one of the most profound theological dialogues known to man. As Henry David Thoreau once said, "In the morning I bathe my intellect in the stupendous and cosmogonal philosophy of the *Bhagavad Gita*, in comparison with which our modern world and its literature seem puny and trivial."

The first message of Lord Krishna's teaching in the *Bhagavad Gita* is that we are not these bodies. The body is constantly changing; we once had the body of a small baby, then that of a child, of an adult, of an old person, and eventually the body will return to the dust from whence it came. Yet when we look in the mirror we think that this body is what we are.

But what are we really? Krishna explains that we are the eternal soul within the body, and what we call death is merely the soul leaving one body and going elsewhere:

Never was there a time when I did not exist, nor you, nor all these kings; nor in the future shall any of these cease to be.

As the embodied soul continuously passes, in this body, from boyhood to youth to old age, the soul similarly passes into another body at the time of death. A sober person is not bewildered by such a change.

For the soul there is neither birth nor death at any time. He has not come into being, does not come into being, and will not come into being. He is unborn, eternal, ever-existing, and primeval. He is not slain when the body is slain.

As a person puts on new garments, giving up old and useless ones, the soul similarly accepts new material bodies, giving up old and useless ones. (2.12–13, 20, 22)

Krishna is explaining that we are not these bodies; we are the soul inside. I am not a twenty-year-old college student about to fail his philosophy course, but rather I am an eternal spirit-soul who, out of ignorance of his true nature, now identifies himself with the temporary forms of this world. When I enter a new body, I remain the same person.

For example, imagine a candle over which a series of filters are placed; the light appears to be changing according to the color of the filter obscuring it—blue, green, etc. But the original source of the light, the flame, is not changing, only the covering is. In the same way, the soul does not change, only the covering, the body, changes.

Sometimes at night we look up at the sky and see that the clouds are luminous. From the glowing of the clouds we can understand that the moon, the clouds themselves appear to be luminous. Similarly, when examining this body we can infer the existence of the soul by its symptoms, consciousness, which pervades the body and gives it the appearance of being alive.

Another basic teaching of the *Bhagavad Gita* is the law of karma, which states that for every action there is a corresponding reaction, or "whatever goes around, comes around." Our situation in this life was caused by the activities and desires of our previous lives. Similarly, our future existence—our body, education, amount of wealth, happiness and distress, etc.—will be determined by how we live now. If we harm others, then we must suffer in return, and if we do good, then we correspondingly enjoy. Moreover, we are given a body that suits our consciousness. If, like an animal, a human spends his life eating, sleeping, mating, and defending, ignoring his higher capacities, then he may be placed into the body of an animal. At the time of death the consciousness we have cultivated during our life will carry us, the soul, to our next body. "Whatever state of being one remembers when he quits his body, that state he will attain without fail" (8.6).

The goal is not to come back to this world at all but to attain the supreme destination:

From the highest planet in the material world down to the lowest, all are places of misery wherein repeated birth and death take place.

But one who attains to My abode . . . never takes birth again. (8.16)

Death is perceived according to the quality of one's existence. The ignorant see death as something to be feared. They have material desires, and death will defeat them. Those who are seeking wisdom understand death as an impetus to live correctly, as a time when their knowledge will be put to test. The most amazing thing in this world is that although everyone knows they are going to die, they still act as though they will live forever. Imagine a person who has received an eviction notice—he must vacate his apartment in two weeks. If he promptly prepared for this and found another place to go, he would not be in anxiety. Unfortunately, even though our eviction notice was given at the time of birth, very few take heed.

Krishna states:

What is night for all living beings is the time of awakening for the self-controlled, and the time of awakening for all beings is the night for the introspective sage. (2.69)

Different types of activities have different values. There are pious activities, which lead to taking birth in a situation of relative enjoyment; there are impious activities, which lead to suffering and ignorance; and there are spiritual activities, which lead one to God. Such spiritual activities are called *yoga*. (*Yoga* does not mean Indian gymnastics but actually refers to the process of reuniting one's self with God.)

This yoga, or real religious life, is not just a passive activity but is an active cultivation. If a farmer wants to harvest crops, he must begin working early in the season; plowing the fields, planting seeds, watering, weeding, etc. The fruits of his labor will manifest themselves at harvest time. Similarly, one who desires to attain to perfection must engage in a cultivation of the soul that will yield the harvest of spiritual perfec-

tion. When death comes, he will taste the fruit of his endeavor.

In this world there is nothing so sublime and pure as transcendental knowledge. Such knowledge is the mature fruit of all mysticism. And one who has become accomplished in the practice of devotional service enjoys this knowledge within himself in due course of time. "That is the way of the spiritual and godly life, after attaining which a person is not bewildered. If one is in this situation even at the hour of death, one can enter into the kingdom of God" (4.38; 2.72).

Death will come. No situation in this world is permanent. All changes. Whether a table, a car, a human body, a civilization, or a mountain, everything comes into being, remains for some time, and then finally dwindles and disappears. What of this world can survive the passage of time? As Krishna says, "One who has been born is sure to die" (2.27). Of this there is no doubt.

Yet many people do not see the urgency of our situation. "Yes, I know one day I will have to die; but for now let me eat, drink, have fun, and get a big bank balance," they think. Dedicated to the pursuit of the temporary phenomena of this world, living a life of vanity, they die like ignorant animals without higher knowledge. They and their fantasies are put to ruin. Their valuable human form of life with its great potential of knowledge and self-realization is wasted.

On the other hand, a thoughtful person understands the reality of this world, and, like a student who knows he must pass a test before he can graduate, prepares himself. This process of preparation begins with inquiry. Who am I? When this body is finished, what happens to me? Why do I exist? How can I be happy? By nature the eternal soul is full of happiness and knowledge. But now that eternal, blissful, fully cognizant being is something like a fish out of water. The lost creature will not be happy until it is placed back into the water. Giving the fish a new car or expensive jewelry will not rectify its problem; it will not become happy in this way. So too, no degree of rearranging this material world will solve our problems; we will not be satisfied until we are back in the spiritual world. Thus, a wise person is not interested in attaining any of the tempting but temporary offerings of this world, knowing that they have a beginning and an end. As the founder of Christianity pointed out, "Seek ye first the kingdom of God, and all these things will be added unto you." Therefore, "The yogis, abandoning attachment, act . . . only for the sake of purification" (5.11).

The sage is not interested in attaining temporary things like fame, adoration, or distinction.

> An intelligent person does not take part in the sources of misery, which are done to contact with the material senses. . . . Such pleasures have a beginning and an end, and so the wise man does not delight in them. (5.22)

He does not mind leaving this world because he is not attached to it. Rather he is interested in things with real value. Krishna lists some qualities that a thoughtful person might cultivate:

> Humility; pridelessness; non-violence; tolerance; simplicity; approaching a bona fide spiritual master; cleanliness; steadiness; self-control; the perception of the evil of birth, death, old age, and disease; detachment; freedom from entanglement with children, wife, home and the rest; evenmindedness amid pleasant and unpleasant events; constant and unalloyed devotion to Me; aspiring to live in a solitary place; detachment from the general mass of people; accepting the importance

of self-realization; and philosophical search for the Absolute Truth. . . . (13.8–12)

A yogi has no desire to fulfill in this world. Thus, he is not attached to it. Thus, he does not mind leaving it. Thus, he has no fear of death.

Since he has no personal desire in this world and has faith in God, he welcomes death in the same way that the kitten welcomes the jaws of the mother cat, whereas they are feared by the mouse. Krishna states:

> To those who are constantly devoted to serving Me with love, I give the understanding by which they can come back to Me.
> To show them special mercy, I, dwelling in their hearts, destroy with the shining lamp of knowledge the darkness born of ignorance. (10.10–11)

For those of us who are not enlightened beings, the fact that we must die can serve as an impetus to reach that higher transcendental state; what have we to lose? If we are wrong in our hopes and death does indeed end all, then have we lost anything by our effort? And if our hopes are correct, then certainly we have all to gain.

A faithful man who is dedicated to transcendental knowledge and who subdues his senses is eligible to achieve such knowledge, and having achieved it he quickly attains the supreme spiritual peace.

When one is enlightened with the knowledge by which [ignorance] is destroyed, then his knowledge reveals everything, as the sun lights up everything in the daytime (4.39, 5.16).

Study Questions

1. What is "the most amazing thing" in all the world?
2. According to Prasannatma Das, what is the Hindu view of life and death? What is the purpose of life?
3. What do Hindus mean by "karma"?
4. Compare the Hindu view with Plato's view of life and death (see Chapter 12 in this volume).

For Further Reading

Cheney, David, and Steven Sanders, eds. *The Meaning of Life*. Englewood Cliffs, N.J.:
    Prentice Hall, 1980.

Kierkegaard, Søren. *Sickness unto Death*. Princeton, N.J.: Princeton University Press, 1973.

Klemke, E. D., ed. *The Meaning of Life*. New York: Oxford University Press, 1981.

"Philosophical Problems of Death," *The Monist*, 59:2 (April 1976).

Rosenberg, Jay. *Thinking Clearly About Death*. Englewood Cliffs, N.J.: Prentice Hall, 1983.

Stace, Walter. *Man Against Nature*. Pittsburgh: University of Pittsburgh Press, 1967.

Part IV

Suicide

Introduction

Suicide is generally recognized as an immoral or insane act, especially by religious people. Hamlet laments, "O that this too sullied flesh would melt, . . . Or that the Everlasting had not fixed His canon 'gainst selfslaughter!" But suicide was not always condemned by society or religion.

On the whole, suicide was tolerated by the ancient Greeks and often commended by them and the Romans. The first recorded opposition to it is in Plato's *Phaedo* (ca. 390 B.C.E.) where Socrates offers the two arguments against suicide: We are sentinels on duty who must not desert our post, and we are the property of the gods and must not destroy property that does not belong to us. Nevertheless, Socrates, being condemned to death, refused an offer of a safe escape and willingly drank the hem lock. Aristotle was the second philosopher to argue against suicide, saying that it was an offense against the state, because it weakened the state by destroying a useful citizen.

On the other hand, Stoic writings abound with exhortations to suicide. "Foolish man," Seneca wrote, "what do you complain about, and what do you fear? Wherever you look there is an end of evils. You see that yawning precipice? It leads to liberty. You see that flood, that river, that well? Liberty houses within them. . . . Do you inquire the road to freedom? You shall find it in every vein in your body." Cato, Seneca, Demosthenes, Lucretius, Brutus, Cassius, Mark Anthony, Cleopatra, and Hannibal all committed suicide. For the most part, they calmly deliberated and took their lives because in some way life had lost its meaning for them.[1]

No word against suicide is found in the Old Testament, where four suicides are recorded without adverse comment, or in the New Testament, where Judas Iscariot hanged himself. At Masada (72 A.C.E.), Eleazar led some 900 Jews in a mass suicide rather than be captured by the Romans. In the first centuries of the Christian church, suicide was tolerated. The leading theologians Tertullian (160–230) and Origen (185–254) regarded Jesus' death as a suicide, noting that he voluntarily "gave up the ghost." Early Christians often embraced martyrdom willingly, sometimes paying strangers to kill them so they might enter heaven immediately. Virgins killed themselves in order to prevent being raped. "Let me enjoy those beasts," exclaimed the Christian martyr Ignatius in the second century, "whom I wish more cruel than they are; for if they will not attack me, I will provoke and draw them by force." Gibbon tells us that the Christian sect, the Donatists, "frequently stopped travellers on the public highways and obliged them to inflict the stroke of martyrdom by promise of a reward, if they consented, and by the threat of instant death, if they refused to grant so very singular a favor."[2]

It was Augustine, Bishop of Hippo (354–430), who in response to the growing loss of Christians in his domain through voluntary martyrdom first proclaimed that it was sinful, a violation of the Sixth Commandment, "Thou shalt not kill." Suicide was first condemned by the Church at the Council of Braga in 562, at which time persons who had committed suicide were denied funeral rites. In the next century, persons who had attempted suicide were excommunicated from the Church and later referred to as "martyrs for Satan." Thomas Aquinas (1225–1274) sets forth the position of the Catholic Church in our first reading, arguing that it is a mortal sin against God because it is against nature and charity, an offense against society and a destruction of God's gift, life—the same arguments found in Plato and Aristotle.

Since the sixth century suicide has been condemned in Western society. In many places it is illegal. However, some voices have always called for tolerance, even justifying rational suicide: Montaigne, Donne, and, most notably, David Hume. Our second reading is Hume's classic essay, "On the Naturalness of Suicide," in which he responds to Aquinas's arguments against suicide.

Our next two essays discuss the morality of suicide. Albert Camus links the issue to the question of whether life has meaning. Richard Brandt first shows that many suicides are not blameworthy because of diminished mental capacity. Second, he argues for grounds for the moral acceptability of some suicides. Finally, he discusses the phenomenon of depression, which often prevents the potential suicide from thinking rationally. His last point may be used to legitimize schemes for suicide prevention.

Our final essay by Margaret Pabst Battin sets the problem within the context of human rights based on a Kantian notion of human dignity. She discusses which kinds of suicide promote this trait and hence are justified and which kinds do not.

Notes

1. John Donne, *Biathanos* (1611) lists three pages of Greek and Roman nobles who killed themselves. For more on this subject, see A. Alvarez, *The Savage God* (New York: Random House, 1973), from which some of this material is taken.

2. Edward Gibbon, *Decline and Fall of the Roman Empire,* Vol. 1, (1776), p. 401.

CHAPTER 18

Suicide Is Unnatural and Immoral

THOMAS AQUINAS

The Dominican monk Thomas Aquinas (1225–1274) is considered by many to be the greatest theologian in Western religion. His systematic theology and comprehensive philosophical thinking is a monument to the human intellect.

In this section from his *magnus opus* the *Summa Theologica*, he argues against five arguments for the morality of suicide and offers three arguments against suicide: It is contrary to natural law and charity, it injures the community, and it destroys God's gift to us.

Note that this article uses the scholastic format of first stating the objection to the author's position and then replying to each objection, showing that the author's thesis is supported by sound reasons.

WE PROCEED THUS to the Fifth Article:

Objection 1. It would seem lawful for a man to kill himself. For murder is a sin in so far as it is contrary to justice. But no man can do an injustice to himself, as is proved in *Ethic* v.11.[1] Therefore no man sins by killing himself.

Obj. 2. Further, It is lawful, for one who exercises public authority, to kill evildoers. Now he who exercises public authority is sometimes an evildoer. Therefore he may lawfully kill himself.

Obj. 3. Further, It is lawful for a man to suffer spontaneously a lesser danger that he may avoid a greater. Thus it is lawful for a man to cut off a decayed limb even from himself, that he may save his whole body. Now sometimes a man, by killing himself, avoids a greater evil, for an example an unhappy life, or the shame of sin. Therefore a man may kill himself.

Obj. 4. Further, Sampson killed himself, as related in Judges xvi, and yet he is numbered among the saints (Heb. xi). Therefore it is lawful for a man to kill himself.

Obj. 5. Further, It is related (2 Mach. xiv. 42) that a certain Razias killed himself, *choosing to die nobly rather than to fall into the hands of the wicked, and to suffer abuses unbecoming his noble birth.* Now nothing that is done nobly and bravely is unlawful. Therefore suicide is not unlawful.

On the contrary, Augustine says (*De Civ. Dei* i. 20): *Hence it follows that the words "Thou shalt not kill" refer to the killing of a man; not another man; therefore, not even thyself. For he who kills himself, kills nothing else than a man.*

I answer that, It is altogether unlawful to kill oneself, for three reasons. First, because everything naturally loves itself, the result being that everything naturally keeps itself in being, and resists corruption so far as it can. Wherefore suicide is contrary to the inclination of nature and to charity, whereby every man should love himself. Hence suicide is always a mortal sin, as being contrary to the natural law and to charity.

From Summa Theologica, *Vol. II, Part II, Question 64, A5. By permission of Benziger Brothers, New York, 1925.*

Secondly, because every part, as such, belongs to the whole. Now every man is part of the community, and so, as such, he belongs to the community. Hence by killing himself he injures the community, as the Philosopher declares (*Ethic* v. ii).

Thirdly, because life is God's gift to man, and is subject to His power, Who kills and makes to live. Hence whoever takes his own life sins against God, even as he who kills another's slave sins against that slave's master, and as he who usurps himself judgment of a matter not entrusted to him. For it belongs to God alone to pronounce sentence of death and life, according to Deut. xxxii. 39, *I will kill and I will make to live.*

Reply Obj. 1. Murder is a sin, not only because it is contrary to justice, but also because it is opposed to charity, which a man should have towards himself; in this respect suicide is a sin in relation to oneself. In relation to the community and to God, it is sinful, by reason also to its opposition to justice.

Reply Obj. 2. One who exercises public authority may lawfully put to death an evildoer, since he can pass judgment on him. But no man is judge of himself. Wherefore it is not lawful for one who exercises public authority to put himself to death for any sin whatever, although he may lawfully commit himself to the judgment of others.

Reply Obj. 3. Man is made master of himself through his free will: wherefore he can lawfully dispose of himself as to those matters which pertain to this life, which is ruled by man's free will. But the passage from this life to another and happier one is subject not to man's free will but to the power of God. Hence it is not lawful for a man to take his own life that he may pass to a happier life, nor that he may escape any unhappiness whatsoever to the present life, because the ultimate and most fearsome evil of this life is death, as the Philosopher states (*Ethic* iii. 6). Therefore to bring death upon oneself in order to escape the other afflictions of this life is to adopt a greater evil in order to avoid a lesser. In like manner it is unlawful to take one's own life on account of one's having committed a sin, both because by so doing one does oneself a very great injury, by depriving oneself of the time needful for repentance, and because it is not lawful to slay an evildoer except by the sentence of the public authority. Again it is unlawful for a woman to kill herself lest she be violated, because she ought not to commit on herself the very great sin of suicide to avoid the lesser sin of another. For she commits no sin in being violated by force, provided she does not consent, since *without consent of the mind there is no stain on the body,* as the Blessed Lucy declared. Now it is evident that fornication and adultery are less grievous sins than taking a man's, especially one's own, life, since the latter is most grievous, because one injures oneself, to whom one owes the greatest love. Moreover it is most dangerous since no time is left wherein to expiate it by repentance. Again it is not lawful for anyone to take his own life for fear he should consent to sin, because *evil must not be done that good may come* (Rom. iii. 8) or that evil maybe avoided, especially if the evil be of small account and an uncertain event, for it is uncertain whether one will at some future time consent to a sin, since God is able to deliver man from sin under any temptation whatever.

Reply Obj. 4. As Augustine says (*De Civ. Dei* i. 21), *not even Samson is to be excused that he crushed himself together with his enemies under the ruins of the house, except the Holy Ghost, Who had wrought many wonders through him, had secretly commanded him to do this.* He assigns the same reason in the case of certain holy women who at the time of persecution took their own lives and who are commemorated by the Church.

Reply Obj. 5. It belongs to fortitude that a man does not shrink from being slain by another, for the sake of the good of virtue and that he may avoid sin. But that a man take his own life in order to avoid penal evils has indeed an appearance of fortitude (for which reason some . . . have killed themselves, thinking to act from fortitude), yet it is not true fortitude, but rather a weakness of soul unable to bear penal evils, as the Philosopher (*Ethic* iii. 7) and Augustine (*De Civ. Dei* i. 22, 23) declare.

Note

1. The reference is to Aristotle, to whom Aquinas frequently refers as "The Philosopher"—ED.

Study Questions

1. What are the five objections that Aquinas seeks to answer in his argument that suicide is morally wrong?
2. What are Aquinas's reasons for prohibiting suicide? Do you agree with him?

CHAPTER 19

On the Naturalness of Suicide

DAVID HUME

The Scottish empiricist and skeptic David Hume (1711–1776) is one of the most brilliant philosophers to live. His classic work *Treatise on Human Nature* was written when he was twenty-seven years old. He was known for his kindness and conviviality.

In this essay Hume responds to the classic arguments against suicide, those given by Aquinas in the previous reading. Hume argues that suicide does not violate natural laws, since no event can violate those laws. Rational suicide does not harm society since it only occurs when the life is of little value, and it does not constitute a sin against the self, since "no man throws away life while it is worth keeping."

So GREAT IS OUR HORROR OF DEATH, that when it presents itself, under any form, besides that to which a man has endeavoured to reconcile his imagination, it acquires new terrors and overcomes his feeble courage: But when the menaces of superstition are joined to this natural timidity, no wonder it quite deprives men of all power over their lives, since even many pleasures and enjoyments, to which we are carried by a strong propensity, are torn from us by this inhuman tyrant. Let us here endeavour to restore men to their native liberty by examining all the common arguments against Suicide, and shewing that that action may be free from every imputation of guilt or blame, according to the sentiments of all the ancient philosophers.

If Suicide be criminal, it must be a transgression of our duty either to God, our neighbour, or ourselves.—To prove that suicide is no transgression of our duty to God, the following considerations may perhaps suffice. In order to govern the material world, the almighty Creator has established general and immutable laws by which all bodies, from the greatest planet to the smallest particle of matter, are maintained in their proper sphere and function. To govern the animal world, he has endowed all living creatures with bodily and mental powers; with senses, passions, appetites, memory and judgement, by which they are impelled or regulated in that course of life to which they are destined. These two distinct principles of the material and animal world, continually encroach upon each other, and mutually retard or forward each other's operations. The powers of men and of all other animals are restrained and directed by the nature and qualities of the surrounding bodies; and the modifications and actions of these bodies are incessantly altered by the operation of all animals. Man is stopt by rivers in his passage over the surface of the earth; and rivers, when properly directed, lend their force to the motion of machines, which serve to the use of man. But tho' the provinces of the material and animal powers are not kept entirely separate, there results from thence no discord or disorder

 From The Standards of Taste and Other Essays *(Bobbs-Merrill, 1965).*

in the creation; on the contrary, from the mixture, union and contrast of all the various powers of inanimate bodies and living creatures, arises that surprising harmony and proportion which affords the surest argument of supreme wisdom. The providence of the Deity appears not immediately in any operation, but governs everything by those general and immutable laws, which have been established from the beginning of time. All events, in one sense, may be pronounced the action of the Almighty; they all proceed from those powers with which he has endowed his creatures. A house which falls by its own weight is not brought to ruin by his providence more than one destroyed by the hands of men; nor are the human faculties less his workmanship, than the laws of motion and gravitation. When the passions play, when the judgement dictates, when the limbs obey; this is all the operation of God, and upon these animate principles, as well as upon the inanimate, has he established the government of the universe. Every event is alike important in the eyes of that infinite being, who takes in at one glance the most distant regions of space and remotest periods of time. There is no event, however important to us, which he has exempted from the general laws that govern the universe, or which he has peculiarly reserved for his own immediate action and operation. The revolution of states and empires depends upon the smallest caprice or passion of single men; and the lives of men are shortened or extended by the smallest accident of air or diet, sunshine or tempest. Nature still continues her progress and operation; and if general laws be ever broke by particular volitions of the Deity, 'tis after a manner which entirely escapes human observation. As, on the one hand, the elements and other inanimate parts of the creation carry on their action without regard to the particular interest and situation of men; so men are entrusted to their own judgement and discretion, in the various shocks of matter, and may employ every faculty with which they are endowed, in order to provide for their ease, happiness, or preservation. What is the meaning then of that principle, that a man who, tired of life, and hunted by pain and misery, bravely overcomes all the natural terrors of death and makes his escape from this cruel scene; that such a man, I say, has incurred the indignation of his Creator by encroaching on the office of divine providence, and disturbing the order of the universe? Shall we assert that the Almighty has reserved to himself in any peculiar manner the disposal of the lives of men, and has not submitted that event, in common with others, to the general laws by which the universe is governed? This is plainly false; the lives of men depend upon the same laws as the lives of all other animals; and these are subjected to the general laws of matter and motion. The fall of a tower, or the infusion of a poison, will destroy a man equally with the meanest creature; an inundation sweeps away every thing without distinction that comes within the reach of its fury. Since therefore the lives of men are for ever dependent on the general laws of matter and motion, is a man's disposing of his life criminal, because in every case it is criminal to encroach upon these laws, or disturb their operation? But this seems absurd; all animals are entrusted to their own prudence and skill for their conduct in the world, and have full authority, as far as their power extends, to alter all the operations of nature. Without the exercise of this authority they could not subsist a moment; every action, every motion of a man, innovates on the order of some parts of matter, and diverts from their ordinary course the general laws of motion. Putting together, therefore, these conclusions, we find that human life depends upon the general laws of matter and motion, and that it is no encroachment on the office of providence to disturb or alter these general laws: Has not every one, of consequence, the free disposal of his own life? And may he not lawfully employ that power with which nature has endowed him? In order to destroy the evidence of this conclusion, we must show a reason, why this particular case is excepted; is it because human life is of so great importance, that 'tis a presumption for human prudence to dispose of it? But the life of a man is of no greater importance to the universe than that of an oyster. And were it of ever so great importance, the order of nature has actually submitted it to human prudence, and reduced us to a necessity in every incident of determining concerning it. Were the disposal of human life so much reserved as the peculiar province of the Almighty that it were an encroachment on his right, for men to dispose of their own lives; it would be equally criminal to act for the preservation of life as for its destruction. If I turn aside a stone which is falling upon my head, I disturb the course of nature, and I invade the peculiar province of the Almighty by lengthening out my life beyond the period which by the general laws of matter and motion he had assigned it.

A hair, a fly, an insect is able to destroy this mighty being whose life is of such importance. Is it an absurdity to suppose that human prudence may lawfully dispose of what depends on such insignificant causes? It would be no crime in me to divert the *Nile* or *Danube* from its course, were I able to effect such purposes. Where then is the crime of turning a few ounces of blood from their natural channel?—Do you imagine that I repine at providence or curse my creation, because I go out of life, and put a period to a being, which, were it to continue, would render me miserable? Far be such sentiments from me; I am only convinced of a matter of fact, which you yourself acknowledge possible, that human life may be unhappy, and that my existence, if further prolonged, would become ineligible: but I thank providence, both for the good which I have already enjoyed, and for the power with which I am endowed of escaping the ill that threatens me.[1] To you it belongs to repine at providence, who foolishly imagine that you have no such power, and who must still prolong a hated life, tho' loaded with pain and sickness, with shame and poverty.—Do

you not teach, that when any ill befalls me; tho' by the malice of my enemies, I ought to be resigned to providence, and that the actions of men are the operations of the Almighty as much as the actions of inanimate beings? When I fall upon my own sword, therefore, I receive my death equally from the hands of the Deity as if it had proceeded from a lion, a precipice, or a fever. The submission which you require to providence, in every calamity that befalls me, excludes not human skill and industry, if possibly by their means I can avoid or escape the calamity: And why may I not employ one remedy as well as another?—If my life be not my own, it were criminal for me to put it in danger, as well as to dispose of it; nor could one man deserve the appellation of *hero* whom glory or friendship transports into the greatest dangers, and another merit the reproach of *wretch* or *miscreant* who puts a period to his life from the same or like motives.—There is no being, which possesses any power or faculty, that it receives not from its Creator, nor is there any one, which by ever so irregular an action can encroach upon the plan of his providence, or disorder the universe. Its operations are his works equally with that chain of events, which it invades, and which ever principle prevails, we may for that very reason conclude it to be most favoured by him. Be it animate, or inanimate, rational, or irrational; 'tis all a case: Its power is still derived from the supreme creator, and is alike comprehended in the order of his providence. When the horror of pain prevails over the love of life; when a voluntary action anticipates the effects of blind causes; 'tis only in consequence of those powers and principles, which he has implanted in his creatures. Divine providence is still inviolate and placed far beyond the reach of human injuries.[2] 'Tis impious, says the old Roman superstition, to divert rivers from their course, or invade the prerogatives of nature. 'Tis impious, says the French superstition, to inoculate for the small-pox, or usurp the business of providence, by voluntarily producing distempers and maladies. 'Tis impious, says the modern *European* superstition, to put a period to our own life, and thereby rebel against our creator; and why not impious, say I, to build houses, cultivate the ground, or sail upon the ocean? In all these actions we employ our powers of mind and body, to reduce some innovation in the course of nature; and in none of them do we any more. They are all of them therefore equally innocent, or equally criminal. *But you are placed by providence, like a centinel in a particular station, and when you desert it without being recalled, you are equally guilty of rebellion against your almighty sovereign, and have incurred his displeasure.*—I ask, why do you conclude that providence has placed me in this station? For my part I find that I owe my birth to a long chain of causes, of which many depended upon voluntary actions of men. *But Providence guided all these Causes, and nothing happens in the universe without its consent and Co-operation.* If so, then neither does my death, however voluntary, happen without its consent; and whenever pain or sorrow so far overcome my patience, as to make me tired of life, I may conclude that I am recalled from my station in the clearest and most express terms. 'Tis Providence surely that has placed me at this present moment in this chamber: but may I not leave it when I think proper, without being liable to the imputation of having deserted my post or station? When I shall be dead, the principles of which I am composed will still perform their part in the universe, and will be equally useful in the grand fabric, as when they composed this individual creature. The difference to the whole will be no greater than betwixt my being in a chamber and in the open air. The one change is of more importance to me than the other: but not more so to the universe.

'Tis a kind of blasphemy to imagine that any created being can disturb the order of the world or invade the business of providence! It supposes, that that Being possesses powers and faculties, which it received not from its creator, and which are not subordinate to his government and authority. A man may disturb society no doubt, and thereby incur the displeasure of the Almighty: But the government of the world is placed far beyond his reach and violence. And how does it appear that the Almighty is displeased with those actions that disturb society? By the principles which he has implanted in human nature, and which inspire us with a sentiment of remorse if we ourselves have been guilty of such actions, and with that of blame and disapprobation, if we ever observe them in orders.—Let us now examine, according to the method proposed, whether Suicide be of this kind of actions, and be a breach of our duty to our *neighbour* and to *society*.

A man, who retires from life, does no harm to society: He only ceases to do good; which, if it is an injury, is of the lowest kind.—All our obligations to do good to society seem to imply something reciprocal. I receive the benefits of society and therefore ought to promote its interests, but when I withdraw myself altogether from society, can I be bound any longer? But, allowing that our obligations to do good were perpetual, they have certainly some bounds; I am not obliged to do a small good to society at the expense of a great harm to myself; why then should I prolong a miserable existence, because of some frivolous advantage which the public may perhaps receive from me? If upon account of age and infirmities I may lawfully resign any office, and employ my time altogether in fencing against these calamities, and alleviating as much as possible the miseries of my future life: Why may I not cut short these miseries at once by an action which is no more prejudicial to society?—But suppose that it is no longer in my power to promote the interest of society; suppose that I am a burthen to it; suppose that my life hinders some person from being much more useful to society. In such cases my resignation of life must not only be innocent but laudable. And most people who lie under any temptation to abandon existence, are in some such situation; those, who have health, or power, or authority, have commonly better reason to be in humour with the world.

A man is engaged in a conspiracy for the public interest; is seized upon suspicion; is threatened with the rack; and knows from his own weakness that the secret will be extorted from him: Could such a one consult the public interest better than by putting a quick period to a miserable life? This was the case of the famous and brave *Strozi* of *Florence.*—Again, suppose a malefactor is justly condemned to a shameful death; can any reason be imagined, why he may not anticipate his punishment, and save himself all the anguish of thinking on its dreadful approaches? He invades the business of providence no more than the magistrate did, who ordered his execution; and his voluntary death is equally advantageous to society by ridding it of a pernicious member.

That suicide may often be consistent with interest and with our duty to ourselves, no one can question, who allows that age, sickness, or misfortune may render life a burden, and make it worse even than annihilation. I believe that no man ever threw away life, while it was worth keeping. For such is our natural horror of death, that small motives will never be able to reconcile us to it; and though perhaps the situation of a man's health or fortune did not seem to require this remedy, we may at least be assured, that any one who, without apparent reason, has had recourse to it, was curst with such an incurable depravity or gloominess of temper as must poison all enjoyment, and render him equally miserable as if he had been loaded with the most grievous misfortunes.—If suicide be supposed a crime, 'tis only cowardice can impel us to it. If it be no crime, both prudence and courage should engage us to rid ourselves at once of existence, when it becomes a burthen. 'Tis the only way that we can then be useful to society, by setting an example, which, if imitated, would preserve to every one his chance for happiness in life and would effectually free him from all danger or misery.

Notes

1. Agamus Deo gratias, quod nemo in vita teneri potest. SEN., Epist. 12.
2. TACIT. Ann. lib. i. 79.

Study Questions

1. Examine Hume's argument in order to see whether he meets each of Aquinas's reasons against the permissibility of suicide.
2. How does Hume reply to the objection that suicide is unnatural?

CHAPTER 20

Life Is Absurd

ALBERT CAMUS

Albert Camus (1913–1960) was born in French colonial Algeria, into a poor working-class family. He was a French journalist, novelist, and philosopher who fought in the French underground during World War II and fought for courage and integrity in public life. He is most famous for his novels *The Stranger* (1942), *The Plague* (1947), and *The Fall* (1957), for which he received a Nobel Prize for literature. He was killed in a car crash in 1960. His rival existentialist, Jean-Paul Sartre, fittingly called it "an absurd death."

In this selection we see Camus's overall assessment that life is absurd, meaningless. The only important philosophical question is, why not commit suicide? Life is compared to the myth of Sisyphus, wherein that man is condemned by the gods to roll a huge stone up a mountain, watch it roll back down, and retrieve it, only to repeat the process again, endlessly.

Absurdity and Suicide

THERE IS BUT ONE TRULY SERIOUS philosophical problem, and that is suicide. Judging whether life is or is not worth living amounts to answering the fundamental question of philosophy. All the rest—whether or not the world has three dimensions, whether the mind has nine or twelve categories—comes afterwards. These are games; one must first answer. And if it is true, as Nietzsche claims, that a philosopher, to deserve our respect, must preach by example, you can appreciate the importance of that reply, for it will precede the definitive act. These are facts the heart can feel; yet they call for careful study before they become clear to the intellect.

If I ask myself how to judge that this question is more urgent than that, I reply that one judges by the actions it entails. I have never seen any-

one die for the ontological argument. Galileo, who held a scientific truth of great importance, abjured it with the greatest of ease as soon as it endangered his life. In a certain sense, he did right.[1] That truth was not worth the stake. Whether the earth or the sun revolves around the other is a matter of profound indifference. To tell the truth, it is a futile question. On the other hand, I see many people die because they judge that life is not worth living. I see others paradoxically getting killed for the ideas or illusions that give them a reason for living (what is called a reason for living is also an excellent reason for dying). I therefore conclude that the meaning of life is the most urgent of questions. How to answer it? On all essential problems (I mean thereby those that run the risk of leading to death or those that intensify the passion of living) there are probably but two methods of thought: the method of La Palisse and the method of Don Quixote. Solely the balance between evidence and lyricism can allow us to achieve simultaneously emotion and lucidity. In a subject at once so humble and so heavy with emotion, the learned and classical dialectic must yield, one can see, to a more modest attitude of mind deriving at one and the same time from common sense and understanding.

Suicide has never been dealt with except as a social phenomenon. On the contrary, we are concerned here, at the outset, with the relationship between individual thought and suicide. An act like this is prepared within the silence of the heart, as is a great work of art. The man himself is ignorant of it. One evening he pulls the trigger or jumps. Of an apartment-building manager who had killed himself I was told that he had lost his daughter five years before, that he had changed greatly since, and that that experience had "undermined" him. A more exact word cannot be imagined. Beginning to think is beginning to be undermined. Society has but little connection with such beginnings. The worm is in man's heart. That is where it must be sought. One must follow and understand this fatal game that leads from lucidity in the face of existence to flight from light. . . .

But it is hard to fix the precise instant, the subtle step when the mind opted for death, it is easier to deduce from the act itself the consequences it implies. In a sense, and as in melodrama, killing yourself amounts to confessing. It is confessing that life is too much for you or that you do not understand it. Let's not go too far in such analogies, however, but rather return to everyday words. It is merely confessing that that "is not worth the trouble." Living, naturally, is never easy. You continue making the gestures commanded by existence for many reasons, the first of which is habit. Dying voluntarily implies that you have recognized, even instinctively, the ridiculous character of that habit, the absence of any profound reason for living, the insane character of that daily agitation, and the uselessness of suffering.

What, then, is that incalculable feeling that deprives the mind of the sleep necessary to life? A world that can be explained even with bad reasons is a familiar world. But, on the other hand, in a universe suddenly divested of illusions and lights, man feels an alien, a stranger. His exile is without remedy since he is deprived of the memory of a lost home or the hope of a promised land. This divorce between man and his life, the actor and his setting, is properly the feeling of absurdity. All healthy men having thought of their own suicide, it can be seen, without further explanation, that there is a direct connection between this feeling and the longing for death.

The subject of this essay is precisely this relationship between the absurd and suicide, the exact degree to which suicide is a solution to the absurd. The principle can be established that for a man who does not cheat, what he believes to be true must determine his action. Belief in the absurdity of existence must then dictate his conduct. It is legitimate to wonder, clearly and without false pathos, whether a conclusion of this importance requires forsaking as rapidly as possible an incomprehensible condition. I am speaking, of course, of men inclined to be in harmony with themselves. . . .

All great deeds and all great thoughts have a ridiculous beginning. Great works are often born on a street-corner or in a restaurant's revolving door. So it is with absurdity. The absurd world more than others derives its nobility from that abject birth. In certain situations, replying "nothing" when asked what one is thinking about may be pretense in a man. Those who are loved are well aware of this. But if that reply is sincere, if it symbolizes that odd state of soul in which the void becomes eloquent, in which the chain of daily gestures is broken, in which the heart vainly seeks the link that will connect it again, then it is as it were the first sign of absurdity.

It happens that the stage sets collapse. Rising, streetcar, four hours in the office or the factory, meal, streetcar, four hours of work, meal, sleep, and Monday Tuesday Wednesday Thursday Friday and Saturday according to the same rhythm—this path is easily followed most of the time. But one day the "why" arises and everything begins in that weariness tinged with amazement. "Begins"—this is important. Weariness comes at the end of the acts of a mechanical life, but at the same time it inaugurates the impulse of consciousness. It awakens consciousness and provokes what follows. What follows is the gradual return into the chain or it is the definitive awakening. At the end of the awakening comes, in time, the consequence: suicide or recovery. In itself weariness has something sickening about it. Here, I must conclude that it is good. For everything begins with consciousness and nothing is worth anything except through it. . . .

But what does life mean in such a universe? Nothing else for the moment but indifference to the future and a desire to use up everything that is given. Belief in the meaning of life always implies a scale of values, a choice, our preferences. Belief in the absurd, according to our definitions, teaches the contrary. But this is worth examining.

Knowing whether or not one can live *without appeal* is all that interests me. I do not want to get out of my depth. This aspect of life being given me, can I adapt myself to it? Now, faced with this particular concern, belief in the absurd is tantamount to substituting the quantity of experiences for the quality. If I convince myself that this life has no other aspect than that of the absurd, if I feel that its whole equilibrium depends on that perpetual opposition between my conscious revolt and the darkness in which it struggles, if I admit that my freedom has no meaning except in relation to its limited fate, then I must say that what counts is not the best of living but the most living. . . .

On the one hand the absurd teaches that all experiences are unimportant, and on the other it urges toward the greatest quantity of experiences. How, then, can one fail to do as so many

of those men I was speaking of earlier—choose the form of life that brings us the most possible of that human matter, thereby introducing a scale of values that on the other hand one claims to reject?

But again it is the absurd and its contradictory life that teaches us. For the mistake is thinking that that quantity of experiences depends on the circumstances of our life when it depends solely on us. Here we have to be over-simple. To two men living the same number of years, the world always provides the same sum of experiences. It is up to us to be conscious of them. Being aware of one's life, one's revolt, one's freedom, and to the maximum, is living, and to the maximum. Where lucidity dominates, the scale of values becomes useless. . . .

The Myth of Sisyphus

The gods had condemned Sisyphus to ceaselessly rolling a rock to the top of a mountain, whence the stone would fall back of its own weight. They had thought with some reason that there is no more dreadful punishment than futile and hopeless labor.

If one believes Homer, Sisyphus was the wisest and most prudent of mortals. According to another tradition, however, he was disposed to practice the profession of highwayman. I see no contradiction in this. Opinions differ as to the reasons why he became the futile laborer of the underworld. To begin with, he is accused of a certain levity in regard to the gods. He stole their secrets. Ægina, the daughter of Æsopus, was carried off by Jupiter. The father was shocked by that disappearance and complained to Sisyphus. He, who knew of the abduction, offered to tell about it on condition that Æsopus would give water to the citadel of Corinth. To the celestial thunderbolts he preferred the benediction of water. He was punished for this in the underworld. Homer tells us also that Sisyphus had put Death in chains. Pluto could not endure the sight of his deserted, silent empire. He dispatched the god of war, who liberated Death from the hands of her conqueror.

It is said also that Sisyphus, being near to death, rashly wanted to test his wife's love. He ordered her to cast his unburied body into the middle of the public square. Sisyphus woke up in the underworld. And there, annoyed by an obedience so contrary to human love, he obtained from Pluto permission to return to earth in order to chastise his wife. But when he had seen again the face of this world, enjoyed water and sun, warm stones and the sea, he no longer wanted to go back to the infernal darkness. Recalls, signs of anger, warnings were of no avail. Many years more he lived facing the curve of the gulf, the sparkling sea, and the smiles of earth. A decree of the gods was necessary. Mercury came and seized the impudent man by the collar and, snatching him from his joys, led him forcibly back to the underworld, where his rock was ready for him.

You have already grasped that Sisyphus is the absurd hero. He *is*, as much through his passions as through his torture. His scorn of the gods, his hatred of death, and his passion for life won him that unspeakable penalty in which the whole being is exerted toward accomplishing nothing. This is the price that must be paid for the passions of this earth. Nothing is told us about Sisyphus in the underworld. Myths are made for the imagination to breathe life into them. As for this myth, one sees merely the whole effort of a body straining to raise the huge stone, to roll it and push it up a slope a hundred times over; one sees the face screwed up, the cheek tight against the stone, the shoulder bracing the clay-covered mass, the foot wedging it, the fresh start with arms outstretched, the wholly human security of two earth-clotted hands. At the very end of his long effort measured by skyless space and time without depth, the purpose is achieved. Then Sisyphus watches the stone rush down in a few moments toward that lower world whence he

will have to push it up again toward the summit. He goes back down to the plain.

It is during, that return, that pause, that Sisyphus interests me. A face that toils so close to stones is already stone itself! I see that man going back down with a heavy yet measured step toward the torment of which he will never know the end. That hour like a breathing-space which returns as surely as his suffering, that is the hour of consciousness. At each of those moments when he leaves the heights and gradually sinks toward the lairs of the gods, he is superior to his fate. He is stronger than his rock.

If this myth is tragic, that is because its hero is conscious. Where would his torture be, indeed, if at every step the hope of succeeding upheld him? The workman of today works every day in his life at the same tasks, and this fate is no less absurd. But it is tragic only at the rare moments when it becomes conscious. Sisyphus, proletarian of the gods, powerless and rebellious, knows the whole extent of his wretched condition: it is what he thinks of during his descent. The lucidity that was to constitute his torture at the same time crowns his victory. There is no fate that cannot be surmounted by scorn.

If the descent is thus sometimes performed in sorrow, it can also take place in joy. This word is not too much. Again I fancy Sisyphus returning toward his rock, and the sorrow was in the beginning. When the images of earth cling too tightly to memory, when the call of happiness becomes too insistent, it happens that melancholy rises in man's heart: this is the rock's victory, this is the rock itself. The boundless grief is too heavy to bear. These are our nights of Gethsemane. But crushing truths perish from being acknowledged. Thus, Œdipus at the outset obeys fate without knowing it. But from the moment he knows, his tragedy begins. Yet at the same moment, blind and desperate, he realizes that the only bond linking him to the world is the cool hand of a girl. Then a tremendous remark rings out: "Despite so many ordeals, my advanced age and the nobility of my soul make me conclude that all is well." Sophocles, Œdipus, like Dostoevsky's Kirilov, thus gives the recipe for the absurd victory. Ancient wisdom confirms modern heroism.

One does not discover the absurd without being tempted to write a manual of happiness. "What! by such narrow ways—?" There is but one world, however. Happiness and the absurd are two sons of the same earth. They are inseparable. It would be a mistake to say that happiness necessarily springs from the absurd discovery. It happens as well that the feeling of the absurd springs from happiness. "I conclude that all is well," says Œdipus, and that remark is sacred. It echoes in the wild and limited universe of man. It teaches that all is not, has not been, exhausted. It drives out of this world a god who had come into it with dissatisfaction and a preference for futile sufferings. It makes of fate a human matter, which must be settled among men.

All Sisyphus' silent joy is contained therein. His fate belongs to him. His rock is his thing. Likewise, the absurd man, when he contemplates his torment, silences all the idols. In the universe suddenly restored to its silence, the myriad wondering little voices of the earth rise up. Unconscious, secret calls, invitations from all the faces, they are the necessary reverse and price of victory. There is no sun without shadow, and it is essential to know the night. The absurd man says yes and his effort will henceforth be unceasing. If there is a personal fate, there is no higher destiny, or at least there is but one which he concludes is inevitable and despicable. For the rest, he knows himself to be the master of his days. At that subtle moment when man glances backward over his life, Sisyphus returning toward his rock, in that slight pivoting he contemplates that series of unrelated actions which becomes his fate, created by him, combined under his memory's eye and soon sealed by his death. Thus, convinced of the wholly human origin of all that is human, a blind man eager to see who knows that the night has no end, he is still on the go. The rock is still rolling.

I leave Sisyphus at the foot of the mountain! One always finds one's burden again. But Sisyphus teaches the higher fidelity that negates the gods and raises rocks. He too concludes that all is well. This universe henceforth without a master seems to him neither sterile nor futile. Each atom of that stone, each mineral flake of that night-filled mountain, in itself forms a world. The struggle itself toward the heights is enough to fill a man's heart. One must imagine Sisyphus happy.

Note

1. From the point of view of the relative value of truth. On the other hand, from the point of view of virile behavior, this scholar's fragility may well make us smile.

Study Questions

1. Is life absurd, as Camus insists? Does Camus give good reasons for this claim? What leads him to this pessimistic conclusion?
2. Is Camus being irreverent in asking the question "Why not commit suicide?"?
3. Why does Camus say Sisyphus must be imagined to be happy?
4. What does Sisyphus symbolize?

CHAPTER 21

On the Morality and Rationality of Suicide

RICHARD BRANDT

Richard Brandt was professor in philosophy at the University of Michigan where he taught for many years. He is one of the most respected moral philosophers in the United States and is the author of several works, including *Ethical Theory* (1959) and *A Theory of the Good and the Right* (1979).

In this essay Brandt first discusses the blameworthiness of suicide, arguing that in many cases the subject may be excused—even if the deed is objectively wrong. Brandt then discusses the major arguments against suicide and finds them weak. Finally, he explores the problem of whether and when suicide is rational for the agent, suggesting that often the depressed person fails to assess the future accurately.

FROM THE POINT OF VIEW of contemporary philosophy, suicide raises the following distinct questions: whether a person who commits suicide (assuming that there is suicide if and only if there is intentional termination of one's own life) is morally blameworthy, reprehensible, sinful in all circumstances; whether suicide is objectively right or wrong, and in what circumstances it is right or wrong, from a moral point of view; and whether, or in which circumstances, suicide is the best or the rational thing to do from the point of view of the agent's personal welfare.

The Moral Blameworthiness of Suicide

In former times the question of whether suicide is sinful was of great interest because the answer to it was considered relevant to how the agent would spend eternity. At present the practical issue is not as great, although a normal funeral service may be denied a person judged to have committed suicide sinfully. The chief practical issue now seems to be that persons may disapprove of a decedent for having committed suicide, and his friends or relatives may wish to defend his memory against moral charges.

The question of whether an act of suicide was sinful or morally blameworthy is not apt to arise unless it is already believed that the agent morally ought not to have done it: for instance, if he really had very poor reason for doing so, and his act foreseeably had catastrophic consequences for his wife and children. But, even if a given suicide is morally wrong, it does not follow that it is morally reprehensible. For, while asserting that a given act of suicide was wrong, we may still think that the act was hardly morally blameworthy or sinful if, say, the agent was in a state of great emotional turmoil at the time. We might then say that, although what he did was

From A Handbook for the Study of Suicide, *edited by Seymour Perlin. Copyright © 1975 by Oxford University Press, Inc. Reprinted by permission.*

wrong, his action is *excusable,* just as in the criminal law it may be decided that, although a person broke the law, he should not be punished because he was *not responsible,* that is, was temporarily insane, did what he did inadvertently, and so on.

The foregoing remarks assume that to be morally blameworthy (or sinful) on account of an act is one thing, and for the act to be wrong is another. But, if we say this, what after all does it *mean* to say that a person is morally blameworthy on account of an action? We cannot say there is agreement among philosophers on this matter, but I suggest the following account as being safe from serious objection: "*X* is morally blameworthy on account of an action *A*" may be taken to mean "*X* did *A*, and *X* would not have done *A* had not his character been in some respect below standard; and in view of this it is fitting or justified for *X* to have some disapproving attitudes including remorse toward himself, and for some other persons *Y* to have some disapproving attitudes toward *X* and to express them in behavior." Traditional thought would include God as one of the "other persons" who might have and express disapproving attitudes.

In case the foregoing definition does not seem obviously correct, it is worthwhile pointing out that it is usually thought that an agent is not blameworthy or sinful for an action unless it is a *reflection on him;* the definition brings this fact out and makes clear why.

If someone charges that a suicide was sinful, we may now properly ask, "What defect of character did it show?" Some writers have claimed that suicide is blameworthy because it is *cowardly,* and since being cowardly is generally conceded to be a defect of character, if an act of suicide is admitted to be both objectively wrong and also cowardly, the claim to blameworthiness might be warranted in terms of the above definition. Of course, many people would hesitate to call taking one's own life a cowardly act, and there will certainly be controversy about which acts are cowardly and which are not. But at least

we can see part of what has to be done to make a charge of blameworthiness valid.

The most interesting question is the general one: which types of suicide in general are ones that, even if objectively wrong (in a sense to be explained below), are not sinful or blameworthy? Or, in other words, when is a suicide *morally excused* even if it is objectively wrong? We can at least identify some types that are morally excusable.

1. Suppose I *think* I am morally bound to commit suicide because I have a terminal illness and continued medical care will ruin my family financially. Suppose, however, that I am mistaken in this belief, and that suicide in such circumstances is not right. But surely I am not morally blameworthy; for I may be doing, out of a sense of duty to my family, what I would personally prefer not to do and is hard for me to do. What defect of character might my action show? Suicide from a genuine sense of duty is not blameworthy, even when the moral conviction in question is mistaken.

2. Suppose that I commit suicide when I am temporarily of unsound mind, either in the sense of the M'Naghten rule that I do not know that what I am doing is wrong, or of the Durham rule that, owing to a mental defect, I am substantially unable to do what is right. Surely, any suicide in an unsound state of mind is morally excused.

3. Suppose I commit suicide when I could not be said to be temporarily of unsound mind, but simply because I am not myself. For instance, I may be in an extremely depressed mood. Now a person may be in a very depressed mood, and commit suicide on account of being in that mood, when there is nothing the matter with his character—or, in other words, his character is not in any relevant way below standard. What are other examples of being "not myself," of emotional states that might be responsible for a person's committing suicide, and that might render the suicide excusable even if wrong? Being frightened; being distraught; being in almost any highly emotional frame of mind (anger,

frustration, disappointment in love); perhaps just being terribly fatigued.

So there are at least three types of suicide which can be morally excused even if they are objectively wrong. The main point is this: Mr. *X* may commit suicide and it may be conceded that he ought not to have done so, but it is another step to show that he is sinful, or morally blameworthy, for having done so. To make out that further point, it must be shown that his act is attributable to some substandard trait of character. So, Mrs. *X* after the suicide can concede that her husband ought not to have done what he did, but she can also point out that it is no reflection on his character. The distinction, unfortunately, is often overlooked. St. Thomas Aquinas, who recognizes the distinction in other places, seems blind to it in his discussion of suicide.

The Moral Reasons for and Against Suicide

Persons who say suicide is morally wrong must be asked which of two positions they are affirming: Are they saying that *every* act of suicide is wrong, *everything considered;* or are they merely saying that there is always *some* moral obligation—doubtless of serious weight—not to commit suicide, so that very often suicide is wrong, although it is possible that there are *countervailing considerations* which in particular situations make it right or even a moral duty? It is quite evident that the first position is absurd; only the second has a chance of being defensible.

In order to make clear what is wrong with the first view, we may begin with an example. Suppose an army pilot's single-seater plane goes out of control over a heavily populated area; he has the choice of staying in the plane and bringing it down where it will do little damage but at the cost of certain death for himself, and of bailing out and letting the plane fall where it will, very possibly killing a good many civilians. Suppose

he chooses to do the former, and so, by our definition, commits suicide. Does anyone want to say that his action is morally wrong? Even Immanuel Kant, who opposed suicide in all circumstances, apparently would not wish to say that it is; he would, in fact, judge that this act is not one of suicide, for he says, "It is no suicide to risk one's life against one's enemies, and even to sacrifice it, in order to preserve one's duties toward oneself."[1] St. Thomas Aquinas, in his discussion of suicide, may seem to take the position that such an act would be wrong, for he says, "It is altogether unlawful to kill oneself," admitting as an exception only the case of being under special command of God. But I believe St. Thomas would, in fact, have concluded that the act is right because the basic intention of the pilot was to save the lives of civilians, and whether an act is right or wrong is a matter of basic intention.[2]

In general, we have to admit that there are things with some moral obligation to avoid which, on account of other morally relevant considerations, it is sometimes right or even morally obligatory to do. There may be some obligation to tell the truth on every occasion, but surely in many cases the consequences of telling the truth would be so dire that one is obligated to lie. The same goes for promises. There is some moral obligation to do what one has promised (with a few exceptions); but, if one can keep a trivial promise only at serious cost to another person (i.e., keep an appointment only by failing to give aid to someone injured in an accident), it is surely obligatory to break the promise.

The most that the moral critic of suicide could hold, then, is that there is *some* moral obligation not to do what one knows will cause one's death; but he surely cannot deny that circumstances exist in which there are obligations to do things which, in fact, will result in one's death. If so, then in principle it would be possible to argue, for instance, that in order to meet my obligation to my family, it might be right for me to take my own life as the only way to avoid catastrophic hospital expenses in a terminal illness. Possibly the main point that critics of suicide on moral grounds would wish to make is that it is never right to take one's own life *for reasons of one's own personal welfare,* of any kind whatsoever. Some of the arguments used to support the immorality of suicide, however, are so framed that if they were supportable at all, they would prove that suicide is *never* moral.

One well-known type of argument against suicide may be classified as *theological.* St. Augustine and others urged that the Sixth Commandment ("Thou shalt not kill.") prohibits suicide, and that we are bound to obey a divine commandment. To this reasoning one might first reply that it is arbitrary exegesis of the Sixth Commandment to assert that it was intended to prohibit suicide. The second reply is that if there is not some consideration which shows on the merits of the case that suicide is morally wrong, God had no business prohibiting it. It is true that some will object to this point, and I must refer them elsewhere for my detailed comments on the divine-will theory of morality.[3]

Another theological argument with wide support was accepted by John Locke, who wrote: ". . . Men being all the workmanship of one omnipotent and infinitely wise Maker; all the servants of one sovereign Master, sent into the world by His order and about His business; they are His property, whose workmanship they are made to last during His, not one another's pleasure. . . . Every one . . . is bound to preserve himself, and not to quit his station wilfully. . . ."[4] And Kant: "We have been placed in this world under certain conditions and for specific purposes. But a suicide opposes the purpose of his Creator; he arrives in the other world as one who has deserted his post; he must be looked upon as a rebel against God. So long as we remember the truth that it is God's intention to preserve life, we are bound to regulate our activities in conformity with it. This duty is upon us until the time comes when God expressly

commands us to leave this life. Human beings are sentinels on earth and may not leave their posts until relieved by another beneficent hand."[5] Unfortunately, however, even if we grant that it is the duty of human beings to do what God commands or intends them to do, more argument is required to show that God does *not* permit human beings to quit this life when their own personal welfare would be maximized by so doing. How does one draw the requisite inference about the intentions of God? The difficulties and contradictions in arguments to reach such a conclusion are discussed at length and perspicaciously by David Hume in his essay "On Suicide," and in view of the unlikelihood that readers will need to be persuaded about these, I shall merely refer those interested to that essay.[6]

A second group of arguments may be classed as arguments *from natural law.* St. Thomas says: "It is altogether unlawful to kill oneself, for three reasons. First, because everything naturally loves itself, the result being that everything naturally keeps itself in being, and resists corruptions so far as it can. Wherefore suicide is contrary to the inclination of nature, and to charity whereby every man should love himself. Hence suicide is always a mortal sin, as being contrary to the natural law and to charity."[7] Here St. Thomas ignores two obvious points. First, it is not obvious why a human being is morally bound to do what he or she has some inclination to do. (St. Thomas did not criticize chastity.) Second, while it is true that most human beings do feel a strong urge to live, the human being who commits suicide obviously feels a stronger inclination to do something else. It is as natural for a human being to dislike, and to take steps to avoid, say, great pain, as it is to cling to life.

A somewhat similar argument by Immanuel Kant may seem better. In a famous passage Kant writes that the maxim of a person who commits suicide is "From self-love I make it my principle to shorten my life if its continuance threatens more evil than it promises pleasure. The only further question to ask is whether this principle of self-love can become a universal law of nature. It is then seen at once that a system of nature by whose law the very same feeling whose function is to stimulate the furtherance of life should actually destroy life would contradict itself and consequently could not subsist as a system of nature. Hence this maxim cannot possibly hold as a universal law of nature and is therefore entirely opposed to the supreme principle of all duty."[8] What Kant finds contradictory is that the motive of self-love (interest in one's own long-range welfare) should sometimes lead one to struggle to preserve one's life, but at other times to end it. But where is the contradiction? One's circumstances change, and, if the argument of the following section in this chapter is correct, one sometimes maximizes one's own long-range welfare by trying to stay alive, but at other times by bringing about one's demise.

A third group of arguments, a form of which goes back at least to Aristotle, has a more modern and convincing ring. These are arguments to show that, in one way or another, a suicide necessarily does harm to other persons, or to society at large. Aristotle says that the suicide treats the *state* unjustly.[9] Partly following Aristotle, St. Thomas says: "Every man is part of the community, and so, as such, he belongs to the community. Hence by killing himself he injures the community."[10] Blackstone held that a suicide is an offense against the king "who hath an interest in the preservation of all his subjects," perhaps following Judge Brown in 1563, who argued that suicide cost the king a subject—"he being the head has lost one of his mystical members."[11] The premise of such arguments is, as Hume pointed out, obviously mistaken in many instances. It is true that Freud would perhaps have injured society had he, instead of finishing his last book, committed suicide to escape the pain of throat cancer. But surely there have been many suicides whose demise was not a noticeable loss to society; an honest man could only say that in some instances society was better off without them.

It need not be denied that suicide is often injurious to other persons, especially the family of a suicide. Clearly it sometimes is. But, we should notice what this fact establishes. Suppose we admit, as generally would be done, that there is some obligation not to perform any action which will probably or certainly be injurious to other people, the strength of the obligation being dependent on various factors, notably the seriousness of the expected injury. Then there is *some* obligation not to commit suicide, when that act would probably or certainly be injurious to other people. But, as we have already seen, many cases of *some* obligation to do something nevertheless are *not* cases of a duty to do that thing, *everything considered*. So it could sometimes be morally justified to commit suicide, even if the act will harm someone. Must a man with a terminal illness undergo excruciating pain because his death will cause his wife sorrow—when she will be caused sorrow a month later anyway, when he is dead of natural causes? Moreover, to repeat, the fact that an individual has some obligation not to commit suicide when that act will probably injure other persons does not imply that, everything considered, it is wrong for him to do it, namely, that in all circumstances suicide *as such* is something there is some obligation to avoid.

Is there any sound argument, convincing to the modern mind, to establish that there is (or is not) *some moral obligation* to avoid suicide *as such*, an obligation, of course, which might be overridden by other obligations in some or many cases? (Captain Oates may have had a moral obligation not to commit suicide as such, but his obligation not to stand in the way of his comrades' getting to safety might have been so strong that, everything considered, he was justified in leaving the polar camp and allowing himself to freeze to death.)

To present all the arguments necessary to answer this question convincingly would take a great deal of space. I shall, therefore, simply state one answer to it which seems plausible to some contemporary philosophers. Suppose it could be shown that it would maximize the long-run welfare of everybody affected if people were taught that there is a moral obligation to avoid suicide—so that people would be motivated to avoid suicide just because they thought it wrong (would have anticipatory guilt feelings at the very idea), and so that other people would be inclined to disapprove of persons who commit suicide unless there were some excuse (such as those mentioned in the first section). One might ask: how could it maximize utility to mold the conceptual and motivational structure of persons in this way? To which the answer might be: feeling in this way might make persons who are impulsively inclined to commit suicide in a bad mood, or a fit of anger or jealousy, take more time to deliberate; hence, some suicides that have bad effects generally might be prevented. In other words, it might be a good thing in its effects for people to feel about suicide in the way they feel about breach of promise or injuring others, just as it might be a good thing for people to feel a moral obligation not to smoke, or to wear seat belts. However, it might be that negative moral feelings about suicide as such would stand in the way of action by those persons whose welfare really is best served by suicide and whose suicide is the best thing for everybody concerned.

When a Decision to Commit Suicide is Rational from the Person's Point of View

The person who is contemplating suicide is obviously making a choice between future world-courses; the world-course that includes his demise, say, an hour from now, and several possible ones that contain his demise at a later point. One cannot have precise knowledge about many features of the latter group of world-courses, but it is certain that they will all end with death some (possibly short) finite time from now.

Why do I say the choice is between *world-courses* and not just a choice between future life-courses of the prospective suicide, the one shorter than the other? The reason is that one's suicide has some impact on the world (and one's continued life has some impact on the world), and that conditions in the rest of the world will often make a difference in one's evaluation of the possibilities. One *is* interested in things in the world other than just oneself and one's own happiness.

The basic question a person must answer, in order to determine which world-course is best or rational for him to choose, is which he *would* choose under conditions of optimal use of information, when *all* of his desires are taken into account. It is not just a question of what we prefer *now*, with some clarification of all the possibilities being considered. Our preferences change, and the preferences of tomorrow (assuming we can know something about them) are just as legitimately taken into account in deciding what to do now as the preferences of today. Since any reason that can be given today for weighting heavily today's preference can be given tomorrow for weighting heavily tomorrow's preference, the preferences of any time-stretch have a rational claim to an equal vote. Now the importance of that fact is this: we often know quite well that our desires, aversions, and preferences may change after a short while. When a person is in a state of despair—perhaps brought about by a rejection in love or discharge from a long-held position—nothing but the thing he cannot have seems desirable; everything else is turned to ashes. Yet we know quite well that the passage of time is likely to reverse all this; replacements may be found or other types of things that are available to us may begin to look attractive. So, if we were to act on the preferences of today alone, when the emotion of despair seems more than we can stand, we might find death preferable to life; but if we allow for the preferences of the weeks and years ahead, when many goals will be enjoyable and attractive, we might find life much preferable to death. So, if a choice of what is best is to be determined by what we want not only now but later (and later desires on an equal basis with the present ones)—as it should be—then what is the best or preferable world-course will often be quite different from what it would be if the choice, or what is best for one, were fixed by one's desires and preferences now.

Of course, if one commits suicide there are no future desires or aversions that may be compared with present ones and that should be allowed an equal vote in deciding what is best. In that respect the course of action that results in death is different from any other course of action we may undertake. I do not wish to suggest the rosy possibility that it is often or always reasonable to believe that next week "I shall be more interested in living than I am today, if today I take a dim view of continued existence." On the contrary, when a person is seriously ill, for instance, he may have no reason to think that the preference-order will be reversed—it may be that tomorrow he will prefer death to life more strongly.

The argument is often used that one can never be *certain* what is going to happen, and hence one is never rationally justified in doing anything as drastic as committing suicide. But we always have to live by probabilities and make our estimates as best we can. As soon as it is clear beyond reasonable doubt not only that death is now preferable to life, but also that it will be every day from now until the end, the rational thing is to act promptly.

Let us not pursue the question of whether it is rational for a person with a painful terminal illness to commit suicide; it is. However, the issue seldom arises, and few terminally ill patients do commit suicide. With such patients matters usually get worse slowly so that no particular time seems to call for action. They are often so heavily sedated that it is impossible for the men-

tal processes of decision leading to action to occur; or else they are incapacitated in a hospital and the very physical possibility of ending their lives is not available. Let us leave this grim topic and turn to a practically more important problem: whether it is rational for persons to commit suicide for some reason other than painful terminal physical illness. Most persons who commit suicide do so, apparently, because they face a nonphysical problem that depresses them beyond their ability to bear.

Among the problems that have been regarded as good and sufficient reasons for ending life, we find (in addition to serious illness) the following: some event that has made a person feel ashamed or lose his prestige and status; reduction from affluence to poverty; the loss of a limb or of physical beauty; the loss of sexual capacity; some event that makes it seem impossible to achieve things by which one sets store; loss of a loved one; disappointment in love; the infirmities of increasing age. It is not to be denied that such things can be serious blows to a person's prospects of happiness.

Whatever the nature of an individual's problem, there are various plain errors to be avoided—errors to which a person is especially prone when he is depressed—in deciding whether, everything considered, he prefers a world-course containing his early demise to one in which his life continues to its natural terminus. Let us forget for a moment the relevance to the decision of preferences that he may have tomorrow, and concentrate on some errors that may infect his preference as of today, and for which correction or allowance must be made.

In the first place, depression, like any severe emotional experience, tends to primitivize one's intellectual processes. It restricts the range of one's survey of the possibilities. One thing that a rational person would do is compare the world-course containing his suicide with his *best* alternative. But his best alternative is precisely a possibility he may overlook if, in a depressed mood, he thinks only of how badly off he is and cannot imagine any way of improving his situation. If a person is disappointed in love, it is possible to adopt a vigorous plan of action that carries a good chance of acquainting him with someone he likes at least as well; and if old age prevents a person from continuing the tennis game with his favorite partner, it is possible to learn some other game that provides the joys of competition without the physical demands.

Depression has another insidious influence on one's planning: it seriously affects one's judgment about probabilities. A person disappointed in love is very likely to take a dim view of himself, his prospects, and his attractiveness; he thinks that because he has been rejected by one person he will probably be rejected by anyone who looks desirable to him. In a less gloomy frame of mind he would make different estimates. Part of the reason for such gloomy probability estimates is that depression tends to repress one's memory of evidence that supports a nongloomy prediction. Thus, a rejected lover tends to forget any cases in which he has elicited enthusiastic response from ladies in relation to whom he has been the one who has done the rejecting. Thus his pessimistic self-image is based upon a highly selected, and pessimistically selected, set of data. Even when he is reminded of the data, moreover, he is apt to resist an optimistic inference.

Another kind of distortion of the look of future prospects is not a result of depression, but is quite normal. Events distant in the future feel small, just as objects distant in space look small. Their prospect does not have the effect on motivational processes that it would have if it were of an event in the immediate future. Psychologists call this the "goal-gradient" phenomenon; a rat, for instance, will run faster toward a perceived food box than a distant unseen one. In the case of a person who has suffered some misfortune, and whose situation now is an unpleasant one, this reduction of the motivational influence of events distant in time has the effect that present unpleasant states weigh far more heavily than

probable future pleasant ones in any choice of world-courses.

If we are trying to determine whether we now prefer, or shall later prefer, the outcome of one world-course to that of another (and this is leaving aside the questions of the weight of the votes of preferences at a later date), we must take into account these and other infirmities of our "sensing" machinery. Since knowing that the machinery is out of order will not tell us what results it would give if it were working, the best recourse might be to refrain from making any decision in a stressful frame of mind. If decisions have to be made, one must recall past reactions, in a normal frame of mind, to outcomes like those under assessment. But many suicides seem to occur in moments of despair. What should be clear from the above is that a moment of despair, if one is seriously contemplating suicide, ought to be a moment of reassessment of one's goals and values, a reassessment which the individual must realize is very difficult to make objectively, because of the very quality of his depressed frame of mind.

A decision to commit suicide may in certain circumstances be a rational one. But a person who wants to act rationally must take into account the various possible "errors" and make appropriate rectification of his initial evaluations.

Notes

1. Immanuel Kant, *Lectures on Ethics* (New York: Harper Torchbook, 1963), p. 150.

2. See St. Thomas Aquinas, *Summa Theologica*, Second Part of the Second Part, Q. 64, Art. 5. In Article 7, he says: "Nothing hinders one act from having two effects, only one of which is intended, while the other is beside the intention. Now moral acts take their species according to what is intended, and not according to what is beside the intention, since this is accidental as explained above" (Q. 43, Art. 3: I–II, Q. 1, Art. 3, as 3). Mr. Norman St. John-Stevas, the most articulate contemporary defender of the Catholic view, writes as follows: "Christian thought allows certain exceptions to its general condemnation of

suicide. That covered by a particular divine inspiration has already been noted. Another exception arises where suicide is the method imposed by the State for the execution of a just death penalty. A third exception is *altruistic* suicide, of which the best known example is Captain Oates. Such suicides are justified by invoking the principles of double effect. The act from which death results must be good or at least morally indifferent; some other good effect must result: The death must not be directly intended or the real means to the good effect: and a grave reason must exist for adopting the course of action" [*Life, Death and the Law* (Bloomington, Ind.: Indiana University Press, 1961), pp. 250–51]. Presumably the Catholic doctrine is intended to allow suicide when this is required for meeting strong moral obligations; whether it can do so consistently depends partly on the interpretation given to "real means to the good effect." Readers interested in pursuing further the Catholic doctrine of double effect and its implications for our problem should read Philippa Foot, "The Problem of Abortion and the Doctrine of Double Effect," *The Oxford Review*, 5 (Trinity 1967), 5–15.

3. R. B. Brandt, *Ethical Theory* (Englewood Cliffs, N.J.: Prentice Hall, Inc., 1959), pp. 61–82.

4. John Locke, *The Second Treatise on Civil Government*, Chap. 2.

5. Kant, *Lectures on Ethics*, p. 154.

6. This essay appears in collections of Hume's works.

7. For an argument similar to Kant's, see also St. Thomas Aquinas, *Summa Theologica*, II, II, Q. 64, Art. 5.

8. Immanuel Kant, *The Fundamental Principles of the Metaphysic of Morals*, trans. H. J. Paton (London: The Hutchinson Group, 1948), Chap. 2.

9. Aristotle, *Nicomachaean Ethics*, Bk. 5, Chap. 10, p. 1138a.

10. St. Thomas Aquinas, *Summa Theologica*, II, II, Q. 64, Art. 5.

11. Sir William Blackstone, *Commentaries*, 4:189; Brown in *Hales* v. *Petit*. I Plow. 253, 75 E.R. 387 (C.B. 1563). Both cited by Norman St. John-Stevas, *Life, Death and the Law*, p. 235.

Study Questions

1. Explain Brandt's position on the blameworthiness of suicide.
2. What are Brandt's arguments for the permissibility of suicide? How does he think suicide can be a rational act?

CHAPTER 22

Suicide: A Fundamental Right?

MARGARET PABST BATTIN

Margaret Pabst Battin is professor of philosophy at the University of Utah. Besides being the author of several articles and books in moral philosophy, especially medical ethics, she has published works in fiction.

In this essay Battin applies the Kantian notion of human dignity to the problem of suicide. She separates cases where dignity is honored from those where it is violated and argues that only in the former does a moral right to suicide exist.

DO PERSONS HAVE THE RIGHT to end their own lives, that is, the right to suicide? Of the philosophical issues concerning suicide, it is perhaps this which is most hotly disputed, and it is this upon which the most diverse claims have been made. Schopenhauer, for instance, says:

> It is quite obvious that there is nothing in the world to which every man has a more unassailable title than to his own life, and person.[1]

Wittgenstein, in contrast, holds:

> If suicide is allowed then everything is allowed. If anything is not allowed then suicide is not allowed. This throws a light on the nature of ethics, for suicide is, so to speak, the elementary sin.[2]

When we are confronted with actual cases, our own views may be equally diverse. Consider, for instance, the real-life case of a woman we shall call Elsie Somerset:

> . . . an 80-year-old woman who had for two years been living in a nursing home. She suffered from glaucoma, which had almost completely blinded

her, and from cancer of the colon, for which she was receiving chemotherapy. Her husband was recently dead. To relieve her chronic pain, and perhaps to mitigate the side effects of chemotherapy, she was being given hydromorphone, a morphine-like drug. In order to save up a week's supply of hydromorphone tablets she suffered through 168 hours of uninterrupted pain. Then she swallowed her hoard and went into coma.
>
> She was rushed to a hospital emergency room and subjected to a variety of procedures to save her life, including the intravenous injection of naloxone, a powerful morphine antagonist. The naloxone worked and she was returned to the nursing home—still suffering from glaucoma and from cancer.[3]

We may be strongly inclined to say that Elsie Somerset had a right to take these pills, and a right to die undisturbed after she had done so. But our intuitions often swing the other way. In St. Paul recently, a fifteen-year-old boy jumped to his death from a bridge, saying that he was doing so because his favorite TV program, "Battlestar Galactica," had been canceled.[4] Here we are very much less inclined to say that such

Reprinted from Suicide: The Philosophical Issues, *edited by Margaret Pabst Battin and David J. Mayo (New York: St. Martin's Press, 1980), by permission.*

people—even if they were able to make a clear-headed choice—have a *right* to end their lives, and certainly not to assistance in so doing. How then, in the face of these two very different cases, do we resolve the issue of whether there can be said to be a right to suicide?[5]

I

There are two general strategies which have traditionally been used to attempt to resolve this issue. The first one attempts to show that although there is some general obligation or moral canon which prohibits suicide, certain sympathetic cases can be allowed as exceptions. For instance, Aristotle said that suicide violates one's obligation to the community; we might argue that exceptions can be made in cases where suicide benefits the community.[6] Plato and Augustine claimed that one has a prior obligation to obey the command of God; both acknowledge as exceptions, however, instances (like Socrates and Samson) in which God directs rather than forbids the ending of one's life.[7] Kant held that suicide is forbidden because one has an obligation to respect the humanity in one's own person; he, too, though otherwise strictly impermissive of suicide, recognized at least one exception: the case of Cato.[8] On this first strategy there is no right to suicide, though certain special cases may be permitted as exceptions to an otherwise general rule.

If, however, one finds the arguments for general obligations against suicide unpersuasive (as many contemporary thinkers have), a second strategy for taking account of our divergent intuitions concerning suicide may suggest itself: to grant that an individual may have a *prima facie* right to suicide, but point out that there are (frequent) circumstances in which this right is overridden. Under this second strategy, suicide is construed as a right in virtue of the individual's general liberty to do as he chooses, pro-

vided, of course, that his choices do not harm the interests or violate the rights of other persons. In other words, suicide, on this second strategy, is construed as a liberty-right (of the sort propounded by John Stuart Mill);[9] one then attempts to do justice to one's initial sense that suicide in some cases is not a matter of right by showing that the liberty-right to suicide is often overridden on the basis of considerations of its effects on others. The emphasis here is typically placed on the injury suicide causes to others, particularly in emotional and psychological ways, but often in financial and social respects as well. Since, it is argued, suicide can frequently be extremely damaging to the survivors of the individual who takes his own life—and clinical studies do show that it can severely distort the lives of spouses, parents, children, and intimate friends[10]—therefore the individual's *prima facie* liberty-right to suicide is often, or almost always, overridden. On this account, suicide ceases to be a right not because of what it does to oneself (since on Mill's notion of liberty-rights one may have a right to choose things which harm oneself), but because of what it does to others.

Like the first approach, I think this second strategy for taking account of our divergent intuitions concerning the issues of rights to suicide also fails. First, an account which restricts one's right to end one's life in cases in which doing so will have bad consequences for others may seem to oblige us to hold, in consistency, that one is obligated to end one's life in cases where the consequences would be good. Second, it leaves the hard work undone: it provides no settled account of what particular circumstances might override the right to suicide.[11] And third, it provides unequal treatment for individuals whose grounds for suicide may be the same but who differ in their surrounding circumstances or their relationships with others. Of two persons afflicted with an identical terminal illness, for instance, one might have a right to suicide and the other not, if one is free from family relationships and the other not, even though the pain and medical degradation—the reasons for the suicide—might be the same. And finally, although this is not fully distinct from the preceding objection, we see in appealing to cases that this way of construing rights to suicide really misses the mark: what is wrong with the suicide of the "Battlestar Galactica" youth is not just that his parents will be grieved; and what allows Elsie Somerset her right to end her life is not simply that no one around her cares.[12]

II

It may be tempting, at this point, to discard the notion that suicide is a matter of rights altogether, and to look for some alternative way of accounting for our sense that some suicide is permissible whereas other cases are not.[13] But I think this move is hasty. After all, persons have at least two sorts of rights:[14] not only liberty-rights of the sort we have described, but more basic, fundamental rights, to be accounted for in a wholly different way. I wish to claim, that the right to suicide is indeed a right, and a right of the fundamental sort.

These more basic rights, as distinct from the liberty-rights one has as a function of one's freedom to do as one chooses, we call natural rights, fundamental rights, or fundamental human rights. They are rights of the sort identified in the classical manifestos: the American Constitution and its Bill of Rights, the French Declaration of the Rights of Man, the Communist Manifesto, and the 1948 U.N. Declaration of Human Rights, among others. The rights listed, of course, vary from one manifesto to another, variously including rights to life, liberty, ownership of property; freedom of assembly, speech, and worship; rights to education, employment, political representation, and medical care. However, although the manifestos vary considerably in their contents, the conception underlying them is similar: they declare that certain universal, general, *fundamental* rights are held by individuals just in virtue of their being human.

I shall suggest, then, as a third strategy for achieving resolution of our conflicting intuitions regarding suicide, that it be construed as a *fundamental human right*. On this view, permissible suicide is not merely an exception to the general rules, nor is it mere exercise of one's liberty-right to harm oneself if one wishes. Rather, it is a fundamental human right, on a par with rights to life,[15] to liberty, to freedom of speech and worship, to education, political representation, and the pursuit of happiness. Although I do not have space here to give an account of the claims against others, both for noninterference and for assistance, which a fundamental right to suicide might generate, it is at least clear that if what had appeared to be a liberty-right to suicide turns out to be a *fundamental* right, the force of ordinary utilitarian arguments against it will collapse.

Of course, there will seem to be a good deal of evidence against this view. For one thing, the "Battlestar Galactica" case reminds us that we intuitively feel that there are cases in which persons have no right to kill themselves at all, let alone a fundamental right. Secondly, although listing in manifestos can not be taken as a reliable index of whether something is a fundamental right, it is nevertheless a conspicuous fact that a "right to suicide" is listed in none, even among manifestos of the most politically diverse sorts.[16] And finally, the fact that we have starkly differing intuitions about rights to suicide in different sorts of cases suggests that if rights of any sort are involved, they surely are not fundamental ones: if suicide were a fundamental right, we should expect all persons to have it, not just some.

Let us consider, however, the way in which fundamental rights are to be accounted for. I do not of course have space here in which to develop a full theory of rights, but I would like to sketch what I think is a correct account, and one which I shall take in this argument as a basic premise. *Individuals have fundamental rights to do certain sorts of things because doing those things tends to be constitutive of human dignity.*[17] ("Human dignity," though it is perhaps difficult to define, is a notion rooted in an ideal conception of human life, human community, and human excellence; I shall have more to say about the concept of human dignity in the course of this paper.) On this view, although we may take ourselves to have a variety of relatively superficial and easily overridden liberty-rights, we also understand ourselves to have more fundamental human rights because we conceive them to establish and promote human dignity. The right freely to associate with others we recognize as a fundamental right because we take free association with others to contribute to our dignity. Alcoholism, on the other hand, does not typically conduce to human dignity; hence, although it may still be a liberty-right, *viz.* when it does not harm other persons, it is not a fundamental right.

While this account of rights may at first seem to be an *ad hoc* device for resolving our conflicts about suicide, I think it may also help explain and resolve some of the more volatile disputes concerning other rights and show why there are no disputes concerning some. It is rarely disputed, for instance, that persons have a right to freedom, since it is very widely assumed that freedom contributes to human dignity. On the other hand, although Lockean liberals defend a fundamental right to private property, Marxists and others in the post-Rousseau tradition deny this right: what is really at issue, beneath this dispute about whether private property is a right, is whether the owning of property contributes to or detracts from human dignity, both for the owner and for others as well.

But although this account of rights succeeds not just for suicide but for fundamental rights in general, it is the particular case of the right to suicide that makes us notice the central way in which it differs from more conventional accounts. On this account, *because fundamental rights are rooted in human dignity, they are not equally distributed.* This claim may well seem initially counterintuitive and perhaps morally offensive as well; although we are of course accustomed to assume that liberty-rights are inequally distributed (since for different individuals different special obligations may override them), we insist that the distribution of fundamental rights is uniform: *all* persons have them, simply in virtue of their being human. But this notion that fundamental rights are equally distributed is an illusion (though I think a necessary and desirable one):[18] it reflects not the uniform nature of fundamental rights, but the fact that the things that they guarantee tend to be constitutive of human dignity equally for all persons. Thus, it appears to be analytic of the notion of fundamental human rights that they are equally distributed; it is precisely the case of suicide that shows us they are not. Some persons in some situations, we shall see, have a fundamental right to suicide; others do not. Of course, the right to suicide, if it is one, is not alone among fundamental rights in being unequally distributed (we recognize this by saying that fundamental rights are abridged or overridden by such circumstances as incompetence or grave public need);[19] it is merely more unequally distributed than most. It is this matter of unequal distribution, I think, that has disguised from us the fact that suicide is a fundamental right.

In practice, of course, there are obstacles to this account of rights. To hold that fundamental rights are not equally distributed can very well invite abuse. And to claim that one has fundamental rights only when the things they guarantee are constitutive of human dignity brings with it problems, much like those in the calculi of utilitarian theory, of ascertaining the characteristics and outcome of the exercise of a given right. Nor is human dignity any easier to quantify than happiness or utility. Nevertheless, I think we must attend to this alternative account of rights if we are to resolve the issue of suicide. The traditional account of rights will not permit us to see *why* there might be a right to suicide; to claim that we do, or do not, have a right to suicide only adds, along with Schopenhauer and Wittgenstein, to the array of unfounded assertions in this regard. What we need to see is that we have a right to suicide (if and when we do) *because* it is constitutive of human dignity, and that this basis is the same as that on which we have all other fundamental human rights. Even though it may be very markedly unequally distributed, the right to suicide is not an "exception" or a "special" right, or a right which is to be accounted for in some different way; it is of a piece with the other fundamental human rights we enjoy.

III

Not all suicide is constitutive of human dignity. If we consider the "Battlestar Galactica" *vs.* Elsie Somerset cases, this may seem quite clear. Surely we can imagine other acts on the part of the youth which would grant more dignity than his furtive leap from the bridge: the futures open to him were varied and numerous, including no doubt love, purposeful occupation, social contribution, and the attainment of ideals. The boy's death lacks utility, of course, in that it does not promote happiness or well-being in the agent or in others, but it also lacks that dignity which might redeem this fault. Elsie Somerset's suicide, on the other hand, seems to be quite a different case. If we consider the futures open to her, at age eighty, we see that they are different indeed from those of the "Battlestar" youth, and a good deal less numerous. An unfortunately realistic picture of old age suggests that she can expect increasing debility, dependence, financial limitation, loss of communication and affection, increasingly poor self-image, increasing depression, isolation, and, due to her glaucoma and cancer, blindness and pain. There are alternative possible futures, of course: one of

them is suicide. Another is that which she no doubt wants: a continuing, pain-free, socially involved, productive, affectionate life. But, given her physical condition and the social conditions of the society in which she lives, this is no longer possible, and so her options are reduced to only two: suicide, or the catalogue of horrors just described. Suicide, then, may be constitutive of human dignity in at least a negative sense; in Elsie Somerset's case it leaves one less example of human degradation in the world.[20]

This kind of observation invites us to establish a procedure for sorting suicide cases into those in which the act surely cannot be constitutive of human dignity (the "Battlestar Galactica" case), and those in which it is (Elsie Somerset)—the category of those who have no right to suicide (or only an overrideable liberty-right),[21] and the category of those whose right is fundamental; this would supply the basis for various practical social policies with respect to such activities as suicide prevention, psychiatric treatment, involuntary commitment, and the like. It may seem intuitively obvious that the first of these categories will include unhappy youths, star-crossed lovers, persons suffering from financial setbacks or bereavement or temporary depression; while the second category will include the so-called rational suicides: those who are painfully terminally ill or suffer from severe disabilities, incurable diseases, other intolerable medical conditions, or who have other good grounds for suicide. But it is just this sort of intuitive classification of suicides that is most dangerous and is the reason we need to be clear about the basis of any alleged right to suicide. To see this, we must examine the notion of dignity.

In one, originally Kantian, sense, all human beings have dignity, or what we might describe as intrinsic human worth. Dignity in this sense is an ideal, a construct which points to ends to be achieved; we might equate dignity with "worthiness of respect." But there is a second, empirical sense of dignity as well, which corrupt or abused persons may not have. In this second sense, we can distinguish observed characteristics of individuals as involving dignity from those which do not.[22] Just as we can observe whether a person is being treated with respect or "as a person"—that is, with dignity—in such situations as the classroom, in commercial relations, or in a bureaucracy, we can distinguish characteristics of the individual himself or herself which show that he or she achieves dignity as a human being. For instance, we can distinguish between the person who bears pain with dignity and the person who, in fright or panic, does not.[23] The ghastly lessons of the Nazi camps provide examples of human beings who suffered unbelievable mistreatment with dignity: and those—the so-called Muselmänner—who did not.

Working from a large range of observed phenomena, we can then begin to formulate the components of dignity;[24] they are probably jointly sufficient for the application of this term, though they do not all seem to be necessary. These characteristics include, to begin with, autonomy vis à vis external events, self-determination, and responsibility for one's acts.[25] Dignity also includes self-awareness and cognizance of one's condition and acts, together with their probable consequences. Dignity usually involves rationality, though this may not always be the case. It can also be said to involve expressiveness, or rather self-expressiveness, an assertion of oneself in the world. It surely also involves self-acceptance and self-respect: an affirmation of who and what one is. We can also suggest what tends to undermine dignity: anonymity, for instance, as in an impersonal institution; alienation of labor, crowding, meaningless and repetitive jobs, segregation, and torture.[26]

But dignity, for all its apparent initial similarity to happiness or other utilitarian desiderata, differs from these conditions of the individual in a crucially important way. Dignity is not simply a characteristic of the individual but a characteristic of the individual in relation to his world. This is what in part makes it so difficult to define. And yet I think we can isolate its most important characteristic: one cannot promote one's own *dignity* by destroying the dignity of someone else, though one can certainly promote one's own interests, happiness, or reputation at another's expense. My happiness may cost your happiness, and that may be a price I am nevertheless willing to force you to pay; despite this morally repugnant choice, I may still achieve happiness. But if I try to elevate my dignity by robbing you of yours, I lose my own as well—even though I may nevertheless gain happiness, satisfaction of my interests, and other utilitarian benefits. Thus the concept of dignity is not wholly empirical, but contains ideal features as well.

To destroy your dignity, of course, is not just to graze your ego or to hurt your feelings, and it is even possible, as the Nazi camps have shown, that I may seriously damage your interests or even kill you without destroying the dignity you have. But where an act of mine would tend to destroy your capacities for such things as autonomy, self-awareness, rationality, self-expressiveness, and self-respect, then we will begin to want to say that I lose my own dignity in doing such an act to you. Dignity, although it is a characteristic inhering primarily in the individual and is not simply a relational property, contains essential reference to the dignity of others where others are involved; no act which undermines the dignity of others can be an act constitutive of one's own human dignity, whatever utility it may produce, for it thus violates that ideal conception of human *community* in which the notion of dignity is in part rooted. Furthermore, although dignity contains essential reference to the dignity of others wherever others are involved, an act may also be an act of dignity even if it affects oneself alone—provided that it honors that ideal conception of human *excellence* in which the notion of dignity is also based.

Thus there can be no dignity tradeoffs, like the interests or happiness tradeoffs which plague utilitarian calculations; the problem of sacrificing the dignity of some for the dignity of others cannot arise. It is in this sense that dignity is both an empirical and an ideal notion, and it may be that the actual acts which contribute to dignity are in fact very few. Nevertheless, I do think it is a conception of dignity of this sort that lies at the basis of our ascriptions of fundamental rights.

But can *suicide* satisfy both the empirical and ideal criteria for dignity, and so be an act to which one has a fundamental right? And does the distinction between apparently irrational suicides and those for which one has good cause reflect that between dignity-constitutive suicides and those which are not?

IV

There are many different kinds of suicide, both in terms of the individual's interior states and the act's effects on others involved, yet they can be divided into two principal groups. On the one hand are the "violent" suicides: desperate, aggressive acts, which display both contempt and hatred for oneself and for others as well. Most common among these perhaps are the "get-even" suicides, which show a desire for revenge upon one's enemies or erstwhile loved ones and often a despising of the world as a whole. Animosity, ambivalence, and agitation are the symptoms here.

Others, in contrast, are "nonviolent": of these, some may be described as involving cessation or surcease rather than obliteration or annihilation, often anticipated and planned in a resigned but purposeful way; others, not always distinct from the surcease suicides, are sacrificial in character and focus centrally on the benefits to some other person or cause. The nonviolent suicides are nonviolent both toward oneself and toward others, at least in the clearest cases; they do not seek to punish oneself or to injure or retaliate against others. Very often these nonviolent suicides contain a component of what we might,

paradoxically perhaps, call self-preservation, a kind of self-respect: "I am what I have been," they sometimes seem to say, "but cannot be anymore." They are based, as it were, on a self-ideal: a conception of one's own value and worth, beneath which one is not willing to slip. Whether the threat to one's self-ideal is from physical illness and pain, as in euthanatic suicide, or from the destruction of other persons or values upon which one's life is centrally focused, as in self-sacrificial suicide, the import is the same: one chooses death instead of further life, because further life would bring with it a compromise of that dignity without which one cannot consent to live.

This distinction between violent, self-aggressive and nonviolent, self-respecting suicides is an intuitive distinction only; it is a distinction not much recognized in clinical practice, though perhaps only because psychiatric clinicians are very much less likely to confront cases of the self-respecting, nonviolent type.[27] It is important to be clear, in addition, that this distinction is not based on the means involved: some deaths by gunshot or jumping are of the nonviolent kind, whereas some deaths by tranquilizers or gas or even refusal to eat are of the violent sort, involving extreme self-aggression and aggression toward others. Nevertheless, it is possible to characterize generally the kinds of suicide that are common among certain groups and in certain kinds of situations. Violence toward oneself and others characterizes a good deal of youthful suicide, even that associated with depression; it is also found among the old. But nonviolent, surcease suicide is much more common in disability and terminal-illness cases, and particularly among the old. Self-death or self-directed death in these latter conditions, of course, we often term voluntary euthanasia or sometimes euthanatic suicide; we frequently attempt to distinguish them both morally and legally from "irrational" suicide in nonterminal conditions, that is, suicide for which one does not have good reason.

In distinguishing between irrational suicide and euthanatic suicide, we do recognize that there are important differences between suicide which precludes indefinitely continuing life and suicide in preference to inevitable death by another more painful or degrading means. But this distinction does *not* precisely coincide with the distinction between those kinds of suicide to which an individual has only liberty-rights or no right at all, and those kinds of suicide to which the individual has a fundamental human right, one which cannot be overridden by any particular obligations or claims. This is because some cases of noneuthanatic suicide may be constitutive of human dignity—Cato's death is a case in point—whereas some genuine euthanasia cases may not be acts of human dignity but acts of cowardice and fear—hasty, terrified measures which preclude any final human dignity rather than contribute to it. Some writers opposed to suicide in general would have us believe that all euthanatic suicides are of this latter sort—acts of cowardice and fear; I think this is false, but I think it is equally wrong to assume that all suicide in the face of terminal illness is a rational, composed, self-dignifying affirmation of one's own highest life-ideal.

It may be that as a practical matter the nearest workable policy is acceptance of the notion of rational suicide, and the devising of selective suicide-prevention and psychiatric-treatment measures to discourage suicide of the irrational sort. If this is the only really practical policy for selectively permitting suicides of fundamental right and prohibiting those which are not,[28] I think on moral grounds we ought to adopt it, in preference either to maintaining the traditional universal suicide prohibitions or adopting indiscriminately permissive policies. We should bear in mind, however, that the rational/irrational distinction does not quite mirror the difference we want.

Now we see why our temptation to classify suicides into dignity-constitutive and non-dignity-constituitive cases on the basis of external characteristics is such a dangerous one, particularly if such a classification is to become the basis for various practical policies: the circumstances under which it occurs do not determine the character of the act. There can be suicides of dignity in conditions of depair; there can be suicides without dignity when the circumstances are such that the individual might have every reason to die.

In his paper "Suicide as Instrument and Expression," David Wood invents a case: the suicide (by jumping) of an architect who pioneered high-rise apartment buildings and realizes too late what he has done. Is this a suicide of dignity, and so one to which he has a fundamental right, or is it a suicide of the violent, non-dignity-promoting sort, one to which he does not have such a right? We can imagine the case either way: as the final, desperate act of self-loathing and self-contempt, occurring as the confused climax of long years of self-reproach; but we can also imagine it as a considered, courageous statement of principle, a dignified final act transcending one's own defeat. If it is a violent suicide of loathing, we can imagine reminding the man that he has obligations to his family, his friends, his gods, and himself, that is, we can imagine treating it as a liberty-right, quickly to be overridden by the claims of others. But if it is a genuine suicide of dignity it is difficult to know what objection we could make, since we must only admire his attainment of a difficult human ideal. That the price of this attainment is high—very high—is perhaps lamentable, but it is not grounds for interfering with his exercise of the right.

V

What of Schopenhauer and Wittgenstein, and the disparate philosophical views with which we began? Perhaps now we can venture some explanation, which, though it is conjectural, may also explain the apparent inconsistency in our own precritical views. When Wittgenstein claims that suicide is "the elementary sin," he is perhaps conceiving (no doubt in an auto-biographical way) of cases in which the act is an act of self-annihilation and the annihilation of one's social world; it is the ultimate act of disrespect and violence. When Schopenhauer, on the other hand, says that man has no "more unassailable title than to his own life and person," it may be that he is drawing upon a notion of suicide as the act of ultimate dignity: the final act of self-determination and self-affirmation in an immoral, unyielding world. In this way both views are correct, and not after all incompatible: individuals in the cases Wittgenstein has in mind have no right, or at most only an overrideable liberty-right, to kill themselves, while individuals in the cases Schopenhauer sees have a basic, nonoverrideable, fundamental human right to end their lives. The only real mistake Schopenhauer and Wittgenstein make is this: they assume that the "right to suicide" is a uniform right, which all individuals either have or do not.

Notes

1. Arthur Schopenhauer, "On Suicide," from *Studies in Pessimism,* in *Complete Essays of Schopenhauer,* trans. T. Bailey Saunders (New York: Wiley Book Co., 1940). Although Schopenhauer grants that man has a right to suicide, he holds that suicide is a moral and metaphysical error, since it results not from an ascetic cessation of the will, but from frustration of it.

2. Ludwig Wittgenstein, *Notebooks 1914–1916,* ed. G. H. von Wright and G. E. M. Anscombe (Oxford: Basil Blackwell, 1961), p. 91e. Wittgenstein continues, however, in this final entry of the notebooks:

> And when one investigates it [suicide], it is like investigating mercury vapour in order to comprehend the nature of vapours. Or is even suicide in itself neither good nor evil?

3. Adapted from Edward M. Brecher, "Opting for Suicide," *The New York Times Magazine,* March 18, l979, quoting from the October 1978 issue of *Hospital Physician.*

4. *Minneapolis Star and Tribune,* Saturday, August 25, 1979, p. 1A.

5. One may be said to have a right to *x,* or a right to do *x:* that to which a person may have a right can be an object, a condition, a state of affairs, or an action. Construing suicide as an action, I shall speak throughout only of the right to (commit ["do"]) suicide, rather than, say the right to the object or condition (death) which suicide brings about.

6. Aristotle, *Nicomachean Ethics* 1138a.

7. Plato, *Phaedo* 6IC–62E; Augustine, *City of God,* Book I Chapters 17–27.

8. Kant, *Lectures on Ethics,* tr. Louis Infield (New York: Harper Torchbooks, 1963), "Suicide," pp. 148–54.

9. Mill, *On Liberty.* It is interesting that Mill does not discuss suicide directly, although it might seem the most crucial case for the application of his views. In *On Liberty* he argues that one may not sell oneself into slavery because this would fail to preserve one's liberty; one might infer from this that Mill would also repudiate suicide on the same grounds. However, one might argue that since after suicide the individual does not exist in an unfree state (but, rather, does not exist at all), Mill provides no basis for an objection to this practice.

10. There is a large sociological and psychological literature on the effects of suicide on those persons surrounding the individual. See e.g., Albert C. Cain, ed , *Survivors of Suicide* (Springfield, Ill.: Charles C. Thomas, 1972).

11. This is not of course a theoretical objection to the liberty-rights' account of suicide, but it does point out that without further elaboration the account is not a particularly helpful or informative one.

12. Paul-Louis Landsberg, in *The Moral Problem of Suicide,* trans. Cynthia Rowland (New York: Philosophical Library, 1953), p. 84, puts the point in this way:

> It is purely and simply antipersonalist to try to decide such an intimately personal question as to whether or not I have the right to kill myself by reference to society. Suppose I die a little sooner or a little later, what has that to do with society, to which, in any case, I belong for so short a space?

13. See e.g., James Bogen, "Suicide and Virtue," p. 286, who claims that an adequate treatment of the morality of suicide cannot be made in terms of obligations, rights, and duties.

14. In addition to liberty-rights and fundamental rights, we also recognize legal rights. Given, however, the very uneven situation of the law with regard to suicide (see in this connection the papers of Alan Sullivan and Leslie Francis, pp. 229 and 254), I have restricted the scope of this paper to moral rights alone.

15. Note that a fundamental right to suicide does not preclude an equally fundamental right to life, since both may be constitutive of human dignity. This is so even in euthanasia cases: there may be dignity in an individual's struggling against the inevitable oncoming of decay, medical degradation, and pain; there may equally well be dignity in his choosing to avoid these by ending his life. In general, one may have fundamental rights to various incompatible actions, as for instance one may have fundamental rights to own private property or to join a communal economic group when either course of action is the kind which can be constitutive of human dignity. Thus, rights are not to be conflated with duties.

16. One might mention "the right to die" now being championed by various patients'-rights groups: this, however, is usually understood as the right to freedom from unwanted medical treatment, or a "right to passive euthanasia." The scope of a "right to suicide" would be considerably broader.

17. This account appears to resemble in some respects that put forward by William T. Blackstone in "Human Rights and Human Dignity," *The Philosophy Forum* 9, Nos. 1/2 (March 1971), and perhaps even the counterthesis in the same volume, Herbert Spiegelberg's "Human Dignity: A Challenge to Contemporary Philosophy." It also resembles one component of the account Arnold S. Kaufman defends in "A Sketch of a Liberal Theory of Fundamental Human Rights," *The Monist* 52 (No. 4), though for Kaufman fundamental human rights may be justified either on the basis of dignity or on the basis of maximum utility together with equality. Also relevant in connection with this issue is Michael S. Pritchard's "Human Dignity and Justice," *Ethics* 82 (No. 4, July 1972).

18. The fiction that fundamental rights are universally distributed is both necessary and desirable for the following reasons. The present account of rights (although I believe it to be correct) is hopelessly particularist, in that it holds that an individual has a fundamental right to do just that sort of act, or just that act, which is conducive to human dignity. But it is extremely difficult to predict whether an act of a given kind will in fact contribute to human dignity, and so be an act of the kind to which that individual has a fundamental right. This may vary from one individual

to the next, or change for a given individual over a period of time. Furthermore, despite certain empirical earmarks of dignity, it is in principle impossible to diagnose with full reliability whether a given individual does or does not achieve complete human dignity. The best we can say is that *on the whole*, certain types of actions or things—e.g., free assembly, free speech, freedom from the quartering of soldiers in one's house, etc.—tend to be constitutive of human dignity, whether or not we can in fact make a reliable, confirmable assessment in any given case. Thus we are forced to assume that fundamental rights are universally or at least very widely distributed; this is the "necessary" feature. But once we have made this assumption, we must then produce justification for any abridgment of those (alleged) fundamental rights; this is the "desirable" part. Because we allow ourselves to assume the right to free assembly, for instance, is a fundamental right, shared by all human beings, we thus compel ourselves to justify any abridgment of that right. Hence protection of these rights is made much more likely. If we were to recognize and honor an individual's fundamental right to, say, free assembly only in cases in which we could establish that the exercise of free assembly would conduce to the dignity of that individual, we would risk abridgments of this right in very, very many cases.

Whether such a fiction is either necessary or desirable in the case of suicide, however, is quite a different question. It is I think intuitively clear that not all persons in all circumstances have a right to suicide, though some persons in some circumstances may: we are not forced to assume that, *on the whole*, suicide is constitutive of human dignity, because we clearly see that it does not. Nor is it clearly desirable to adopt a fiction which, in practice, would place the burden of justification on those who would interfere with a suicide rather than on those who plan suicide for whatever reason.

19. Conventional theories of rights hold that fundamental rights are overridden in circumstances such as incompetence (e.g., the right of a severely retarded person to freedom of travel may be abridged) or requirements of community interest (the felon's right to freedom of travel may also be abridged); on the present account, fundamental rights are never overridden, but in cases such as these simply do not apply. It is silly to insist that the seriously retarded individual has a "fundamental right to freedom of travel" when travel (at least without assistance) can mean nothing but helpless wandering in an unfriendly world, or that the recidivist felon has a right to freedom of his person when exercise of that right conduces to anything but human dignity. Since this is so, nonvoluntary in-

stitutionalization of such persons does not genuinely represent an abridgment of their fundamental rights, though institutionalization in a cruel environment, or without facilities for special education, etc., might do so.

20. Human degradation in the empirical sense, of course. The dual concept of human dignity suggests that all human beings continue to have dignity in the ideal sense, that is, all human beings remain worthy of respect, regardless of how degrading the conditions and circumstances in which they are forced to live.

21. We cannot attempt here to resolve the issue of whether suicide, in cases in which it does not conduce to dignity and hence is not a fundamental right, is nevertheless a liberty-right, or is, rather, no right at all. If it were a liberty-right, it would of course be subject to overriding on the basis of a variety of considerations. If it is a fundamental right, it is a liberty-right and should be a legal right as well.

22. This dual account of the concept of human dignity is developed in several of the papers mentioned in note 17.

23. See Abraham Edel, "Humanist Ethics and the Meaning of Human Dignity," *Moral Problems in Contemporary Society: Essays in Humanistic Ethics,* ed.

Paul Kurtz (Englewood Cliffs, N.J.: Prentice-Hall, 1969), p. 234.

24. This is done here, of course, only in a somewhat a priori and very tentative way. But it is the sort of task we might wish philosophers will do.

25. This is the concept of dignity used by B. F. Skinner in *Beyond Freedom and Dignity,* especially in Chapter 3, and also the second sense of dignity for Marvin Kohl, "Voluntary Beneficent Euthanasia," in Kohl, ed., *Beneficent Euthanasia* (Buffalo: Prometheus Books, 1975), p. 133.

26. The list is Spiegelberg's, "Human Dignity," p. 60.

27. Surcease suicide in terminal illness is almost never reported as suicide, and is not recorded in that way by the coroner or by insurance companies. It is believed, however, that the practice of surcease suicide in terminal illness, often with the assistance of the physician in providing lethal drugs, is fairly common.

28. Criminal prohibitions, of course, would be most plausibly directed against suicides exhibiting violence against others.

Study Questions

1. What is a human right, according to Battin?
2. How does the notion of human dignity function in Battin's arguments? How does it affect whether one has a moral right to commit suicide?

For Further Reading

Alvarez, A. *The Savage God. A Study of Suicide.* New York: Random House, 1973.
Battin, Margaret Pabst, and David J. Mayo, eds. *Suicide: The Philosophical Issues.* New York: St. Martin's Press, 1980. A set of contemporary essays.
Donnelly, John, ed. *Suicide.* Buffalo, N.Y.: Prometheus Books, 1980.
Perlin, Seymour, ed. *A Handbook for the Study of Suicide.* Oxford: Oxford University Press, 1975. A helpful series of articles.
Wallace, Samuel, and Albin Eser. *Suicide and Euthanasia.* Knoxville: University of Tennessee Press, 1981.

Part V

Euthanasia

Introduction

The intentional termination of the life of one human being by another—mercy killing—is contrary to that for which the medical profession stands and is contrary to the policy of the American Medical Association.

The cessation of the employment of extraordinary means to prolong the life of the body when there is irrefutable evidence that biological death is imminent is the decision of the patient and/or his immediate family. The advice and judgment of the physician should be freely available to the patient and/or his immediate family.

(American Medical Association policy statement on voluntary euthanasia)

On April 14, 1975, Karen Ann Quinlan, a twenty-one-year-old woman, lapsed into a coma from which she never emerged. Thus began the most famous case in the history of American medical ethics. The combination of Valium, aspirin, and three gin and tonics at a party may have deprived her brain of oxygen, causing extensive damage and a state of persistent vegetation, which lasted ten years; meanwhile, the family, the hospital, and the courts angrily fought over her body. The national media caught every breath and blow in the action.

After months of watching their adopted daughter's body curled up in a fetal position and maintained by life supports, Joseph and Julia Quinlan despaired of hope, and with the approval of their priest they asked the physicians at St. Clare's Hospital in Danville, New Jersey, to disconnect the ventilator. They were told that since Karen was twenty-one, they needed a court order appointing Mr. Quinlan as Karen's legal guardian before the ventilator could be switched off. Karen was not brain dead under New Jersey law. There was some electroencephalogram activity, though neurologists agreed that her comatose condition was irreversible. Meanwhile, Medicare was paying the medical costs of $450 per day.

The case was brought to court, and the Quinlans lost. The presiding judge stated that the family's anguish over their comatose daughter was clouding their judgment.[1]

In Rome, a Vatican theologian, Gino Concetti, condemned the act of removing Karen from life support. "A right to death does not exist. Love for life, even a life reduced to a ruin, drives one to protect life with every possible care."[2]

The case was appealed, and on January 26, 1976, the New Jersey Supreme Court overruled Judge Muir. It set aside all criminal liability in removing Karen from a respirator. The respirator was detached, and she was taken to the Morris View Nursing Home, where for nine years she lay in a comatose state on a waterbed, being artificially fed via a feeding tube. On June 11, 1985, Karen died.

The *New York Times* has reported that presently over 10,000 people in the nation are in the condition in which Karen had been. The most notable of these is Nancy Cruzan. In July, 1990, the United States Supreme Court decided that unless there is a prior, clear proof of intent, the matter of allowing patients in a persistent vegetative state to die should be left up to individual states.[3]

The term *euthanasia* comes from the Greek and means "good death." *Webster's Dictionary* defines it as "a quiet and easy death" or "the action of inducing a quiet and easy death." Euthanasia can refer to inducing death either *passively* or *actively*—that is, either by withdrawing treatment or actively putting to death. It can also be divided into two types of patient intentions, where the patient has given consent and where the patient is not able to do so—that is, *voluntarily* and *involuntarily* (or *nonvoluntarily*). If we take these categories and combine them, we end up with four distinct types of euthanasia:

	Voluntary	*Involuntary*
Passive	Refusal of treatment No extraodinary means or 　heroic treatment	Withdrawing of treatment primarily of 　defective neonates, incompetent 　patients, and those in a persistant 　vegetative state
	Induce death with consent	Induce without consent
Active	Mercy killing (allocide) of hopeless 　cases with pain	Mercy killing of incompetent patients 　or deformed neonates

Active euthanasia is illegal throughout the United States, though under considerable debate. Passive euthanasia has long been practiced. Its application under modern conditions is accepted in some contexts, such as withdrawing life support from the terminally ill, and under debate in other conditions, such as allowing newborns to starve to death when a decision has been made not to operate on Down's syndrome babies who have intestinal obstructions.

The official American Medical Association (AMA) position, quoted at the beginning of this section, condemns active euthanasia but permits passive euthanasia, especially the withholding of extraordinary means of support or heroic measures from the patient.

Cases of voluntary passive euthanasia happen every day. When a doctor respects the wishes of a Jehovah's Witness or Christian Science patient and refrains from giving the believer a lifesaving blood transfusion, the doctor is practicing passive voluntary euthanasia. When the doctor withdraws a life-support machine from a patient in a persistent vegetative state or from a seriously defective neonate or refuses to use extraordinary means to save these patients' lives, he or she is practicing involuntary passive euthanasia. In the case of the permanently comatose patients, like Karen Ann Quinlan and Nancy Cruzan, lawyers and doctors argued whether it was right to practice passive involuntary euthanasia and withdraw the life-support system.

Cases of voluntary active euthanasia are at the center of the debate. The celebrated journalist Stewart Alsop relates an incident that took place while he was a patient in the cancer ward of the National Institutes of Health in Bethesda, Maryland. His roommate was a twenty-eight-year-old man he called Jack. Jack had a malignant tumor in his stomach about the size of a softball, which had metastasized and was beyond control. Jack was in constant pain. His physicians prescribed an intravenous shot of a synthetic opiate every four hours, but it was impossible to control the pain that long. After a few hours Jack would begin to moan or whimper, "then he would begin to howl like a dog." A nurse would come and administer codeine, but it did little good.

"The third night of this routine," Alsop writes, "the terrible thought occurred to me, 'If Jack were a dog . . . what would be done with him?' The answer was obvious: the pound and chloroform. No human being with a spark of pity could let a living thing suffer so, to no good end."[4]

Alsop's experience with Jack raises important questions. Should the terminally ill be given the option of choosing to be put to death? Do patients have a right to die if they so choose? What would be the consequences of making voluntary euthanasia legal?

In our first reading, Yale Kamisar argues that, although moral grounds may exist in favor of permitting voluntary euthanasia for some individuals, to legalize euthanasia would be disastrous. He sets forth several considerations—some of them, utilitarian reasons—to make his case. In our second reading, Glanville Williams responds to Kamisar and argues that none of his conclusions are warranted by the facts. The principles of avoiding cruelty and respecting one's liberty override any utilitarian reasons against legalizing voluntary euthanasia. Next, James Rachels takes issue with the stance of the AMA that permits passive euthanasia but forbids active euthanasia. Rachels argues that this distinction is bankrupt. In our fourth reading, Thomas Sullivan takes issue with Rachels, arguing that the original distinction is founded on the difference between intending some evil and merely foreseeing that it will occur as a by-product of a morally acceptable act.

Notes

1. Gregory Pence, *Classic Cases in Medical Ethics* (New York: McGraw-Hill, 1990), p. 11.
2. Quoted in ibid., p. 13.
3. *New York Times* (June 26, 1990).
4. Stewart Alsop, "The Right to Die with Dignity," *Good Housekeeping* (August 1974).

CHAPTER 23

Against Legalizing Euthanasia

YALE KAMISAR

Born in 1929, Yale Kamisar is professor of law at the University of Michigan. He has served on several national commissions and has coauthored such books as *Criminal Justice in Our Time* (1965) and *Constitutional Law: Cases, Comments and Questions* (1980).

In this debate with Glanville Williams, Kamisar argues against the legalization of voluntary euthanasia. He agrees that, although a moral case can be made for euthanasia in the abstract, there are overriding reasons against legalizing the practice. Four arguments against the legalization of euthanasia are set forth: (1) Ascertaining whether consent is voluntary is difficult; (2) there is a risk of an incorrect diagnosis; (3) there is a risk of killing a patient for whom a cure may be found; and (4) accepting voluntary euthanasia may lead to the acceptance of involuntary euthanasia; this is known as the wedge argument.

A BOOK BY GLANVILLE WILLIAMS, *The Sanctity of Life and the Criminal Law*,[1] once again brought to the fore the controversial topic of euthanasia, more popularly known as 'mercy-killing'. In keeping with the trend of the euthanasia movement over the past generation, Williams concentrates his efforts for reform on the *voluntary* type of euthanasia, for example the cancer victim begging for death, as opposed to the *involuntary* variety—that is, the case of the congenital idiot, the permanently insane or the senile. . . .

The existing law on euthanasia is hardly perfect. But if it is not too good, neither, as I have suggested, is it much worse than the rest of the criminal law. At any rate, the imperfections of existing law are not cured by Williams's proposal. Indeed, I believe adoption of his views would add more difficulties than it would remove.

Williams strongly suggests that 'euthanasia can be condemned only according to a religious opinion.' He tends to view the opposing camps as Roman Catholics versus Liberals. Although this has a certain initial appeal to me, a non-Catholic and self-styled liberal, I deny that this is the only way the battle lines can, or should, be drawn. I leave the religious arguments to the theologians. I share the view that 'those who hold the faith may follow its precepts without requiring those who do not hold it to act as if they did'. But I do find substantial utilitarian obstacles on the high road to euthanasia. I am not enamoured of the *status quo* on mercy-killing. But while I am not prepared to defend it against all comers, I am prepared to defend it against the proposals for change which have come forth to date.

As an ultimate philosophical proposition, the case for voluntary euthanasia is strong. What-

Reprinted from the Minnesota Law Review *42: 6 (May 1958) by permission. Edited.*

ever may be said for and against suicide generally, the appeal of death is immeasurably greater when it is sought not for a poor reason or just any reason, but for 'good cause', so to speak; when it is invoked not on behalf of a 'socially useful' person, but on behalf of, for example, the pain-racked 'hopelessly incurable' cancer victim. *If* a person is *in* fact (1) presently incurable, (2) beyond the aid of any respite which may come along in his life expectancy, suffering (3) intolerable and (4) unmitigable pain and of a (5) fixed and (6) rational desire to die, I would hate to have to argue that the hand of death should be stayed. But abstract propositions and carefully formed hypotheticals are one thing; specific proposals designed to cover everyday situations are something else again.

In essence, Williams's specific proposal is that death be authorized for a person in the above situation 'by giving the medical practitioner a wide discretion and trusting to his good sense'. This, I submit, raises too great a risk of abuse and mistake to warrant a change in the existing law. That a proposal entails risk of mistake is hardly a conclusive reason against it. But neither is it irrelevant. Under any euthanasia programme the consequences of mistake, of course, are always fatal. As I shall endeavour to show, the incidence of mistake of one kind or another is likely to be quite appreciable. If this indeed be the case, unless the need for the authorized conduct is compelling enough to override it, I take it the risk of mistake *is* a conclusive reason against such authorization. I submit, too, that the possible radiations from the proposed legislation—for example, involuntary euthanasia of idiots and imbeciles (the typical 'mercy-killings' reported by the press)—and the emergence of the legal precedent that there are lives not 'worth living', give additional cause for reflection.

I see the issue, then, as the need for voluntary euthanasia versus (1) the incidence of mistake and abuse; and (2) the danger that legal machinery initially designed to kill those who are a nuisance to themselves may some day engulf those who are a nuisance to others. . . .

The 'Choice'

Under current proposals to establish legal machinery, elaborate or otherwise, for the administration of a quick and easy death, it is not enough that those authorized to pass on the question decide that the patient, in effect, is 'better off dead'. The patient must concur in this opinion. Much of the appeal in the current proposal lies in this so-called 'voluntary' attribute.

But is the adult patient really in a position to concur? Is he truly able to make euthanasia a 'voluntary' act? There is a good deal to be said, is there not, for Dr. Frohman's pithy comment that the 'voluntary' plan is supposed to be carried out 'only if the victim is both sane and crazed by pain'.[2]

By hypothesis, voluntary euthanasia is not to be resorted to until narcotics have long since been administered and the patient has developed a tolerance to them. *When*, then, does the patient make the choice? While heavily drugged? Or is narcotic relief to be withdrawn for the time of decision? But if heavy dosage no longer deadens pain, indeed, no longer makes it bearable, how overwhelming is it when whatever relief narcotics offer is taken away too?

'Hypersensitivity to pain after analgesia has worn off is nearly always noted'. Moreover, 'the mental side-effects of narcotics, unfortunately for anyone wishing to suspend them temporarily without unduly tormenting the patient, appear to outlast the analgesic effect' and 'by many hours'.[3] The situation is further complicated by the fact that 'a person in terminal stages of cancer who had been given morphine steadily for a matter of weeks would certainly be dependent upon it physically and would

[handwritten margin note: when do you make the choice?]

probably be addicted to it and react with the addict's response'.[4]

The narcotics problem aside, Dr. Benjamin Miller, who probably has personally experienced more pain than any other commentator on the euthanasia scene, observes:

> Anyone who has been severely ill knows how distorted his judgment became during the worst moments of the illness. Pain and the toxic effect of disease, or the violent reaction to certain surgical procedures may change our capacity for rational and courageous thought.[5]

Undoubtedly, some euthanasia candidates will have their lucid moments. How they are to be distinguished from fellow-sufferers who do not, or how these instances are to be distinguished from others when the patient is exercising an irrational judgment, is not an easy matter. Particularly is this so under Williams's proposal, where no specially qualified persons, psychiatrically trained or otherwise, are to assist in the process.

Assuming, for purposes of argument, that the occasion when a euthanasia candidate possesses a sufficiently clear mind can be ascertained and that a request for euthanasia is then made, there remain other problems. The mind of the pain-racked may occasionally be clear, but is it not also likely to be uncertain and variable? This point was pressed hard by the great physician, Lord Horder, in the House of Lords debates:

> During the morning depression he [the patient] will be found to favour the application under this Bill, later in the day he will think quite differently, or will have forgotten all about it. The mental clarity with which noble Lords who present this Bill are able to think and to speak must not be thought to have any counterpart in the alternating moods and confused judgments of the sick man.[6]

The concept of 'voluntary' in voluntary euthanasia would have a great deal more substance to it if, as is the case with voluntary admission statutes for the mentally ill, the patient retained the right to reverse the process within a specified number of days after he gives written notice of his desire to do so—but unfortunately this cannot be. The choice here, of course, is an irrevocable one.

The likelihood of confusion, distortion or vacillation would appear to be serious drawbacks to any voluntary plan. Moreover, Williams's proposal is particularly vulnerable in this regard, since as he admits, by eliminating the fairly elaborate procedure of the American and British Societies' plans, he also eliminates a time period which would furnish substantial evidence of the patient's settled intention to avail himself of euthanasia. . . .

Professor Williams states that where a pre-pain desire for 'ultimate euthanasia' is 'reaffirmed' under pain, 'there is the best possible proof of full consent'. Perhaps. But what if it is alternately renounced and reaffirmed under pain? What if it is neither affirmed or renounced? What if it is only renounced? Will a physician be free to go ahead on the ground that the prior desire was 'rational', but the present desire 'irrational'? Under Williams's plan, will not the physician frequently 'be walking in the margin of the law'—just as he is now? Do we really accomplish much more under this proposal than to put the euthanasia principle on the books?

Even if the patient's choice could be said to be 'clear and incontrovertible', do not other difficulties remain? Is this the kind of choice, assuming that it can be made in a fixed and rational manner, that we want to offer a gravely ill person? Will we not sweep up, in the process, some who are not really tired of life, but think others are tired of them; some who do not really want to die, but who feel they should not live on, because to do so when there looms the legal alternative of euthanasia is to do a selfish or a cowardly act? Will not some feel an obligation to have themselves 'eliminated' in order that funds allocated for their terminal care might be better used by their families or, financial worries aside, in order to relieve their families of the emotional strain involved?

It would not be surprising for the gravely ill person to seek to inquire of those close to him whether he should avail himself of the legal alternative of euthanasia. Certainly, he is likely to wonder about their attitude in the matter. It is quite possible, is it not, that he will not exactly be gratified by any inclination on their part—however noble their motives may be in fact—that he resort to the new procedure? At this stage, the patient-family relationship may well be a good deal less than it ought to be.

And what of the relatives? If their views will not always influence the patient, will they not at least influence the attending physician? Will a physician assume the risks to his reputation, if not his pocketbook, by administering the *coup de grâce* over the objection—however irrational—of a close relative. Do not the relatives, then, also have a 'choice'? Is not the decision on their part to do nothing and say nothing *itself* a 'choice'? In many families there will be some, will there not, who will consider a stand against euthanasia the only proof of love, devotion and gratitude for past events? What of the stress and strife if close relatives differ over the desirability of euthanatizing the patient?

At such a time, members of the family are not likely to be in the best state of mind, either, to make this kind of decision. Financial stress and conscious or unconscious competition for the family's estate aside,

> The chronic illness and persistent pain in terminal carcinoma may place strong and excessive stresses upon the family's emotional ties with the patient. The family members who have strong emotional attachment to start with are most likely to take the patient's fears, pains and fate personally. Panic often strikes them. Whatever guilt feelings they may have toward the patient emerge to plague them.
>
> If the patient is maintained at home, many frustrations and physical demands may be im-

posed on the family by the advanced illness. There may develop extreme weakness, incontinence and bad odors. The pressure of caring for the individual under these circumstances is likely to arouse a resentment and, in turn, guilt feelings on the part of those who have to do the nursing.[7]

Nor should it be overlooked that while Professor Williams would remove the various procedural steps and personnel contemplated in the British and American Bills and bank his all on the 'good sense' of the general practitioner, no man is immune to the fear, anxieties and frustrations engendered by the apparently helpless, hopeless patient. Not even the general practitioner. . . .

The 'Hopelessly Incurable' Patient and the Fallible Doctor

Professor Williams notes as 'standard argument' the plea that 'no sufferer from an apparently fatal illness should be deprived of his life because there is always the possibility that the diagnosis is wrong, or else that some remarkable cure will be discovered in time,'. . . .

Until the Euthanasia Societies of Great Britain and America had been organized and a party decision reached, shall we say, to advocate euthanasia only for incurables on their request, Dr. Abraham L. Wolbarst, one of the most ardent supporters of the movement, was less troubled about putting away 'insane or defective people [who] have suffered mental incapacity and tortures of the mind for many years' than he was about the 'incurables'.[8] He recognized the 'difficulty involved in the decision as to incurability' as one of the 'doubtful aspects of euthanasia': 'Doctors are only human beings, with few if any supermen among them. They make honest mistakes, like other men, because of the limitations of the human mind.'

He noted further that 'it goes without saying that, in recently developed cases with a possibility of cure, euthanasia should not even be considered', that 'the law might establish a limit of, say, ten years in which there is a chance of the patient's recovery'.

Dr. Benjamin Miller is another who is unlikely to harbour an ulterior theological motive. His interest is more personal. He himself was left to die the death of a 'hopeless' tuberculosis victim, only to discover that he was suffering from a rare malady which affects the lungs in much the same manner but seldom kills. Five years and sixteen hospitalizations later, Dr. Miller dramatized his point by recalling the last diagnostic clinic of the brilliant Richard Cabot, on the occasion of his official retirement:

> He was given the case records [complete medical histories and results of careful examinations] of two patients and asked to diagnose their illnesses. . . . The patients had died and only the hospital pathologist knew the exact diagnosis beyond doubt, for he had seen the descriptions of the post-mortem findings. Dr. Cabot, usually very accurate in his diagnosis, that day missed both.
>
> The chief pathologist who had selected the cases was a wise person. He had purposely chosen two of the most deceptive to remind the medical students and young physicians that even at the end of a long and rich experience one of the greatest diagnosticians of our time was still not infallible.[9]

Richard Cabot was the John W. Davis, the John Lord O'Brian, of his profession. When one reads the account of his last clinic, one cannot help but think how fallible the *average* general practitioner must be, how fallible the *young doctor just starting practice* must be—and this, of course, is all that some small communities have in the way of medical care—how fallible the *worst* practitioner, young or old, must be. If the range of skill and judgment among licensed physicians approaches the wide gap between the very best and the very worst members of the bar—and I have no reason to think it does not—then the minimally competent physician is hardly the man to be given the responsibility for ending another's life. Yet, under Williams's proposal at least, the marginal physician, as well as his more distinguished brethren, would have legal authorization to make just such decisions. Under Williams's proposal, euthanatizing a patient or two would all be part of the routine day's work. . . .

Faulty diagnosis is only one ground for error. Even if the diagnosis is correct, a second ground for error lies in the possibility that some measure of relief, if not a full cure, may come to the fore within the life expectancy of the patient. Since Glanville Williams does not deign this objection to euthanasia worth more than a passing reference, it is necessary to turn elsewhere to ascertain how it has been met. One answer is: 'It must be little comfort to a man slowly coming apart from multiple sclerosis to think that fifteen years from now, death might not be his only hope.'[10]

To state the problem this way is of course, to avoid it entirely. How do we know that fifteen *days* or fifteen *hours* from now, 'death might not be [the incurable's] only hope'?

A second answer is: '[N]o cure for cancer which might be found "tomorrow" would be of any value to a man or woman "so far advanced in cancerous toxemia as to be an applicant for euthanasia."'[11]

As I shall endeavour to show, this approach is a good deal easier to formulate than it is to apply. For one thing, it presumes that we know today *what* cures will be found tomorrow. For another, it overlooks that if such cases can be said to exist, the patient is likely to be *so far* advanced in cancerous toxemia as to be no longer capable of understanding the step he is taking and hence *beyond* the stage when euthanasia ought to be administered.

Thirty-six years ago, Dr. Haven Emerson, then President of the American Public Health Association, made the point that 'no one can say today what will be incurable tomorrow. No one can predict what disease will be fatal or permanently incurable until medicine becomes stationary and sterile,'[12]. . . .

Voluntary Versus Involuntary Euthanasia

Ever since the 1870s, when what was probably the first euthanasia debate of the modern era took place, most proponents of the movement—at least when they are pressed—have taken considerable pains to restrict the question to the plight of the unbearably suffering incurable who *voluntarily seeks* death, while most of their opponents have striven equally hard to frame the issue in terms which would encompass certain involuntary situations as well, e.g. the 'congenital idiots', the 'permanently insane', and the senile. . . .

The boldness and daring which characterize most of Glanville Williams's book dim perceptibly when he comes to involuntary euthanasia proposals. As to the senile, he states:

> At present the problem has certainly not reached the degree of seriousness that would warrant an effort being made to change traditional attitudes towards the sanctity of life of the aged. Only the grimmest necessity could bring about a change that, however cautious in its approach, would probably cause apprehension and deep distress to many people, and inflict a traumatic injury upon the accepted code of behaviour built up by two thousand years of the Christian religion. It may be, however, that as the problem becomes more acute it will itself cause a reversal of generally accepted values.

To me, this passage is the most startling one in the book. On page 310 Williams invokes 'traditional attitudes towards the sanctity of life' and 'the accepted code of behaviour built up by two thousand years of the Christian religion' to check the extension of euthanasia to the senile, but for 309 pages he had been merrily rolling along debunking both. Substitute 'cancer victim' for 'the aged' and Williams's passage is essentially the argument of many of his *opponents* on the voluntary euthanasia question.

The unsupported comment that 'the problem [of senility] has certainly not reached the

degree of seriousness' to warrant euthanasia is also rather puzzling, particularly coming as it does after an observation by Williams on the immediately preceding page that 'it is increasingly common for men and women to reach an age of "second childishness and mere oblivion", with a loss of almost all adult faculties except that of digestion'.

How 'serious' does a problem have to be to warrant a change in these 'traditional attitudes'? If, as the statement seems to indicate, 'seriousness' of the problem is to be determined numerically, the problem of the cancer victim does not appear to be as substantial as the problem of the senile. For example, taking just the 95,837 first admissions to 'public prolonged-care hospitals' for mental diseases in the United States in 1955, 23,561—or one-fourth—were cerebral arteriosclerosis or senile brain disease cases. I am not at all sure that there are twenty thousand cancer victims per year who die *unbearably painful* deaths. Even if there were, I cannot believe that among their ranks are some twenty thousand per year who, when still in a rational state, so long for a quick and easy death that they would avail themselves of legal machinery for euthanasia.

If the problem of the incurable cancer victim has reached 'the degree of seriousness that would warrant an effort being made to change traditional attitudes towards the sanctity of life', as Williams obviously thinks it has, then so has the problem of senility. In any event, the senility problem will undoubtedly soon reach even Williams's requisite degree of seriousness:

> A decision concerning the senile may have to be taken within the next twenty years. The number of old people are increasing by leaps and bounds. Pneumonia, 'the old man's friend', is now checked by antibiotics. The effects of hardship, exposure, starvation and accident are now minimized. Where is this leading us? . . . What of the drooling, helpless, disorientated old man or the doubly incontinent old woman lying log-like in bed? Is it here that the real need for euthanasia exists?[13]

If, as Williams indicates, 'seriousness' of the problem is a major criterion for euthanatizing a category of unfortunates, the sum total of mentally deficient persons would appear to warrant high priority, indeed.

When Williams turns to the plight of the 'hopelessly defective infants', his characteristic vim and vigour are, as in the senility discussion, conspicuously absent:

While the Euthanasia Society of England has never advocated this, the Euthanasia Society of America did include it in its original programme. The proposal certainly escapes the chief objection to the similar proposal for senile dementia: it does not create a sense of insecurity in society, because infants cannot, like adults, feel anticipatory dread of being done to death if their condition should worsen. Moreover, the proposal receives some support on eugenic grounds, and more importantly on humanitarian grounds—both on account of the parents, to whom the child will be a burden all their lives, and on account of the handicapped child itself. (It is not, however, proposed that any child should be destroyed against the wishes of its parents.) Finally, the legalization of euthanasia for handicapped children would bring the law into closer relation to its practical administration, because juries do not regard parental mercy-killing as murder. For these various reasons the proposal to legalize humanitarian infanticide is put forward from time to time by individuals. They remain in a very small minority, and the proposal may at present be dismissed as politically insignificant.

It is understandable for a reformer to limit his present proposals for change to those with a real prospect of success. But it is hardly reassuring for Williams to cite the fact that only 'a very small minority' has urged euthanasia for 'hopelessly defective infants' as the *only* reason for not pressing for such legislation now. If, as Williams sees it, the only advantage voluntary euthanasia has over the involuntary variety lies in the organized movements on its behalf, that advantage can readily be wiped out.

In any event, I do not think that such 'a very small minority' has advocated 'humanitarian infanticide'. Until the organization of the British and American societies led to a concentration on the voluntary type, and until the by-products of the Nazi euthanasia programme somewhat embarrassed, if only temporarily, most proponents of involuntary euthanasia, about as many writers urged one type as another. Indeed, some euthanasiasts have taken considerable pains to demonstrate the superiority of defective infant euthanasia over incurably ill euthanasia.

As for dismissing euthanasia of defective infants as 'politically insignificant', the only poll that I know of which measured the public response to both types of euthanasia revealed that *45 per cent favoured euthanasia for defective infants under certain conditions while only 37.3 per cent approved euthanasia for the incurably and painfully ill under any conditions,*[14] Furthermore, of those who favoured the mercy-killing cure for incurable adults, some 40 per cent would require only family permission or medical board approval, but not the patient's permission.

Nor do I think it irrelevant that while public resistance caused Hitler to yield on the adult euthanasia front, the killing of malformed and idiot children continued unhindered to the end of the war, the definition of 'children' expanding all the while. Is it the embarrassing experience of the Nazi euthanasia programme which has rendered destruction of defective infants presently 'politically insignificant'? If so, is it any more of a jump from the incurably and painfully ill to the unorthodox political thinker than it is from the hopelessly defective infant to the same 'unsavoury character'? Or is it not so much that the euthanasiasts are troubled by the Nazi experience as it is that they are troubled that the public is troubled by the Nazi experience?

I read Williams's comments on defective infants for the proposition that there are some very good reasons for euthanatizing defective infants, but the time is not yet ripe. When will it be? When will the proposal become politically significant? After a voluntary euthanasia law is on the books and public opinion is sufficiently 'educated'?

Williams's reasons for not extending euthanasia—once we legalize it in the narrow 'voluntary' area—to the *senile and the defective* are much less forceful and much less persuasive than his arguments for legalizing voluntary euthanasia in the first place. I regard this as another reason for not legalizing voluntary euthanasia in the first place.

Notes

1. First published in the U.S. in 1957, by arrangement with the Columbia Law School. Page references in the notes following relate to the British edition (Faber & Faber, 1958).

2. Frohman, 'Vexing Problems in Forensic Medicine: A Physician's View', *New York Univ. Law Review*, 31 (1956), 1215, 1222.

3. Sharpe, 'Medication as a Threat to Testamentary Capacity', *N. Carolina Law Review*, 35 (1957), 380, 392, and medical authorities cited therein.

4. Sharpe, op. cit., 384.

5. 'Why I Oppose Mercy Killings', *Woman's Home Companion* (June 1950), pp. 38, 103.

6. *House of Lords Debates,* 103, 5th series (1936), vols. 466, 492–3.

7. Zarling, 'Psychological Aspects of Pain in Terminal Malignancies', *Management of Pain in Cancer* (Schiffrin edn. 1956), pp. 211–12.

8. Wolbarst, 'Legalize Euthanasia!' *The Forum,* 94 (1935), 330, 332. But see Wolbarst, 'The Doctor Looks at Euthanasia,' *Medical Record,* 149 (1939), 354.

9. Op. Cit. (*n.* 5 above), p. 39.

10. 'Pro & Con: Shall We Legalize "Mercy Killing"?' *Reader's Digest* (Nov. 1938), pp. 94, 96.

11. James, 'Euthanasia—Right or Wrong?' *Survey Graphic* (May 1948), pp. 241, 243; Wolbarst, 'The Doctor Looks at Euthanasia', *Medical Record,* 149 (1939), 354, 355.

12. Emerson, 'Who Is Incurable? A Query and a Reply', *New York Times* (Oct. 22, 1933) Sec. 8, p. 5 col. 1.

13. Banks, 'Euthanasia', *Bulletin of New York Academy of Medicine,* 26 (1950), 297, 305.

14. The Fortune Quarterly Survey: IX, *Fortune Magazine* (July 1937), pp. 96, 106.

Study Questions

1. Does Kamisar think that voluntary euthanasia is always morally wrong? Explain.
2. Examine each of Kamisar's four arguments against voluntary euthanasia and discuss whether they are sound.

Chapter 24

For Legalizing Euthanasia: A Rejoinder

GLANVILLE WILLIAMS

Born in 1911, Glanville Williams was for many years a fellow of Jesus College, Cambridge University, and a member of the Standing Committee on Criminal Law Revision in England. He has been a leading advocate of the legalization of voluntary euthanasia. His *Sanctity of Life and the Criminal Law* (1957) sparked a strong debate on the issue of euthanasia, witnessed by the preceding essay by Yale Kamisar. Williams bases his support for voluntary euthanasia on two grounds: (1) it is cruel to refuse a terminally ill patient who is in agony the right to die; and (2) the principle of liberty overrides any utilitarian or social considerations against permitting voluntary euthanasia.

Williams responds to all four of Kamisar's objections to the legalization of voluntary euthanasia.

I WELCOME Professor Kamisar's reply to my argument for voluntary euthanasia, because it is on the whole a careful, scholarly work, keeping to knowable facts and accepted human values. It is, therefore, the sort of reply that can be rationally considered and dealt with. In this short rejoinder I shall accept most of Professor Kamisar's valuable notes, and merely submit that they do not bear out his conclusion.

The argument in favour of voluntary euthanasia in the terminal stages of painful diseases is a quite simple one, and is an application of two values that are widely recognized. The first value is the prevention of cruelty. Much as men differ in their ethical assessments, all agree that cruelty is an evil—the only difference of opinion residing in what is meant by cruelty. Those who plead for the legalization of euthanasia think that it is cruel to allow a human being to linger for months in the last stages of agony, weakness and decay, and to refuse him his demand for

merciful release. There is also a second cruelty involved—not perhaps quite so compelling, but still worth consideration: the agony of the relatives in seeing their loved one in his desperate plight. Opponents of euthanasia are apt to take a cynical view of the desires of relatives, and this may sometimes be justified. But it cannot be denied that a wife who has to nurse her husband through the last stages of some terrible disease may herself be so deeply affected by the experience that her health is ruined, either mentally or physically. Whether the situation can be eased for such a person by voluntary euthanasia I do not know; probably it depends very much upon the individuals concerned, which is as much as to say no solution in terms of a general regulatory law can be satisfactory. The conclusion should be in favour of individual discretion.

The second value involved is that of liberty. The criminal law should not be invoked to repress conduct unless this is demonstrably neces-

Reprinted from the Minnesota Law Review *43: 1 (1958) by permission.*

sary on social grounds. What social interest is there in preventing the sufferer from choosing to accelerate his death by a few months? What positive value does his life still possess for society, that he is to be retained in it by the terrors of the criminal law?

And, of course, the liberty involved is that of the doctor as well as that of the patient. It is the doctor's responsibility to do all he can to prolong worth-while life, or, in the last resort, to ease his patient's passage. If the doctor honestly and sincerely believes that the best service he can perform for his suffering patient is to accede to his request for euthanasia, it is a grave thing that the law should forbid him to do so.

This is the short and simple case for voluntary euthanasia, and, as Kamisar admits, it cannot be attacked directly on utilitarian grounds. Such an attack can only be by finding possible evils of an indirect nature. These evils, in the view of Professor Kamisar, are (1) the difficulty of ascertaining consent, and arising out of that the danger of abuse; (2) the risk of an incorrect diagnosis; (3) the risk of administering euthanasia to a person who could later have been cured by developments in medical knowledge; (4) the 'wedge' argument. . . .

Kamisar's first objection, under the heading 'The Choice', is that there can be no such thing as truly voluntary euthanasia in painful and killing diseases. He seeks to impale the advocates of euthanasia on an old dilemma. Either the victim is not yet suffering pain, in which case his consent is merely an uninformed and anticipatory one—and he cannot bind himself by contract to be killed in the future—or he is crazed by pain and stupefied by drugs, in which case he is not of sound mind. I have dealt with this problem in my book; Kamisar has quoted generously from it, and I leave the reader to decide. As I understand Kamisar's position, he does not really persist in the objection. With the laconic 'perhaps', he seems to grant me, though unwillingly, that there are cases where one be sure of the patient's consent. But having thus abandoned

his own point, he then goes off to a different horror, that the patient may give his consent only in order to relieve his relatives of the trouble of looking after him.

On this new issue, I will return Kamisar the compliment and say: 'Perhaps'. We are certainly in an area where no solution is going to make things quite easy and happy for everybody, and all sorts of embarrassments may be conjectured. But these embarrassments are not avoided by keeping to the present law: we suffer from them already. If a patient, suffering pain in a terminal illness, wishes for euthanasia partly because of his pain and partly because he sees his beloved ones breaking under the strain of caring for him, I do not see how this decision on his part, agonizing though it may be, is necessarily a matter of discredit either to the patient himself or to his relatives. The fact is that, whether we are considering the patient or his relatives, there are limits to human endurance.

Kamisar's next objection rests on the possibility of mistaken diagnosis. . . . I agree with him that, before deciding on euthanasia in any particular case, the risk of mistaken diagnosis would have to be considered. Everything that is said in the essay would, therefore, be most relevant when the two doctors whom I propose in my suggested measure come to consult on the question of euthanasia; and the possibility of mistake might most forcefully be brought before the patient himself. But have these medical questions any true relevance to the legal discussion?

Kamisar, I take it, notwithstanding his wide reading in medical literature, is by training a lawyer. He has consulted much medical opinion in order to find arguments against changing the law. I ought not to object to this, since I have consulted the same opinion for the opposite purpose. But what we may well ask ourselves is this: is it not a trifle bizarre that we should be doing so at all? Our profession is the law, not medicine. How does it come about that lawyers have to examine medical literature to assess the advantages and disadvantages of a medical practice?

If the import of this question is not immediately clear, let me return to my imaginary state of Ruritania. Many years ago, in Ruritania as elsewhere, surgical operations were attended with great risk. Lister had not discovered antisepsis, and surgeons killed as often as they cured. In this state of things, the legislature of Ruritania passed a law declaring all surgical operations to be unlawful in principle, but providing that each specific type of operation might be legalized by a statute specially passed for the purpose. The result is that, in Ruritania, as expert medical opinion sees the possibility of some new medical advance, a pressure group has to be formed in order to obtain legislative approval for it. Since there is little public interest in these technical questions, and since, moreover, surgical operations are thought in general to be inimical to the established religion, the pressure group has to work for many years before it gets a hearing. When at last a proposal for legalization is seriously mooted, the lawyers and politicians get to work upon it, considering what possible dangers are inherent in the new operation. Lawyers and politicians are careful people, and they are perhaps more prone to see the dangers than the advantages in a new departure. Naturally they find allies among some of the more timid or traditional or less knowledgeable members of the medical profession, as well as among the priesthood and the faithful. Thus it is small wonder that whereas appendectomy has been practised in civilized countries since the beginning of the present century, a proposal to legalize it has still not passed the legislative assembly of Ruritania.

It must be confessed that on this particular matter the legal prohibition has not been an unmixed evil for the Ruritanians. During the great popularity of the appendix operation in much of the civilized world during the 'twenties and 'thirties of this century, large numbers of these organs were removed without adequate cause, and the citizens of Ruritania have been spared this inconvenience. On the other hand, many citizens of that country have died of appendicitis, who would have been saved if they had lived elsewhere. And whereas in other countries the medical profession has now learned enough to be able to perform this operation with wisdom and restraint, in Ruritania it is still not being performed at all. Moreover, the law has destroyed scientific inventiveness in that country in the forbidden fields.

Now, in the United States and England we have no such absurd general law on the subject of surgical operations as they have in Ruritania. In principle, medical men are left free to exercise their best judgment, and the result has been a brilliant advance in knowledge and technique. But there are just two—or possibly three—operations which are subject to the Ruritanian principle. These are abortion, euthanasia, and possibly sterilization of convenience. In these fields we, too, must have pressure groups, with lawyers and politicians warning us of the possibility of inexpert practitioners and mistaken diagnosis, and canvassing medical opinion on the risk of an operation not yielding the expected results in terms of human happiness and the health of the body politic. In these fields we, too, are forbidden to experiment to see if the foretold dangers actually come to pass. Instead of that, we are required to make a social judgment on the probabilities of good and evil before the medical profession is allowed to start on its empirical tests.

This anomaly is perhaps more obvious with abortion than it is with euthanasia. Indeed, I am prepared for ridicule when I describe euthanasia as a medical operation. Regarded as surgery it is unique, since its object is not to save or prolong life but the reverse. But euthanasia has another object which it shares with many surgical operations—the saving of pain. And it is now widely recognized, as Lord Dawson said in the debate in the House of Lords, that the saving of pain is a legitimate aim of medical practice. The question whether euthanasia will effect a net saving of pain and distress is, perhaps, one that we can attempt to answer only by trying it. But it is obscurantist to forbid the experiment on the ground that until it is performed we cannot certainly know its results. Such an attitude, in any other field of medical endeavour, would have inhibited progress.

The argument based on mistaken diagnosis leads into the argument based on the possibility of dramatic medical discoveries. Of course, a new medical discovery which gives the opportunity of remission or cure will almost at once put an end to mercy-killings in the particular group of cases for which the discovery is made. On the other hand, the discovery cannot affect patients who have already died from their disease. The argument based on mistaken diagnosis is therefore concerned only with those patients who have been mercifully killed just before the discovery becomes available for use. The argument is that such persons may turn out to have been 'mercy-killed' unnecessarily, because if the physician had waited a bit longer they would have been cured. Because of this risk for this tiny fraction of the total number of patients, patients who are dying in pain must be left to do so, year after year, against their entreaty to have it ended.

Just how real is the risk? When a new medical discovery is claimed, some time commonly elapses before it becomes tested sufficiently to justify large-scale production of the drug, or training in the techniques involved. This is a warning period when euthanasia in the particular class of case would probably be halted anyway. Thus it is quite probable that when the new discovery becomes available, the euthanasia process would not in fact show any mistakes in this regard.

Kamisar says that in my book I 'did not deign this objection to euthanasia more than a passing reference'. I still do not think it is worth any more than that.

He advances the familiar but hardly convincing arguments that the quantitative need for euthanasia is not large. As one reason for this argument, he suggests that not many patients would wish to benefit from euthanasia, even if it were allowed. I am not impressed by the argument. It may be true, but it is irrelevant. So long as there are *any* persons dying in weakness and grief who are refused their request for a speeding of their end, the argument for legalizing euthanasia remains. Next, he suggests that there is no great need for euthanasia because of the advances made with pain-killing drugs. He has made so many quotations from my book that I cannot complain that he has not made more, but there is one relevant point that he does not mention. In my book, recognizing that medical science does manage to save many dying patients from the extreme of physical pain, I pointed out that it often fails to save them from an artificial, twilight existence, with nausea, giddiness, and extreme restlessness, as well as the long hours of consciousness of a hopeless condition. A dear friend of mine, who died of cancer of the bowel, spent his last months in just this state, under the influence of morphine, which deadened pain, but vomiting incessantly, day in and day out. The question that we have to face is whether the unintelligent brutality of such an existence is to be imposed on one who wishes to end it. . . .

The last part of the essay is devoted to the ancient 'wedge' argument which I have already examined in my book. It is the trump card of the traditionalist, because no proposal for reform, however strong the arguments in its favour, is immune from the wedge objection. In fact, the stronger the arguments in favour of a reform, the more likely it is that the traditionalist will take the wedge objection—it is then the only one he has. C. M. Cornford put the argument in its proper place when he said that the wedge objection means this: that you should not act justly today, for fear that you may be asked to act still more justly tomorrow.

We heard a great deal of this type of argument in England in the nineteenth century, when it was used to resist almost every social and economic change. In the present century we have had less of it, but it is still accorded an exaggerated importance in some contexts. When lecturing on the law of torts in an American university a few years ago, I suggested that just as compulsory liability insurance for automobiles had spread practically throughout the civilized world, so we should in time see the law of tort superseded in this field by a system of state insurance for traffic accidents, administered independently of proof of fault. The suggestion was immediately met by one student with a horrified reference to 'creeping socialism.' That is the standard objection made by many people to any proposal for a new department of state activity. The implication is that you must resist every proposal, however admirable in itself, because otherwise you will never be able to draw the line. On the particular question of socialism, the fear is belied by the experience of a number of countries which have extended state control of the economy without going the whole way to socialistic state regimentation.

Kamisar's particular bogey, the racial laws of Nazi Germany, is an effective one in the democratic countries. Any reference to the Nazis is a powerful weapon to prevent change in the traditional taboo on sterilization as well as euthanasia. The case of sterilization is particularly interesting on this; I dealt with it at length in my book, though Kamisar does not mention its bearing on the argument. When proposals are made for promoting voluntary sterilization on eugenic and other grounds, they are immediately condemned by most people as the thin end of a wedge leading to involuntary sterilization; and then they point to the practices of the Nazis. Yet a more persuasive argument pointing in the other direction can easily be found. Several American states have sterilization laws, which for the most part were originally drafted in very wide terms to cover desexualization as well as sterilization, and authorizing involuntary as well as voluntary operations. This legislation goes back long before the Nazis; the earliest statute was in Indiana in 1907. What has been its practical effect? In several American states it has

hardly been used. A few have used it, but in practice they have progressively restricted it until now it is virtually confined to voluntary sterilization. This is so, at least, in North Carolina, as Mrs. Woodside's study strikingly shows. In my book I summed up the position as follows:

> The American experience is of great interest because it shows how remote from reality in a democratic community is the fear—frequently voiced by Americans themselves—that voluntary sterilization may be the 'thin end of the wedge', leading to a large-scale violation of human rights as happened in Nazi Germany. In fact, the American experience is the precise opposite—starting with compulsory sterilization, administrative practice has come to put the operation on a voluntary footing.

But it is insufficient to answer the 'wedge' objection in general terms; we must consider the particular fears to which it gives rise. Kamisar professes to fear certain other measures that the Euthanasia Societies may bring up if their present measure is conceded to them. Surely these other measures, if any, will be debated on their merits? Does he seriously fear that anyone in the United States or in Great Britain is going to propose the extermination of people of a minority race or religion? Let us put aside such ridiculous fancies and discuss practical politics.

Kamisar is quite right in thinking that a body of opinion would favour the legalization of the involuntary euthanasia of hopelessly defective infants, and some day a proposal of this kind may be put forward. The proposal would have distinct limits, just as the proposal for voluntary euthanasia of incurable sufferers has limits. I do not think that any responsible body of opinion would now propose the euthanasia of insane adults, for the perfectly clear reason that any such practice would greatly increase the sense of insecurity felt by the borderline insane and by the large number of insane persons who have sufficient understanding on this particular matter.

Kamisar expresses distress at a concluding remark in my book in which I advert to the possibility of old people becoming an overwhelming burden on mankind. I share his feeling that there are profoundly disturbing possibilities here; and if I had been merely a propagandist, intent upon securing agreement for a specific measure of law reform, I should have done wisely to have omitted all reference to this subject. Since, however, I am merely an academic writer, trying to bring such intelligence as I have to bear on moral and social issues, I deemed the topic too important and threatening to leave without a word. I think I have made it clear, in the passages cited, that I am not for one moment proposing any euthanasia of the aged in present society; such an idea would shock me as much as it shocks Kamisar and would shock everybody else. Still, the fact that we may one day have to face is that medical science is more successful in preserving the body than in preserving the mind. It is not impossible that, in the foreseeable future, medical men will be able to preserve the mindless body until the age, say, of a thousand, while the mind itself will have lasted only a tenth of that time. What will mankind do then? It is hardly possible to imagine that we shall establish huge hospital-mausolea where the aged are kept in a kind of living death. Even if it is desired to do this, the cost of the undertaking may make it impossible.

This is not an immediately practical problem, and we need not yet face it. The problem of maintaining persons afflicted with senile dementia is well within our economic resources as the matter stands at present. Perhaps some barrier will be found to medical advance which will prevent the problem becoming more acute. Perhaps, as time goes on, and as the alternatives become more clearly realized, men will become more resigned to human control over the mode of termination of life. Or the solution may be that after the individual has reached a certain age, or a certain degree of decay, medical science will hold its hand, and allow him to be carried off by natural causes. But what if these natural causes are themselves painful? Would it not then be kinder to substitute human agency?

In general, it is enough to say that we do not have to know the solutions to these problems. The only doubtful moral question upon which we have to make an immediate decision in relation to involuntary euthanasia is whether we owe a moral duty to terminate the life of an insane person who is suffering from a painful and incurable disease. Such a person is left unprovided for under the legislative proposal formulated in my book. The objection to any system of involuntary euthanasia of the insane is that it may cause a sense of insecurity. It is because I think that the risk of this fear is a serious one that a proposal for the reform of the law must exclude its application to the insane.

Study Questions

1. Examine Williams's main arguments in favor of voluntary euthanasia. Do you agree with them?
2. How does Williams reply to Kamisar's four arguments against the legalization of voluntary euthanasia? Who is closer to what you believe?
3. Should voluntary euthanasia be legalized?

CHAPTER 25

Active and Passive Euthanasia

JAMES RACHELS

James Rachels is professor of philosophy at the University of Alabama at Birmingham and the author of several articles and books in ethics, among them are *The End of Life* (1986) and *Created from Animals* (1990).

The debate for and against the legalization of euthanasia often appeals to a well-known distinction between passive and active euthanasia: Passive is considered moral, and active is considered immoral. Rachels challenges that distinction, arguing that the distinction between killing and letting die, upon which the active-passive distinction is founded, is morally irrelevant.

THE DISTINCTION BETWEEN active and passive euthanasia is thought to be crucial for medical ethics. The idea is that it is permissible, at least in some cases, to withhold treatment and allow a patient to die, but it is never permissible to take any direct action designed to kill the patient. This doctrine seems to be accepted by most doctors, and it is endorsed in a statement adopted by the House of Delegates of the American Medical Association on 4 December 1973:

The intentional termination of the life of one human being by another—mercy killing—is contrary to that for which the medical profession stands and is contrary to the policy of the American Medical Association.

The cessation of the employment of extraordinary means to prolong the life of the body when there is irrefutable evidence that biological death is imminent is the decision of the patient and/or his immediate family. The advice and judgement of the physician should be freely available to the patient and/or his immediate family.

However, a strong case can be made against this doctrine. In what follows I will set out some of the relevant arguments, and urge doctors to reconsider their views on this matter.

To begin with a familiar type of situation, a patient who is dying of incurable cancer of the throat is in terrible pain, which can no longer be satisfactorily alleviated. He is certain to die within a few days, even if present treatment is continued, but he does not want to go on living for those days since the pain is unbearable. So he asks the doctor for an end to it, and his family joins in the request.

Suppose the doctor agrees to withhold treatment, as the conventional doctrine says he may. The justification for his doing so is that the patient is in terrible agony, and since he is going to die anyway, it would be wrong to prolong his suffering needlessly. But now notice this. If one simply withholds treatment, it may take the patient longer to die, and so he may suffer more than he would if more direct action were taken and a lethal injection given. This fact provides strong reason for thinking that, once the initial

 Reprinted from The New England Journal of Medicine *292: 2 (1975) by permission.*

decision not to prolong his agony has been made, active euthanasia is actually preferable to passive euthanasia, rather than the reverse. To say otherwise is to endorse the option that leads to more suffering rather than less, and is contrary to the humanitarian impulse that prompts the decision not to prolong his life in the first place.

Part of my point is that the process of being 'allowed to die' can be relatively slow and painful, whereas being given a lethal injection is relatively quick and painless. Let me give a different sort of example. In the United States about one in 600 babies is born with Down's syndrome. Most of these babies are otherwise healthy—that is, with only the usual pediatric care, they will proceed to an otherwise normal infancy. Some, however, are born with congenital defects such as intestinal obstructions that require operations if they are to live. Sometimes, the parents and the doctor will decide not to operate, and let the infant die. Anthony Shaw describes what happens then:

> When surgery is denied [the doctor] must try to keep the infant from suffering while natural forces sap the baby's life away. As a surgeon whose natural inclination is to use the scalpel to fight off death, standing by and watching a salvageable baby die is the most emotionally exhausting experience I know. It is easy at a conference, in a theoretical discussion to decide that such infants should be allowed to die. It is altogether different to stand by in the nursery and watch as dehydration and infection wither a tiny being over hours and days. This is a terrible ordeal for me and the hospital staff—much more so than for the parents who never set foot in the nursery.[1]

I can understand why some people are opposed to all euthanasia, and insist that such infants must be allowed to live. I think I can also understand why other people favour destroying these babies quickly and painlessly. But why should anyone favour letting 'dehydration and infection wither a tiny being over hours and days'? The doctrine that says a baby may be allowed to dehydrate and wither, but may not be given an injection that would end its life without suffering, seems so patently cruel as to require no further refutation. The strong language is not intended to offend, but only to put the point in the clearest possible way.

My second argument is that the conventional doctrine leads to decisions concerning life and death made on irrelevant grounds.

Consider again the case of the infants with Down's syndrome who need operations for congenital defects unrelated to the syndrome in order to live. Sometimes, there is no operation, and the baby dies, but when there is no such defect, the baby lives on. Now, an operation such as that to remove an intestinal obstruction is not prohibitively difficult. The reason why such operations are not performed in these cases is, clearly, that the child has Down's syndrome and the parents and the doctor judge that because of that fact it is better for the child to die.

But notice that this situation is absurd, no matter what view one takes of the lives and potentials of such babies. If the life of such an infant is worth preserving what does it matter if it needs a simple operation? Or, if one thinks it better that such a baby should not live on, what difference does it make that it happens to have an unobstructed intestinal tract? In either case, the matter of life and death is being decided on irrelevant grounds. It is the Down's syndrome, and not the intestines, that is the issue. The matter should be decided, if at all, on that basis, and not be allowed to depend on the essentially irrelevant question of whether the intestinal tract is blocked.

What makes this situation possible, of course, is the idea that when there is an intestinal blockage, one can 'let the baby die', but when there is no such defect there is nothing that can be done, for one must not 'kill' it. The fact that this idea leads to such results as deciding life or death on irrelevant grounds is another good reason why the doctrine would be rejected.

One reason why so many people think that there is an important moral difference between active and passive euthanasia is that they think killing someone is morally worse than letting someone die. But is it? Is killing, in itself, worse than letting die? To investigate this issue, two cases may be considered that are exactly alike except that one involves killing whereas the other involves letting someone die. Then, it can be asked whether this difference makes any difference to the moral assessments. It is important that the cases be exactly alike, except for this one difference, since otherwise one cannot be confident that it is this difference and not some other that accounts for any variation in the assessments of the two cases. So, let us consider this pair of cases:

In the first, Smith stands to gain a large inheritance if anything should happen to his six-year-old cousin. One evening while the child is taking his bath, Smith sneaks into the bathroom and drowns the child, and then arranges things so that it will look like an accident.

In the second, Jones also stands to gain if anything should happen to his six-year-old cousin. Like Smith, Jones sneaks in planning to drown the child in his bath. However, just as he enters the bathroom Jones sees the child slip and hit his head, and fall face down in the water. Jones is delighted; he stands by, ready to push the child's head back under if it is necessary, but it is not necessary. With only a little thrashing about, the child drowns all by himself, 'accidentally', as Jones watches and does nothing.

Now Smith killed the child, whereas Jones 'merely' let the child die. That is the only difference between them. Did either man behave better, from a moral point of view? If the difference between killing and letting die were in itself a morally important matter, one should say that Jones's behaviour was less reprehensible than Smith's. But does one really want to say that? I think not. In the first place, both men acted from the same motive, personal gain, and both

had exactly the same end in view when they acted. It may be inferred from Smith's conduct that he is a bad man, although that judgement may be withdrawn or modified if certain further facts are learned about him—for example, that he is mentally deranged. But would not the very same thing be inferred about Jones from his conduct? And would not the same further considerations also be relevant to any modification of this judgement? Moreover, suppose Jones pleaded, in his own defence, 'After all, I didn't do anything except just stand there and watch the child drown. I didn't kill him; I only let him die. 'Again, if letting die were in itself less bad than killing, this defence should have at least some weight. But it does not. Such a 'defence' can only be regarded as a grotesque perversion of moral reasoning. Morally speaking, it is no defence at all.

Now, it may be pointed out, quite properly, that the cases of euthanasia with which doctors are concerned are not like this at all. They do not involve personal gain or the destruction of normal healthy children. Doctors are concerned only with cases in which the patient's life is of no further use to him, or in which the patient's life has become or will soon become a terrible burden. However, the point is the same in these cases: the bare difference between killing and letting die does not, in itself, make a moral difference. If a doctor lets a patient die, for humane reasons, he is in the same moral position as if he had given the patient a lethal injection for humane reasons. If his decision was wrong— if, for example, the patient's illness was in fact curable—the decision would be equally regrettable no matter which method was used to carry it out. And if the doctor's decision was the right one, the method used is not in itself important.

The AMA policy statement isolates the crucial issue very well; the crucial issue is 'the intentional termination of the life of one human being by another'. But after identifying this issue, and forbidding 'mercy killing', the statement goes on to deny that the cessation of treatment is the intentional termination of a life. This is where the mistake comes in, for what is the cessation of treatment, in these circumstances, if it is not 'the intentional termination of the life of one human being by another'? Of course it is exactly that, and if it were not, there would be no point to it.

Many people will find this judgement hard to accept. One reason, I think, is that it is very easy to conflate the question of whether killing is, in itself, worse than letting die, with the very different question of whether most actual cases of killing are more reprehensible than most actual cases of letting die. Most actual cases of killing are clearly terrible (think, for example, of all the murders reported in the newspapers), and one hears of such cases every day. On the other hand, one hardly ever hears of a case of letting die, except for the actions of doctors who are motivated by humanitarian reasons. So one learns to think of killing in a much worse light than of letting die. But this does not mean that there is something about killing that makes it in itself worse than letting die, for it is not the bare difference between killing and letting die that makes the difference in these cases. Rather, the other factors—the murderer's motive of personal gain, for example, contrasted with the doctor's humanitarian motivation—account for different reactions to the different cases.

I have argued that killing is not in itself any worse than letting die; if my contention is right, it follows that active euthanasia is not any worse than passive euthanasia. What arguments can be given on the other side? The most common, I believe, is the following:

> The important difference between active and passive euthanasia is that, in passive euthanasia, the doctor does not do anything to bring about the patient's death. The doctor does nothing, and the patient dies of whatever ills already afflict him. In active euthanasia, however, the doctor does something to bring about the patient's death: he kills him. The doctor who gives the patient with cancer a lethal injection has himself caused his patient's death; whereas if he merely ceases treatment, the cancer is the cause of the death.

A number of points need to be made here. The first is that it is not exactly correct to say that in passive euthanasia the doctor does nothing, for he does do one thing that is very important: he lets the patient die. 'Letting someone die' is certainly different, in some respects, from other types of action—mainly in that it is a kind of action that one may perform by way of not performing certain other actions. For example, one may let a patient die by way of not giving medication, just as one may insult someone by way of not shaking his hand. But for any purpose of moral assessment, it is a type of action none the less. The decision to let a patient die is subject to moral appraisal in the same way that a decision to kill him would be subject to moral appraisal: it may be assessed as wise or unwise, compassionate or sadistic, right or wrong. If a doctor deliberately lets a patient die who was suffering from a routinely curable illness, the doctor would certainly be to blame for what he had done, just as he would be to blame if he had needlessly killed the patient. Charges against him would then be appropriate. If so, it would be no defence at all for him to insist that he didn't 'do anything'. He would have done something very serious indeed, for he let his patient die.

Fixing the cause of death may be very important from a legal point of view, for it may determine whether criminal charges are brought against the doctor. But I do not think that this notion can be used to show a moral difference between active and passive euthanasia. The reason why it is considered bad to be the cause of someone's death is that death is regarded as a great evil—and so it is. However, if it has been decided that euthanasia—even passive euthanasia—is desirable in a given case, it has also been decided that in this instance death is no greater an evil than the patient's continued existence. And if this is true, the usual reason for not wanting to be the cause of someone's death simply does not apply.

Finally, doctors may think that all of this is only of academic interest—the sort of thing that philosophers may worry about but that has no practical bearing on their own work. After all, doctors must be concerned about the legal consequences of what they do, and active euthanasia is clearly forbidden by the law. But even so, doctors should also be concerned with the fact that the law is forcing upon them a moral doctrine that may be indefensible, and has a considerable effect on their practices. Of course, most doctors are not now in the position of being coerced in this matter, for they do not regard themselves as merely going along with what the law requires. Rather, in statements such as the AMA policy statement that I have quoted, they are endorsing this doctrine as a central point of medical ethics. In that statement, active eutha-nasia is condemned not merely as illegal but as 'contrary to that for which the medical profession stands', whereas passive euthanasia is approved. However, the preceding considerations suggest that there is really no moral difference between the two, considered in themselves (there may be important moral differences in some cases in their *consequences*, but, as I pointed out, these differences may make active euthanasia, and not passive euthanasia, the morally preferable option). So, whereas doctors may have to discriminate between active and passive euthanasia to satisfy the law, they should not do any more than that. In particular, they should not give the distinction any added authority and weight by writing it into official statements of medical ethics.

Note

1. Shaw, Anthony, 'Doctor, Do We Have a Choice?' *The New York Times Magazine,* 30 Jan. 1972, p. 54.

Study Questions

1. Examine Rachels's argument against the passive-active distinction. Is Rachels correct that the distinction is morally irrelevant?
2. How does Rachels explain why many people believe that killing is worse than letting die?
3. What should be done to defective neonates? Suppose you were a physician and one of your patients had given birth to a baby with Down's syndrome who also had an intestinal blockage. The parents do not want the baby, since it will be an abnormal, retarded child. If you do nothing, the baby will slowly starve to death. If you kill the baby, you would save it from some suffering. What should you do? Should you save the baby's life against the wishes of the parents? How would Rachels treat this case?

CHAPTER 26

Active and Passive Euthanasia:
An Impertinent Distinction?

THOMAS D. SULLIVAN

Thomas D. Sullivan is professor of philosophy at the College of St. Thomas, St. Paul, Minnesota, and the author of *Between Thoughts and Things: The Status of Meaning*. In this article, Sullivan responds to Rachels's attack on the passive-active distinction and defends the standard account. Emphasizing the difference between intending and foreseeing, he argues that the traditional view forbids the intentional termination of life, whether by killing or letting die, but not the withholding of extraordinary means.

BECAUSE OF RECENT ADVANCES in medical technology, it is today possible to save or prolong the lives of many persons who in an earlier era would have quickly perished. Unhappily, however, it often is impossible to do so without committing the patient and his or her family to a future filled with sorrows. Modern methods of neurosurgery can successfully close the opening at the base of the spine of a baby born with severe myelomeningocoele, but do nothing to relieve the paralysis that afflicts it from the waist down or to remedy the patient's incontinence of stool and urine. Antibiotics and skin grafts can spare the life of a victim of severe and massive burns, but fail to eliminate the immobilizing contractions of arms and legs, the extreme pain, and the hideous disfigurement of the face. It is not surprising, therefore, that physicians and moralists in increasing number recommend that assistance should not be given to such patients, and that some have even begun to advocate the deliberate hastening of death by medical means, provided informed consent has been given by the appropriate parties.

The latter recommendation consciously and directly conflicts with what might be called the "traditional" view of the physician's role. The traditional view, as articulated, for example, by the House of Delegates of the American Medical Association in 1973, declared:

> The intentional termination of the life of one human being by another—mercy killing—is contrary to that for which the medical profession stands and is contrary to the policy of the American Medical Association.
>
> The cessation of the employment of extraordinary means to prolong the life of the body when there is irrefutable evidence that biological death is imminent is the decision of the patient and/or his immediate family. The advice and judgement of the physician should be freely available to the patient and/or his immediate family.

Basically this view involves two points: (1) that it is impermissible for the doctor or anyone else to terminate intentionally the life of a patient, but (2) that it is permissible in some cases to cease

From Human Life Review *3: 3 (summer 1977), pp. 40–46. Reprinted with permission from The* Human Life Foundation, Inc., *150 East 35th Street, New York, NY 10016.*

the employment of "extraordinary means" of preserving life, even though the death of the patient is a foreseeable consequence.

Does this position really make sense? Recent criticism charges that it does not. The heart of the complaint is that the traditional view arbitrarily rules out all cases of intentionally acting to terminate life, but permits what is in fact the moral equivalent, letting patients die. This accusation has been clearly articulated by James Rachels in a widely read article that appeared in a recent issue of the *New England Journal of Medicine*, entitled "Active and Passive Euthanasia."[1] By "active euthanasia" Rachels seems to mean *doing something* to bring about a patient's death, and by "passive euthanasia" not doing anything, i.e., just letting the patient die. Referring to the A.M.A. statement, Rachels sees the traditional position as always forbidding active euthanasia but permitting passive euthanasia. Yet, he argues, passive euthanasia, may be in some cases morally indistinguishable from active euthanasia, and in other cases even worse. To make his point he asks his readers to consider the case of a Down's syndrome baby with an intestinal obstruction that easily could be remedied through routine surgery. Rachels comments:

> I can understand why some people are opposed to all euthanasia, and insist that such infants must be allowed to live. I think I can also understand why other people favor destroying these babies quickly and painlessly. But why should anyone favor letting 'dehydration and infection wither a tiny being over hours and days?' The doctrine that says that a baby may be allowed to dehydrate and wither, but may not be given an injection that would end its life without suffering, seems so patently cruel as to require no further refutation.[2]

Rachels' point is that decisions such as the one he describes as "patently cruel" arise out of a misconceived moral distinction between active and passive euthanasia, which in turn rests upon a distinction between killing and letting die that itself has no moral importance.

One reason why so many people think that there is an important moral difference between active and passive euthanasia is that they think killing someone is morally worse than letting someone die. But is it? . . . To investigate this issue, two cases may be considered that are exactly alike except that one involves killing whereas the other involves letting someone die. Then, it can be asked whether this difference makes any difference to the moral assessments. . . .

In the first, Smith stands to gain a large inheritance if anything should happen to his six-year-old cousin. One evening while the child is taking his bath, Smith sneaks into the bathroom and drowns the child, and then arranges things so that it will look like an accident.

In the second, Jones also stands to gain if anything should happen to his six-year-old cousin. Like Smith, Jones sneaks in planning to drown the child in his bath. However, just as he enters the bathroom Jones sees the child slip and hit his head, and fall face down in the water. Jones is delighted: he stands by, ready to push the child's head back under if it is necessary, but it is not necessary. With only a little thrashing about the child drowns all by himself, "accidentally," as Jones watches and does nothing.[3]

Rachels observes that Smith killed the child, whereas Jones "merely" let the child die. If there's an important moral distinction between killing and letting die, then, we should say that Jones' behavior from a moral point of view is less reprehensible than Smith's. But while the law might draw some distinctions here, it seems clear that the acts of Jones and Smith are not different in any important way, or, if there is a difference, Jones' action is even worse.

In essence, then, the objection to the position adopted by the A.M.A. of Rachels and those who argue like him is that it endorses a highly questionable moral distinction between killing and letting die, which, if accepted, leads to indefensible medical decisions. Nowhere does Rachels quite come out and say that he favors active euthanasia in some cases, but the implication is clear. Nearly everyone holds that it is sometimes pointless to prolong the process of dying and that in those cases it is morally permissible to let a patient die even though a few hours or days could be salvaged by procedures that would also increase the agonies of the dying. But if it is impossible to defend a general distinction between letting people die and acting to terminate their lives directly, then it would seem that active euthanasia also may be morally permissible.

Now what shall we make of all this? It *is* cruel to stand by and watch a Down's baby die an agonizing death when a simple operation would remove the intestinal obstruction, but to offer the excuse that in failing to operate we didn't *do* anything to bring about death is an example of moral evasiveness comparable to the excuse Jones would offer for his action of "merely" letting his cousin die. Furthermore, it is true that if someone is trying to bring about the death of another human being, then it makes little difference from the moral point of view if his purpose is achieved by action or by malevolent omission, as in the cases of Jones and Smith.

But if we acknowledge this, are we obliged to give up the traditional view expressed by the A.M.A. statement? Of course not. To begin with, we are hardly obliged to assume the Jones-like role Rachels assigns the defender of the traditional view. We have the option of operating on the Down's baby and saving its life. Rachels mentions that possibility only to hurry past it as if that is not what his opposition would do. But, of course, that is precisely the course of action most defenders of the traditional position would choose.

Secondly, while it may be that the reason some rather confused people give for upholding the traditional view is that they think killing someone is always worse than letting them die, nobody who gives the matter much thought puts it that way. Rather they say that killing someone is clearly morally worse than not killing them, and killing them can be done by acting to

bring about their death or by refusing ordinary means to keep them alive in order to bring about the same goal.

What I am suggesting is that Rachels' objections leave the position he sets out to criticize untouched. It is worth noting that the jargon of active and passive euthanasia—and it is jargon—does not appear in the resolution. Nor does the resolution state or imply the distinction Rachels attacks, a distinction that puts a moral premium on overt behavior—moving or not moving one's parts—while totally ignoring the intentions of the agent. That no such distinction is being drawn seems clear from the fact that the A.M.A. resolution speaks approvingly of ceasing to use extraordinary means in certain cases, and such withdrawals might easily involve bodily movement, for example unplugging an oxygen machine.

In addition to saddling his opposition with an indefensible distinction it doesn't make, Rachels proceeds to ignore one that it does make—one that is crucial to a just interpretation of the view. Recall the A.M.A. allows the withdrawal of what it calls extraordinary means of preserving life; clearly the contrast here is with ordinary means. Though in its short statement those expressions are not defined, the definition Paul Ramsey refers to as standard in his book, *The Patient as Person,* seems to fit.

> Ordinary means of preserving life are all medicines, treatments, and operations, which offer a reasonable hope of benefit for the patient and which can be obtained and used without excessive expense, pain, and other inconveniences.
>
> Extra-ordinary means of preserving life are all those medicines, treatments, and operations which cannot be obtained without excessive expense, pain, or other inconvenience, or which, if used, would not offer a reasonable hope of benefit.[4]

Now with this distinction in mind, we can see how the traditional view differs from the position Rachels mistakes for it. The traditional view is that the intentional termination of human life is impermissible, irrespective of whether this goal is brought about by action or inaction. Is the action or refraining *aimed* at producing a death? Is the termination of life *sought, chosen or planned*? Is the intention deadly? If so, the act or omission is wrong.

But we all know it is entirely possible that the unwillingness of a physician to use extra-ordinary means for preserving life may be prompted not by a determination to bring about death, but by other motives. For example, he may realize that further treatment may offer little hope of reversing the dying process and/or be excruciating, as in the case when a massively necrotic bowel condition in a neonate is out of control. The doctor who does what he can to comfort the infant but does not submit it to further treatment or surgery may foresee that the decision will hasten death, but it certainly doesn't follow from that fact that he intends to bring about its death. It is, after all, entirely possible to foresee that something will come about as a result of one's conduct without intending the consequence or side effect. If I drive downtown, I can foresee that I'll wear out my tires a little, but I don't drive downtown with the intention of wearing out my tires. And if I choose to forego my exercises for a few days, I may think that as a result my physical condition will deteriorate a little, but I don't omit my exercise with a view to running myself down. And if you have to fill a position and select Green, who is better qualified for the post than her rival Brown, you needn't appoint Mrs. Green with the intention of hurting Mr. Brown, though you may foresee that Mr. Brown will feel hurt. And if a country extends its general education programs to its illiterate masses, it is predictable the suicide rate will go up, but even if the public officials are aware of this fact, it doesn't follow that they initiate the program with a view to making the suicide rate go up. In general, then, it is not the case that all the foreseeable consequences and side effects of our conduct are necessarily

intended. And it is because the physician's withdrawal of extra-ordinary means can be otherwise motivated than by a desire to bring about the predictable death of the patient that such action cannot categorically be ruled out as wrong.

But the refusal to use ordinary means is an altogether different matter. After all, what is the point of refusing assistance which offers reasonable hope of benefit to the patient without involving excessive pain or other inconvenience? How could it be plausibly maintained that the refusal is not motivated by a desire to bring about the death of the patient? The traditional position, therefore, rules out not only direct actions to bring about death, such as giving a patient a lethal injection, but malevolent omissions as well, such as not providing minimum care for the newborn.

The reason the A.M.A. position sounds so silly when one listens to arguments such as Rachels' is that he slights the distinction between ordinary and extra-ordinary means and then drums on cases where *ordinary* means are refused. The impression is thereby conveyed that the traditional doctrine sanctions omissions that are morally indistinguishable in a substantive way from direct killings, but then incomprehensibly refuses to permit quick and painless termination of life. If the traditional doctrine would approve of Jones' standing by with a grin on his face while his young cousin drowned in a tub, or letting a Down's baby wither and die when ordinary means are available to preserve its life, it would indeed be difficult to see how anyone could defend it. But so to conceive the traditional doctrine is simply to misunderstand it. It is not a doctrine that rests on some supposed distinction between "active" and "passive euthanasia," whatever those words are supposed to mean, nor on a distinction between moving and not moving our bodies. It is simply a prohibition against intentional killing, which includes both direct actions and malevolent omissions.

To summarize—the traditional position represented by the A.M.A. statement is not incoherent. It acknowledges, or more accurately, insists upon the fact that withholding ordinary means to sustain life may be tantamount to killing. The traditional position can be made to appear incoherent only by imposing upon it a crude idea of killing held by none of its more articulate advocates.

Thus the criticism of Rachels and other reformers, misapprehending its target, leaves the traditional position untouched. That position is simply a prohibition of murder. And it is good to remember, as C. S. Lewis once pointed out:

> No man, perhaps, ever at first described to himself the act he was about to do as Murder, or Adultery, or Fraud, or Treachery. . . . And when he hears it so described by other men he is (in a way) sincerely shocked and surprised. Those others "don't understand." If they knew what it had really been like for him, they would not use those crude "stock" names. With a wink or a titter, or a cloud of muddy emotion, the thing has slipped into his will as something not very extraordinary, something of which, rightly understood in all of his peculiar circumstances, he may even feel proud.[5]

I fully realize that there are times when those who have the noble duty to tend the sick and the dying are deeply moved by the sufferings of their patients, especially of the very young and the very old, and desperately wish they could do more than comfort and companion them. Then, perhaps, it seems that universal moral principles are mere abstractions having little to do with the agony of the dying. But of course we do not see best when our eyes are filled with tears.

Notes

1. *The New England Journal of Medicine,* vol. 292 (Jan. 9, 1975), pp. 78–80. [Rachels's article precedes this reading.—Ed.]
2. Ibid., pp. 78–79.
3. Ibid., p. 79.
4. Paul Ramsey, *The Patient as Person* (New Haven and London: Yale University Press, 1970), p. 122. Ramsey abbreviates the definition first given by Gerald Kelly, S.J., *Medico-Moral Problems* (St. Louis, Mo.: The Catholic Hospital Association, 1958), p. 129.
5. C.S. Lewis, *The Abolition of Man* (New York: Collier Books, 1986).

Study Questions

1. Why does Sullivan believe that euthanasia is immoral?
2. How does Sullivan respond to Rachels's argument? Explain his view on the difference between intending and foreseeing and how this affects the morality of terminating life.
3. What are "extraordinary means"? Is this concept morally relevant in this debate?

CHAPTER 27

The Oregon Law on the Right to Die

In 1995, following the Supreme Court rule that allowed states to devise their own guidelines regarding assisted suicide, the state of Oregon put forth the following death with dignity act.

The Death with Dignity Act

1. The patient must be at least 18, terminally ill (having less than 6 months to live), and an Oregon resident.

2. The patient must voluntarily make an oral request to the attending medical/osteopathic physician for a prescription for medication to end his or her life. A 15-day waiting period then begins.

3. The attending physician ensures the patient understands the diagnosis and prognosis. The patient is informed of all options, including pain control, hospice care, and comfort care, as well as the risks and expected result of taking the medication.

4. The attending physician (a) determines whether the patient is capable of making health care decisions and is acting voluntarily; (b) encourages the patient to notify his or her next of kin; (c) informs the patient that he or she can withdraw the request for medication at any time and in any manner; and (d) refers the patient to a consulting physician who is asked to confirm the attending physician's diagnosis and prognosis.

5. The consulting physician also decides whether the patient is capable of making the decision and is acting voluntarily. If either or both physicians believe the patient is suffering from a psychiatric illness or depression that causes impaired judgment, the patient will be referred for counseling.

6. Once the preceding steps have been satisfied, the patient voluntarily signs a written request witnessed by two people. At least one witness cannot be a relative or an heir of the patient.

7. The patient then makes a second oral request to the attending physician for medication to end his or her life.

8. The attending physician again informs the patient that he or she can withdraw the request for medication at any time and in any manner.

9. No sooner than 15 days after the first oral request and 48 hours after the written request, the patient may receive a prescription for medicine to end his or her life. The attending physician again verifies at this time that the patient is making an informed decision.

For Further Reading

Beauchamp, Tom L., and James F. Childress, *Principles of Biomedical Ethics*. New York: Oxford University Press, 1994.

Beauchamp, Tom L., and Seymour Perlin, eds. *Ethical Issues in Death and Dying.* Englewood Cliffs, N.J.: Prentice Hall, 1978.

Devine, Philip E. *The Ethics of Homicide.* Ithaca, N.Y.: Cornell University Press, 1978.

Kohl, Marvin, ed. *Beneficent Euthanasia.* Buffalo, N.Y.: Prometheus Books, 1975.

Mappes, Thomas, and Jane Zembaty, eds. *Biomedical Ethics,* 2d ed. New York: McGraw-Hill, 1986.

Munson, Ronald, ed. *Intervention and Reflection.* Belmont, Calif.: Wadsworth, 1987.

Rachels, James. *The End of Life.* New York: Oxford University Press, 1986.

Singer, Peter. *Practical Ethics.* Cambridge: Cambridge University Press, 1979.

Veatch, Robert M. *Death, Dying and the Biological Revolution.* New Haven, Conn.: Yale University Press, 1976.

Part VI

What Is Death? The Crisis of Criteria

On May 24, 1968, in Richmond, Virginia, a worker named Bruce Tucker fell, sustaining a severe head injury. When the ambulance delivered him to the emergency ward of the Medical College of Virginia Hospital, he was found to be bleeding within his brain. He was put on a ventilator and an operation was performed to relieve the strain on the brain. It was unsuccessful, and Tucker was described by the physician in charge as "mechanically alive . . . [his] prognosis for recovery is nil and death imminent."

At the same time a patient named Joseph Klett was in a ward waiting for a donor heart. When the electroencephalogram (EEG) attached to Tucker showed a flat line, the doctors concluded that he was "brain dead." They operated and transplanted his heart to Klett. Tucker's kidneys were also removed for transplantation.

Although Tucker's wallet contained his brother's business card, including a telephone number and address only fifteen blocks away from the hospital, no attempt was made to contact him. William Tucker, the brother, brought suit against the doctors who performed the operation, but the doctors were exonerated in court, even though Virginia law defined death as total cessation of all bodily functions. William Tucker, disappointed with the verdict, exclaimed, "There's nothing they can say to make me believe they didn't kill [my brother]."[1]

When is someone dead? Until the mid-twentieth century this was seldom a serious question. If someone failed to have a pulse and stopped breathing, this determined that he or she was dead. But in the middle of this century biomedical technology developed ways to keep the body alive almost indefinitely, causing us to reflect anew on the meaning of death. Moreover, this same technology can transplant organs from one patient to another, so that we need a definition of death to guide us when to remove the organs from the person declared dead.

Several physicians, philosophers, and medical ethicists, led by Henry Beecher and Robert M. Veatch, have called for a redefinition of death in terms of brain function, "brain death." Others, like Paul Ramsey and Hans Jonas, have opposed this move.

Four definitions of death appear in the literature: (1) the departure of the soul from the body; (2) the irreversible loss of the flow of vital fluids or the irreversible cessation of cardiovascular pulmonary function; (3) whole brain death; and (4) neocortical brain death.

Loss of Soul

The first major philosopher to hold that death occurred with the departure of the soul was Plato, but the view is found in the Orthodox Jewish and Christian traditions and in René Descartes (1596–1650), who believed that the soul resided in the pineal gland at the base of the brain and left the body at death. The sign of the departure was the cessation of breathing. Orthodox Jews say that a person is dead only when the last breath is drawn.[2] Note that the Hebrew word for spirit, *ruach*, is the same word used for breath, and the Greek word *pneuma* has the same double meaning.

This view is beset with problems. First, it is difficult to know what the soul is, let alone whether we are endowed with one or more. Second, neurological science can explain much of human behavior by appeal to brain function, so the notion of a separate spiritual entity seems irrelevant. Third, if a soul is in us and if it only leaves us after we have breathed our last, medical technology can keep the soul in the body for scores of years after the brain has ceased to function and, as far as we can tell, all consciousness has long disappeared. Unless we are really convinced that God has revealed this doctrine to us, we should dismiss it as unsupported by the best evidence available.

The Cardiopulmonary View

When the heart and lungs stop functioning, the person is dead. This has been the traditional medical definition. *Black's Law Dictionary* puts it this way: "The cessation of life: the ceasing to exist; defined by physicians as a total stoppage of the circulation of the blood, and a cessation of the animal and vital functions consequent thereupon, such as respiration, pulsation, etc." In *Thomas* v. *Anderson*, a California District Court in 1950 quoted Black and added, "Death occurs precisely when life ceases and does not occur until the heart stops beating and respiration ends. Death is not a continuous event and is an event that takes place at a precise time."[3]

This standard definition is problematic in that it goes against the intuitions of many people that irreversibly comatose patients, like Karen Ann Quinlan or Nancy Cruzan, are not alive at all. Bodily functions alone do not constitute human life. We need to be sentient and self-conscious.

The Whole Brain View

As Roland Puccetti puts it, "Where the brain goes, there the person goes."[4] In the same year that Bruce Tucker had his heart and lungs removed, the Ad Hoc Committee of the Harvard Medical School, under the chairmanship of Dr. Henry K. Beecher, met to decide on criteria for declaring a person dead. The study was a response to the growing confusion over the uses of biomedical technology in being able to keep physical life going for an indefinite period of time after consciousness has been irretrievably lost. It also was a response to the desire to obtain organs from "donors" who were permanently comatose but whose organs were undamaged, because of the ability of technology to keep the vital fluids flowing.

The committee came up with four criteria that together would enable the examiner to pronounce a person dead:

1. Unreceptivity and unresponsivity (i.e., no awareness of externally applied stimuli)
2. No movement or breathing without the use of artificial mechanisms
3. No reflexes; the pupil is fixed and dilated and will not respond to bright light
4. A flat electroencephalogram (EEG), which indicates no cerebral activity

The tests must be repeated at least twenty-four hours later in order to rule out rare false positives.

The Harvard committee's criteria have been widely accepted as a safe set, allowing medical practitioners to detach patients from artificial respirators and to transfer organs to needy recipients. Of thousands of patients tested, no one has regained consciousness who has met the criteria.

But critics have objected that the Harvard criteria are too conservative. By its norms, patients who are permanently comatose or in persistent vegetative states, like Karen Ann Quinlan and Nancy Cruzan, would be considered alive, since their lower brain stems continued to function. Indeed, people have been recorded as living as long as thirty-seven years in such an unconscious state. Since they are alive and can be fed intravenously, or via gastric feeding tubes, we have an obligation to continue to maintain them. The worry is that hospitals and nursing homes could turn into mausoleums for the comatose. So a fourth view of death has arisen.

Neocortical Brain Death

What is vital to human existence? Henry Beecher, head of the Harvard Ad Hoc Committee, says it is consciousness. Robert M. Veatch says it is our capacity for social interaction, involving the power of thought, speech, and consciousness. These higher functions are located in the neocortex of the cerebrum or upper brain; when a sufficient part of this section of the brain is destroyed, the patient is dead. An electroencephalogram (EEG) can determine when the cerebrum has ceased to function.

Beecher and Veatch see human death as the loss of what is significant for human life. Veatch, in our first reading, defines death this way: "Death means a complete change in the status of a living entity characterized by the irreversible loss of those characters that are essentially significant to it." By this reasoning, Karen Ann Quinlan would have been declared dead as soon as she was discovered to be in a persistent vegetative state.

In our second reading David Mayo and Daniel Wikler oppose the redefinition of death, arguing that a comatose human being whose lower brain stem is still functioning and whose heart is beating is still a living organism. According to them, death is an event, not a process, in which the biological organism ceases to function. If Mayo and Winkler are right, we should give up our notion of the sanctity of biological life and recognize that some lives are not worth living, including life as an organism in a persistent vegetative state. Although the irreversibly comatose being is biologically alive, it is no longer a life possessing any quality. If we see that personhood involves being self-conscious, we may say in these cases that although the body is alive the *person* is dead. Not only should the body be detached from expensive lifesaving machines, but its organs should be removed for use on the living. Organs are a precious medical resource that can be used to enable people to live longer and better lives.

Notes

1. Cited in Robert M. Veatch, *Death, Dying, and the Biological Revolution* (New Haven, Conn.: Yale University Press, 1976), pp. 21–24.

2. Immanuel Jakobovitz, *Jewish Medical Ethics* (Philadelphia: Block, 1959), p. 277.

3. Quoted in Tom Beauchamp and Seymour Perlin, eds., *Ethical Issues in Death and Dying* (Englewood Cliffs, N.J.: Prentice Hall, 1978), p. 14.

4. Roland Puccetti, "Brain Transplantation and Personal Identity," *Analysis* 29 (1969), p. 65.

CHAPTER 28

Defining Death Anew

ROBERT M. VEATCH

Robert M. Veatch is associate for medical ethics at the Kennedy Institute of Society, Ethics and Life Sciences at Georgetown University in Washington, D.C. He is the author of numerous works on questions of medical ethics, including *Death, Dying, and the Biological Revolution* from which the following selection is taken.

Veatch argues that in the light of the technological revolution in medicine, a better definition of death is needed. He sets forth four levels in the definition of death and argues that the Harvard committee's redefinition does not go far enough. Veatch advocates the notion that the irreversible loss of functioning in the cerebral neocortex rather than in the whole brain should be the basic criterion for the determination of death.

FOUR SEPARATE LEVELS in the definition of death debate must be distinguished. First, there is the purely formal analysis of the term *death*, an analysis that gives the structure and specifies the framework that must be filled in with content. Second, the *concept* of death is considered, attempting to fill the content of the formal definition. At this level the question is, What is so essentially significant about life that its loss is termed *death*? Third, there is the question of the locus of death: where in the organism ought one to look to determine whether death has occurred? Fourth, one must ask the question of the criteria of death: what technical tests must be applied at the locus to determine if an individual is living or dead?

Serious mistakes have been made in slipping from one level of the debate to another and in presuming that expertise on one level necessarily implies expertise on another. For instance, the Report of the Ad Hoc Committee of the Harvard Medical School to Examine the Defini-tion of Brain Death is titled "A Definition of Irreversible Coma."[1] The report makes clear that the committee members are simply reporting empirical measures which are criteria for predicting an irreversible coma. (I shall explore later the possibility that they made an important mistake even at this level.) Yet the name of the committee seems to point more to the question of locus, where to look for measurement of death. The committee was established to examine the death of the brain. The implication is that the empirical indications of irreversible coma are also indications of "brain death." But by the first sentence of the report the committee claims that "Our primary purpose is to define irreversible coma as a new criterion for death." They have now shifted so that they are interested in "death." They must be presuming a philosophical concept of death—that a person in irreversible coma should be considered dead—but they nowhere argue this or even state it as a presumption.

Reprinted from Death, Dying, and the Biological Revolution *(New Haven, Conn.: Yale University Press, 1976) by permission.*

Even the composition of the Harvard committee membership signals some uncertainty of purpose. If empirical criteria were their concern, the inclusion of nonscientists on the panel was strange. If the philosophical concept of death was their concern, medically trained people were overrepresented. As it happened, the committee did not deal at all with conceptual matters. The committee and its interpreters have confused the questions at different levels. The remainder of this [essay] will discuss the meaning of death at these four levels.

The Formal Definition of Death

A strictly formal definition of death might be the following: "Death means a complete change in the status of a living entity characterized by the irreversible loss of those characteristics that are essentially significant to it." Such a definition would apply equally well to a human being, a nonhuman animal, a plant, an organ, a cell, or even metaphorically to a social phenomenon like a society or to any temporally limited entity like a research project, a sports event, or a language. To define the death of a human being, we must recognize the characteristics that are essential to humanness. It is quite inadequate to limit the discussion to the death of the heart or the brain.

Henry Beecher, the distinguished physician who chaired the Harvard committee that proposed a "definition of irreversible coma," has said that "at whatever level we *choose* . . . , it is an arbitrary decision" [italics added].[2] But he goes on, "It is *best* to choose a level where although the brain is dead, usefulness of other organs is still present" [italics added]. Now, clearly he is not making an "arbitrary decision" any longer. He recognizes that there are policy payoffs. He, like the rest of us, realizes that death already has a well-established meaning. It is the task of the current debate to clarify that meaning for a few rare and difficult cases. We use the term *death* to

mean the loss of what is essentially significant to an entity—in the case of man, the loss of humanness. The direct link of a word *death* to what is "essentially significant" means that the task of defining it in this sense is first and foremost a philosophical, theological, ethical task.

The Concept of Death

To ask what is essentially significant to a human being is a philosophical question—a question of ethical and other values. Many elements make human beings unique—their opposing thumbs, their possession of rational souls, their ability to form cultures and manipulate symbol systems, their upright postures, their being created in the image of God, and so on. Any concept of death will depend directly upon how one evaluates these qualities. Four choices seem to me to cover the most plausible approaches.

Irreversible Loss of Flow of Vital Fluids

At first it would appear that the irreversible cessation of heart and lung activity would represent a simple and straightforward statement of the traditional understanding of the concept of death in Western culture. Yet upon reflection this proves otherwise. If patients simply lose control of their lungs and have to be permanently supported by a mechanical respirator, they are still living persons as long as they continue to get oxygen. If modern technology produces an efficient, compact heart–lung machine capable of being carried on the back or in a pocket, people using such devices would not be considered dead, even though both heart and lungs were permanently nonfunctioning. Some might consider such a technological man an affront to human dignity; some might argue that such a device should never be connected to a human; but even they would, in all likelihood, agree that such people are alive.

What the traditional concept of death centered on was not the heart and lungs as such, but the flow of vital fluids, that is, the breath and the blood. It is not without reason that these fluids are commonly referred to as "vital." The nature of man is seen as related to this vitality—or vital activity of fluid flow—which man shares with other animals. This fluidity, the movement of liquids and gases at the cellular and organismic level, is a remarkable biological fact. High school biology students are taught that the distinguishing characteristics of "living" things include respiration, circulation of fluids, movement of fluids out of the organism, and the like. According to this view the human organism, like other living organisms, dies when there is an irreversible cessation of the flow of these fluids.

Irreversible Loss of the Soul from the Body

There is a longstanding tradition, sometimes called vitalism, that holds the essence of man to be independent of the chemical reactions and electrical forces that account for the flow of the bodily fluids. Aristotle and the Greeks spoke of the soul as the animating principle of life. The human being, according to Aristotle, differs from other living creatures in possessing a rational soul as well as vegetative and animal souls. This idea later became especially pronounced in the dualistic philosophy of gnosticism, where salvation was seen as the escape of the enslaved soul from the body. Christianity in its Pauline and later Western forms shares the view that the soul is an essential element in the living man. While Paul and some later theologian-scholars including Erasmus and Luther sometimes held a tripartite anthropology that included spirit as well as body and soul, a central element in all their thought seems to be animation of the body by a noncorporeal force. In Christianity, however, contrasting to the gnostic tradition, the body is a crucial element—not a prison from which the soul escapes, but a significant part of the person. This will become important later in this discussion. The soul remains a central element in the concept of man in most folk religion today.

The departure of the soul might be seen by believers as occurring at about the time that the fluids stop flowing. But it would be a mistake to equate these two concepts of death, as according to the first fluid stops from natural, if unexplained, causes, and death means nothing more than that stopping of the flow which is essential to life. According to the second view, the fluid stops flowing at the time the soul departs, and it stops because the soul is no longer present. Here the essential thing is the loss of the soul, not the loss of the fluid flow.

The Irreversible Loss of the Capacity for Bodily Integration

In the debate between those who held a traditional religious notion of the animating force of the soul and those who had the more naturalistic concept of the irreversible loss of the flow of bodily fluids, the trend to secularism and empiricism made the loss of fluid flow more and more the operative concept of death in society. But man's intervention in the dying process through cardiac pacemakers, respirators, intravenous medication and feeding, and extravenous purification of blood has forced a sharper examination of the naturalistic concept of death. It is now possible to manipulate the dying process so that some parts of the body cease to function while other parts are maintained indefinitely. This has given rise to disagreements within the naturalistic camp itself. In its report, published in 1968, the interdisciplinary Harvard Ad Hoc Committee to Examine the Definition of Brain Death gave two reasons for their undertaking. First, they argued that improvements in resuscitative and supportive measures had sometimes had only partial success, putting a great burden on "patients who suffer permanent loss of intellect, on their families, on the hospitals, and on those in need of hospital beds already occupied by these comatose patients." Second, they argued that "obsolete criteria for the definition of death can lead to controversy in obtaining organs for transplantation."

These points have proved more controversial than they may have seemed at the time. In the first place, the only consideration of the patient among the reasons given for changing the definition of death was the suggestion that a comatose patient can feel a "great burden." If the committee is right, however, in holding that the person is in fact dead despite continued respiration and circulation, then all the benefits of the change in definition will come to other individuals or to society at large. For those who hold that the primary ethical consideration in the care of the patient should be the patient's own interest, this is cause for concern.

In the second place, the introduction of transplant concerns into the discussion has attracted particular criticism. Paul Ramsey, among others, has argued against making the issue of transplant a reason for updating the definition of death: "If no person's death should *for this purpose* be hastened, then the definition of death should not *for this purpose* be updated, or the procedures for stating that a man has died be revised as a means of affording easier access to organs."[3]

At first it would appear that the irreversible loss of brain activity is the concept of death held by those no longer satisfied with the vitalistic concept of the departure of the soul or the animalistic concept of the irreversible cessation of fluid flow. This is why the name *brain death* is frequently given to the new proposals, but the term is unfortunate for two reasons.

First, as we have seen, it is not the heart and lungs as such that are essentially significant but rather the vital functions—the flow of fluids—which we believe according to the best empirical human physiology to be associated with these organs. An "artificial brain" is not a present-day possibility but a walking, talking, thinking individual who had one would certainly be considered living. It is not the collection of physical tissues called the brain, but rather their functions—consciousness; motor control; sensory feeling; ability to reason; control over bodily functions including respiration and circulation; major integrating reflexes controlling blood pressure, ion levels, and pupil size; and so forth—which are given essential significance by those who advocate adoption of a new concept of death or clarification of the old one. In short they see the body's capacity for integrating its functions as the essentially significant indication of life.

Second, as suggested earlier, we are not interested in the death of particular cells, organs, or organ systems but in the death of the person as a whole—the point at which the person as a whole undergoes a quantum change through the loss of characteristics held to be essentially significant, the point at which "death behavior" becomes appropriate. Terms such as *brain death* or *heart death* should be avoided because they tend to obscure the fact that we are searching for the meaning of the death of the person as a whole. At the public policy level, this has very practical consequences. A statute adopted in Kansas specifically refers to "alternative definitions of death" and says that they are "to be used for all purposes in this state. . . ." According to this language, which has resulted from talking of brain and heart death, a person in Kansas may be simultaneously dead according to one definition and alive according to another. When a distinction must be made, it should be made directly on the basis of the philosophical significance of the functions mentioned above rather than on the importance of the tissue collection called the brain. For purposes of simplicity we shall use the phrase *the capacity for bodily integration* to refer to the total list of integrating mechanisms possessed by the body. The case for these mechanisms being the ones that are essential to humanness can indeed be made. Man is more than the flowing of fluids. He is a complex, integrated organism with capacities for internal regulation. With and only with these integrating mechanisms is *Homo sapiens* really a human person.

There appear to be two general aspects to this concept of what is essentially significant: first, a capacity for integrating one's internal bodily environment (which is done for the most part unconsciously through highly complex homeostatic, feedback mechanisms) and, secondly, a capacity for integrating one's self, including one's body, with the social environment through consciousness, which permits interaction with other persons. Clearly these taken together offer a more profound understanding of the nature of man than does the simple flow of bodily fluids. Whether or not it is more a profound concept of man than that which focuses simply on the presence or absence of the soul, it is clearly a very different one. The ultimate test between the two is that of meaningfulness and plausibility. For many in the modern secular society, the concept of loss of capacity for bodily integration seems much more meaningful and plausible, that is, we see it as a much more accurate description of the essential significance of man and of what is lost at the time of death. According to this view, when individuals lose all of these "truly vital" capacities we should call them dead and behave accordingly.

At this point the debate may just about have been won by the defenders of the neurologically oriented concept. For the most part the public sees the main dispute as being between partisans of the heart and the brain. Even court cases like the Tucker suit and the major articles in the scientific and philosophical journals have for the most part confined themselves to contrasting these two rather crudely defined positions. If these were the only alternatives, the discussion probably would be nearing an end. There are, however, some critical questions that are just beginning to be asked. This new round of discussion was provoked by the recognition that it may be possible in rare cases for a person to have the higher brain centers destroyed but still retain lower brain functions, including spontaneous respiration.[4] This has led to the question of just what brain functions are essentially significant to man's nature. A fourth major concept of death thus emerges.

The Irreversible Loss of the Capacity for Social Interaction

The fourth major alternative for a concept of death draws on the characteristics of the third concept and has often been confused with it. Henry Beecher offers a summary of what he considers to be essential to man's nature: "the individual's personality, his conscious life, his uniqueness, his capacity for remembering, judging, reasoning, acting, enjoying, worrying, and so on. . . ."[5]

Beecher goes on immediately to ask the anatomical question of locus. He concludes that these functions reside in the brain and that when the brain no longer functions, the individual is dead. We shall take up the locus question later in this [essay]. What is remarkable is that Beecher's list, with the possible exception of "uniqueness," is composed entirely of functions explicitly related to consciousness and the capacity to relate to one's social environment through interaction with others. All the functions which give the capacity to integrate one's internal bodily environment through unconscious, complex, homeostatic reflex mechanisms—respiration, circulation, and major integrating reflexes—are omitted. In fact, when asked what was essentially significant to man's living, Beecher replied simply, "Consciousness."

Thus a fourth concept of death is the irreversible loss of the capacity for consciousness or social integration. This view of the nature of man places even more emphasis on social character. Even, given a hypothetical human being with the full capacity for integration of bodily function, if he had irreversibly lost the capacity for consciousness and social interaction, he would have lost the essential character of humanness and, according to this definition, the person would be dead.

Even if one moves to the so-called higher functions and away from the mere capacity to integrate bodily functions through reflex mechanisms, it is still not clear precisely what is ultimately valued. We must have a more careful specification of "consciousness or the capacity for social integration." Are these two capacities synonymous and, if not, what is the relationship between them? Before taking up that question, we must first make clear what is meant by capacity.

Holders of this concept of death and related concepts of the essence of man specifically do not say that individuals must be valued by others in order to be human. This would place life at the mercy of other human beings who may well be cruel or insensitive. Nor does this concept imply that the essence of man is the fact of social interaction with others, as this would also place a person at the mercy of others. The infant raised in complete isolation from other human contact would still be human, provided that the child retained the mere capacity for some form of social interaction. This view of what is essentially significant to the nature of man makes no quantitative or qualitative judgments. It need not, and for me could not, lead to the view that those who have more capacity for social integration are more human. The concepts of life and death are essentially bipolar, threshold concepts. Either one has life or one does not. Either a particular type of death behavior is called for or it is not. One does not pronounce death half-way or read a will half-way or become elevated from the vice presidency to the presidency half-way.

One of the real dangers of shifting from the third concept of death to the fourth is that the fourth, in focusing exclusively on the capacity for consciousness or social interaction, lends itself much more readily to quantitative and qualitative considerations. When the focus is on the complete capacity for bodily integration, including the ability of the body to carry out spontaneous respiratory activity and major reflexes, it is

quite easy to maintain that if any such integrating function is present the person is alive. But when the question begins to be, "What kinds of integrating capacity are really significant?" one finds oneself on the slippery slope of evaluating kinds of consciousness or social interaction. If consciousness is what counts, it might be asked if a long-term catatonic schizophrenic or a patient with extreme senile dementia really has the capacity for consciousness. To position oneself for such a slide down the slope of evaluating the degree of capacity for social interaction is extremely dangerous. It seems to me morally obligatory to stay off the slopes.

Precisely what are the functions considered to be ultimately significant to human life according to this concept? There are several possibilities.

The capacity for rationality is one candidate. *Homo sapiens* is a rational animal, as suggested by the name. The human capacity for reasoning is so unique and so important that some would suggest that it is the critical element in man's nature. But certainly infants lack any such capacity and they are considered living human beings. Nor is possession of the potential for reasoning what is important. Including potential might resolve the problem of infants, but does not explain why those who have no potential for rationality (such as the apparently permanent backward psychotic or the senile individual) are considered to be humanly living in a real if not full sense and to be entitled to the protection of civil and moral law.

Consciousness is a second candidate that dominates much of the medical and biological literature. If the rationalist tradition is reflected in the previous notion, then the empiricalist philosophical tradition seems to be represented in the emphasis on consciousness. What may be of central significance is the capacity for experience. This would include the infant and the individual who lacks the capacity for rationality, and focuses attention on the ability for sensory activity summarized as consciousness. Yet, this is a very individualistic understanding of man's nature. It describes what is essentially significant to the human life without any reference to other human beings.

Social interaction is a third candidate. At least in the Western tradition, man is seen as an essentially social animal. Perhaps it is man's capacity or potential for social interaction that has such ultimate significance that its loss is considered death. Is this in any sense different from the capacity for experience? Certainly it is conceptually different and places a very different emphasis on man's essential role. Yet it may well be that the two functions, experience and social interaction, are completely coterminous. It is difficult to conceive a case where the two could be separated, at least if social interaction is understood in its most elementary form. While it may be important for a philosophical understanding of man's nature to distinguish between these two functions, it may not be necessary for deciding when a person has died. Thus, for our purposes we can say that the fourth concept of death is one in which the essential element that is lost is the capacity for consciousness or social interaction or both.

The concept presents one further problem. The Western tradition which emphasizes social interaction also emphasizes, as we have seen, the importance of the body. Consider the admittedly remote possibility that the electrical impulses of the brain could be transferred by recording devices onto magnetic computer tape. Would that tape together with some kind of minimum sensory device be a living human being and would erasure of the tape be considered murder? If the body is really essential to man, then we might well decide that such a creature would not be a living human being.

Where does this leave us? The alternatives are summarized in the table at the end of the [essay]. The earlier concepts of death—the irreversible loss of the soul and the irreversible stopping of the flow of vital body fluids—strike me as quite implausible. The soul as an independent nonphysical entity that is necessary and

sufficient for a person to be considered alive is a relic from the era of dichotomized anthropologies. Animalistic fluid flow is simply too base a function to be the human essence. The capacity for bodily integration is more plausible, but I suspect it is attractive primarily because it includes those higher functions that we normally take to be central—consciousness, the ability to think and feel and relate to others. When the reflex networks that regulate such things as blood pressure and respiration are separated from the higher functions, I am led to conclude that it is the higher functions which are so essential that their loss ought to be taken as the death of the person. While consciousness is certainly important, man's social nature and embodiment seem to me to be the truly essential characteristics. I therefore believe that death is most appropriately thought of as the irreversible loss of the embodied capacity for social interaction.

The Locus of Death

Thus far I have completely avoided dealing with anatomy. Whenever the temptation arose to formulate a concept of death by referring to organs or tissues such as the heart, lungs, brain, or cerebral cortex, I have carefully resisted. Now finally I must ask, "Where does one look if one wants to know whether a person is dead or alive?" This question at last leads into the field of anatomy and physiology. Each concept of death formulated in the previous section (by asking what is of essential significance to the nature of man) raises a corresponding question of where to look to see if death has occurred. This level of the definitional problem may be called the locus of death.

The term *locus* must be used carefully. I have stressed that we are concerned about the death of the individual as a whole, not a specific part. Nevertheless, differing concepts of death will lead us to look at different body functions and structures in order to diagnose the death of the person as a whole. This task can be undertaken only after the conceptual question is resolved, if what we really want to know is where to look to determine if a person is dead rather than where to look to determine simply if the person has irreversibly lost the capacity for vital fluid flow or bodily integration or social interaction. What then are the different loci corresponding to the different concepts?

The *loci* corresponding to the irreversible loss of vital fluid flow are clearly the heart and blood vessels, the lungs and respiratory tract. At least according to our contemporary empirical knowledge of physiology and anatomy, in which we have good reason to have confidence, these are the vital organs and organ systems to which the tests should have applied to determine if a person has died. Should a new Harvey reveal evidence to the contrary, those who hold to the concept of the irreversible loss of vital fluid flow would probably be willing to change the site of their observations in diagnosing death.

The locus, or the "seat," of the soul has not been dealt with definitively since the day of Descartes. In his essay "The Passions of the Soul," Descartes pursues the question of the soul's dwelling place in the body. He argues that the soul is united to all the portions of the body conjointly, but, nevertheless, he concludes:

> There is yet . . . a certain part in which it exercises its functions more particularly than in all the others; and it is usually believed that this part is the brain, or possibly the heart: the brain, because it is with it that the organs of sense are connected, and the heart because it is apparently in it that we experience the passions. But in examining the matter with care, it seems as though I had clearly ascertained that the part of the body in which the soul exercises its functions immediately is in no wise the heart, not the whole of the brain, but merely the most inward of all its parts, to wit, a certain very small gland which is situated in the middle of its substance. . . .[6]

Descartes is clearly asking the question of locus. His anatomical knowledge is apparently sound, but his conclusion that the soul resides primarily and directly in the pineal body raises physiological and theological problems which most of us are unable to comprehend today. What is significant is that he seemed to hold that the irreversible loss of the soul is the critical factor in determining death, and he was asking the right kind of question about where to look to determine whether a man is dead.

The fact that the Greek term *pneuma* has the dual meaning of both breath and soul or spirit could be interpreted to imply that the presence of this animating force is closely related to (perhaps synonymous with) breath. This gives us another clue about where holders of the irreversible loss of the soul concept of death might look to determine the presence or absence of life.

The locus for loss of capacity for bodily integration is a more familiar concept today. The anatomist and physiologist would be sure that the locus of the integrating capacity is the central nervous system, as Sherrington has ingrained into the biomedical tradition. Neurophysiologists asked to find this locus might reasonably request a more specific concept, however. They are aware that the autonomic nervous system and spinal cord play a role in the integrating capacity, both as transmitters of nervous impulses and as the central analyzers for certain simple acts of integration (for example, a withdrawal reflex mediated through the spinal cord); they would have to know whether one was interested in such simple reflexes.

Beecher gives us the answer quite specifically for his personal concept of death: he says spinal reflexes are to be omitted.[7] This leaves the brain as essentially the place to look to determine whether a man is dead according to the third concept of death. The brain's highly complex circuitry provides the minimal essentials for the body's real integrating capacity. This third concept quite specifically includes unconscious homeostatic and higher reflex mechanisms such as spontaneous respiration and pupil reflexes. Thus, anatomically, according to our reading of neurophysiology, we are dealing with the whole brain, including the cerebellum, medulla, and brainstem. This is the basis for calling the third concept of death *brain death,* and we already discussed objections to this term.

Where to seek the locus for irreversible loss of the capacity for social interaction, the fourth conception of death, is quite another matter. We have eliminated unconscious reflex mechanisms. The answer is clearly not the whole brain—it is much too massive. Determining the locus of consciousness and social interaction certainly requires greater scientific understanding, but evidence points strongly to the neocortex or outer surface of the brain as the site.[8] Indeed, if this is the locus of consciousness, the presence or absence of activity in the rest of the brain will be immaterial to the holder of this view.

The Criteria of Death

Having determined a concept of death, which is rooted in a philosophical analysis of the nature of man, and a locus of death, which links this philosophical understanding to the anatomy and physiology of the human body, we are finally ready to ask the operational question, What tests or measurements should be applied to determine if an individual is living or dead? At this point we have moved into a more technical realm in which the answer will depend primarily on the data gathered from the biomedical sciences.

Beginning with the first concept of death, irreversible loss of vital fluid flow, what criteria can be used to measure the activity of the heart and lungs, the blood vessels and respiratory track? The methods are simple: visual observation of respiration, perhaps by the use of the classic mirror held at the nostrils; feeling the pulse; and listening for the heartbeat. More technical measures are also now available to the trained clinician: the electrocardiogram and direct measures of oxygen and carbon dioxide levels in the blood.

If Descartes' conclusion is correct that the locus of the soul is in the pineal body, the logical question would be "How does one know when the pineal body has irreversibly ceased to function?" or more precisely "How does one know when the soul has irreversibly departed from the gland?" This matter remains baffling for the modern neurophysiologist. If, however, holders of the soul-departing concept of death associate the soul with the breath, as suggested by the word *pneuma,* this might give us another clue. If respiration and specifically breath are the locus of the soul, then the techniques discussed above as applying to respiration might also be the appropriate criteria for determining the loss of the soul.

We have identified the (whole) brain as the locus associated with the third concept of death, the irreversible loss of the capacity for bodily integration. The empirical task of identifying criteria in this case is to develop accurate predictions of the complete and irreversible loss of brain activity. This search for criteria was the real task carried out by the Ad Hoc Committee to Examine the Definition of Brain Death of Harvard Medical School; the simple criteria they proposed have become the most widely recognized in the United States:

1. Unreceptivity and unresponsitivity
2. No movements or breathing
3. No reflexes
4. Flat electroencephalogram

The report states that the fourth criterion is "of great confirmatory value." It also calls for the repetition of these tests twenty-four hours later. Two types of cases are specifically excluded: hypothermia (body temperature below 90°F) and the presence of central nervous system depressants such as barbiturates.[9]

Other criteria have been proposed to diagnose the condition of irreversible loss of brain function. James Toole, a neurologist at the Bowman Gray School of Medicine, has suggested that metabolic criteria such as oxygen consumption of the brain or the measure of metabolic products in the blood or cerebrospinal fluid could possibly be developed as well.[10]

European observers seem to place more emphasis on demonstrating the absence of circulation in the brain. This is measured by angiography, radioisotopes, or sonic techniques.[11] In Europe sets of criteria analogous to the Harvard criteria have been proposed. G. P. J. Alexandre, a surgeon who heads a Belgian renal transplant department, reports that in addition to absence of reflexes as criteria of irreversible destruction of the brain, he uses lack of spontaneous respiration, a flat EEG, complete bilateral mydriasis, and falling blood pressure necessitating increasing amounts of vasopressive drugs.[12] J. P. Revillard, a Frenchman, reportedly uses these plus angiography and absence of reaction to atropine.[13] Even among those who agree on the types of measure, there may still be disagreement on the levels of measurement. This is especially true for the electroencephalogram, which can be recorded at varying sensitivities and for different time periods. The Harvard-proposed twenty-four-hour period is now being questioned as too conservative.

While these alternate sets of criteria are normally described as applicable to measuring loss of brain function (or "brain death" as in the name of the Harvard committee), it appears that many of these authors, especially the earlier ones, have not necessarily meant to distinguish them from criteria for measuring the narrower loss of cerebral function.

The criteria for irreversible loss of the capacity for social interaction are far more selective. It should be clear from the above criteria that they measure loss of all brain activity, including spontaneous respiration and higher reflexes and not simply loss of consciousness. This raises a serious problem about whether the Harvard criteria re-

ally measure "irreversible coma" as the report title indicates. Exactly what is measured is an entirely empirical matter. In any case, convincing evidence has been cited by the committee and more recently by a committee of the Institute of Society, Ethics and the Life Sciences that no one will falsely be pronounced in irreversible coma. In 128 patients who underwent autopsy, the brain was found to be "obviously destroyed" in each case.[14] Of 2,650 patients with isoelectric EEGs of twenty-four hours' duration, not one patient recovered ("excepting three who had received anesthetic doses of CNS depressants, and who were, therefore, outside the class of patients covered by the report").[15]

What then is the relationship between the more inclusive Harvard criteria and the simple use of electrocerebral silence as measured by an isoelectric or flat electroencephalogram? The former might be appropriate for those who associate death with the disappearance of any neurological function of the brain. For those who hold the narrower concept based simply on consciousness or capacity for social interaction, however, the Harvard criteria may suffer from exactly the same problem as the old heart- and lung-oriented criteria. With those criteria, every patient whose circulatory and respiratory function had ceased was indeed dead, but the criteria might be too conservative, in that some patients dead according to the "loss of bodily integrating capacity" concept of death (for which the brain is the corresponding locus) would be found alive according to heart- and lung-oriented criteria. It might also happen that some patients who should be declared dead according to the irreversible loss of consciousness and social interaction concept would be found to be alive according to the Harvard criteria.[16] All discussions of the neurological criteria fail to consider that the criteria might be too inclusive, too conservative. The criteria might, therefore, give rise to classifying patients as dead according to the consciousness or social interaction conception, but as alive according to the full Harvard criteria.

A report in *Lancet* by the British physician J. B. Brierley and his colleagues implies this may indeed be the case.[17] In two cases in which patients had undergone cardiac arrest resulting in brain damage, they report, "the electroencephalogram (strictly defined) was isoelectric throughout. Spontaneous respiration was resumed almost at once in case 2, but not until day 21 in case l."[18] They report that the first patient did not "die" until five months later. For the second patient they report, "The patient died on day 153." Presumably in both cases they were using the traditional heart and lung locus and correlated criteria for death as they pronounced it. They report that subsequent detailed neuropathological analysis confirmed that the "neocortex was dead while certain brainstem and spinal centers remained intact." These intact centers specifically involved the functions of spontaneous breathing and reflexes: eye-opening, yawning, and "certain reflex activities at brainstem and spinal cord levels." As evidence that lower brain activity remained, they report that an electroretinogram (measuring electrical activity of the eye) in patient 1 was normal on day 13. After day 49 there still remained reactivity of the pupils to light in addition to spontaneous respiration.

If this evidence is sound, it strongly suggests that it is empirically as well as theoretically possible to have irreversible loss of cortical function (and therefore loss of consciousness) while lower brain functions remain intact.

This leaves us with the empirical question of the proper criteria for the irreversible loss of consciousness which is thought to have its locus in the neocortex of the cerebrum. Brierley and his colleagues suggest that the EEG alone (excluding the other three criteria of the Harvard report) measures the activity of the neocortex.[19] Presumably this test must also meet the carefully specified conditions of amplifier gain, repeat of the test after a given time period, and exclusion of the exceptional cases, if it is to be used as the criterion for death according to our fourth concept, irreversible loss of capacity for social interaction. The empirical evidence is not all in, but

it would seem that the 2,650 cases of flat EEG without recovery which are cited to support the Harvard criteria would also be persuasive preliminary empirical evidence for the use of the EEG alone as empirical evidence for the irreversible loss of consciousness and social interaction which (presumably) have their locus in the neocortex. What these 2,650 cases would have to include for the data to be definitive would be a significant number of Brierley-type patients where the EEG criteria were met without the other Harvard criteria being met. This is a question for the neurophysiologists to resolve.

There is another problem with the use of electroencephalogram, angiography, or other techniques for measuring cerebral function as a criterion for the irreversible loss of consciousness. Once again we must face the problem of a false positive diagnosis of life. The old heart and lung criteria may provide a false positive diagnosis for a holder of the bodily integrating capacity concept, and the Harvard criteria may give false positive indications for a holder of the consciousness or social interaction concept. Could a person have electroencephalographic activity but still have no capacity for consciousness or social interaction? Whether this is possible empirically is difficult to say, but at least theoretically there are certainly portions of the neocortex which could be functioning and presumably be recorded on an electroencephalogram without the individual having any capacity for consciousness. For instance, what if through an accident or vascular occlusion the motor cortex remained viable but the sensory cortex did not? Even the most narrow criterion of the electroencephalogram alone may still give false positive diagnoses of living for holders of the social interaction concept.

Notes

1. Ad Hoc Committee of the Harvard Medical School to Examine the Definition of Brain Death, "A Definition of Irreversible Coma," *Journal of the American Medical Association* (1968), 205:337–340.

Table 28.1 Levels of the Definition of Death

Formal Definition: Death means a complete change in the status of a living entity characterized by the irreversible loss of those characteristics that are essentially significant to it.

Concept of death:	Locus of death:	Criteria of death:
Philosophical or theological judgment of the essentially significant change at death	Place to look to determine if a person has died	Measurements physicians or other officials use to determine whether a person is dead—to be determined by scientific empirical study
1. The irreversible stopping of the flow of "vital" body fluids, i.e., the blood and breath	Heart and lungs	1. Visual observation of respiration, perhaps with the use of a mirror 2. Feeling of the pulse, possibly supported by electrocardiogram
2. The irreversible loss of the soul from the body	The pineal body? (according to Descartes) The respiratory tract?	Observation of breath?
3. The irreversible loss of the capacity for bodily integration and social interaction	The brain	1. Unreceptivity and responsivity 2. No movements or breathing 3. No reflexes (except spinal reflexes) 4. Flat electroencephalogram (to be used as confirmatory evidence) —All tests to be repeated 24 hours later (excluded conditions: hypothermia and central nervous system drug depression)
4. Irreversible loss of consciousness or the capacity for social interaction	Probably the neocortex	Electroencephalogram

Note: The possible concepts, loci, and criteria of death are much more complex than the ones given here. These are meant to be simplified models of types of positions being taken in the current debate. It is obvious that those who believe that death means the irreversible loss of the capacity for bodily integration (3) or the irreversible loss of consciousness (4) have no reservations about pronouncing death when the heart and lungs have ceased to function. This is because they are willing to use loss of heart and lung activity as shortcut criteria for death, believing that once heart and lungs have stopped, the brain or neocortex will necessarily stop as well.

2. Henry K. Beecher, "The New Definition of Death, Some Opposing Views," paper presented at the meeting of the American Association for the Advancement of Science, December 1970, p. 2.

3. Paul Ramsey, "On Updating Procedures for Stating That a Man Has Died," in *The Patient as Person* (New Haven, Conn.: Yale University Press, 1970), p. 103.

4. J. B. Brierley, J. A. H. Adams, D. I. Graham, and J. A. Simpson, "Neocortical Death after Cardiac Arrest," *Lancet*, September 11, 1971, pp. 560–565.

5. Beecher, "The New Definition of Death," p. 4.

6. René Descartes, "The Passions of the Soul," in *The Philosophical Works of Descartes* (Cambridge, England: Cambridge University Press, 1911), 1:345.

7. Beecher, "The New Definition of Death," p. 2.

8. Brierley et al., "Neocortical Death."

9. Ad Hoc Committee of the Harvard Medical School," A Definition of Irreversible Coma," pp. 337–338. See also F. Mellerio, "Clinical and EEG Study of a Case of Acute Poisoning with Cerebral Electrical Silence, Followed by Recovery," *Electroencephalography Clinical Neurophysiology* (1971), 30:270–271.

10. James F. Toole, "The Neurologist and the Concept of Brain Death," *Perspectives in Biology and Medicine* (Summer 1971), p. 602.

11. See, for example, A. A. Hadijidimos, M. Brock, P. Baum, and K. Schurmann, "Cessation of Cerebral Blood Flow in Total Irreversible Loss of Brain Function," in M. Brock, C. Fieschi, D. H. Ingvar, N. A. Lassen, and K. Schurmann, eds., *Cerebral Blood Flow* (Berlin: Springer-Verlag, 1969), pp. 209–212; A. Beis et al., "Hemodynamic and Metabolic Studies in 'Coma Depassé,'" *ibid.*, pp. 213–215.

12. G. E. W. Wolstenholme and Maeve O'Connor, eds., *Ethics in Medical Progress: With Special Reference to Transplantation* (Boston: Little, Brown, 1966), p. 69.

13. *Ibid.*, p. 71.

14. Task Force on Death and Dying of the Institute of Society, Ethics and the Life Sciences, "Refinements in Criteria for the Determination of Death: An Appraisal," *Journal of the American Medical Association* (1972), 221:50–51.

15. Daniel Silverman, Richard L. Masland, Michael G. Saunders, and Robert S. Schwab, "Irreversible Coma Associated with Electrocerebral Silence," *Neurology* (1970), 20:525–533.

16. The inclusion of absence of breathing and reflexes in the criteria suggests this, but does not necessarily lead to this. It might be that, empirically, it is necessary for lower brain reflexes and breathing to be absent for twenty-four hours in order to be sure that the patient not only will never regain these functions but will never regain consciousness.

17. Brierley et al., "Neocortical Death." See also Ricardo Ceballos and Samuel C. Little, "Progressive Electroencephalographic Changes in Laminar Necrosis of the Brain," *Southern Medical Journal* (1971), 64:1370–1376.

18. *Ibid.*, p. 560.

19. Brierley et al., "Neocortical Death."

Study Questions

1. What are the four conceptions of death? Which conception seems most plausible to you?
2. What is the Harvard Ad Hoc Committee's view on the notion of brain death? What is Veatch's view on their report?
3. What is Veatch's view on the concept of death? Do you agree?

CHAPTER 29

Euthanasia and the Transition from Life to Death

DAVID J. MAYO AND DANIEL WIKLER

David J. Mayo is associate professor of philosophy at the University of Minnesota, Duluth, and the coeditor of *Suicide: The Philosophical Issues* (1980). Daniel Wikler is associate professor of philosophy at the University of Wisconsin and is the author of several articles in medical ethics.

Mayo and Wikler distinguish four possible states of the human organism. Beginning with death proper, the states are

State 4 All principal life systems of the organism (cardiovascular, central nervous, and pulmonary) irreversibly cease functioning. This is death proper.

State 3 The patient is irreversibly comatose because the entire brain ceases functioning, but cardiovascular pulmonary functions continue because they are maintained by artificial life-support systems.

State 2 The patient is irreversibly comatose because the cerebral cortex has ceased functioning, but the brain stem is still active so that the cardiovascular pulmonary functions continue.

State 1 The dying patient is conscious and in pain and desires to be in state 4.

Next, Mayo and Wikler separate the biological from the valuational or moral dimension. That persons in States 1–3 are alive is a biological fact. But the value question is whether we should keep them alive. Only State 4 constitutes death, properly understood, but our respect for the patient's autonomy should place the burden of proof on those who would paternalistically intervene in preventing the patient from going from State 1 to State 4. In State 2, the case of irreversible coma, we are absolved of any duty to preserve life since it has lost what is valuable about humanity. The same goes for State 3: The patient should be detached from the artificial maintenance and left to die.

IN DISCUSSIONS OF MEDICAL ETHICS, euthanasia is sometimes referred to as if it involved a single issue. But the problems involved are numerous: Must any attempt to justify euthanasia refer exclusively to the interests of the patient? Must death be requested by the patient? Who has the right to make the decision? Is there a moral difference between killing and letting die?[1] The list goes on. One difficulty facing anyone who is discussing euthanasia generally is

Reprinted from "Euthanasia and the Transition from Life to Death," in Medical Responsibility, *edited by Wade L. Robison and Michael Prichard (Clifton, N.J.: Humana Press, 1979).*

that of finding a way to relate all of these questions, particularly since their answers may be interdependent.

The advent of modern life-saving technology has made the situation even more complex. Previously, the issue concerned the propriety of acquiescing to a clear and unmistakable transition from life to death. That transition is no longer so clear, and we must now consider transitions from and to various states. The moral acceptability of any position on euthanasia may vary, depending on whether the transition under consideration involves full consciousness, coma independent of life-support systems, coma dependent on life-support systems, or functional decomposition. Since medicine now has the ability to sustain patients in many cases in any of these states, it must develop moral policies which are appropriate to each. Extant views of euthanasia which were conceived with only the transition from the first to the last of these states in mind may fail for lack of specificity. The problem must be addressed anew.

In Part I of this essay, we will give brief descriptions of the four states just mentioned, and we will proceed to examine some aspects of the euthanasia question as they apply to transitions from each of the first three to the fourth. Part II is concerned with the matter of the definition of death itself. The definition of death has been regarded as having significant logical and moral relationships to the question we are considering. By labeling these states neutrally in Part I, we postpone any discussion on this matter until Part II. Since the disposition of a body after death is not considered to be as serious a moral issue in medical ethics as that of euthanasia, the claim that any one of the states we define is death would imply that any transitions to subsequent states were not really matters of major moral importance. We will argue, however, that death is properly construed as the last of these states only, and hence that it is appropriate to regard the acquiescence to any transition to the final state as euthanasia. And we find fault with

recent "redefinitions" of death, in part because they seem to be motivated by the mistaken notion that substantive moral issues can be sidestepped by simply clarifying or reinterpreting our concept of "death."

I. Transitions

This section highlights some of the moral considerations which are relevant to assessing the moral desirability of transitions between various states occurring near the end of human life. We begin with rough and ready descriptions of four possible states of human organism, which are described in terms which do not pre-suppose an answer to the question, to be explored in Part II, of how death is to be defined.

State 4: Most or all principal life systems—cardiovascular, central-nervous, and pulmonary—have irreversibly ceased functioning.

State 3: The cortex and brain stem have ceased functioning irreversibly; the patient is irreversibly comatose. Metabolic processes in the patient's body continue only because cardiovascular and pulmonary functions are sustained by artificial life-support systems.

State 2: The cortex has permanently ceased functioning, and the patient is irreversibly comatose; but principal life functions continue without artificial support due to brain stem activity.

State 1: The patient is moving quickly and inexorably to subsequent states; however, the patient is conscious and suffering pain, and wishes to be in state 4, rather than in pain.

For patients in any of the first three states, the transition to state 4 is usually more or less imminent, with no significant chance of transition in the direction of regained health. There are three fundamental moral principles which usually bear on the question of whether the inevitable transition to state 4 should always be resisted as long as possible, at whatever cost, or whether there may be circumstances under which one should acquiesce to such a transition:

The Primacy of Life Principle: The preservation of human life is not only valuable, but something the value of which so exceeds any other values we may have that it must never be subordinated to them.

The Principle of Beneficence: A doctor ought to do what is in the best interests of the patient's well-being.

The Principle of Autonomy: Whenever possible, individuals should themselves be the ones to make decisions in matters which involve primarily their own welfare (unless of course their proposed courses of action might infringe on the rights of others).

The fact that each of these principles has an air of plausibility to it, combined with the fact that any two of them may come into conflict, accounts in large measure for the moral difficulty of decisions which confront modern medicine in the treatment of persons in states 1, 2 or 3, and it is to specific consideration of these cases that we now turn.

Patients in State 1

The conflict of principles is straightforward enough in the case of patients in state 1: the Principle of Autonomy supports the view that patients' wishes to acquiesce to the transition to state 4 should be respected. Similarly, the Principle of Beneficence would dictate that patients should be spared unnecessary suffering, and the terminal nature of their condition suggests their suffering may be useless and hence unnecessary. However, the Primacy of Life Principle would dictate that patients' lives must be preserved as long as possible, since the value of life overrides competing values, including the values we place on beneficence and autonomy.

Since the Primacy of Life Principle figures prominently in much popular thinking about these issues, it is worth taking time here to scrutinize this principle carefully. Specifically, we argue against this principle by pointing out that anyone who consistently acted on it would lead an outrageously eccentric and unattractive life. We then deal with the question of what might have seduced anyone in the first place into thinking they should accept a principle, the implications of which are so obviously objectionable.

The Primacy of Life Principle claims that the value of preserving human life is so great that it should never be subordinated to competing values. Reflection suggests that this is a very strong principle, for the force of the word "never" precludes the possibility of compromise, or of weighing life-sustaining considerations against other pressing concerns we may have. In this it differs, for instance, from the much weaker but ultimately more defensible principle that human life has *some* value. Adherence to the Primacy of Life Principle would require that people never do anything which involved risking their lives in any way if they could avoid doing so, however valuable the risk-taking activity might be in other respects. But everyone takes avoidable risks with their lives. Nearly all of us ride in cars and planes and cross streets when we could avoid doing so, and pursue careers in fields in spite of actuarial evidence indicating other vocations would be safer from the point of view of longevity. Many of us live in polluted metropolitan areas, smoke, keep ourselves in less than peak physical shape, and indulge in cuisine proscribed by considerations of taste as well as by considerations of diet. Some people even seek out risks by mountain climbing, sky diving, motorcycling or space exploration. Nor is such behavior universally regarded as irrational; while different people draw the line between courage and foolhardiness at different points, most of us tend to admire certain persons precisely because they do take such risks. Conversely, people who consistently opted only for behavior which involved no avoidable risk to life would be viewed as terribly odd, and rightly so, for they would lead very dull and eccentric lives. Such persons would have to forgo not only aspiration to high public office, but even passionate, emotional involvements with other human beings, since both increase the risk of being murdered. And any woman who accepted the principle with respect to her own life or even all existing lives would have to forgo childbearing.

We believe these considerations show the Primacy of Life Principle is unacceptable. But if this is so, the question arises of how sensible people could ever have come to espouse it? The most obvious answer is that usually we place a very high value on preserving lives, and in the absence of critical scrutiny this *high* value might mistakenly be thought to be an *absolute* one. Some, doubtless, have accepted it on religious grounds. Religious dispute is well beyond the scope of this essay, but it is perhaps relevant to note that many contemporary Western religious authorities in fact endorse acquiescence to death under certain circumstances, and hence do not accept the Primacy of Life Principle. Anyone who did endorse the Primacy of Life Principle on religious grounds, it seems, would also be obliged to lead the very bizarre risk-free life we have sketched previously in our critique of the principle.

A somewhat subtler argument is sometimes given for the Primacy of Life Principle: people value many things, including being alive. But since people must be alive before they can pursue any of their other values, and before they can experience any of the experiences they value, the value on life assumes a special significance. Pursuing the value one places on being alive is a prerequisite for pursuing any other values one may hold. This tempting argument seems to yield the Primacy of Life Principle, which in effect holds that preserving life is to be valued above all other things. But this argument embodies two confusions: the first identifies valuing something with valuing the experience of

that something. This mistaken identification may go undetected because *many* of the things we value *are* experiences. But this is not always the case. People may have values which can be satisfied without their experiencing these values being satisfied, and, indeed, which can be satisfied only without their lives being preserved; the most obvious case of this sort may be the value terminally ill patients in state 1 place on the end of their suffering. (Others would be the value people place on having their estates distributed as they wished after their death, or of being fondly remembered, or of being buried in such-and-such a place.)

The second confusion identifies the requirement that one be alive at one time in order to experience something one values experiencing, with a requirement that one be alive as long as possible afterwards. Even though one may value some kind of experience, it does not follow that that value could not lead the person to act in a way which would ultimately speed death. There would be no logical blunder, nor indeed even any irrationality, in people placing such a high value on the cultural advantages of a big city that they opt to live in cities, even though they realized that they would probably die a few years earlier because of their accompanying tensions and pollution.

The Primacy of Life Principle must be rejected as too strong, and it is clear that some weaker principle must be substituted. Even though we do not place an *uncompromisable* value on preserving human life, we still place a *very high* value on doing so as a rule. A reasonable alternative to the Primacy of Life Principle is this weaker, but more realistic one:

The Preservation of Life Principle: Unless there are overriding considerations to the contrary, human life should be preserved whenever possible.

We suggest there are such considerations in the medical context. The first has to do with the fact that while human life is generally of value, some lives are of greater value than others, and just how valuable a particular life may be depends on a number of things. That different lives are of different values *to others,* or to society at large, is evidenced by some of the considerations that go into triage policies. That different lives are of different value to the persons whose lives they are, is evidenced by the fact that some persons wish their lives would end as soon as possible. Thus lives of unmitigated suffering which are the lot of persons in state 1 are reasonably held to be of less value than healthy lives. That some such persons wish to die because of the pain and hopelessness of their situation certainly shows that their lives are held *by them* to have negative value *for them,* all things considered.

We feel this consideration significantly strengthens the case in favor of acquiescing to the transition from state 1 to state 4, particularly in light of the relatively high value we place on treating others beneficently and on respecting personal autonomy. In our view, these considerations add up to a strong *prima facie* case in favor of respecting the wishes of an individual to acquiesce to the transition from state 1 to state 4, in many cases.

However, this is only a *prima facie* case, for in certain situations, the relevance of beneficence and respect for autonomy may not be so straightforward. For instance, imagine persons whose conditions are terminal and who are suffering greatly at the moment, but for whom the best prognosis is that they will have some relatively pain-free months ahead before they finally succumb. Here, one may feel the Principle of Beneficence requires that such persons be kept alive through the passing period of pain, and even in spite of their present pleas for the release death would bring. A more general doubt may be raised about the relevance of the Principle of Autonomy. All but the most ardent libertarians, for instance, concede that a person's autonomy should not be absolute, and that if people are

"not in control of themselves"—whether from fear, anger, depression, pain or some other form of stress—it may be right to intervene to prevent them from doing significant and irreparable harm to themselves. Of course, persons who are in pain and who are told their condition is terminal may very well "lose control" in this sense—or else be so drugged as to be unable to appraise their situation realistically or reasonably. In such cases, the Principle of Autonomy hardly requires that we respect their stated wishes. Indeed, their stated wishes may even fluctuate wildly from one moment to the next.

The seriousness of this problem should not be underestimated; virtually all serious euthanasia legislation has been sensitive to it. Legislation considered in Great Britain involved a provision whereby persons in state 1 who requested active euthanasia would be given a "cooling off" period during which they could reconsider their request before being killed. The Euthanasia Educational Council's "Living Will" is a document which they urge people to consider and discuss with those who will be involved in decision making, *prior* to finding themselves in the grips of a terminal illness.

On the basis of such considerations, some have argued that the wishes of a person in state 1 should *never* be respected. It is the feeling of the present authors, however, that no such simplistic conclusion is legitimate. Rather, we believe the conclusion to be drawn is that these matters must be considered on a case-by-case basis, in light of the three principles that we have been discussing, along with any others which may apply in particular cases—for instance, those which may involve rights or special interests of other parties. It is our suspicion that in many cases the difficulties cited above are not sufficient to warrant paternalistic intervention, and that to some extent wholesale resistance to respecting the wishes of patients in such situations stems more from an uncritical commitment to the Primacy of Life Principle than it does from any legitimate appeal to considerations which would justify overriding benefi-cence and the autonomy of the individual.[2]

The conclusion which emerges regarding persons in state 1 is that there is no general rea-son why all should be denied the transition they wish for to state 4, and that in cases where their wishes are denied, the burden of proof should be on those who feel such paternalistic inter-vention is warranted. Viewed in this light, the problem of persons in state 1 comes to be seen as a special case of the problem determining the conditions under which it is proper to intervene paternalistically at the expense of someone else's autonomy. A more general point also emerges, however, and that is that any simple principle which would stipulate a standard han-dling of all cases is highly suspect, for the con-siderations which are relevant to such cases are moral considerations, the proper weighing of which depends upon the specifics of individual cases.

Patients in State 2

State 2 is the state in which the cessation of cor-tex function results in irreversible coma, but life functions continue without the aid of artificial support due to brain stem activity. What consid-erations are relevant in this case to the morality of acquiescing to a transition to state 4?

It seems clear enough that here the Principle of Beneficence is irrelevant. The comatose expe-rience no pleasure or pain, and hence the ques-tion of what is conducive to their well-being is moot; in an important sense, such individuals really have no "well-being."

The relevance of the Principle of Autonomy may at first seem likewise negated. In a very straightforward sense, persons in state 2 have and will continue to have no decision-making capacity, and to that extent they lack autonomy. (This is surely one consideration behind the fre-quently made claim that such individuals are no longer "persons.") Thus on first blush it seems that neither acquiescing nor refusing to acqui-

esce to the death of such patients could consti-tute a violation of their autonomy.

By the same token, irreversible coma may well be the most straightforward case of a special circumstance which absolves us from the general obligation imposed by the Preservation of Life Principle, since the factors which normally prompt us to attribute value to human life are completely absent. Surely, it would be wrong to claim that a person's continued existence in state 2 has value from *that person's* point of view; in fact, it seems difficult to make sense of the claim that that person even continues to embody a "point of view." At the very least, the obligation imposed by the Preservation of Life Principle seems drastically weakened.

Within the Hippocratic tradition, it is gener-ally held that peoples' medical care should be dictated by considerations having to do with their well-being, the value their life has for them, their wishes and their autonomy. If, however, all of these considerations become moot at the on-set of irreversible coma, medicine then seems justified in departing from the traditional Hippo-cratic orientation which focuses on these patient-oriented considerations, and in turning instead to considerations having to do with the welfare or well-being of others. While one can imagine circumstances in which the continued mainte-nance of a person in state 2 is most desirable from the point of view of the welfare of others, this surely is not the standard case. Normally there are various stiff costs involved in maintain-ing individuals in state 2, as well as important benefits which are lost. The most obvious are the actual costs of the medical care. Next may be the "emotional costs" to relatives. Then come the indirect "costs" or loss of benefits which oth-ers might have received if scarce medical re-sources had been used on them instead of being tied up in the maintenance of "hopelessly" co-matose patients. The final indirect cost—and surely an underlying consideration behind cer-tain proposed redefinitions of death—is the cost in lives which could have been saved if organs of individuals in state 2 had been available for transplant. With the advent of transplant technology, parts of the comatose individuals themselves come to be regarded as "scarce medical resources" just as legitimately as the hospital beds and medical attention which are required to sustain them in state 2.

In our view, these considerations add up to an impressive case in favor of acquiescing to a transition from state 2 to state 4, unless there are special considerations to the contrary. Unfortunately, however, the matter is not quite this simple. Considerable philosophical complexity is injected into the above analysis, by the fact noted previously, that a person's interests may post-date that person's being interested in them, and even that person's death. Persons may have interests in events, and indeed are routinely granted decision-making autonomy over matters, which they themselves will never experience, because these events occur after their deaths. The most obvious example of this is found in the institution of wills. It is generally recognized that people are entitled to stipulate what is to be done with their property following their death, and that these stipulations will be respected. Similarly, organs to be used for transplant purposes must be donated, not just in the trivial sense that they were previously part of some other body, but in the stronger sense that someone—ideally the person they previously belonged to—must agree to their use by another.

This difficulty is compounded by the fact the survivors frequently invoke not only the expressed wishes of deceased persons in these matters, but also hypothetical wishes. Thus the claim that someone would have wanted his or her organs made available for transplant (had he or she gotten around to considering the matter) might well figure in the proxy decision by a relative to authorize the harvesting of organs and transplant.

There are a number of philosophical complexities surrounding the issue of posthumous interests. Is our respect for wills to be justified in terms of autonomy and posthumous interests, as we suggest above, or is it rather to be justified in terms of the comfort and security the living find in the belief that their wills will in turn be respected? Does the Principle of Autonomy really have any bearing on what becomes of one's kidneys, once one is dead? It is obviously not an issue which bears on the *life* of the deceased person. At what point do appeals to what a dead person wanted, or would have wanted, rely on sentimentality rather than on legitimate respect for the dead person's autonomy? These are all difficult issues, which have received little attention in the literature, and they will not be resolved here. Suffice to say at this point that in any event, unless we are particularly wealthy or particularly sentimental, most of us place some limits on the extent to which we feel the lives of the living are determined by the wishes of the dead, and we do so for the very sound reason that what we do is of no consequence to the dead, in the sense that it does not alter their experience in any way. Because the irreversibly comatose (even if they are alive) at least resemble the dead in this respect, it seems appropriate, in determining whether to acquiesce to the transition to state 4 of a patient in state 2, to at least weigh alongside any actual or hypothetical interest of the comatose patient those considerations having to do with the interests and welfare of others which were mentioned earlier.

As this is done in individual cases, the outcome may be far from clear. At one extreme, it would seem completely unreasonable to sustain a patient in state 2 who had never considered the possibility of being in that condition, if by doing so severe financial hardship were imposed on the family, and scarce medical resources were tied up which otherwise might make an important difference for other patients. At the other extreme, it might seem quite reasonable to sustain in state 2 a patient who had expressed a clear desire to be maintained in the event of having become irreversibly comatose, if the family had sufficient funds, and if doing so did not require scarce medical resources which would be readily available for others if they were not being used in maintaining the comatose patient. Although the vast majority of actual cases doubtless lie closer to the former of these cases than to the latter, difficult intermediate cases exist, and that is in part responsible for the fact that present medical practice is by no means consistent in handling cases of this type. Perhaps philosophical analysis might clear away some of the present confusion, with the result that increasing numbers of persons will clearly assert their own wishes in the matter—hopefully in the direction of acquiescing, in light of the stiff social costs which others must bear if a person is to be maintained in state 2.

Patients in State 3

The state of these patients differs from state 2 in that these patients have suffered irreversible loss of function of the entire brain, with the result that they are not only irreversibly comatose, but in addition they require artificial life-support systems to be maintained. Virtually all of the considerations relevant to the previous case derived from the fact that the patients were in irreversible coma, and hence apply to patients in state 3 as well. The only additional consideration which is relevant to patients in state 3 is that such persons require more in the way of scarce medical resources—the artificial life-support systems and the supervision required for their operation—and this, of course, becomes an additional reason for acquiescing to the transition to state 4. Even here, however, this does not strike us as absolutely decisive; there still remains the possibility that the various social costs might be small or could be easily met, and also that the patient might have expressed vigorous interest in being sustained in the event of irreversible coma. We feel that such cases would be rare, however, and that in the absence of such special circumstances, it would be morally desirable to acquiesce to the transition to state 4.

Mention should be given to a final consideration in favor of maintaining patients in either stages 2 or 3, which is quite different from any of the previous ones. When organs are transplanted, there is frequently some lapse of time between the time a person is selected as a suitable donor, and the time the donated organ is harvested for transplant. During this time, the individual is maintained in state 2 or 3, not for any of the reasons mentioned above, but simply in order to maintain the organ so it will be suitable when it is time to transplant. Of course, the need to preserve an organ for transplant would justify maintaining a patient for the brief period of time in question. However, it is important to note that in this case, the decision to "maintain" a patient in state 2 or 3 until the organ is needed for transplant already presupposes a decision to acquiesce to the transition to state 4 at the moment when the organ finally is needed, so this is a case of a "decision to maintain" only in the most trivial sense.

II. The Redefinition of Death

Throughout the previous discussion we have spoken in the clumsy idiom of "transitions between states" in order to avoid prejudging the question of which state(s) constitute death. It is to this question which we now must turn. To begin, it should be noted that the above discussion would not have strained common sense if it had been conducted in the language of euthanasia. Bearing in mind the literal meaning of the term "euthanasia—good death"—the discussion would then have been presented as dealing with the circumstances under which the transition from life to death would be a good thing rather than a bad one, and hence of the circumstances under which moral agents might acquiesce to death.

That issue, of course, is not an academic one. At this moment, there are in this country alone literally thousands of persons in state 3, as well as some in state 2, and thousands more—friends, relatives, and medical staff—who are presently agonizing over the questions of when these patients will undergo the transition to state 4, and what role, if any, they should play in speeding or delaying that transition. Some of these people (the medical staff) will continue to charge substantial fees for their services until that transition is complete, while others (the friends, relatives, and insurance companies) will doubtless pay those bills, firm in the belief that they are making payment for services rendered to someone who was dying. This belief is obviously shared by the medical staff, who do not as a rule knowingly minister and devote their closest attentions to the dead.

Dying is a process engaged in by the living. Death marks the end of the dying process, not the beginning or middle of it. Just as it is clear to all that someone in state 4 is dead, so it is clear to the vast majority of us that persons who are in states 2 and 3 are dying, and hence not yet dead. The transitions to state 4 from 2 and 3 constitute dying just as clearly as the transition to state 4 from state 1. Although different moral considerations are relevant to acquiescing to death depending on whether the patient is in state 1, or 2 or 3, it seems indisputable that the considerations which are relevant are moral ones in the latter cases just as clearly as in the first. In fact, while in practice it may be psychologically less trying to opt for death in the case of the irreversibly comatose than in the case of the terminal patient who is suffering and wants to die, the case of the comatose is perhaps the more difficult in theory, precisely because it involves the extremely subtle and difficult issues of the limits of a person's autonomy, as well as the shift from the Hippocratic mode of decision-making focusing on patient-related considerations, to a perspective which includes appeals to the welfare of others as well.

Nevertheless, there are those who insist that we are simply wasting our moral energy if we construe the problem of continued treatment of comatose patients as a moral issue. Their view is that it is not really a moral issue at all, but rather a conceptual or scientific one, having to do with the definition of death. If this view is sound, it is certainly of central significance, for it promises a way out of moral choices which are difficult by almost anyone's reckoning. It is to an examination of this strategy, then, that we must now turn our attention.

Several different definitions of death have recently been proposed, calculated to pluck us from the grips of a difficult moral decision to acquiesce to death, by the easy mechanism of redefinition of death. Although the so-called "Harvard definition" of death is only one such definition, it is the one which has presently received the widest attention and acceptance. Accordingly, it will be our central focus here, although one other redefinition of death which has similar objectives will be mentioned in passing.

The substance of the Harvard proposal is well known.[3] The report spells out tests designed to tell whether the patient's cortex and brain stem have irreversibly ceased to function; the tests range from reflex-tests to examination by EEG. It is an empirical claim that a patient who meets these criteria is in fact in state 3 and irreversibly comatose, and medical scientists are obviously qualified to make such a claim if anyone is.

The crux of the Harvard proposal is that persons who meet these conditions should be considered (and pronounced) dead.[4] Thus, for those who accept the proposal, the question of acquiescing to the death of a comatose patient in state 3 is not *answered*, but rather *dismissed* as a logically mistaken question, with no need for any moral deliberation at all. According to the proposal, there really is no question here of "acquiescing to the death" of such patients, for one can only acquiesce to the death of someone who is living, and to accept the Harvard proposal is to accept the claim that patients in state 3 are already dead—and hence, presumably, that they are *not* dying. What has previously struck doctors, concerned relatives, and moral philosophers as a grim and weighty moral issue is in effect made to vanish.

We believe, however, that this is only conceptual sleight of hand, which obscures the inevitable moral component of the problem of the continued maintenance of the irreversibly comatose. The most that can be claimed in the name of cold, hard science is that certain conditions inevitably indicate irreversible coma and loss of brain function. The additional step of claiming that patients in state 3 are dead (and hence of course can be treated as dead people) is surely not cold hard fact at all. It seems, rather, to be a claim which grows out of conceptual confusion, and which appears plausible only because it seduces with a promise of deliverance from the clutches of difficult moral decisions.

The conceptual confusion implicit in the Harvard proposal grows out of confusing value judgments with biological ones. It is enormously plausible to suggest that one of the conditions for a human life *having value* is the possibility of consciousness. But, while the possibility of consciousness seems quite clearly to be a condition of human life *having value*, that is not to say that it is a condition of a human being *having life*.

This might be illustrated by a somewhat facetious analogy. Imagine oil shortages reaching the point where neither heating oil nor synthetics for clothing are available, as a result of which we turn again to animal furs for clothing. Suppose further that rabbits come to be especially valued both because of their warm fur and because of their legendary breeding habits. If, for some reason, a rabbit should have the misfortune of being both bald and sterile, he would *not* be a valuable rabbit. But that is of course not to say that he would be a dead rabbit. In the case of both rabbits and persons, a creature having life is one matter, and that life having value is quite another. "Death" is not a value notion, but a biological notion to be made sense of in

terms of the absence of life, not in terms of the absence of value.

A similar confusion has prompted even more radical proposals for redefining death. While the Harvard proposal focuses on state 3, Robert Veatch[5] notes that state 2 is also an identifiable state: a person may suffer irreversible coma (through the death of the neo-cortex of the brain) even though lower brain stem activity makes spontaneous breathing and heartbeat possible. Such people are not in state 3 and do not meet the Harvard criteria for death, but Veatch argues that this is a defect of the Harvard proposal. The rationale Veatch provides for this is as follows: first, that death is the "irreversible loss of that which is essentially significant to the nature of man," and second, that what is essentially significant to the nature of man is the capacity for experience and social interaction. When these are lost, Veatch argues the person should be regarded as dead. An integral part of Veatch's position is the identification of what is essential to being human, with what is essential to a human being being alive. But of course this too is a confusion, for those are two very different things. Humans are only one kind of living thing: what is essential to being human is something that *differentiates* us from other living things, something which we *do not* share with dogs or trees or mosquitoes. Being alive, on the other hand, is something we *do* share with other living things. To extend our rabbit analogy, suppose we singled out as particularly valuable those rabbits which were especially fertile and whose offspring were particularly furry, and labeled them "schmabbits." Then, a rabbit who first made the status of schmabbit and then became sterile would no longer manifest what was "essentially significant to the nature of schmabbits"—that is, it would not longer be a schmabbit. But that, again, does not mean that it would properly be considered a dead schmabbit, much less that it would be dead *simpliciter*.

More generally, the death of a rabbit, a schmabbit, or of a human being has nothing to do with the loss of those characteristics which differentiate each of them from other kinds of living things, but rather with loss of what they have in common with other living things. Biologists have a concept of life, or of when an organism is alive, that does not appeal to what is unique to some particular living species, but which appeals instead to features common to all living things. It is only because biology has some notion of what life is, apart from the specifics of any species, that it was possible to ask meaningfully "Is there life on Mars, and if so, what is it like?" Being alive is something we have in common with our pets and the lawns and trees in front of our houses; we are all living things. The proper place to turn for a definition of death is not to the kinds of considerations which make this or that life valuable, or which make it different from other forms of life, but rather to the kinds of general biological considerations which justify saying that something is alive.

An adequate definition of life is beyond the scope of this essay, but a few preliminary remarks may be in order. Since life is a process, or rather a structured group of processes, an adequate definition of life will presumably be in terms of the occurrence of life processes, and the definition of death will then be in terms of the cessation of these processes. The matter is not simple, for these processes go on at different levels, and, of course, do not stop all at once. Specifically, being alive cannot mean that all parts are functioning normally (they don't in a deaf, sterile or blind person), or that no parts are machine- or drug-dependent (the diabetic and pacemaker patients are alive). When a biologist says an organism is dead, he or she surely means something like "principal life systems have irreversibly ceased to function." Of course, this raises a series of difficult issues, including the questions of which life systems are the principal ones, how many of them have shut down, and how completely. No biological sophistication is required to realize that they may shut down by degrees—this strikes us as obvious in the case of

large plants such as trees, because the processes shut down over long periods of time. Unfortunately, for many purposes we need—or at least presently feel we need—to be be able to speak of the "moment of death," and if modern medicine continues to refine its techniques for prolonging the process of dying, it is possible that our present notion of death will prove to be inadequate. Our thesis is not that a redefinition of death will never be needed. Our only concern is to argue that when and if such a time arrives, two very different questions must be kept distinct. The question of when the life of an organism has ended is a conceptual question—one focusing on the central concept in biology—and it obviously must be answered in terms of our biological concepts and theory, for that theory embodies our understanding of what life *is*.

The question of when an organism's life *ought* to be terminated, on the other hand, is not a scientific question, nor a conceptual one, but a moral one. Unless these are seen to be very different questions, decisions about whether or not to acquiesce to a person's death—tough and important moral decisions which deserve all the honesty and precision our moral thinking can give them—will come to be regarded as "purely medical judgments," or "purely scientific" judgments, and moral debate and argument will be dismissed as irrelevant to them.

In the course of the Harvard proposal, it is urged that once it has been established that the patient is in an irreversible coma, the patient should be pronounced dead, and then the respirator turned off. It goes on to say:

> The decision to do this and the responsibility for it are to be taken by the physician-in-charge, in consultation with one or more physicians who have been directly involved in the case. It is unsound and undesirable to force the family to make the decision.[6]

While this eagerness to exclude non-professionals spares relatives from having to make a morally difficult decision, it also denies them their rightful role in such decision-making. But even more troubling is the fact that the Harvard proposal would spare even the doctors the realization that they are in fact deciding that someone should die. Some such decisions are correct ones we believe, but all ought to be faced honestly for what they are—decisions to end someone's life.

Notes

1. The killing/letting die distinction is a very difficult issue, one which we wish to avoid here. In order to keep our language neutral with respect to this issue, we will speak about the moral desirability of "acquiescing" to certain transitions from one state to another, and thereby leave open for further discussion the question of whether the moral acceptability of "acquiescing" might depend on whether, in a particular case, it was a matter of accelerating the transition, or of merely not acting to decelerate it.

2. The medical context generates some curious paradoxes with respect to our usual thinking about autonomy. Many of our decisions in life—whom to marry, whether to go mountain climbing—are made on impulse, even in confusion. They may have irreversible consequences. But no one makes us prove that we are in a rational frame of mind before we are allowed to act in these matters. Similarly, sick persons may decide not to see doctors, and that, too, is their privilege. Once the patient is in the doctor's care, however, the requirements for free action are made more stringent. Patients must show that they are rational before their wish to die is respected—and it may not be respected even then. The patient, who may be suffering from cancer or other physical disease, is treated as a psychiatric patient. We do not want to claim that obviously confused or irrationally depressed patients should be allowed to order their own deaths. The issue is much subtler, and our own intuitions are mixed. Yet, we wish to point out the inconsistency: perhaps physicians' fealty to the principle that they must do all they can for their patients should not lead them to forget that this principle merely sets the limit on what may be asked of them by their patients. If the patients' autonomy is strictly respected, perhaps they must be free to ask for less.

3. Ad Hoc Committee of the Harvard Medical School to Examine the Definition of Brain Death, "A Definition of Irreversible Coma," *J.A.M.A.* 205, No. 6, pp. 337–340, 1968.

4. It is not entirely clear whether the Ad Hoc Committee proposed its tests as new tests for the same condition tested for by previous criteria, or whether a new condition was being defined; we will assume the latter here.

5. Robert M. Veatch, "The Whole-Brain-Oriented Concept of Death: An Outmoded Philosophical Formulation," *J. Thanat.* 3, pp. 13–30, No. 1 for 1975.

6. Ad Hoc Committee, *op. cit.,* p. 338.

Study Questions

1. How do Mayo and Wikler differ from Veatch on the definition of death?
2. What are their four states of the human organism with regard to death and dying?
3. What is their view on keeping irreversibly comatose persons alive by artificial maintenance? Do you agree with them?

For Further Reading

Culver, Charles, and Bernard Gert. *Philosophy in Medicine.* New York: Oxford University Press, 1982.

Engelhardt, H. Tristram, Jr. *The Foundations of Bioethics.* New York: Oxford University Press, 1986. Chapter 6.

President's Commission for the Study of Ethical Problems in Medicine and Biomedical and Behavioral Research: Defining Death (1981).

Veatch, Robert M. *Death, Dying, and the Biological Revolution.* New Haven, Conn.: Yale University Press, 1976.

Part VII

Abortion

Introduction

A major social issue before us today that divides our nation as does no other issue is that of the moral and legal status of the human fetus and the corresponding question of the moral permissibility of abortion. On the one hand, such organizations as the Roman Catholic Church and the Right to Life movement, appalled by the more than 1.5 million abortions that take place in this country each year, have exerted significant political pressure toward introducing a constitutional amendment that would grant full legal rights to fetuses. These movements have in some cases made the abortion issue the single issue in political campaigns. On the other hand, pro-choice groups such as the National Organization of Women (NOW), the National Abortion Rights Action League (NARAL), and feminist organizations have exerted enormous pressure on politicians to support pro-abortion legislation. The Republican and Democratic political platforms of the last two elections took diametrically opposite sides on this issue.

Why is abortion a moral issue? Take a fertilized egg—a zygote, a tiny sphere of cells. By itself it is hard to see what is so important about such an inconspicuous piece of matter. It is virtually indistinguishable from other clusters of cells or zygotes of other animals. Now take an adult human being, a class of beings that we all intuitively feel to be worthy of high respect and having rights, including the right to life. To kill an innocent human being is an act of murder and universally condemned. Yet no obvious line separates that single-cell zygote from the adult it will become. Hence, the problem of abortion.

John Noonan begins his argument against abortion with this sort of analysis. He argues that since it is always wrong to kill innocent human beings and since fetuses are innocent human beings, it is wrong to kill fetuses. He makes an exception when the mother's life is in danger, because something of comparable worth is at stake. Noonan argues that conception is the only nonarbitrary cutoff place between nonpersonhood and personhood.

In our second essay Judith Jarvis Thomson grants for the sake of argument that fetuses are persons. With the use of an ingenious analogy about a famous violin player who requires your kidneys for nine months, she argues that just as you have a right to unplug yourself from the violinist, so a woman has a right to an abortion even if the fetus is a person.

Next, Baruch Brody takes issue with Thomson. He argues that the right to self-defense does not work in the way Thomson suggests, because she fails to distinguish between our duty to save X's life and our duty not to take X's life. When we take that distinction into consideration, the mother has no right to abort the fetus in order to regain control over her life. In the last part of his paper Brody sets forth a more moderate approach.

In our fourth reading Mary Anne Warren argues against Noonan that fetuses are not persons because persons must have such characteristics as self-consciousness and rationality, which fetuses do not have.

In our fifth reading Harry Gensler appeals to the Golden Rule to argue that abortion is wrong.

In our sixth reading Don Marquis argues that abortion is immoral because it robs a being of a future like ours. In our last reading Gerald Paske contends that Marquis's argument fails.

CHAPTER 30

Abortion Is Morally Wrong

JOHN T. NOONAN, JR.

John T. Noonan, Jr., is professor of law at the University of California, Berkeley. He is a Roman Catholic philosopher who has written several works on moral issues, including *Contraception: A History of Its Treatment by the Catholic Theologians and Canonists* (1965) and *A Private Choice: Abortion in America in the Seventies* (1979). In this selection Noonan defends the conservative view that an entity becomes a person at conception and that abortion, except to save the mother's life, is morally wrong. He uses an argument from probabilities to show that his criterion of humanity is objectively based.

THE MOST FUNDAMENTAL QUESTION involved in the long history of thought on abortion is: How do you determine the humanity of a being? To phrase the question that way is to put in comprehensive humanistic terms what the theologians either dealt with as an explicitly theological question under the heading of "ensoulment" or dealt with implicitly in their treatment of abortion. The Christian position as it originated did not depend on a narrow theological or philosophical concept. It had no relation to theories of infant baptism. It appealed to no special theory of instantaneous ensoulment. It took the world's view on ensoulment as that view changed from Aristotle to Zacchia. There was, indeed, theological influence affecting the theory of ensoulment finally adopted, and, of course, ensoulment itself was a theological concept, so that the position was always explained in theological terms. But the theological notion of ensoulment could easily be translated into humanistic language by substituting "human" for "rational soul"; the problem of knowing when a man is a man is common to theology and humanism.

If one steps outside the specific categories used by the theologians, the answer they gave can be analyzed as a refusal to discriminate among human beings on the basis of their varying potentialities. Once conceived, the being was recognized as man because he had man's potential. The criterion for humanity, thus, was simple and all-embracing: if you are conceived by human parents, you are human.

The strength of this position may be tested by a review of some of the other distinctions offered in the contemporary controversy over legalizing abortion. Perhaps the most popular distinction is in terms of viability. Before an age of so many months, the fetus is not viable, that is, it cannot be removed from the mother's womb and live apart from her. To that extent, the life of the fetus is absolutely dependent on the life of the mother. This dependence is made the basis of denying recognition to its humanity.

There are difficulties with this distinction. One is that the perfection of artificial incubation may make the fetus viable at any time: it may be removed and artificially sustained. Experiments with animals already show that such a procedure is possible. This hypothetical extreme case relates to an actual difficulty: there is considerable elasticity to the idea of viability. Mere length of life is not an exact measure. The viability of the fetus depends on the extent of its anatomical and functional development. The weight and length of the fetus are better guides to the state of its development than age, but weight and length vary. Moreover, different racial groups have different ages at which their fetuses are viable. Some evidence, for example, suggests that Negro fetuses mature more quickly than white fetuses. If viability is the norm, the standard would vary with race and with many individual circumstances.

The most important objection to this approach is that dependence is not ended by viability. The fetus is still absolutely dependent on someone's care in order to continue existence; indeed a child of one or three or even five years of age is absolutely dependent on another's care for existence; uncared for, the older fetus or the younger child will die as surely as the early fetus detached from the mother. The unsubstantial lessening in dependence at viability does not seem to signify any special acquisition of humanity.

A second distinction has been attempted in terms of experience. A being who has had experience, has lived and suffered, who possesses memories, is more human than one who has not. Humanity depends on formation by experience. The fetus is thus "unformed" in the most basic human sense.

This distinction is not serviceable for the embryo which is already experiencing and reacting. The embryo is responsive to touch after eight weeks and at least at that point is experiencing. At an earlier stage the zygote is certainly alive and responding to its environment. The distinction may also be challenged by the rare case where aphasia has erased adult memory: has it erased humanity? More fundamentally, this distinction leaves even the older fetus or the

younger child to be treated as an unformed inhuman thing. Finally, it is not clear why experience as such confers humanity. It could be argued that certain central experiences such as loving or learning are necessary to make a man human. But then human beings who have failed to love or to learn might be excluded from the class called man.

A third distinction is made by appeal to the sentiments of adults. If a fetus dies, the grief of the parents is not the grief they would have for a living child. The fetus is an unnamed "it" till birth, and is not perceived as personality until at least the fourth month of existence when movements in the womb manifest a vigorous presence demanding joyful recognition by the parents.

Yet feeling is notoriously an unsure guide to the humanity of others. Many groups of humans have had difficulty in feeling that persons of another tongue, color, religion, sex, are as human as they. Apart from reactions to alien groups, we mourn the loss of a ten-year-old boy more than the loss of his one-day-old brother or his 90-year-old grandfather. The difference felt and the grief expressed vary with the potentialities extinguished, or the experience wiped out; they do not seem to point to any substantial difference in the humanity of baby, boy, or grandfather.

Distinctions are also made in terms of sensation by the parents. The embryo is felt within the womb only after about the fourth month. The embryo is seen only at birth. What can be neither seen nor felt is different from what is tangible. If the fetus cannot be seen or touched at all, it cannot be perceived as man.

Yet experience shows that sight is even more untrustworthy than feeling in determining humanity. By sight, color became an appropriate index for saying who was a man, and the evil of racial discrimination was given foundation. Nor can touch provide the test; a being confined by sickness, "out of touch" with others, does not thereby seem to lose his humanity. To the extent that touch still has appeal as a criterion, it appears to be a survival of the old English idea of "quickening"—a possible mistranslation of the Latin *animatus* used in the canon law. To that extent touch as a criterion seems to be dependent on the Aristotelian notion of ensoulment, and to fall when this notion is discarded.

Finally, a distinction is sought in social visibility. The fetus is not socially perceived as human. It cannot communicate with others. Thus, both subjectively and objectively, it is not a member of society. As moral rules are rules for the behavior of members of society to each other, they cannot be made for behavior toward what is not yet a member. Excluded from the society of men, the fetus is excluded from the humanity of men.

By force of the argument from the consequences, this distinction is to be rejected. It is more subtle than that founded on an appeal to physical sensation, but it is equally dangerous in its implications. If humanity depends on social recognition, individuals or whole groups may be dehumanized by being denied any status in their society. Such a fate is fictionally portrayed in *1984* and has actually been the lot of many men in many societies. In the Roman empire, for example, condemnation to slavery meant the practical denial of most human rights; in the Chinese Communist world, landlords have been classified as enemies of the people and so treated as nonpersons by the state. Humanity does not depend on social recognition, though often the failure of society to recognize the prisoner, the alien, the heterodox as human has led to the destruction of human beings. Anyone conceived by a man and a woman is human. Recognition of this condition by society follows a real event in the objective order, however imperfect and halting the recognition. Any attempt to limit humanity to exclude some group runs the risk of furnishing authority and precedent for excluding other groups in the name of the consciousness or perception of the controlling group in the society.

A philosopher may reject the appeal to the humanity of the fetus because he views "humanity" as a secular view of the soul and because he doubts the existence of anything real and objective which can be identified as humanity. One answer to such a philosopher is to ask how he reasons about moral questions without supposing that there is a sense in which he and the others of whom he speaks are human. Whatever group is taken as the society which determines who may be killed is thereby taken as human. A second answer is to ask if he does not believe that there is a right and wrong way of deciding moral questions. If there is such a difference, experience may be appealed to: to decide who is human on the basis of the sentiment of a given society has led to consequences which rational men would characterize as monstrous.

The rejection of the attempted distinctions based on viability and visibility, experience and feeling, may be buttressed by the following considerations: Moral judgments often rest on distinctions, but if the distinctions are not to appear arbitrary fiat, they should relate to some real difference in probabilities. There is a kind of continuity in all life, but the earlier stages of the elements of human life possess tiny probabilities of development. Consider for example, the spermatozoa in any normal ejaculate: There are about 200,000,000 in any single ejaculate, of which one has a chance of developing into a zygote. Consider the oocytes which may become ova: there are 100,000 to 1,000,000 oocytes in a female infant, of which a maximum of 390 are ovulated. But once spermatozoon and ovum meet and the conceptus is formed, such studies as have been made show that roughly in only 20 percent of the cases will spontaneous abortion occur. In other words, the chances are about 4 out of 5 that this new being will develop. At this stage in the life of the being there is a sharp shift in probabilities, an immense jump in potentialities. To make a distinction between the rights of spermatozoa and the rights of the fertilized ovum is to respond to an enormous shift in possibilities. For about twenty days after conception the egg may split to form twins or combine with another egg to form a chimera, but the probability of either event happening is very small.

It may be asked, What does a change in biological probabilities have to do with establishing humanity? The argument from probabilities is not aimed at establishing humanity but at establishing an objective discontinuity which may be taken into account in moral discourse. As life itself is a matter of probabilities, as most moral reasoning is an estimate of probabilities, so it seems in accord with the structure of reality and the nature of moral thought to found a moral judgment on the change in probabilities at conception. The appeal to probabilities is the most commonsensical of arguments, to a greater or smaller degree all of us base our actions on probabilities, and in morals, as in law, prudence and negligence are often measured by the account one has taken of the probabilities. If the chance is 200,000,000 to 1 that the movement in the bushes into which you shoot is a man's, I doubt if many persons would hold you careless in shooting; but if the chances are 4 out of 5 that the movement is a human being's, few would acquit you of blame. Would the argument be different if only one out of ten children conceived came to term? Of course this argument would be different. This argument is an appeal to probabilities that actually exist, not to any and all states of affairs which may be imagined.

The probabilities as they do exist do not show the humanity of the embryo in the sense of a demonstration in logic any more than the probabilities of the movement in the bush being a man demonstrate beyond all doubt that the being is a man. The appeal is a "buttressing" consideration, showing the plausibility of the standard adopted. The argument focuses on the decisional factor in any moral judgment and assumes that part of the business of a moralist is drawing lines. One evidence of the nonarbitrary character of the line drawn is the difference of probabilities on either side of it. If a spermatozoon is destroyed, one destroys a being which had a chance of far less than 1 in 200 million of developing into a reasoning being, possessed of the genetic code, a heart and other organs, and

capable of pain. If a fetus is destroyed, one destroys a being already possessed of the genetic code, organs, and sensitivity to pain, and one which had an 80 percent chance of developing further into a baby outside the womb who, in time, would reason.

The positive argument for conception as the decisive moment of humanization is that at conception the new being receives the genetic code. It is this genetic information which determines his characteristics, which is the biological carrier of the possibility of human wisdom, which makes him a self-evolving being. A being with a human genetic code is man.

This review of current controversy over the humanity of the fetus emphasizes what a fundamental question the theologians resolved in asserting the inviolability of the fetus. To regard the fetus as possessed of equal rights with other humans was not, however, to decide every case where abortion might be employed. It did decide the case where the argument was that the fetus should be aborted for its own good. To say a being was human was to say it had a destiny to decide for itself which could not be taken from it by another man's decision. But human beings with equal rights often come in conflict with each other, and some decision must be made as whose claims are to prevail. Cases of conflict involving the fetus are different only in two respects: the total inability of the fetus to speak for itself and the fact that the right of the fetus regularly at stake is the right to life itself.

The approach taken by the theologians to these conflicts was articulated in terms of "direct" and "indirect." Again, to look at what they were doing from outside their categories, they may be said to have been drawing lines or "balancing values." "Direct" and "indirect" are spatial metaphors; "line-drawing" is another. "To weigh" or "to balance" values is a metaphor of a more complicated mathematical sort hinting at the process which goes on in moral judgments. All the metaphors suggest that, in the moral judgments made, comparisons were necessary, that no value completely controlled. The principle of double effect was no doctrine fallen from heaven, but a method of analysis appropriate where two relative values were being compared. In Catholic moral theology, as it developed, life even of the innocent was not taken as an absolute. Judgments on acts affecting life issued from a process of weighing. In the weighing, the fetus was always given a value greater than zero, always a value separate and independent from its parents. This valuation was crucial and fundamental in all Christian thought on the subject and marked it off from any approach which considered that only the parents' interests needed to be considered.

Even with the fetus weighed as human, one interest could be weighed as equal or superior: that of the mother in her own life. The casuists between 1450 and 1895 were willing to weigh this interest as superior. Since 1895, that interest was given decisive weight only in the two special cases of the cancerous uterus and the ectopic pregnancy. In both of these cases the fetus itself had little chance of survival even if the abortion were not performed. As the balance was once struck in favor of the mother when ever her life was endangered, it could be so struck again. The balance reached between 1895 and 1930 attempted prudentially and pastorally to forestall a multitude of exceptions for interests less than life.

The perception of the humanity of the fetus and the weighing of fetal rights against other human rights constituted the work of the moral analysts. But what spirit animated their abstract judgments? For the Christian community it was the injunction of Scripture to love your neighbor as yourself. The fetus as human was a neighbor; his life had parity with one's own. The commandment gave life to what otherwise would have been only rational calculation.

The commandment could be put in humanistic as well as theological terms: Do not injure your fellow man without reason. In these terms, once the humanity of the fetus is perceived, abortion is never right except in self-defense. When life must be taken to save life, reason alone cannot say that a mother must prefer a child's life to her own. With this exception, now of great rarity, abortion violates the rational humanist tenet of the equality of human lives.

For Christians the commandment to love had received a special imprint in that the exemplar proposed of love was the love of the Lord for his disciples. In the light given by this example, self-sacrifice carried to the point of death seemed in the extreme situations not without meaning. In the less extreme cases, preference for one's own interests to the life of another seemed to express cruelty or selfishness irreconcilable with the demands of love.

Study Questions

1. Where does Noonan draw the line between being human and nonhuman? Do you agree with him? Explain.
2. Has Noonan successfully argued that abortion is immoral? How would he argue against abortion in cases of rape?
3. Examine Noonan's argument from the relevance of probabilities in determining whether a fetus will become a fully formed human person. What are the implications of this suggestion? Is it sound?

Chapter 31

A Defense of Abortion

JUDITH JARVIS THOMSON

Judith Jarvis Thomson is professor of philosophy at Massachusetts Institute of Technology and the author of several books and articles in moral and political philosophy, including *Rights, Restitution and Risk* (1986).

In the following article Thomson argues that a woman has a right to an abortion even if the fetus is a human being, a person. Using a series of examples, including the imagined case of a famous violinist who needs your kidney for nine months, she argues that just as you have a right to unplug yourself from the violinist, the pregnant woman has a right to an abortion. Although she rejects the idea that the fetus has a right to life that overrides the mother's right to her own body, Thomson distinguishes cases where it would be a good thing for a woman to refrain from having an abortion.

MOST OPPOSITION TO ABORTION relies on the premise that the foetus is a human being, a person, from the moment of conception. The premiss is argued for, but, as I think, not well. Take, for example, the most common argument. We are asked to notice that the development of a human being from conception through birth into childhood is continuous; then it is said that to draw a line, to choose a point in this development and say 'before this point the thing is not a person, after this point it is a person' is to make an arbitrary choice, a choice for which in the nature of things no good reason can be given. It is concluded that the foetus is, or anyway that we had better say it is, as a person from the moment of conception. But this conclusion does not follow. Similar things might be said about the development of an acorn into an oak tree, and it does not follow that acorns are oak trees, or that we had better say they are. Arguments of this form are sometimes called 'slippery slope arguments'—the phrase is perhaps self-explanatory—and it is dismaying that opponents of abortion rely on them so heavily and uncritically.

I am inclined to agree, however, that the prospects for 'drawing a line' in the development of the foetus look dim. I am inclined to think also that we shall probably have to agree that the foetus has already become a human person well before birth. Indeed, it comes as a surprise when one first learns how early in its life it begins to acquire human characteristics. By the tenth week, for example, it already has a face, arms and legs, fingers and toes; it has internal organs, and brain activity is detectable. On the other hand, I think that the premiss is false, that the foetus is not a person from the moment of conception. A newly fertilized ovum, a newly implanted clump of cells, is no more a person than an acorn is an oak tree. But I shall not discuss any of this. For it seems to me to be of

Reprinted from Philosophy and Public Affairs *1: 1 (1971) by permission of Princeton University Press. Footnotes edited.*

great interest to ask what happens if, for the sake of argument, we allow the premiss. How, precisely, are we supposed to get from there to the conclusion that abortion is morally impermissible? Opponents of abortion commonly spend most of their time establishing that the foetus is a person, and hardly any time explaining the step from there to the impermissibility of abortion. Perhaps they think the step too simple and obvious to require much comment. Or perhaps instead they are simply being economical in argument. Many of those who defend abortion rely on the premiss that the foetus is not a person, but only a bit of tissue that will become a person at birth; and why pay out more arguments than you have to? Whatever the explanation, I suggest that the step they take is neither easy nor obvious, that it calls for closer examination than it is commonly given, and that when we do give it this closer examination we shall feel inclined to reject it.

I propose, then, that we grant that the foetus is a person from the moment of conception. How does the argument go from here? Something like this, I take it. Every person has a right to life. So the foetus has a right to life. No doubt the mother has a right to decide what shall happen in and to her body; everyone would grant that. But surely a person's right to life is stronger and more stringent than the mother's right to decide what happens in and to her body, and so outweighs it. So the foetus may not be killed; an abortion may not be performed.

It sounds plausible. But now let me ask you to imagine this. You wake up in the morning and find yourself back to back in bed with an unconscious violinist. A famous unconscious violinist. He has been found to have a fatal kidney ailment, and the Society of Music Lovers has canvassed all the available medical records and found that you alone have the right blood type to help. They have therefore kidnapped you, and last night the violinist's circulatory system was plugged into yours, so that your kidneys can be used to extract poisons from his blood as well as your own. The director of the hospital now

tells you, 'Look, we're sorry the Society of Music Lovers did this to you—we would never have permitted it if we had known. But still, they did it, and the violinist now is plugged into you. To unplug you would be to kill him. But never mind, it's only for nine months. By then he will have recovered from his ailment, and can safely be unplugged from you.' Is it morally incumbent on you to accede to this situation? No doubt it would be very nice of you if you did, a great kindness. But do you *have* to accede to it? What if it were not nine months, but nine years? Or longer still? What if the director of the hospital says, 'Tough luck, I agree, but you've now got to stay in bed, with the violinist plugged into you, for the rest of your life. Because remember this. All persons have a right to life, and violinists are persons. Granted you have a right to decide what happens in and to your body, but a person's right to life outweighs your right to decide what happens in and to your body. So you cannot ever be unplugged from him.' I imagine you would regard this as outrageous, which suggests that something really is wrong with that plausible-sounding argument I mentioned a moment ago.

In this case, of course, you were kidnapped; you didn't volunteer for the operation that plugged the violinist into your kidneys. Can those who oppose abortion on the ground I mentioned make an exception for a pregnancy due to rape? Certainly. They can say that persons have a right to life only if they didn't come into existence because of rape; or they can say that all persons have a right to life, but that some have less of a right to life than others, in particular, that those who came into existence because of rape have less. But these statements have a rather unpleasant sound. Surely the question of whether you have a right to life at all, or how much of it you have, shouldn't turn on the question of whether or not you are the product of a rape. And in fact the people who oppose abortion on the ground I mentioned do not make this distinction, and hence do not make an exception in case of rape.

Nor do they make an exception for a case in which the mother has to spend the nine months of her pregnancy in bed. They would agree that would be a great pity, and hard on the mother; but all the same, all persons have a right to life, the foetus is a person, and so on. I suspect, in fact, that they would not make an exception for a case in which, miraculously enough, the pregnancy went on for nine years, or even the rest of the mother's life.

Some won't even make an exception for a case in which continuation of the pregnancy is likely to shorten the mother's life; they regard abortion as impermissible even to save the mother's life. Such cases are nowadays very rare, and many opponents of abortion do not accept this extreme view. All the same, it is a good place to begin: a number of points of interest come out in respect to it.

1. Let us call the view that abortion is impermissible even to save the mother's life 'the extreme view'. I want to suggest first that it does not issue from the argument I mentioned earlier without the addition of some fairly powerful premises. Suppose a woman has become pregnant, and now learns that she has a cardiac condition such that she will die if she carries the baby to term. What may be done for her? The foetus, being a person, has a right to life, but as the mother is a person too, so has she a right to life. Presumably they have an equal right to life. How is it supposed to come out that an abortion may not be performed? If mother and child have an equal right to life, shouldn't we perhaps flip a coin? Or should we add to the mother's right to life her right to decide what happens in and to her body, which everybody seems to be ready to grant—the sum of her rights now outweighing the foetus's right to life?

The most familiar argument here is the following. We are told that performing the abortion would be directly killing[1] the child, whereas doing nothing would not be killing the mother, but only letting her die. Moreover, in killing the child, one would be killing an inno-

cent person, for the child has committed no crime, and is not aiming at his mother's death. And then there are a variety of ways in which this might be continued. (1) But as directly killing an innocent person is always and absolutely impermissible, an abortion may not be performed. Or, (2) as directly killing an innocent person is murder, and murder is always and absolutely impermissible, an abortion may not be performed.[2] Or, (3) as one's duty to refrain from directly killing an innocent person is more stringent than one's duty to keep a person from dying, an abortion may not be performed. Or, (4) if one's only options are directly killing an innocent person or letting a person die, one must prefer letting the person die, and thus an abortion may not be performed.[3]

Some people seem to have thought that these are not further premises which must be added if the conclusion is to be reached, but that they follow from the very fact that an innocent person has a right to life.[4] But this seems to me to be a mistake, and perhaps the simplest way to show this is to bring out that while we must certainly grant that innocent persons have a right to life, the theses in (1) to (4) are all false. Take (2), for example. If directly killing an innocent person is murder, and thus is impermissible, then the mother's directly killing the innocent person inside her is murder, and thus is impermissible. But it cannot seriously be thought to be murder if the mother performs an abortion on herself to save her life. It cannot seriously be said that she *must* refrain, that she *must* sit passively by and wait for her death. Let us look again at the case of you and the violinist. There you are, in bed with the violinist, and the director of the hospital says to you, 'It's all most distressing, and I deeply sympathize, but you see this is putting an additional strain on your kidneys, and you'll be dead within the month. But you *have* to stay where you are all the same. Because unplugging you would be directly killing an innocent violinist, and that's murder, and that's impermissible.' If anything in the world is true, it is that you do not commit murder, you do not do what is impermissible, if you reach around to your back and unplug yourself from that violinist to save your life.

The main focus of attention in writings on abortion has been on what a third party may or may not do in answer to a request from a woman for an abortion. This is in a way understandable. Things being as they are, there isn't much a woman can safely do to abort herself. So the question asked is what a third party may do, and what the mother may do, if it is mentioned at all, is deduced, almost as an afterthought, from what it is concluded that third parties may do. But it seems to me that to treat the matter in this way is to refuse to grant to the mother that very status of person which is so firmly insisted on for the foetus. For we cannot simply read off what a person may do from what a third party may do. Suppose you find yourself trapped in a tiny house with a growing child. I mean a very tiny house, and a rapidly growing child—you are already up against the wall of the house and in a few minutes you'll be crushed to death. The child on the other hand won't be crushed to death; if nothing is done to stop him from growing he'll be hurt, but in the end he'll simply burst open the house and walk out a free man. Now I could well understand it if a bystander were to say, 'There's nothing we can do for you. We cannot choose between your life and his, we cannot be the ones to decide who is to live, we cannot intervene.' But it cannot be concluded that you too can do nothing, that you cannot attack it to save your life. However innocent the child may be, you do not have to wait passively while it crushes you to death. Perhaps a pregnant woman is vaguely felt to have the status of house, to which we don't allow the right of self-defence. But if the woman houses the child, it should be remembered that she is a person who houses it.

I should perhaps stop to say explicitly that I am not claiming that people have a right to do anything whatever to save their lives. I think, rather, that there are drastic limits to the right of self-defence. If someone threatens you with death unless you torture someone else to death, I think you have not the right, even to save your life, to do so. But the case under consideration here is very different. In our case there are only two people involved, one whose life is threatened, and one who threatens it. Both are innocent: the one who is threatened is not threatened because of any fault, the one who threatens does not threaten because of any fault. For this reason we may feel that we bystanders cannot intervene. But the person threatened can.

In sum, a woman surely can defend her life against the threat to it posed by the unborn child, even if doing so involves its death. And this shows not merely that the theses in (1) to (4) are false; it shows also that the extreme view of abortion is false, and so we need not canvass any other possible ways of arriving at it from the argument I mentioned at the outset.

2. The extreme view could of course be weakened to say that while abortion is permissible to save the mother's life, it may not be performed by a third party, but only by the mother herself. But this cannot be right either. For what we have to keep in mind is that the mother and the unborn child are not like two tenants in a small house which has, by an unfortunate mistake, been rented to both: the mother *owns* the house. The fact that she does adds to the offensiveness of deducing that the mother can do nothing from the supposition that third parties can do nothing. But it does more than this: it casts a bright light on the supposition that third parties can do nothing. Certainly it lets us see that a third party who says 'I cannot choose between you' is fooling himself if he thinks this is impartiality. If Jones has found and fastened on a certain coat, which he needs to keep him from freezing, but which Smith also needs to keep him from freezing, then it is not impartiality that says 'I cannot choose between you' when Smith owns the coat. Women have said again and again 'This body is *my* body!' and they have

reason to feel angry, reason to feel that it has been like shouting into the wind. Smith, after all, is hardly likely to bless us if we say to him, 'Of course it's your coat, anybody would grant that it is. But no one may choose between you and Jones who is to have it.'

We should really ask what it is that says 'no one may choose' in the face of the fact that the body that houses the child is the mother's body. It may be simply a failure to appreciate this fact. But it may be something more interesting, namely the sense that one has a right to refuse to lay hands on people, even where it would be just and fair to do so, even where justice seems to require that somebody do so. Thus justice might call for somebody to get Smith's coat back from Jones, and yet you have a right to refuse to be the one to lay hands on Jones, a right to refuse to do physical violence to him. This, I think, must be granted. But then what should be said is not 'no one may choose', but only '*I* cannot choose', and indeed not even this, but '*I* will not *act*', leaving it open that somebody else can or should, and in particular that anyone in a position of authority, with the job of securing people's rights, both can and should. So this is no difficulty. I have not been arguing that any given third party must accede to the mother's request that he perform an abortion to save her life, but only that he may.

I suppose that in some views of human life the mother's body is only on loan to her, the loan not being one which gives her any prior claim to it. One who held this view might well think it impartiality to say 'I cannot choose'. But I shall simply ignore this possibility. My own view is that if a human being has any just, prior claim to anything at all, he has a just, prior claim to his own body. And perhaps this needn't be argued for here anyway, since, as I mentioned, the arguments against abortion we are looking at do grant that the woman has a right to decide what happens in and to her body.

But although they do grant it, I have tried to show that they do not take seriously what is

done in granting it. I suggest the same thing will reappear even more clearly when we turn away from cases in which the mother's life is at stake, and attend, as I propose we now do, to the vastly more common cases in which a woman wants an abortion for some less weighty reason than preserving her own life.

3. Where the mother's life is not at stake, the argument I mentioned at the outset seems to have a much stronger pull. 'Everyone has a right to life, so the unborn person has a right to life.' And isn't the child's right to life weightier than anything other than the mother's own right to life, which she might put forward as ground for an abortion?

This argument treats the right to life as if it were unproblematic. It is not, and this seems to me to be precisely the source of the mistake.

For we should now, at long last, ask what it comes to, to have a right to life. In some views having a right to life includes having a right to be given at least the bare minimum one needs for continued life. But suppose that what in fact *is* the bare minimum a man needs for continued life is something he has no right at all to be given? If I am sick unto death, and the only thing that will save my life is the touch of Henry Fonda's cool hand on my fevered brow, then all the same, I have no right to be given the touch of Henry Fonda's cool hand on my fevered brow. It would be frightfully nice of him to fly in from the West Coast to provide it. It would be less nice, though no doubt well meant, if my friends flew out to the West Coast and carried Henry Fonda back with them. But I have no right at all against anybody that he should do this for me. Or again, to return to the story I told earlier, the fact that for continued life that violinist needs the continued use of your kidneys does not establish that he has a right to be given the continued use of your kidneys. He certainly has no right against you that *you* should give him continued use of your kidneys. For nobody has any right to use your kidneys unless you give him such a right; and nobody has the right against you that you shall give him this right—if you do allow him to go on using your kidneys, this is a kindness on your part, and not something he can claim from you as his due. Nor has he any right against anybody else that *they* should give him continued use of your kidneys. Certainly he had no right against the Society of Music Lovers that they should plug him into you in the first place. And if you now start to unplug yourself, having learned that you will otherwise have to spend nine years in bed with him, there is nobody in the world who must try to prevent you, in order to see to it that he is given something he has a right to be given.

Some people are rather stricter about the right to life. In their view, it does not include the right to be given anything, but amounts to, and only to, the right not to be killed by anybody. But here a related difficulty arises. If everybody is to refrain from killing that violinist, then everybody must refrain from doing a great many different sorts of things. Everybody must refrain from slitting his throat, everybody must refrain from shooting him—and everybody must refrain from unplugging you from him. But does he have a right against everybody that they shall refrain from unplugging you from him? To refrain from doing this is to allow him to continue to use your kidneys. It could be argued that he has a right against us that *we* should allow him to continue to use your kidneys. That is, while he had no right against us that we should give him the use of your kidneys, it might be argued that he anyway has a right against us that we shall not now intervene and deprive him of the use of your kidneys. I shall come back to third-party interventions later. But certainly the violinist has no right against you that *you* shall allow him to continue to use your kidneys. As I said, if you do allow him to use them, it is a kindness on your part, and not something you owe him.

The difficulty I point to here is not peculiar to the right to life. It reappears in connection with all the other natural rights; and it is something which an adequate account of rights must

deal with. For present purposes it is enough just to draw attention to it. But I would stress that I am not arguing that people do not have a right to life—quite to the contrary, it seems to me that the primary control we must place on the acceptability of an account of rights is that it should turn out in that account to be a truth that all persons have a right to life. I am arguing only that having a right to life does not guarantee having either a right to be given the use of or a right to be allowed continued use of another person's body—even if one needs it for life itself. So the right to life will not serve the opponents of abortion in the very simple and clear way in which they seem to have thought it would.

4. There is another way to bring out the difficulty. In the most ordinary sort of case, to deprive someone of what he has a right to is to treat him unjustly. Suppose a boy and his small brother are jointly given a box of chocolates for Christmas. If the older boy takes the box and refuses to give his brother any of the chocolates, he is unjust to him, for the brother has been given a right to half of them. But suppose that, having learned that otherwise it means nine years in bed with that violinist, you unplug yourself from him. You surely are not being unjust to him, for you gave him no right to use your kidneys, and no one else can have given him any such right. But we have to notice that in unplugging yourself, you are killing him; and violinists, like everybody else, have a right to life, and thus in the view we were considering just now, the right not to be killed. So here you do what he supposedly has a right you shall not do, but you do not act unjustly to him in doing it.

The emendation which may be made at this point is this: the right to life consists not in the right not to be killed, but rather in the right not to be killed unjustly. This runs a risk of circularity, but never mind: it would enable us to square the fact that the violinist has a right to life with the fact that you do not act unjustly toward him in unplugging yourself, thereby killing him. For if you do not kill him unjustly, you do not violate his right to life, and so it is no wonder you do him no injustice.

But if this emendation is accepted, the gap in the argument against abortion stares us plainly in the face: it is by no means enough to show that the foetus is a person, and to remind us that all persons have a right to life—we need to be shown also that killing the foetus violates its right to life, i.e. that abortion is unjust killing. And is it?

I suppose we may take it as a datum that in a case of pregnancy due to rape the mother has not given the unborn person a right to the use of her body for food and shelter. Indeed, in what pregnancy could it be supposed that the mother has given the unborn person such a right? It is not as if there were unborn persons drifting about the world, to whom a woman who wants a child says 'I invite you in'.

But it might be argued that there are other ways one can have acquired a right to the use of another person's body than by having been invited to use it by that person. Suppose a woman voluntarily indulges in intercourse, knowing of the chance it will issue in pregnancy, and then she does become pregnant; is she not in part responsible for the presence, in fact the very existence, of the unborn person inside her? No doubt she did not invite it in. But doesn't her partial responsibility for its being there itself give it a right to the use of her body? If so, then her aborting it would be more like the boy's taking away the chocolates, and less like your unplugging yourself from the violinist—doing so would be depriving it of what it does have a right to, and thus would be doing it an injustice.

And then, too, it might be asked whether or not she can kill it even to save her own life: If she voluntarily called it into existence, how can she now kill it, even in self-defence?

The first thing to be said about this is that it is something new. Opponents of abortion have been so concerned to make out the independence of the foetus, in order to establish that it has a right to life, just as its mother does, that they have tended to overlook the possible support they might gain from making out that the foetus is *dependent* on the mother, in order to establish that she has a special kind of responsibility for it, a responsibility that gives it rights against her which are not possessed by any independent person—such as an ailing violinist who is a stranger to her.

On the other hand, this argument would give the unborn person a right to its mother's body only if her pregnancy resulted from a voluntary act, undertaken in full knowledge of the chance a pregnancy might result from it. It would leave out entirely the unborn person whose existence is due to rape. Pending the availability of some further argument, then we would be left with the conclusion that unborn persons whose existence is due to rape have no right to the use of their mothers' bodies, and thus that aborting them is not depriving them of anything they have a right to and hence is not unjust killing.

And we should also notice that it is not at all plain that this argument really does go even as far as it purports to. For there are cases and cases, and the details make a difference. If the room is stuffy, and I therefore open a window to air it, and a burglar climbs in, it would be absurd to say, 'Ah, now he can stay, she's given him a right to the use of her house—for she is partially responsible for his presence there, having voluntarily done what enabled him to get in, in full knowledge that there are such things as burglars, and that burglars burgle.' It would be still more absurd to say this if I had had bars installed outside my windows, precisely to prevent burglars from getting in, and a burglar got in only because of a defect in the bars. It remains equally absurd if we imagine it is not a burglar who climbs in, but an innocent person who blunders or falls in. Again, suppose it were like this: people-seeds drift about in the air like pollen, and if you open your windows, one may drift in and take root in your carpets or upholstery. You don't want children, so you fix up your windows with fine mesh screens, the very best you can buy. As can happen, however, and on very, very rare occasions does happen, one of the screens is defective; and a seed drifts in and takes root. Does the person-plant who now develops have a right to the use of your house? Surely not—despite the fact that you voluntarily opened your windows, you knowingly kept carpets and upholstered furniture, and you knew that screens were sometimes defective. Someone may argue that you are responsible for its rooting, that it does have a right to your house, because after all you *could* have lived out your life with bare floors and furniture, or with sealed windows and doors. But this won't do—for by the same token anyone can avoid a pregnancy due to rape by having a hysterectomy, or anyway by never leaving home without a (reliable!) army.

It seems to me that the argument we are looking at can establish at most that there are *some* cases in which the unborn person has a right to the use of its mother's body, and therefore *some* cases in which abortion is unjust killing. There is room for much discussion and argument as to precisely which, if any. But I think we should side-step this issue and leave it open, for at any rate the argument certainly does not establish that all abortion is unjust killing.

5. There is room for yet another argument here, however. We surely must all grant that there may be cases in which it would be morally indecent to detach a person from your body at the cost of his life. Suppose you learn that what the violinist needs is not nine years of your life but only one hour: all you need do to save his life is to spend one hour in that bed with him. Suppose also that letting him use your kidneys for that one hour would not affect your health in the slightest. Admittedly you were kidnapped. Admittedly you did not give anyone permission to plug him into you. Nevertheless it seems to me plain you *ought* to allow him to use your kidneys for that hour—it would be indecent to refuse.

Again, suppose pregnancy lasted only an hour, and constituted no threat to life or health. And suppose that a woman becomes pregnant as a result of rape. Admittedly she did not voluntarily do anything to bring about the existence of a child. Admittedly she did nothing at all which would give the unborn person a right to the use of her body. All the same it might well be said, as in the newly emended violinist story, that she *ought* to allow it to remain for that hour—that it would be indecent of her to refuse.

Now some people are inclined to use the term 'right' in such a way that it follows from the fact that you ought to allow a person to use your body for the hour he needs, that he has a right to use your body for the hour he needs, even though he has not been given that right by any person or act. They may say that it follows also that if you refuse, you act unjustly toward him. This use of the term is perhaps so common that it cannot be called wrong; nevertheless it seems to me to be an unfortunate loosening of what we would do better to keep a tight rein on. Suppose that box of chocolates I mentioned earlier had not been given to both boys jointly, but was given only to the older boy. There he sits, stolidly eating his way through the box, his small brother watching enviously. Here we are likely to say 'You ought not to be so mean. You ought to give your brother some of those chocolates.' My own view is that it just does not follow from the truth of this that the brother has any right to any of the chocolates. If the boy refuses to give his brother any, he is greedy, stingy, callous—but not unjust. I suppose that the people I have in mind will say it does follow that the brother has a right to some of the chocolates, and thus that the boy does act unjustly if he refuses to give his brother any. But the effect of saying this is to obscure what we should keep distinct, namely the difference between the boy's refusal in this case and the boy's refusal in the earlier case, in which the box was given to both boys jointly, and in which the small brother thus had what was from any point of view clear title to half.

A further objection to so using the term 'right' that from the fact that *A* ought to do a thing for *B*, it follows that *B* has a right against

A that *A* do it for him, is that it is going to make the question of whether or not a man has a right to a thing turn on how easy it is to provide him with it; and this seems not merely unfortunate, but morally unacceptable. Take the case of Henry Fonda again. I said earlier that I had no right to the touch of his cool hand on my fevered brow, even though I needed it to save my life. I said it would be frightfully nice of him to fly in from the West Coast to provide me with it, but that I had no right against him that he should do so. But suppose he isn't on the West Coast. Suppose he has only to walk across the room, place a hand briefly on my brow—and lo, my life is saved. Then surely he ought to do it, it would be indecent to refuse. Is it to be said 'Ah, well, it follows that in this case she has a right to the touch of his hand on her brow, and so it would be an injustice in him to refuse?' So that I have a right to it when it is easy for him to provide it, though no right when it's hard? It's rather a shocking idea that anyone's rights should fade away and disappear as it gets harder and harder to accord them to him.

So my own view is that even though you ought to let the violinist use your kidneys for the one hour he needs, we should not conclude that he has a right to do so—we should say that if you refuse, you are, like the boy who owns all the chocolates and will give none away, self-centred and callous, indecent in fact, but not unjust. And similarly, that even supposing a case in which a woman pregnant due to rape ought to allow the unborn person to use her body for the hour he needs, we should not conclude that he has a right to do so; we should conclude that she is self-centred, callous, indecent, but not unjust, if she refuses. The complaints are no less grave; they are just different. However, there is no need to insist on this point. If anyone does wish to deduce 'he has a right' from 'you ought,' then all the same he must surely grant that there are cases in which it is not morally required of you that you allow that violinist to use your kidneys, and in which he does not have a right to use them, and so also for mother and unborn child. Except in such cases as the unborn person has a right to demand it—and we were leaving open the possibility that there may be such cases—nobody is morally *required* to make large sacrifices, of health, of all other interests and concerns, of all other duties and commitments, for nine years, or even for nine months, in order to keep another person alive.

6. We have in fact to distinguish between two kinds of Samaritan: the Good Samaritan and what we might call the Minimally Decent Samaritan. The story of the Good Samaritan, you will remember, goes like this:

> A certain man went down from Jerusalem to Jericho, and fell among thieves, which stripped him of his raiment, and wounded him, and departed, leaving him half dead.
>
> And by chance there came down a certain priest that way; and when he saw him, he passed by on the other side.
>
> And likewise a Levite, when he was at the place, came and looked on him, and passed by on the other side.
>
> But a certain Samaritan, as he journeyed, came where he was; and when he saw him he had compassion on him.
>
> And went to him, and bound up his wounds, pouring in oil and wine, and set him on his own beast, and brought him to an inn, and took care of him.
>
> And on the morrow, when he departed, he took out two pence, and gave them to the host, and said unto him, 'Take care of him; and whatsoever thou spendest more, when I come again, I will repay thee.'
>
> (LUKE 10: 30–5)

The Good Samaritan went out of his way, at some cost to himself, to help one in need of it. We are not told what the options were, that is, whether or not the priest and the Levite could have helped by doing less than the Good Samaritan did, but assuming they could have, then the fact they did nothing at all shows they were not even Minimally Decent Samaritans, not because they were not Samaritans, but because they were not even minimally decent.

These things are a matter of degree, of course, but there is a difference, and it comes out perhaps most clearly in the story of Kitty Genovese, who, as you will remember, was murdered while thirty-eight people watched or listened, and did nothing at all to help her. A Good Samaritan would have rushed out to give direct assistance against the murderer. Or perhaps we had better allow that it would have been a Splendid Samaritan who did this, on the ground that it would have involved a risk of death for himself. But the thirty-eight not only did not do this, they did not even trouble to pick up a phone to call the police. Minimally Decent Samaritanism would call for doing at least that, and their not having done it was monstrous.

After telling the story of the Good Samaritan, Jesus said 'Go, and do thou likewise.' Perhaps he meant that we are morally required to act as the Good Samaritan did. Perhaps he was urging people to do more than is morally required of them. At all events it seems plain that it was not morally required of any of the thirty-eight that he rush out to give direct assistance at the risk of his own life, and that it is not morally required of anyone that he give long stretches of his life— nine years or nine months—to sustaining the life of a person who has no special right (we were leaving open the possibility of this) to demand it.

Indeed, with one rather striking class of exceptions, no one in any country in the world is *legally* required to do anywhere near as much as this for anyone else. The class of exceptions is obvious. My main concern here is not the state of the law in respect to abortion, but it is worth drawing attention to the fact that in no state in this country is any man compelled by law to be even a Minimally Decent Samaritan to any person; there is no law under which charges could be brought against the thirty-eight who stood by while Kitty Genovese died. By contrast, in most states in this country women are compelled by law to be not merely Minimally Decent Samaritans, but Good Samaritans to unborn persons inside them. This doesn't by itself

settle anything one way or the other, because it may well be argued that there should be laws in this country—as there are in many European countries—compelling at least Minimally Decent Samaritanism. But it does show that there is a gross injustice in the existing state of the law. And it shows also that the groups currently working against liberalization of abortion laws, in fact working toward having it declared unconstitutional for a state to permit abortion, had better start working for the adoption of Good Samaritan laws generally, or earn the charge that they are acting in bad faith.

I should think, myself, that Minimally Decent Samaritan laws would be one thing, Good Samaritan laws quite another, and in fact highly improper. But we are not here concerned with the law. What we should ask is not whether anybody should be compelled by law to be a Good Samaritan, but whether we must accede to a situation in which somebody is being compelled—by nature, perhaps—to be a Good Samaritan. We have, in other words, to look now at third-party interventions. I have been arguing that no person is morally required to make large sacrifices to sustain the life of another who has no right to demand them, and this even where the sacrifices do not include life itself; we are not morally required to be Good Samaritans or anyway Very Good Samaritans to one another. But what if a man cannot extricate himself from such a situation? What if he appeals to us to extricate him? It seems to me plain that there are cases in which we can, cases in which a Good Samaritan would extricate him. There you are, you were kidnapped, and nine years in bed with that violinist lie ahead of you. You have your own life to lead. You are sorry, but you simply cannot see giving up so much of your life to the sustaining of his. You cannot extricate yourself, and ask us to do so. I should have thought that—in light of his having no right to the use of your body—it was obvious that we do not have to accede to your being forced to give up so much. We can do what you ask. There is no injustice to the violinist in our doing so.

7. Following the lead of the opponents of abortion, I have throughout been speaking of the foetus merely as a person, and what I have been asking is whether or not the argument we began with, which proceeds only from the foetus's being a person, really does establish its conclusion. I have argued that it does not.

But of course there are arguments and arguments, and it may be said that I have simply fastened on the wrong one. It may be said that what is important is not merely the fact that the foetus is a person, but that it is a person for whom the woman has a special kind of responsibility issuing from the fact that she is its mother. And it might be argued that all my analogies are therefore irrelevant—for you do not have that special kind of responsibility for that violinist, Henry Fonda does not have that special kind of responsibility for me. And our attention might be drawn to the fact that men and women both *are* compelled by law to provide support for their children.

I have in effect dealt (briefly) with this argument in section 4 above; but a (still briefer) recapitulation now may be in order. Surely we do not have any such 'special responsibility' for a person unless we have assumed it, explicitly or implicitly. If a set of parents do not try to prevent pregnancy, do not obtain an abortion, and then at the time of birth of the child do not put it out for adoption, but rather take it home with them, then they have assumed responsibility for it, they have given it rights, and they cannot *now* withdraw support from it at the cost of its life because they now find it difficult to go on providing for it. But if they have taken all reasonable precautions against having a child, they do not simply by virtue of their biological relationship to the child who comes into existence have a special responsibility for it. They may wish to assume responsibility for it, or they may not wish to. And I am suggesting that if assuming responsibility for it would require large sacrifices, then they may refuse. A Good Samaritan would not refuse—or anyway, a Splendid Samaritan, if the sacrifices that had to be made

were enormous. But then so would a Good Samaritan assume responsibility for that violinist; so would Henry Fonda, if he is a Good Samaritan, fly in from the West Coast and assume responsibility for me.

8. My argument will be found unsatisfactory on two counts by many of those who want to regard abortion as morally permissible. First, while I do argue that abortion is not impermissible, I do not argue that it is always permissible. There may well be cases in which carrying the child to term requires only Minimally Decent Samaritanism of the mother, and this is a standard we must not fall below. I am inclined to think it a merit of my account precisely that it does *not* give a general yes or a general no. It allows for and supports our sense that, for example, a sick and desperately frightened fourteen-year-old schoolgirl, pregnant due to rape, may *of course* choose abortion, and that any law which rules this out is an insane law. And it also allows for and supports our sense that in other cases resort to abortion is even positively indecent. It would be indecent in the woman to request an abortion, and indecent in a doctor to perform it, if she is in her seventh month, and wants the abortion just to avoid the nuisance of postponing a trip abroad. The very fact that the arguments I have been drawing attention to treat all cases of abortion, or even all cases of abortion in which the mother's life is not at stake, as morally on a par ought to have made them suspect at the outset.

Secondly, while I am arguing for the permissibility of abortion in some cases, I am not arguing for the right to secure the death of the unborn child. It is easy to confuse these two things in that up to a certain point in the life of the foetus it is not able to survive outside the mother's body; hence removing it from her body guarantees its death. But they are importantly different. I have argued that you are not morally required to spend nine months in bed, sustaining the life of that violinist; but to say this is by no means to say that if, when you unplug yourself, there is a miracle and he survives, you then have a right to turn round and slit his throat. You may detach yourself even if this costs him his life; you have no right to be guaranteed his death, by some other means, if unplugging yourself does not kill him. There are some people who will feel dissatisfied by this feature of my argument. A woman may be utterly devastated by the thought of a child, a bit of herself, put out for adoption and never seen or heard of again. She may therefore want not merely that the child be detached from her, but more, that it die. Some opponents of abortion are inclined to regard this as beneath contempt—thereby showing insensitivity to what is surely a powerful source of despair. All the same, I agree that the desire for the child's death is not one which anybody may gratify, should it turn out to be possible to detach the child alive.

At this place, however, it should be remembered that we have only been pretending throughout that the foetus is a human being from the moment of conception. A very early abortion is surely not the killing of a person, and so is not dealt with by anything I have said here.

Notes

1. The term 'direct' in the arguments I refer to is a technical one. Roughly, what is meant by 'direct killing' is either killing as an end in itself, or killing as a means to some end, for example, the end of saving someone else's life. See note 4, below, for an example of its use.

2. Cf. *Encyclical Letter of Pope Pius XI on Christian Marriage,* St. Paul Editions (Boston, n.d.), p. 32: 'however much we may pity the mother whose health and even life is gravely imperiled in the performance of the duty allotted to her by nature, nevertheless what could ever be a sufficient reason for excusing in any way the direct murder of the innocent? This is precisely what we are dealing with here.' Noonan (*The Morality of Abortion,* p. 43) reads this as follows: 'What cause can ever avail to excuse in any way the direct killing of the innocent? For it is a question of that.'

3. The thesis in (2) is in an interesting way weaker than those in (1), (2), and (3): they rule out abortion even in cases in which both mother *and* child will die if the abortion is not performed. By contrast, one who held the view expressed in (2) could consistently say that one needn't prefer letting two persons die to killing one.

4. Cf. the following passage from Pius XII, *Address to the Italian Catholic Society of Midwives:* 'The baby in the maternal breast has the right to life immediately from God.—Hence there is no man, no human authority, no science, no medical, eugenic, social, economic or moral "indication" which can establish or grant a valid juridical ground for a direct deliberate disposition of an innocent human life, that is a disposition which looks to its destruction either as an end or as a means to another end perhaps in itself not illicit.—The baby, still not born, is a man in the same degree and for the same reason as the mother' (quoted in Noonan, *The Morality of Abortion,* p. 45).

Study Questions

1. What is Thomson's argument for the permissibility of abortion? How effective is the analogy comparing abortion to detaching oneself from the world famous violinist?
2. Under what conditions, if any, does the violinist have a right to use your kidney? If he only needs it for five minutes, does he have a right to your kidney? Should you allow him to use it? Explain.
3. Thomson's argument seems relevant to cases of rape, where the woman did not voluntarily have sex. Does it apply to cases where the woman voluntarily had sex?

CHAPTER 32

Against an Absolute Right to Abortion

BARUCH BRODY

Baruch Brody is professor of philosophy at Rice University and the Baylor College of Medicine in Houston. In the following reading, Brody attacks Thomson's position that a woman always has a right to an abortion even if the fetus is a person. He argues that Thomson has "not sufficiently attended to the distinction between our duty to save X's life and our duty not to take it." When this is seen, it turns out that the mother does not have a right to kill the fetus, if it is a person, simply to regain control of her life. In a section not included in this selection, Brody does allow that when both the fetus and the mother will die unless an abortion is performed, it may be performed. In the last section of this essay Brody sets forth his "brain-death" theory of personhood. Just as a human being may be alive but not a person when his or her brain ceases to function, so a fetus is not a person until its brain begins to function. Brody explores just when the brain is fully functioning and sets the time between the sixth and twelfth week after conception. The mother, then, has the right to have an abortion up to the time when the fetus has a functioning brain, though we must still decide when that occurs.

1. Does a Woman Have a Right to Kill Her Fetus?

IT IS A COMMON CLAIM that a woman ought to be in control of what happens to her body to the greatest extent possible, that she ought to be able to use her body in ways that she wants to and refrain from using it in ways that she does not want to. This right is particularly pressed where certain uses of her body have deep and lasting effects upon the character of her life, personal, social, and economic. Therefore, it is argued, a woman should be free either to carry her fetus to term, thereby using her body to support it, or to abort the fetus, thereby not using her body for that purpose.

In some contexts in which this argument is advanced, it is clear that it is not addressed to the issue of the morality of abortion at all. Rather, it is made in opposition to laws against abortion on the ground that the choice to abort or not is a moral decision that should belong only to the mother. But that specific direction of the argument is irrelevant to our present purposes; I will consider it [later] when I deal with the issues raised by laws prohibiting abortions. For the moment, I am concerned solely with the use of this principle as a putative ground tending

From "Fetal Humanity and the Theory of Essentialism," in Philosophy and Sex, *edited by Robert Baker and Frederick Elliston (Buffalo, N.Y.: Prometheus Books, 1984).*

to show the permissibility of abortion, with the claim that because it is the woman's body that carries the fetus and upon which the fetus depends, she has certain rights to abort the fetus that no one else may have.

We may begin by remarking that it is obviously correct that, as carrier of the fetus, the mother has it within her power to choose whether or not to abort the fetus. And, as an autonomous and responsible agent, she must make this choice. But let us notice that this in no way entails either that whatever choice she makes is morally right or that no one else has the right to evaluate the decision that she makes.

At first glance, it would seem that this argument cannot be used by anyone who supposes, as we do for the moment, that there is a point in fetal development from which time on the fetus is a human being. After all, people do not have the right to do anything whatsoever that may be necessary for them to retain control over the uses of their bodies. In particular, it would seem wrong for them kill another human being in order to do so.

In a recent article, Professor Judith Thomson has, in effect, argued that this simple view is mistaken. How does Professor Thomson defend her claim that the mother has a right to abort the fetus, even if it is a human being, whether or not her life is threatened and whether or not she has consented to the act of intercourse in which the fetus is conceived? At one point, discussing just the case in which the mother's life is threatened, she makes the following suggestion:

> In [abortion], there are only two people involved, one whose life is threatened and one who threatens it. Both are innocent: the one who is threatened is not threatened because of any fault, the one who threatens does not threaten because of any fault. For this reason, we may feel that we bystanders cannot intervene. But the person threatened can.

But surely this description is equally applicable to the following case: *A* and *B* are adrift on a lifeboat, *B* has a disease that he can survive, but *A*, if he contracts it, will die, and the only way that *A* can avoid that is by killing *B* and pushing him overboard. Surely, *A* has no right to do this. So there must be some special reason why the mother has, if she does, the right to abort the fetus.

There is, to be sure, an important difference between our lifeboat case and abortion, one that leads us to the heart of Professor Thomson's argument. In the case that we envisaged, both *A* and *B* have equal rights to be in the lifeboat, but the mother's body is hers and not the fetus's and she has first rights to its use. The primacy of these rights allow an abortion whether or not her life is threatened. Professor Thomson summarizes this argument in the following way:

> I am arguing only that having a right to life does not guarantee having either a right to be given the use of, or a right to be allowed continued use of, another person's body—even if one needs it for life itself.

One part of this claim is clearly correct. I have no duty to *X* to save *X*'s life by giving him the use of my body (or my life savings, or the only home I have, and so on), and *X* has no right, even to save his life, to any of those things. Thus, the fetus conceived in the laboratory that will perish unless it is implanted into a woman's body has in fact no right to any woman's body. But this portion of the claim is irrelevant to the abortion issue, for in abortion of the fetus that is a human being the mother must kill *X* to get back the sole use of her body, and that is an entirely different matter.

This point can also be put as follows: . . . we must distinguish the taking of *X*'s life from the saving of *X*'s life, even if we assume that one has a duty not to do the former and to do the latter. Now that latter duty, if it exists at all, is much weaker than the first duty; many circumstances may relieve us from the latter duty that will not relieve us from the former one. Thus, I am certainly relieved from my duty to save *X*'s life by the fact that fulfilling it means the loss of my life savings. It may be noble for me to save *X*'s life at the cost of everything I have, but I certainly have no duty to do that. And the same observation may be made about cases in which I can save *X*'s life by giving him the use of my body for an extended period of time. However, I am not relieved of my duty not to take *X*'s life by the fact that fulfilling it means the loss of everything I have and not even by the fact that fulfilling it means the loss of my life. . . .

At one point in her paper, Professor Thomson does consider this objection. She has previously imagined the following case: a famous violinist, who is dying from a kidney ailment, has been, without your consent, plugged into you for a period of time so that his body can use your kidneys:

> Some people are rather stricter about the right to life. In their view, it does not include the right to be given anything, but amounts to, and only to, the right not to be killed by anybody. But here a related difficulty arises. If everybody is to refrain from killing that violinist, then everybody must refrain from doing a great many different sorts of things . . . everybody must refrain from unplugging you from him. But does he have a right against everybody that they shall refrain from unplugging you from him? To refrain from doing this is to allow him to continue to use your kidneys . . . certainly the violinist has no right against you that you shall allow him to continue to use your kidneys.

Applying this argument to the case of abortion, we can see that Professor Thomson's argument would run as follows:

1. Assume that the fetus's right to life includes the right not to be killed by the woman carrying him.
2. But to refrain from killing the fetus is to allow him the continued use of the woman's body.

3. So our first assumption entails that the fetus's right to life includes the right to the continued use of the woman's body.
4. But we all grant that the fetus does not have the right to the continued use of the woman's body.
5. Therefore, the fetus's right to life cannot include the right not to be killed by the woman in question.

And it is also now clear what is wrong with this argument. When we granted that the fetus has no right to the continued use of the woman's body, all that we meant was that he does not have this right merely because the continued use saves his life. But, of course, there may be other reasons why he has this right. One would be that the only way to take the use of the woman's body away from the fetus is by killing him, and that is something that neither she nor we have the right to do. So, I submit, the way in which Assumption 4 is true is irrelevant, and cannot be used by Professor Thomson, for Assumption 4 is true only in cases where the saving of the life of the fetus is at stake and not in cases where the taking of his life is at stake.

I conclude therefore that Professor Thomson has not established the truth of her claims about abortion, primarily because she has not sufficiently attended to the distinction between our duty to save *X*'s life and our duty not to take it. Once one attends to that distinction, it would seem that the mother, in order to regain control over her body, has no right to abort the fetus from the point at which it becomes a human being.

It may also be useful to say a few words about the larger and less rigorous context of the argument that the woman has a right to her own body. It is surely true that one way in which women have been oppressed is by their being denied authority over their own bodies. But it seems to me that, as the struggle is carried on for meaningful amelioration of such oppression, it ought not to be carried so far that it violates the steady responsibilities all people have to one another. Parents may not desert their children, one class may not oppress another, one race or nation may not exploit another. For parents, powerful groups in society, races or nations in ascendancy, there are penalties for refraining from these wrong actions, but those penalties can in no way be taken as the justification for such wrong actions. Similarly, if the fetus is a human being, the penalty of carrying it cannot, I believe, be used as the justification for destroying it. . . .

2. Abortion to Save the Mother

Let us begin by considering the case in which the continued existence of the fetus threatens the life of the mother. This would seem to be the case in which she has the strongest claim for the right to abort the fetus even if it is a human being with a right to life. . . .

Why would not it be permissible for the mother to have an abortion in order to save her life even after that point at which the fetus becomes a human being? After all, the fetus's continued existence poses a threat to the life of the mother, and why can't she void that threat by taking the life of the fetus, as an ultimate act of defense?

To be sure, it may be the physician, or other agent, who will cause the abortion, and not the mother herself, but that difference seems to be irrelevant. Our intuition is that the person whose life is threatened (call that person *A*) may either take the life of the person (*B*) who threatens his life or call upon someone else (*C*) to do so. And more important, it seems permissible (and perhaps even obligatory in some cases) for *C* to take *B*'s life in order to save *A*'s life. Put in traditional terms, we are really speaking of the mother's right as the pursued, or anyone else's right as an onlooker, to take the life of the fetus who is the pursuer.

Pope Pius XI observed, in objecting to this argument from self-defense, that in the paradigm case of killing the pursuer *B* is unjustly attempting to take *A*'s life and is responsible for this attempt. It is the resulting guilt, based in part on *B*'s intention (found in the attempt to kill *A*), together with the fact that *A* will die unless *B* is stopped, which permits the taking of *B*'s life. The reader will notice that the abortion situation is quite different. Leaving aside for now—we shall return to it later on—the question as to whether the fetus can properly be described as attempting to take the mother's life, we can certainly agree that the fetus is not responsible for such an attempt (if it is occurring), that the fetus is therefore innocent, not guilty, and that the taking of fetal life cannot be compared to the paradigm case of killing the pursuer.

There is another way of putting Pope Pius' point. Consider the following case: there is, let us imagine, a medicine that *A* needs to stay alive, *C* owns some, and *C* will give it to *A* only if *A* kills *B*. Moreover, *A* has no other way of getting the medicine. In this case, the continued existence of *B* certainly poses a threat to the life of *A*; *A* can survive only if *B* does not survive. Still, it is not permissible for *A* to kill *B* in order to save *A*'s life. Why not? How does this case differ from the paradigm case of killing the pursuer? The simplest answer is that in this case, while *B*'s continued existence poses a threat to the life of *A*, *B* is not guilty of attempting to take *A*'s life because there is no attempt to be guilty about it in the first place. Now if we consider the case of a fetus whose continued existence poses a threat to the life of the mother, we see that it is like the medicine case and not like the paradigm case of killing the pursuer. The fetus does pose (in our imagined situation) a threat to the life of its mother, but it is not guilty of attempting to take its mother's life. Consequently, in an analogue to the medicine case, the mother (or her agent) could not justify destroying the fetus on the ground that it would be a permissible act of killing the pursuer.

The persuasiveness of both of the preceding arguments indicates that we have to analyze the whole issue of pursuit far more carefully before we can definitely decide whether an abortion to save the life of the mother could be viewed as a permissible act of killing the pursuer. If we look again at a paradigm case of pursuit, we see that there are three factors involved:

1. The continued existence of B poses a threat to the life of A, a threat that can be met only by the taking of B's life (we shall refer to this as the condition of danger).
2. B is unjustly attempting to take A's life (we shall refer to this as the condition of *attempt*).
3. B is responsible for his attempt to take A's life (we shall refer to this as the condition of *guilt*).

In the medicine case, only the danger condition was satisfied. Our intuitions that it would be wrong for A to take B's life in that case reflects our belief that the mere fact that B is a danger to A is not sufficient to establish that killing B will be a justifiable act of killing a pursuer. But it would be rash to conclude, as Pope Pius did, that all three conditions must be satisfied before the killing of B will be a justifiable act of killing a pursuer. What would happen, for example, if the first two conditions, but not the guilt condition, were satisfied?

There are good reasons for supposing that the satisfaction of the first two conditions is sufficient justification for taking B's life as an act of killing the pursuer. Consider, for example, a variation of the pursuit paradigm—one in which B is about to shoot A, and the only way by which A can stop him is by killing him first—but one in which B is a minor who is not responsible for his attempt to take A's life. In this case, the only condition not satisfied is the condition of guilt. Still, despite that fact, it seems that A may

justifiably take B's life as a permissible act of killing a pursuer. The guilt of the pursuer, then, is not a requirement for legitimacy in killing the pursuer. . . .

To summarize, then, our general discussion of killing the pursuer, we can say the following: the mere satisfaction of the danger condition is not sufficient to justify the killing of the pursuer. If, in addition . . . the attempt condition . . . is satisfied, then one would be justified in killing the pursuer to save the life of the pursued. In any case, the condition of guilt, arising from full knowledge and intent, need not be satisfied. . . .

Is, then, the aborting of the fetus, when necessary to save the life of the mother, a permissible act of killing a pursuer? It is true that in such cases the fetus is a danger to his mother. But it is also clear that the condition of attempt is not satisfied. The fetus has neither the beliefs nor the intentions to which we have referred. Furthermore, there is on the part of the fetus no action that threatens the life of the mother. . . . It seems to follow, therefore, that aborting the fetus could not be a permissible act of killing a pursuer. . . .

3. Two Other Cases Considered

All of the arguments that we have looked at so far are attempts to show that there is something special about abortion that justifies its being treated differently from other cases of the taking of human life. We shall now consider claims that are confined to certain special cases of abortion: the case in which the mother has been raped . . . and the case in which having the child may cause a problem for the rest of her family (the latter case is a particular case of the societal argument). In addressing these issues, we shall see whether there is any point to the permissibility of abortions in some of the cases covered by the Model Penal Code proposals.

When the expectant mother has conceived after being raped, there are two different sorts of considerations that might support the claim that she has the right to take the life of the fetus. They are the following: (A) the woman in question has already suffered immensely from the act of rape and the physical and/or psychological aftereffects of that act. It would be particularly unjust, the argument runs, for her to have to live through an unwanted pregnancy owing to that act of rape. Therefore, even if we are at a stage at which the fetus is a human being, the mother has the right to abort it; (B) the fetus in question has no right to be in that woman. It was put there as a result of an act of aggression upon her by the rapist, and its continued presence is an act of aggression against the mother. She has a right to repel that aggression by aborting the fetus.

The first argument is very compelling. We can all agree that a terrible injustice has been committed on the woman who is raped. The question that we have to consider, however, is whether it follows that it is morally permissible for her to abort the fetus. We must make that consideration reflecting that, however unjust the act of rape, it was not the fetus who committed or commissioned it. The injustice of the act, then, should in no way impinge upon the rights of the fetus, for it is innocent. What remains is the initial misfortune of the mother (and the injustice of her having to pass through the pregnancy, and, further, to assume responsibility of at least giving the child over for adoption or assuming the burden of its care). However unfortunate that circumstance, however unjust, the misfortune and the injustice are not sufficient cause to justify the taking of the life of an innocent human being as a means of mitigation.

It is at this point that Argument B comes in, for its whole point is that the fetus, by its mere presence in the mother, is committing an act of aggression against her, one over and above the one committed by the rapist, and one that the mother has a right to repel by abortion. But . . . (1) the fetus is certainly innocent (in the sense of not responsible) for any act of aggression against the mother and that (2) the mere presence of the fetus in the mother, no matter how unfortunate for her, does not constitute an act of aggression by the fetus against the mother. Argument B fails then at just that point at which Argument A needs its support, and we can therefore conclude that the fact that pregnancy is the result of rape does not give the mother the right to abort the fetus. . . .

We come finally to those cases in which the continuation of the pregnancy would cause serious problems for the rest of the family. There are a variety of cases that we have to consider here together. Perhaps the health of the mother will be affected in such a way that she cannot function effectively as a wife and mother during, or even after, the pregnancy. Or perhaps the expenses incurred as a result of the pregnancy would be utterly beyond the financial resources of the family. The important point is that the continuation of the pregnancy raises a serious problem for other innocent people involved besides the mother and the fetus, and it may be argued that the mother has the right to abort the fetus to avoid that problem.

By now, the difficulties with this argument should be apparent. We have seen earlier that the mere fact that the continued existence of the fetus threatens to harm the mother does not, by itself, justify the aborting of the fetus. Why should anything be changed by the fact that the threatened harm will accrue to the other members of the family and not to the mother? Of course, it would be different if the fetus were committing an act of aggression against the other members of the family. But, once more, this is certainly not the case.

We conclude, therefore, that none of these special circumstances justifies an abortion from that point at which the fetus is a human being. . . .

4. Fetal Humanity and Brain Function

The question which we must now consider is the question of fetal humanity. Some have argued that the fetus is a human being with a right to life (or, for convenience, just a human being) from the moment of conception. Others have argued that the fetus only becomes a human being at the moment of birth. Many positions in between these two extremes have also been suggested. How are we to decide which is correct?

The analysis which we will propose here rests upon certain metaphysical assumptions which I have defended elsewhere. These assumptions are: (a) the question is when has the fetus acquired all the properties essential (necessary) for being a human being, for when it has, it is a human being; (b) these properties are such that the loss of any one of them means that the human being in question has gone out of existence and not merely stopped being a human being; (c) human beings go out of existence when they die. It follows from these assumptions that the fetus becomes a human being when it acquires all those characteristics which are such that the loss of any one of them would result in the fetus's being dead. We must, therefore, turn to the analysis of death. . . .

We will first consider the question of what properties are essential to being human if we suppose that death and the passing out of existence occur only if there has been an irreparable cessation of brain function (keeping in mind that that condition itself, as we have noted, is a matter of medical judgment). We shall then consider the same question on the supposition that [Paul] Ramsey's more complicated theory of death (the modified traditional view) is correct.

According to what is called the brain-death theory, as long as there has not been an irreparable cessation of brain function the person in question continues to exist, no matter what else has happened to him. If so, it seems to follow that there is only one property—leaving aside those entailed by this one property—that is essential to humanity, namely, the possession of a brain that has not suffered an irreparable cessation of function.

Several consequences follow immediately from this conclusion. We can see that a variety of often advanced claims about the essence of humanity are false. For example, the claim that movement, or perhaps just the ability to move, is essential for being human is false. A human being who has stopped moving, and even one who has lost the ability to move, has not therefore stopped existing. Being able to move, and a fortiori moving, are not essential properties of human beings and therefore are not essential to being human. Similarly, the claim that being perceivable by other human beings is essential for being human is also false. A human being who has stopped being perceivable by other humans (for example, someone isolated on the other side of the moon, out of reach even of radio communication) has not stopped existing. Being perceivable by other human beings is not an essential property of human beings and is not essential to being human. And the same point can be made about the claims that viability is essential for being human, that independent existence is essential for being human, and that actual interaction with other human beings is essential for being human. The loss of any of these properties would not mean that the human being in question had gone out of existence, so none of them can be essential to that human being and none of them can be essential for being human.

Let us now look at the following argument: (1) A functioning brain (or at least, a brain that, if not functioning, is susceptible of function) is a property that every human being must have because it is essential for being human. (2) By the time an entity acquires that property, it has all the other properties that are essential for being human. Therefore, when the fetus acquires that property it becomes a human being. It is clear that the property in question is, according to the brain-death theory, one that is had essentially by all human beings. The question that we have to consider is whether the second premise is true. It might appear that its truth does follow from the brain-death theory. After all, we did see that the theory entails that only one property (together with those entailed by it) is essential for being human. Nevertheless, rather than relying solely on my earlier argument, I shall adopt an alternative approach to strengthen the conviction that this second premise is true: I shall note the important ways in which the fetus resembles and differs from an ordinary human being by the time it definitely has a functioning brain (about the end of the sixth week of development). It shall then be evident, in light of our theory of essentialism, that none of these differences involves the lack of some property in the fetus that is essential for its being human.

Structurally, there are few features of the human being that are not fully present by the end of the sixth week. Not only are the familiar external features and all the internal organs present, but the contours of the body are nicely rounded. More important, the body is functioning. Not only is the brain functioning, but the heart is beating sturdily (the fetus by this time has its own completely developed vascular system), the stomach is producing digestive juices, the liver is manufacturing blood cells, the kidney is extracting uric acid from the blood, and the nerves and muscles are operating in concert, so that reflex reactions can begin.

What are the properties that a fetus acquires after the sixth week of its development? Certain structures do appear later. These include the fingernails (which appear in the third month), the completed vocal chords (which also appear then), taste buds and salivary glands (again, in the third month), and hair and eyelashes (in the fifth month). In addition, certain functions begin later than the sixth week. The fetus begins to urinate (in the third month), to move spontaneously (in the third month), to respond to external stimuli (at least in the fifth month), and to breathe (in the sixth month). Moreover, there is

a constant growth in size. And finally, at the time of birth the fetus ceases to receive its oxygen and food through the placenta and starts receiving them through the mouth and nose.

I will not examine each of these properties (structures and functions) to show that they are not essential for being human. The procedure would be essentially the one used previously to show that various essentialist claims are in error. We might, therefore, conclude, on the supposition that the brain-death theory is correct, that the fetus becomes a human being about the end of the sixth week after its development.

There is, however, one complication that should be noted here. There are, after all, progressive stages in the physical development and in the functioning of the brain. For example, the fetal brain (and nervous system) does not develop sufficiently to support spontaneous motion until some time in the third month after conception. There is, of course, no doubt that that stage of development is sufficient for the fetus to be human. No one would be likely to maintain that a spontaneously moving human being has died; and similarly, a spontaneously moving fetus would seem to have become human. One might, however, want to claim that the fetus does not become a human being until the point of spontaneous movement. So then, on the supposition that the brain-death theory is correct, one ought to conclude that the fetus becomes a human being at some time between the sixth and twelfth week after its conception.

But what if we reject the brain-death theory, and replace it with its equally plausible contender, Ramsey's theory of death? According to that theory—which we can call the brain, heart, and lung theory of death—the human being does not die, does not go out of existence, until such time as the brain, heart, and lungs have irreparably ceased functioning naturally. What are the essential features of being human according to this theory?

Actually, the adoption of Ramsey's theory requires no major modifications. According to that theory, what is essential to being human, what each human being must retain if he is to continue to exist, is the possession of a functioning (actually or potentially) heart, lung, or brain. It is only when a human being possesses none of these that he dies and goes out of existence; and the fetus comes into humanity, so to speak, when he acquires one of these.

On Ramsey's theory, the argument would now run as follows: (1) The property of having a functioning brain, heart, or lungs (or at least organs of the kind that, if not functioning, are susceptible of function) is one that every human being must have because it is essential for being human. (2) By the time that an entity acquires that property it has all the other properties that are essential for being human. Therefore, when the fetus acquires that property it becomes a human being. There remains, once more, the problem of the second premise. Since the fetal heart starts operating rather early, it is not clear that the second premise is correct. Many systems are not yet operating, and many structures are not yet present. Still, following our theory of essentialism, we should conclude that the fetus becomes a human being when it acquires a functioning heart (the first of the organs to function in the fetus).

There is, however, a further complication here, and it is analogous to the one encountered if we adopt the brain-death theory: When may we properly say that the fetal heart begins to function? At two weeks, when occasional contractions of the primitive fetal heart are present? In the fourth to fifth week, when the heart, although incomplete, is beating regularly and pumping blood cells through a closed vascular system, and when the tracings obtained by an ECG exhibit the classical elements of an adult tracing? Or after the end of the seventh week, when the fetal heart is functioning complete and "normal"?

We have not reached a precise conclusion in our study of the question of when the fetus becomes a human being. We do know that it does so some time between the end of the second week and the end of the third month. But it surely is not a human being at the moment of conception and it surely is one by the end of the third month. Though we have not come to a final answer to our question, we have narrowed the range of acceptable answers considerably.

[In summary] we have argued that the fetus becomes a human being with a right to life some time between the second and twelfth week after conception. We have also argued that abortions are morally impermissible after that point except in rather unusual circumstances. What is crucial to note is that neither of these arguments appeal to any theological considerations. We conclude, therefore, that there is a human-rights basis for moral opposition to abortions. . . .

Study Questions

1. How does Brody argue against Thomson's position on abortion? What is the distinction that, according to Brody, Thomson fails to take into consideration?
2. In Brody's estimation, what are the necessary conditions to justify killing an innocent person in self-defense? Does a fetus meet these conditions?
3. When, according to Brody, does a fetus become a person or a human being with a right to life? Do you agree with Brody? Explain.

CHAPTER 33

The Personhood Argument in Favor of Abortion

MARY ANNE WARREN

Mary Anne Warren teaches philosophy at San Francisco State University and has written in the area of feminism, including *The Nature of Woman: An Encyclopedia and Guide to the Literature* (1980). In the following paper she defends the liberal view that abortion is always morally permissible. She attacks Noonan's argument on the basis of an ambiguity in using the term *human being,* showing that the term has a biological and moral sense. What is crucial is the moral sense that presupposes certain characteristics, such as self-consciousness and rationality that a fetus does not have. At the end of her article she addresses the issue of infanticide.

THE QUESTION WHICH WE MUST answer in order to produce a satisfactory solution to the problem of the moral status of abortion is this: How are we to define the moral community, the set of beings with full and equal moral rights, such that we can decide whether a human fetus is a member of this community or not? What sort of entity, exactly, has the inalienable rights to life, liberty, and the pursuit of happiness? Jefferson attributed these rights to all *men,* and it may or may not be fair to suggest that he intended to attribute them *only* to men. Perhaps he ought to have attributed them to all human beings. If so, then we arrive, first, at Noonan's problem of defining what makes a being human, and, second, at the equally vital question which Noonan does not consider, namely, What reason is there for identifying the moral community with the set of all human beings, in whatever way we have chosen to define that term?

1. On the Definition of "Human"

One reason why this vital second question is so frequently overlooked in the debate over the moral status of abortion is that the term "human" has two distinct, but not often distinguished, senses. This fact results in a slide of meaning, which serves to conceal the fallaciousness of the traditional argument that since (1) it is wrong to kill innocent human beings, and (2) fetuses are innocent human beings, then (3) it is wrong to kill fetuses. For if "human" is used in the same sense in both (1) and (2) then, whichever of the two senses is meant, one of these premises is question-begging. And if it is used in two different senses then of course the conclusion doesn't follow.

Thus, (1) is a self-evident moral truth,[1] and avoids begging the question about abortion, only if "human being" is used to mean something like "a full-fledged member of the moral community." (It may or may not also be meant to refer exclusively to members of the species *Homo sapiens.*) We may call this the *moral* sense of "human." It is not to be confused with what we will call the *genetic* sense, i.e., the sense in which *any* member of the species is a human being, and no member of any other species could be. If (1) is acceptable only if the moral sense is intended, (2) is non-question-begging only if what is intended is the genetic sense.

In "Deciding Who Is Human," Noonan argues for the classification of fetuses with human beings by pointing to the presence of the full genetic code, and the potential capacity for rational thought.[2] It is clear that what he needs to show, for his version of the traditional argument to be valid, is that fetuses are human in the moral sense, the sense in which it is analytically true that all human beings have full moral rights. But, in the absence of any argument showing that whatever is genetically human is also morally human, and he gives none, nothing more than genetic humanity can be demonstrated by the presence of the human genetic code. And, as we will see, the *potential* capacity for rational thought can at most show that an entity has the potential for *becoming* human in the moral sense.

2. Defining the Moral Community

Can it be established that genetic humanity is sufficient for moral humanity? I think that there are very good reasons for not defining the moral community in this way. I would like to suggest an alternative way of defining the moral community, which I will argue for only to the extent of explaining why it is, or should be, self-evident. The suggestion is simply that the moral community consists of all and only *people,* rather than all and only human beings;[3] and probably the best way of demonstrating its self-evidence is by considering the concept of personhood, to

see what sorts of entities are and are not persons, and what the decision that a being is or is not a person implies about its moral rights.

What characteristics entitle an entity to be considered a person? This is obviously not the place to attempt a complete analysis of the concept of personhood, but we do not need such a fully adequate analysis just to determine whether and why a fetus is or isn't a person. All we need is a rough and approximate list of the most basic criteria of personhood, and some idea of which, or how many, of these an entity must satisfy in order to properly be considered a person.

In searching for such criteria, it is useful to look beyond the set of people with whom we are acquainted, and ask how we would decide whether a totally alien being was a person or not. (For we have no right to assume that genetic humanity is necessary for personhood.) Imagine a space traveler who lands on an unknown planet and encounters a race of beings utterly unlike any he has ever seen or heard of. If he wants to be sure of behaving morally toward these beings, he has to somehow decide whether they are people, and hence have full moral rights, or whether they are the sort of thing which he need not feel guilty about treating as, for example, a source of food.

How should he go about making this decision? If he has some anthropological background, he might look for such things as religion, art, and the manufacturing of tools, weapons, or shelters, since these factors have been used to distinguish our human from our prehuman ancestors, in what seems to be closer to the moral than the genetic sense of "human." And no doubt he would be right to consider the presence of such factors as good evidence that the alien beings were people, and morally human. It would, however, be overly anthropocentric of him to take the absence of these things as adequate evidence that they were not, since we can imagine people who have progressed beyond, or evolved without ever developing, these cultural characteristics.

I suggest that the traits which are most central to the concept of personhood, or humanity in the moral sense, are, very roughly, the following:

1. consciousness (of objects and events external and/or internal to the being), and in particular the capacity to feel pain;

2. reasoning (the *developed* capacity to solve new and relatively complex problems);

3. self-motivated activity (activity which is relatively independent of either genetic or direct external control);

4. the capacity to communicate, by whatever means, messages of an indefinite variety of types, that is, not just with an indefinite number of possible contents, but on indefinitely many possible topics;

5. the presence of self-concepts, and self-awareness, either individual or racial, or both.

Admittedly, there are apt to be a great many problems involved in formulating precise definitions of these criteria, let alone in developing universally valid behavioral criteria for deciding when they apply. But I will assume that both we and our explorer know approximately what (1)–(5) mean, and that he is also able to determine whether or not they apply. How, then, should he use his findings to decide whether or not the alien beings are people? We needn't suppose that an entity must have *all* of these attributes to be properly considered a person; (1) and (2) alone may well be sufficient for personhood, and quite probably (1)–(3) are sufficient. Neither do we need to insist that any one of these criteria is *necessary* for personhood, although once again (1) and (2) look like fairly good candidates for necessary conditions, as does (3), if "activity" is construed so as to include the activity of reasoning.

All we need to claim, to demonstrate that a fetus is not a person, is that any being which satisfies *none* of (1)–(5) is certainly not a person. I consider this claim to be so obvious that I think anyone who denied it, and claimed that a being which satisfied none of (1)–(5) was a person all the same, would thereby demonstrate that he had no notion at all of what a person is—perhaps because he had confused the concept of a person with that of genetic humanity. If the opponents of abortion were to deny the appropriateness of these five criteria, I do not know what further arguments would convince them. We would probably have to admit that our conceptual schemes were indeed irreconcilably different, and that our dispute could not be settled objectively.

I do not expect this to happen, however, since I think that the concept of a person is one which is very nearly universal (to people), and that it is common to both proabortionists and antiabortionists, even though neither group has fully realized the relevance of this concept to the resolution of their dispute. Furthermore, I think that on reflection even the antiabortionists ought to agree not only that (1)–(5) are central to the concept of personhood, but also that it is a part of this concept that all and only people have full moral rights. The concept of a person is in part a moral concept; once we have admitted that *x* is a person we have recognized, even if we have not agreed to respect, *x's* right to be treated as a member of the moral community. It is true that the claim that *x is a human being* is more commonly voiced as part of an appeal to treat *x* decently than is the claim that *x* is a person, but this is either because "human being" is here used in the sense which implies personhood, or because the genetic and moral senses of "human" have been confused.

Now if (1)–(5) are indeed the primary criteria of personhood, then it is clear that genetic humanity is neither necessary nor sufficient for establishing that an entity is a person. Some human beings are not people, and there may well be people who are not human beings. A man or woman whose consciousness has been permanently obliterated but who remains alive is a human being which is no longer a person; defective human beings, with no appreciable mental capacity, are not and presumably never will be people; and a fetus is a human being which is not yet a person, and which therefore cannot coherently be said to have full moral rights. Citizens of the next century should be prepared to recognize highly advanced, self-aware robots or computers, should such be developed, and intelligent inhabitants of other worlds, should such be found, as people in the fullest sense, and to respect their moral rights. But to ascribe full moral rights to an entity which is not a person is as absurd as to ascribe moral obligations and responsibilities to such an entity.

3. Fetal Development and the Right to Life

Two problems arise in the application of these suggestions for the definition of the moral community to the determination of the precise moral status of a human fetus. Given that the paradigm example of a person is a normal adult human being, then (1) How like this paradigm, in particular how far advanced since conception, does a human being need to be before it begins to have a right to life by virtue, not of being fully a person as of yet, but of being *like* a person? and (2) To what extent, if any, does the fact that a fetus has the *potential* for becoming a person endow it with some of the same rights? Each of these questions requires some comment.

In answering the first question, we need not attempt a detailed consideration of the moral rights of organisms which are not developed enough, aware enough, intelligent enough, etc., to be considered people, but which resemble people in some respects. It does seem reasonable to suggest that the more like a person, in the relevant respects, a being is, the stronger is the case for regarding it as having a right to life, and in-

deed the stronger its right to life is. Thus we ought to take seriously the suggestion that, insofar as "the human individual develops biologically in a continuous fashion . . . the rights of a human person might develop in the same way."[4] But we must keep in mind that the attributes which are relevant in determining whether or not an entity is enough like a person to be regarded as having some of the same moral rights are no different from those which are relevant to determining whether or not it is fully a person— i.e., are no different from (1)–(5)—and that being genetically human, or having recognizably human facial and other physical features, or detectable brain activity, or the capacity to survive outside the uterus, are simply not among these relevant attributes.

Thus it is clear that even though a seven- or eight-month fetus has features which make it apt to arouse in us almost the same powerful protective instinct as is commonly aroused by a small infant, nevertheless it is not significantly more personlike than is a very small embryo. It is *somewhat* more personlike; it can apparently feel and respond to pain, and it may even have a rudimentary form of consciousness, insofar as its brain is quite active. Nevertheless, it seems safe to say that it is not fully conscious, in the way that an infant of a few months is, and that it cannot reason, or communicate messages of indefinitely many sorts, does not engage in self-motivated activity, and has no self-awareness. Thus, in the *relevant* respects, a fetus, even a fully developed one, is considerably less personlike than is the average mature mammal, indeed the average fish. And I think that a rational person must conclude that if the right to life of a fetus is to be based upon its resemblance to a person, then it cannot be said to have any more right to life than, let us say, a newborn guppy (which also seems to be capable of feeling pain), and that a right of that magnitude could never override a woman's right to obtain an abortion, at any stage of her pregnancy.

There may, of course, be other arguments in favor of placing legal limits upon the stage of pregnancy in which an abortion may be performed. Given the relative safety of the new techniques of artificially inducing labor during the third trimester, the danger to the woman's life or health is no longer such an argument. Neither is the fact that people tend to respond to the thought of abortion in the later stages of pregnancy with emotional repulsion, since mere emotional responses cannot take the place of moral reasoning in determining what ought to be permitted. Nor, finally, is the frequently heard argument that legalizing abortion, especially late in the pregnancy, may erode the level of respect for human life, leading, perhaps, to an increase in unjustified euthanasia and other crimes. For this threat, if it is a threat, can be better met by educating people to the kinds of moral distinctions which we are making here than by limiting access to abortion (which limitation may, in its disregard for the rights of women, be just as damaging to the level of respect for human rights).

Thus, since the fact that even a fully developed fetus is not personlike enough to have any significant right to life on the basis of its personlikeness shows that no legal restrictions upon the stage of pregnancy in which an abortion may be performed can be justified on the grounds that we should protect the rights of the older fetus, and since there is no other apparent justification for such restrictions, we may conclude that they are entirely unjustified. Whether or not it would be *indecent* (whatever that means) for a woman in her seventh month to obtain an abortion just to avoid having to postpone a trip to Europe, it would not, in itself, be *immoral*, and therefore it ought to be permitted.

4. Potential Personhood and the Right to Life

We have seen that a fetus does not resemble a person in any way which can support the claim that it has even some of the same rights. But

what about its *potential*, the fact that if nurtured and allowed to develop naturally it will very probably become a person? Doesn't that alone give it at least some right to life? It is hard to deny that the fact that an entity is a potential person is a strong prima facie reason for not destroying it; but we need not conclude from this that a potential person has a right to life, by virtue of that potential. It may be that our feeling that it is better, other things being equal, not to destroy a potential person is better explained by the fact that potential people are still (felt to be) an invaluable resource, not to be lightly squandered. Surely, if every speck of dust were a potential person, we would be much less apt to conclude that every potential person has a right to become actual.

Still, we do not need to insist that a potential person has no right to life whatever. There may well be something immoral, and not just imprudent, about wantonly destroying potential people, when doing so isn't necessary to protect anyone's rights. But even if a potential person does have some prima facie right to life, such a right could not possibly outweigh the right of a woman to obtain an abortion, since the rights of any actual person invariably outweigh those of any potential person, whenever the two conflict. Since this may not be immediately obvious in the case of a human fetus, let us look at another case.

Suppose that our space explorer falls into the hands of an alien culture, whose scientists decide to create a few hundred thousand or more human beings, by breaking his body into its component cells, and using these to create fully developed human beings, with, of course, his genetic code. We may imagine that each of these newly created men will have all of the original man's abilities, skills, knowledge, and so on, and also have an individual self-concept, in short that each of them will be a bona fide (though hardly unique) person. Imagine that the whole project will take only seconds, and that its chances of success are extremely high, and that our explorer knows all of this, and also knows that these people will be treated fairly. I maintain that in such a situation he would have every right to escape if he could, and thus to deprive all of these potential people of their potential lives; for his right to life outweighs all of theirs together, in spite of the fact that they are all genetically human, all innocent, and all have a very high probability of becoming people very soon, if only he refrains from acting.

Indeed, I think he would have a right to escape even if it were not his life which the alien scientists planned to take, but only a year of his freedom, or, indeed, only a day. Nor would he be obligated to stay if he had gotten captured (thus bringing all these people-potentials into existence) because of his own carelessness, or even if he had done so deliberately, knowing the consequences. Regardless of how he got captured, he is not morally obligated to remain in captivity for *any* period of time for the sake of permitting any number of potential people to come into actuality, so great is the margin by which one actual person's right to liberty outweighs whatever right to life even a hundred thousand potential people have. And it seems reasonable to conclude that the rights of a woman will outweigh by a similar margin whatever right to life a fetus may have by virtue of its potential personhood.

Thus, neither a fetus's resemblance to a person, nor its potential for becoming a person provides any basis whatever for the claim that it has any significant right to life. Consequently, a woman's right to protect her health, happiness, freedom, and even her life, by terminating an unwanted pregnancy, will always override whatever right to life it may be appropriate to ascribe to a fetus, even a fully developed one. And thus, in the absence of any overwhelming social need for every possible child, the laws which restrict the right to obtain an abortion, or limit the period of pregnancy during which an abortion may be performed, are a wholly unjustified violation of a woman's most basic moral and constitutional rights.

Postscript on Infanticide

Since the publication of this article, many people have written to point out that my argument appears to justify not only abortion, but infanticide as well. For a newborn infant is not significantly more personlike than an advanced fetus, and consequently it would seem that if the destruction of the latter is permissible so too must be that of the former. Inasmuch as most people, regardless of how they feel about the morality of abortion, consider infanticide a form of murder, this might appear to represent a serious flaw in my argument.

Now, if I am right in holding that it is only people who have a full-fledged right to life, and who can be murdered, and if the criteria of personhood are as I have described them, then it obviously follows that killing a newborn infant isn't murder. It does *not* follow, however, that infanticide is permissible, for two reasons. In the first place, it would be wrong, at least in this country and in this period of history, and other things being equal, to kill a newborn infant, because even if its parents do not want it and would not suffer from its destruction, there are other people who would like to have it, and would, in all probability, be deprived of a great deal of pleasure by its destruction. Thus, infanticide is wrong for reasons analogous to those which make it wrong to wantonly destroy natural resources, or great works of art.

Secondly, most people, at least in this country, value infants and would much prefer that they be preserved, even if foster parents are not immediately available. Most of us would rather be taxed to support orphanages than allow unwanted infants to be destroyed. So long as there are people who want an infant preserved, and who are willing and able to provide the means of caring for it, under reasonably humane conditions, it is *ceteris paribus*, wrong to destroy it.

But, it might be replied, if this argument shows that infanticide is wrong, at least at this time and in this country, doesn't it also show that abortion is wrong? After all, many people value fetuses, are disturbed by their destruction, and would much prefer that they be preserved, even at some cost to themselves. Furthermore, as a potential source of pleasure to some foster family, a fetus is just as valuable as an infant. There is, however, a crucial difference between the two cases: so long as the fetus is unborn, its preservation, contrary to the wishes of the pregnant woman, violates her rights to freedom, happiness, and self-determination. Her rights override the rights of those who would like the fetus preserved, just as if someone's life or limb is threatened by a wild animal, his right to protect himself by destroying the animal overrides the rights of those who would prefer that the animal not be harmed.

The minute the infant is born, however, its preservation no longer violates any of its mother's rights, even if she wants it destroyed, because she is free to put it up for adoption. Consequently, while the moment of birth does not mark any sharp discontinuity in the degree to which an infant possesses the right to life, it does mark the end of its mother's right to determine its fate. Indeed, if abortion could be performed without killing the fetus, she would never possess the right to have the fetus destroyed, for the same reasons that she has no right to have an infant destroyed.

On the other hand, it follows from my argument that when an unwanted or defective infant is born into a society which cannot afford and/or is not willing to care for it, then its destruction is permissible. This conclusion will, no doubt, strike many people as heartless and immoral; but remember that the very existence of people who feel this way, and who are willing and able to provide care for unwanted infants, is reason enough to conclude that they should be preserved.

Notes

1. Of course, the principle that it is (always) wrong to kill innocent human beings is in need of many other modifications, e.g., that it may be permissible to do so to save a greater number of other innocent human beings, but we may safely ignore these complications here.

2. John Noonan, "Deciding Who Is Human," *Natural Law Forum,* 13 (1968), 135.

3. From here on, we will use "human" to mean genetically human, since the moral sense seems closely connected to, and perhaps derived from, the assumption that genetic humanity is sufficient for membership in the moral community.

4. Thomas L. Hayes, "A Biological View," *Commonweal,* 85 (March 17, 1967), 677–78; quoted by Daniel Callahan, in *Abortion: Law, Choice and Morality* (London: Macmillan & Co., 1970).

Study Questions

1. In what way is the term *human being* ambiguous? How does this ambiguity affect the conservative argument against abortion?
2. According to Warren, what characteristics make an entity a person with a right to life? Do you agree with Warren?
3. According to Warren, when does a woman have a right to an abortion?
4. What are the implications for Warren's position for the morality of infanticide? Does this affect the central argument in your eyes?

CHAPTER 34

The Golden Rule Argument Against Abortion

HARRY J. GENSLER

Harry J. Gensler is professor of philosophy at Loyola College in Chicago. In the article that follows, Gensler does three things. First, he analyzes the meaning of *human* and the question of when human life begins. Second, he examines the major arguments in favor of abortion and concludes that none of them are successful. Third, he uses a Kantian argument based on consistency (a version of the Golden Rule) to show that normally abortion is morally wrong. In closing, he responds to six objections against his position.

IF YOU ASKED TEN YEARS AGO for my view on the morality of abortion, I would have said "I don't have a view—the issue confuses me." But now I think that abortion is wrong and that certain Kantian consistency requirements more or less force us into thinking this. Part III will present my reasoning. But first, in Parts I and II, I will show why various traditional and recent arguments on abortion do not work.

I. A Traditional Anti-Abortion Argument

One common traditional argument goes this way:

The killing of innocent human life is wrong.
The fetus is innocent human life.
Therefore, the killing of the fetus is wrong.

This seemingly simple argument raises some difficult questions:

It is "always wrong" or "normally wrong"? And if the latter, how do we decide the difficult cases?

Is the fetus "innocent" if it is attacking the life or health or social well-being of the woman?

Is there a clear and morally-weighty distinction between "killing" and "letting die"— or between "direct killing" and "indirect killing"?

I will not discuss these important questions; a short essay on abortion must leave many questions unanswered. But I will discuss this one: "What does the term 'human life' in the abortion argument mean?" People sometimes presume that the meaning of the term is clear and that the major problem is the factual one of whether the fetus is "human life" (in some clear sense). But I think that the term in this context is fuzzy and could be used in different senses.

Suppose we found a Martian who could discuss philosophy; would he be "human"? We need to make distinctions: the Martian would be "human" in the sense of "animal capable of rea-

From "A Kantian Argument Against Abortion," Philosophical Studies 49 (1986), pp. 83–98.
Reprinted by permission of Kluwer Academic Publishers.

soning" ("rational animal") but not in the sense of "member of the species *Homo sapiens*"—so the Martian is "human" in one sense but not in another. Which of these senses should be used in the abortion argument? The fetus is not yet an "animal capable of reasoning." Is it a "member of the species *Homo sapiens*"? That depends on whether the unborn are to be counted as "members" of a species—ordinary language can use the term either way. In the biology lab we all (regardless of our views on abortion) distinguish between "human" fetuses and "mouse" fetuses—so in this sense (the "genetic sense") the fetus is human. But in counting the number of mice or humans in the city of Chicago we all (regardless of our views on abortion) count only the born—so in this sense ("the population-study sense") the fetus is not a human. So is the fetus a "human"? In two senses of this term that we have distinguished the answer would be NO while in a third sense the answer would be YES; whether the fetus is "human" depends on what is meant by "human."

Human life has been claimed to begin at various points:

(1) at conception.
(2) when individuality is assured (and the zygote cannot split or fuse with another).
(3) when the fetus exhibits brain waves.
(4) when the fetus could live apart.
(5) at birth.
(6) when the being becomes self-conscious and rational.

Here we do not have a factual disagreement over when there emerges, in the same clear sense of the term, a "human", rather we have six ways to use the term. Answer (1) is correct for the "genetic sense," (5) for the "population-study sense," and (6) for the "rational animal sense"; answers (2) to (4) reflect other (possibly idiosyncratic) senses. And there are likely other senses of "human" besides these six. Which of these are we to use in the first premise ("The killing of innocent *human* life is wrong")? We get different principles depending on which sense of the term "human" we use.

Can we decide which sense to use by appealing to scientific data? No, we cannot. Scientific data can help us judge whether a specific individual is "human" in some specified sense (e.g., sense [3] or sense [4]) but it can not tell us which sense of "human" to use in our principle.

Can we decide by "intuition"—by following the principle that *seems* most correct? Note that moral intuitions depend greatly on upbringing and social milieu. Most Catholics were brought up to have intuitions in line with sense (1) (the "genetic sense"). Many ancient Romans and Greeks were trained to have sense (6) intuitions (allowing abortion *and* infanticide). And many Americans today are being brought up to have sense (5) intuitions (allowing abortion but not infanticide). Is there any way to resolve this clash—other than simply praising our own intuitions and insulting contrary ones? Can we carry on the argument further? I think we can and that the Kantian appeal to consistency provides a way to resolve the issue rationally.

II. Some Recent Pro-Abortion Arguments

Before getting to the Kantian approach, let us consider three arguments in defense of abortion. A common utilitarian argument goes this way:

> Anything having a balance of good results (considering everyone) is morally permissible.
> Abortion often has a balance of good results (considering everyone).
> Therefore, abortion often is morally permissible.

Here "good results" is most commonly interpreted in terms of pleasure and pain ("hedonistic act utilitarianism") or the satisfaction of desires ("preference act utilitarianism").

The second premise (on the good results of abortion) is controversial. People defending the premise say that abortion often avoids difficulties such as the financial burden of a child on poor parents or on society, the disruption of schooling or a career, and the disgrace of an unwed mother; that where these problems or probable birth defects exist, the child-to-be would have less chance for happiness; and that abortion provides a "second chance" to prevent a birth when contraceptives fail or people want to rethink an earlier choice. But opponents say that we can have equally good results without abortion, by using better social structures (more social support toward unwed mothers and poor families, better adoption practices, wiser use of contraceptives, etc.) and scientific advances (better contraceptives, artificial wombs, etc.); and they say that abortion can harm the woman psychologically and promote callous attitudes toward human life.

I think the weaker link is the first premise—the argument's utilitarian basis. This premise would often justify killing, not just fetuses, but also infants and the sick or handicapped or elderly; many utilitarian reasons for not wanting a child around the house would also apply to not wanting grandmother around. And the premise would justify these killings, not just when they have great utilitarian benefits, but even when the utilitarian benefits are slight. Utilitarianism says that the killing of an innocent human being is justified whenever it brings even a slight increase in the sum-total of pleasure (or desire-satisfaction). This is truly bizarre.

Imagine a town where lynchings give the people pleasure (or satisfy their desires) and the utilitarian sheriff lynches an innocent person each week because the pleasure (or desire) of the masses slightly outweighs the misery (or frustration of desire) of the person to be lynched—and so the action has a slight gain in "good results." If the utilitarian principle is correct then the sheriff's lynchings are morally justified! But could anyone really believe that these lynchings would be morally justified?

I could pile up further examples of strange and unbelievable implications of utilitarianism. Utilitarians try to weasel out of these examples but I think not with ultimate success. So my verdict on utilitarianism is that it would justify so many bizarre actions (including so many killings) that we would not accept this principle if we were consistent and realized its logical consequences.

My second pro-abortion argument is from Michael Tooley.[1] Tooley recognizes that humans have a right to life—presumably a greater right than utilitarians would recognize; but only humans in sense (6) ("rational animals"—or, as he puts it, "persons") have such a right. The human fetus, while it might develop into a being with a right to life, presently has no more right to life than a mouse fetus. A fetus lacks a right to life because "rights" connect with "desires" conceptually—so that you can have rights only if you have desires. Tooley's argument is roughly this:

A being has a right to X only if it desires X.
No fetus desires its continued existence [because then the fetus would have to have a concept of itself as a continuing subject of experiences—a concept it cannot as yet have].
Therefore, no fetus has a right to its continued existence.

Tooley claims that the first premise is not correct as it stands; we must add three qualifications to make the premise harmonize with our intuitions regarding rights:

A being has a right to X only if either it desires X or else it would desire X were it not (a) emotionally unbalanced or (b) temporarily unconscious or (c) conditioned otherwise.

He thinks the revised first premise will serve equally well (assuming obvious changes in the second premise); so he concludes that fetuses (and infants) do not have a right to life.

But we need further exceptions to make the first premise correspond to our intuitions. If we think that the dead have rights (e.g., to have their wills followed), then we need to add "or (d) the being did desire *X* when it was alive." If we think that a child who lacks the concept "hepatitis" (and thus cannot desire not to be given this disease) does not thereby lose his right not to be given hepatitis, then we need to add "or (e) the being would desire *X* if it had the necessary concepts." If we think (as I do) that trees and canyons have the right not to be destroyed without good reason, then we would have to add some exception for this. And if we think that the fetus (or infant) has a right to life, then we need to add something like "or (f) if the being were to grow up to be an adult member of the rational species to which it belongs then it would desire to have had *X*" (presumably if the fetus were to grow up to be an adult member of *Homo sapiens* then it would desire to have had continued life—and this, with (f), allows the fetus to have a right to life).[2] The trouble with Tooley's argument is that disagreements over the main issue of the right to life of the fetus translate into disagreements over how to qualify the first premise to make it mesh with "our" intuitions; so the argument cannot decide the main issue.

The third argument in defense of abortion comes from Judith Jarvis Thomson and presumes that the fetus is a "person" (in some undefined sense):[3]

One who has voluntarily assumed no special obligation toward another person has no obligation to do anything requiring great personal cost to preserve the life of the other.
Often a pregnant woman has voluntarily assumed no special obligation toward the unborn child (a person), and to preserve its life by continuing to bear the unborn child would require great personal cost.
Therefore, often a pregnant woman has no obligation to continue to bear the unborn child.

The first premise here seems acceptable. Normally you have no obligation to risk your life to save a drowning stranger; if you risk your life then you do more than duty requires. But it is different if you are a lifeguard who has assumed a special obligation—then you have to try to save the person, even at the risk of your own life. Thomson thinks that a woman getting pregnant intending to have a child is voluntarily accepting a special obligation toward the child. However if the pregnancy is accidental (the result of a contraceptive failure or rape) then the woman has assumed no such special obligation and, if continuing to bear the child requires great personal cost, the woman has no obligation to continue to bear it; the woman would do no wrong if she has an abortion—but if she continues to bear the child in spite of personal cost then she is doing something heroic, something beyond what duty requires.

Thomson gives an analogy. Suppose you wake up and find yourself in bed with an unconscious violinist attached to your circulatory system (his friends attached him to you because this was needed to save his life); if you disconnect him before nine months, he will die—otherwise he will live. Even though it might be praiseworthy to make the sacrifice and leave him plugged in for nine months, still you have no obligation to do so; it would be morally right for you to disconnect him, even though he will die. So also if you are pregnant under the conditions mentioned above, then, even though it might be praiseworthy to make the sacrifice and bear the child for nine months, still you have no obligation to do so; it would be morally right for you to have the child removed, even though it will die.

The first premise of Thomson's argument is slightly misstated. A motorist has a special obligation toward a person he has injured in an accident, even though he has not voluntarily assumed this obligation any clear way (the accident happened against his will and despite all reasonable precautions—just like an accidental pregnancy). Similarly a child has a special obligation towards his parents—even though he has not voluntarily assumed this obligation. Not all special obligations toward others are "voluntarily assumed"—so these two words should be crossed out in the premises.

My main objection to the argument can be put as a dilemma. Utilitarianism is either true or false. If it is *true*, then the first premise is false (because then the person has an obligation to do whatever has the best consequences—despite personal cost); and so the pro-abortion utilitarian Peter Singer rejects this premise, since it conflicts with utilitarianism. But if utilitarianism is *false*, then presumably Sir David Ross was right in claiming it to be morally significant that others:

> . . . stand to me in relation of promisee to promiser, of creditor to debtor, of wife to husband, *of child to parent* [my emphasis], of friend to friend, of fellow countryman to fellow countryman, and the like; and each of these relations is the foundation of *a prima facie* duty, which is more or less incumbent on me according to the circumstances of the case.[4]

If utilitarianism is *false*, then likely a person has greater obligations toward his or her offspring than toward a violinist stranger—and so the second premise, which claims that the pregnant woman has no special responsibility toward her own child, begins to look doubtful (recall that we crossed out the words "voluntarily assumed").

III. A Kantian Argument

My Kantian approach to abortion stresses consistency. In discussing utilitarianism I appealed to simple logical consistency (not accepting a principle without accepting its recognized logical consequences). Here I will use two further consistency requirements (based on the universalizability and prescriptivity principles) and a third consistency requirement derived from these two (a version of the golden rule). The following argument displays these three requirements and how the third follows from the first two:

> If you are consistent and think that it would be all right for someone *to do A to X*, then you will think that it would be all right for someone *to do A to you* in similar circumstances.
>
> If you are consistent and think that it would be *all right for* someone to do A to you in similar circumstances, then you will *consent* to the idea of someone doing A to you in similar circumstances.
>
> Therefore, if you are consistent and think that it would be *all right to do A to X*, then you will *consent* to the idea of someone *doing A to you* in similar circumstances. (GR [Golden Rule])

The first premise can be justified by the "universalizability principle," which demands that we make similar ethical judgments about the same sort of situation (regardless of the individuals involved); so if I think it would be all right to rob *Jones* but I don't think it would be all right for someone to rob *me* in an imagined exactly similar situation, then I violate universalizability and am inconsistent. The second premise can be justified by the "prescriptivity principle," which demands that we keep our ethical beliefs in harmony with the rest of our lives (our actions, intentions, desires, and so forth); so if I think an act would be all right but I don't consent to it being done, then I violate prescriptivity and am inconsistent. These and further derived requirements can be formulated and justified in a rigorous way; but I won't do that here. The conclusion GR is a form of the golden rule; if I think it would be all right to rob Jones but yet I don't consent to (or approve of) the idea of someone robbing me in similar circumstances, then I violate GR and am inconsistent.[5]

The following argument combines an instance of GR with an empirical premise about your desires:

> If you are consistent and think that *stealing is normally permissible,* then you will consent to the idea of *people stealing from you* in normal circumstances. (From GR)
>
> You do not consent to the idea of people stealing from you in normal circumstances.
>
> Therefore, if you are consistent then you will not think that stealing is normally permissible.

Most of us do not consent to the idea of people stealing from us in normal circumstances; so we would not be consistent if we held "Stealing is normally permissible" (since then we would violate consistency principle GR). This argument shows that, given that a person has a certain desire (one that most people can be presumed to have), he would not be consistent if he held a given ethical view. The conclusion here concerns the consistency of holding the ethical judgment and not the judgment's truth. A person could escape this conclusion if he did not care if people robbed him; then the second premise would be false. Throughout the rest of this essay I will generally assume that the reader desires not to be robbed or blinded or killed; if you would love people to rob or blind or kill you (or you don't care whether they do this to you)—then most of my further conclusions will not apply to you.

It might seem easy to argue similarly on abortion. How would you like it if someone had aborted you? Should we say that you don't like the idea and so you can't consistently hold that abortion is permissible? Or should we say that as an ignorant fetus you would not have known

enough to have been against the abortion—so that this argument won't work?

Let us slow down and try to understand GR more clearly before applying it to abortion. Properly understood, GR has to do with my *present reaction* toward a hypothetical case—not with how I *would react if I were* in the hypothetical case. A few examples may clarify things. Consider this chart:

Issue	Right Question	Wrong Question
Do I think it permissible to rob *X* while *X* is asleep?	Do I now consent to the idea of my being robbed while asleep?	If I were robbed while I was asleep, would I then (while asleep) consent to this action?

(In the "Right Question" and "Wrong Question" I presume implicit "in relevantly or exactly similar circumstances" qualifiers). The point of this chart is that, by GR, to be consistent in answering YES to the ISSUE I must also answer yes to the *right question*—but I need not answer *yes* to the *wrong question.* Presumably I would answer *no* to the *right questions;* when I consider the hypothetical case of my-being-robbed-while asleep, I find that I now (while awake) do not consent to or approve of this action. But the *wrong question* has to do with what I, if I were robbed while asleep, would consent to or approve of while thus asleep (and thus ignorant of the robbery); GR, correctly understood, has nothing to do with the *wrong question.* Let me give another example:

Issue	Right Question	Wrong Question
Do I think it permissible to violate *X*'s will after his death?	Do I now consent to the idea of my will being violated after my death?	If my will is violated after my death, would I then (while dead) consent to this action?

Again GR has to do with my *present reaction* toward a hypothetical case in which I may imagine myself as asleep or dead or even a fetus—but not with how I *would* react *while* asleep or dead or a fetus *in* the hypothetical situation.

But is it legitimate to apply the golden rule to our treatment of a fetus? Consider a case not involving abortion:

Issue	Right Question	Wrong Question
Do I think it permissible to blind X while X is a fetus?	Do I now consent to the idea of my having been blinded while a fetus?	If I were blinded while a fetus, would I then (while a fetus) consent to this action?

Suppose you had a sadistic mother who, while pregnant with you, contemplated injecting herself with a blindness-drug which would have no effect on her but which would cause the fetus (you) to be born blind and remain blind all its (your) life. Your mother could have done this to you. Do you think this would have been all right—and do you consent to the idea of her having done this? The answer is a clear *no*—and an equally clear *no* regardless of the time of pregnancy that we imagine the injection taking place. We could then argue as we did concerning stealing:

If you are consistent and think that *blinding a fetus is normally permissible,* then you will consent to the idea of *your having been blinded while a fetus* in normal circumstances. (From GR)
You do not consent to the idea of your having been blinded while a fetus in normal circumstances.
Therefore, if you are consistent then you will not think that blinding a fetus is normally permissible.

Again, with most people the second premise will be true—most people can be presumed not to

consent to (or approve of) the idea of this act having been done to them.

It is legitimate to apply the golden rule to our treatment of a fetus? Surely it is—the above reasoning makes good sense. If a pregnant woman is about to do something harmful to the fetus (like taking drugs or excessive alcohol or cigarettes), it seems appropriate for her to ask, "How do I now react to the idea of my mother having done this same thing while she was pregnant with me?" Applying the golden rule to a fetus raises no special problems.

But someone might object as follows:

Seemingly your view forces us to accept that the fetus has rights (e.g., not to be blinded by the drug), even though you avoid saying it is human. But your question about *"my* having been blinded *while a fetus"* presupposes that the fetus and my present self are identical—the *same human being.* So aren't you presupposing (despite your earlier discussion on the many senses of "human") that the fetus is "human"?

While my way of phrasing the question may presuppose this, I put my question this way only for the sake of convenience; I could rephrase my question so that it doesn't presuppose this:

Do I now consent to the idea of:

- my having been blinded while a fetus?
- the fetus that developed into my present self having been blinded?
- Helen E. Gensler having taken the blindness-drug while pregnant in 1945?

The second and third ways to phrase the question do not presuppose that the fetus and my present self are identical or the same human being; if you wish, you may rephrase my comments thusly (I will keep to the first way of speaking for the sake of brevity). I am against the idea of the drug having been given, not because I think that the fetus was in some metaphysical sense the *same human being* as I, but rather because if this drug had been given then I would be blind all my life.

The application of GR to abortion is similar—we need only switch from a blindness-drug (which blinds the fetus) to a death-drug (which kills the fetus). Your mother could have killed you through such a death-drug (or other means of abortion). Do you think this would have been all right—and do you consent to (or approve of) the idea of her having done this? Again the answer is a clear *no*—and an equally clear *no* regardless of the time of pregnancy that we imagine the killing taking place. We can argue as we did concerning blinding:

> If you are consistent and think that *abortion is normally permissible,* then you will consent to the idea of *your having been aborted* in normal circumstances. (From GR)
>
> You do not consent to the idea of your having been aborted in normal circumstances.
>
> Therefore, if you are consistent then you will not think that abortion is normally permissible.

Again with most people the second premise will be true—most people can be presumed not to consent to (or approve of) the idea of this act having been done to them. So insofar as most people take a consistent position they will not think that abortion is normally permissible.

IV. Six Objections

(1) Surely a utilitarian would see your two drug cases as very different—the blindness-drug inflicts needless future suffering while the death-drug simply eliminates a life. Why wouldn't a utilitarian, moved by the greatest total happiness principle, approve of the death-drug having been given to him if this would have led to a greater total happiness?

Wouldn't such a person be a consistent upholder of the view that abortion is normally permissible?

My answer is that utilitarianism leads to so many strange moral implications that, even *if* the utilitarian could be consistent on this one case, still he would likely be inconsistent in his overall position. I previously claimed that utilitarianism would justify so many bizarre actions (including so many killings) that we would not accept this principle if we were consistent and realized its logical consequences. But if there are few (if any) consistent utilitarians then there would be few (if any) consistent utilitarian upholders of the view that abortion is normally permissible.

(2) Let us consider a *nonutilitarian* who approves of abortion but not infanticide or the blindness-drug. Why couldn't such a person consent to the idea of himself having been aborted under imagined or actual normal circumstances—and hence be consistent?

Such a person could be consistent, but only with bizarre desires about how he himself is to be treated. Let us suppose that someone combined these three judgments (as many are being brought up to do in our society today):

(a) It is wrong to blind an adult or child or infant or fetus.

(b) It is wrong to kill an adult or child or infant

(c) It is permissible to kill a fetus.

To be consistent the person would have to answer these questions as follows:

Do you consent to the idea of my *blinding* you now?—NO!
Do you consent to the idea of my having blinded you yesterday?—NO!

Do you consent to the idea of my *killing* you now?—NO!
Do you consent to the idea of my having *killed* you yesterday?—NO!

...when you were five years old?—NO!	...when you were five years old?—NO!
...when you were one day old?—NO!	...when you were one day old?—NO!
...before you were born?—NO!	...before you were born?—*YES!!!*

It is strange that the person *disapproves equally* of being *blinded* at the various times—and *disapproves equally* of being *killed* at the first four times—and yet *approves* of being *killed* at the last time. He opposes the blindings because, regardless of their timing, the effect would be the same—he would be blind. He opposes the killings at the first four times because, again, the effect would be the same—he would not be alive; but killing at the fifth time has the same effect—why should he not oppose this killing also? The *yes* here seems rather strange. Of course one who thinks his life not worth living could give a *yes* to the idea of his having been killed while a fetus—but then we would expect *yes* answers to the idea of his being killed at the other times as well (which would make him inconsistent if he held that it is wrong to kill an adult or child or infant). So while a nonutilitarian who combines the three judgments above *could* in principle have such desires and be consistent, still this is unlikely to happen very often—to be consistent the person would have to have very bizarre desires.[6]

(3) Are you saying that the desires that most people have are good while unusual (or "bizarre") desires are bad? How would you establish this?

I am not saying that common desires are good while unusual desires are bad—often the reverse is true; and sometimes when we notice a conflict between our moral beliefs and our desires we come to change our desires and not our moral beliefs. Rather I am appealing to desires that most people have because I am trying to develop a consistency argument to show that most

people who adopt the pro-abortion view are inconsistent. In effect I am challenging those who adopt such a view by saying, "Look at what you would have to desire in order to be consistent in your position—go and think about it and see whether you really are consistent!" I claim that most of the times the pro-abortionist will find that he is indeed inconsistent—he is supporting certain moral principles about the treatment of others that he would not wish to have been followed in their actions toward him.

(4) You question the consistency of one who holds that abortion is permissible but infanticide is wrong. But let us see whether you are consistent. If it would have been wrong for your parents to have aborted you, wouldn't it have been equally wrong for your parents not to have conceived you? The result would have been the same—there would be no YOU!

My answer here is complicated. My first reaction is to disapprove of the idea of my parents not having conceived me—to think it would have been wrong for them to have abstained or used contraceptives; but the universalizing requirement forces me to change my reactions (whereas it doesn't do this in the abortion case). If I hold "It is wrong to have an abortion in this (my) case," then I have to make the same judgment in all similar cases; but I can easily hold (consistently) that it is in general wrong to have an abortion. But if I hold "It is wrong to prevent conception (by, e.g., abstinence or contraceptives) in this (my) case," then I again have to make the same judgment in all similar cases; but I cannot hold (consistently) that it is in general wrong to prevent conception—since this would commit me to desiring a policy which would bring about a greatly overpopulated world of starving people at a very low level of human life. So, in order to be consistent, I change my first reaction and come to judge that it would have been morally permissible for my parents not to have conceived (me) on August 5, 1944—but instead perhaps to have conceived (someone else) on September 5, 1944—and I come, though with hesitation, to consent to the possibility of their having done this. To sum up: the universalizing requirement points to an important difference between *aborting* and *not conceiving*—I can "will as a universal law" a general prohibition against *aborting*, but not one against *nonconceiving*.

(5) Suppose that reason does force us into thinking that abortion is *normally* wrong. What does "normal" here mean? And aren't the "abnormal" or "unusual" cases the more important and difficult ones to deal with? So isn't your conclusion unimportant?

My claim that abortion is *normally* wrong means that it is wrong in at least the great majority of cases but perhaps not in every conceivable case (e.g., in the imagined case where Dr. Evil will destroy the world if we do not do an abortion). The question of what unusual conditions (if any) would justify abortion is indeed important and difficult. But I think that, in light of the very great number of "convenience abortions" going on today, the issue of the general moral status of abortion is at the present time far more important.

(6) Suppose that *if I am consistent* I cannot hold that abortion is normally permissible. What if I do not care about being consistent? Can you prove to me that I ought to care? Or can you prove to me that abortion is wrong without appealing to consistency?

You ask too much. Suppose I give you an argument proving that abortion is wrong (or that you ought to care about being consistent). If you do not already care about consistency, why should you not accept the premises of my argument and yet reject the conclusion? This would be inconsistent—but you don't care about this!

So you presumably wouldn't care about any argument I might give—in effect you are saying that you have a closed mind. If you don't care about consistency then I am wasting my time when I try to reason with you.

Notes

1. Tooley's original argument was in "Abortion and Infanticide," *Philosophy and Public Affairs* 2 (1972), pages 37–65. He added refinements to his view in *Philosophy and Public Affairs* 2 (1973), pages 419–432; in a postscript to a reprint of his article in *The Rights and Wrongs of Abortion*, edited by Marshall Cohen, Thomas Nagel, and Thomas Scanlon (Princeton, 1974), pages 80–84; and in "In Defense of Abortion and Infanticide," in *The Problem of Abortion* (second edition), edited by Joel Feinberg (Belmont, Calif., 1984), pages 120–134. (The weak link in the latest version of the argument seems to be this premise: 'An individual existing at one time cannot have desires at other times unless there is at least one time at which it possesses the concept of a continuing self or mental substance'; this entails the incredible 'Your pet kitten cannot yesterday have had a desire to eat unless at some time it possesses the concept of a continuing self or mental substance.') Peter Singer's defense of abortion and infanticide rests partially on Tooley's earlier argument but mainly on his preference utilitarianism; see chapter 4 and 6 of his *Practical Ethics* (Cambridge, 1979).

2. Clause (f) was phrased to skirt the issue of Tooley's "superkittens" who become rational if given a certain drug; my intuitions on the superkitten (and Frankenstein) cases are not very clear. Clause (f) may require further refinement.

3. "A Defense of Abortion," in *Philosophy and Public Affairs* 1 (1971), pages 47–66.

4. *The Right and the Good* (Oxford, 1930), page 19.

5. In arguing the abortion issue, I use some ideas from the theory of R. M. Hare, as developed in his *Freedom and Reason* (Oxford, 1963). Hare once wrote an article on "Abortion and the Golden Rule" (*Philosophy and Public Affairs* 4 (1975), pages 201–222); but his approach differs from mine. Hare rests his case on 'We should do to others what we are glad was done to us' and on the fact that we are glad that we were conceived, not aborted, and not killed as infants; hence we too ought to conceive, not abort, and not kill infants (but contraception, abortion, and

infanticide turn out to have only a weak *prima facie* wrongness which is easy to override by other considerations). Hare's formulation of the golden rule here is defective; if I am *glad* my parents gave me hundreds of gifts each Christmas, then perhaps to be consistent I must hold that it would be good to do this same thing in similar circumstances—but I need not hold that one *should* do this (that it is a *duty*). Also my conclusions differ from Hare's—I view abortion and infanticide (but not failing-to-conceive) as seriously wrong; I think my conclusions are what Hare's theory should lead to.

6. On the Tooley/Singer view the cut-off point for killing is not birth but rather when the child comes to desire its continued existence as a continuing subject of experiences. (It is unclear at what age this happens.) My response to this view would be much like the above, except that the killing side of the chart would now have one more *yes*.

Study Questions

1. Is Gensler fair to the positions he criticizes, the utilitarians, Michael Tooley, and Judith Jarvis Thomson? Can you think of ways to strengthen their positions? How would Mary Anne Warren respond to the Golden Rule argument?
2. Do you see any weaknesses in the Golden Rule argument? Can you think of any counterexamples to it? Consider this one. A convicted criminal serving time in prison says to the warden, "Do you believe in the Golden Rule, Sir?" The warden replies, "Yes, I try to live my life by it." "Then," responds the prisoner, "if you were in my place, wouldn't you want me to set you free? So you should set me free."

   Or try this application of Gensler's principle. I say to myself, "Do I, rock'n'roll lover that I am, now consent to listen to rock music played at 140 decibels?" If I say yes, does that mean I am permitted to play it that loud whether or not my roommate and neighbors can stand it?

   How would Gensler respond to these counterexamples? Do they affect Gensler's argument?

CHAPTER 35

Why Abortion Is Immoral

DON MARQUIS

Don Marquis is professor of philosophy at the University of Kansas. In this essay he argues that both anti-abortionists and pro-choicers arrive at a standoff when they resort to arguments about whether the fetus is a person or a "human life." What is needed is a deeper understanding of what makes killing itself wrong. Marquis argues that what makes killing someone wrong is the fact that he or she has a future good (or "a future like ours"). He considers objections to his position, especially the objection that his arguments would entail that contraception is wrong, and argues that none of them defeats his proposal.

Why Abortion Is Immoral

THE VIEW THAT ABORTION IS, with rare exceptions, seriously immoral has received little support in the recent philosophical literature. No doubt most philosophers affiliated with secular institutions of higher education believe that the anti-abortion position is either a symptom of irrational religious dogma or a conclusion generated by seriously confused philosophical argument. The purpose of this essay is to undermine this general belief. This essay sets out an argument that purports to show, as well as any argument in ethics can show, that abortion is, except possibly in rare cases, seriously immoral, that it is in the same moral category as killing an innocent adult human being.

The argument is based on a major assumption. Many of the most insightful and careful writers on the ethics of abortion—such as Joel Feinberg, Michael Tooley, Mary Anne Warren, H. Tristam Engelhardt, Jr., L. W. Sumner, John T. Noonan, Jr., and Philip Devine—believe that whether or not abortion is morally permissible stands or falls on whether or not a fetus is the sort of being whose life it is seriously wrong to end. In this essay, I will assume, but not argue, that they are correct.

Also, this essay will neglect issues of great importance to a complete ethics of abortion. Some anti-abortionists will allow that certain abortions, such as abortion before implantation or abortion when the life of a woman is threatened by pregnancy or abortion after rape, may be morally permissible. This essay will not explore the casuistry of these hard cases. My purpose is to develop a general argument for the claim that the overwhelming majority of deliberate abortions are seriously immoral.

I

A sketch of standard anti-abortion and pro-choice arguments exhibits how those arguments possess certain symmetries that explain why partisans of those positions are so convinced of the correctness of their own positions, why they are not successful in convincing their opponents,

Reprinted from The Journal of Philosophy *86 (April 1989), by permission.*

and why, to others, this issue seems to be unresolvable. An analysis of the nature of this standoff suggests a strategy for surmounting it.

Consider the way a typical anti-abortionist argues. She will argue or assert that life is present from the moment of conception or that fetuses look like babies or that fetuses possess a characteristic such as a genetic code that is both necessary and sufficient for being human. Anti-abortionists seem to believe that (1) the truth of all these claims is quite obvious, and (2) establishing any of these claims is sufficient to show that abortion is morally akin to murder.

A standard pro-choice strategy exhibits similarities. The pro-choicer will argue or assert that fetuses are not persons or that fetuses are not rational agents or that fetuses are not social beings. Pro-choicers seem to believe that (1) the truth of any of these claims is quite obvious, and (2) establishing any of these claims is sufficient to show that an abortion is not a wrongful killing.

In fact, both the pro-choice and the anti-abortion claims do seem to be true, although the "it looks like a baby" claim is more difficult to establish the earlier the pregnancy is. We seem to have a standoff. How can it be resolved?

As everyone who has taken a bit of logic knows, if any of these arguments concerning abortion is a good argument, that argument requires not only some claim characterizing fetuses, but also some general moral principle that ties a characteristic of fetuses to having or not having the right to life or to some other moral characteristic that will generate the obligation or the lack of obligation not to end the life of a fetus. Accordingly, the arguments of the anti-abortionist and the pro-choicer need a bit of filling in to be regarded as adequate.

Note what each partisan will say. The anti-abortionist will claim that her position is supported by such generally accepted moral principles as "It is always prima facie seriously wrong to take a human life" or "It is always prima facie seriously wrong to end the life of a baby." Since these are generally accepted moral principles,

her position is certainly not obviously wrong. The pro-choicer will claim that her position is supported by such plausible moral principles as "Being a person is what gives an individual intrinsic moral worth" or "It is only seriously prima facie wrong to take the life of a member of the human community." Since these are generally accepted moral principles, the pro-choice position is certainly not obviously wrong. Unfortunately, we have again arrived at a standoff.

Now, how might one deal with this standoff? The standard approach is to try to show how the moral principles of one's opponent lose their plausibility under analysis. It is easy to see how this is possible. On the one hand, the anti-abortionist will defend a moral principle concerning the wrongness of killing that tends to be broad in scope such that even fetuses at an early stage of pregnancy will fall under it. The problem with broad principles is that they often embrace too much. In this particular instance, the principle "It is always prima facie wrong to take a human life" seems to entail that it is wrong to end the existence of a living human cancer-cell culture, on the grounds that the culture is both living and human. Therefore, it seems that the anti-abortionist's favored principle is too broad.

On the other hand, the pro-choicer wants to find a moral principle concerning the wrongness of killing that tends to be narrow in scope such that fetuses will *not* fall under it. The problem with narrow principles is that they often do not embrace enough. Hence, the needed principles such as "it is prima facie seriously wrong to kill only persons" or "It is prima facie wrong to kill only rational agents" do not explain why it is wrong to kill infants or young children or the severely retarded or even perhaps the severely mentally ill. Therefore, we seem again to have a standoff. The anti-abortionist charges, not unreasonably, that pro-choice principles concerning killing are too narrow to be acceptable; the pro-choicer charges, not unreasonably, that anti-abortionist principles concerning killing are too broad to be acceptable.

Attempts by both sides to patch up the difficulties in their positions run into further difficulties. The anti-abortionist will try to remove the problem in her position by reformulating her principle concerning killing in terms of human beings. Now we end up with "It is always prima facie seriously wrong to end the life of a human being." This principle has the advantage of avoiding the problem of the human cancer-cell culture counterexample. But this advantage is purchased at a high price. For although it is clear that a fetus is both human and alive, it is not at all clear that a fetus is a human *being*. There is at least something to be said for the view that something becomes a human being only after a process of development, and that therefore first trimester fetuses and perhaps all fetuses are not yet human beings. Hence, the anti-abortionist, by this move, has merely exchanged one problem for another.

The pro-choicer fares no better. She may attempt to find reasons why killing infants, young children, and the severely retarded is wrong that are independent of her major principle that is supposed to explain the wrongness of taking human life, but that will not also make abortion immoral. This is no easy task. Appeals to social utility will seem satisfactory only to those who resolve not to think of the enormous difficulties with a utilitarian account of the wrongness of killing and the significant social costs of preserving the lives of the unproductive. A pro-choice strategy that extends the definition of "person" to infants or even to young children seems just as arbitrary as an anti-abortion strategy that extends the definition of "human being" to fetuses. Again, we find symmetries in the two positions and we arrive at a standoff.

There are even further problems that reflect symmetries in the two positions. In addition to counterexample problems, or the arbitrary application problems that can be exchanged for them, the standard anti-abortionist principle "It is prima facie seriously wrong to kill a human being," or one of its variants, can be objected to on the grounds of ambiguity. If "human being" is taken to be a *biological* category, then the anti-abortionist is left with the problem of explaining why a merely biological category should make a moral difference. Why, it is asked, is it any more reasonable to base a moral conclusion on the number of chromosomes in one's cells than on the color of one's skin? If "human being," on the other hand, is taken to be a *moral* category, then the claim that a fetus is a human being cannot be taken to be a premise in the anti-abortion argument, for it is precisely what needs to be established. Hence, either the anti-abortionist's main category is a morally irrelevant, merely biological category, or it is of no use to the anti-abortionist in establishing (noncircularly, of course) that abortion is wrong.

Although this problem with the anti-abortionist position is often noticed, it is less often noticed that the pro-choice position suffers from an analogous problem. The principle "Only persons have the right to life" also suffers from an ambiguity. The term "person" is typically defined in terms of psychological characteristics, although there will certainly be disagreement concerning which characteristics are most important. Supposing that this matter can be settled, the pro-choicer is left with the problem of explaining why *psychological* characteristics should make a *moral* difference. If the pro-choicer should attempt to deal with this problem by claiming that an explanation is not necessary, that in fact we do treat such a cluster of psychological properties as having moral significance, the sharp-witted anti-abortionist should have a ready response. We do treat being both living and human as having moral significance. If it is legitimate for the pro-choicer to demand that the anti-abortionist provide an explanation of the connection between the biological character of being a human being and the wrongness of being killed (even though people accept this connection), then it is legitimate for the anti-abortionist to demand that the pro-choicer provide an explanation of the connection between psychological criteria for being a person and the wrongness of being killed (even though that connection is accepted).

Feinberg has attempted to meet this objection (he calls psychological personhood "commonsense personhood"):

> The characteristics that confer commonsense personhood are not arbitrary bases for rights and duties, such as race, sex, or species membership; rather they are traits that make sense out of rights and duties and without which those moral attributes would have no point or function. It is because people are conscious; have a sense of their personal identities; have plans, goals, and projects; experience emotions; are liable to pains, anxieties, and frustrations; can reason and bargain, and so on—it is because of these attributes that people have values and interests, desires, and expectations of their own, including a stake in their own futures, and a personal well-being of a sort we cannot ascribe to unconscious or nonrational beings. Because of their developed capacities they can assume duties and responsibilities and can have and make claims on one another. Only because of their sense of self, their life plans, their value hierarchies, and their stakes in their own futures can they be ascribed fundamental rights. There is nothing arbitrary about these linkages. . . .

The plausible aspects of this attempt should not be taken to obscure its implausible features. There is a great deal to be said for the view that being a psychological person under some description is a necessary condition for having duties. One cannot have a duty unless one is capable of behaving morally, and a being's capability of behaving morally will require having a certain psychology. It is far from obvious, however, that having rights entails consciousness or rationality, as Feinberg suggests. We speak of the rights of the severely retarded or the severely mentally ill, yet some of these persons are not rational. We speak of the rights of the temporarily unconscious. The New Jersey Supreme

Court based their decision in the Quinlan case on Karen Ann Quinlan's right to privacy, and she was known to be permanently unconscious at that time. Hence, Feinberg's claim that having rights entails being conscious is, on its face, obviously false.

Of course, it might not make sense to attribute rights to a being that would never in its natural history have certain psychological traits. This modest connection between psychological personhood and moral personhood will create a place for Karen Ann Quinlan and the temporarily unconscious. But then it makes a place for fetuses also. Hence, it does not serve Feinberg's pro-choice purposes. Accordingly, it seems that the pro-choicer will have as much difficulty bridging the gap between psychological personhood and personhood in the moral sense as the anti-abortionist has bridging the gap between being a biological human being and being a human being in the moral sense.

Furthermore, the pro-choicer cannot any more escape her problem by making person a purely moral category than the anti-abortionist could escape by the analogous move. For if person is a moral category, then the pro-choicer is left without the resources for establishing (non-circularly, of course) the claim that a fetus is not a person, which is an essential premise in her argument. Again, we have both a symmetry and a standoff between pro-choice and anti-abortion views.

Passions in the abortion debate run high. There are both plausibilities and difficulties with the standard positions. Accordingly, it is hardly surprising that partisans of either side embrace with fervor the moral generalizations that support the conclusions they preanalytically favor and reject with disdain the moral generalizations of their opponents as being subject to inescapable difficulties. It is easy to believe that the counterexamples to one's own moral principles are merely temporary difficulties that will dissolve in the wake of further philosophical research and that the counterexamples to the principles of one's opponents are as straight-forward as the contradiction between *A* and *O* propositions in traditional logic. This might suggest to an impartial observer (if there are any) that the abortion issue is unresolvable.

There is a way out of this apparent dialectical quandary. The moral generalizations of both sides are not quite correct. The generalizations hold for the most part, for the usual cases. This suggests that they are all *accidental* generalizations, that the moral claims made by those on both sides of the dispute do not touch on the *essence* of the matter.

This use of the distinction between essence and accident is not meant to invoke obscure metaphysical categories. Rather, it is intended to reflect the rather atheoretical nature of the abortion discussion. If the generalization a partisan in the abortion dispute adopts was derived from the reason why ending the life of a human being is wrong, then there could not be exceptions to that generalization unless some special case obtains in which there are even more powerful countervailing reasons. Such generalizations would not be merely accidental generalizations; they would point to, or be based on, the essence of the wrongness of killing—what it is that makes killing wrong. All this suggests that a necessary condition of resolving the abortion controversy is a more theoretical account of the wrongness of killing. After all, if we merely believe, but do not understand, why killing adult human beings such as ourselves is wrong, how could we conceivably show that abortion is either immoral or permissible?

II

To develop such an account, we can start from the following unproblematic assumption concerning our own case: It is wrong to kill us. Why is it wrong? Some answers can be easily eliminated. It might be said that what makes killing us wrong is that a killing brutalizes the one who kills. But the brutalization consists of being inured to the performance of an act that is hideously immoral; hence, the brutalization does not explain the immorality. It might be said that what makes killing us wrong is the great loss others would experience because of our absence. Although such hubris is understandable, such an explanation does not account for the wrongness of killing hermits, or those whose lives are relatively independent and whose friends find it easy to make new friends.

A more obvious answer is better. What primarily makes killing wrong is neither its effect on the murderer nor its effect on the victim's friends and relatives, but its effect on the victim. The loss of one's life is one of the greatest losses one can suffer. The loss of one's life deprives one of all the experiences, activities, projects, and enjoyments that would otherwise have constituted one's future. Therefore, killing someone is wrong, primarily because the killing inflicts (one of) the greatest possible losses on the victim. To describe this as the loss of life can be misleading, however. The change in my biological state does not by itself make killing me wrong. The effect of the loss of my biological life is the loss to me of all those activities, projects, experiences, and enjoyments that would otherwise have constituted my future personal life. These activities, projects, experiences, and enjoyments are either valuable for their own sakes or are means to something else that is valuable for its own sake. Some parts of my future are not valued by me now, but will come to be valued by me as I grow older and as my values and capacities change. When I am killed, I am deprived both of what I now value that would have been part of my future personal life, and what I would come to value. Therefore, when I die, I am deprived of all the value of my future. Inflicting this loss on me is ultimately what makes killing me wrong. This being the case, it would seem that what makes killing *any* adult human being prima facie seriously wrong is the loss of his or her future.

How should this rudimentary theory of the wrongness of killing be evaluated? It cannot be faulted for deriving an "ought" from an "is," for it does not. The analysis assumes that killing me (or you, reader) is prima facie seriously wrong. The point of the analysis is to establish which natural property ultimately explains the wrongness of the killing, given that it is wrong. A natural property will ultimately explain the wrongness of killing only if (1) the explanation fits our intuitions about the matter and (2) there is no other natural property that provides a better explanation of the wrongness of killing. This analysis rests on the intuition that what makes killing a particular human or animal wrong is what it does to that particular human or animal. What makes killing wrong is some natural effect or other of the killing. Some would deny this. For instance, a divine-command theorist in ethics would deny it. Surely this denial is, however, one of those features of divine-command theory that renders it so implausible.

The claim that what makes killing wrong is the loss of the victim's future is directly supported by two considerations. In the first place, this theory explains why we regard killing as one of the worst of crimes. Killing is especially wrong because it deprives the victim of more than perhaps any other crime. In the second place, people with AIDS or cancer who know they are dying believe, of course, that dying is a very bad thing for them. They believe that the loss of a future to them that they would otherwise have experienced is what makes their premature death a very bad thing for them. A better theory of the wrongness of killing would require a different natural property associated with killing that better fits with the attitudes of the dying. What could it be?

The view that what makes killing wrong is the loss to the victim of the value of the victim's future gains additional support when some of its implications are examined. In the first place, it is incompatible with the view that it is wrong to kill only beings who are biologically human. It is

possible that there exists a different species from another planet whose members have a future like ours. Since having a future like that is what makes killing someone wrong, this theory entails that it would be wrong to kill members of such a species. Hence, this theory is opposed to the claim that only life that is biologically human has great moral worth, a claim that many anti-abortionists have seemed to adopt. This opposition, which this theory has in common with personhood theories, seems to be a merit of the theory.

In the second place, the claim that the loss of one's future is the wrong-making feature of one's being killed entails the possibility that the futures of some actual nonhuman mammals on our own planet are sufficiently like ours that it is seriously wrong to kill them also. Whether some animals do have the same right to life as human beings depends on adding to the account of the wrongness of killing some additional account of just what it is about my future or the futures of other adult human beings that makes it wrong to kill us. No such additional account will be offered in this essay. Undoubtedly, the provision of such an account would be a very difficult matter. Undoubtedly, any such account would be quite controversial. Hence, it surely should not reflect badly on this sketch of an elementary theory of the wrongness of killing that it is indeterminate with respect to some very difficult issues regarding animal rights.

In the third place, the claim that the loss of one's future is the wrong-making feature of one's being killed does not entail, as sanctity of human life theories do, that active euthanasia is wrong. Persons who are severely and incurably ill, who face a future of pain and despair, and who wish to die will not have suffered a loss if they are killed. It is, strictly speaking, the value of a human's future that makes killing wrong in this theory. This being so, killing does not necessarily wrong some persons who are sick and dying. Of course, there may be other reasons for a prohibition of active euthanasia, but that is another matter. Sanctity-of-human-life theories seem to hold that active euthanasia is seriously wrong even in an individual case where there seems to be good reason for it independently of public policy considerations. This consequence is most implausible, and it is a plus for the claim that the loss of a future of value is what makes killing wrong that it does not share this consequence.

In the fourth place, the account of the wrongness of killing defended in this essay does straightforwardly entail that it is prima facie seriously wrong to kill children and infants, for we do presume that they have futures of value. Since we do believe that it is wrong to kill defenseless little babies, it is important that a theory of the wrongness of killing easily account for this. Personhood theories of the wrongness of killing, on the other hand, cannot straightforwardly account for the wrongness of killing infants and young children. Hence, such theories must add special ad hoc accounts of the wrongness of killing the young. The plausibility of such ad hoc theories seems to be a function of how desperately one wants such theories to work. The claim that the primary wrong-making feature of a killing is the loss to the victim of the value of its future accounts for the wrongness of killing young children and infants directly; it makes the wrongness of such acts as obvious as we actually think it is. This is a further merit of this theory. Accordingly, it seems that this value of a future-like-ours theory of the wrongness of killing shares strengths of both sanctity-of-life and personhood accounts while avoiding weaknesses of both. In addition, it meshes with a central intuition concerning what makes killing wrong.

The claim that the primary wrong-making feature of a killing is the loss to the victim of the value of its future has obvious consequences for the ethics of abortion. The future of a standard fetus includes a set of experiences, projects, activities, and such that are identical with the futures of adult human beings and are identical with the futures of young children. Since the reason that is sufficient to explain why it is wrong to kill human beings after the time of birth is a reason that also applies to fetuses, it follows that abortion is prima facie seriously morally wrong.

This argument does not rely on the invalid inference that, since it is wrong to kill persons, it is wrong to kill potential persons also. The category that is morally central to this analysis is the category of having a valuable future like ours; it is not the category of personhood. The argument to the conclusion that abortion is prima facie seriously morally wrong proceeded independently of the notion of person or potential person or any equivalent. Someone may wish to start with this analysis in terms of the value of a human future, conclude that abortion is, except perhaps in rare circumstances, seriously morally wrong, infer that fetuses have the right to life, and then call fetuses "persons" as a result of their having the right to life. Clearly, in this case, the category of person is being used to state the *conclusion* of the analysis rather than to generate the *argument* of the analysis.

The structure of this anti-abortion argument can be both illuminated and defended by comparing it to what appears to be the best argument for the wrongness of the wanton infliction of pain on animals. This latter argument is based on the assumption that it is prima facie wrong to inflict pain on me (or you, reader). What is the natural property associated with the infliction of pain that makes such infliction wrong? The obvious answer seems to be that the infliction of pain causes suffering and that suffering is a misfortune. The suffering caused by the infliction of pain is what makes the wanton infliction of pain on me wrong. The wanton infliction of pain on other adult humans causes suffering. The wanton infliction of pain on animals causes suffering. Since causing suffering is what makes the wanton infliction of pain wrong and since the wanton infliction of pain on animals causes suffering, it follows that the wanton infliction of pain on animals is wrong,

This argument for the wrongness of the wanton infliction of pain on animals shares a number of structural features with the argument for the serious prima facie wrongness of abortion. Both arguments start with an obvious assumption concerning what it is wrong to do to me (or you, reader). Both then look for the characteristic or the consequence of the wrong action that makes the action wrong. Both recognize that the wrong-making feature of these immoral actions is a property of actions sometimes directed at individuals other than postnatal human beings. If the structure of the argument for the wrongness of the wanton infliction of pain on animals is sound, then the structure of the argument for the prima facie serious wrongness of abortion is also sound, for the structure of the two arguments is the same. The structure common to both is the key to the explanation of how the wrongness of abortion can be demonstrated without recourse to the category of person. In neither argument is that category crucial.

This defense of an argument for the wrongness of abortion in terms of a structurally similar argument for the wrongness of the wanton infliction of pain on animals succeeds only if the account regarding animals is the correct account. Is it? In the first place, it seems plausible. In the second place, its major competition is Kant's account. Kant believed that we do not have direct duties to animals at all because they are not persons. Hence, Kant had to explain and justify the wrongness of inflicting pain on animals on the grounds that "he who is hard in his dealings with animals becomes hard also in his dealing with men." The problem with Kant's account is that there seems to be no reason for accepting this latter claim unless Kant's account is rejected. If the alternative to Kant's account is accepted, then it is easy to understand why someone who is indifferent to inflicting pain on animals is also indifferent to inflicting pain on humans, for one is indifferent to what makes inflicting pain wrong in both cases. But, if Kant's account is accepted, there is no intelligible reason why one who is hard in his dealings with animals (or crabgrass or stones) should also be hard in his dealings with men. After all, men are persons; animals are no more persons than are crabgrass or stones. Persons are Kant's crucial moral category. Why, in short, should a Kantian accept the basic claim in Kant's argument?

Hence, Kant's argument for the wrongness of inflicting pain on animals rests on a claim that, in a world of Kantian moral agents, is demonstrably false. Therefore, the alternative analysis, being more plausible anyway, should be accepted. Since this alternative analysis has the same structure as the anti-abortion argument being defended here, we have further support for the argument for the immorality of abortion being defended in this essay.

Of course, this value of a future-like-ours argument, if sound, shows only that abortion is prima facie wrong, not that it is wrong in any and all circumstances. Since the loss of the future to a standard fetus, if killed, is, however, at least as great a loss as the loss of the future to a standard adult human being who is killed, abortion, like ordinary killing, could be justified only by the most compelling reasons. The loss of one's life is almost the greatest misfortune that can happen to one. Presumably abortion could be justified in some circumstances, only if the loss consequent on failing to abort would be at least as great. Accordingly, morally permissible abortions will be rare indeed unless, perhaps, they occur so early in pregnancy that a fetus is not yet definitely an individual. Hence, this argument should be taken as showing that abortion is presumptively very seriously wrong, where the presumption is very strong—as strong as the presumption that killing another adult human being is wrong.

III

How complete an account of the wrongness of killing does the value of a future-like-ours account have to be in order that the wrongness of abortion is a consequence? This account does not have to be an account of the necessary conditions for the wrongness of killing. Some persons in nursing homes may lack valuable human futures, yet it may be wrong to kill them for other reasons. Furthermore, this account does not obviously have to be the sole reason killing is wrong where the victim did have a valuable future. This analysis claims only that, for any killing where the victim did have a valuable future like ours, having that future by itself is sufficient to create the strong presumption that the killing is seriously wrong.

One way to overturn the value of a future-like-ours argument would be to find some account of the wrongness of killing that is at least as intelligible and that has different implications for the ethics of abortion. Two rival accounts possess at least some degree of plausibility. One account is based on the obvious fact that people value the experience of living and wish for that valuable experience to continue. Therefore, it might be said, what makes killing wrong is the discontinuation of that experience for the victim. Let us call this the *discontinuation account.* Another account is based on the obvious fact that people strongly desire to continue to live. This suggests that what makes killing us so wrong is that it interferes with the fulfillment of a strong and fundamental desire, the fulfillment of which is necessary for the fulfillment of any other desires we might have. Let us call this the *desire account.*

Consider first the desire account as a rival account of the ethics of killing that would provide the basis for rejecting the anti-abortion position. Such an account will have to be stronger than the value of a future-like-ours account of the wrongness of abortion if it is to do the job expected of it. To entail the wrongness of abortion, the value of a future-like-ours account has only to provide a sufficient, but not a necessary, condition for the wrongness of killing. The desire account, on the other hand, must provide us also with a necessary condition for the wrongness of killing to generate a pro-choice conclu-

sion on abortion. The reason for this is that presumably the argument from the desire account moves from the claim that what makes killing wrong is interference with a very strong desire to live to the claim that abortion is not wrong because the fetus lacks a strong desire to live. Obviously, this inference fails if someone's having the desire to live is not a necessary condition of its being wrong to kill that individual.

One problem with the desire account is that we do regard it as seriously wrong to kill persons who have little desire to live or who have no desire to live or, indeed, have a desire not to live. We believe it is seriously wrong to kill the unconscious, the sleeping, those who are tired of life, and those who are suicidal. The value-of-a-human-future account renders standard morality intelligible in these cases; these cases appear to be incompatible with the desire account.

The desire account is subject to a deeper difficulty. We desire life, because we value the goods of this life. The goodness of life is not secondary to our desire for it. If this were not so, the pain of one's own premature death could be done away with merely by an appropriate alteration in the configuration of one's desires. This is absurd. Hence, it would seem that it is the loss of the goods of one's future, not the interference with the fulfillment of a strong desire to live, that accounts ultimately for the wrongness of killing.

It is worth noting that, if the desire account is modified so that it does not provide a necessary, but only a sufficient, condition for the wrongness of killing, the desire account is compatible with the value of a future-like-ours account. The combined accounts will yield an anti-abortion ethic. This suggests that one can retain what is intuitively plausible about the desire account without a challenge to the basic argument of this paper.

It is also worth noting that, if future desires have moral force in a modified desire account of the wrongness of killing, one can find support for an anti-abortion ethic even in the absence of a value of a future-like-ours account. If one decides that a morally relevant property, the possession of which is sufficient to make it wrong to kill some individual, is the desire at some future time to live—one might decide to justify one's refusal to kill suicidal teenagers on these grounds, for example—then, since typical fetuses will have the desire in the future to live, it is wrong to kill typical fetuses. Accordingly, it does not seem that a desire account of the wrongness of killing can provide a justification of a pro-choice ethic of abortion that is nearly as adequate as the value of a human future justification of an anti-abortion ethic.

The discontinuation account looks more promising as an account of the wrongness of killing. It seems just as intelligible as the value of a future-like-ours account, but it does not justify an anti-abortion position. Obviously, if it is the continuation of one's activities, experiences, and projects, the loss of which makes killing wrong, then it is not wrong to kill fetuses for that reason, for fetuses do not have experiences, activities, and projects to be continued or discontinued. Accordingly, the discontinuation account does not have the anti-abortion consequences that the value of a future-like-ours account has. Yet, it seems as intelligible as the value of a future-like-ours account, for when we think of what would be wrong, with our being killed, it does seem as if it is the discontinuation of what makes our lives worthwhile that makes killing us wrong.

Is the discontinuation account just as good an account as the value of a future-like-ours account? The discontinuation account will not be adequate at all if it does not refer to the *value* of the experience that may be discontinued. One does not want the discontinuation account to make it wrong to kill a patient who begs for death and who is in severe pain that cannot be relieved short of killing. (I leave open the question of whether it is wrong for other reasons.) Accordingly, the discontinuation account must be more than a bare discontinuation account. It must make some reference to the positive value of the patient's experiences. But, by the same

token, the value of a future-like-ours account cannot be a bare future account either. Just having a future surely does not itself rule out killing this patient. This account must make some reference to the value of the patient's future experiences and projects also. Hence, both accounts involve the value of experiences, projects, and activities. So far we still have symmetry between the accounts.

The symmetry fades, however, when we focus on the time period of the value of the experiences, and so forth that has moral consequences. Although both accounts leave open the possibility that the patient in our example may be killed, this possibility is left open only by virtue of the utterly bleak future for the patient. It makes no difference whether the patient's immediate past contains intolerable pain, or consists of being in a coma (which we can imagine is a situation of indifference), or consists of a life of value. If the patient's future is a future of value, we want our account to make it wrong to kill the patient. If the patient's future is intolerable, whatever his or her immediate past, we want our account to allow killing the patient. Obviously, then, it is the value of that patient's future that is doing the work in rendering the morality of killing the patient intelligible.

This being the case, it seems clear that whether one has immediate past experiences or not does not work in the explanation of what makes killing wrong. The addition the discontinuation account makes to the value of a human future account is otiose. Its addition to the value-of-a-future account plays no role at all in rendering intelligible the wrongness of killing. Therefore, it can be discarded with the discontinuation account of which it is a part.

IV

The analysis of the previous section suggests that alternative general accounts of the wrongness of killing are either inadequate or unsuccessful in getting around the anti-abortion consequences of the value of a future-like-ours argument. A different strategy for avoiding these anti-abortion consequences involves limiting the scope of the value of a future argument. More precisely, the strategy involves arguing that fetuses lack a property that is essential for the value-of-a-future argument (or for any anti-abortion argument) to apply to them.

One move of this sort is based on the claim that a necessary condition of one's future being valuable is that one values it. Value implies a valuer. Given this, one might argue that, since fetuses cannot value their futures, their futures are not valuable to them. Hence, it does not seriously wrong them deliberately to end their lives.

This move fails, however, because of some ambiguities. Let us assume that something cannot be of value unless it is valued by someone, This does not entail that my life is of no value unless it is valued by me. I may think, in a period of despair, that my future is of no worth whatsoever, but I may be wrong because others rightly see value—even great value—in it. Furthermore, my future can be valuable to me even if I do not value it. This is the case when a young person attempts suicide but is rescued and goes on to significant human achievements. Such young people's futures are ultimately valuable to them, even though such futures do not seem to be valuable to them at the moment of attempted suicide. A fetus's future can be valuable to it in the same way. Accordingly, this attempt to limit the anti-abortion argument fails.

Another similar attempt to reject the anti-abortion position is based on Tooley's claim that an entity cannot possess the right to life unless it has the capacity to desire its continued existence. It follows that, since fetuses lack the conceptual capacity to desire to continue to live, they lack the right to life. Accordingly, Tooley concludes that abortion cannot be seriously prima facie wrong. . . .

What could be the evidence for Tooley's basic claim? Tooley once argued that individuals have

a prima facie right to what they desire and that the lack of the capacity to desire something undercuts the basis of one's right to it. . . . This argument plainly will not succeed in the context of the analysis of this essay, however, since the point here is to establish the fetus's right to life on other grounds. Tooley's argument assumes that the right to life cannot be established in general on some basis other than the desire for life. This position was considered and rejected in the preceding section of this paper.

One might attempt to defend Tooley's basic claim on the grounds that, because a fetus cannot apprehend continued life as a benefit, its continued life cannot be a benefit or cannot be something it has a right to or cannot be something that is in its interest. This might be defended in terms of the general proposition that, if an individual is literally incapable of caring about or taking an interest in some *X*, then one does not have a right to *X* or *X* is not a benefit or *X* is not something that is in one's interest.

Each member of this family of claims seems to be open to objections. As John C. Stevens has pointed out, one may have a right to be treated with a certain medical procedure (because of a health insurance policy one has purchased), even though one cannot conceive of the nature of the procedure. And, as Tooley himself has pointed out, persons who have been indoctrinated, or drugged, or rendered temporarily unconscious may be literally incapable of caring about or taking an interest in something that is in their interest or to which they have a right, or that benefits them. Hence, the Tooley claim that would restrict the scope of the value of a future-like-ours argument is undermined by counterexamples.

Finally, Paul Bassen has argued that, even though the prospects of an embryo might seem to be a basis for the wrongness of abortion, an embryo cannot be a victim and therefore cannot be wronged. An embryo cannot be a victim, he says, because it lacks sentience. His central argument for this seems to be that, even though plants and the permanently unconscious are alive, they clearly cannot be victims. What is the explanation of this? Bassen claims that their lives consist of mere metabolism and mere metabolism is not enough to ground victimizability. Mentation is required.

The problem with this attempt to establish the absence of victimizability is that both plants and the permanently unconscious clearly lack what Bassen calls "prospects" or what I have called "a future life like ours." Hence, it is surely open to argument whether the real reason we believe plants and the permanently unconscious cannot be victims is that killing them cannot deprive them of a future life like ours; the real reason is not their absence of present mentation.

Bassen recognizes that his view is subject to this difficulty, and he recognizes that the case of children seems to support this difficulty, for "much of what we do for children is based on prospects." He argues, however, that, in the case of children and in other such cases, "potentiality comes into play only where victimizability has been secured on other grounds". . . .

Bassen's defense of his view is patently question-begging, since what is adequate to secure victimizability is exactly what is at issue. His examples do not support his own view against the thesis of this essay. Of course, embryos can be victims: When their lives are deliberately terminated, they are deprived of their futures of value, their prospects. This makes them victims, for it directly wrongs them.

The seeming plausibility of Bassen's view stems from the fact that paradigmatic cases of imagining someone as a victim involve empathy, and empathy requires mentation of the victim. The victims of flood, famine, rape, or child abuse are all persons with whom we can empathize. That empathy seems to be part of seeing them as victims.

In spite of the strength of these examples, the attractive intuition that a situation in which there is victimization requires the possibility of empathy is subject to counterexamples. Consider a case that Bassen himself offers: "Posthu-mous obliteration of an author's work constitutes a misfortune for him only if he had wished his work to endure". . . . The conditions Bassen wishes to impose upon the possibility of being victimized here seem far too strong. Perhaps this author, due to his unrealistic standards of excellence and his low self-esteem, regarded his work as unworthy of survival, even though it possessed genuine literary merit. Destruction of such work would surely victimize its author. In such a case, empathy with the victim concerning the loss is clearly impossible.

Of course, Bassen does not make the possibility of empathy a necessary condition of victimizability; he requires only mentation. Hence, on Bassen's actual view, this author, as I have described him, can be a victim. The problem is that the basic intuition that renders Bassen's view plausible is missing in the author's case. In order to attempt to avoid counterexamples, Bassen has made his thesis too weak to be supported by the intuitions that suggested it.

Even so, the mentation requirement on victimizability is still subject to counterexamples. Suppose a severe accident renders me totally unconscious for a month, after which I recover. Surely killing me while I am unconscious victimizes me, even though I am incapable of mentation during that time. It follows that Bassen's thesis falls. Apparently, attempts to restrict the value of a future-like-ours argument so that fetuses do not fall within its scope do not succeed.

V

In this essay, I have argued that the correct ethic of the wrongness of killing can be extended to fetal life and used to show that there is a strong presumption that any abortion is morally impermissible. If the ethic of killing adopted here entails, however, that contraception is also seriously immoral, then there would appear to be a difficulty with the analysis of this essay.

But this analysis does not entail that contraception is wrong. Of course, contraception prevents the actualization of a possible future of value. Hence, it follows from the claim that futures of value should be maximized that contraception is prima facie immoral. This obligation to maximize does not exist, however; furthermore, nothing in the ethics of killing in this paper entails that it does. The ethics of killing in this essay would entail that contraception is wrong only if something were denied a human future of value by contraception. Nothing at all is denied such a future by contraception, however.

Candidates for a subject of harm by contraception fall into four categories: (1) some sperm or other, (2) some ovum or other, (3) a sperm and an ovum separately, and (4) a sperm and an ovum together. Assigning the harm to some sperm is utterly arbitrary, for no reason can be given for making a sperm the subject of harm rather than an ovum. Assigning the harm to some ovum is utterly arbitrary, for no reason can be given for making an ovum the subject of harm rather than a sperm. One might attempt to avoid these problems by insisting that contraception deprives both the sperm and the ovum separately of a valuable future like ours. On this alternative, too many futures are lost. Contraception was supposed to be wrong because it deprived us of one future of value, not two. One might attempt to avoid this problem by holding that contraception deprives the combination of sperm and ovum of a valuable future-like-ours. But here the definite article misleads. At the time of contraception, there are hundreds of millions of sperm, one (released) ovum and millions of possible combinations of all these. There is no actual combination at all. Is the subject of the loss to be a merely possible combination? Which one? This alternative does not yield an actual subject of harm either. Accordingly, the immorality of contraception is not entailed by the loss of a future-like-ours argument simply because there is no nonarbitrarily identifiable subject of the loss in the case of contraception.

VI

The purpose of this essay has been to set out an argument for the serious presumptive wrongness of abortion subject to the assumption that the moral permissibility of abortion stands or falls on the moral status of the fetus. Since a fetus possesses a property, the possession of which in adult human beings is sufficient to make killing an adult human being wrong, abortion is wrong. This way of dealing with the problem of abortion seems superior to other approaches to the ethics of abortion because it rests on an ethics of killing which is close to self-evident, because the crucial morally relevant property clearly applies to fetuses, and because the argument avoids the usual equivocations on "human life:' "human being," or "person." The argument rests neither on religious claims nor on Papal dogma. It is not subject to the objection of "speciesism." Its soundness is compatible with the moral permissibility of euthanasia and contraception. It deals with our intuitions concerning young children.

Finally, this analysis can be viewed as resolving a standard problem—indeed, *the* standard problem—concerning the ethics of abortion. Clearly, it is wrong to kill adult human beings. Clearly, it is not wrong to end the life of some arbitrarily chosen single human cell. Fetuses seem to be like arbitrarily chosen human cells in some respects and like adult humans in other respects. The problem of the ethics of abortion is the problem of determining the fetal property that settles this moral controversy. The thesis of this essay is that the problem of the ethics of abortion, so understood, is solvable.

Study Questions

1. Why does Marquis think that the debate between the anti-abortionists and the pro-choicers over abortion has come to a standoff? Do you agree?
2. Explain Marquis's notion of a future good. What sort of entities can have a future good? Does he exclude trees and cars from that classification? Does he exclude animals? Discuss his conditions.
3. Is Marquis against all abortions? If not, which kinds would he permit? Is he correct?
4. Why does Marquis believe that his thesis avoids condemning the use of contraceptive devices as immoral?

CHAPTER 36

Abortion and the Neo-Natal Right to Life

A Critique of Marquis's Futurist Argument

GERALD H. PASKE

Gerald H. Paske is professor of philosophy at Wichita State University. The abstract he wrote for his essay follows.

Abstract

IN HIS "WHY ABORTION IS IMMORAL," Don Marquis has presented a serious challenge to the pro-choice position. Marquis's argument is based on the following three claims: (1) Personhood is an inadequate foundation for the right to life. (2) The right to life is based on having a future-like-ours. (3) Normal fetuses have a future-like-ours and, hence, normal fetuses have a right to life.

I argue that (a) Marquis's own position presupposes the concept of personhood, (b) that having a future-like-ours is neither a sufficient nor a necessary condition for having a right to life, and (c) that given the concept of personhood, neonates, infants, and children have a right to life. This later point requires a discussion of a fetal right to care.

In an influential but misleadingly entitled paper, Don Marquis has presented a serious challenge to the pro-choice position.[1] Although the paper is entitled "Why Abortion Is Immoral," Marquis's argument actually allows for abortions of severely mentally defective fetuses. Marquis, thus, is on the conservative end of the pro-choice spectrum.

Marquis's challenge remains serious, however, because his argument, if sound, would show that from conception onward all abortions of normal fetuses are seriously immoral. Marquis's argument is based on the following three claims: (1) Personhood is an inadequate foundation for the right to life. (2) The right to life is based on having a future-like-ours. (3) Normal fetuses have a future-like-ours and, hence, normal fetuses have a right to life. Marquis also claims that the personhood concept provides an inadequate basis for the right to life of infants and children, and he takes this to constitute an additional serious challenge to the standard pro-choice position.[2]

I shall argue (a) that Marquis's own position presupposes the concept of personhood, (b) that having a future-like-ours is neither a sufficient nor a necessary condition for having a right to life, and (c) that given the concept of personhood, neonates, infants, and children have a right to life.[3]

Marquis summarizes his argument as follows:

> In order to develop (my) account, we can start from the following unproblematic assumption concerning our own case: It is wrong to kill *us*. . . . The loss of one's life is one of the greatest

This essay was commissioned for the first edition of The Abortion Controversy, *edited by Louis P. Pojman and Frank Beckwith (Boston: Jones & Bartlett, 1994), by permission.*

losses one call suffer. The loss of one's life deprives one of all the experiences, activities, projects, and enjoyments that would otherwise have constituted one's future. . . . To describe this as the loss of life can be misleading, however. The change in my biological state does not by itself make killing me wrong. The effect of the loss of my biological life is the loss to me of all those activities, projects, experiences, and enjoyments that would otherwise have constituted my future personal life. . . . Therefore, when I die I am deprived of all of the value of my future. Inflicting this loss on me is ultimately what makes killing me wrong. This being the case, it would seem that what makes killing *any* adult human being prima facie seriously wrong is the loss of his or her future.

Marquis applies this "deprivation argument" to the abortion issue as follows:

The claim that the primary wrong-making feature of a killing is the loss to the victim of the value of its future has obvious consequences for the ethics of abortion. The future of a standard fetus includes a set of experiences, projects, activities, and such that are identical with the futures of adult human beings and are identical with the futures of young children. Since the reason that is sufficient to explain why it is wrong to kill human beings after the time of birth is a reason that also applies to fetuses, it follows that abortion is prima facie seriously morally wrong.

While granting the appeal of Marquis's argument, I shall nevertheless attack it at its foundation: the claim that having a future-like-ours is a sufficient condition for a right to life.[4] Since Marquis's positive argument is entwined with his negative claims about personhood, I shall begin with the concept of personhood.

Marquis is correct when he offers the "unproblematic assumption" that "it is wrong to kill *us*." But though the assumption is unproblematic it requires explication. Indeed, if we are to avoid "human chauvinism" and "species bias,"

this unproblematic assumption must be explicated.[5] Why is it that a future-like-ours is the one that counts and not—say—the future of a pig or a cow?[6] The answer lies in the concept of personhood.

The concept of personhood is both complex and controversial. I will discuss it in some detail later, but first I shall appeal to intuitions. Given the popularity of the television show *Star Trek* and of the movie *E. T.*, most of us are comfortable with the notion of nonhuman rational beings and it is easy to ascribe a right to life to such beings. We do so because, no matter how much they differ physically, their mental lives are very similar to ours. Intuitively, then, personhood is that set of mental characteristics which hypothetical nonhuman rational beings share with humans, but which neither they nor humans share with pigs and cows. It is this personhood which makes a future-like-ours possible and it is, hence, personhood which underlies Marquis's right to life. This becomes quite clear when one examines Marquis's defense of his own position. He offers the following as points in support of his thesis:

In the first place, (my theory) is incompatible with the view that it is wrong to kill only human beings who are biologically human. . . . In the second place, the claim that the loss of one's future is the wrong-making feature of one's being killed entails the possibility that the futures of some actual nonhuman mammals on our own planet are sufficiently like ours that it is seriously wrong to kill them also. . . . In the third place, the claim that the loss of one's future is the wrong-making feature of one's being killed does not entail . . . that active euthanasia is wrong.

Since Marquis offers these points in support of his thesis, one assumes that these points are more basic than the thesis itself. But, in response to his first point, if we ask what differentiates those nonhumans who have a right to life from those nonhumans who lack such a right, the answer is clear. Those nonhumans who have a right to life are persons, as are we, and those nonhumans who lack a right to life also lack personhood. With regard to Marquis's second point, the nonhuman mammals on our own planet that have something like a future-like-ours are the higher apes, and they come closest to being persons. And finally, what could justify active euthanasia except that the human *person* is either gone (comatose) or overwhelmed by excruciating pain?

Despite the fact that the Marquis thesis presupposes personhood, Marquis explicitly rejects the personhood criterion when he says that those who accept the personhood criteria are "left with the problem of explaining why *psychological* characteristics should make a *moral* difference." Insofar as this is offered as an argument it commits the *ad ignorantiam* fallacy. One is tempted, therefore, to offer the *ad hominem* response that Marquis has exactly the same problem with regard to explaining why human futures are more important than other futures. But I will not base my case on fallacies. Rather, I will provide an explanation of why certain psychological characteristics make a moral difference.

It is a basic moral principle that harming sentient life requires justification.[7] It is also an empirical fact that different kinds of harm can be done to various forms of sentient life depending on the nature of their consciousness. For example, you can cause a snake physical pain, but you cannot cause it psychological pain by insulting it. Persons can grasp and use many concepts that cannot be understood by nonpersons. Such concepts can generate attitudes and expectations that can be frustrated. Since such frustrations constitute an emotional harm, persons can be harmed in ways that nonpersons cannot. Some of these harms are the most serious that can be done to humans. Thus, what is special about human or person consciousness is that persons are capable of experiencing *conceptually based emotions.*

Conceptually based emotions are feeling states that can be experienced only if one is capable of understanding a variety of quite abstract concepts. Some examples of conceptually based emotions are the feelings of moral guilt, regret, indignation, hope, and pride. We can feel moral guilt only if we have a concept of moral wrong. We can feel indignant only if we have a concept of justice and fairness. We can feel hope only if we can foresee a variety of possible futures.

The conceptually based emotions are the basis of the demand that human beings be treated differently from other animals. For example, the desire to be an autonomous individual is a desire that can be had only by persons, and thus it is only persons whose autonomy can be violated. Also, there is nothing wrong with taking a cat's kittens away from her because, after a brief period, the cat will not and cannot miss the kittens. This is because she has no significant sense of self, nor does she have any prolonged memory of her kittens. If she were able to look forward to raising her kittens, to anticipate eventual grandkittens, and to feel a lifelong despair over the loss of her kittens, then to take her kittens from her would be immoral. But then she would be a person, a cat-person to be sure, but a person nonetheless.

Persons, and only persons, can conceptualize a distant future in which they are a participant. Only persons can anticipate and deliberately shape their own future. Only persons can desire and possess the freedom to shape their own self, their own life, their own future. Only persons can have their long-term plans frustrated by their untimely death. One aspect of the seriousness of death for a person is the loss of an anticipated, intended, longed-for future. No nonperson can be harmed in this way. It is the loss of this sort of a future that constitutes a common—but not a universal—harm arising from death. Thus, the harm constituted by the loss of *our* future presupposes that we are persons. This, in brief, is the explanation of why psychological states have moral importance.

But, for a person, what is an even more serious loss than the loss of a possible future is the loss of the actual, existent person. It is this immediate loss of personhood which constitutes the basic harm in killing. It is this loss that makes the murder of persons even on their deathbeds a serious harm. One more minute of being a living person is of great value—even if that minute is an innocuous one—and taking that minute is a great harm. The loss of a future increases the harm of a killing, but the primary harm of a killing is the loss of the life of the person. This is a serious harm even when the person has no future.

It might be replied that even if one's future amounts to no more than one more minute, it is nevertheless the loss of that minute, and not the loss of personhood, that constitutes the harm. This reply is certainly plausible, but it gets its plausibility from confusing two distinct harms that result from murder: the loss of one's personhood and the loss of one's future. If, as the reply suggests, the loss of one's future is the only harm, then the badness of the murder under discussion would arise from the harm done by the loss of the last minute of life. But surely, the difference between a life of—say—89 years and a life of 89 years and one minute, given that the minute is an innocuous one, is not sufficient to account for the serious wrongness of a deathbed murder.

Were we to derive the wrongness of a murder solely from the loss of one's future, the degree of wrongness would vary inversely with life expectancy. Murdering the elderly would be less wrong than murdering the young. While such a consequence might be appealing to some, it goes against legal practice and, I believe, it goes against moral intuition. Thus, if all murders, *qua* murder, are equally bad, it is the loss of personhood that accounts for the intrinsic wrongness of murder, and it is the failure to recognize this that constitutes the basic error involved in Marquis's deprivation thesis. However, this error is both understandable and alluring.

Having a future-like-ours and being a person are conceptually independent but empirically related properties. All persons, insofar as they retain their personhood, have a future-like-ours. Thus, whenever a person is killed, there is the simultaneous destruction of a future-like-ours.[8] This empirical entwining of personhood and having a future-like-ours makes it difficult to ascertain whether it is the loss of personhood, the loss of a future-like-ours, or the loss of both that constitutes the definitive harm done by the killing of a person.

However, consider a situation where, because of limited resources, one must choose between saving the life of a 9-year-old and saving the life of an 89-year-old. The differences in their expected futures (as well as their pasts) is surely relevant with regard to who should be saved. Surely one ought to save the child. This indicates that the value of a future-like-ours can vary in degree, one parameter being the expected length of the specific future-like-ours. It is this that makes premature death sadder than death at the end of a normal life-span.

Contrast the difference between premature and "normal" death with the difference between the murders of a 9-year-old and an 89-year-old. It is *not* the case that one murder is less wrong than the other. Both are equally wrong *qua* murder. The murders are equally wrong even though the murder of the 9-year-old causes a greater loss of a future-like-ours than does the murder of an 89-year-old. The degree of loss, the degree of harm, is not relevant to the wrongness of the murder *per se*. Rather, it is the destruction of personhood that makes all murders, *qua* murder, equally wrong.[9]

Given that we can detach the harm of the loss of personhood from the harm of the loss of a future-like-ours, we can now consider the importance of the loss of a future-like-ours when the entity undergoing the loss has not attained personhood.

Imagine that a kitten is injected with a serum that will have no significant effect on the kitten for nine months but that will, after nine months, instantaneously cause the kitten to become a person and hence, to have both a present and a future-like-ours.[10] Suppose further that an antidote to the serum is available. Would it be morally permissible to give the antidote before the kitten becomes a person? More important, would there be any moral difference between giving the antidote before the kitten becomes a person and giving the antidote after the kitten becomes a person (assuming that the antidote will then return the kitten to a normal cat state)? Giving the antidote before the acquisition of personhood changes the biological state of the kitten, but giving the antidote after the acquisition of personhood destroys an existing person. Marquis, presumably, would have to conclude that the antidote should never be given. I, on the other hand, believe that the antidote could be given before the kitten becomes a person, but not after.

Perhaps this difference merely reduces to a difference in intuitions, but I think not. It is appropriate to ask what underlies the different intuitions. Marquis and I agree that—for normal adult humans—the loss of a future-like-ours is a tragic loss. But—for normal adult humans—such a loss is simultaneous with the loss of personhood. That is, it is the simultaneous loss of personhood that underlies the tragedy of the loss of a future.

Insofar as this is correct, and insofar as killing a dying patient against their conscious will is wrong, having a future-like-ours is not a necessary condition for having a right to life. Furthermore, insofar as giving our hypothetical kitten the antidote before it becomes a person is morally permissible, having a future-like-ours is not a sufficient condition for having a right to life. What is a sufficient condition for having a right to life is *being* a person. What is wrong with killing us is not the destruction of a future but the destruction of a person.

Marquis recognizes this possibility and he discusses it under the rubric of the "discontinu-ation account" of the wrongness of killing. This account, he says, seems just as intelligible as the value of a future-like-ours account, but, since it does not justify an anti-abortion position, Marquis feels compelled to argue against it. His argument is as follows:

> The discontinuation account will not be adequate at all, if it does not refer to the *value of* the experience that may be discontinued. One does not want the discontinuation account to make it wrong to kill a patient who begs for death and who is in severe pain that cannot be relieved short of killing. . . . If the patient's future is a future of value, we want our account to make it wrong to kill the patient. If the patient's future is intolerable, whatever his or her immediate past, we want our account to allow killing the patient. Obviously, then, it is the value of that patient's future that is doing the work in rendering the morality of killing the patient intelligible.
>
> This being the case, it seems clear that whether one has immediate past experiences or not does no work in the explanation of what makes killing wrong. The addition the discontinuation account makes to the value of a human future account is otiose. Its addition to the value-of-a-future account plays no role at all in rendering intelligible the wrongness of killing.

Contrary to Marquis, what the discontinuation account is asserting is that the immediate existence of a person has great value. It is significant that in his purported refutation of this account Marquis refers to both the past and future of a person, but says absolutely nothing about the value of the instantaneous present. Thus he says: "If the patient's future is intolerable, whatever his or her immediate past, we want our account to allow killing the patient." But this is surely a mistake. Even if one is faced with a future life of intolerable pain, one ought not be killed *now*. If possible, euthanasia should be postponed until one's life *is* intolerable. Ideally, euthanasia should not be performed merely because one's life will become intolerable in the future.

In summary, Marquis's deprivation thesis acquires some initial plausibility because a full explanation of all the harms involved in a killing usually must refer to the future, for the loss of a future is *usually* part of the harm. But even if one has no (significant) future, killing one is still wrong. It is the immediate death of a person, the immediate snuffing out of personhood, that constitutes the evil of killing. The loss of a valuable future, when it accompanies the loss of personhood, is a significant *additional* loss. But it is not the loss of the future that is crucial vis-à-vis the killing. What is crucial is the loss of personhood.

The personhood account of the wrongness of killing, explicated by the concept of the conceptually based emotions, can explain the wrongness of killing, including the killing of persons who have no significant future. It is therefore superior to the future-like-ours account. However, the personhood account is still vulnerable to Marquis's claim that it cannot adequately account for the right to life of neonates. This is so, he argues, because neonates are not persons and hence would have no right to life.

Marquis's argument is unsound. His argument rests on the false assumption that a neonatal right to life must arise from the same source that generates an adult right to life. But there are many types of right. Human, or more accurately *person* rights are those rights that each person has by virtue of being a person. Social rights are those rights that are fundamental to the well functioning of a morally acceptable society. The right to life (of persons) is a human or person right. The right to—say—property is a social right. Both types of rights can be important enough to justify sacrificing ones life in their defense.

All persons have a right to life as a result of being persons. But other entities might also have a right to life, a social right to life. Indeed, I shall argue that neonates should have a social right to life. This is not a right that springs *de novo* into existence. It is rather a right that grows out of a specific fetal right, the right to care (to be cared for).

The recognition that the right to care is an increasing, dynamic right makes possible a rational defense of the widespread intuition that late abortions require more justification than early abortions. In addition, the right to care accounts for and is compatible with the equally widespread intuition that some moral significance should be attributed to conception since it is at conception that each of us as a unique biological entity first came into being.

The right to care has four sources that can be divided into two groups: those *intrinsic* to the developing entity and those that relate the entity to others, the *relational* sources. The intrinsic sources are genetic humanness and potentiality of personhood. The relational sources are both the degree to which the fetus is cared about and whether or not a decision has been made to allow it to develop.

Genetic humanness is instantaneously present at conception, and the potentiality for personhood (for normal fetuses) is generated at conception also. This is what underlies the intuition that conception is a morally significant point. Nevertheless, conception is not sufficient to generate a right to life. Conception is the beginning of a biological entity that, after extensive development, may result in the beginnings of a person, but the beginning of personhood is better thought of as occurring when sentience begins and not with mere biological existence.

The concept of brain death is relevant to this point. Brain death clearly indicates that mere genetic humanness does not generate a right to life. Indeed, biologically alive genetic human beings are humanly dead if lacking the possibility of consciousness. Brain dead individuals are biologically living human organisms, but since they permanently lack consciousness they are not living *persons*. They are biological living organisms that, because they have been persons, are now dead people.

Of course the brain dead not only lack consciousness, they also lack the potential for consciousness and, hence, are crucially different from fetuses. It is the fact that most human fetuses are potential persons that generates a minimal right to care at conception. This right is generated as follows: First, we are human and, hence, have both a right and an obligation to treat human entities in a special way even if those entities are not persons. In a sense this is species bias, but if it is thought of on the analogy of a family—the human family—it is quite plausible. If the right to care is kept within legitimate bounds, the species bias that underlies it is quite reasonable. We may legitimately treat the members of our own family in special ways so long as our doing so does not violate the rights of other entities. Family members have claims on one another that others do not. So too with the human family. Exactly what claims our family members have on us, and what responsibilities we have toward them, is a subject for another paper. Nevertheless, if human beings exist whose conceptual abilities are no more than those of a cat, we should not treat them just as we treat cats. They are one of ours, and on that basis we may and ought to treat them as one of ours. We ought to care for them.

The role of *potentiality*, though significant, is minimal. It is significant enough so that the loss of the entity is at least unfortunate, but since a potential person is not a person, its loss is not equivalent to the loss of a person. The loss of an early fetus is less sad than the loss of a more developed fetus because more of the potential becomes actualized as time passes. But at no stage is the fetus a person, and hence its loss is never the equivalent of the loss of a person. The two intrinsic properties of fetuses, therefore, generate a minimal right to care. This right can be strengthened by the relational properties of the fetus.

This first relational property is that of being cared about. Reflection dispels any doubt that merely caring about something can give it value. If we think of a family heirloom we can recognize that the objective value of the heirloom can be quite small compared with the subjective value family members attach to it. This difference in value does not mean that the family

members do not know the heirloom's objective value. Its value to the family, however, grows out of the history of the object, a history that they as family members share. This subjective value transcends the mere objective value of the object.

A conceptus, like an heirloom, can acquire a great deal of relational value depending on the response to it by others, primarily its biological progenitors. If the biological progenitors want to have a child the relational value of the fetus can be enormous. Yet this relational value is contingent on the attitude of the biological progenitors. If the pregnancy is not wanted, then the conceptus gains no relational value from this source.

The second source of relational value is possible only in situations where abortions are legally permissible. In such cases, the continuation of a pregnancy is a matter of choice and the decision to continue the pregnancy increases the responsibility of the woman and thereby increases the right to care of the fetus. If a woman decides to continue her pregnancy even though she does not really want a child, that decision nevertheless increases her responsibility towards the fetus. If she decides to continue the pregnancy, the fetus will (most likely) become a person. Hence the woman's support for the continuation of the pregnancy increases the fetal right to care since the well-being of the person-to-be depends on the care given to the fetus. If you allow a process that will result in a person to continue, you acquire some responsibility toward that future person and, hence, for the fetus which will become that person. The woman's decision to continue the pregnancy gives the fetus an additional degree of the right to care. She cannot morally continue the pregnancy and neglect the fetus. If she decides to remain pregnant, she has an obligation to take care of herself for the good of the fetus, and the fetus has a right to such care.[11]

The right to care increases throughout the pregnancy because the woman's voluntary assumption of responsibility increases the longer she continues the pregnancy and the potentiality of the fetus becomes more actualized. Thus late term abortions are justifiable only to prevent the death of or serious harm to the woman. Since this final "threat" ends with birth, the neonate has a full (social) right to life.

In conclusion, personhood is the primary source of the right to life. Until a human passes through the fetal and neonatal stages and develops personhood its rights depend on the other four sources of rights. Those sources generate a range of rights beginning with a minimal and easily defeasible right to care during the early stages of the pregnancy, through an increasingly significant right to care, and culminating in a full social right to life for neonates.

Notes

1. Marquis, Don, "Why Abortion Is Immoral," *The Journal of Philosophy*, 86, 4 (April 1989), 183–202. This article is reprinted in the following: (1) *Midwest Medical Ethics*, 5, Summer 1989. (2) *Social Ethics*, Mappes and Zembaty, eds., 4th ed., 1992. (3) *Taking Sides: Clashing Views on Controversial Moral Issues*, Stephen Satris, ed., 3rd ed., 1992. (4) *Today's Moral Issues*, Daniel Bonevac, ed., 1st ed., 1992. (5) *Social and Personal Ethics*, William H. Shaw, ed., 1st ed., 1992. (6) *Personal Values: Moral Problems in Daily Life*, Eric H. Gampel, ed., 1992. (7) *Gender Basics*, Anne Minas, ed., 1993. (8) *Moral Controversies: Race, Gender and Class*, Steven Gold, ed., 1993. (9) *Arguing About Abortion*, Lewis M. Schwartz, ed., 1st ed., 1993.

2. There are several concepts of personhood but the relevant notion vis-à-vis the abortion debate is that persons are capable of highly abstract thought. It is generally agreed that some higher mammals may be capable of such thought but mammals such as cows and pigs are not. It is also generally assumed that human fetuses and neonates lack this capacity.

3. In the rest of the paper I shall use "fetus" to mean "normal fetus." The question of whether seriously defective fetuses and neonates have a right to life complicates matters but cannot be discussed here.

4. For other points of attack see McInerney, Peter K., "Does a Fetus Already Have a Future-Like-Ours" and Norcross, Alastair, "Killing, Abortion, and Contraception: A Reply to Marquis," both in the *Journal of Philosophy*, 87, 5 (May 1990). I believe that Mar-

quis has met these attacks in his unpublished paper "Abortion and the Deprivation of a Future: A Reply."

5. See, for example, Routley, R. and Routley, V., "Against the Inevitability of Human Chauvinism," *Ethics and Problems of the 21st Century*, K. E. Goodpaster, and K. M. Sayre, eds., Notre Dame, Ind.: University of Notre Dame Press, 1979. For a discussion of species bias see Regan, Tom, *The Case for Animal Rights*, Berkeley: University of California Press, 1983.

6. For the purposes of this paper I assume that cows and pigs have no right to life. I make no such assumption with regard to the higher apes. For a discussion of animal rights, see Paske, Gerald H., "Why Animals Have No Right to Life," *Australasian Journal of Philosophy*, 66, 4 (December 1988).

7. For an argument that sentience is a necessary condition for a right to life, see Paske, Gerald H., "The Life Principle: A (metaethical) Rejection," *Journal of Applied Philosophy*, 6, 2 (1989).

8. At first glance it may appear that the reverse is not true, that the loss of future-like-ours by a person does not entail the loss of that person. However, this is a mistake. Consider a person who is struck in the head and, although not killed, is so brain damaged that he or she no longer has a future-like-ours. In such cases personhood has been destroyed even though biological life continues The extreme forms of this are cases of brain death where the loss of personhood, despite the continuation of biological life, is explicitly recognized as constituting human (or person) death. Unfortunately there are intermediate cases with which the law has not yet adequately dealt. A discussion of such cases, of which higher brain death is one, is beyond the scope of this paper.

9. Some may feel, contrary to my intuition, that there is a difference in the degree of wrongness of the murders. Even so, the difference in degree of harm between the murder of a 9-year-old and an 89-year-old, such that there is much less harm done to the 89-year-old, does not correspond to any plausible difference in the wrongness of the two murders. To claim otherwise would be to trivialize murdering the elderly.

10. This distinction has already been drawn by Michael Tooley with his well-known cat example. See his "Abortion and Infanticide," *Philosophy and Public Affairs*, 2, 1, (Fall 1972), 60–62. However, because the animal rights movement has become influential since Tooley's article first appeared, I have modified the example so that the kitten need not be killed.

11. I have restricted my discussion to the decision of the woman. Men also can participate in the decision to continue a pregnancy, and by doing so they can affect the relational value of the fetus. However, the role of men in this regard is secondary to my thesis and is too complex to be integrated into this article.

Study Questions

1. According to Paske, why does Marquis's concept of a future-like-ours depend on the notion of personhood? Is he correct?
2. Do you agree with Paske that having conceptually based emotions is a necessary condition for personhood? Explain your answer.
3. According to Paske, do neonates and infants have a right to life? Do they have conceptually based emotions?
4. Paske states that being wanted gives the fetus some right to life. What if an infant is not wanted? What if one parent (or grandparent) wants the fetus to live and the other doesn't? Can Paske successfully solve these problems?

For Further Reading

Brody, Baruch. *Abortion and the Sanctity of Life: A Philosophical View.* Cambridge, Mass.: MIT Press, 1975.

Devine, Philip E. *The Ethics of Homicide.* Ithaca, N.Y.: Cornell University Press, 1978, Chapters 2–4.

Feinberg, Joel, ed. *The Problem of Abortion.* Belmont, Calif.: Wadsworth, 1973.

Grisez, Germaine. *Abortion: The Myths, the Realities, and the Arguments.* New York: Corpus Books, 1970.

Noonan, John T., ed. *The Morality of Abortion: Legal and Historical Perspectives.* Cambridge, Mass.: Harvard University Press, 1970.

Sumner, L. W. *Abortion and Moral Theory.* Princeton, N.J.: Princeton University Press, 1981.

Tooley, Michael. *Abortion and Infanticide.* Oxford: Oxford University Press, 1983.

Part VIII

Human Cloning

My own view is that human cloning would have to raise deep concerns given our most cherished concepts of faith and humanity. Each human life is unique, born of a miracle that reaches beyond laboratory science. I believe we must respect this profound gift and resist the temptation to replicate ourselves. . . .

What this legislation will do is to reaffirm our most cherished belief about the miracle of human life and the God-given individuality each person possesses. It will ensure that we do not fall prey to the temptation to replicate ourselves at the expense of those beliefs. . . . Banning human cloning reflects our humanity. It is the right thing to do. Creating a child through this new method calls into question our most fundamental beliefs.[1]

(PRESIDENT WILLIAM CLINTON)

The Cloning of Dolly and the Implications for Humanity

In Huxley's *Brave New World,* sexuality is divorced from procreation. Sexual intercourse—"feelies"—is recreational, occurring promiscuously and daily. Children are genetically manufactured by the "Bokanovsky Process" in state hatcheries according to eugenic principles (Alpha Plus Intellectuals, Beta, Delta workers . . . Epsilon Minus Morons) to fill various state functions. Individualism, especially personal commitments like those of family loyalty, were viewed as repugnant, giving way to the social motto: *Community, Identity, Stability.* This separation of sex from procreation typically struck people as the most implausible feature of Aldous Huxley's 1932 fantasy. But today it is close to a possibility. We have the technological knowledge to be able to produce or manufacture babies with specific genomes. Science fiction may become science.

On February 24, 1997, the front-page story all over the world was about a lamb named Dolly that had been cloned at the Roslin Institute in Scotland by a team led by Ian Wilmut. The implications for cloning humans was immediately realized.

Within hours, thousands of statements condemning that prospect were hurled from leaders throughout the world. In New York, legislator John Marchi introduced a bill to make human cloning illegal in his state. An official of the Catholic Bishops Conference of England and Wales urged a ban on human cloning because "each human being has a right to two biological parents." President Clinton condemned human cloning and set up a commission, the National Bioethics Advisory Commission (NBAC), to look into the advisability of cloning. After ninety days of study the NBAC agreed, urging federal legislation to ban human cloning (excerpts of this report constitute our second reading).[2] France's President Jacques Chirac called for the European Commonwealth to ban the technology. On January 12, 1998, nineteen European nations signed an agreement prohibiting the genetic replication of humans. Freelance activist Jeremy Rifkin said, "It's a horrendous crime to make a Xerox of someone. . . . You're putting a human into a genetic straightjacket." He demanded a worldwide ban on human cloning, with penalties for transgressors similar to rape and murder.[3] Medical ethicist Daniel Callahan was quoted as saying, "I think we have a right to our own individual genetic identity. . . . I think this could well violate that right."[4] A *Time*/CNN poll conducted a few days after the announcement showed that 93% of Americans disapproved of cloning humans.[5] Ian Wilmut himself condemned human cloning.

How should reflective moral people react to the news of cloning? As noted above, the first reactions of the religious leaders, politicians, medical ethicists, and the public at large were overwhelmingly negative. However, though this should be noted, in itself it should not influence us too much.

One ought to take the initial public reaction to cloning with a grain of salt. Such gut-level reactions are not good reasons to approve or disapprove a policy. I can remember when in the 1950s it was proposed that we send a man to the Moon. People were appalled that we should play God in this way ("If God wanted us to live on the Moon, he would have put us there!"), and even the eminent philosopher Ludwig Wittgenstein said it was in principle impossible to do this. When the U.S. Supreme Court in *Roe v. Wade* asserted that the Constitution supported abortion up through the second trimester, a huge public outcry reverberated throughout the land. Only twenty-seven years later, most Americans approve of such a permissive policy (though, to be sure, they do not think it ideal). Similarly, when the first test-tube baby, Louise Brown, was born in England on July 25, 1978, a public outcry expressed itself with only 15% approving of it. Just twenty-two years later, over 24,000 American children have been produced this way, and the sky hasn't fallen, nor is there evidence that the children so created are any worse for it. It has a 70% approval rating. Louise seems a normal, healthy young adult, unharmed by the experience.[6] What seems more important than how a baby comes into the world is how he or she is cared for.

A more important question than what the public and the experts think is, What are the moral issues connected with cloning, specifically human cloning? They include the following:

1. The question of human dignity: to what extent does natural procreation, leading to a unique genome, endow us with a special dignity?

2. The problem of the misuse and abuse of technology: there seem no limits to what science and technology could do in creating monsters—Frankensteins, multiple Hitlers, and *Brave New World* scenarios come to mind. Rich people could clone multiple selves and spread their genomes throughout society.

3. What could be the long-range effects of asexual procreation? Is there something fundamentally basic about the heterosexual act in procreation?

4. Eugenics: should we use genetic information to create more perfect persons (e.g., genomes selected for longevity, health, intelligence, self-control, and physical prowess)?

5. Commercialization: should we permit clones to be sold on the open market? Wouldn't this cheapen human life, or do people have a right to sell their genomes?

Our readings deal with these issues.

What Is Cloning?

Before we attempt a moral assessment of cloning, we should understand what it is. Cloning, or more accurately, nuclear somatic transfer (NST) is a type of asexual reproduction, artificially induced. Cloning, as related to mammals, is the process of removing the nucleus of an adult cell and implanting it in an *enucleated* egg (i.e., an ovum from which the original nucleus has been removed). Most people, like bioethicist Leon Kass in our first reading, accept cloning of nonhuman animals. Currently, the agriculture industry is engaged in nuclear transfer to produce better livestock. Changes in the *phenotype* of livestock are accomplished by bombarding their embryos with genes that will produce livestock with desired traits. Scientists are also engaged in *transgenic* processes in pigs, in which genetic manipulation of porcine embryos can produce tissue suitable for replacement of human tissue. Transgenics involves the exchange of genetic information among plant, animal, and microbial species. In mice embryo experiments, a key gene in the morphological development is knocked out at an early stage. This results in a fetus with no head. All other organs of the mice fetus develop normally, except the brain. Hence, the resulting mouse cannot live long after birth and has no ability to perceive or act. However, tissue from headless mice may eventually be used for human tissue replacement. The potential uses and abuses of transgenics are enormous.

The Promise of Cloning

Here are a few of the positive *possibilities* human cloning would offer:

1. Suppose we admired someone—say the movie stars Gregory Peck, Charlton Heston, Audrey Hepburn, or Julie Andrews; or saintly people like Gandhi, Mother Teresa, or the Dalai Lama; or athletes like Michael Jordan or Mark McGwire. We

could buy their genome and clone it, bringing up their identical twin—only much younger. Similarly, societies might one day be able to use cloning to develop a group of outstanding political and moral leaders.

2. One spouse might have a genetic disposition toward a serious disease—for example, spina bifida, Tay-Sachs disease, Down's Syndrome, cystic fibrosis, or heart disease—so we could clone the other spouse's genome. Suppose the husband has the bad genes. We would clone the mother who would give birth to her own identical twin. She would be both mother and sister to her child. Or if the man was cloned, he would be both father and brother to the child. Suppose that you, an only child, and your father were killed in an accident. Your mother, deeply distraught at this earthshaking dual loss, asks her scientist doctor to harvest a cell from your body to clone you, so that you would live on through your clone.

3. A couple could freeze an embryo clone of each of their children so that should any of the children die their genetic twin could be developed from the embryo. Applying this process to the example of your being cloned (in 2), one of your cell nuclei would have been transplanted into one of your mother's enucleated ova and frozen in a medical storage plant.

4. We could freeze embryonic clones of an individual so that if the person later needed a bone marrow, liver or kidney transplant, the clone could be implanted in a gestational surrogate and developed. The tissue match from the clone would be exact, so that the vexing problem of tissue rejection would not arise.

5. One could not only perpetuate a family line but also an exact gene line. Person A might be 90 years old while his or her next twin is 50 years old and next twin is only 5 years old. Suppose it turns out that you are the clone of one of the healthiest, happiest, long-lived people who has inhabited this planet—a person who lived 110 years. Given even better nutrition and health standards, you could make it to a happy 150 years. Would you regret the fact that you were cloned? How would you react to the news? Who would you be if you weren't cloned?

These five positive possibilities may have tremendous financial costs and unknown societal costs attached to them, but in themselves they seem morally acceptable. Let us turn to our readings.

Our first reading, "The Wisdom of Repugnance" is by Leon Kass, professor at the University of Chicago. Kass testified to the NBAC that human cloning was "morally repugnant," so dangerous that the NBAC should act "as if the future of humanity may lie in the balance."[7] His article is a scathing denunciation of cloning, calling for an unequivocal ban on human cloning.

> We should declare that human cloning is unethical in itself and dangerous in its likely consequences. In so doing, we shall have the backing of the overwhelming majority of our fellow Americans, and of the human race, and (I believe) of most practicing scientists. Next we should do all that we can to prevent the cloning of human beings. We should do this by means of an international legal ban, at a minimum.[8]

Kass gives a range of arguments, beginning with an appeal to *Natural Law,* then arguing that cloning is a culmination of contemporary narcissism, and ending with an argument that cloned beings will not be independent and may not even be moral agents.

Our second reading is a selection from the eighteen-member National Bioethics Advisory Commission's (NBAC) report on cloning human beings. It assesses the arguments for and against human cloning, sets forth the positive and negative possibilities, and sets forth its conclusions. Its main conclusion calls for a three- to five-year ban on human cloning and calls on Congress to pass a law making it a federal crime to produce a child by cloning.

Our third reading, Richard Lewontin's "The Confusion over Cloning," examines the arguments in the NBAC report and argues that most of the arguments against cloning are confused. He is especially critical of its overemphasis on the religious emphasis of its arguments, which, he thinks, should have been replaced by ethical considerations.

In our final reading, Gregory Pence examines the main argument against cloning, that it will unnecessarily harm the resulting person. He sets forth several considerations undermining this thesis.

Notes

1. President Bill Clinton, a speech replayed on PBS's *Newshour,* quoted in Patrick Hopkins, "Bad Copies: How Popular Media Represent Cloning as an Ethical Problem," *Hastings Center Report* 28: 2 (1998), p. 9. Clinton went on to announce a ban on cloning. Similarly, U.S. Congressman Vernon Ehlers of Michigan urged Congress to pass a law making human cloning a federal crime. He wrote, "Human life is sacred. The good Lord ordained a time-honored method of creating human life, commensurate with substantial responsibility on the part of the parents, the responsibility to raise a child appropriately. Creating life in the laboratory is totally inappropriate and so far removed from the process of marriage and parenting that has been instituted upon this planet that we must rebel against the very concept of human cloning. It is simply wrong to experiment with the creation of human life in this way." Quoted in Gregory E. Pence, *Who's Afraid of Human Cloning?* (Lanham, Md.: Rowman & Littlefield, 1998), p. 39. This is the best book on the subject of cloning, and this part of the book is indebted to it.

2. Gregory E. Pence, *Who's Afraid,* p. 1.

3. *Time,* (March 10, 1997), p. 70. Quoted in Hopkins, "Bad Copies," pp. 6–13; and in Pence, *Who's Afraid,* p. 27.

4. *Time,* (November 8, 1993), p. 68. Quoted in Hopkins, "Bad Copies."

5. Pence, *Who's Afraid,* p. 2.

6. Pence, *Who's Afraid,* pp. 4–5.

7. Quoted in Pence, *Who's Afraid,* p. 5.

8. Kass "The Wisdom of Repugnance," *New Republic,* (June 2, 1997), p. 25.

CHAPTER 37

The Wisdom of Repugnance

LEON R. KASS

Leon R. Kass is the Addie Clark Harding professor in the College and the Committee on Social Thought at the University of Chicago. He is a molecular biologist who
works mainly in bioethics. Known for his opposition to in vitro fertilization, Kass
extends his criticisms of that form of reproduction to human cloning. He offers
what is widely regarded in the literature as the strongest attack on human cloning.
His arguments include the allegation that human cloning violates natural moral law,
that it represents a form of narcissism, and that the cloned being will be severely
harmed by the process.

OUR HABIT OF DELIGHTING in news of
scientific and technological breakthroughs has
been sorely challenged by the birth announcement of a sheep named Dolly. Though Dolly
shares with previous sheep the "softest clothing,
woolly, bright," William Blake's question,
"Little Lamb, who made thee?" has for her a
radically different answer: Dolly was, quite literally, made. She is the work not of nature or
nature's God but of man, an Englishman, Ian
Wilmut, and his fellow scientists. What's more,
Dolly came into being not only asexually—ironically, just like "He [who] calls Himself a
Lamb"—but also as the genetically identical
copy (and the perfect incarnation of the form or
blueprint) of a mature ewe, of whom she is a
clone. This long-awaited yet not quite expected
success in cloning a mammal raised immediately
the prospect—and the specter—of cloning human beings: "I a child and Thou a lamb," despite our differences, have always been equal
candidates for creative making, only now, by
means of cloning, we may both spring from the
hand of man playing at being God.

After an initial flurry of expert comment and
public consternation, with opinion polls showing overwhelming opposition to cloning human
beings, President Clinton ordered a ban on all
federal support for human cloning research
(even though none was being supported) and
charged the National Bioethics Advisory Commission to report in ninety days on the ethics of
human cloning research. The commission (an
eighteen-member panel, evenly balanced between scientists and nonscientists, appointed by
the president and reporting to the National Science and Technology Council) invited testimony from scientists, religious thinkers and bioethicists, as well as from the general public. It is
now deliberating about what it should recommend, both as a matter of ethics and as a matter
of public policy.

Congress is awaiting the commission's report, and is poised to act. Bills to prohibit the
use of federal funds for human cloning research
have been introduced in the House of Representatives and the Senate; and another bill, in the
House, would make it illegal "for any person to

use a human somatic cell for the process of producing a human clone." A fateful decision is at hand. To clone or not to clone a human being is no longer an academic question.

Taking Cloning Seriously, Then and Now

Cloning first came to public attention roughly thirty years ago, following the successful asexual production, in England, of a clutch of tadpole clones by the technique of nuclear transplantation. The individual largely responsible for bringing the prospect and promise of human cloning to public notice was Joshua Lederberg, a Nobel Laureate geneticist and a man of large vision. In 1966, Lederberg wrote a remarkable article in *The American Naturalist* detailing the eugenic advantages of human cloning and other forms of genetic engineering, and the following year he devoted a column in *The Washington Post*, where he wrote regularly on science and society, to the prospect of human cloning. He suggested that cloning could help us overcome the unpredictable variety that still rules human reproduction, and allow us to benefit from perpetuating superior genetic endowments. These writings sparked a small public debate in which I became a participant. At the time a young researcher in molecular biology at the National Institutes of Health (NIH), I wrote a reply to the *Post*, arguing against Lederberg's amoral treatment of this morally weighty subject and insisting on the urgency of confronting a series of questions and objections, culminating in the suggestion that "the programmed reproduction of man will, in fact, dehumanize him."

Much has happened in the intervening years. It has become harder, not easier, to discern the true meaning of human cloning. We have in some sense been softened up to the idea—through movies, cartoons, jokes and intermittent commentary in the mass media, some serious, most lighthearted. We have become accustomed to new practices in human reproduction: not just in vitro fertilization, but also embryo manipulation, embryo donation and surrogate pregnancy. Animal biotechnology has yielded transgenic animals and a burgeoning science of genetic engineering, easily and soon to be transferable to humans.

Even more important, changes in the broader culture make it now vastly more difficult to express a common and respectful understanding of sexuality, procreation, nascent life, family, and the meaning of motherhood, fatherhood and the links between the generations. Twenty-five years ago, abortion was still largely illegal and thought to be immoral, the sexual revolution (made possible by the extramarital use of the pill) was still in its infancy, and few had yet heard about the reproductive rights of single women, homosexual men and lesbians. (Never mind shameless memoirs about one's own incest!) Then one could argue, without embarrassment, that the new technologies of human reproduction—babies without sex—and their confounding of normal kin relations—who's the mother: the egg donor, the surrogate who carries and delivers, or the one who rears?—would "undermine the justification and support that biological parenthood gives to the monogamous marriage." Today, defenders of stable, monogamous marriage risk charges of giving offense to those adults who are living in "new family forms" or to those children who, even without the benefit of assisted reproduction, have acquired either three or four parents or one or none at all. Today, one must even apologize for voicing opinions that twenty-five years ago were nearly universally regarded as the core of our culture's wisdom on these matters. In a world whose once-given natural boundaries are blurred by technological change and whose moral boundaries are seemingly up for grabs, it is much more difficult to make persuasive the still compelling case against cloning human beings. As Raskolnikov put it, "man gets used to everything—the beast!"

Indeed, perhaps the most depressing feature of the discussions that immediately followed the news about Dolly was their ironical tone, their genial cynicism, their moral fatigue: "AN UDDER WAY OF MAKING LAMBS" (*Nature*), "WHO WILL CASH IN ON BREAKTHROUGH IN CLONING?" (*The Wall Street Journal*), "IS CLONING BAAAAAAAAD?" (*The Chicago Tribune*). Gone from the scene are the wise and courageous voices of Theodosius Dobzhansky (genetics), Hans Jonas (philosophy) and Paul Ramsey (theology) who, only twenty-five years ago, all made powerful moral arguments against ever cloning a human being. We are now too sophisticated for such argumentation; we wouldn't be caught in public with a strong moral stance, never mind an absolutist one. We are all, or almost all, post-modernists now.

Cloning turns out to be the perfect embodiment of the ruling opinions of our new age. Thanks to the sexual revolution, we are able to deny in practice, and increasingly in thought, the inherent procreative teleology of sexuality itself. But, if sex has no intrinsic connection to generating babies, babies need have no necessary connection to sex. Thanks to feminism and the gay rights movement, we are increasingly encouraged to treat the natural heterosexual difference and its preeminence as a matter of "cultural construction." But if male and female are not normatively complementary and generatively significant, babies need not come from male and female complementarity. Thanks to the prominence and the acceptability of divorce and out-of-wedlock births, stable, monogamous marriage as the ideal home for procreation is no longer the agreed-upon cultural norm. For this new dispensation, the clone is the ideal emblem: the ultimate "single-parent child."

Thanks to our belief that all children should be *wanted* children (the more high-minded principle we use to justify contraception and abortion), sooner or later only those children who fulfill our wants will be fully acceptable. Through cloning, we can work our wants and wills on the very identity of our children, exercising control as never before. Thanks to modern notions of individualism and the rate of cultural change, we see ourselves not as linked to ancestors and defined by traditions, but as projects for our own self-creation, not only as self-made men but also man-made selves; and self-cloning is simply an extension of such rootless and narcissistic self-re-creation.

Unwilling to acknowledge our debt to the past and unwilling to embrace the uncertainties and the limitations of the future, we have a false relation to both: cloning personifies our desire fully to control the future, while being subject to no controls ourselves. Enchanted and enslaved by the glamour of technology, we have lost our awe and wonder before the deep mysteries of nature and of life. We cheerfully take our own beginnings in our hands and, like the last man, we blink.

Part of the blame for our complacency lies, sadly, with the field of bioethics itself, and its claim to expertise in these moral matters. Bioethics was founded by people who understood that the new biology touched and threatened the deepest matters of our humanity: bodily integrity, identity and individuality, lineage and kinship, freedom and self-command, eros and aspiration, and the relations and strivings of body and soul. With its capture by analytic philosophy, however, and its inevitable routinization and professionalization, the field has by and large come to content itself with analyzing moral arguments, reacting to new technological developments and taking on emerging issues of public policy, all performed with a naïve faith that the evils we fear can all be avoided by compassion, regulation and a respect for autonomy. Bioethics has made some major contributions in the protection of human subjects and in other areas where personal freedom is threatened; but its practitioners, with few exceptions, have turned the big human questions into pretty thin gruel.

One reason for this is that the piecemeal formation of public policy tends to grind down large questions of morals into small questions of procedure. Many of the country's leading bioethicists have served on national commissions or state task forces and advisory boards, where, understandably, they have found utilitarianism to be the only ethical vocabulary acceptable to all participants in discussing issues of law, regulation and public policy. As many of these commissions have been either officially under the aegis of NIH or the Health and Human Services Department, or otherwise dominated by powerful voices for scientific progress, the ethicists have for the most part been content, after some "values clarification" and wringing of hands, to pronounce their blessings upon the inevitable. Indeed, it is the bioethicists, not the scientists, who are now the most articulate defenders of human cloning: the two witnesses testifying before the National Bioethics Advisory Commission in favor of cloning human beings were bioethicists, eager to rebut what they regard as the irrational concerns of those of us in opposition. One wonders whether this commission, constituted like the previous commissions, can tear itself sufficiently free from the accommodationist pattern of rubber-stamping all technical innovation, in the mistaken belief that all other goods must bow down before the gods of better health and scientific advance.

If it is to do so, the commission must first persuade itself, as we all should persuade ourselves, not to be complacent about what is at issue here. Human cloning, though it is in some respects continuous with previous reproductive technologies, also represents something radically new, in itself and in its easily foreseeable consequences. The stakes are very high indeed. I exaggerate, but in the direction of the truth, when I insist that we are faced with having to decide nothing less than whether human procreation is going to remain human, whether children are going to be made rather than begotten, whether it is a good thing, humanly speaking, to say yes in principle to the road which leads (at best) to the dehumanized rationality of *Brave New World*. This is not business as usual, to be fretted about for a while but finally to be given our seal of approval. We must rise to the occasion and make our judgments as if the future of our humanity hangs in the balance. For so it does.

The State of the Art

If we should not underestimate the significance of human cloning, neither should we exaggerate its imminence or misunderstand just what is involved. The procedure is conceptually simple. The nucleus of a mature but unfertilized egg is removed and replaced with a nucleus obtained from a specialized cell of an adult (or fetal) organism (in Dolly's case, the donor nucleus came from mammary gland epithelium). Since almost all the hereditary material of a cell is contained within its nucleus, the renucleated egg and the individual into which this egg develops are genetically identical to the organism that was the source of the transferred nucleus. An unlimited number of genetically identical individuals— clones—could be produced by nuclear transfer. In principle, any person, male or female, newborn or adult, could be cloned, and in any quantity. With laboratory cultivation and storage of tissues, cells outliving their sources make it possible even to clone the dead.

The technical stumbling block, overcome by Wilmut and his colleagues, was to find a means of reprogramming the state of the DNA in the donor cells, reversing its differentiated expression and restoring its full totipotency, so that it could again direct the entire process of producing a mature organism. Now that this problem has been solved, we should expect a rush to develop cloning for other animals, especially livestock, in order to propagate in perpetuity the champion meat or milk producers. Though exactly how soon someone will succeed in cloning a human being is anybody's guess, Wilmut's technique, almost certainly applicable to humans, makes *attempting* the feat an imminent possibility.

Yet some cautions are in order and some possible misconceptions need correcting. For a start, cloning is not Xeroxing. As has been reassuringly reiterated, the clone of Mel Gibson though his genetic double, would enter the world hairless, toothless and peeing in his diapers, just like any other human infant. Moreover, the success rate, at least at first, will probably not be very high: the British transferred 277 adult nuclei into enucleated sheep eggs, and implanted twenty-nine clonal embryos, but they achieved the birth of only one live lamb clone. For this reason, among others, it is unlikely that, at least for now, the practice would be very popular, and there is no immediate worry of mass-scale production of multicopies. The need of repeated surgery to obtain eggs and, more crucially, of numerous borrowed wombs for implantation will surely limit use, as will the expense; besides, almost everyone who is able will doubtless prefer nature's sexier way of conceiving.

Still, for the tens of thousands of people already sustaining over 200 assisted-reproduction clinics in the United States and already availing themselves of in vitro fertilization, intracytoplasmic sperm injection and other techniques of assisted reproduction, cloning would be an option with virtually no added fuss (especially when the success rate improves). Should commercial interests develop in "nucleus-banking," as they have in sperm-banking; should famous athletes or other celebrities decide to market their DNA the way they now market their autographs and just about everything else; should techniques of embryo and germline genetic testing and manipulation arrive as anticipated, increasing the use of laboratory assistance in order to obtain "better" babies—should all this come to pass, then cloning, if it is permitted, could become more than a marginal practice simply on the basis of free reproductive choice, even without any

social encouragement to upgrade the gene pool or to replicate superior types. Moreover, if laboratory research on human cloning proceeds, even without any intention to produce cloned humans, the existence of cloned human embryos in the laboratory, created to begin with only for research purposes, would surely pave the way for later baby-making implantations.

In anticipation of human cloning, apologists and proponents have already made clear possible uses of the perfected technology, ranging from the sentimental and compassionate to the grandiose. They include: providing a child for an infertile couple; "replacing" a beloved spouse or child who is dying or has died; avoiding the risk of genetic disease; permitting reproduction for homosexual men and lesbians who want nothing sexual to do with the opposite sex; securing a genetically identical source of organs or tissues perfectly suitable for transplantation; getting a child with a genotype of one's own choosing, not excluding oneself; replicating individuals of great genius, talent or beauty—having a child who really could "be like Mike"; and creating large sets of genetically identical humans suitable for research on, for instance, the question of nature versus nurture, or for special missions in peace and war (not excluding espionage), in which using identical humans would be an advantage. Most people who envision the cloning of human beings, of course, want none of these scenarios. That they cannot say why is not surprising. What is surprising, and welcome, is that, in our cynical age, they are saying anything at all.

The Wisdom of Repugnance

"Offensive." "Grotesque." "Revolting." "Repugnant." "Repulsive." These are the words most commonly heard regarding the prospect of human cloning. Such reactions come both from the man or woman in the street and from the intellectuals, from believers and atheists, from humanists and scientists. Even Dolly's creator has said he "would find it offensive" to clone a human being.

People are repelled by many aspects of human cloning. They recoil from the prospect of mass production of human beings, with large clones of look-alikes, compromised in their individuality; the idea of father-son or mother-daughter twins; the bizarre prospects of a woman giving birth to and rearing a genetic copy of herself, her spouse or even her deceased father or mother; the grotesqueness of conceiving a child as an exact replacement for another who has died; the utilitarian creation of embryonic genetic duplicates of oneself, to be frozen away or created when necessary, in case of need for homologous tissues or organs for transplantation; the narcissism of those who would clone themselves and the arrogance of others who think they know who deserves to be cloned or which genotype any child-to-be should be thrilled to receive; the Frankensteinian hubris to create human life and increasingly to control its destiny; man playing God. Almost no one finds any of the suggested reasons for human cloning compelling; almost everyone anticipates its possible misuses and abuses. Moreover, many people feel oppressed by the sense that there is probably nothing we can do to prevent it from happening. This makes the prospect all the more revolting.

Revulsion is not an argument; and some of yesterday's repugnances are today calmly accepted—though, one must add, not always for the better. In crucial cases, however, repugnance is the emotional expression of deep wisdom, beyond reason's power fully to articulate it. Can anyone really give an argument fully adequate to the horror which is father-daughter incest (even with consent), or having sex with animals, or mutilating a corpse, or eating human flesh, or even just (just!) raping or murdering another human being? Would anybody's failure to give full rational justification for his or her revulsion

at these practices make that revulsion ethically suspect? Not at all. On the contrary, we are suspicious of those who think that they can rationalize away our horror, say, by trying to explain the enormity of incest with arguments only about the genetic risks of inbreeding.

The repugnance at human cloning belongs in this category. We are repelled by the prospect of cloning human beings not because of the strangeness or novelty of the undertaking, but because we intuit and feel, immediately and without argument, the violation of things that we rightfully hold dear. Repugnance, here as elsewhere, revolts against the excesses of human willfulness, warning us not to transgress what is unspeakably profound. Indeed, in this age in which everything is held to be permissible so long as it is freely done, in which our given human nature no longer commands respect, in which our bodies are regarded as mere instruments of our autonomous rational wills, repugnance may be the only voice left that speaks up to defend the central core of our humanity. Shallow are the souls that have forgotten how to shudder.

The goods protected by repugnance are generally overlooked by our customary ways of approaching all new biomedical technologies. The way we evaluate cloning ethically will in fact be shaped by how we characterize it descriptively, by the context into which we place it, and by the perspective from which we view it. The first task for ethics is proper description. And here is where our failure begins.

Typically, cloning is discussed in one or more of three familiar contexts, which one might call the technological, the liberal and the meliorist. Under the first, cloning will be seen as an extension of existing techniques for assisting reproduction and determining the genetic makeup of children. Like them, cloning is to be regarded as a neutral technique, with no inherent meaning or goodness, but subject to multiple uses, some good, some bad. The morality of cloning thus depends absolutely on the goodness or badness of the motives and intentions of the cloners: as one bioethicist defender of cloning puts it, "the ethics must be judged [only] by the way the parents nurture and rear their resulting child and whether they bestow the same love and affection on a child brought into existence by a technique of assisted reproduction as they would on a child born in the usual way."

The liberal (or libertarian or liberationist) perspective sets cloning in the context of rights, freedoms and personal empowerment. Cloning is just a new option for exercising an individual's right to reproduce or to have the kind of child that he or she wants. Alternatively, cloning enhances our liberation (especially women's liberation) from the confines of nature, the vagaries of chance, or the necessity for sexual mating. Indeed, it liberates women from the need for men altogether, for the process requires only eggs, nuclei and (for the time being) uteri—plus, of course, a healthy dose of our (allegedly "masculine") manipulative science that likes to do all these things to mother nature and nature's mothers. For those who hold this outlook, the only moral restraints on cloning are adequately informed consent and the avoidance of bodily harm. If no one is cloned without her consent, and if the clonant is not physically damaged, then the liberal conditions for licit, hence moral, conduct are met. Worries that go beyond violating the will or maiming the body are dismissed as "symbolic"—which is to say, unreal.

The meliorist perspective embraces valetudinarians and also eugenicists. The latter were formerly more vocal in these discussions, but they are now generally happy to see their goals advanced under the less threatening banners of freedom and technological growth. These people see in cloning a new prospect for improving human beings—minimally, by ensuring the perpetuation of healthy individuals by avoiding the risks of genetic disease inherent in the lottery of sex, and maximally, by producing "optimum babies," preserving outstanding genetic material, and (with the help of soon-to-come techniques for precise genetic engineering) enhancing inborn human capacities on many fronts. Here the morality of cloning as a means is justified solely by the excellence of the end, that is, by the outstanding traits or individuals cloned—beauty, or brawn, or brains.

These three approaches, all quintessentially American and all perfectly fine in their places, are sorely wanting as approaches to human procreation. It is, to say the least, grossly distorting to view the wondrous mysteries of birth, renewal and individuality, and the deep meaning of parent-child relations, largely through the lens of our reductive science and its potent technologies. Similarly, considering reproduction (and the intimate relations of family life!) primarily under the political-legal, adversarial and individualistic notion of rights can only undermine the private yet fundamentally social, cooperative and duty-laden character of childbearing, child-rearing and their bond to the covenant of marriage. Seeking to escape entirely from nature (in order to satisfy a natural desire or a natural right to reproduce!) is self-contradictory in theory and self-alienating in practice. For we are erotic beings only because we are embodied beings, and not merely intellects and wills unfortunately imprisoned in our bodies. And, though health and fitness are clearly great goods, there is something deeply disquieting in looking on our prospective children as artful products perfectible by genetic engineering, increasingly held to our willfully imposed designs, specifications and margins of tolerable error.

The technical, liberal and meliorist approaches all ignore the deeper anthropological, social and, indeed, ontological meanings of bringing forth new life. To this more fitting and profound point of view, cloning shows itself to be a major alteration, indeed, a major violation, of our given nature as embodied, gendered and engendering beings—and of the social relations built on this natural ground. Once this perspective is recognized, the ethical judgment on cloning can no longer be reduced to a matter of motives and intentions, rights and freedoms, benefits and harms, or even means and ends. It must be regarded primarily as a matter of meaning: Is cloning a fulfillment of human begetting and belonging? Or is cloning rather, as I contend, their pollution and perversion? To pollution and perversion, the fitting response can only be horror and revulsion; and conversely, generalized horror and revulsion are prima facie evidence of foulness and violation. The burden of moral argument must fall entirely on those who want to declare the widespread repugnances of humankind to be mere timidity or superstition.

Yet repugnance need not stand naked before the bar of reason. The wisdom of our horror at human cloning can be partially articulated, even if this is finally one of those instances about which the heart has its reasons that reason cannot entirely know.

The Profundity of Sex

To see cloning in its proper context, we must begin not, as I did before, with laboratory technique, but with the anthropology—natural and social—of sexual reproduction.

Sexual reproduction—by which I mean the generation of new life from (exactly) two complementary elements, one female, one male, (usually) through coitus—is established (if that is the right term) not by human decision, culture or tradition, but by nature; it is the natural way of all mammalian reproduction. By nature, each child has two complementary biological progenitors. Each child thus stems from and unites exactly two lineages. In natural generation, moreover, the precise genetic constitution of the resulting offspring is determined by a combination of nature and chance, not by human design: each human child shares the common natural human species genotype, each child is genetically (equally) kin to each (both) parent(s), yet each child is also genetically unique.

These biological truths about our origins foretell deep truths about our identity and about our human condition altogether. Every one of us is at once equally human, equally enmeshed in a particular familial nexus of origin, and equally individuated in our trajectory from birth to death—and, if all goes well, equally capable (despite our mortality) of participating, with a complementary other, in the very same renewal of such human possibility through procreation. Though less momentous than our common humanity, our genetic individuality is not humanly trivial. It shows itself forth in our distinctive appearance through which we are everywhere recognized; it is revealed in our "signature" marks of fingerprints and our self-recognizing immune system; it symbolizes and foreshadows exactly the unique, never-to-be-repeated character of each human life.

Human societies virtually everywhere have structured child-rearing responsibilities and systems of identity and relationship on the bases of these deep natural facts of begetting. The mysterious yet ubiquitous "love of one's own" is everywhere culturally exploited, to make sure that children are not just produced but well cared for and to create for everyone clear ties of meaning, belonging and obligation. But it is wrong to treat such naturally rooted social practices as mere cultural constructs (like left- or right-driving, or like burying or cremating the dead) that we can alter with little human cost. What would kinship be without its clear natural grounding? And what would identity be without kinship? We must resist those. who have begun to refer to sexual reproduction as the "traditional method of reproduction," who would have us regard as merely traditional, and by implication arbitrary, what is in truth not only natural but most certainly profound.

Asexual reproduction, which produces "single-parent" offspring, is a radical departure from the natural human way, confounding all normal understandings of father, mother, sibling, grandparent, etc., and all moral relations tied thereto. It becomes even more of a radical departure when the resulting offspring is a clone derived not from an embryo, but from a mature adult to whom the clone would be an identical twin; and when the process occurs not by natural accident (as in natural twinning), but by deliberate human design and manipulation; and when the child's (or children's) genetic constitution is preselected by the parent(s) (or scientists). Accordingly, as we will see, cloning is vulnerable to three kinds of concerns and objections, related to these three points: cloning threatens confusion of identity and individuality, even in small-scale cloning; cloning represents a giant step (though not the first one) toward transforming procreation into manufacture, that is, toward the increasing depersonalization of the process of generation and, increasingly, toward the "production" of human children as artifacts, products of human will and design (what others have called the problem of "commodification" of new life); and cloning—like other forms of eugenic engineering of the next generation—represents a form of despotism of the cloners over the cloned, and thus (even in benevolent cases) represents a blatant violation of the inner meaning of parent–child relations, of what it means to have a child, of what it means to say "yes" to our own demise and "replacement."

Before turning to these specific ethical objections, let me test my claim of the profundity of the natural way by taking up a challenge recently posed by a friend. What if the given natural human way of reproduction were asexual, and we now had to deal with a new technological innovation—artificially induced sexual dimorphism and the fusing of complementary gametes—whose inventors argued that sexual reproduction promised all sorts of advantages, including hybrid vigor and the creation of greatly increased individuality? Would one then be forced to defend natural asexuality because it was natural? Could one claim that it carried deep human meaning?

The response to this challenge broaches the ontological meaning of sexual reproduction. For it is impossible, I submit, for there to have been human life—or even higher forms of animal life—in the absence of sexuality and sexual reproduction. We find asexual reproduction only in the lowest forms of life: bacteria, algae, fungi, some lower invertebrates. Sexuality brings with it a new and enriched relationship to the world. Only sexual animals can seek and find complementary others with whom to pursue a goal that transcends their own existence. For a sexual being, the world is no longer an indifferent and largely homogeneous *otherness*, in part edible, in part dangerous. It also contains some very special and related and complementary beings, of the same kind but of opposite sex, toward whom one reaches out with special interest and intensity. In higher birds and mammals, the outward gaze keeps a lookout not only for food and predators, but also for prospective mates; the beholding of the many splendored world is suffused with desire for union, the animal antecedent of human eros and the germ of sociality. Not by accident is the human animal both the sexiest animal—whose females do not go into heat but are receptive throughout the estrous cycle and whose males must therefore have greater sexual appetite and energy in order to reproduce successfully—and also the most aspiring, the most social, the most open and the most intelligent animal.

The soul-elevating power of sexuality is, at bottom, rooted in its strange connection to mortality, which it simultaneously accepts and tries to overcome. Asexual reproduction may be seen as a continuation of the activity of self-preservation. When one organism buds or divides to become two, the original being is (doubly) preserved, and nothing dies. Sexuality, by contrast, means perishability and serves replacement; the two that come together to generate one soon will die. Sexual desire, in human beings as in animals, thus serves an end that is partly hidden from, and finally at odds with, the self-serving individual. Whether we know it or not, when we are sexually active we are voting with our genitalia for our own demise. The salmon swimming upstream to spawn and die tell the universal story: sex is bound up with death, to which it holds a partial answer in procreation.

The salmon and the other animals evince this truth blindly. Only the human being can understand what it means. As we learn so powerfully from the story of the Garden of Eden, our humanization is coincident with sexual self-consciousness, with the recognition of our sexual nakedness and all that it implies: shame at our needy incompleteness, unruly self-division and finitude; awe before the eternal; hope in the self-transcending possibilities of children and a relationship to the divine. In the sexually self-conscious animal, sexual desire can become eros, lust can become love. Sexual desire humanly regarded is thus sublimated into erotic longing for wholeness, completion and immortality, which drives us knowingly into the embrace and its generative fruit—as well as into all the higher human possibilities of deed, speech and song.

Through children, a good common to both husband and wife, male and female achieve some genuine unification (beyond the mere sexual "union," which fails to do so). The two become one through sharing generous (not needy) love for this third being as good. Flesh of their flesh, the child is the parents' own commingled being externalized, and given a separate and persisting existence. Unification is enhanced also by their commingled work of rearing. Providing an opening to the future beyond the grave, carrying not only our seed but also our names, our ways and our hopes that they will surpass us in goodness and happiness, children are a testament to the possibility of transcendence. Gender duality and sexual desire, which first draws our love upward and outside of ourselves, finally provide for the partial overcoming of the confinement and limitation of perishable embodiment altogether.

Human procreation, in sum, is not simply an activity of our rational wills. It is a more complete activity precisely because it engages us bodily, erotically and spiritually, as well as rationally. There is wisdom in the mystery of nature that has joined the pleasure of sex, the inarticulate longing for union, the communication of the loving embrace and the deep-seated and only partly articulate desire for children in the very activity by which we continue the chain of human existence and participate in the renewal of human possibility. Whether or not we know it, the severing of procreation from sex, love and intimacy is inherently dehumanizing, no matter how good the product.

We are now ready for the more specific objections to cloning.

The Perversities of Cloning

First, an important if formal objection: any attempt to clone a human being would constitute an unethical experiment upon the resulting child-to-be. As the animal experiments (frog and sheep) indicate, there are grave risks of mishaps and deformities. Moreover, because of what cloning means, one cannot presume a future cloned child's consent to be a clone, even a healthy one. Thus, ethically speaking, we cannot even get to know whether or not human cloning is feasible.

I understand, of course, the philosophical difficulty of trying to compare a life with defects against nonexistence. Several bioethicists, proud of their philosophical cleverness, use this conundrum to embarrass claims that one can injure a child in its conception, precisely because it is only thanks to that complained-of conception that the child is alive to complain. But common sense tells us that we have no reason to fear such philosophisms. For we surely know that people can harm and even maim children in the very act of conceiving them, say, by paternal transmission of the AIDS virus, maternal transmission of heroin dependence or, arguably, even by bringing them into being as bastards or with no capacity or willingness to look after them properly. And we believe that to do this intentionally, or even negligently, is inexcusable and clearly unethical.

The objection about the impossibility of presuming consent may even go beyond the obvious and sufficient point that a clonant, were he subsequently to be asked, could rightly resent having been made a clone. At issue are not just benefits and harms, but doubts about the very independence needed to give proper (even retroactive) consent, that is, not just the capacity to choose but the disposition and ability to choose freely and well. It is not at all clear to what extent a clone will truly be a moral agent. For, as we shall see, in the very act of cloning, and of rearing him as a clone, his makers subvert the cloned child's independence, beginning with that aspect that comes from knowing that one was an unbidden surprise, a gift, to the world, rather than the designed result of someone's artful project.

Cloning creates serious issues of identity and individuality. The cloned person may experience concerns about his distinctive identity not only because he will be in genotype and appearance identical to another human being, but, in this case, because he may also be twin to the person who is his "father" or "mother"—if one can still call them that. What would be the psychic burdens of being the "child" or "parent" of your twin? The cloned individual, moreover, will be saddled with a genotype that has already lived. He will not be fully a surprise to the world. People are likely always to compare his performances in life with that of his alter ego. True, his nurture and his circumstance in life will be different; genotype is not exactly destiny. Still, one

must also expect parental and other efforts to shape this new life after the original—or at least to view the child with the original version always firmly in mind. Why else did they clone from the star basketball player, mathematician and beauty queen—or even dear old dad—in the first place?

Since the birth of Dolly, there has been a fair amount of doublespeak on this matter of genetic identity. Experts have rushed in to reassure the public that the clone would in no way be the same person, or have any confusions about his or her identity: as previously noted, they are pleased to point out that the clone of Mel Gibson would not be Mel Gibson. Fair enough. But one is shortchanging the truth by emphasizing the additional importance of the intrauterine environment, rearing and social setting: genotype obviously matters plenty. That, after all, is the only reason to clone, whether human beings or sheep. The odds that clones of Wilt Chamberlain will play in the NBA are, I submit, infinitely greater than they are for clones of Robert Reich.

Curiously, this conclusion is supported, inadvertently, by the one ethical sticking point insisted on by friends of cloning: no cloning without the donor's consent. Though an orthodox liberal objection, it is in fact quite puzzling when it comes from people (such as Ruth Macklin) who also insist that genotype is not identity or individuality, and who deny that a child could reasonably complain about being made a genetic copy. If the clone of Mel Gibson would not be Mel Gibson, why should Mel Gibson have grounds to object that someone had been made his clone? We already allow researchers to use blood and tissue samples for research purposes of no benefit to their sources: my falling hair, my expectorations, my urine and even my biopsied tissues are "not me" and not mine. Courts have held that the profit gained from uses to which scientists put my discarded tissues do not legally belong to me. Why, then, no cloning without consent—including, I assume, no cloning from the body of someone who just died? What harm is done the donor, if genotype is "not me"? Truth to tell, the only powerful justification for objecting is that genotype really does have something to do with identity, and everybody knows it. If not, on what basis could Michael Jordan object that someone cloned "him," say, from cells taken from a "lost" scraped-off piece of his skin? The insistence on donor consent unwittingly reveals the problem of identity in all cloning.

Genetic distinctiveness not only symbolizes the uniqueness of each human life and the independence of its parents that each human child rightfully attains. It can also be an important support for living a worthy and dignified life. Such arguments apply with great force to any large-scale replication of human individuals. But they are sufficient, in my view, to rebut even the first attempts to clone a human being. One must never forget that these are human beings upon whom our eugenic or merely playful fantasies are to be enacted.

Troubled psychic identity (distinctiveness), based on all-too-evident genetic identity (sameness), will be made much worse by the utter confusion of social identity and kinship ties. For, as already noted, cloning radically confounds lineage and social relations, for "offspring" as for "parents." As bioethicist James Nelson has pointed out, a female child cloned from her "mother" might develop a desire for a relationship to her "father," and might understandably seek out the father of her "mother," who is after all also her biological twin sister. Would "grandpa," who thought his paternal duties concluded, be pleased to discover that the clonant looked to him for paternal attention and support?

Social identity and social ties of relationship and responsibility are widely connected to, and supported by, biological kinship. Social taboos on incest (and adultery) everywhere serve to keep clear who is related to whom (and especially which child belongs to which parents), as well as to avoid confounding the social identity of parent-and-child (or brother-and-sister) with the social identity of lovers, spouses and co-parents. True, social identity is altered by adoption (but as a matter of the best interest of already living children: we do not deliberately produce children for adoption). True, artificial insemination and in vitro fertilization with donor sperm, or whole embryo donation, are in some way forms of "prenatal adoption"—a not altogether unproblematic practice. Even here, though, there is in each case (as in all sexual reproduction) a known male source of sperm and a known single female source of egg—a genetic father and a genetic mother—should anyone care to know (as adopted children often do) who is genetically related to whom.

In the case of cloning, however, there is but one "parent." The usually sad situation of the "single-parent child" is here deliberately planned, and with a vengeance. In the case of self-cloning, the "offspring" is, in addition, one's twin; and so the dreaded result of incest—to be parent to one's sibling—is here brought about deliberately, albeit without any act of coitus. Moreover, all other relationships will be confounded. What will father, grandfather, aunt, cousin, sister mean? Who will bear what ties and what burdens? What sort of social identity will someone have with one whole side—"father's" or "mother's"—necessarily excluded? It is no answer to say that our society, with its high incidence of divorce, remarriage, adoption, extramarital child-bearing and the rest, already confounds lineage and confuses kinship and responsibility for children (and everyone else), unless one also wants to argue that this is, for children, a preferable state of affairs.

Human cloning would also represent a giant step toward turning begetting into making, procreation into manufacture (literally, something "handmade"), a process already begun with in vitro fertilization and genetic testing of embryos. With cloning, not only is the process in hand, but the total genetic blueprint of the cloned individual is selected and determined by the human artisans. To be sure, subsequent development will take place according to natural processes; and the resulting children will still be recognizably human. But we here would be taking a major step into making man himself simply another one of the man-made things. Human nature becomes merely the last part of nature to succumb to the technological project, which turns all of nature into raw material at human disposal, to be homogenized by our rationalized technique according to the subjective prejudices of the day.

How does begetting differ from making? In natural procreation, human beings come together, complementarily male and female, to give existence to another being who is formed, exactly as we were, *by what we are:* living, hence perishable, hence aspiringly erotic, human beings. In clonal reproduction, by contrast, and in the more advanced forms of manufacture to which it leads, we give existence to a being not by what we are but by what we intend and design. As with any product of our making, no matter how excellent, the artificer stands above it, not as an equal but as a superior, transcending it by his will and creative prowess. Scientists who clone animals make it perfectly clear that they are engaged in instrumental making; the animals are, from the start, designed as means to serve rational human purposes. In human cloning, scientists and prospective "parents" would be adopting the same technocratic mentality to human children: human children would be their artifacts.

Such an arrangement is profoundly dehumanizing, no matter how good the product. Mass-scale cloning of the same individual makes the point vividly; but the violation of human equality, freedom and dignity are present even in a single planned clone. And procreation dehumanized into manufacture is further degraded by commodification, a virtually inescapable result of allowing baby-making to proceed under the banner of commerce. Genetic and reproductive biotechnology companies are already growth industries, but they will go into commercial orbit once the Human Genome Project nears completion. Supply will create enormous demand. Even before the capacity for human cloning arrives, established companies will have invested in the harvesting of eggs from ovaries obtained at autopsy or through ovarian surgery, practiced embryonic genetic alteration, and initiated the stockpiling of prospective donor tissues. Through the rental of surrogate-womb services, and through the buying and selling of tissues and embryos, priced according to the merit of the donor, the commodification of nascent human life will be unstoppable.

Finally, and perhaps most important, the practice of human cloning by nuclear transfer—like other anticipated forms of genetic engineering of the next generation—would enshrine and aggravate a profound and mischievous misunderstanding of the meaning of having children and of the parent-child relationship. When a couple now chooses to procreate, the partners are saying yes to the emergence of new life in its novelty, saying yes not only to having a child but also, tacitly, to having whatever child this child turns out to be. In accepting our finitude and opening ourselves to our replacement, we are tacitly confessing the limits of our control In this ubiquitous way of nature, embracing the future by procreating means precisely that we are relinquishing our grip, in the very activity of taking up our own share in what we hope will be the immortality of human life and the human species. This means that our children are not *our* children: they are not our property, not our possessions. Neither are they supposed to live our lives for us, or anyone else's life but their own. To be sure, we seek to guide them on their way, imparting to them not just life but nurturing, love, and a way of life; to be sure, they bear our hopes that they will live fine and flourishing lives, enabling us in small measure to transcend our own limitations. Still, their genetic distinctiveness and independence are the natural fore-shadowing of the deep truth that they have their own and never-before-enacted life to live. They are sprung from a past, but they take an uncharted course into the future.

Much harm is already done by parents who try to live vicariously through their children. Children are sometimes compelled to fulfill the broken dreams of unhappy parents; John Doe Jr. or the III is under the burden of having to live up to his forebear's name. Still, if most parents have hopes for their children, cloning parents will have expectations. In cloning, such overbearing parents take at the start a decisive step which contradicts the entire meaning of the open and forward-looking nature of parent-child relations. The child is given a genotype that has already lived, with full expectation that this blueprint of a past life ought to be controlling of the life that is to come. Cloning is inherently despotic, for it seeks to make one's children (or someone else's children) after one's own image (or an image of one's choosing) and their future according to one's will. In some cases, the despotism may be mild and benevolent. In other cases, it will be mischievous and downright tyrannical. But despotism—the control of another through one's will—it inevitably will be.

Meeting Some Objections

The defenders of cloning, of course, are not wittingly friends of despotism. Indeed, they regard themselves mainly as friends of freedom: the freedom of individuals to reproduce, the freedom of scientists and inventors to discover and devise and to foster "progress" in genetic knowledge and technique. They want large-scale cloning only for animals, but they wish to preserve cloning as a human option for exercising our "right to reproduce"—our right to have children, and children with "desirable genes." As law professor John Robertson points out, un-

der our "right to reproduce" we already practice early forms of unnatural, artificial and extramarital reproduction, and we already practice early forms of eugenic choice. For this reason, he argues, cloning is no big deal.

We have here a perfect example of the logic of the slippery slope, and the slippery way in which it already works in this area. Only a few years ago, slippery slope arguments were used to oppose artificial insemination and in vitro fertilization using unrelated sperm donors. Principles used to justify these practices, it was said, will be used to justify more artificial and more eugenic practices, including cloning. Not so, the defenders retorted, since we can make the necessary distinctions. And now, without even a gesture at making the necessary distinctions, the continuity of practice is held by itself to be justificatory.

The principle of reproductive freedom as currently enunciated by the proponents of cloning logically embraces the ethical acceptability of sliding down the entire rest of the slope—to producing children ectogenetically from sperm to term (should it become feasible) and to producing children whose entire genetic makeup will be the product of parental eugenic planning and choice. If reproductive freedom means the right to have a child of one's own choosing, by whatever means, it knows and accepts no limits.

But, far from being legitimated by a "right to reproduce," the emergence of techniques of assisted reproduction and genetic engineering should compel us to reconsider the meaning and limits of such a putative right. In truth, a "right to reproduce" has always been a peculiar and problematic notion. Rights generally belong to individuals, but this is a right which (before cloning) no one can exercise alone. Does the right then inhere only in couples? Only in married couples? Is it a (woman's) right to carry or deliver or a right (of one or more parents) to nurture and rear? Is it a right to have your own biological child? Is it a right only to attempt reproduction, or a right also to succeed? Is it a right to acquire the baby of one's choice?

The assertion of a negative "right to reproduce" certainly makes sense when it claims protection against state interference with procreative liberty, say, through a program of compulsory sterilization. But surely it cannot be the basis of a tort claim against nature, to be made good by technology, should free efforts at natural procreation fail. Some insist that the right to reproduce embraces also the right against state interference with the free use of all technological means to obtain a child. Yet such a position cannot be sustained: for reasons having to do with the means employed, any community may rightfully prohibit surrogate pregnancy, or polygamy, or the sale of babies to infertile couples, without violating anyone's basic human "right to reproduce." When the exercise of a previously innocuous freedom now involves or impinges on troublesome practices that the original freedom never was intended to reach, the general presumption of liberty needs to be reconsidered.

We do indeed already practice negative eugenic selection, through genetic screening and prenatal diagnosis. Yet our practices are governed by a norm of health. We seek to prevent the birth of children who suffer from known (serious) genetic diseases. When and if gene therapy becomes possible, such diseases could then be treated, in utero or even before implantation—I have no ethical objection in principle to such a practice (though I have some practical worries), precisely because it serves the medical goal of healing existing individuals. But therapy, to be therapy, implies not only an existing "patient." It also implies a norm of health. In this respect, even germline gene "therapy," though practiced not on a human being but on egg and sperm, is less radical than cloning, which is in no way therapeutic. But once one blurs the distinction between health promotion and genetic enhancement, between so-called negative and positive eugenics, one opens the door to all future eugenic designs. "To make sure that a child will be healthy and have good chances in life": this is

Robertson's principle, and owing to its latter clause it is an utterly elastic principle, with no boundaries. Being over eight feet tall will likely produce some very good chances in life, and so will having the looks of Marilyn Monroe, and so will a genius-level intelligence.

Proponents want us to believe that there are legitimate uses of cloning that can be distinguished from illegitimate uses, but by their own principles no such limits can be found. (Nor could any such limits be enforced in practice.) Reproductive freedom, as they understand it, is governed solely by the subjective wishes of the parents-to-be (plus the avoidance of bodily harm to the child). The sentimentally appealing case of the childless married couple is, on these grounds, indistinguishable from the case of an individual (married or not) who would like to clone someone famous or talented, living or dead. Further, the principle here endorsed justifies not only cloning but, indeed, all future artificial attempts to create (manufacture) "perfect" babies.

A concrete example will show how, in practice no less than in principle, the so-called innocent case will merge with, or even turn into, the more troubling ones. In practice, the eager parents-to-be will necessarily be subject to the tyranny of expertise. Consider an infertile married couple, she lacking eggs or he lacking sperm, that wants a child of their (genetic) own, and propose to clone either husband or wife. The scientist-physician (who is also co-owner of the cloning company) points out the likely difficulties—a cloned child is not really their (genetic) child, but the child of only *one* of them; this imbalance may produce strains on the marriage; the child might suffer identity confusion; there is a risk of perpetuating the cause of sterility; and so on—and he also points out the advantages of choosing a donor nucleus. Far better than a child of their own would be a child of their own choosing. Touting his own expertise in selecting healthy and talented donors, the doctor presents the couple with his latest catalog containing the pictures, the health records and the accomplishments of his stable of cloning donors, samples of whose tissues are in his deep freeze. Why not, dearly beloved, a more perfect baby?

The "perfect baby," of course, is the project not of the infertility doctors, but of the eugenic scientists and their supporters. For them, the paramount right is not the so-called right to reproduce but what biologist Bentley Glass called, a quarter of a century ago, "the right of every child to be born with a sound physical and mental constitution, based on a sound genotype . . . the inalienable right to a sound heritage." But to secure this right, and to achieve the requisite quality control over new human life, human conception and gestation will need to be brought fully into the bright light of the laboratory, beneath which it can be fertilized, nourished, pruned, weeded, watched, inspected, prodded, pinched, cajoled, injected, tested, rated, graded, approved, stamped, wrapped, sealed and delivered. There is no other way to produce the perfect baby.

Yet we are urged by proponents of cloning to forget about the science fiction scenarios of laboratory manufacture and multiple-copied clones, and to focus only on the homely cases of infertile couples exercising their reproductive rights. But why, if the single cases are so innocent, should multiplying their performance be so off-putting? (Similarly, why do others object to people making money off this practice, if the practice itself is perfectly acceptable?) When we follow the sound ethical principle of universalizing our choice—"would it be right if everyone cloned a Wilt Chamberlain (with his consent, of course)? Would it be right if everyone decided to practice asexual reproduction?"—we discover what is wrong with these seemingly innocent cases. The so-called science fiction cases make vivid the meaning of what looks to us, mistakenly, to be benign.

Though I recognize certain continuities between cloning and, say, in vitro fertilization, I believe that cloning differs in essential and important ways. Yet those who disagree should be reminded that the "continuity" argument cuts both ways. Sometimes we establish bad precedents, and discover that they were bad only when we follow their inexorable logic to places we never meant to go. Can the defenders of cloning show us today how, on their principles, we will be able to see producing babies ("perfect babies") entirely in the laboratory or exercising full control over their genotypes (including so-called enhancement) as ethically different, in any essential way, from present forms of assisted reproduction? Or are they willing to admit, despite their attachment to the principle of continuity, that the complete obliteration of "mother" or "father," the complete depersonalization of procreation, the complete manufacture of human beings and the complete genetic control of one generation over the next would be ethically problematic and essentially different from current forms of assisted reproduction? If so, where and how will they draw the line, and why? I draw it at cloning, for all the reasons given.

Ban the Cloning of Humans

What, then, should we do? We should declare that human cloning is unethical in itself and dangerous in its likely consequences. In so doing, we shall have the backing of the overwhelming majority of our fellow Americans, and of the human race, and (I believe) of most practicing scientists. Next, we should do all that we can to prevent the cloning of human beings. We should do this by means of an international legal ban if possible, and by a unilateral national ban, at a minimum. Scientists may secretly undertake to violate such a law, but they will be deterred by not being able to stand up proudly to claim the credit for their technological bravado and success. Such a ban on clonal baby-making, moreover, will not harm the progress of basic genetic science and technology. On the contrary, it will reassure the public that scientists are happy to proceed without violating the deep ethical norms and intuitions of the human community.

This still leaves the vexed question about laboratory research using early embryonic human clones, specially created only for such research purposes, with no intention to implant them into a uterus. There is no question that such research holds great promise for gaining fundamental knowledge about normal (and abnormal) differentiation, and for developing tissue lines for transplantation that might be used, say, in treating leukemia or in repairing brain or spinal cord injuries—to mention just a few of the conceivable benefits. Still, unrestricted clonal embryo research will surely make the production of living human clones much more likely. Once the genies put the cloned embryos into the bottles, who can strictly control where they go (especially in the absence of legal prohibitions against implanting them to produce a child)?

I appreciate the potentially great gains in scientific knowledge and medical treatment available from embryo research, especially with cloned embryos. At the same time, I have serious reservations about creating human embryos for the sole purpose of experimentation. There is something deeply repugnant and fundamentally transgressive about such a utilitarian treatment of prospective human life. This total, shameless exploitation is worse, in my opinion, than the "mere" destruction of nascent life. But I see no added objections, as a matter of principle, to creating and using *cloned* early embryos for research purposes, beyond the objections that I might raise to doing so with embryos produced sexually.

And yet, as a matter of policy and prudence, any opponent of the manufacture of cloned humans must, I think, in the end oppose also the creating of cloned human embryos. Frozen embryonic clones (belonging to whom?) can be shuttled around without detection. Commercial ventures in human cloning will be developed without adequate oversight. In order to build a

fence around the law, prudence dictates that one oppose—for this reason alone—all production of cloned human embryos, even for research purposes. We should allow all cloning research on animals to go forward, but the only safe trench that we can dig across the slippery slope, I suspect, is to insist on the inviolable distinction between animal and human cloning.

Some readers, and certainly most scientists, will not accept such prudent restraints, since they desire the benefits of research. They will prefer, even in fear and trembling, to allow human embryo cloning research to go forward.

Very well. Let us test them. If the scientists want to be taken seriously on ethical grounds, they must at the very least agree that embryonic research may proceed if and only if it is preceded by an absolute and effective ban on all attempts to implant into a uterus a cloned human embryo (cloned from an adult) to produce a living child. Absolutely no permission for the former without the latter.

The National Bioethics Advisory Commission's recommendations regarding this matter should be watched with the greatest care. Yielding to the wishes of the scientists, the commission will almost surely recommend that cloning human embryos for research be permitted. To allay public concern, it will likely also call for a temporary moratorium—not a legislative ban—on implanting cloned embryos to make a child, at least until such time as cloning techniques will have been perfected and rendered "safe" (precisely through the permitted research with cloned embryos). But the call for a moratorium rather than a legal ban would be a moral and a practical failure. Morally, this ethics commission would (at best) be waffling on the main ethical question, by refusing to declare the production of human clones unethical (or ethical). Practically, a moratorium on implantation cannot provide even the minimum protection needed to prevent the production of cloned humans.

Opponents of cloning need therefore to be vigilant. Indeed, no one should be willing even to consider a recommendation to allow the embryo research to proceed unless it is accompanied by a call for *prohibiting* implantation and until steps are taken to make such a prohibition effective.

Technically, the National Bioethics Advisory Commission can advise the president only on federal policy, especially federal funding policy. But given the seriousness of the matter at hand, and the grave public concern that goes beyond federal funding, the commission should take a broader view. (If it doesn't, Congress surely will.) Given that most assisted reproduction occurs in the private sector, it would be cowardly and insufficient for the commission to say, simply, "no federal funding" for such practices. It would be disingenuous to argue that we should allow federal funding so that we would then be able to regulate the practice; the private sector will not be bound by such regulations. Far better, for virtually everyone concerned, would be to distinguish between research on embryos and baby-making, and to call for a complete national and international ban (effected by legislation and treaty) of the latter, while allowing the former to proceed (at least in private laboratories).

The proposal for such a legislative ban is without American precedent, at least in technological matters, though the British and others have banned cloning of human beings, and we ourselves ban incest, polygamy and other forms of "reproductive freedom." Needless to say, working out the details of such a ban, especially a global one, would be tricky, what with the need to develop appropriate sanctions for violators. Perhaps such a ban will prove ineffective; perhaps it will eventually be shown to have been a mistake. But it would at least place the burden of practical proof where it belongs: on the proponents of this horror, requiring them to show very clearly what great social or medical good can be had only by the cloning of human beings.

We Americans have lived by, and prospered under, a rosy optimism about scientific and technological progress. The technological imperative—if it can be done, it must be done—has probably served us well, though we should admit that there is no accurate method for weighing benefits and harms. Even when, as in the cases of environmental pollution, urban decay or the lingering deaths that are the unintended by-products of medical success, we recognize the unwelcome outcomes of technological advance, we remain confident in our ability to fix all the "bad" consequences—usually by means of still newer and better technologies. How successful we can continue to be in such post hoc repairing is at least an open question. But there is very good reason for shifting the paradigm around, at least regarding those technological interventions into the human, body and mind that will surely effect fundamental (and likely irreversible) changes in human nature, basic human relationships, and what it means to be a human being. Here we surely should not be willing to risk everything in the naïve hope that, should things go wrong, we can later set them right.

The president's call for a moratorium on human cloning has given us an important opportunity. In a truly unprecedented way, we can strike a blow for the human control of the technological project, for wisdom, prudence and human dignity. The prospect of human cloning, so repulsive to contemplate, is the occasion for deciding whether we shall be slaves of unregulated progress, and ultimately its artifacts, or whether we shall remain free human beings who guide our technique toward the enhancement of human dignity. If we are to seize the occasion, we must, as the late Paul Ramsey wrote,

> raise the ethical questions with a serious and not a frivolous conscience. A man of frivolous conscience announces that there are ethical quandaries ahead that we must urgently consider before the future catches up with us. By this he often means that we need to devise a new ethics that will provide the rationalization for doing in the

future what men are bound to do because of new actions and interventions science will have made possible. In contrast a man of serious conscience means to say in raising urgent ethical questions that there may be some things that men should never do. The good things that men do can be made complete only by the things they refuse to do.

Study Questions

1. Why does Kass think that cloning is "the perfect embodiment of the ruling opinions of our new age"? What does he find objectionable about these opinions? Is he correct? Why or why not?
2. Kass suggests that those who reject his position and accept cloning are moral relativists. Could one accept cloning for objective moral reasons? Explain.
3. Why does Kass think that the urge for human cloning is an expression of rootless narcissism? How strong are his arguments?
4. What does Kass say about the potential independence of a cloned human? Would he or she be a fully moral agent, according to him? Compare Kass's argument on this point with Lewontin's discussion of cloned persons in our third reading.
5. Why does Kass believe that we should take seriously the intuitions of the ordinary citizen, even though they lack expertise in matters related to the technology of cloning?

CHAPTER 38

Against Cloning Human Beings

NATIONAL BIOETHICS ADVISORY COMMISSION

In the wake of the news of Dolly's cloning, President Clinton asked his bioethics commission, the National Bioethics Advisory Commission (NBAC), to investigate the ethical and policy issues connected with human cloning. They summed up the positive and negative aspects of the prospect of human cloning and concluded that the dangers outweigh the advantages. The commission recommended a three- to five-year ban on all research involving human cloning. Their reasons are given in the selection that follows.

Ethical Considerations

THE PROSPECT OF CREATING children through somatic cell nuclear transfer has elicited widespread concern, much of it in the form of fears about harms to the children who may be born as a result. There are concerns about possible physical harms from the manipulations of ova, nuclei, and embryos which are parts of the technology, and also about possible psychological harms, such as a diminished sense of individuality and personal autonomy. There are ethical concerns as well about a degradation of the quality of parenting and family life if parents are tempted to seek excessive control over their children's characteristics, to value children according to how well they meet overly detailed parental expectations, and to undermine the acceptance and openness that typify loving families. Virtually all people agree that the current risks of physical harm to children associated with somatic cell nuclear transplantation cloning justify a prohibition at this time on such experimentation. In addition to concerns about specific harms to children, people have frequently expressed fears that a widespread practice of such cloning would undermine important social values, such as opening the door to a form of eugenics or by tempting some to manipulate others as if they were objects instead of persons, and exceeding the moral boundaries inherent in the human condition. Arrayed against these concerns are other important social values, such as protecting personal choice, maintaining privacy and the freedom of scientific inquiry, and encouraging the possible development of new biomedical breakthroughs. As somatic cell nuclear transfer cloning could represent a means of human reproduction for some people, limitations on that choice must be made only when the societal benefits of prohibition clearly outweigh the value of maintaining the private nature of such highly personal decisions. Especially in light of some arguably compelling cases for attempting to create a child through somatic cell nuclear transfer, the ethics of policy making must strike a balance between the values we, as a society, wish to reflect and

From Cloning Human Beings: Report and Recommendations of the National Bioethics Advisory Commission. *Rockville, MD: United States National Bioethics Advisory Commission, 1997. Notes deleted.*

the freedom of individual choice and any liberties we propose to limit.

The unique prospect, vividly raised by Dolly, is the creation of a new individual genetically identical to an existing (or previously existing) person—a "delayed" genetic twin. This prospect has been the source of the overwhelming public concern about such cloning. While the creation of embryos for research purposes alone always raises serious ethical questions, the use of somatic cell nuclear transfer to create embryos raises no new issues in this respect. The unique and distinctive ethical issues raised by the use of somatic cell nuclear transfer to create children relate to, for example, serious safety concerns, individuality, family integrity, and treating children as objects. Consequently, the Commission focused its attention on the use of such techniques for the purpose of creating an embryo which would then be implanted in a woman's uterus and brought to term. It also expanded its analysis of this particular issue to encompass activities in both the public and private sector.

Potential for Physical Harms

There is one basis of opposition to somatic cell nuclear transfer cloning on which almost everyone can agree. For reasons outlined [earlier], there is virtually universal concern regarding the current safety of attempting to use this technique in human beings. Even if there were a compelling case in favor of creating a child in this manner, it would have to yield to one fundamental principle of both medical ethics and political philosophy—the injunction, as it is stated in the Hippocratic canon, to "first do no harm." In addition, the avoidance of physical and psychological harm was established as a standard for research in the Nuremberg Code, 1946–49. At this time, the significant risks to the fetus and physical well-being of a child created by somatic cell nuclear transplantation cloning outweigh arguably beneficial uses of the technique.

It is important to recognize that the technique that produced Dolly the sheep was successful in only 1 of 277 attempts. If attempted in humans, it would pose the risk of hormonal manipulation in the egg donor; multiple miscarriages in the birth mother; and possibly severe developmental abnormalities in any resulting child. Clearly the burden of proof to justify such an experimental and potentially dangerous technique falls on those who would carry out the experiment. Standard practice in biomedical science and clinical care would never allow the use of a medical drug or device on a human being on the basis of such a preliminary study and without much additional animal research. Moreover, when risks are taken with an innovative therapy, the justification lies in the prospect of treating an illness in a patient, whereas, here no patient is at risk until the innovation is employed. Thus, no conscientious physician or Institutional Review Board should approve attempts to use somatic cell nuclear transfer to create a child at this time. For these reasons, prohibitions are warranted on all attempts to produce children through nuclear transfer from a somatic cell at this time.

Even on this point, however, NBAC has noted some difference of opinion. Some argue, for example, that prospective parents are already allowed to conceive, or to carry a conception to term, when there is a significant risk—or even certainty—that the child will suffer from a serious genetic disease. Even when others think such conduct is morally wrong, the parents' right to reproductive freedom takes precedence. Since many of the risks believed to be associated with somatic cell nuclear transfer may be no greater than those associated with genetic disorders, some contend that such cloning should be subject to no more restriction than other forms of reproduction (Brock, 1997).

And, as in any new and experimental clinical procedure, harms cannot be accurately determined until trials are conducted in humans. Law professor John Robertson noted before NBAC on March 13, 1997 that:

[The] first transfer [into a uterus] of a human [embryo] clone [will occur] before we know whether it will succeed. . . . [Some have argued therefore] that the first transfers are somehow unethical . . . experimentation on the resulting child, because one does not know what is going to happen, and one is . . . possibly leading to a child who could be disabled and have developmental difficulties. . . . [But the] child who would result would not have existed but for the procedure at issue, and [if] the intent there is actually to benefit that child by bringing it into being . . . [this] should be classified as experimentation for [the child's] benefit and thus it would fall within recognized exceptions. . . . We have a very different set of rules for experimentation intended to benefit [the experimental subject].

(Robertson, 1997)

But the argument that somatic cell nuclear transfer cloning experiments are "beneficial" to the resulting child rests on the notion that it is a "benefit" to be brought into the world as compared to being left unconceived and unborn. This metaphysical argument, in which one is forced to compare existence with non-existence, is problematic. Not only does it require us to compare something unknowable—non-existence—with something else, it also can lead to absurd conclusions if taken to its logical extreme. For example, it would support the argument that there is no degree of pain and suffering that cannot be inflicted on a child, provided that the alternative is never to have been conceived. Even the originator of this line of analysis rejects this conclusion.

In addition, it is true that the actual risks of physical harm to the child born through somatic cell nuclear transfer cannot be known with certainty unless and until research is conducted on human beings. It is likewise true that if we insisted on absolute guarantees of no risk before we permitted any new medical intervention to be attempted in humans, this would severely hamper if not halt completely the introduction of new therapeutic interventions, including new methods of responding to infertility. The assertion that we should regard attempts at human cloning as "experimentation for [the child's] benefit" is not persuasive.

Cloning and Individuality

In addition to physical harms, many worry about psychological harms associated with such cloning. One of the forms of psychological harm most frequently mentioned is the possible loss of a sense of uniqueness.

Many argue that somatic cell nuclear transfer cloning creates serious issues of identity, and individuality and forces us to reconsider how we define ourselves. In his testimony before NBAC March 13, 1997, Gilbert Meilaender commented on the importance of genetic uniqueness not only for individuals but in the eyes of their parents:

Our children begin with a kind of genetic independence of us, their parents. They replicate neither their father nor their mother. That is a reminder of the independence that we must eventually grant to them and for which it is our duty to prepare them. To lose even in principle this sense of the child as gift will not be good for children.

(Meilaender, 1997)

The concept of creating a genetic twin, although separated in time, is one aspect of somatic cell nuclear transfer cloning that most find both troubling and fascinating. The phenomenon of identical twins has intrigued human cultures across the globe, and throughout history (Schwartz, 1996). It is easy, to understand why identical twins hold such fascination. Common experience demonstrates how distinctly different twins are, both in personality and in personhood. At the same time, observers cannot help but imbue identical bodies with some expectation that identical persons occupy those bodies, since body and personality remain intertwined in human intuition. With the prospect of somatic cell nuclear transfer cloning comes a scientifically inaccurate but nonetheless instinctive fear of multitudes of identical bodies, each housing personalities that are somehow less than distinct, less unique, and less autonomous than usual.

Is there a moral or human right to a unique identity, and if so would it be violated by this manner of human cloning? For such somatic cell nuclear transfer cloning to violate a right to a unique identity, the relevant sense of identity would have to be genetic identity, that is a right to a unique unrepeated genome. Even with the same genes, two individuals—for example homozygous twins—are distinct and not identical, so what is intended must be the various properties and characteristics that make each individual qualitatively unique and different than others. Does having the same genome as another person undermine that unique qualitative identity?

Along these lines of inquiry some question whether reproduction using somatic cell nuclear transfer would violate what philosopher Hans Jonas called a right to ignorance, or what philosopher Joel Feinberg called a right to an open future, or what Martha Nussbaum called the quality of "separateness" (Jonas, 1974; Feinberg, 1980; Nussbaum, 1990). Jonas argued that human cloning, in which there is a substantial time gap between the beginning of the lives of the earlier and later twin, is fundamentally different from the simultaneous beginning of the lives of homozygous twins that occur in nature. Although contemporaneous twins begin their lives with the same genetic inheritance, they also begin their lives or biographies at the same time, in ignorance of what the twin who shares the same genome will by his or her choices make of his or her life. To whatever extent one's genome determines one's future, each life begins ignorant of what that determination will be, and so remains as free to choose a future as are individuals who do not have a twin. In this line of reasoning, ignorance of the effect of one's genome on one's future is necessary for the spontaneous, free, and authentic construction of a life and self.

A later twin created by cloning, Jonas argues, knows, or at least believes he or she knows, too much about him or herself. For there is already in the world another person, one's earlier twin, who from the same genetic starting point has made the life choices that are still in the later twin's future. It will seem that one's life has already been lived and played out by another, that one's fate is already determined, and so the later twin will lose the spontaneity of authentically creating and becoming his or her own self. One will lose the sense of human possibility in freely creating one's own future. It is tyrannical, Jonas claims, for the earlier twin to try to determine another's fate in this way.

And even if it is a mistake to believe such crude genetic determinism according to which one's genes determine one's fate, what is important for one's experience of freedom and ability to create a life for oneself is whether one thinks one's future is open and undetermined, and so still to be largely determined by one's own choices. One might try to interpret Jonas' objection so as not to assume either genetic determinism, or a belief in it. A later twin might grant that he or she is not destined to follow in his or her earlier twin's footsteps, but that nevertheless the earlier twin's life would always haunt the later twin, standing as an undue influence on the latter's life, and shaping it in ways to which others' lives are not vulnerable.

In a different context, and without applying it to human cloning, Feinberg has argued for a child's right to an open future. This requires that others raising a child not close off the future possibilities that the child would otherwise have by constructing his or her own life. One way this right to an open future would be violated is to deny even a basic education to a child, and another way might be to create the child as a later twin so that he or she will believe its future has already been set by the choices made and the life lived by the earlier twin.

On the other hand, all of these concerns are not only quite speculative, but are directly related to certain specific cultural values. Someone created through the use of somatic cell nuclear transfer techniques may or may not believe that their future is relatively constrained. Indeed, they may, believe the opposite. In addition, quite normal parenting usually involves many constraints on a child's behavior that children may resent. Moreover, Feinberg's argument does not apply, if the belief is false and it can be shown to be false.

Thus, a central difficulty in evaluating the implications for somatic cell nuclear transfer cloning of a right either to ignorance or to an open future, is whether the right is violated merely because the later twin may be likely to believe that its future is already determined, even if that belief is clearly false and supported only by the crudest genetic determinism. Moreover, what such a twin is likely to believe will depend on the facts that emerge and what scientists and ethicists claim.

Cloning and the Family

Among those concerns that are not focused on arguments about harm to the child are a set of worries about use of such cloning as a means of control. There are concerns, for example, about possibly generating large numbers of people whose life choices are limited by their own constrained self-image or by the constraining expectations of others. From this image of less-than-autonomous children comes the fear, however misplaced, of technology creating armies of cloned soldiers, each diminished in his or her physical individuality and thereby diminished in their psychological autonomy. Similarly, this expectation of diminished autonomy underlies the eugenic arguments that have led many to speculate about the possibility of cloning "desirable" or "evil" people, ranging from actors to dictators of various stripes to distinguished religious leaders. Complicating matters even further, this misplaced belief in the ability of genes to fully determine behavior and personality amplifies the

image, so that in the end one imagines being able to make either armies of complacent workers, crazed soldiers, brilliant musicians, or beatific saints.

Although such fears are based . . . on gross misunderstandings of human biology, and psychology, they are nonetheless fears that have been voiced. In addition, these same concerns also manifest themselves in fears that underlie the characterization of somatic cell nuclear transfer cloning as a form of "making" children rather than "begetting" children. With cloning, the total genetic blueprint of the cloned individual is selected and determined by the human artisans. This, according to Kass:

> . . . would be taking a major step into making man himself simply another one of the man made things. Human nature becomes merely the last part of nature to succumb to the technological project which turns all of nature into raw material at human disposal. . . . As with any product of our making, no matter how excellent, the artificer stands above it, not as an equal but as a superior, transcending it by his will and creative prowess.
> (Kass, 1997)

For many, this kind of relationship is inconsistent with an ideal of parenting in which parents embrace not only the similarities between themselves and their children but also the differences, and in which they accept not only the developments they sought to bring about through care and teaching but also the serendipitous developments they never planned for or anticipated (Rothenberg, 1997).

Of course, parents already exercise great control over their offspring, through means as varied as contraception to control of the timing and spacing of births, to genetic screening and use of donor gametes to avoid genetic disorders, to organized medical and educational interventions to guide physical and intellectual development. These interventions exist along a spectrum of control over development. Somatic cell nuclear transfer cloning, some fear, offers the possibility of virtually complete control over one important aspect of a child's development, his or her genome, and it is the completeness of this control, even if only over this partial aspect of human development, that is alarming to many people and invokes images of manufacturing children according to specification. The lack of acceptance this implies for children who fail to develop according to expectations, and the dominance it introduces into the parent-child relationship, is viewed by many as fundamentally at odds with the acceptance, unconditional love, and openness characteristic of good parenting. Meilaender addressed both the mystery of reproduction and fears about it veering toward a means of production in his testimony before NBAC:

> But whatever we say of [other reproductive technologies], surely human cloning would be a new and decisive turn on this road. Far more emphatically a kind of production. Far less a surrender to the mystery of the genetic lottery which is the mystery of the child who replicates neither Father nor Mother but incarnates their union. Far more an understanding of the child as a product of human will.
>
> (Meilaender, 1997)

Questions are raised, as well, about the effect such interventions will have on a particular child. Will the child himself or herself feel less independent from the nucleus donor than a child ordinarily would from a parent? Will the knowledge of how one's genetic profile developed in another person at another time leave the child feeling that his character is as predetermined as his eye or hair color? Even if the child feels completely independent of the nucleus donor, will others regard the child as a copy or a successor to that donor? If so, will such expectations on the part of others warp the child's emerging self-understanding?

Finally, some critics of such cloning are concerned that the legal or social status of the child arising from nuclear transfer of somatic cells may be uncertain. For some, the disparity between the child's genetic and social identity threatens the stability of the family. Is the child who results from somatic cell nuclear transfer the sibling or the child of its parents? The child or the grandchild of its grandparents? From this perspective the child's psychological and social well-being may be in doubt or even endangered. Ambiguity over parental roles may undermine the child's sense of identity. It may be harder for a child to achieve independence from a parent who is also his or her twin.

At the same time, others are not persuaded by such objections. Children born through assisted reproductive technologies may also have complicated relationships to genetic, gestational, and rearing parents. Skeptics of this point of view note that there is no evidence that confusion over family roles has harmed children born through assisted reproductive technologies, although the subject has not been carefully studied.

Potential Harms to Important Social Values

Those with grave reservations about somatic cell nuclear transfer cloning ask us to imagine a world in which cloning human beings via somatic cell nuclear transfer were permitted and widely practiced. What kind of people, parents, and children would we become in such a world? Opponents fear that such cloning to create children may disrupt the interconnected web of social values, practices, and institutions that support the healthy growth of children. The use of such cloning techniques might encourage the undesirable attitude that children are to be valued according to how closely they meet parental expectations, rather than loved for their own sake. In this way of looking at families and parenting, certain values are at the heart of those relationships, values such as love, nurturing, loyalty, and steadfastness. In contrast, a world in which such cloning were widely practiced would give, the critics claim, implicit approval to vanity, narcissism, and avarice. To these critics, changes that undermine those deeply prized values should be avoided if possible. At a minimum, such undesirable changes should not be fostered by public policies.

On the other hand, others are not persuaded by these objections. First, many social observers point out that if strongly held moral values are in decline, there are likely many complex reasons for this, which would not be addressed by a ban on cloning in this fashion. Furthermore, skeptics argue that people can, and do, adapt in socially redeeming ways, to new technologies. In their view, a child born through somatic cell nuclear transfer could be loved and accepted like any other child, and not disrupt important family and kinship relations.

The strength of public reaction, however, reflects a deep concern that somehow many important social values could be harmed in a society where such cloning were widely used. In his testimony before the Commission on March 13, 1997, bioethicist Leon Kass summarized many of the widely held concerns regarding the possibility of cloning human beings via somatic cell nuclear transfer when he noted:

> Almost no one sees any compelling reason for human cloning. Almost everyone anticipates its possible misuses and abuses. Many feel oppressed by the sense that there is nothing we can do to prevent it from happening and this makes the prospect seem all the more revolting. Revulsion is surely not an argument. . . . But . . . in crucial cases repugnance is often the emotional bearer of deep wisdom beyond reason's power fully to articulate it.
>
> (Kass, 1997)

But some people, however, argue against relying on moral intuition to set public policy. While it is certainly true that repugnance may be the bearer of wisdom, it may also be the bearer of simple and thoughtless prejudice. In her testimony before NBAC on March 14, 1997, bioethicist Ruth Macklin challenged the inclination to take as axiomatic the proposition that to be born as a result of using these techniques is to be harmed or at least to be wronged:

> Intuition has never been a reliable epistemological method, especially since people notoriously disagree in their moral intuitions. . . . If objectors to cloning can identify no greater harm than a supposed affront to the dignity of the human species, that is a flimsy basis on which to erect barriers to scientific research and its applications.
>
> (Macklin, 1997)

Nevertheless, opponents assert that this new type of cloning tempts human beings to transgress moral boundaries and to grasp for powers that are properly outside human control. Ancient Greek literature and many Biblical interpretations emphasize that human beings occupy a moral position between other forms of life and the divine. In particular, humans should not consider themselves as omnipotent over nature. From this perspective, respecting limits is to respect the appropriate place of humankind in the universe and to ensure that technology is not allowed to push aside critical social and moral commitments. This view need not be tied to a single religious doctrine, a particular view of God, or even a belief in God. However, these objections are often expressed in religious terms. For example, critics talk of how the ability to create children through somatic cell nuclear transfer may tempt us to seek immortality, to usurp the role of God, or to violate divine commands.

On the other hand, some observers do not see this type of cloning as dramatically new or extreme, especially when compared to other assisted reproductive technologies. Robertson notes:

> In an important sense cloning is not the most radical thing on the horizon. Much more significant, I think, would be the ability to actually alter

or manipulate the genome of offspring. Cloning takes a genome as it is . . . and might replicate it. . . . [T]hat is much less ominous than having an ability to take a given genome and either add or take out a gene which could then lead to a child being born with characteristics other than it would have had with the genome it started with.
(Robertson, 1997).

Finally, critics have also raised questions about an inappropriate use of scarce resources. The generation of children through somatic cell nuclear transfer would divert scarce resources, including the skills of researchers and clinicians, from more pressing social and medical needs. These considerations about allocation of resources are particularly pertinent if public funds would be involved. In the words of theologian Nancy Duff:

When considering research into human cloning we must look at the responsible use of limited resources. . . . [I]t is mandatory to ask whether other research projects will serve a greater number of people than research on human cloning and take the answer to that seriously.

Treating People as Objects

Some opponents of somatic cell nuclear cloning fear that the resulting children will be treated as objects rather than as persons. This concern often underlies discussions of whether such cloning amounts to "making" rather than "begetting" children, or whether the child who is created in this manner will be viewed as less than a fully independent moral agent. In sum, will being cloned from the somatic cell of an existing person result in the child being regarded as less of a person whose humanity and dignity would not be fully respected.

One reason this discussion can be hard to capture and to articulate is that certain terms, such as "person," are used differently by different people. What is common to these various views, however, is a shared understanding that being a "person" is different from being the manipulated "object" of other people's desires and expectations. Writes legal scholar Margaret Radin,

The person is a subject, a moral agent, autonomous and self-governing. An object is a nonperson, not treated as a self-governing moral agent. . . . [By] "objectification of persons," we mean, roughly, "what Kant would not want us to do."

That is, to objectify a person is to act towards the person without regard for his or her own desires or well-being, as a thing to be valued according to externally imposed standards, and to control the person rather than to engage her or him in a mutually respectful relationship. Objectification, quite simply, is treating the child as an object—a creature less deserving of respect for his or her moral agency. Commodification is sometimes distinguished from objectification and concerns treating persons as commodities, including treating them as a thing that can be exchanged, bought or sold in the marketplace. To those who view the intentional choice by another of one's genetic makeup as a form of manipulation by others, somatic cell nuclear transfer cloning represents a form of objectification or commodification of the child.

Some may deny that objectification is any more a danger in somatic cell nuclear transfer cloning than in current practices such as genetic screening or, in the future perhaps, gene therapy. These procedures aim either to avoid having a child with a particular condition, or to compensate for a genetic abnormality. But to the extent that the technology is used to benefit the child by, for example, allowing early preventive measures with phenylketonuria, no objectification of the child takes place.

When such cloning is undertaken not for any purported benefit of the child himself or herself, but rather to satisfy the vanity of the nucleus donor, or even to serve the need of someone else, such as a dying child in need of a bone marrow donor, then some would argue that it goes yet another step toward diminishing the personhood of the child created in this fashion. The final insult, opponents argue, would come if the child created through somatic cell nuclear transfer is regarded as somehow less than fully equal to the other human beings, due to his or her diminished physical uniqueness and the diminished mystery surrounding some aspects of his or her future physical development.

Eugenic Concerns

The desire to improve on nature is as old as humankind. It has been played out in agriculture through the breeding of special strains of domesticated animals and plants. With the development of the field of genetics over the past 100 years came the hope that the selection of advantageous inherited characteristics—called eugenics, from the Greek *eugenes* meaning wellborn or noble in heredity—could be as beneficial to humankind as selective breeding in agriculture.

The transfer of directed breeding practices from plants and animals to human beings is inherently problematic, however. To begin, eugenic proposals require that several dubious and offensive assumptions be made. First, that most, if not all people would mold their reproductive behavior to the eugenic plan; in a country that values reproductive freedom, this outcome would be unlikely absent compulsion. Second, that means exist for deciding which human traits and characteristics would be favored, an enterprise that rests on notions of selective human superiority that have long been linked with racist ideology.

Equally important, the whole enterprise of "improving" humankind by eugenic programs oversimplifies the role of genes in determining human traits and characteristics. Little is known about correlation between genes and the sorts of complex, behavioral characteristics that are associated with successful and rewarding human lives; moreover, what little is known indicates that most such characteristics result from complicated interactions among a number of genes and the environment. While cows can be bred to produce more milk and sheep to have softer fleece, the idea of breeding humans to be superior would belong in the realm of science fiction even if one could conceive how to establish the metric of superiority, something that turns not only on the values and prejudices of those who construct the metric but also on the sort of a world they predict these specially bred persons would face.

Nonetheless, at the beginning of this century eugenic ideas were championed by scientific and political leaders and were very popular with the American public. It was not until they were practiced in such a grotesque fashion in Nazi Germany that their danger became apparent. Despite this sordid history and the very real limitations in what genetic selection could be expected to yield, the lure of "improvement" remains very real in the minds of some people. In some ways, creating people through somatic cell nuclear transfer offers eugenicists a much more powerful tool than any before. In selective breeding programs, such as the "germinal choice" method urged by the geneticist H. J. Muller a generation ago (Kevles, 1995), the outcome depended on the usual "genetic lottery" that occurs each time a sperm fertilizes an egg, fusing their individual genetic heritages into a new individual. Cloning, by contrast, would allow the selection of a desired genetic prototype which would be replicated in each of the "offspring," at least on the level of the genetic material in the cell nucleus.

It might be enough to object to the institution of a program of human eugenic cloning—even a voluntary program—that it would rest on false scientific premises and hence be wasteful and misguided. But that argument might not be sufficient to deter those people who want to push the genetic traits of a population in a particular direction. While acknowledging that a particular set of genes can be expressed in variety of ways and therefore that cloning (or any other form of eugenic selection) does not guarantee a particular phenotypic manifestation of the genes, they might still argue that certain genes provide a better starting point for the next generation than other genes.

The answer to any who would propose to exploit the science of cloning in this way is that the moral problems with a program of human eugenics go far beyond practical objections of infeasibility. Some objections are those that have already been discussed in connection with the possible desire of individuals to use somatic cell nuclear transfer that the creation of a child under such circumstances could result in the child being objectified, could seriously undermine the value that ought to attach to each individual as an end in themselves, and could foster inappropriate efforts to control the course of the child's life according to expectations based on the life of the person who was cloned.

In addition to such objections are those that arise specifically because what is at issue in eugenics is more than just an individual act, it is a collective program. Individual acts may be undertaken for singular and often unknown or even unknowable reasons, whereas a eugenics program would propagate dogma about the sorts of people who are desirable and those who are dispensable. That is a path that humanity has tread before, to its everlasting shame. And it is a path to whose return the science of cloning should never be allowed to give even the slightest support. . . .

Recommendations of the Commission

With the announcement that an apparently quite normal sheep had been born in Scotland as a result of somatic cell nuclear transfer cloning came the realization that, as a society, we must yet again collectively decide whether and how to use what appeared to be a dramatic new technological power. The promise and the peril of this scientific advance was noted immediately around the world, but the prospects of creating human beings through this technique mainly elicited widespread resistance and/or concern. Despite this reaction, the scientific significance of the accomplishment, in terms of improved understanding of cell development and cell differentiation, should not be lost. The challenge to public policy is to support the myriad beneficial applications of this new technology, while simultaneously guarding against its more questionable uses.

Much of the negative reaction to the potential application of such cloning in humans can be attributed to fears about harms to the children who may result, particularly psychological harms associated with a possibly diminished sense of individuality and personal autonomy. Others express concern about a degradation in the quality of parenting and family life. And virtually all people agree that the current risks of physical harm to children associated with somatic cell nuclear transplantation cloning justify a prohibition at this time on such experimentation.

In addition to concerns about specific harms to children, people have frequently expressed fears that a widespread practice of somatic cell nuclear transfer cloning would undermine important social values by opening the door to a form of eugenics or by tempting some to manipulate others as if they were objects instead of persons. Arrayed against these concerns are other important social values, such as protecting personal choice, particularly in matters pertaining to procreation and child rearing, maintaining privacy and the freedom of scientific inquiry, and encouraging the possible development of new biomedical breakthroughs.

As somatic cell nuclear transfer cloning could represent a means of human reproduction for some people, limitations on that choice must be made only when the societal benefits of prohibition clearly outweigh the value of maintaining the private nature of such highly personal decisions. Especially in light of some arguably compelling cases for attempting to clone a human being using somatic cell nuclear transfer, the ethics of policy making must strike a balance between the values society wishes to reflect and issues of privacy and the freedom of individual choice.

To arrive at its recommendations concerning the use of somatic cell nuclear transfer techniques, NBAC also examined long-standing religious traditions that often influence and guide citizens' responses to new technologies. Religious positions on human cloning are pluralistic in their premises, modes of argument, and conclusions. Nevertheless, several major themes are prominent in Jewish, Roman Catholic, Protestant, and Islamic positions, including responsible human dominion over nature, human dignity and destiny, procreation, and family life. Some religious thinkers argue that the use of somatic cell nuclear transfer cloning to create a child would be intrinsically immoral and thus could never be morally justified; they usually propose a ban on such human cloning. Other religious thinkers contend that human cloning to create a child could be morally justified under some circumstances but hold that it should be strictly regulated in order to prevent abuses.

The public policies recommended with respect to the creation of a child using somatic cell nuclear transfer reflect the Commission's best judgments about both the ethics of attempting such an experiment and our view of traditions regarding limitations on individual actions in the name of the common good. At present, the use of this technique to create a child would be a premature experiment that exposes the developing child to unacceptable risks. This in itself is sufficient to justify a prohibition on cloning human beings at this time, even if such efforts were to be characterized as the exercise of a fundamental right to attempt to procreate. More speculative psychological harms to the child, and effects on the moral, religious, and cultural values of society may be enough to justify contin-

ued prohibitions in the future, but more time is needed for discussion and evaluation of these concerns.

Beyond the issue of the safety of the procedure, however, NBAC found that concerns relating to the potential psychological harms to children and effects on the moral, religious, and cultural values of society merited further reflection and deliberation. Whether upon such further deliberation our nation will conclude that the use of cloning techniques to create children should be allowed or permanently banned is, for the moment, an open question. Time is an ally in this regard, allowing for the accrual of further data from animal experimentation, enabling an assessment of the prospective safety and efficacy of the procedure in humans, as well as granting a period of fuller national debate on ethical and social concerns. The Commission therefore concluded that there should be imposed a period of time in which no attempt is made to create a child using somatic cell nuclear transfer.

Within this overall framework the Commission came to the following conclusions and recommendations.

I. The Commission concludes that at this time it is morally unacceptable for anyone in the public or private sector, whether in a research or clinical setting, to attempt to create a child using somatic cell nuclear transfer cloning. We have reached a consensus on this point because current scientific information indicates that this technique is not safe to use in humans at this time. Indeed, we believe it would violate important ethical obligations were clinicians or researchers to attempt to create a child using these particular technologies, which are likely to involve unacceptable risks to the fetus and/or potential child. Moreover, in addition to safety concerns, many other serious ethical concerns have been identified, which require much more widespread and careful public deliberation before this technology may be used.

The Commission, therefore, recommends the following for immediate action:

- A continuation of the current moratorium on the use of federal funding in support of any attempt to create a child by somatic cell nuclear transfer.

- An immediate request to all firms, clinicians, investigators, and professional societies in the private and non-federally funded sectors to comply voluntarily with the intent of the federal moratorium. Professional and scientific societies should make clear that any attempt to create a child by somatic cell nuclear transfer and implantation into a woman's body would at this time be an irresponsible, unethical, and unprofessional act.

II. The Commission further recommends that:

- Federal legislation should be enacted to prohibit anyone from attempting, whether in a research or clinical setting, to create a child through somatic cell nuclear transfer cloning. It is critical, however, that such legislation include a sunset clause to ensure that Congress will review the issue after a specified time period (three to five years) in order to decide whether the prohibition continues to be needed. If state legislation is enacted, it should also contain such a sunset provision. Any such legislation or associated regulation also ought to require that at some point prior to the expiration of the sunset period, an appropriate oversight body will evaluate and report on the current status of somatic cell nuclear transfer technology and on the ethical and social issues that its potential use to create human beings would raise in light of public understandings at that time.

III. The Commission also concludes that:

- Any regulatory or legislative actions undertaken to effect the foregoing prohibition on creating a child by somatic cell nuclear transfer should be carefully written so as not to interfere with other important areas of scientific research. In particular, no new regulations are required regarding the cloning of human DNA sequences and cell lines, since neither activity raises the scientific and ethical issues that arise from the attempt to create children through somatic cell nuclear transfer, and these fields of research have already provided important scientific and biomedical advances. Likewise, research on cloning animals by somatic cell nuclear transfer does not raise the issues implicated in attempting to use this technique for human cloning, and its continuation should only be subject to existing regulations regarding the humane use of animals and review by institution-based animal protection committees.

- If a legislative ban is not enacted, or if a legislative ban is ever lifted, clinical use of somatic cell nuclear transfer techniques to create a child should be preceded by research trials that are governed by the twin protections of independent review and informed consent, consistent with existing norms of human subjects protection.

- The United States Government should cooperate with other nations and international organizations to enforce any common aspects of their respective policies on the cloning of human beings.

IV. The Commission also concludes that different ethical and religious perspectives and traditions are divided on many of the important moral issues that surround any attempt to create a child using somatic cell nuclear transfer techniques. Therefore, we recommend that;

- The federal government, and all interested and concerned parties, encourage widespread and continuing deliberation on these issues in order to further our understanding of the ethical and social implications of this technology and to enable society to produce appropriate long-term policies regarding this technology should the time come when present concerns about safety have been addressed.

V. Finally, because scientific knowledge is essential for all citizens to participate in a full and informed fashion in the governance of our complex society, the Commission recommends that:

- Federal departments and agencies concerned with science should cooperate in seeking out and supporting opportunities to provide information and education to the public in the area of genetics, and on other developments in the biomedical sciences, especially where these affect important cultural practices, values, and beliefs.

References

Brock, Dan. "Cloning Human Beings: An Assessment," (1997), unpublished.

Feinberg, J. "The child's right to an open future," in *Whose Child? Children's Rights, Parental Authority, and State Power,* W. Aiken and H. LaFollette (eds.) (Totowa, NJ: Rowman & Littlefield, 1980).

Jonas, H. *Philosophical Essays: From Ancient Creed to Technological Man* (Englewood Cliffs, NJ: Prentice-Hall, 1974).

Kass, L. "Why We Should Ban the Cloning of Human Beings," Testimony presented to the National Bioethics Advisory Commission, March 13, 1997.

Kevles, D. J. *In the Name of Eugenics* (Cambridge, MA: Harvard University Press, 1995).

Macklin, R. "Why We Should Regulate—But Not Ban—the Cloning of Human Beings," Testimony presented to the National Bioethics Advisory Commission, March 14, 1997.

Meilaender, G. "Remarks on Human Cloning to the National Bioethics Advisory Commission," Testimony presented to the National Bioethics Advisory Commission, March 13, 1997.

Nussbaum, M. C. "Aristotelian social democracy," in *Liberalism and the Good* 203, R. Bruce Douglass, et al. (eds.), pp. 217–226, 1990.

Radin, M. "Reflections on Objectification," 65 *Southern California Law Review* 341 (November 1991).

Radin, M. "The Colin Ruagh Thomas O'Fallon Memorial Lecture on Personhood," 74 *Oregon Law Review* 423 (Summer 1995).

Robertson, J. A. "A Ban on Cloning and Cloning Research is Unjustified," Testimony Presented to the National Bioethics Advisory Commission, March 14, 1997.

Rothenberg, K. Testimony before the Senate Committee on Labor and Human Resources, March 12, 1997.

Schwartz, H. *The Culture of Copy* (New York: Zone Books, 1996).

Study Questions

1. Examine the arguments discussed by the NBAC against cloning humans. Which are the most compelling? Which are the weakest?
2. Do you agree with the NBAC assessment of public opinion, that virtually everyone agrees to a ban on cloning of humans at this time? How important is public opinion? What if it is simply misinformed and frightened of novel technological processes? What should be our attitude toward innovative technology?
3. Examine the conclusions set forth by the report. Did it fulfill its task in striking a balance "between the values we, as a society, wish to reflect and the freedom of the individual choice and any liberties we propose to limit"?
4. Consider the argument against human cloning based on unnecessary harm. How strong is it? The next two articles will take up this problem, so you might want to come back to the NBAC report on this point.

CHAPTER 39

The Confusion over Cloning

RICHARD LEWONTIN

Richard Lewontin is Alexander Agassiz professor of zoology and biology at Harvard University. He is the author of The Genetic Basis of Evolutionary Change *(1974). In this article, Lewontin argues that many of the arguments against human cloning are confused, since a clone is really no different than an identical twin removed in time from its mate. He criticizes the NBAC report, especially for its overemphasis on religious perspectives. Focusing more on the moral aspects would have resulted in a different report.*

THERE IS NOTHING like sex or violence for capturing the immediate attention of the state. Only a day after Franklin Roosevelt was told in October 1939 that both German and American scientists could probably make an atom bomb, a small group met at the President's direction to talk about the problem and within ten days a committee was undertaking a full-scale investigation of the possibility. Just a day after the public announcement on February 23, 1997, that a sheep, genetically identical to another sheep, had been produced by cloning, Bill Clinton formally requested that the National Bioethics Advisory Commission "undertake a thorough review of the legal and ethical issues associated with the use of this technology. . . ."

The President had announced his intention to create an advisory group on bioethics eighteen months before, on the day that he received the disturbing report of the cavalier way in which ionizing radiation had been administered experimentally to unsuspecting subjects.[1] The commission was finally formed, after a ten-month delay, with Harold Shapiro, President of Princeton, as chair and a membership consisting largely of academics from the fields of philosophy, medicine,

public health, and law, a representation from government and private foundations, and the chief business officer of a pharmaceutical company. In his letter to the commission the President referred to "serious ethical questions, particularly with respect to the possible use of this technology to clone human embryos" and asked for a report within ninety days. The commission missed its deadline by only two weeks.

In order not to allow a Democratic administration sole credit for grappling with the preeminent ethical issue of the day, the Senate held a day-long inquiry on March 12, a mere three weeks after the announcement of Dolly. Lacking a body responsible for any moral issues outside the hanky-panky of its own membership, the Senate assigned the work to the Subcommittee on Public Health and Safety of the Committee on Labor and Human Resources, perhaps on the grounds that cloning is a form of the production of human resources. The testimony before the subcommittee was concerned not with issues of the health and safety of labor but with the same ethical and moral concerns that preoccupied the bioethics commission. The witnesses representing the biotechnology industry were

---

especially careful to assure the senators that they would not dream of making whole babies and were interested in cloning solely as a laboratory method for producing cells and tissues that could be used in transplantation therapies.

It seems pretty obvious why, just after the Germans' instant success in Poland, Roosevelt was in a hurry. The problem, as he said to Alexander Sachs, who first informed him about the possibility of the Bomb, was to "see that the Nazis don't blow us up." The origin of Mr. Clinton's sense of urgency is not so clear. After all, it is not as if human genetic clones don't appear every day of the week, about thirty a day in the United States alone, given that there are about four million births a year with a frequency of identical twins of roughly 1 in 400.[2] So it cannot be the mere existence of doppelgänger that creates urgent problems (although I will argue that parents of twins are often guilty of a kind of psychic child abuse). And why ask the commission on bioethics rather than a technical committee of the National Institutes of Health or the National Research Council? Questions of individual autonomy and responsibility for one's own actions, of the degree to which the state ought to interpose itself in matters of personal decision, are all central to the struggle over smoking, yet the bioethics commission has not been asked to look into the bioethics of tobacco, a matter that would certainly be included in its original purpose.

The answer is that the possibility of human cloning has produced a nearly universal anxiety over the consequences of hubris. The testimony before the bioethics commission speaks over and over of the consequences of "playing God." We have no responsibility for the chance birth of genetically identical individuals, but their deliberate manufacture puts us in the Creation business, which, like extravagant sex, is both seductive and frightening. Even Jehovah botched the job despite the considerable knowledge of biology that He must have possessed, and we have suffered the catastrophic consequences ever

since. According to Haggadic legend, the Celestial Cloner put a great deal of thought into technique. In deciding on which of Adam's organs to use for Eve, He had the problem of finding tissue that was what the biologist calls "totipotent," that is, not already committed in development to a particular function. So He cloned Eve

> not from the head, lest she carry her head high in arrogant pride, not from the eye, lest she be wanton-eyed, not from the ear lest she be an eavesdropper, not from the neck lest she be insolent, not from the mouth lest she be a tattler, not from the heart lest she be inclined to envy, not from the hand lest she be a meddler, not from the foot lest she be a gadabout

but from the rib, a "chaste portion of the body." In spite of all the care and knowledge, something went wrong, and we have been earning a living by the sweat of our brows ever since. Even in the unbeliever, who has no fear of sacrilege, the myth of the uncontrollable power of creation has a resonance that gives us all pause. It is impossible to understand the incoherent and unpersuasive document produced by the National Bioethics Advisory Commission except as an attempt to rationalize a deep cultural prejudice, but it is also impossible to understand it without taking account of the pervasive error that confuses the genetic state of an organism with its total physical and psychic nature as a human being.

After an introductory chapter placing the issue of cloning in a general historical and social perspective, the commission begins with an exposition of the technical details of cloning and with speculations on the reproductive, medical, and commercial applications that are likely to be found for the technique. Some of these applications involve the clonal reproduction of genetically engineered laboratory animals for research or the wholesale propagation of commercially desirable livestock; but these raised no ethical issues for the commission, which, wisely, avoided questions of animal rights.

Specifically human ethical questions are raised by two possible applications of cloning. First, there are circumstances in which parents may want to use techniques of assisted reproduction to produce children with a known genetic makeup for reasons of sentiment or vanity or to serve practical ends. Second, there is the possibility of producing embryos of known genetic constitution whose cells and tissues will be useful for therapeutic purposes. Putting aside, for consideration in a separate chapter, religious claims that human cloning violates various scriptural and doctrinal prescriptions about the correct relation between God and man, men and women, husbands and wives, parents and children, or sex and reproduction, the commission then lists four ethical issues to be considered: individuality and autonomy, family integrity, treating children as objects, and safety.

The most striking confusion in the report is in the discussion of individuality and autonomy. Both the commission report and witnesses before the Senate subcommittee were at pains to point out that identical genes do not make identical people. The fallacy of genetic determinism is to suppose that the genes "make" the organism. It is a basic principle of developmental biology that organisms undergo a continuous development from conception to death, a development that is the unique consequence of the interaction of the genes in their cells, the temporal sequence of environments through which the organisms pass, and random cellular processes that determine the life, death, and transformations of cells. As a result, even the fingerprints of identical twins are not identical. Their temperaments, mental processes, abilities, life choices, disease histories, and deaths certainly differ despite the determined efforts of many parents to enforce as great a similarity as possible.

Frequently twins are given names with the same initial letter, dressed identically with identical hair arrangements, and given the same books, toys, and training. There are twin conventions at which prizes are offered for the most similar pairs. While identical genes do indeed contribute to a similarity between them, it is the pathological compulsion of their parents to create an inhuman identity between them that is most threatening to the individuality of genetically identical individuals.

But even the most extreme efforts to turn genetic clones into human clones fail. As a child I could not go to the movies or look at a picture magazine without being confronted by the genetically identical Dionne quintuplets, identically dressed and coiffed, on display in "Quintland" by Dr. Dafoe and the Province of Ontario for the amusement of tourists. This enforced homogenization continued through their adolescence, when they were returned to their parents' custody. Yet each of their unhappy adulthoods was unhappy in its own way, and they seemed no more alike in career or health than we might expect from five girls of the same age brought up in a rural working-class French Canadian family. Three married and had families. Two trained as nurses, two went to college. Three were attracted to a religious vocation, but only one made it a career. One died in a convent at age twenty, suffering from epilepsy, one at age thirty-six, and three remain alive at sixty-three. So much for the doppelgänger phenomenon. The notion of "cloning Einstein" is a biological absurdity.

The Bioethics Advisory Commission is well aware of the error of genetic determinism, and the report devotes several pages to a sensible and nuanced discussion of the difference between genetic and personal identity. Yet it continues to insist on the question of whether cloning violates an individual human being's "unique qualitative identity."

> And even if it is a mistake to believe such crude genetic determinism according to which one's genes determine one's fate, what is important for oneself is whether one *thinks* one's future is open and undetermined, and so still to be largely determined by one's own choices. [p. A8, emphasis added]

Moreover, the problem of self-perception may be worse for a person cloned from an adult than it is for identical twins, because the already fully formed and defined adult presents an irresistible persistent model for the developing child. Certainly for the general public the belief is widely expressed that a unique problem of identity is raised by cloning that is not already present for twins. The question posed by the commission, then, is not whether genetic identity per se destroys individuality, but whether the erroneous state of public understanding of biology will undermine an individual's own sense of uniqueness and autonomy.

Of course it will, but surely the commission has chosen the wrong target of concern. If the widespread genomania propagated by the press and by vulgarizers of science produces a false understanding of the dominance that genes have over our lives, then the appropriate response of the state is not to ban cloning but to engage in a serious educational campaign to correct the misunderstanding. It is not Dr. Wilmut and Dolly who are a threat to our sense of uniqueness and autonomy, but popularizers like Richard Dawkins who describes us as "gigantic lumbering robots" under the control of our genes that have "created us, body and mind."

Much of the motivation for cloning imagined by the commission rests on the same mistaken synecdoche that substitutes "gene" for "person." In one scenario a self-infatuated parent wants to reproduce his perfection or a single woman wants to exclude any other contribution to her offspring. In another, morally more appealing, story a family suffers an accident that kills the father and leaves an only child on the point of death. The mother wishing to have a child who is the biological offspring of her dead husband, uses cells from the dying infant to clone a baby. Or what about the sterile man whose entire family has been exterminated in Auschwitz and who wishes to prevent the extinction of his genetic patrimony?

Creating variants of these scenarios is a philosopher's parlor game. All such stories appeal to the same impetus that drives adopted children to search for their "real," i.e., biological, parents in order to discover their own "real" identity. They are modern continuations of an earlier preoccupation with blood as the carrier of an individual's essence and as the mark of legitimacy. It is not the possibility of producing a human being with a copy of someone else's genes that has created the difficulty or that adds a unique element to it. It is the fetishism of "blood" which, once accepted, generates an immense array of apparent moral and ethical problems. Were it not for the belief in blood as essence, much of the motivation for the cloning of humans would disappear.

The cultural pressure to preserve a biological continuity as the form of immortality and family identity is certainly not a human universal. For the Romans, as for the Japanese, the preservation of family interest was the preeminent value, and adoption was a satisfactory substitute for reproduction. Indeed, in Rome the foster child (*alumnus*) was the object of special affection by virtue of having been adopted, i.e., acquired by an act of choice.

The second ethical problem cited by the commission, family integrity, is neither unique to cloning nor does it appear in its most extreme form under those circumstances. The contradictory meanings of "parenthood" were already made manifest by adoption and the old-fashioned form of reproductive technology, artificial insemination from anonymous semen donors. Newer technology like in vitro fertilization and implantation of embryos into surrogate mothers has already raised issues to which the possibility of cloning adds nothing. A witness before the Senate subcommittee suggested that the "replication of a human by cloning would radically alter the definition of a human being by producing the world's first human with a single genetic parent."[3] Putting aside the possible priority of the case documented in Matthew 1:23, there is a confusion here. A child by cloning has a full double set of chromosomes like anyone else, half of which were derived from a mother and half from a father. It happens that these chromosomes were passed through another individual, the cloning donor, on their way to the child. That donor is certainly not the child's "parent" in any biological sense, but simply an earlier offspring of the original parents. Of course this sibling may *claim* parenthood over its delayed twin, but it is not obvious what juridical or ethical principle would impel a court or anyone else to recognize that claim.

There is one circumstance, considered by the commission, in which cloning is a biologically realistic solution to a human agony. Suppose that a child, dying of leukemia, could be saved by a bone marrow replacement. Such transplants are always risky because of immune incompatibilities between the recipient and the donor, and these incompatibilities are a direct consequence of genetic differences. The solution that presents itself is to use bone marrow from a second, genetically, identical, child who has been produced by cloning from the first.[4] The risk to a bone marrow donor is not great, but suppose it were a kidney that was needed. There is, moreover, the possibility that the fetus itself is to be sacrificed in order to provide tissue for therapeutic purposes. This scenario presents in its starkest form the third ethical issue of concern to the commission, the objectification of human beings. In the words of the commission:

> To objectify a person is to act towards the person without regard for his or her own desires or well-being, as a thing to be valued according to externally imposed standards, and to control the person rather than to engage her or him in a mutually respectful relationship.

We would all agree that it is morally repugnant to use human beings as mere instruments of our deliberate ends. Or would we? That's what I do when I call in the plumber. The very words "employment" and "employee" are descriptions of an objectified relationship in which human beings are "thing(s) to be valued according to

externally imposed standards." None of us escapes the objectification of humans that arises in economic life. Why has no National Commission on Ethics been called into emergency action to discuss the conceptualization of human beings as "factory hands" or "human capital" or "operatives"? The report of the Bioethics Advisory Commission fails to explain how cloning would significantly increase the already immense number of children whose conception and upbringing were intended to make them instruments of their parents' frustrated ambitions, psychic fantasies, desires for immortality, or property calculations.

Nor is there a simple relation between those motivations and the resulting family relations. I myself was conceived out of my father's desire for a male heir, and my mother, not much interested in maternity, was greatly relieved when her first and only child filled the bill. Yet, in retrospect, I am glad they were my parents. To pronounce a ban on human cloning because sometimes it will be used for instrumental purposes misses both the complexity of human motivation and the unpredictability of developing personal relationships. Moreover, cloning does not stand out from other forms of reproductive technology in the degree to which it is an instrument of parental fulfillment. The problem of objectification permeates social relations. By loading all the weight of that sin on the head of one cloned lamb, we neatly avoid considering our own more general responsibility.

The serious ethical problems raised by the prospect of human cloning lie in the fourth domain considered by the bioethics commission, that of safety. Apparently, these problems arise because cloned embryos may not have a proper set of chromosomes. Normally a sexually reproduced organism contains in all its cells two sets of chromosomes, one received from its mother through the egg and one from the father through the sperm. Each of these sets contains a complete set of the different kinds of genes necessary for normal development and adult function. Even though each set has a complete repertoire of genes, for reasons that are not well understood we must have two sets and only two sets to complete normal development. If one of the chromosomes should accidentally be present in only one copy or in three, development will be severely impaired.

Usually we have exactly two copies in our cells because in the formation of the egg and sperm that combined to produce us, a special form of cell division occurs that puts one and only one copy of each chromosome into each egg and each sperm. Occasionally, however, especially in people in their later reproductive years, this mechanism is faulty and a sperm or egg is produced in which one or another chromosome is absent or present more than once. An embryo conceived from such a faulty gamete will have a missing or extra chromosome. Down's syndrome, for example, results from an extra Chromosome 21, and Edward's syndrome, almost always lethal in the first few weeks of life, is produced by an extra Chromosome 18.

After an egg is fertilized in the usual course of events by a sperm, cell division begins to produce an embryo, and the chromosomes, which were in a resting state in the original sperm and egg, are induced to replicate new copies by signals from the complex machinery of cell division. The division of the cells and the replication of more chromosome copies are in perfect synchrony so every new cell gets a complete exact set of chromosomes just like the fertilized egg. When clonal reproduction is performed, however, the events are quite different. The nucleus containing the egg's chromosomes are removed and the egg cell is fused with a cell containing a nucleus from the donor that already contains a full duplicate set of chromosomes. These chromosomes are not necessarily in the resting state and so they may divide out of synchrony with the embryonic cells. The result will be extra and missing chromosomes so that the embryo will be abnormal and will usually, but not necessarily, die.

The whole trick of successful cloning is to make sure that the chromosomes of the donor are in the right state. However, no one knows how to make sure. Dr. Wilmut and his colleagues know the trick in principle, but they produced only one successful Dolly out of 277 tries. The other 276 embryos died at various stages of development. It seems pretty obvious that the reason the Scottish laboratory did not announce the existence of Dolly until she was a full-grown adult sheep is that they were worried that her postnatal development would go awry. Of course, the technique will get better, but people are not sheep and there is no way to make cloning work reliably in people except to experiment on people. Sheep were chosen by the Scottish group because they had turned out in earlier work to be unusually favorable animals for growing fetuses cloned from embryonic cells. Cows had been tried but without success. Even if the methods could be made eventually to work as well in humans as in sheep, how many human embryos are to be sacrificed, and at what stage of their development?[5] Ninety percent of the loss of the experimental sheep embryos was at the so-called "morula" stage, hardly more than a ball of cells. Of the twenty-nine embryos implanted in maternal uteruses, only one showed up as a fetus after fifty days in utero, and that lamb was finally born as Dolly.

Suppose we have a high success rate of bringing cloned human embryos to term. What kinds of developmental abnormalities would be acceptable? Acceptable to whom? Once again, the moral problems said to be raised by cloning are not unique to that technology. Every form of reproductive technology raises issues of lives worth living, of the stage at which an embryo is thought of as human, as having rights including the juridical right to state protection. Even that most benign and widespread prenatal intervention, amniocentesis, has a non-negligible risk of damaging the fetus. By concentrating on the acceptability of cloning, the commission again tried to finesse the much wider issues.

They may have done so, however, at the peril of legitimating questions about abortion and reproductive technology that the state has tried to avoid, questions raised from a religious standpoint. Despite the secular basis of the American polity, religious forces have over and over played an important role in influencing state policy. Churches and religious institutions were leading actors in the abolitionist movement and the Underground Railroad,[6] the modern civil rights movement and the resistance to the war in Vietnam. In these instances religious forces were part of, and in the case of the civil rights movement leaders of, wider social movements intervening on the side of the oppressed against then-reigning state policy They were both liberatory and representative of a widespread sentiment that did not ultimately depend upon religious claims.

The present movements of religious forces to intervene in issues of sex, family structure, reproductive behavior, and abortion are of a different character. They are perceived by many people, both secular and religious, not as liberatory but as restrictive, not as intervening on the side of the wretched of the earth but as themselves oppressive of the widespread desire for individual autonomy. They seem to threaten the stable accommodation between Church and State that has characterized American social history. The structure of the commission's report reflects this current tension in the formation of public policy. There are two separate chapters on the moral debate, one labelled "Ethical Considerations" and the other "Religious Perspectives." By giving a separate and identifiable voice to explicitly religious views the commission has legitimated religious conviction as a front on which the issues of sex, reproduction, the definition of the family, and the status of fertilized eggs and fetuses are to be fought.

The distinction made by the commission between "religious *perspectives*" and "ethical *considerations*" is precisely the distinction between theological hermeneutics—interpretation of sacred texts—and philosophical inquiry. The religious problem is to recognize God's truth. If a natural family were defined as one man, one woman, and such children as they have produced through loving procreation; if a human life, imbued by God with a soul, is definitively initiated at conception; if sex, love, and the begetting of children are by revelation morally inseparable; then the work of bioethics commissions becomes a great deal easier. Of course, the theologians who testified were not in agreement with each other on the relevant matters, in part because they depend on different sources of revelation and in part because the meaning of those sources is not unambiguous. So some theologians, including Roman Catholics, took human beings to be "stewards" of a fixed creation, gardeners tending what has already been planted. Others, notably Jewish and Islamic scholars, emphasized a "partnership" with God that includes improving on creation. One Islamic authority thought that there was a positive imperative to intervene in the works of nature, including early embryonic development, for the sake of health.

Some Protestant commentators saw humans as "co-creators" with God and so certainly not barred from improving on present nature. In the end, some religious scholars thought cloning was definitively to be prohibited, while others thought it could be justified under some circumstances. As far as one can tell, fundamentalist Protestants were not consulted, an omission that rather weakens the usefulness of the proceedings for setting public policy. The failure to engage directly the politically most active and powerful American religious constituency, while soliciting opinions from a much safer group of "religious scholars," can only be understood as a tactic of defense of an avowedly secular state against pressure for a yet greater role for religion. Perhaps the commission was already certain of what Pat Robertson would say.

The immense strength of a religious viewpoint is that it is capable of abolishing hard ethical problems if only we can correctly decipher the meaning of what has been revealed to us.[7] It is a question of having the correct "perspective." Philosophical "considerations" are quite another matter. The painful tensions and contradictions that seem to the secular moral philosopher to be unresolvable in principle, but that demand de facto resolution in public and private action, did not appear in the testimony of any of the theologians. While they disagreed with one another, they did not have to cope with internal contradictions in their own positions. That, of course, is a great attraction of the religious perspective. It is not only poetry that tempts us to a willing suspension of disbelief.

Notes

1. Report of the specially created Advisory Committee on Human Radiation Experiments (October 3, 1995).

2. In fact, identical twins are genetically *more* identical than a cloned organism is to its donor. All the biologically inherited information is not carried in the genes of a cell's nucleus. A very small number of genes, sixty out of a total of 100,000 or so, are carried by intracellular bodies, the mitochondria. These mitochondrial genes specify certain essential enzyme proteins, and defects in these genes can lead to a variety of disorders. The importance of this point for cloning is that the egg cell that has had its nucleus removed to make way for the genes of the donor cell has not had its mitochondria removed. The results of the cell fusion that will give rise to the cloned embryo is then a mixture of mitochondrial genes from the donor and the recipient. Thus, it is not, strictly speaking, a perfect genetic clone of the donor organism. Identical twins, however, *are* the result of the splitting of a fertilized egg arid have the same mitochondria as well as the same nucleus.

3. G. J. Annas, "Scientific discoveries and cloning: Challenges for public policy," testimony of March 12, 1997.

4. There is always the possibility, of course, that gene mutations have predisposed the child to leukemia, in which case the transplant from a genetic clone only propagates the defect.

5. It has recently been announced that success in cloning in cows is almost at hand, but by an indirect method that, if applied in humans, raises the following ethical problem. The method involves cloning embryos from adult cells, but then breaking up the embryos to use their cells for a second round of cloning. No cloned calf was yet born as of August 1, but ten are well established *en ventre leurs mères*. Even if they all reach an unimpaired adulthood, they will owe their lives to many destroyed embryos.

6. An example was the resistance to the Fugitive Slave Acts by the pious Presbyterians of Oberlin, Ohio, an excellent account of which may be found in Nat Brandt, *The Town that Started the Civil War* (Syracuse University Press, 1990).

7. Once, impelled by a love of contradiction, I asked a friend learned in the Talmud whether meat from a cow into which a single pig gene had been genetically engineered would be kosher. His reply was that the problem would not arise for the laws of *kashruth* because to make any mixed animal was already a prohibited thing.

Study Questions

1. What is the significance of Lewontin's comparison between President Roosevelt's decision to form a commission on the possibility of constructing an atomic bomb and President Clinton's decision to form a commission to look into the matter of human cloning? We can understand the dangers of the first type of technology, but what are the reasons for alarm over the second type?

2. What does Lewontin think is the "most striking confusion in the [NBAC] report," and why does he think it is a confusion? Is he correct?

3. How does Lewontin deal with the charge that "replication of a human by cloning would radically alter the definition of a human being by producing the world's first human with a single genetic parent"?

4. One concern of the NBAC report is that cloning would involve treating humans as means, not ends in themselves. How does Lewontin respond to this charge? Evaluate the difference.

CHAPTER 40

Will Cloning Harm People?

GREGORY E. PENCE

Gregory E. Pence is a medical ethicist and professor of philosophy at the University of Alabama, Birmingham. He is the author of several works in medical ethics, including *Who's Afraid of Human Cloning?* (1998). In this essay he responds to the report of the National Bioethics Advisory Board (Chapter 38), which called for a three- to five-year moratorium on research dealing with human cloning on the basis that it could have harmful effects on people. Pence argues that the board's recommendation is wrong and that their arguments can be answered.

THE MOST IMPORTANT MORAL objection to originating a human by cloning is the claim that the resulting person may be unnecessarily harmed, either by something in the process of cloning or by the unique expectations placed upon the resulting child. This essay considers this kind of objection.

By now the word "cloning" has so many bad associations from science fiction and political demagoguery that there is no longer any good reason to continue to use it. A more neutral phrase, meaning the same thing, is "somatic cell nuclear transfer" (SCNT), which refers to the process by which the genotype of an adult, differentiated cell can be used to create a new human embryo by transferring its nucleus to an enucleated human egg. The resulting embryo can then be gestated to create a baby who will be a delayed twin of its genetic ancestor.

For purposes of clarity and focus, I will only discuss the simple case where a couple wants to originate a single child by SCNT and not the cases of multiple origination of the same genotype. I will also not discuss questions of who would regulate reproduction of genotypes and processes of getting consent to reproduce genotypes.

Parallels with In Vitro Fertilization: Repeating History?

Any time a new method of human reproduction may occur, critics try to prevent it by citing possible harm to children. The implicit premise: before it is allowed, any new method must prove that only healthy children will be created. Without such proof, the new method amounts to "unconsented to" experimentation on the unborn. So argued the late conservative, Christian bioethicist Paul Ramsey in the early 1970s about in vitro fertilization (IVF).[1]

Of course, ordinary sexual reproduction does not guarantee healthy children every time. Nor can a person consent until he is born. Nor can he really consent until he is old enough to understand consent. The requirement of "consent to be born" is silly.

Reprinted from Gregory E. Pence, Flesh of My Flesh: The Ethics of Cloning Humans *(Lanham, Md.: Rowman & Littlefield, 1998), by permission.*

Jeremy Rifkin, another critic of IVF in the early 1970s, seemed to demand that new forms of human reproduction be risk-free.[2] Twenty years later, Rifkin predictably bolted out the gate to condemn human cloning, demanding its world-wide ban, with penalties for transgressions as severe as those for rape and murder: "It's a horrendous crime to make a Xerox of someone," he declared ominously. "You're putting a human into a genetic straitjacket. For the first time, we've taken the principles of industrial design—quality control, predictability—and applied them to a human being."[3]

Daniel Callahan, a philosopher who had worked in the Catholic tradition and who founded the Hastings Center for research in medical ethics, argued in 1978 that the first case of IVF was "probably unethical" because there was no possible guarantee that Louise Brown would be normal.[4] Callahan added that many medical breakthroughs are unethical because we cannot know (using the philosopher's strong sense of "know") that the first patient will not be harmed. Two decades later, he implied that human cloning would also be unethical: "We live in a culture that likes science and technology very much. If someone wants something, and the rest of us can't prove they are going to do devastating harm, they are going to do it."[5]

Leon Kass, a social conservative and biologist-turned-bioethicist, argued strenuously in 1971 that babies created by artificial fertilization might be deformed: "It doesn't matter how many times the baby is tested while in the mother's womb," he averred, "they will never be certain the baby won't be born without defect."[6]

What these critics overlooked is that no reasonable approach to life avoids all risks. Nothing in life is risk-free, including having children. Even if babies are born healthy, they do not always turn out as hoped. Taking such chances is part of becoming a parent.

Without some risk, there is no progress, no advance. Without risk, pioneers don't cross prairies, astronauts don't walk on the moon, and Freedom Riders don't take buses to integrate the South. The past critics of assisted reproduction demonstrated a psychologically normal but nevertheless unreasonable tendency to magnify the risk of a harmful but unlikely result. Such a result—even if very bad—still represents a very small risk. A baby born with a lethal genetic disease is an extremely bad but unlikely result; nevertheless, the risk shouldn't deter people from having children.

Humanity Will Not Be Harmed

Human SCNT is even more new and strange-sounding than in vitro fertilization (IVF). All that means is that it will take longer to get used to. Scaremongers have predicted terrible harm if children are born by SCNT, but in fact very little will change. Why is that?

First, to create a child by SCNT, a couple must use IVF, which is an expensive process, costing about $8,000 per attempt. Most American states do not require insurance companies to cover IVF, so IVF is mostly a cash-and-carry operation. Second, most IVF attempts are unsuccessful. The chances of any couple taking home a baby is quite low—only about 15%.

Only about 40,000 IVF babies have been born in America since the early 1980s. Suppose 50,000 such babies are born over the next decade. How many of these couples would want to originate a child by SCNT? Very few—at most, perhaps, a few hundred.

These figures are important because they tamp down many fears. As things now stand, originating humans by SCNT will never be common. Neither evolution nor old-fashioned human sex is in any way threatened. Nor is the family or human society. Most fears about human cloning stem from ignorance.

Similar fears linking cloning to dictatorship or the subjugation of women are equally ignorant. There are no artificial wombs (predictions, yes;

realities, no—otherwise we could save premature babies born before 20 weeks). A healthy woman must agree to gestate any SCNT baby and such a woman will retain her right to abort. Women's rights to abortion are checks on evil uses of any new reproductive technology.

New Things Make Us Fear Harms Irrationally

SCNT isn't really so new or different. Consider some cases on a continuum. In the first, the human embryo naturally splits in the process of twinning and produces two genetically-identical twins. Mothers have been conceiving and gestating human twins for all of human history. Call the children who result from this process Rebecca and Susan.

In the second case a technique is used where a human embryo is deliberately twinned in order to create more embryos for implantation in a woman who has been infertile with her mate. Instead of a random quirk in the uterus, now a physician and an infertile couple use a tiny electric current to split the embryo. Two identical embryos are created. All embryos are implanted and, as sometimes happens, rather than no embryo implanting successfully or only one, both embryos implant. Again, Rebecca and Susan are born.

In the third case, one of the twinned embryos is frozen (Susan) along with other embryos from the couple and the other embryo is implanted. In this case, although several embryos were implanted, only the one destined to be Rebecca is successful. Again, Rebecca is born.

Two years pass, and the couple desires another child. Some of their frozen embryos are thawed and implanted in the mother. The couple knows that one of the implanted embryos is the twin of Rebecca. In this second round of reproductive assistance, the embryo destined to be Susan successfully implants and a

twin is born. Now Susan and Rebecca exist as twins, but born two years apart. Susan is the delayed twin of Rebecca. (Rumors abound that such births have already occurred in American infertility clinics.)

Suppose now that the "embryo that could become Susan" was twinned, and the "non-Susan" embryo is frozen. The rest of the details are then the same as the last scenario, but now two more years pass and the previously-frozen embryo is now implanted, gestated, and born. Susan and Rebecca now have another identical sister, Samantha. They would be identical triplets, born two and four years apart. In contrast to SCNT, where the mother's contribution of mitochondrial genes introduces small variations in nearly-identical genotypes, these embryos would have identical genomes.

Next, suppose that the embryo that could have been Rebecca miscarried and never became a child. The twinned embryo that could become Susan still exists. So the parents implant this embryo and Susan is born. Query to National Bioethics Advisory Commission: have the parents done something illegal? A child has been born who was originated by reproducing an embryo with a unique genotype. Remember, the embryo-that-could-become Rebecca existed first. So Susan only exists as a "clone" of the non-existent Rebecca.

Now, as bioethicist Leroy Walters emphasizes, let us consider an even thornier but more probable scenario.[7] Suppose we took the embryo-that-could-become Susan and transferred its nucleus to an enucleated egg of Susan's mother. Call the person who will emerge from this embryo "Suzette," because she is like Susan but different, because of her new mitochondrial DNA. Although the "Susan" embryo was created sexually, Suzette's origins are through somatic cell nuclear transfer. It is not clear that this process is illegal. The NBAC *Report* avoids taking a stand on this kind of case.[8]

Now compare all the above cases to originating Susan asexually by SCNT from the genotype of the adult Rebecca. Susan would again have a nearly-identical genome with Rebecca (identical except for mitochondrial DNA contributed by the gestating woman). Here we have nearly identical female gonotypes, separated in time, created by choice. But how is this so different from choosing to have a delayed twin-child? Originating a child by SCNT is not a break-through in kind but a matter of degree along a continuum involving twins and a special kind of reproductive choice.

Comparing the Harms of Human Reproduction

The question of multiple copies of one genome and its special issues of harm are ones that will not be discussed in this essay, but one asymmetry in our moral intuitions should be noticed.

The increasing use of fertility drugs has expanded many times the number of humans born who are twins, triplets, quadruplets, quintuplets, sextuplets, and even (in November of 1997 to the McCaugheys of Iowa) septuplets. If an entire country can rejoice about seven humans who are gestated in the same womb, raised by the same parents, and simultaneously created randomly from the same two sets of chromosomes, why should the same country fear deliberately originating copies of the same genome, either at once or over time? Our intuitions are even more skewed when we rejoice in the statistically-unlikely case of the seven healthy McCaughey children and ignore the far more likely cases where several of the multiply-gestated fetuses are disabled or dead.

People exaggerate the fears of the unknown and downplay the very real dangers of the familiar. In a very important sense, driving a car each day is far more dangerous to children than the new form of human reproduction under discussion here. Many, many people are hurt and killed every day in automobile wrecks, yet few people consider not driving.

In SCNT, there are possible dangers of telomere shortening, inheritance of environmental effects on adult cells passed to embryonic cells, and possible unknown dangers. Mammalian animal studies must determine if such dangers will occur in human SCNT origination. Once such studies prove that there are no special dangers of SCNT, the crucial question will arise: how safe must we expect human SCNT to be before we allow it?

In answering this question, it is very important to ask about the baseline of comparison. How safe is ordinary, human sexual reproduction? How safe is assisted reproduction? Who or what counts as a subject of a safety calculation about SCNT?

At least 40% of human embryos fail to implant in normal sexual reproduction.[9] Although this fact is not widely known, it is important because some discussions tend to assume that every human embryo becomes a human baby unless some extraordinary event occurs such as abortion. But this is not true. Nature seems to have a genetic filter, such that malformed embryos do not implant. About 50% of the rejected embryos are chromosomally abnormal, meaning that if they were somehow brought to term, the resulting children would be mutants or suffer genetic dysfunction.

A widely-reported but misleading aspect of Ian Wilmut's work was that it took 277 embryos to produce one live lamb. In fact, Wilmut started with 277 eggs, fused nuclei with them to create embryos, and then allowed them to become the best 29 embryos, which were allowed to gestate further. He had three lambs almost live, with one true success, Dolly. Subsequent work may easily bring the efficiency rate to 25%. When the calves "Charlie" and "George" were born in 1998, four live-born calves were created from an initial batch of only 50 embryos.[10]

Wilmut's embryo-to-birth ratio only seems inefficient or unsafe because the real inefficiency fate of accepted forms of human assisted reproduction is so little known. In in vitro fertilization, a woman is given drugs to stimulate superovulation so that physicians can remove as many eggs as possible. At each cycle of attempted in vitro fertilization, three or four embryos are implanted. Most couples make several attempts, so as many as nine to twelve embryos are involved for each couple. As noted, only about 15–20% of couples undergoing such attempts ever take home a baby.

Consider what these numbers mean when writ large. Take a hundred couples attempting assisted reproduction, each undergoing (on average) three attempts. Suppose there are unusually good results and that 20% of these couples eventually take home a baby. Because more than one embryo may implant, assume that among these 20 couples, half have non-identical twins. But what is the efficiency rate here? Assuming a low number of three embryos implanted each time for the 300 attempts, it will take 900 embryos to produce 30 babies, for an efficiency rate of 1 in 30.

Nor is it true that all the loss of human potential occurred at the embryonic stage. Unfortunately, some of these pregnancies will end in miscarriages of fetuses, some well along in the second trimester.

Nevertheless, such loss of embryos and fetuses is almost universally accepted as morally permissible. Why is that? Because the infertile parents are trying to conceive their own children, because everyone thinks that is a good motive, and because few people object to the loss of embryos and fetuses *in this context of trying to conceive babies*. Seen in this light, what Wilmut did, starting out with a large number of embryos to get one successful lamb at birth, is not so novel or different from what now occurs in human assisted reproduction.

Subjects and Non-Subjects of Harm

One premise that seems to figure in discussions of the safety of SCNT and other forms of as-

sisted reproduction is that loss of human embryos morally matters. That premise should be rejected.

As the above discussion shows, loss of human embryos is a normal part of human conception and, without this process, humanity might suffer much more genetic disease. This process essentially involves the loss of human embryos as part of the natural state of things. Indeed, some researchers believe that for every human baby successfully born, there has been at least one human embryo lost along the way.

In vitro fertilization is widely-accepted as a great success in modern medicine. As said, over 40,000 American babies have been born this way. But calculations indicate that as many as a million human embryos may have been used in creating such successes.

Researchers often create embryos for subsequent cycles of implantation, only to learn that a pregnancy has been achieved and that such stored embryos are no longer needed. Thousands of such embryos can be stored indefinitely in liquid nitrogen. No one feels any great urgency about them and, indeed, many couples decline to pay fees to preserve their embryos.

The above considerations point to the obvious philosophical point that embryos are not persons with rights to life. Like an acorn, their value is all potential, little actual. Faced with a choice between paying a thousand dollars to keep two thousand embryos alive for a year in storage, or paying for an operation to keep a family pet alive for another year, no one will choose to pay for the embryos. How people actually act says much about their real values.

Thus an embryo cannot be harmed by being brought into existence and then being taken out of existence. An embryo is generally considered such until nine weeks after conception, when it is called a "fetus" (when it is born, it is called a "baby"). Embryos are not sentient and cannot experience pain. They are thus not the kind of subjects that can be harmed or benefitted.

As such, whether it takes one embryo to create a human baby or a hundred does not matter morally. It may matter aesthetically, financially, emotionally, or in time spent trying to reproduce, but it does not matter morally. As such, new forms of human reproduction such as IVF and SCNT that involve significant loss of embryos cannot be morally criticized on this charge.

Finally, because embryos don't count morally, they could be tested in various ways to eliminate defects in development or genetic mishaps. Certainly, if four or five SCNT embryos were implanted, only the healthiest one should be brought to term. As such, the risk of abnormal SCNT babies could be minimized.

Setting the Standard about the Risk of Harm

Animal tests have not yet shown that SCNT is safe enough to try in humans, and extensive animal testing should be done over the next few years. That means that, before we attempt SCNT in humans, we will need to be able to routinely produce healthy offspring by SCNT in lambs, cattle, and especially non-human primates. After this testing is done, the time will come when a crucial question must be answered: how safe must human SCNT be before it is allowed? This is probably the most important, practical question before us now.

Should we have a very high standard, such that we take virtually no risk with a SCNT child? Daniel Callahan and Paul Ramsey, past critics of IVF, implied that unless a healthy baby could be guaranteed the first time, it was unethical to try to produce babies in a new way. At the other extreme, a low standard would allow great risks.

What is the appropriate standard? How high should be the bar over which scientists must be made to jump before they are allowed to try to originate a SCNT child? In my opinion, the standard of Callahan and Ramsey is too high. In reality, only God can meet that Olympian standard. It is also too high for those physicians trying to help infertile couples. If this high standard had been imposed on these people in the past, no form of assisted reproduction—including in vitro fertilization—would ever have been allowed.

On the other end of the scale, one could look at the very worst conditions for human gestation, where mothers are drug-dependent during pregnancy or exposed to dangerous chemicals. Such worst-case conditions include parents with a 50% chance of passing on a lethal genetic disease. The lowest standard of harm allows human reproduction even if there is such a high risk of harm ("harm" in the sense that the child would likely have a sub-normal future). One could argue that since society allows such mothers and couples to reproduce sexually, it could do no worse by allowing a child to be originated by SCNT.

I believe that the low standard is inappropriate to use with human SCNT. There is no reason to justify down to the very worst conditions under which society now tolerates humans being born. If the best we can do by SCNT is to produce children as good as those born with fetal-maternal alcohol syndrome, we shouldn't originate children this way.

Between these standards, there is the normal range of risk that is accepted by ordinary people in sexual reproduction. Human SCNT should be allowed when the predicted risk from animal studies falls within this range. "Ordinary people" refers to those who are neither alcoholic nor dependent on an illegal drug and where neither member of the couple knowingly passes on a high risk for a serious genetic disease.

This standard seems reasonable. It does not require a guarantee of a perfect baby, but it also rejects the "anything goes" view. For example, if the rate of serious deformities in normal human reproduction is 1%, and if the rate of chimpanzee SCNT reproduction were brought down to this rate, and if there were no reason to think that SCNT in human primates would be any higher, it should be permissible to attempt human SCNT.

We Already Allow More Dangerous Forms of Familiar Things

Consider the case of an infertility researcher trying to increase the chances of older women successfully giving birth by using eggs of younger women. The practice of using an egg of a younger woman increases the chances of a 44-year-old woman giving birth from the 3.5% chance of IVF to 50%.[11] The problem with this practice is that the gestating older woman does not have a genetic connection to the resulting child.

But there is a new, possible way to solve this problem. Researcher James Grifo, chief of New York University's infertility clinic, proposes to enucleate an egg of a younger woman and insert the sexually-mixed chromosomes into it from an embryo of an older couple.[12] The older woman will gestate the new SCNT-created embryo, an embryo that may successfully implant because it has the outer cytoplasm and mitochondria of a younger woman's egg. Creating an embryo by such a SCNT process is not "cloning," not asexual reproduction, because the chromosomes randomly mixed when sperm met egg. Nevertheless, the process of creating a human embryo (created sexually) by SCNT here is obviously very close to the process of creating a human embryo by *asexual* SCNT.

This new, nucleus-transferring procedure is controversial but permitted under existing law. It undoubtedly is experimental and risks possible harm to any resulting child, but because this procedure does not have the emotional associations of "cloning," it will probably pass unnoticed in the general world. This is exactly what happened with intracytoplasmic sperm injection—where only one sperm is used to fertilize an egg—despite its unknown safety record when first attempted.[13] Such new procedures, and the possible harm of doing them, are very close to those of SCNT. We say the sky will fall if we try SCNT while we ignore the fact that very similar risks are being taken all around us.

Finally, we are already doing things far more radical than human SCNT. Putting human genes in pigs to create possible organ transplants from such altered pigs is far more radical than human SCNT. Transplants from such pig organs open up the possibility of a two-way travel of porcine viruses to humans and vice-versa (of concern to those who think that AIDS came from simian–human contact). In 1987, we allowed Harvard University to patent its oncomouse (aka the "Harvard oncomouse"). Since then over a thousand applications for such patents have been filed and over 50 patents on genetically-altered or genetically-created animals have been issued by the U.S. Patent Office.[14] Overall, from genetically-altered tomatoes to pig-grown livers for transplanting into humans, we are doing radically new things to save human lives, crossing natural barriers all the time, and hardly blinking an eye about it. Why, then, are we so concerned about SCNT?

Psychological Harm to the Child

Another concern is about psychological harm to a child originated by SCNT. According to this objection, choosing to have a child is not like choosing a car or house. It is a moral decision because another being is affected. Having a child should be a careful, responsible choice and focused on what's best for the child. Having a child originated by SCNT is not morally permissible because it is not best for the child.

The problem with this argument is the last six words of the last sentence, which assumes bad motives on the part of parents. Unfortunately, SCNT is associated with bad motives in science fiction, but until we have evidence that it will be used this way, why assume the worst about people?

Certainly, if someone deliberately brought a child into the world with the intention of causing him harm, that would be immoral. Unfortunately, the concept of harm is a continuum and some people have very high standards, such that not providing a child a stay-at-home parent constitutes harming the child. But there is nothing about SCNT per se that is necessarily linked to bad motives. True, people would have certain expectations of a child created by SCNT, but parents-to-be already have certain expectations about children.

Too many parents are fatalistic and just accept whatever life throws at them. The very fact of being a parent for many people is something they must accept (because abortion was not a real option). Part of this acceptance is to just accept whatever genetic combination comes at birth from the random assortment of genes.

But why is such acceptance a good thing? It is a defeatist attitude in medicine against disease; it is a defeatist attitude toward survival when one's culture or country is under attack; and it is a defeatist attitude toward life in general. "The expectations of parents will be too high!" critics repeat. "Better to leave parents in ignorance and to leave their children as randomness decrees." The silliness of that view is apparent as soon as it is made explicit.

If we are thinking about harm to the child, an objection that comes up repeatedly might be called the argument for an open future. "In the case of cloning," it is objected, "the expectations are very specifically tied to the life of another person. So in a sense, the child's future is denied to him because he will be expected to be like his ancestor. But part of the wonder of having children is surprise at how they turn out. As such, some indeterminacy should remain a part of childhood. Human SCNT deprives a person of an open future because when we know how his previous twin lived, we will know how the new child will live."

It is true that the adults choosing this genotype rather than that one must have some expectations. There has to be some reason for choosing one genotype over another. But these expectations are only half based in fact. As we know, no person originated by SCNT will be identical to his ancestor because of mitochondrial DNA, because of his different gestation, because of his different parents, because of his different time in history, and perhaps, because of his different country and culture. Several famous pairs of conjoined twins, such as Eng and Chang, with both identical genotypes and identical uterine/childhood environments, have still had different personalities.[15] To assume that a SCNT child's future is not open is to assume genetic reductionism.

Moreover, insofar as parents have specific expectations about children created by SCNT, such expectations will likely be no better or worse than the normal expectations by parents of children created sexually. As said, there is nothing about SCNT per se that necessitates bad motives on the part of parents.

Notice that most of the expected harm to the child stems *from the predicted, prejudicial attitudes of other people to the SCNT child*. ("Would you want to be a cloned child? Can you imagine being called a freak and having only one genetic parent?") As such, it is important to remember that social expectations are *merely* social expectations. They are malleable and can change quickly. True, parents might initially have expectations that are too high and other people might regard such children with prejudice. But just as such inappropriate attitudes faded after the first cases of in vitro fertilization, they will fade here too.

Ron James, the Scottish millionaire who funded much of Ian Wilmut's research, points out that social attitudes change fast. Before the announcement of Dolly, polls showed that people thought that cloning animals and gene transfer to animals were "morally problematic," whereas germ-line gene therapy fell in the category of "just wrong." Two months after the announcement of Dolly, and after much discussion of human cloning, people's attitudes had shifted to accepting animal cloning and gene transfer to humans as "morally permissible," whereas germ-line gene therapy had shifted to being merely "morally problematic."[16]

James Watson, the co-discoverer of the double helix, once opposed in vitro fertilization by claiming that prejudicial attitudes of other people would harm children created this way. . . .[17] In that piece, the prejudice was really in Watson, because the way that he was stirring up fear was doing more to create the prejudice than any normal human reaction. Similarly, Leon Kass's recent long essay in *The New Republic* (see this volume), where he calls human asexual reproduction "repugnant" and a "horror," creates exactly the kind of prejudiced reaction that he predicts.[18] Rather than make a priori, self-fulfilling prophecies, wouldn't it be better to be empirical about such matters? To be more optimistic about the reactions of ordinary parents?

Children created by SCNT would not *look* any different from other children. Nobody at age two looks like he does at age 45 and, except for his parents, nobody knows what the 45-year-old man looked liked at age two. And since ordinary children often look like their parents, know one would be able to tell a SCNT child from others until he had lived a decade.

Kass claims that a child originated by SCNT will have "a troubled psychic identity" because he or she will be "utterly" confused about his social, genetic, and kinship ties.[19] At worst, this child will be like a child of "incest" and may, if originated as a male from the father, have the same sexual feelings towards the wife as the father. An older male might in turn have strong

sexual feelings toward a young female with his wife's genome.

Yet if this were so, any husband of any married twin might have an equally troubled psychic identity because he might have the same sexual feelings toward the twin as his wife. Instead, those in relationships with twins claim that the individuals are very different.

Much of the above line of criticism simply begs the question and assumes that humans created by SCNT will be greeted by stigma or experience confusion. It is hard to understand why, once one gets beyond the novelty, because a child created asexually would know *exactly* who his ancestor was. No confusion there. True, prejudicial expectations could damage children, but why make public policy based on that?

Besides, isn't this kind of argument hypocritical in our present society? Where no one is making any serious effort to ban divorce, despite the overwhelming evidence that divorce seriously damages children, even teenage children. It is always far easier to concentrate on the dramatic, far-off harm than the ones close-at-hand. When we are really concerned about minimizing harm to children, we will pass laws requiring all parents wanting to divorce to go through counseling sessions or to wait a year. We will pass a federal law compelling child-support from fathers who flee to other states, and make it impossible to renew a professional license or get paid in a public institution in another state until all child-support is paid. After that is done, then we can non-hypocritically talk about how much our society cares about not harming children who may be originated in new ways.

In conclusion, the predicted harms of SCNT to humans are wildly exaggerated, lack a comparative baseline, stem from irrational fears of the unknown, overlook greater dangers of familiar things, and are often based on the armchair psychological speculation of amateurs. Once studies prove SCNT as safe as normal sexual reproduction in non-human mammals, the harm objection will disappear. Given other arguments that SCNT could substantially benefit many children, the argument that SCNT would harm children is a weak one that needs to be weighed against its many potential benefits.[20]

Notes

1. Paul Ramsey, *Fabricated Man: The Ethics of Genetic Control* (New Haven, Conn.: Yale University Press, 1970).

2. "What are the psychological implications of growing up as a specimen, sheltered not by a warm womb but by steel and glass, belonging to no one but the lab technician who joined together sperm and egg? In a world already populated with people with identity crises, what's the personal identity of a test-tube baby?" J. Rifkin and T. Howard, *Who Shall Play God?* (New York: Dell, 1977), 15.

3. Ehsan Massod, "Cloning Technique 'Reveals Legal Loophole'," *Nature* 38, 27 February 1987.

4. *New York Times,* 27 July 1978, A16.

5. Knight-Ridder newspapers, 10 March 1997.

6. Leon Kass, "The New Biology: What Price Relieving Man's Estate?" *Journal of the American Medical Association,* vol. 174, 19 November 1971, 779–788.

7. Leroy Walters, "Biomedical Ethics and Their Role in Mammalian Cloning," Conference on Mammalian Cloning: Implications for Science and Society, 27 June 1997, Crystal City Marriott, Crystal City, Virginia.

8. National Bioethics Advisory Commission (NBAC), *Cloning Human Beings: Report and Recommendations of the National Bioethics Advisory Commission,* Rockville, Md., June 1997.

9. A. Wilcox et al., "Incidence of Early Loss of Pregnancy," *New England Journal of Medicine* 319, no. 4, 28 July 1988, 189–194. See also J. Grudzinskas and A. Nysenbaum, "Failure of Human Pregnancy after Implantation," *Annals of New York Academy of Sciences* 442, 1985, 39–44; J. Muller et al., "Fetal Loss after Implantation," *Lancet* 2, 1980, 554–556.

10. Rick Weiss, "Genetically Engineered Calves Cloned," 21 January 1998, *Washington Post,* A3.

11. Lisa Belkin, "Pregnant with Complications," *New York Times Magazine,* October 26, 1997, 38.

12. ABC News report, October 27, 1997.

13. Axel Kahn, "Clone Animals . . . Clone Man?" specially-commissioned article to accompany articles from *Nature* on cloning on the web site of *Nature.* . . .

14. See the web site of a leading law firm in this area, Elman & Associates, at http://www.elman.com/elman.

15. David R. Collins, *Eng and Chang: The Original Siamese Twins* (New York: Dillon Press, 1994). Elaine Landau, *Joined at Birth: The Lives of Conjoined Twins* (New York: Grolier Publishing, 1997). See also Geoffrey A. Machin, "Conjoined Twins: Implications for Blastogenesis," *Birth Defects: Original Articles Series* 20, no. 1, 1993, March of Dimes Foundation, 142.

16. Ron James, Managing Director, PPL Therapeutics, "Industry Perspective: The Promise and Practical Applications," Conference on Mammalian Cloning: Implications for Science and Society, 27 June 1997, Crystal City Marriott, Crystal City, Virginia.

17. James D. Watson, "Moving Towards the Clonal Man," *Atlantic,* May 1971, 50–53.

18. Leon Kass, "The Wisdom of Repugnance," *The New Republic,* 2 June 1997.

19. Kass, "The Wisdom of Repugnance," 22–23.

20. Thanks to Mary Litch for comments on this essay.

Study Questions

1. Explain the parallel between cloning and in vitro fertilization. How does Pence use this to defend cloning of humans?

2. Go over the scenarios involving Rebecca and Susan (etc.). How does Pence use these to defend his argument? How successful is he? Can you see any problems in this kind of argument?

3. Examine Pence's discussion of levels of risk in experimentation. Do you agree with his middle path?

4. Examine Pence's arguments to the effect that the case that SCNT (cloning) would harm children is a weak one. Evaluate his reasoning.

For Further Reading

Hopkins, Patrick. "Bad Copies: How Popular Media Represent Cloning as an Ethical Problem," *Hastings Center Report* 28:2 (1998). A revealing essay on how the media influences public opinion on ethical issues and specifically human cloning.

Kass, Leon. " The Wisdom of Repugnance." *New Republic* (June 2, 1997). A blistering attack on the idea of human cloning.

Pence, Gregory E. *Who's Afraid of Human Cloning?* Lanham, Md.: Rowman & Littlefield, 1998. A timely, well-written work supporting human cloning.

———, ed. *Flesh of My Flesh.* Lanham, Md.: Rowman & Littlefield, 1998. An anthology on human cloning, just published.

———. *Classic Cases in Medical Ethics,* 3d ed. New York: McGraw-Hill, 1999. The best single-authored text on medical ethics.

Singer, Peter, and Deane Wells. *The Reproductive Revolution: New Ways of Making Babies.* New York: Oxford University Press, 1984. Still worth reading.

Steinbok, Bonnie, and Ron McClamrock, "When Is Birth Unfair to the Child?" *Hastings Center Report* 24:6 (1994). A good discussion of the issue.

Part IX

The Death Penalty

Introduction

When, if ever, is the state morally permitted to execute a criminal? In executing a murderer does the state itself become a criminal, a murderer? Does the death penalty fulfill the demands of justice, or is it an affront to the inherent dignity in every person, even the criminal? Does the death penalty deter would-be criminals, or are criminals who commit capital offenses beyond the pale of deterrence? Is the death penalty a violation of the Eighth Amendment of the U.S. Constitution, which forbids cruel and unusual punishment? These are the questions we address in this part of our book.

On August 15, 1990, Angel Diaz, age nineteen, was sentenced in the Bronx for the murder of an Israeli immigrant who had employed one of Diaz's friends. After strangling the man with a shoelace and stabbing him, Diaz and four friends donned Halloween masks to rob, beat, and gang-rape the man's wife and sixteen-year-old daughter. The women were then sexually tortured while the murdered man's three-year-old daughter watched from her crib.

Angel Diaz already had been convicted of burglary four times before he was sixteen years old. Diaz's lawyer, Paul Auerbach, said that Diaz was an honest boy forced by poverty to do bad things. Diaz was sentenced to prison for thirty-eight and one-third years to life on thirteen counts of murder, robbery, burglary, and conspiracy. His accomplice, Victor Sanchez, age twenty-one, who worked for the murdered man and planned the murder, had already been sentenced to fifteen years to life.[1]

The National Center of Health Statistics has reported that the homicide rate for young men in the United States is four to seventy-three times the rate of other industrialized countries. In 1994, 23,330 murders were committed in the United States. Whereas killings per 100,000 by men aged fifteen through twenty-four years old in 1987 was 0.3 in Austria and 0.5 in Japan, the figure was 21.9 in the United States and as high as 232 per 100,000 for Blacks in some states. The nearest nation to the United States was Scotland, with a 5.0 homicide rate. In some central city areas, the rate is 732 times that of men in Austria. In 1994 the rate was 37 per 100,000 men between the ages of fifteen and twenty-four.[2] The homicide rate in New York City broke the 2,000 mark in 1990. Black males in Harlem are said to have a lower life expectancy than males in Bangladesh. Escalating crime has caused an erosion in the quality of urban living. It is threatening the fabric of our social life.

Homo sapiens is the only species in which it is common for one member to kill another. In most species when there is a conflict between individuals, the weaker party submits to the stronger through some ritual gesture and is then permitted to depart in peace. Only in captivity, where the defeated animal cannot get away, will it be killed. Only human beings deliberately kill other individuals and groups of their own species. Perhaps it is not that we are more aggressive than other species but that our drives have been made more lethal by the use of weapons. A weapon, such as a gun or bomb, allows us to harm or kill without actually making physical contact with our victim. A person with a gun need not even touch his or her victim. Someone who sends a letter bomb through the mail may never have even laid eyes on the victim. The inhibition against killing is undermined by the trigger's power, a point to be kept in mind when discussing gun-control legislation. Airplane bomber pilots need not even see their victims as they press the button unleashing destruction. We are a violent race whose power of destruction has increased in proportion to our technology.

Naturally, the subject of punishment should receive increased attention, as should the social causes of crime. As a radical student activist in the 1960s, I once opposed increased police protection for my neighborhood in Morningside Heights, New York City, arguing that we must get to the causes of crime rather than deal only with the symptoms. I later realized that this was like refusing firefighters the use of water hoses to put out fires because they only dealt with the symptoms rather than the causes of the fire.

The truth is that we do not know the exact nature of what causes crimes of violence. Males commit a disproportionate number of violent crimes in our country, over 90%. Why is this? In fact, young Black males (between the ages of fifteen and twenty-four) constitute the group with the greatest tendency toward violent crimes.[3] Many people in the United States believe that *poverty causes crime*, but this is false. Poverty is a terrible condition and surely contributes to crime, but it is not a necessary or sufficient condition for violent crime. The majority of people in India are far poorer than most of the American poor, yet a person, male or female, can walk through the worst slum of Calcutta or New Delhi at any time of the day or night without fearing molestation. As a student I lived in a very poor neighborhood in a city in England that was safer than the Midwestern middle-class neighborhood in which I grew up. The use and trafficking of illegal drugs contributes to a great deal of crime, and the turn from heroin to crack as the "drug of choice" has exacerbated the matter, but plenty of crime occurred in our society before drugs became the problem it now is. Thus, we leave the subject of the causes of crime for psychologists and sociologists to solve and turn to the nature of punishment.

Punishment

To be responsible for a past act is to be liable to praise or blame. If the act was especially good, we go further than praise. We reward it. If it was especially evil, we go further than blame. We punish it. To examine the notion of punishment and then that of capital punishment, we first need to inquire under what conditions, if any, criminal punishment is justified. We will look at three approaches to this problem: the retributivist, the utilitarian, and the rehabilitationist.

Even though few of us will ever become criminals or be indicted on criminal charges, most of us feel very strongly about the matter of criminal punishment. Something about crime touches the deepest nerves of our imagination. Take the following situations, which are based on newspaper reports from the mid-1990s:

1. A drug addict in New York City stabs to death a vibrant, gifted twenty-two-year-old graduate student who has dedicated her life to helping others.
2. A sex pervert lures young children into his home, sexually abuses them, and then kills them. Over twenty bodies are discovered on his property.
3. A man sends his wife and daughter on an airplane trip, puts a time bomb into their luggage, and takes out $1 million insurance policy on them. The money will be used to pay off his gambling debts and for prostitutes.
4. A bomb explodes outside the Alfred P. Murrah Federal Building in Oklahoma City, killing over 160 people and injuring many others.

What is it within us that rises up in indignation at the thought of these atrocities? What should happen to the criminals in these cases? How can the victims (or their loved ones) ever be compensated for these crimes? We feel conflicting emotional judgments of harsh vengeance toward the criminal and, at the same time, concern that we don't ourselves become violent and irrational in our quest for revenge.

The Definition of Punishment

We may define "punishment," or more precisely "institutional or legal punishment" as *an evil inflicted by a person in a position of authority upon another person who is judged to have violated a rule.*[4] It can be analyzed into five concepts:

1. *An evil:* To punish is to inflict harm, unpleasantness, or suffering (not necessarily pain). Regarding this concept, the question is: Under what conditions is it right to cause harm or inflict suffering?
2. *For a violation:* The violation is either a moral or a legal offense. The pertinent questions are: Should we punish everyone who commits a moral offense? Need the offense already have been committed, or may we engage in prophylactic punishment where we have good evidence that the agent will commit a crime?

3. *Done to the offender:* The offender must be judged or believed to be guilty of a crime. Does this rule out the possibility of punishing innocent people? What should we call the process of "framing" the innocent and "punishing" them?

4. *Carried out by a personal agency.*

5. *Imposed by an authority.*

Let us spend a moment examining each of these points and the questions they raise.

1. Punishment is an evil. It may involve corporal punishment, loss of rights or freedom, or even loss of life. These are things we normally condemn as immoral. How does what is normally considered morally wrong suddenly become morally right? To quote H. L. A. Hart, former Oxford University professor of jurisprudence, What is this "mysterious piece of moral alchemy in which the combination of two evils of moral wickedness and suffering are transmuted into good"?[5] Theories of punishment bear the burden of proof to justify why punishment is required. The three classical theories have been retribution, deterrence, and rehabilitation (or reform of the criminal). (We examine each of these below.) These theories attempt not only to justify types of punishment but also to provide guidance on the degrees of punishment to be given for various crimes and persons.

2. Punishment is given for an offense, but must it be for a violation of a legal statute or may it also be for any moral failure? Most legal scholars agree that the law should have a moral basis, but it is impractical to make laws against every moral wrong. If we had a law against lying, for example, our courts would be cluttered beyond our ability. Also some laws may be immoral (e.g., anti-abortionists believe that the laws permitting abortion are immoral), but they still are laws, carrying with them coercive measures.

Whether we should punish only offenses already committed or also crimes that are intended is a difficult question. If I know or have good evidence that Smith is about to kill some innocent child (but not which one) and the only way to prevent this is by incarcerating Smith (or killing him), why isn't this morally acceptable? Normally, we don't have certainty about people's intentions, so we can't be certain that Smith really means to kill the child. But what if we do have strong evidence in this case? Nations sometimes launch preemptive strikes when they have strong evidence of an impending attack (e.g., Israel in the Six-Day War in 1967 acted on reliable information that Arab nations were going to attack it; it launched a preemptive strike that probably saved many Israeli lives). Although preemptive strikes are about defense, not punishment per se, could the analogy carry over? After all, part of the role of punishment is defense against future crimes.

This is a difficult subject, and I can conceive of conditions under which we would incapacitate would-be criminals before they commit their crimes, but the opportunity for abuse is so enormous here that one needs to tread carefully. In general our laws permit punishing only the guilty, relying on the principle that every dog may have its first bite—or, at least, an attempt at a first bite.

3. Punishment is done to the offender. No criminologist justifies punishing the innocent, but classic cases of framing the innocent in order to maximize utility exist. Sometimes Caiaphus's decision to frame and execute Jesus of Nazareth (John

10:50) is cited. "It were better that one man should die for a nation than that the whole nation perish." Utilitarians seem to be vulnerable to such practices, but every utilitarian philosopher of law eschews such egregious miscarriages of justice. Why this is so is a point I will discuss below.

This stipulation, "done to an offender," also rules out other uses of the word *punish,* as when, for instance, we say that boxer Mike Tyson "punished" his opponent with a devastating left to the jaw. Such metaphorical or nonlegal uses of the term are excluded from our analysis. Similarly, we quarantine confirmed or potential disease carriers, but we would not call this imposed suffering "punishment," for our intention is not to cause suffering (but to prevent it) and the carrier is innocent of any wrongdoing.

4. Punishment is carried out by a personal agency. Punishment is not the work of natural forces but of people. Lightning may strike and kill a criminal, but only people (or conscious beings) can punish other people.

5. Punishment is imposed by an authority. Punishment is conferred through institutions that have to do with maintaining laws or social codes. This rules out vigilante executions as punishments. Only a recognized authority, such as the state, can carry out legal punishment for criminal behavior.

Traditionally, we have had two main theories of punishment: retributivism and deterrence. Retributivism is typically held by deontologists. The idea appears in the Bible (Exodus 21) where we read that appropriate punishment should consist in "a life for a life, an eye for an eye, a tooth for a tooth, a hand for a hand, a foot for a foot," (the *lex talionis,* "law of the claw"), and it receives its classic philosophical treatment by Kant, who treats punishment as just desert. Justice demands that the criminal be punished in proportion to the gravity of his or her offense. Retributive theories are *backward* looking, focusing on the evil deed rather than on future consequences of the punishment. Deterrent theories are generally held by utilitarians who focus on *future* considerations, using punishment in order to correct, deter, or prevent future crimes. The proper amount of punishment to be inflicted upon the offender is that amount that will do the most good to all those who will be affected by it.

The death penalty, the ultimate sanction, has been used widely throughout history for just about every crime imaginable. In the Bible, sorcerers, kidnappers, worshipers of false gods, children disrespectful of parents, and murderers are to be executed. In the seventh century B.C.E., Draco's Athenian code prescribed the death penalty even for stealing fruit salad. Later Athenians were executed for idleness and for making misleading political speeches. Socrates was executed on the charges of corrupting youth by putting dangerous ideas into their minds and for not believing in the gods. The criminal code of the Holy Roman Empire and later Europe punished sorcery, arson, blasphemy, sodomy, and counterfeiting by burning at the stake. In England during the Tudor and Stuart dynasties, 50 offenses were subject to capital punishment, and in 1819, 233 capital offenses were listed, including poaching and pick-pocketing of twelve pence or more. In North Carolina in 1837, the death penalty was required for rape, stealing bank notes, slave stealing, sodomy, burning of a public building, robbery, concealing a slave with the intent to free him, and bigamy. Hugo Adam Bedau points out that "this harsh code persisted so long in North Carolina partly because the state had no penitentiary and thus had no suitable alternative to the death penalty."[6]

Most people agree that many of these uses of the death penalty are barbaric misuses. But *abolitionists* (those who believe that the death penalty ought to be abolished) argue that all uses of the death penalty are barbaric, "cruel and unusual" punishments, which only degrade humankind.

Proponents of capital punishment (*retentionists*) attempt to justify it either from a retributive or a utilitarian framework, though we can use both theories for a combined justification. Abolitionists deny that these arguments for capital punishment are valid. They argue that the sanctity of human life, which gives each person a right to life, is inconsistent with the practice of putting criminals to death.

In our first reading Immanuel Kant sets forth the classic expression of retributivism. He argues that universal justice requires that criminals be punished in exact proportion to the heinousness of their deeds so that the balance of justice may be restored. We are to punish the criminal, not because it will deter others, but because he or she deserves it. As a person of dignity, the victim of a capital offense deserves to have the offender harmed in proportion to the gravity of the crime, and as a person of dignity and responsibility, the offender shows himself deserving of the death penalty.

In our second reading, Supreme Court Justice Thurgood Marshall's dissenting opinion in *Gregg v. Georgia,* Marshall argues just the opposite of Kant. Capital punishment violates human dignity that the criminal does not relinquish in his misdeed, and it is unnecessary (more humane ways of dealing with crime exist). It violates the Eighth Amendment, which prohibits cruel and unusual punishments.

In the next selection Burton Leiser responds to Justice Marshall's assertion that the death penalty is a violation of the essential dignity of the wrongdoer. Taking the Kantian perspective, Leiser argues just the reverse—the death penalty affirms the wrongdoer's worth as a free, responsible agent who must be held accountable for doing wrong.

Next, Hugo Adam Bedau defends the abolitionist position, arguing that it is consistent with retributivism. Capital punishment does demean the human spirit, it is unnecessary, and there are better ways to punish offenders—for example, with life imprisonment without parole.

In our fifth reading Sidney Hook argues for the use of capital punishment in cases where the convicted criminal prefers death to imprisonment and where a convicted murderer has murdered again.

Our final selection is a set of interviews with Ernest van den Haag and Louis Schwartz, emphasizing the utilitarian and pragmatic aspects of the death penalty. Van den Haag cites studies that show that the death penalty does deter and offers his "Best-Bet" argument—in executing the criminal, we bet that it will deter would-be murderers and so save innocent people. Schwartz argues that the presence of the death penalty makes the judicial process difficult and actually works against the execution of justice.

Notes

1. "Jail for Crime That Shocked Even the Jaded," *New York Times* (August 16, 1990).

2. Statistics are from the National Center of Health Statistics and are available from the Centers for Disease Control. The National Center for Injury Prevention and Control reports that 8116 young people aged fifteen to twenty-four were victims of homicide in 1994 . This amounts to an average of twenty-two youth-victims per day in the United States. This homicide rate is ten times higher than Canada's, fifteen times higher than Australia's, and twenty-eight times higher than France's and Germany's. In 1994 in the United States, 102,220 rapes and 618,950 robberies were reported.

3. The United States 1994 *Uniform Crime Report* states that 1,864,168 violent crimes occurred in 1994, and 25,052 offenders were listed. "Of those whom sex and age were reported 91% of the offenders were males, and 84% were persons 18 years of age or older. . . . Of offenders for whom race was known, 56% were black, 42% white, and the remainder were persons of other races" (p. 14).

4. In the following analysis, I am indebted to Anthony Flew, "Justification of Punishment," *Philosophy* (1954); Joel Feinberg, "Punishment," *Philosophy of Law,* 2d ed., edited by Joel Feinberg and Hyman Gross (Belmont, Calif: Wadsworth, 1980); and Herbert Morris, "Persons and Punishment," *The Monist* 52 (October 1968). See also Tziporah Kasachkoff, "The Criteria of Punishment: Some Neglected Considerations," *Canadian Journal of Philosophy,* 2: 3 (March 1973).

5. H. L. A. Hart, *Punishment and Responsibility* (Oxford: Oxford University Press, 1968), p. 234.

6. From the "Introduction" of Hugo Adam Bedau, ed., *The Death Penalty in America: An Anthology* (New York: Doubleday, 1967).

References

Pojman, Louis, and Jeffrey Reiman. *The Death Penalty.* Lanham, Md.: Rowman & Littlefield, 1998.

Sorell, Tom. *Moral Theory and Capital Punishment.* Oxford: Blackwell, 1987.

Szumski, Bonnie, Lynn Hall, and Susan Bursell, eds. *The Death Penalty: Opposing Viewpoints.* St. Paul: Greenhaven Press, 1986. Contains short accessible articles.

CHAPTER 41

Retributivism: The Right to Capital Punishment

IMMANUEL KANT

Immanuel Kant (1724–1804) gives the classic argument for retributivism (*jus talionis*). The moral law states that a moral principle is such only if every rational person would will it to be a universal law. While criminals usually do not actually will their own punishment, their rational selves affirm the system of laws that involves the punishment that they deserve, a punishment in exact proportion to the seriousness of their wrongdoing. Punishment restores the balance of justice in the universe. It is our sacred duty to execute the person guilty of a capital offense.

THE RIGHT OF ADMINISTERING punishment, is the right of the sovereign as the supreme power to inflict pain upon a subject on account of a crime committed by him. The head of the state cannot therefore be punished; but his supremacy may be withdrawn from him. Any transgression of the public law which makes him who commits it incapable of being a citizen, constitutes a crime, either simply as a private crime, or also as a *public* crime. Private crimes are dealt with by a civil court; public crimes by a criminal court.—Embezzlement or peculation of money or goods entrusted in trade, fraud in purchase or sale, if done before the eyes of the party who suffers, are private crimes. On the other hand, coining false money or forging bills of exchange, theft, robbery, etc., are public crimes, because the commonwealth, and not merely some particular individual, is endangered thereby. Such crimes may be divided into those of a *base* character and those of a *violent* character.

Judicial or juridical punishment is to be distinguished from natural punishment, in which crime as vice punishes itself, and does not as such come within the cognizance of the legislator. Juridical punishment can never be administered merely as a means for promoting another good, either with regard to the criminal himself or to civil society, but must in all cases be imposed only because the individual on whom it is inflicted *has committed a crime*. For one man ought never to be dealt with merely as a means subservient to the purpose of another, nor be mixed up with the subjects of real right. Against such treatment his inborn personality has a right to protect him, even although he may be condemned to lose his civil personality. He must first be found guilty and *punishable*, before there can be any thought of drawing from his punishment any benefit for himself or his fellow-citizens. The penal law is a categorical imperative; and woe to him who creeps through the serpent-windings of utilitarianism to discover some advantage that may discharge him from the justice of punishment, or even from the due measure of it, according to the pharisaic maxim: 'It is better that *one* man should die than that

Immanuel Kant, The Philosophy of Law, *Part II, translated by W. Hastie (Edinburgh: Clark, 1887), pp. 194–198. Latin words have been deleted where they were provided for comparison with translated words.*

once you have committed to crime, you must then be punished.

the whole people should perish.' For if justice and righteousness perish, human life would no longer have any value in the world.—What, then, is to be said of such a proposal as to keep a criminal alive who has been condemned to death, on his being given to understand that if he agreed to certain dangerous experiments being performed upon him, he would be allowed to survive if he came happily through them? It is argued that physicians might thus obtain new information that would be of value to the commonweal. But a court of justice would repudiate with scorn any proposal of this kind if made to it by the medical faculty; for justice would cease to be justice, if it were bartered away for any consideration whatever.

But what is the mode and measure of punishment which public justice takes as its principle and standard? It is just the principle of equality, by which the pointer of the scale of justice is made to incline no more to the one side than the other. It may be rendered by saying that the undeserved evil which any one commits on another is to be regarded as perpetrated on himself. Hence it may be said: 'If you slander another, you slander yourself; if you steal from another, you steal from yourself; if you strike another, you strike yourself; if you kill another, you kill yourself.' This is the right of retaliation (*jus talionis*); and properly understood, it is the only principle which in regulating a public court, as distinguished from mere private judgment, can definitely assign both the quality and the quantity of a just penalty. All other standards are wavering and uncertain; and on account of other considerations involved in them, they contain no principle conformable to the sentence of pure and strict justice. It may appear, however, that difference of social status would not admit the application of the principle of retaliation, which is that of 'like with like.' But although the application may not in all cases be possible according to the letter, yet as regards the effect it may always be attained in practice, by due regard being given to the disposition and sentiment of the parties in the higher social sphere.

Thus a pecuniary penalty on account of a verbal injury, may have no direct proportion to the injustice of slander; for one who is wealthy may be able to indulge himself in this offence for his own gratification. Yet the attack committed on the honour of the party aggrieved may have its equivalent in the pain inflicted upon the pride of the aggressor, especially if he is condemned by the judgment of the court, not only to retract and apologize, but to submit to some meaner ordeal, as kissing the hand of the injured person. In like manner, if a man of the highest rank has violently assaulted an innocent citizen of the lower orders, he may be condemned not only to apologize but to undergo a solitary and painful imprisonment, whereby, in addition to the discomfort endured, the vanity of the offender would be painfully affected, and the very shame of his position would constitute an adequate retaliation after the principle of 'like with like.' But how then would we render the statement: 'If you *steal* from another, you steal from yourself'? In this way, that whoever steals anything makes the property of all insecure; he therefore robs himself of all security in property, according to the right of retaliation. Such a one has nothing, and can acquire nothing, but he has the will to live; and this is only possible by others supporting him. But as the state should not do this gratuitously, he must for this purpose yield his powers to the state to be used in penal labour; and thus he falls for a time, or it may be for life, into a condition of slavery. —But whoever has committed murder, must *die*. There is, in this case, no juridical substitute or surrogate, that can be given or taken for the satisfaction of justice. There is no *likeness* or proportion between life, however painful, and death; and therefore there is no equality between the crime of murder and the retaliation of it but what is judicially accomplished by the execution of the criminal. His death, however, must be kept free from all maltreatment that would make the humanity suffering in his person loathsome or abominable. Even if a civil society resolved to dissolve itself with the consent of all its members—as might be supposed in the case of a people inhabiting an island resolving to separate and scatter themselves throughout the whole world—the last murderer lying in the prison ought to be executed before the resolution was carried out. This ought to be done in order that every one may realize the desert of his deeds, and that bloodguiltiness may not remain upon the people; for otherwise they might all be regarded as participators in the murder as a public violation of justice.

The equalization of punishment with crime, is therefore only possible by the cognition of the judge extending even to the penalty of death, according to the right of retaliation.

If you do not punish by death then society would seem to condone murder. (human dignity)

Study Questions

1. What is Kant's version of punishment?
2. What does Kant mean when he says that crime causes the scale of justice to be imbalanced and that punishment restores the balance? Do you see any problems with this argument?
3. Does Kant have a place for mercy or pardon for the capital offender? How strict is his position? Do you agree with Kant? Why or why not?

Chapter 42

The Death Penalty Is a Denial of Human Dignity

THURGOOD MARSHALL *dissent based on the denial of human dignity.*

Until his retirement in the summer of 1991, Thurgood Marshall, the first African American to be appointed to the Supreme Court, was the most outspoken opponent of capital punishment on the United States Supreme Court. He gained national prominence in his role as the counsel for the plaintiff in the landmark civil rights case, *Brown v. Board of Education* (1954).

The following is Justice Marshall's dissenting opinion in *Gregg v. Georgia* (1976), the Supreme Court's decision that capital punishment did not violate the Constitution. Marshall argues that capital punishment is excessive and that if the American people were fully informed as to the purposes of the death penalty, they would find it morally unacceptable. It is a violation of the Eighth Amendment, which forbids cruel and unusual punishment.

IN *FURMAN V. GEORGIA* (1972) (concurring opinion), I set forth at some length my views on the basic issue presented to the Court in [this case]. The death penalty, I concluded, is a cruel and unusual punishment prohibited by the Eighth and Fourteenth Amendments. That continues to be my view.

I have no intention of retracing the "long and tedious journey" that led to my conclusion in *Furman*. My sole purposes here are to consider the suggestion that my conclusion in *Furman* has been undercut by developments since then, and briefly to evaluate the basis for my Brethren's holding that the extinction of life is a permissible form of punishment under the Cruel and Unusual Punishments Clause.

In *Furman* I concluded that the death penalty is constitutionally invalid for two reasons. First, the death penalty is excessive. And second, the American people, fully informed as to the purposes of the death penalty and its liabilities, would in my view reject it as morally unacceptable.

Since the decision in *Furman*, the legislatures of 35 States have enacted new statutes authorizing the imposition of the death sentence for certain crimes, and Congress has enacted a law providing the death penalty for air piracy resulting in death. I would be less than candid if I did not acknowledge that these developments have a significant bearing on a realistic assessment of the moral acceptability of the death penalty to the American people. But if the constitutionality of the death penalty turns, as I have urged, on the opinion of an *informed* citizenry, then even the enactment of new death statutes cannot be viewed as conclusive. In *Furman*, I observed that the American people are largely unaware of the information critical to a judgment on the morality of the death penalty, and concluded that if they were better informed they would consider it shocking, unjust, and unacceptable.

United States Supreme Court. 428 U.S. 153 (1976).

A recent study, conducted after the enactment of the post-*Furman* statutes, has confirmed that the American people know little about the death penalty, and that the opinions of an informed public would differ significantly from those of a public unaware of the consequences and effects of the death penalty.

Even assuming, however, that the post-*Furman* enactment of statutes authorizing the death penalty renders the prediction of the views of an informed citizenry an uncertain basis for a constitutional decision, the enactment of those statutes has no bearing whatsoever on the conclusion that the death penalty is unconstitutional because it is excessive. An excessive penalty is invalid under the Cruel and Unusual Punishments Clause "even though popular sentiment may favor" it. The inquiry here, then, is simply whether the death penalty is necessary to accomplish the legitimate legislative purposes in punishment, or whether a less severe penalty—life imprisonment—would do as well.

The two purposes that sustain the death penalty as nonexcessive in the Court's view are general deterrence and retribution. In *Furman*, I canvassed the relevant data on the deterrent effect of capital punishment. The state of knowledge at that point, after literally centuries of debate, was summarized as follows by a United Nations Committee:

> It is generally agreed between the retentionists and abolitionists, whatever their opinions about the validity of comparative studies of deterrence, that the data which now exist show no correlation between the existence of capital punishment and lower rates of capital crime.

The available evidence, I concluded in *Furman*, was convincing that "capital punishment is not necessary as a deterrent to crime in our society."...

... The evidence I reviewed in *Furman* remains convincing, in my view, that "capital punishment is not necessary as a deterrent to crime

in our society." The justification for the death penalty must be found elsewhere.

The other principal purpose said to be served by the death penalty is retribution. The notion that retribution can serve as a moral justification for the sanction of death finds credence in the opinion of my Brothers Stewart, Powell, and Stevens. ... It is this notion that I find to be the most disturbing aspect of today's unfortunate [decision].

The concept of retribution is a multifaceted one, and any discussion of its role in the criminal law must be undertaken with caution. On one level, it can be said that the notion of retribution or reprobation is the basis of our insistence that only those who have broken the law be punished, and in this sense the notion is quite obviously central to a just system of criminal sanctions. But our recognition that retribution plays a crucial role in determining who may be punished by no means requires approval of retribution as a general justification for punishment. It is the question whether retribution can provide a moral justification for punishment—in particular, capital punishment—that we must consider.

My Brothers Stewart, Powell, and Stevens offer the following explanation of the retributive justification for capital punishment:

> The instinct for retribution is part of the nature of man, and channeling that instinct in the administration of criminal justice serves an important purpose in promoting the stability of a society governed by law. When people begin to believe that organized society is unwilling or unable to impose upon criminal offenders the punishment they "deserve," then there are sown the seeds of anarchy—of self-help, vigilante justice, and lynch law.

This statement is wholly inadequate to justify the death penalty. As my Brother Brennan stated in *Furman*, "[t]here is no evidence whatever that utilization of imprisonment rather than death encourages private blood feuds and other disorders." It simply defies belief to suggest that the death penalty is necessary to prevent the American people from taking the law into their own hands.

In a related vein, it may be suggested that the expression of moral outrage through the imposition of the death penalty serves to reinforce basic moral values—that it marks some crimes as particularly offensive and therefore to be avoided. The argument is akin to a deterrence argument, but differs in that it contemplates the individual's shrinking from antisocial conduct, not because he fears punishment, but because he has been told in the strongest possible way that the conduct is wrong. This contention, like the previous one, provides no support for the death penalty. It is inconceivable that any individual concerned about conforming his conduct to what society says is "right" would fail to realize that murder is "wrong" if the penalty were simply life imprisonment.

The foregoing contentions—that society's expression of moral outrage through the imposition of the death penalty pre-empts the citizenry from taking the law into its own hands and reinforces moral values—are not retributive in the purest sense. They are essentially utilitarian in that they portray the death penalty as valuable because of its beneficial results. These justifications for the death penalty are inadequate because the penalty is, quite clearly I think, not necessary to the accomplishment of those results.

There remains for consideration, however, what might be termed the purely retributive justification for the death penalty—that the death penalty is appropriate, not because of its beneficial effect on society, but because the taking of the murderer's life is itself morally good. Some of the language of the opinion of my Brothers Stewart, Powell, and Stevens . . . appears positively to embrace this notion of retribution for its own sake as a justification for capital punishment. They state:

> [T]he decision that capital punishment may be the appropriate sanction in extreme cases is an expression of the community's belief that certain crimes are themselves so grievous an affront to humanity that the only adequate response may be the penalty of death.

They then quote with approval from Lord Justice Denning's remarks before the British Royal Commission on Capital Punishment:

> The truth is that some crimes are so outrageous that society insists on adequate punishment, because the wrong-doer deserves it, irrespective of whether it is a deterrent or not.

Of course, it may be that these statements are intended as no more than observations as to the popular demands that it is thought must be responded to in order to prevent anarchy. But the implication of the statements appears to me to be quite different—namely, that society's judgment that the murderer "deserves" death must be respected not simply because the preservation of order requires it, but because it is appropriate that society make the judgment and carry it out. It is this latter notion, in particular, that I consider to be fundamentally at odds with the Eighth Amendment. The mere fact that the community demands the murderer's life in return for the evil he has done cannot sustain the death penalty, for as Justices Stewart, Powell, and Stevens remind us, "the Eighth Amendment demands more than that a challenged punishment be acceptable to contemporary society." To be sustained under the Eighth Amendment, the death penalty must "compor[t] with the basic concept of human dignity at the core of the Amendment"; the objective in imposing it must be "[consistent] with our respect for the dignity of [other] men." Under these standards, the taking of life "because the wrongdoer deserves it" surely must fail, for such a punishment has as its very basis the total denial of the wrongdoer's dignity and worth.

The death penalty, unnecessary to promote the goal of deterrence or to further any legitimate notion of retribution, is an excessive penalty forbidden by the Eighth and Fourteenth Amendments. I respectfully dissent from the Court's judgment upholding the [sentence] of death imposed upon the [petitioner in this case].

Study Questions

1. What are Marshall's arguments against the death penalty?
2. Do you agree with his statement that the American people, if fully informed, would find the death penalty morally unacceptable?

→ grounds for opposing the death penalty.

CHAPTER 43

A Retributivist Justification of the Death Penalty

BURTON LEISER *Discussion of the Constitution- ality of the death penalty*

Burton Leiser is professor of philosophy at Pace University and the author of several books and articles in the areas of law, morality, and religion, among them *Liberty, Justice and Morals* from which this selection is taken.

Leiser responds directly to Justice Marshall's claim that the death penalty constitutes a denial of the criminal's worth and dignity. Just the reverse, argues Leiser. The death penalty, based on retributivism, actually affirms the offender's dignity and worth, for it treats him or her as a fully responsible person. In the last part of the essay Leiser discusses the limits of the death penalty.

Retribution

Vengeance and Vigilante Justice

IN HIS OPINION for the majority in *Gregg v. Georgia,* upholding the death penalty as constitutionally permissible, Justice Potter Stewart observed that capital punishment "is an expression of society's moral outrage at particularly offensive conduct," and that even though this function may be unappealing to many, "it is essential in an ordered society that asks its citizens to rely on legal processes rather than self-help to vindicate their wrongs." Without orderly means of imposing penalties upon offenders proportionate to what the aggrieved parties feel is deserved, society runs the risk of anarchy, vigilante justice, and lynch law. Even if retribution is not the dominant objective of the criminal law, he said, it is neither forbidden by the Constitution nor inconsistent with the dignity of men. Indeed, he went on, capital punishment "may be the appropriate sanction in extreme cases [as] an expression of the community's belief that certain crimes are themselves so grievous that the only

adequate response may be the penalty of death." As Lord Justice Denning told the British Royal Commission on Capital Punishment, "Some crimes are so outrageous that society insists on capital punishment, because the wrong-doer deserves it, irrespective of whether it is a deterrent or not."

In a report on "vicious youth gangs" in Detroit, the *New York Times* quoted a black resident as saying, "If I know who steals or breaks into my home, I'm going to get my gun. I'm going to hunt him. They can lock me up, but that's the only thing left. The police, they're not doing the job." Following another report on violent juvenile crime, a reader wrote to the *Times,* "Sudden death for a young man who does not want to surrender his wallet is cruel and unusual punishment. Why not let the punishment fit the crime, even if we have to amend the Constitution? The bleeding-heart mentality has caused too much bloodshed." And in a small town in the Midwest, after the residents concluded that the authorities would do nothing to relieve them of the violent behavior of a ferocious bully, a large group

Reprinted from Liberty, Justice and Morals, *3d ed. (New York: Macmillan, 1986) by permission of Prentice-Hall, Inc.*

waylaid him and fatally shot him. Afterward, no one in the community could be found who was willing to cooperate with the authorities in their attempt to solve his murder. It is clear that their sense of justice was so outraged that they considered his death to be justifiable homicide, and not murder.

These sentiments are clearly consistent with those theories of government which declare that when people agree to lay down their rights to self-help, transferring their right to avenge themselves on those who harm them to their common sovereign (the government), the sovereign assumes the duty to see that justice is done. By conferring exclusive jurisdiction over criminal sanctions upon the government, the people prevent blood feuds from developing and bring order to the fixing of guilt and the exacting of retribution, which they would otherwise have done informally and summarily. As public frustration grows, as more and more innocent persons feel that they are direct or indirect victims of vicious criminals, and as more people become convinced that their demand for retribution will not be met by those into whose hands they placed the responsibility of exacting appropriate penalties from wrongdoers, the danger of vigilante justice grows. Thus, the move from orderly processes of exacting public retribution toward the arbitrary process of private vengeance gains greater momentum until it is finally translated into action, as it was in that Midwestern town.

Retribution and Human Dignity.

In his dissent in *Gregg v. Georgia,* Justice Thurgood Marshall said that "it simply defies belief to suggest that the death penalty is necessary to prevent the American people from taking the law into their hands." He went on to assert that Lord Denning's contention that some crimes are so outrageous as to deserve the death penalty, regardless of its deterrent effects, is at odds

with the Eighth Amendment. "The mere fact that the community demands the murderer's life for the evil he has done," he said, "cannot sustain the death penalty," for

> the Eighth Amendment demands more than that a challenged punishment be acceptable to contemporary society. To be sustained under the Eighth Amendment, the death penalty must [comport] with the basic concept of human dignity at the core of the Amendment; the objective in imposing it must be [consistent] with our respect for the dignity of [other] men. Under these standards, the taking of life "because the wrongdoer deserves it" surely must fail, for such a punishment has as its very basis the total denial of the wrongdoer's dignity and worth. The death penalty, unnecessary to promote the goal of deterrence or to further any legitimate notion of retribution, is an excessive penalty forbidden by the Eighth and Fourteenth Amendments.

Robert A. Pugsley has argued that the principle of retribution demands that the death penalty *not* be invoked. Capital punishment, he says, is symbolically the ultimate ostracization of an individual. It "emphatically transgresses the inviolability of the executed" and also "destroys those bonds of community which criminal punishment should strive to reaffirm." It is difficult, he says, to reconcile the "respect required for the individual's dignity and moral capacity," which he believes to be the essential point of retributivism, with the practice of execution. The executed criminal is not treated as a human being, but as an object to be discarded. Execution is dehumanizing. It is the "total negation of the moral worth of the person to be executed."

A more proper retributivist response, he says, may be derived from the following considerations:

> Even if [the convicted murderer] is sentenced to a life term without possibility of parole, he retains his membership in the community, and has had

that status reaffirmed by the process of adjudication and punishment. His formal bond with the community *is* the punishment bond. It is that which signifies the community's recognition of him as a responsible moral agent and deserving of its respect, expressed of necessity through penalty and censure. He in turn accepts, if only tacitly, his punishment as justified; he acknowledges that he *ought* to feel guilty and suffer for his violative behavior. In the instance of the life term, particularly, there is this paradox: The community has "cared enough to give the very worst" punishment which, by abolishing the death penalty, it has permitted itself to impose.

As Justice Brennan put it in supporting the abolition of the death penalty, capital punishment treats members of the human race "as nonhumans, as objects to be toyed with and discarded." As such, it is inconsistent with the fundamental principle that "even the vilest criminal remains a human being possessed of common human dignity," whereas capital punishment is "uniquely degrading to human dignity."

Cruel and Unusual Punishment

The Eighth Amendment, which proscribed cruel and unusual punishments, was not intended to outlaw capital punishment as such. This is particularly evident if one considers that the Fifth Amendment, written and adopted at the same time, provides that "no person shall be held to answer for a capital . . . crime, unless on a presentment or indictment of a Grand Jury," and that no person "shall be deprived of life, liberty, or property, without due process of law." It is evident, then, that with a grand jury indictment, and with due process, a person may be deprived of his life, just as he may be deprived of his liberty or property. The cruel and unusual punishments that were banned by the Eighth Amendment were those that involved torture or

a lingering death and those that were disproportionate to the offenses being punished. Later Courts have found, on the same basic principle, that *any* punishment for the mere status of being a drug addict is cruel and unusual, just as a single day in prison would be a cruel and unusual punishment for the "crime" of having a common cold.

The Court found that although the Eighth Amendment was dynamic, evolving over the years as public moral perceptions changed, capital punishment was not cruel and unusual as that term stands in the Constitution. As the liberal Chief Justice Earl Warren had once said, "the death penalty has been employed throughout our history, and, in a day when it is still widely accepted, it cannot be said to violate the constitutional concept of cruelty." Earlier Courts had found that that concept implied "something inhuman and barbarous, something more than the mere extinguishment of life," and that the suffering necessarily involved in any execution was not banned by the Eighth Amendment, though a cruel form of execution was. The Court noted that at least 35 state legislatures had enacted new statutes after *Furman*, providing for the death penalty, as had the Congress. It noted also that the people of California had amended their constitution, by referendum, so as to negate a decision by that state's highest court banning capital punishment. Juries, too, are a measure of public morality, and in March, 1976, more than 460 persons were subject to death sentences.

Arguing that the traditional justifications for capital punishment (deterrence and retribution) were sufficiently well founded, despite the reservations that some people have about them, to continue to play a role in penal policy, the Court concluded that the death penalty is not unreasonable, that it is consistent with contemporary moral standards, and that it is not a cruel and unusual punishment as that term is used in the Constitution. In view of the safeguards erected around defendants accused of capital offenses in

Georgia and other states, the Court concluded that previous reservations about the death penalty being imposed in an arbitrary and capricious manner no longer applied and that it could therefore be imposed whenever similar safeguards existed.

The Limits of Capital Punishment

The death penalty has historically been employed for such diverse offenses as murder, espionage, treason, kidnapping, rape, arson, robbery, burglary, and theft. Except for the most serious crimes, it is now agreed that lesser penalties are sufficient.

The distinction between first- and second-degree murder does not permit fine lines to be drawn between (for example) murder for hire and the killing of a husband by his jealous wife. Many murders committed in the United States are of a domestic nature—spouses or other close relatives becoming involved in angry scenes that end in homicide. Such crimes, usually committed in the heat of a momentary passion, seem inappropriate for the supreme penalty. Although they are premeditated in the legal sense (for it takes no more than an instant for a person to form the intent that is necessary for the legal test to be satisfied), there seems to be a great difference between such crimes and those committed out of a desire for personal gain or for political motives, between a crime committed in an instant of overwrought emotion and one carefully charted and planned in advance. It is reasonable, therefore, to suggest that the vast majority of murders not be regarded as capital crimes, because the penalty may be disproportionate to the crime committed.

Only the most heinous offenses against the state and against individual persons seem to deserve the ultimate penalty. If the claim that life is sacred has any meaning at all, it must be that no man may deliberately cause another to lose his life without some compelling justification.

Such a justification appears to exist when individuals or groups employ wanton violence against others in order to achieve their ends, whatever those ends might be. However appealing the cause, however noble the motives, the deliberate, systematic destruction of innocent human beings is one of the gravest crimes any person can commit and may justify the imposition of the harshest available penalty, consistent with the principles of humanity, decency, and compassion. Some penalties, such as prolonged torture, may in fact be worse than death, and may be deemed such even by the intended victims. Civilized societies reject them as being too barbarous and too cruel to the victims, and too dehumanizing to those who must carry them out.

Perpetrators of such crimes as genocide (the deliberate extermination of entire peoples, racial, religious, or ethnic groups) deserve a penalty no less severe than death on purely retributive grounds. Those who perpetrate major war crimes, crimes against peace, or crimes against humanity, deliberately and without justification plunging nations into violent conflicts that entail widespread bloodshed or causing needless suffering on a vast scale, deserve no less.

Because of the reckless manner in which they endanger the lives of innocent citizens and their clear intention to take human lives on a massive scale in order to achieve their ends, terrorists should be subject to the death penalty, on retributive grounds, on the ground that it serves as the ultimate form of incapacitation—guaranteeing that terrorists who are executed will never again deprive an innocent person of his life, and on the ground that no other penalty can reasonably be expected to serve as a deterrent to persons whose colleagues are likely to engage in further acts of terrorism in order to achieve their release from prison.

Major crimes against the peace, security, and integrity of the state constitute particularly heinous offenses, for they shake the very foundations upon which civilization rests and endanger the lives, the liberties, and the fundamental rights of all the people who depend upon the state for protection. Treason, espionage, and sabotage, particularly during times of great danger (as in time of war), ought to be punishable by death.

Murder for personal gain and murder committed in the course of the commission of a felony that is being committed for personal gain or out of a reckless disregard for the lives or fundamental rights and interests of potential victims ought to be punishable by death.

Murder committed by a person who is serving a life sentence ought to be punishable by death, both because of the enormity of the crime itself and because no other penalty is likely to deter such crimes.

Needless to say, if a person is so deranged as to be legally insane, neither death nor any other punishment is appropriate. The very concept of punishment entails the assumption that the person being punished had the capacity, at the time he committed the act for which he is being punished, to act or refrain from acting, and of behaving at least in a minimally rational way. A person who commits a homicide while insane has not, strictly speaking, committed a murder or, for that matter, any crime at all; for no crime *can* (logically or legally) be committed without *mens rea*, the *intention* or *will* to carry it out.

The mere fact, however, that a person has carried out a homicide in a particularly vile, wanton, or malicious way is not sufficient to establish that that person is insane, for such a fact is consistent with many other explanations (e.g., that the perpetrator, making shrewd and calculated judgments as to what would most likely enable him to succeed without being caught, concluded that it would be in his own best interests if the crime *appeared* to be the act of an insane person who happened to be in the neighborhood).

Bearing these caveats in mind, we may conclude that any murder (as opposed to a mere homicide) committed in a particularly vile, wanton, or malicious way ought to be punishable by death.

One of the principal justifications for the state's existence is the protection it offers those who come under its jurisdiction against violations of their fundamental rights. Those who are entrusted with the responsibility for carrying out the duties of administering the state's functions, enforcing its laws, and seeing that justice is done carry an onerous burden and are particularly likely to become the targets of hostile, malicious, or rebellious individuals or groups. Their special vulnerability entitles them to special protection. Hence, any person guilty of murdering a policeman, a fireman, a judge, a governor, a president, a lawmaker, or any other person holding a comparable position while that person is carrying out his official duties or because of the office he holds has struck at the very heart of government and thus at the foundations upon which the state and civilized society depend. The gravity of such a crime warrants imposition of the death penalty.

From the fact that some persons who bring about the deaths of fellow humans do so under conditions that just and humane men would consider sufficient to justify either complete exculpation or penalties less than death, it does not follow that all of them do. If guilt is clearly established beyond a reasonable doubt under circumstances that guarantee a reasonable opportunity for the defendant to confront his accusers, to cross-examine witnesses, to present his case with the assistance of professional counsel, and in general to enjoy the benefits of due process of law; if in addition he has been given the protection of laws that prevent the use of torture to extract confessions and is provided immunity against self-incrimination; if those who are authorized to pass judgment find there were no excusing or mitigating circumstances; if he is found to have committed a wanton, brutal, callous murder or some other crime that is subversive of the very foundations of an ordered society; and if, finally, the representatives of the people, exercising the people's sovereign authority have prescribed death as the penalty for that crime; then the judge and jury are fully justified in imposing that penalty, and the proper authorities are justified in carrying it out.

Study Questions

1. How does Leiser respond to Marshall's point that the death penalty is a denial of the wrongdoer's dignity and worth?
2. What are the moral limits of the use of the death penalty?

CHAPTER 44

Against the Retributivist Justification of the Death Penalty

HUGO ADAM BEDAU *Wants to abolish capital punishment*

Hugo Adam Bedau is professor of philosophy at Tufts University and past president of the American League to Abolish Capital Punishment. He has been a leading spokesman for the abolitionist movement and is editor of *The Death Penalty in America* (1982) and the author of *The Courts, the Constitution and Capital Punishment* (1977).

In this selection Bedau first draws an analogy between self-defense and the death penalty. Just as in defending ourselves we are to use no more force than is necessary to prevent harm, so in punishing criminals we are to use no more violence than is necessary to adequately punish the criminal. Bedau then argues that the idea of retributive justice does not necessarily entail the death penalty, that the literal application of the *lex talionis* is barbaric, and that long-term imprisonment is adequate punishment.

Self interest
Benevolence for others

Capital Punishment and Social Defense

The Analogy with Self-Defense

CAPITAL PUNISHMENT, it is sometimes said, is to the body politic what self-defense is to the individual. If the latter is not morally wrong, how can the former be morally wrong? In order to assess the strength of this analogy, we need to inspect rather closely the morality of self-defense.

Except for the absolute pacifists, who believe it is morally wrong to use violence even to defend themselves or others from unprovoked and undeserved aggression, most of us believe that it is not morally wrong and may even be our moral duty to use violence to prevent aggression. The law has long granted persons the right to defend themselves against the unjust aggressions of others, even to the extent of killing a would-be assailant. It is very difficult to think of any convincing argument that would show it is never rational to risk the death of another in order to prevent death or grave injury to oneself or to others. Certainly self-interest dictates the legitimacy of self-defense. So does concern for the well-being of others. So also does justice. If it is unfair for one person to attempt violence on another, then it is hard to see why morality compels the victim to acquiesce in the attempt by another to hurt him or her, rather than to resist it, even if that resistance may involve injury to the assailant.

Reprinted from Tom Regan, ed., Matters of Life and Death: New Introductory Essays in Moral Philosophy *(New York: Random House, 1980) by permission of McGraw-Hill Publishing Company.*

the law allows equal force

(verbal attack does not allow a physical attack

The foregoing account assumes that the person acting in self-defense is innocent of any provocation of the assailant. It also assumes that there is no alternative to victimization except resistance. In actual life, both assumptions—especially the second—are often false, because there may be a third alternative: escape, or removing oneself from the scene of danger and imminent aggression. Hence, the law imposes on us the so-called "duty to retreat." Before we use violence to resist aggression, we must try to get out of the way, lest unnecessary violence be used to resist aggression. Now suppose that unjust aggression is imminent, and there is no path open for escape. How much violence may justifiably be used to ward off aggression? The answer is: No more violence than is necessary to prevent the aggressive assault. Violence beyond that is unnecessary and therefore unjustified. We may restate the principle governing the use of violence in self-defense in terms of the use of "deadly force" by the police in the discharge of their duties. The rule is this: Use of deadly force is justified only to prevent loss of life in immediate jeopardy where a lesser use of force cannot reasonably be expected to save the life that is threatened.

In real life, violence in self-defense in excess of the minimum necessary to prevent aggression is often excusable. One cannot always tell what will suffice to deter or prevent becoming a victim, and the law looks with a certain tolerance upon the frightened and innocent would-be victim who turns upon a vicious assailant and inflicts a fatal injury even though a lesser injury would have been sufficient. What is not justified is deliberately using far more violence than is necessary to prevent becoming a victim. It is the deliberate, not the impulsive, use of violence that is relevant to the death-penalty controversy, since the death penalty is enacted into law and carried out in each case only after ample time to weigh alternatives. Notice that we are assuming that the act of self-defense is to protect one's

person or that of a third party. The reasoning outlined here does not extend to the defense of one's property. Shooting a thief to prevent one's automobile from being stolen cannot be excused or justified in the way that shooting an assailant charging with a knife pointed at one's face can be. In terms of the concept of "deadly force," our criterion is that deadly force is never justified to prevent crimes against property or other violent crimes not immediately threatening the life of a person.

The rationale for self-defense as set out above illustrates two moral principles of great importance to our discussion. One is that if a life is to be risked, then it is better that it be the life of someone who is guilty (in our context, the initial assailant) rather than the life of someone who is not (the innocent potential victim). It is not fair to expect the innocent prospective victim to run the added risk of severe injury or death in order to avoid using violence in self-defense to the extent of possibly killing his assailant. It is only fair that the guilty aggressor run the risk.

The other principle is that taking life deliberately is not justified so long as there is any feasible alternative. One does not expect miracles, of course, but in theory, if shooting a burglar through the foot will stop the burglary and enable one to call the police for help, then there is no reason to shoot to kill. Likewise, if the burglar is unarmed, there is no reason to shoot at all. In actual life, of course, burglars are likely to be shot at by aroused householders because one does not know whether they are armed, and prudence may dictate the assumption that they are. Even so, although the burglar has no right to commit a felony against a person or a person's property, the attempt to do so does not give the chosen victim the right to respond in whatever way he or she pleases in retaliation, and then to excuse or justify such conduct on the ground that he or she was "only acting in self-defense." In these ways the law shows a tacit regard for the life of even a felon and discourages the use of unnecessary violence even by the innocent; morality can hardly do less.

Capital Punishment and Retributive Justice

As we have noticed earlier in several contexts, there are two leading principles of retributive justice relevant to the capital-punishment controversy. One is the principle that crimes should be punished. The other is the principle that the severity of a punishment should be proportional to the gravity of the offense. (A corollary to the latter principle is the judgment that nothing so fits the crime of murder as the punishment of death.) Although these principles do not seem to stem from any concern over the worth, value, dignity, or rights of persons, they are moral principles of recognized weight and no discussion of the morality of capital punishment would be complete without them. Leaving aside all questions of social defense, how strong a case for capital punishment can be made on the basis of these principles? How reliable and persuasive are these principles themselves?

Crime Must Be Punished

Given the general rationale for punishment sketched earlier, there cannot be any dispute over this principle. In embracing it, of course, we are not automatically making a fetish of "law and order," in the sense that we would be if we thought that the most important single thing society can do with its resources is to punish crimes. In addition, this principle is not likely to be in dispute between proponents and opponents of the death penalty. Only those who completely oppose punishment for murder and other erstwhile capital crimes would appear to disregard this principle. Even defenders of the death penalty must admit

that putting a convicted murderer in prison for years is a punishment of that criminal. The principle that crime must be punished is neutral to our controversy, because both sides acknowledge it and comply with it.

It is the other principle of retributive justice that seems to be a decisive one. Under the principle of retaliation, *lex talionis,* it must always have seemed that murderers ought to be put to death. Proponents of the death penalty, with rare exceptions, have insisted on this point, and it seems that even opponents of the death penalty must give it grudging assent. The strategy for opponents of the death penalty is to show either (a) that this principle is not really a principle of justice after all, or (b) that although it is, other principles outweigh or cancel, its dictates. As we shall see, both these objections have merit.

Is Murder Alone to Be Punished by Death?

Let us recall, first, that not even the Biblical world limited the death penalty to the punishment of murder. Many other nonhomicidal crimes also carried this penalty (e.g., kidnapping, witchcraft, cursing one's parents). In our own recent history, persons have been executed for aggravated assault, rape, kidnapping, armed robbery, sabotage, and espionage. It is not possible to defend any of these executions (not to mention some of the more bizarre capital statutes, like the one in Georgia that used to provide an optional death penalty for desecration of a grave) on grounds of just retribution. This entails either that such executions are not justified or that they are justified on some ground other than retribution. In actual practice, few if any defenders of the death penalty have ever been willing to rest their case entirely on the moral principle of just retribution as formulated in terms of "a life for a life." Kant seems to have been a conspicuous exception. Most defenders of the death penalty have implied by their willingness to use executions to defend limb and property, as well as life, that they did not place much value on the lives of criminals when compared to the value of both lives and things belonging to innocent citizens.

Are All Murders to Be Punished by Death?

Our society for several centuries has endeavored to confine the death penalty to some criminal homicides. Even Kant took a casual attitude toward a mother's killing of her illegitimate child. ("A child born into the world outside marriage is outside the law . . . , and consequently it is also outside the protection of the law.")[1] In our society, the development nearly 200 years ago of the distinction between first- and second-degree murder was an attempt to narrow the class of criminal homicides deserving of the death penalty. Yet those dead owing to manslaughter, or to any kind of unintentional, accidental, unpremeditated, unavoidable, unmalicious killing are just as dead as the victims of the most ghastly murder. Both the law in practice and moral reflection show how difficult it is to identify all and only the criminal homicides that are appropriately punished by death (assuming that any are). Individual judges and juries differ in the conclusions they reach. The history of capital punishment for homicides reveals continual efforts, uniformly unsuccessful, to identify before the fact those homicides for which the slayer should die. Benjamin Cardozo, a justice of the United States Supreme Court fifty years ago, said of the distinction between degrees of murder that it was

> . . . so obscure that no jury hearing it for the first time can fairly be expected to assimilate and understand it. I am not at all sure that I understand it myself after trying to apply it for many years and after diligent study of what has been written in the books. Upon the basis of this fine distinction with its obscure and mystifying psychology, scores of men have gone to their death.[2]

Similar skepticism has been registered on the reliability and rationality of death-penalty statutes that give the trial court the discretion to sentence to prison or to death. As Justice John Marshall Harlan of the Supreme Court observed a decade ago,

> Those who have come to grips with the hard task of actually attempting to draft means of channeling capital sentencing discretion have confirmed the lesson taught by history. . . . To identify before the fact those characteristics of criminal homicide and their perpetrators which call for the death penalty, and to express these characteristics in language which can be fairly understood and applied by the sentencing authority, appear to be tasks which are beyond present human ability.[3]

The abstract principle that the punishment of death best fits the crime of murder turns out to be extremely difficult to interpret and apply.

If we look at the matter from the standpoint of the actual practice of criminal justice, we can conclude only that "a life for a life" plays little or no role whatever. Plea bargaining (by means of which one of the persons involved in a crime agrees to accept a lesser sentence in exchange for testifying against the others to enable the prosecutor to get them all convicted), even where murder is concerned, is widespread. Studies of criminal justice reveal that what the courts (trial or appellate) decide on a given day is first-degree murder suitably punished by death in a given jurisdiction could just as well be decided in a neighboring jurisdiction on another day either as second-degree murder or as first-degree murder but without the death penalty. The factors that influence prosecutors in determining the charge under which they will prosecute go far beyond the simple principle of "a life for a life." Nor can it be objected that these facts show that our society does not care about justice. To put it succinctly, either justice in punishment does not consist of retribution, because there are other principles of justice; or there are other moral considerations besides justice that must be honored; or retributive justice is not adequately expressed in the idea of "a life for a life."

Is Death Sufficiently Retributive?

Given the reality of horrible and vicious crimes, one must consider whether there is not a quality of unthinking arbitrariness in advocating capital punishment for murder as the retributively just punishment. Why does death in the electric chair or the gas chamber or before a firing squad or on a gallows meet the requirements of retributive justice? When one thinks of the savage, brutal, wanton character of so many murders, how can retributive justice be served by anything less than equally savage methods of execution for the murderer? From a retributive point of view, the oft-heard exclamation, "Death is too good for him!" has a certain truth. Yet few defenders of the death penalty are willing to embrace this consequence of their own doctrine.

The reason they do not and should not is that, if they did, they would be stooping to the methods and thus to the squalor of the murderer. Where criminals set the limits of just methods of punishment, as they will do if we attempt to give exact and literal implementation to *lex talionis,* society will find itself descending to the cruelties and savagery that criminals employ. But society would be deliberately authorizing such acts, in the cool light of reason, and not (as is often true of vicious criminals) impulsively or in hatred and anger or with an insane or unbalanced mind. Moral restraints, in short, prohibit us from trying to make executions perfectly retributive. Once we grant the role of these restraints, the principle of "a life for a life" itself has been qualified and no longer suffices to justify the execution of murderers.

Other considerations take us in a different direction. Few murders, outside television and movie scripts, involve anything like an execution. An execution, after all, begins with a solemn pronouncement of the death sentence from

a judge, is followed by long detention in maximum security awaiting the date of execution, various appeals, perhaps a final sanity hearing, and then "the last mile" to the execution chamber itself. As the French writer Albert Camus remarked,

> For there to be an equivalence, the death penalty would have to punish a criminal who had warned his victim of the date at which he would inflict a horrible death on him and who, from that moment onward, had confined him at his mercy for months. Such a monster is not encountered in private life.[4]

Differential Severity Does Not Require Executions

What, then, emerges from our examination of retributive justice and the death penalty? If retributive justice is thought to consist in *lex talionis,* all one can say is that this principle has never exercised more than a crude and indirect effect on the actual punishments meted out. Other principles interfere with a literal and single-minded application of this one. Some murders seem improperly punished by death at all; other murders would require methods of execution too horrible to inflict; in still other cases any possible execution is too deliberate and monstrous given the nature of the motivation culminating in the murder. Proponents of the death penalty rarely confine themselves to reliance on this principle of just retribution and nothing else, since they rarely confine themselves to supporting the death penalty only for all murders.

But retributive justice need not be thought to consist of *lex talionis.* One may reject that principle as too crude and still embrace the retributive principle that the severity of punishments should be graded accordingly to the gravity of the offense. Even though one need not claim that life imprisonment (or any kind of punishment other than death) "fits" the crime of murder, one can claim that this punishment is the proper one for murder. To do this, the schedule of punishments accepted by society must be arranged so that this mode of imprisonment is the most severe penalty used. Opponents of the death penalty need not reject this principle of retributive justice, even though they must reject a literal *lex talionis*.

Equal Justice and Capital Punishment

During the past generation, the strongest practical objection to the death penalty has been the inequities with which it has been applied. As Supreme Court Justice William O. Douglas once observed, "One searches our chronicles in vain for the execution of any member of the affluent strata of this society."[5] One does not search our chronicles in vain for the crime of murder committed by the affluent. Every study of the death penalty for rape has confirmed that black male rapists (especially where the victim is a white female) are far more likely to be sentenced to death (and executed) than white male rapists. Half of all those under death sentence during 1976 and 1977 were black, and nearly half of all those executed since 1930 were black. All the sociological evidence points to the conclusion that the death penalty is the poor man's justice; as the current street saying has it, "Those without the capital get the punishment."

Let us suppose that the factual basis for such a criticism is sound. What follows for the morality of capital punishment? Many defenders of the death penalty have been quick to point out that since there is nothing intrinsic about the crime of murder or rape that dictates that only the poor or racial-minority males will commit it, and since there is nothing overtly racist about the statutes that authorize the death penalty for murder or rape, it is hardly a fault in the idea of capital punishment if in practice it falls with unfair impact on the poor and the black. There is, in short, nothing in the death penalty that requires it to be applied unfairly and with arbitrary or discriminatory results. It is at worst a fault in

the system of administering criminal justice (and some, who dispute the facts cited above, would deny even this).

Presumably, both proponents and opponents of capital punishment would concede that it is a fundamental dictate of justice that a punishment should not be unfairly—inequitably or unevenly—enforced and applied. They should also be able to agree that when the punishment in question is the extremely severe one of death, then the requirement to be fair in using such a punishment becomes even more stringent. Thus, there should be no dispute in the death penalty controversy over these principles of justice. The dispute begins as soon as one attempts to connect these principles with the actual use of this punishment.

In this country, many critics of the death penalty have argued, we would long ago have got rid of it entirely if it had been a condition of its use that it be applied equally and fairly. In the words of the attorneys who argued against the death penalty in the Supreme Court during 1972, "It is a freakish aberration, a random extreme act of violence, visibly arbitrary and discriminatory—a penalty reserved for unusual application because, if it were usually used it would affront universally shared standards of public decency."[6] It is difficult to dispute this judgment, when one considers that there have been in the United States during the past fifty years about half a million criminal homicides but only about 4,000 executions (all but 50 of which were of men).

We can look at these statistics in another way to illustrate the same point. If we could be assured that the 4,000 persons executed were the worst of the worst, repeated offenders without exception, the most dangerous murderers in captivity—the ones who had killed more than once and were likely to kill again, and the least likely to be confined in prison without imminent danger to other inmates and the staff—then one might accept half a million murders and a few thousand executions with a sense that rough justice had been done. But the truth is otherwise.

Persons are sentenced to death and executed not because they have been found to be uncontrollably violent, hopelessly poor parole and release risks, or for other reasons. Instead, they are executed for entirely different reasons. They have a poor defense at trial; they have no funds to bring sympathetic witnesses to court; they are immigrants or strangers in the community where they were tried; the prosecuting attorney wants the publicity that goes with "sending a killer to the chair"; they have inexperienced or overworked counsel at trial; there are no funds for an appeal or for a transcript of the trial record; they are members of a despised racial minority. In short, the actual study of why particular persons have been sentenced to death and executed does not show any careful winnowing of the worst from the bad. It shows that the executed were usually unlucky victims of prejudice and discrimination, the losers in an arbitrary lottery that could just as well have spared them as killed them, the victims of the disadvantages that almost always go with poverty. A system like this does not enhance respect for human life; it cheapens and degrades it. However heinous murder and other crimes are, the system of capital punishment does not compensate for or erase those crimes. It tends only to add new injuries of its own to the catalogue of our inhumanity to each other.

Conclusion

Our discussion of the death penalty from the moral point of view shows that there is no one moral principle the validity of which is paramount and that decisively favors one side of the controversy. Rather, we have seen how it is possible to argue either for or against the death penalty, and in each case to be appealing to moral principles that derive from the worth, value, or dignity of human life. We have also seen how it is impossible to connect any of these abstract principles with the actual practice of

capital punishment without a close study of sociological, psychological, and economic factors. By themselves, the moral principles that are relevant are too abstract and uncertain in application to be of much help. Without the guidance of such principles, of course, the facts (who gets executed, and why) are of little use, either.

My own view of the controversy is that on balance, given the moral principles we have identified in the course of our discussion (including the overriding value of human life), and given the facts about capital punishment and crimes against the person, the side favoring abolition of the death penalty has the better of the argument. And there is an alternative to capital punishment: long-term imprisonment. Such a punishment is retributive and can be made appropriately severe to reflect the gravity of the crime for which it is the punishment. It gives adequate (though hardly perfect) protection to the public. It is free of the worst defect to which the death penalty is liable: execution of the innocent. It tacitly acknowledges that there is no way for a criminal, alive or dead, to make amends for murder or other grave crimes against the person. Finally, it has symbolic significance. The death penalty, more than any other kind of killing, is done in the name of society and on its behalf. Each of us has a hand in such a killing, and unless such killings are absolutely necessary they cannot really be justified. Thus, abolishing the death penalty represents extending the hand of life even to those who by their crimes have "forfeited" any right to live. It is a tacit admission that we must abandon the folly and pretence of professing to secure perfect justice in an imperfect world.

Searching for an epigram suitable for our times, in which governments have launched vast campaigns of war and suppression of internal dissent by means of methods that can be described only as savage and criminal, Camus was prompted to admonish: "Let us be neither victims nor executioners." Perhaps better than any other, this exhortation points the way between forbidden extremes if we are to respect the humanity in each of us without trespassing on the humanity of others.

Notes

1. Immanuel Kant, *The Metaphysical Elements of Justice* (1797), tr. John Ladd, p. 106.

2. Benjamin Cardozo, "What Medicine Can Do for Law" (1928), reprinted in Margaret E. Hall, ed., *Selected Writings of Benjamin Nathan Cardozo* (1947), p. 204.

3. *McGautha v. California,* 402 U.S. 183 (1971), at p. 204.

4. Albert Camus, *Resistance, Rebellion, and Death* (1961), p. 199.

5. *Furman v. Georgia,* 408 U.S. 238 (1972), at pp. 251–252.

6. NAACP Legal Defense and Educational Fund, Brief for Petitioner in *Aikens v. California,* O.T. 1971, No. 68–5027, reprinted in Philip English Mackey, ed., *Voices Against Death: American Opposition to Capital Punishment, 1787–1975* (1975), p. 288.

Study Questions

1. Analyze Bedau's arguments against capital punishment. How compelling are they?
2. What is the analogy between self-defense and capital punishment?
3. Does Bedau think that the threat of the death penalty deters would-be murderers better than other forms of punishment?
4. Do you agree with Bedau that the death penalty "only tends to add new injuries of its own to the catalogue of our inhumanity to each other"?
5. Would long-term prison sentences without parole for capital offenses serve us better than the death penalty?

CHAPTER 45

The Death Sentence: Limited Use

SIDNEY HOOK

Sidney Hook (1902–1989), professor of philosophy at New York University for forty years, was a philosopher who frequently entered the great debates facing society. He was the author of numerous books and articles on moral, political, and legal philosophy, among them *Political Power and Freedom* (1959) and *The Paradoxes of Freedom* (1965).

In this essay Hook defends the use of the death penalty in two cases: (1) when the criminal sentenced to imprisonment prefers to die and (2) when a convicted murderer commits a second murder.

SINCE I AM NOT A FANATIC or absolutist, I do not wish to go on record as being categorically opposed to the death sentence in all circumstances. I should like to recognize two exceptions. A defendant convicted of murder and sentenced to life should be permitted to choose the death sentence instead. Not so long ago a defendant sentenced to life imprisonment made this request and was rebuked by the judge for his impertinence. I can see no valid grounds for denying such a request out of hand. It may sometimes be denied, particularly if a way can be found to make the defendant labor for the benefit of the dependents of his victim as is done in some European countries. Unless such considerations are present, I do not see on what reasonable ground the request can be denied, particularly by those who believe in capital punishment. Once they argue that life imprisonment is either a more effective deterrent or more justly punitive, they have abandoned their position.

In passing, I should state that I am in favor of permitting *any* criminal defendant, sentenced to life imprisonment, the right to choose death. I can understand why certain jurists, who believe that the defendant wants thereby to cheat the state out of its mode of punishment, should be indignant at the idea. They are usually the ones who believe that even the attempt at suicide should be deemed a crime—in effect saying to the unfortunate person that if he doesn't succeed in his act of suicide, the state will punish him for it. But I am baffled to understand why the absolute abolitionist, dripping with treacly humanitarianism, should oppose this proposal. I have heard some people actually oppose capital punishment in certain cases on the ground that: "Death is too good for the vile wretch! Let him live and suffer to the end of his days." But the absolute abolitionist should be the last person in the world to oppose the wish of the lifer, who regards this form of punishment as torture worse than death, to leave our world.

My second class of exceptions consists of those who having been sentenced once to prison for premeditated murder, murder again. In these particular cases we have evidence that imprisonment is not a sufficient deterrent for the

Reprinted from "The Death Sentence" in The Death Penalty in America, *rev. ed., edited by Hugo Adam Bedau (Garden City, N.Y.: Doubleday, 1967).*

individual in question. If the evidence shows that the prisoner is so psychologically constituted that, without being insane, the fact that he can kill again with impunity may lead to further murderous behavior, the court should have the discretionary power to pass the death sentence if the criminal is found guilty of a second murder.

In saying that the death sentence should be *discretionary* in cases where a man has killed more than once, I am *not* saying that a murderer who murders again is more deserving of death than the murderer who murders once. Bluebeard was not twelve times more deserving of death when he was finally caught. I am saying simply this: that in a sub-class of murderers, i.e., those who murder several times, there may be a special group of sane murderers who, knowing that they will not be executed, will not hesitate to kill again and again. For *them* the argument from deterrence is obviously valid. Those who say that there must be no exceptions to the abolition of capital punishment cannot rule out the existence of such cases on *a priori* grounds. If they admit that there is a reasonable probability that such murderers will murder again or attempt to murder again, a probability which usually grows with the number of repeated murders, and still insist they would *never* approve of capital punishment, I would conclude that they are indifferent to the lives of the human beings doomed, on their position, to be victims. What fancies itself as a humanitarian attitude is sometimes an expression of sentimentalism. The reverse coin of sentimentalism is often cruelty.

Our charity for all human beings must not deprive us of our common sense. Nor should our charity be less for the future or potential victims of the murderer than for the murderer himself. There are crimes in this world which are, like acts of nature, beyond the power of men to anticipate or control. But not all or most crimes are of this character. So long as human beings are responsible and educable, they will respond to praise and blame and punishment. It is hard to imagine it but even Hitler and Stalin were once infants. Once you *can* imagine them as infants, however, it is hard to believe that they were already monsters in their cradles. Every confirmed criminal was once an amateur. The existence of confirmed criminals testifies to the defects of our education—where they can be reformed—and of our penology—where they cannot. That is why we are under the moral obligation to be intelligent about crime and punishment. Intelligence should teach us that the best educational and penological system is the one which prevents crimes rather than punishes them; the next best is one which punishes crime in such a way as to prevent it from happening again.

Study Questions

1. In which cases does Hook support the retention of the death penalty?
2. Do you agree with Hook that prisoners condemned to life imprisonment ought to be permitted to choose the death penalty?
3. Can the death penalty be defended on the grounds that it prevents dangerous criminals from committing further crimes?

CHAPTER 46

The Death Penalty: Pro and Con

ERNEST VAN DEN HAAG AND LOUIS SCHWARTZ *opposed*

In favor of Death Penalty

Ernest van den Haag is professor of jurisprudence and public policy at Fordham University, as well as a psychoanalyst. Among his many works are *Political Violence and Civil Disobedience* (1972) and *Punishing Criminals: Concerning a Very Old and Painful Question* (1975). Louis Schwartz is a prominent American attorney.

In this set of interviews van den Haag gives the utilitarian argument in favor of the death penalty as a supplement to the argument from justice. Schwartz opposes the death penalty on practical grounds: it makes obtaining convictions difficult and probably does not deter most criminals.

Q: Professor van den Haag, why do you favor the use of the death penalty?

A: For certain kinds of crimes it is indispensable.

Thus: The federal prisons now have custody of a man sentenced to life imprisonment who, since he has been in prison, has committed three more murders on three separate occasions—both of prison guards and inmates. There is no further punishment that he can receive. In effect, he has a license to murder.

Take another case: When a man is threatened with life imprisonment for a crime he has already committed, what reason has he not to kill the arresting officer in an attempt to escape? His punishment would be the same.

In short, there are many cases where the death penalty is the only penalty available that could possibly deter.

I'll go a step further. I hold life sacred. Because I hold it sacred, I feel that anyone who takes someone else's life should know that thereby he forsakes his own and does not just suffer an inconvenience about being put into prison for some time.

Q: Could the same effect be achieved by putting the criminal in prison for life?

A: At present, "life imprisonment" means anything from six months—after which the parole board in Florida can release the man—to 12 years in some States. But even if it were real life imprisonment, its deterrent effect will never be as great as that of the death penalty. The death penalty is the only actually irrevocable penalty. Because of that, it is the one that people fear most. And because it is feared most, it is the one that is most likely to deter.

Q: Authorities seem to differ as to whether the death sentence really does deter crime—

A: Usually the statistics quoted were compiled more than 10 years ago and seem to indicate that the absence or presence of the death penalty made no difference in murder rates.

However, in the last 10 years there have been additional investigations. The results indicate, according to Isaac Ehrlich's recent article in the *American Economic Review:* Over the period 1933 to 1969, "an additional execution per year . . . may have resulted on the average in seven or eight fewer murders."

In New York in the last six years, the murder rate went up by 60 percent. Previous to the abolition of the death penalty, about 80 percent of all murders committed in New York were so-called crimes of passion, defined as crimes in which the victim and the murderer were in some way involved with each other. Right now, only 50 percent of all murders in New York are crimes of passion.

Q: How do you interpret those figures?

A: As long as the death penalty existed, largely only people in the grip of passion could not be deterred by the threat of the death penalty. Now that there's no death penalty, people who previously were deterred—who are not in the grip of passion—are no longer deterred from committing murder for the sake of gain. Murder is no longer an irrational act, least of all for juveniles for whom it means at most a few months of inconvenience.

Even if you assume the evidence for the deterrent effect of the death penalty is not clear—I make this point in my book *Punishing Criminals*—you have two risks. Risk 1: If you impose the death penalty and it doesn't have an additional deterrent effect, you have possibly lost the life of a convicted murderer without adding to deterrence and thereby sparing future victims. Risk 2: If you fail to execute the convicted murderer and execution would have had an additional deterrent effect, you have failed to spare the lives of a number of future victims.

Between the two risks, I'd much rather execute the convicted murderer than risk the lives of innocent people who could have been saved.

Q: You noted that the death penalty is irrevocable once it is imposed. Does this make death such a different penalty that it should not be used?

A: It makes it a different penalty. This is why it should be used when the crime is different—so heinous and socially dangerous to call for this extreme measure. When you kill a man with premeditation, you do something very different from stealing from him. I think the punishment should be appropriate. I favor the death penalty as a matter of justice and human dignity even apart from deterrence. The penalty must be appropriate to the seriousness of the crime.

Q: Can you elaborate on your statement that the penalty should match the seriousness of the crime?

A: Our system of punishment is based not just on deterrence but also on what is called "justice"—namely that we feel a man who has committed a crime must be punished in proportion to the seriousness of the crime. Since the crime that takes a life is irrevocable, so must be the punishment.

All religions that I'm aware of feel that human life is sacred and that its sacredness must be enforced by depriving of life anyone who deprives another person of life. Once we make it clear to a person that if he deprives someone else of life he will suffer only minor inconvenience, we have cheapened human life. We are at that point today.

Q: Some argue that capital punishment tends to brutalize and degrade society. Do you agree?

A: Many of the same people also argue that the death penalty is legalized murder because it inflicts on the criminal the same situation that he inflicted on his victim. Yet most punishments inflict on the criminal what he inflicted on the victim. The difference between the punishment and the crime is that one is a legal measure and the other is not.

As for brutalizing, I think that people are more brutalized by their daily TV fare. At any rate, people are not so much brutalized by punishment as they are brutalized by our failure to seriously punish brutal acts.

Q: Professor Schwartz, why do you oppose the death penalty?

A: For a number of reasons. In the first place, mistakes do occur in our trial system. And, if the victim of a mistake has been executed, that mistake is irremediable.

For example: I myself once represented a man who had been frightened into confessing a murder. He was afraid he'd get the electric chair if he stood trial. So he pleaded guilty and got life imprisonment. Twelve years later I was able to prove he was innocent. That would have been too late if he had been executed.

In the second place—and, for me, very important—the death penalty, rarely administered as it is, distorts the whole penal system. It makes the criminal procedure so complex that it turns the public off.

Q: How does it do that?

A: People are so reluctant to administer the death penalty until every last doubt is eliminated that the procedural law gets encumbered with a lot of technical rules of evidence. You not only get this in the trial, but you get habeas corpus proceedings after the trial.

This highly technical procedure is applied not only to capital cases but to other criminal cases as well. So it makes it hard to convict anybody.

I believe the death penalty actually does more harm to security in this country than it does good. Without it, we would be safer from criminals than with it.

Q: Do you think the death penalty is a deterrent to crime?

A: The evidence is inconclusive about that. The best studies I know, done by Thorsten Sellin, Marvin Wolfgang and their students at the University of Pennsylvania, would indicate that there is no deterrent effect. This study compared States using the death penalty with next-door States that did not use it. They also compared the homicide rates in the same State during periods when it used the death penalty and when it did not. And they found no statistical differences in homicide rates—with or without the death penalty.

I agree that there may be cases where a robber will not shoot because he doesn't want to risk "the hot seat." But, in my opinion, there are also situations where the death penalty stimulates a criminal to kill. I'm talking about cases, for instance, where a kidnapper decides to kill the only witness who could identify him, or where witnesses or informers get wiped out because the criminal says: "If I'm convicted, I'm going to get the chair anyway, and I'm safer if I kill him."

So if the death penalty is not demonstrably helpful in saving innocent lives, I don't think we

ought to use it—especially considering the risk of mistakes.

Q: Are there no criminals who commit crimes so heinous that they ought to be executed for society's safety?

A: My view is that society is not well enough organized to make a list of those people who ought to be executed. Sometimes I think if I were permitted to make up the list of those to be executed I wouldn't mind eliminating some people. But the list that society or the Government might make would probably not be the same as my list. Who is to decide who should live and who should die?

Now we're getting to the essential basis of what the Supreme Court must decide. This is whether the processes for choosing the ones to be killed are inevitably irrational, arbitrary and capricious.

Q: Do you think this element of arbitrariness or capriciousness can ever be eliminated—even by making the death penalty mandatory for certain crimes, as many States have?

A: No, I don't. No society has ever been able to make the death-penalty system operate fairly, even by making it mandatory. Look at the British system which operated for a century with mandatory death penalties. They found juries just wouldn't convict in many cases where the conviction meant execution. And even if the death penalty was imposed, the Home Office eventually decided who would actually be killed by granting or withholding clemency.

Taking human nature as it is, I know of no way of administering a death penalty which would be fair. Not every problem has a solution, you know—and I think this is one of those insoluble problems.

Q: Have we given the death penalty a chance to prove its deterrent effect? It hasn't been applied in this country in recent years—

A   Not just in recent years. Use of the death penalty has been declining for decades. In 1933, there were something like 233 people executed in the United States. Since then, the figures have been going down steadily. And, of course, there haven't been any executions since 1967 because of the litigation over the death penalty's legality. But even before that, the American public was turning against the death penalty.

If you take a poll, you find people overwhelmingly in favor of the death penalty. But when you ask a person to sit on a jury and vote to execute a defendant, you find a great reluctance—increasingly so in the modern era.

Q: It has been suggested that jurors and judges who impose a death penalty be required to push the buttons that would carry out the execution—

A: Of course, society would reject that at once. You couldn't get 12 or 13 people who would do it. They may be willing to vote for it to be done, but they don't want to be a part of it. If you really want to make execution a deterrent, make it public—put it on TV—so people can see what it can be like if they kill someone. But, of course, we won't do that. We keep it hidden away from ourselves.

Q: Do you regard it as immoral to execute a criminal?

A: I steer away from that question because I know people's views on the morality of it are varied—and almost unchangeable. I'm a pragmatist. I just don't think it can be made fair or workable.

Study Questions

1. Compare van den Haag's and Schwartz's arguments. Which do you agree with?
2. How does van den Haag deal with the argument that the death penalty does not deter would-be murderers?
3. How does Schwartz argue that the death penalty is actually counterproductive?

For Further Reading

Bedau, Hugo Adam, ed. *The Death Penalty in America,* 3d ed. New York: Oxford University Press, 1982.

Berns, Walter. *For Capital Punishment: The Inevitability of Caprice and Mistake.* New York: Norton, 1974.

Gerber, Rudolph, and Patrick McAnany, eds. *Contemporary Punishment.* Notre Dame, Ind.: University of Notre Dame Press, 1972.

Menninger, Karl. *The Crime of Punishment.* New York: Viking Press, 1968.

Murphy, Jeffrie, ed. *Punishment and Rehabilitation,* 2d ed. Belmont, Calif.: Wadsworth, 1985. A collection of articles on the theory of punishment.

Pojman, Louis P., and Jeffrey Reiman. *The Death Penalty: For and Against.* Lanham, Md.: Rowman and Littlefield, 1998.

Sorell, Tom. *Moral Theory and Capital Punishment.* Oxford: Blackwell, 1987.

Szumski, Bonnie, Lynn Hall, and Susan Bursell, eds. *The Death Penalty: Opposing Viewpoints.* St. Paul: Greenhaven Press, 1986. Contains short, accessible articles.

Part X

Animal Rights

Introduction

How ought we to treat animals? Do they have moral rights? Is their suffering to be equated with human suffering? Should experimentation on animals cease? Should large-scale, commercial "factory" farms be abolished because they tend to cause animals great suffering? Do we have a moral duty to become vegetarians? What exactly is the moral status of animals?

In 1975 a book appeared that opened with "This book is about the tyranny of human over non-human animals. This tyranny has caused and today is still causing an amount of pain and suffering that can only be compared with that which resulted from the centuries of tyranny by white humans over black humans." Thus, Peter Singer began his *Animal Liberation,* which launched the modern animal rights movement. Today thousands of people in every state of the Union and every province of Canada are part of a committed animal rights movement. Some campaign against animal factories, others against animal experimentation, still others against wearing fur, dissecting animals in science classes, hunting, and keeping animals in zoos. While the meat industry quakes and animal experimenters worry whether their laboratories will be dismantled, Americans, for the most part, continue to devour large quantities of meat while millions of animals are put to death for experimental purposes each year.

There are two separate defenses of animal rights: the utilitarian and the deontological arguments. Peter Singer is the main representative of the utilitarians who follow Jeremy Bentham in asserting that what makes all sentient creatures morally considerable is not their rationality or moral capacity but their ability to suffer. All creatures have interests, and the frustration of those interests leads to suffering. Utilitarianism seeks to maximize the satisfaction of interests whether they be those of humans or animals. In some cases human interests will make special claims on us; for example, humans but not mice or pigs will need schools and books. But if a pig and a child are in pain and you only have one pain reliever, you may have a moral dilemma regarding who should receive the pain reliever. Utilitarians will generally allow some animal experimentation; for example, if experimenting on chimpanzees promises to help us find a cure for AIDS, it's probably justified. But a utilitarian animal liberationist like Singer would also be willing to experiment on retarded children if it maximized utility.

The second type of defense of animals is the deontological *rights* position of which Tom Regan is the foremost proponent. The equal rights position on animal rights contends that the same essential psychological properties—desires, memory, intelligence, and so on—link all animals with humans and thereby give us all equal intrinsic value upon which equal rights are founded. These rights are inalienable and cannot be forfeited. Contrary to Singer, we have no right to experiment on chimpanzees in order to maximize satisfaction of interests—that's exploitation. Animals, like people, are "ends in themselves" persons, so that utility is not sufficient to override these rights. Regan is thus more radical than Singer. He calls for not reform but the total dissolution of commercial animal farming, the total elimination of hunting and trapping, and the total abolition of animal experiments. Just as we would condemn a scientist who took children and performed dangerous experiments on them for the good of others, so we must condemn the institutions that use animals.

Both utilitarian and deontological animal rights proponents have been attacked on their own ground. In our readings R. G. Frey, Singer's classmate at Oxford, argues that utilitarianism does not justify the sweeping indictments or proposals that Singer advocates. Because of the greater complexity of the human psyche and its social system, utility will be maximized by exploiting animals. What is needed is an amelioration of existing large-scale farms and safeguards in animal experimentation to prevent and ensure against unnecessary suffering.

Likewise, Mary Anne Warren and Carl Cohen attack Regan's deontological position for failing to see important differences between human beings and even higher animals, especially our ability to reason. Warren, who agrees that we do have duties to be kind to animals, not to kill them without good reason, and to do what we can to make their lives enjoyable, points out that Regan's notion of inherent value is obscure. Cohen goes even further and defends a Kantian perspective that denies we have direct duties to animals. The idea of rights does not apply to animals since "rights" is a concept appropriate only to members of the moral community and animals cannot make moral decisions. Humans are of far greater value than animals. Cohen readily admits that gratuitous suffering should be prohibited, but animal experimentation is needed to ameliorate human suffering, and, as such, it is justified. Robert White also argues for the benefits of using animals for experimentation, yet James Rachels advocates vegetarianism.

One other major position which we have discussed is the contractualist (or "contractarian," as Regan calls it). For contractarians like Hobbes, morality emerges when self-interested parties agree to live by a set of rules. The rules do not apply, however, to those not a part of the contract, between them and us a state of nature exists in which might is right.

Hence, since animals cannot communicate, they cannot be part of the contract. Therefore, they are not morally considerable. Being a contractualist is one way to dissolve the animal rights issue, but contractualism is beset by problems, some of which are discussed by Regan in our readings. Many thinkers find contractualism too narrowly egoistic, not a morality at all, but attempts have been made recently, especially by David Gauthier, to revive it.

We begin our readings with Kant's view that since animals are not self-conscious rational agents capable of forming the moral law, they are not directly morally considerable.

CHAPTER 47

We Have Only Indirect Duties to Animals

IMMANUEL KANT

Immanuel Kant (see Chapter 1 for a biographical sketch) argues that animals are not persons because they are not rational, self-conscious beings capable of grasping the moral law. Since they are not part of the kingdom of moral legislators, we do not owe them anything. But we should be kind to them since that will help develop good character in us and help us treat our fellow human beings with greater consideration. That is, our duties to animals are simply indirect duties to other human beings.

BAUMGARTEN SPEAKS OF DUTIES towards beings which are beneath us and beings which are above us. But so far as animals are concerned, we have no direct duties. Animals are not self-conscious and are there merely as a means to an end. That end is man. We can ask, "Why do animals exist?" But to ask, "Why does man exist?" is a meaningless question. *Our duties towards animals are merely indirect duties towards humanity.* Animal nature has analogies to human nature, and by doing our duties to animals in respect of manifestations of human nature, we indirectly do our duty towards humanity. Thus, if a dog has served his master long and faithfully, his service, on the analogy of human service, deserves reward, and when the dog has grown too old to serve, his master ought to keep him until he dies. Such action helps to support us in our duties towards human beings, where they are bounden duties. If then any acts of animals are analogous to human acts and spring from the same principles, we have duties towards the animals because thus we cultivate the corresponding duties towards human beings. If a man shoots his dog because the animal is no longer capable of service, he does not fail in his duty to the dog, for the dog cannot judge, but his *act is inhuman and damages in himself that humanity which it is his duty to show towards mankind.* If he is not to stifle his human feelings, he must practise kindness towards animals, for he who is cruel to animals becomes hard also in his dealing with men. We can judge the heart of a man by his treatment of animals. Hogarth depicts this in his engravings. He shows how cruelty grows and develops. He shows the child's cruelty to animals, pinch the tail of a dog or a cat; he then depicts the grown man in his cart running over a child; and lastly, the culmination of cruelty in murder. He thus brings home to us in a terrible fashion the rewards of cruelty, and this should be an impressive lesson to children. The more we come in contact with animals and observe their behaviour, the more we love them, for we see how great is their care for their young. It is then difficult for us to be cruel in thought even to a wolf. Leibnitz used a tiny worm for purposes of observation, and then carefully replaced it with its leaf on the tree so that it should not come to harm through any act

From Immanuel Kant, *"Duties to Animals and Spirits,"* in Lectures on Ethics, *translated by Louis Infield (New York: Harper & Row, 1963), pp. 239–41.*

of his. He would have been sorry—a natural feeling for a humane man—to destroy such a creature for no reason. Tender feelings towards dumb animals develop humane feelings towards mankind. In England butchers and doctors do not sit on a jury because they are accustomed to the sight of death and hardened. Vivisectionists, who use living animals for their experiments, certainly act cruelly, although their aim is praiseworthy, and they can justify their cruelty, since animals must be regarded as man's instruments; but any such cruelty for sport cannot be justified. A master who turns out his ass or his dog because the animal can no longer earn its keep manifests a small mind. The Greeks' ideas in this respect were highminded, as can be seen from the fable of the ass and the bell of ingratitude. Our duties towards animals, then, are indirect duties towards mankind.

Study Questions

1. According to Kant, do animals have rights? What capacity do they lack that deprives them of rights?
2. Why should we be kind to animals? Do you agree with Kant? How would an opponent respond to Kant's arguments?

CHAPTER 48

All Animals Are Equal

PETER SINGER

Peter Singer did his graduate work at Oxford University and is a member of the Philosophy Department at La Trobe University in Australia. His book, *Animal Liberation* (1975), from which the following selection is taken, is one of the most influential books ever written on the subject. It has converted many to the animal rights movement. Singer argues that animal liberation today is analogous to racial and gender justice in the past. Just as people once thought it incredible that women or Blacks should be treated as equal to white men, so now speciesists mock the idea that all animals should be given equal consideration. Singer defines *speciesism* (a term devised by Richard Ryder) as the prejudice (unjustified bias) that favors one's own species over every other. What equalizes all sentient beings is our ability to suffer. In that, we and animals are equal and deserving equal consideration of interests. Singer's argument is a utilitarian one having as its goal the maximization of interest satisfaction.

IN RECENT YEARS a number of oppressed groups have campaigned vigorously for equality. The classic instance is the Black Liberation movement, which demands an end to the prejudice and discrimination that has made blacks second-class citizens. The immediate appeal of the black liberation movement and its initial, if limited, success made it a model for other oppressed groups to follow. We became familiar with liberation movements for Spanish-Americans, gay people, and a variety of other minorities. When a majority group—women—began their campaign, some thought we had come to the end of the road. Discrimination on the basis of sex, it has been said, is the last universally accepted form of discrimination, practiced without secrecy or pretense even in those liberal circles that have long prided themselves on their freedom from prejudice against racial minorities.

One should always be wary of talking of "the last remaining form of discrimination." If we have learnt anything from the liberation movements, we should have learnt how difficult it is to be aware of latent prejudice in our attitudes to particular groups until this prejudice is forcefully pointed out.

A liberation movement demands an expansion of our moral horizons and an extension or reinterpretation of the basic moral principle of equality. Practices that were previously regarded as natural and inevitable come to be seen as the result of an unjustifiable prejudice. Who can say with confidence that all his or her attitudes and practices are beyond criticism? If we wish to avoid being numbered amongst the oppressors, we must be prepared to re-think even our most fundamental attitudes. We need to consider them from the point of view of those most dis-

Reprinted from Animal Rights and Human Obligation *(Englewood Cliffs, N.J.: Prentice Hall, 1976) by permission of Peter Singer.*

advantaged by our attitudes, and the practices that follow from these attitudes. If we can make this unaccustomed mental switch we may discover a pattern in our attitudes and practices that consistently operates so as to benefit one group—usually the one to which we ourselves belong—at the expense of another. In this way we may come to see that there is a case for a new liberation movement. My aim is to advocate that we make this mental switch in respect of our attitudes and practices towards a very large group of beings: members of species other than our own—or, as we popularly though misleadingly call them, animals. In other words, I am urging that we extend to other species the basic principle of equality that most of us recognize should be extended to all members of our own species.

All this may sound a little far-fetched, more like a parody of other liberation movements than a serious objective. In fact, in the past the idea of "The Rights of Animals" really has been used to parody the case for women's rights. When Mary Wollstonecroft, a forerunner of later feminists, published her *Vindication of the Rights of Women* in 1792, her ideas were widely regarded as absurd, and they were satirized in an anonymous publication entitled *A Vindication of the Rights of Brutes*. The author of this satire (actually Thomas Taylor, a distinguished Cambridge philosopher) tried to refute Wollstonecroft's reasonings by showing that they could be carried one stage further. If sound when applied to women, why should the arguments not be applied to dogs, cats, and horses? They seemed to hold equally well for these "brutes"; yet to hold that brutes had rights was manifestly absurd; therefore the reasoning by which this conclusion had been reached must be unsound, and if unsound when applied to brutes, it must also be unsound when applied to women, since the very same arguments had been used in each case.

One way in which we might reply to this argument is by saying that the case for equality between men and women cannot validly be extended to nonhuman animals. Women have a right to vote, for instance, because they are just as capable of making rational decisions as men are; dogs, on the other hand, are incapable of understanding the significance of voting, so they cannot have the right to vote. There are many other obvious ways in which men and women resemble each other closely, while humans and other animals differ greatly. So, it might be said, men and women are similar beings, and should have equal rights, while humans and nonhumans are different and should not have equal rights.

The thought behind this reply to Taylor's analogy is correct up to a point, but it does not go far enough. There *are* important differences between humans and other animals, and these differences must give rise to *some* differences in the rights that each have. Recognizing this obvious fact, however, is no barrier to the case for extending the basic principle of equality to nonhuman animals. The differences that exist between men and women are equally undeniable, and the supporters of Women's Liberation are aware that these differences may give rise to different rights. Many feminists hold that women have the right to an abortion on request. It does not follow that since these same people are campaigning for equality between men and women they must support the right of men to have abortions too. Since a man cannot have an abortion, it is meaningless to talk of his right to have one. Since a pig can't vote, it is meaningless to talk of its right to vote. There is no reason why either Women's Liberation or Animal Liberation should get involved in such nonsense. The extension of the basic principle of equality from one group to another does not imply that we must treat both groups in exactly the same way, or grant exactly the same rights to both groups. Whether we should do so will depend on the nature of the members of the two groups. The basic principle of equality, I shall argue, is equality of consideration; and equal consideration for different beings may lead to different treatment and different rights.

So there is a different way of replying to Taylor's attempt to parody Wollstonecroft's arguments, a way which does not deny the differences between humans and nonhumans, but goes more deeply into the question of equality, and concludes by finding nothing absurd in the idea that the basic principle of equality applies to so-called "brutes." I believe that we reach this conclusion if we examine the basis on which our opposition to discrimination on grounds of race or sex ultimately rests. We will then see that we would be on shaky ground if we were to demand equality for blacks, women, and other groups of oppressed humans while denying equal consideration to nonhumans.

When we say that all human beings, whatever their race, creed or sex, are equal, what is it that we are asserting? Those who wish to defend a hierarchical, inegalitarian society have often pointed out that by whatever test we choose, it simply is not true that all humans are equal. Like it or not, we must face the fact that humans come in different shapes and sizes; they come with differing moral capacities, differing intellectual abilities, differing amounts of benevolent feeling and sensitivity to the needs of others, differing abilities to communicate effectively, and differing capacities to experience pleasure and pain. In short, if the demand for equality were based on the actual equality of all human beings, we would have to stop demanding equality. It would be an unjustifiable demand.

Still, one might cling to the view that the demand for equality among human beings is based on the actual equality of the different races and sexes. Although humans differ as individuals in various ways, there are no differences between the races and sexes *as such*. From the mere fact that a person is black, or a woman, we cannot infer anything else about that person. This, it may be said, is what is wrong with racism and sexism. The white racist claims that whites are superior to blacks, but this is false—although there are differences between individuals, some blacks are superior to some whites in all of the capacities and abilities that could conceivably be relevant. The opponent of sexism would say the

same: a person's sex is no guide to his or her abilities, and this is why it is unjustifiable to discriminate on the basis of sex.

This is a possible line of objection to racial and sexual discrimination. It is not, however, the way that someone really concerned about equality would choose, because taking this line could, in some circumstances, force one to accept a most inegalitarian society. The fact that humans differ as individuals, rather than as races or sexes, is a valid reply to someone who defends a hierarchical society like, say, South Africa, in which all whites are superior in status to all blacks. The existence of individual variations that cut across the lines of race or sex, however, provides us with no defence at all against a more sophisticated opponent of equality, one who proposes that, say, the interests of those with I.Q. ratings above 100 be preferred to the interests of those with I.Q.s below 100. Would a hierarchical society of this sort really be so much better than one based on race or sex? I think not. But if we tie the moral principle of equality to the factual equality of the different races or sexes, taken as a whole, our opposition to racism and sexism does not provide us with any basis for objecting to this kind of inegalitarianism.

There is a second important reason why we ought not to base our opposition to racism and sexism on any kind of factual equality, even the limited kind which asserts that variations in capacities and abilities are spread evenly between the different races and sexes: we can have no absolute guarantee that these abilities and capacities really are distributed evenly, without regard to race or sex, among human beings. So far as actual abilities are concerned, there do seem to be certain measurable differences between both races and sexes. These differences do not, of course, appear in each case, but only when averages are taken. More important still, we do not yet know how much is really due to the different genetic endowments of the various races and sexes, and how much is due to environmental differences that are the result of past and continuing discrimination. Perhaps all of the important differences will eventually prove to be environmental rather than genetic. Anyone opposed to racism and sexism will certainly hope that this will be so, for it will make the task of ending discrimination a lot easier; nevertheless it would be dangerous to rest the case against racism and sexism on the belief that all significant differences are environmental in origin. The opponent of, say, racism who takes this line will be unable to avoid conceding that if differences in ability did after all prove to have some genetic connection with race, racism would in some way be defensible.

It would be folly for the opponent of racism to stake his whole case on a dogmatic commitment to one particular outcome of a difficult scientific issue which is still a long way from being settled. While attempts to prove that differences in certain selected abilities between races and sexes are primarily genetic in origin have certainly not been conclusive, the same must be said of attempts to prove that these differences are largely the result of environment. At this stage of the investigation we cannot be certain which view is correct, however much we may hope it is the latter.

Fortunately, there is no need to pin the case for equality to one particular outcome of this scientific investigation. The appropriate response to those who claim to have found evidence of genetically based differences in ability between the races or sexes is not to stick to the belief that the genetic explanation must be wrong, whatever evidence to the contrary may turn up: instead we should make it quite clear that the claim to equality does not depend on intelligence, moral capacity, physical strength, or similar matters of fact. Equality is a moral ideal, not a simple assertion of fact. There is no logically compelling reason for assuming that a factual difference in ability between two people justifies any *difference in the amount of consideration we give to satisfying their needs and interests.* The principle of the equality of human

beings is not a description of an alleged actual equality among humans: it is a prescription of how we should treat humans.

Jeremy Bentham incorporated the essential basis of moral equality into his utilitarian system of ethics in the formula: "Each to count for one and none for more than one." In other words, the interests of every being affected by an action are to be taken into account and given the same weight as the like interests of any other being. A later utilitarian, Henry Sidgwick, put the point in this way: "The good of any one individual is of no more importance, from the point of view (if I may say so) of the Universe, than the good of any other."[1] More recently, the leading figures in contemporary moral philosophy have shown a great deal of agreement in specifying as a fundamental presupposition of their moral theories some similar requirement which operates so as to give everyone's interests equal consideration—although they cannot agree on how this requirement is best formulated.[2]

It is an implication of this principle of equality that our concern for others ought not to depend on what they are like, or what abilities they possess—although precisely what this concern requires us to do may vary according to the characteristics of those affected by what we do. It is on this basis that the case against racism and the case against sexism must both ultimately rest; and it is in accordance with this principle that speciesism is also to be condemned. If possessing a higher degree of intelligence does not entitle one human to use another for his own ends, how can it entitle humans to exploit non-humans?

Many philosophers have proposed the principle of equal consideration of interests, in some form or other, as a basic moral principle; but, as we shall see in more detail shortly, not many of them have recognised that this principle applies to members of other species as well as to our own. Bentham was one of the few who did realize this. In a forward-looking passage, written at a time when black slaves in the British dominions were still being treated much as we now treat nonhuman animals, Bentham wrote:

> The day *may* come when the rest of the animal creation may acquire those rights which never could have been witholden from them but by the hand of tyranny. The French have already discovered that the blackness of the skin is no reason why a human being should be abandoned without redress to the caprice of a tormentor. It may one day come to be recognized that the number of the legs, the villosity of the skin, or the termination of the *os sacrum,* are reasons equally insufficient for abandoning a sensitive being to the same fate. What else is it that should trace the insuperable line? Is it the faculty of reason, or perhaps the faculty of discourse? But a full-grown horse or dog is beyond comparison a more rational, as well as a more conversable animal, than an infant of a day, or a week, or even a month, old. But suppose they were otherwise, what would it avail? The question is not, Can they reason? nor Can they *talk?* but, *Can they suffer?*[3]

In this passage Bentham points to the capacity for suffering as the vital characteristic that gives a being the *right* to equal consideration. The capacity for suffering—or more strictly, for suffering and/or enjoyment or happiness—is not just another characteristic like the capacity for language, or for higher mathematics. Bentham is not saying that those who try to mark "the insuperable line" that determines whether the interests of a being should be considered happen to have selected the wrong characteristic. The capacity for suffering and enjoying things is a prerequisite for having interests at all, a condition that must be satisfied before we can speak of interests in any meaningful way. It would be nonsense to say that it was not in the interests of a stone to be kicked along the road by a schoolboy. A stone does not have interests because it cannot suffer. Nothing that we can do to it could possibly make any difference to its welfare. A mouse, on the other hand, does have an interest in not being tormented, because it will suffer if it is.

If a being suffers, there can be no moral justification for refusing to take that suffering into consideration. No matter what the nature of the being, the principle of equality requires that its suffering be counted equally with the like suffering—in so far as rough comparisons can be made—of any other being. If a being is not capable of suffering, or of experiencing enjoyment or happiness, there is nothing to be taken into account. This is why the limit of sentience (using the term as a convenient, if not strictly accurate, shorthand for the capacity to suffer or experience enjoyment or happiness) is the only defensible boundary of concern for the interests of others. To mark this boundary by some characteristic like intelligence or rationality would be to mark it in an arbitrary way. Why not choose some other characteristic, like skin color?

The racist violates the principle of equality by giving greater weight to the interests of members of his own race, when there is a clash between their interests and the interests of those of another race. Similarly the speciesist allows the interests of his own species to override the greater interests of members of other species.[4] The pattern is the same in each case. Most human beings are speciesists. I shall now very briefly describe some of the practices that show this.

For the great majority of human beings, especially in urban, industrialized societies, the most direct form of contact with members of other species is at meal-times: we eat them. In doing so we treat them purely as means to our ends. We regard their life and well-being as subordinate to our taste for a particular kind of dish. I say "taste" deliberately—this is purely a matter of pleasing our palate. There can be no defence of eating flesh in terms of satisfying nutritional needs, since it has been established beyond doubt that we could satisfy our need for protein and other essential nutrients far more efficiently with a diet that replaced animal flesh by soy beans, or products derived from soy beans, and other high-protein vegetable products.[5]

It is not merely the act of killing that indicates what we are ready to do to other species in order to gratify our tastes. The suffering we inflict on the animals while they are alive is perhaps an even clearer indication of our speciesism than the fact that we are prepared to kill them. In order to have meat on the table at a price that people can afford, our society tolerates methods of meat production that confine sentient animals in cramped, unsuitable conditions for the entire durations of their lives. Animals are treated like machines that convert fodder into flesh, and any innovation that results in a higher "conversion ratio" is liable to be adopted. As one authority on the subject has said, "cruelty is acknowledged only when profitability ceases."[6] . . .

Since, as I have said, none of these practices cater for anything more than our pleasures of taste, our practice of rearing and killing other animals in order to eat them is a clear instance of the sacrifice of the most important interests of other beings in order to satisfy trivial interests of our own. To avoid speciesism we must stop this practice, and each of us has a moral obligation to cease supporting the practice. Our custom is all the support that the meat-industry needs. The decision to cease giving it that support may be difficult, but it is no more difficult than it would have been for a white Southerner to go against the traditions of his society and free his slaves: if we do not change our dietary habits, how can we censure those slaveholders who would not change their own way of living?

The same form of discrimination may be observed in the widespread practice of experimenting on other species in order to see if certain substances are safe for human beings, or to test some psychological theory about the effect of severe punishment on learning, or to try out various new compounds just in case something turns up. . . .

In the past, argument about vivisection has often missed this point, because it has been put in absolutist terms: Would the abolitionist be prepared to let thousands die if they could be saved by experimenting on a single animal? The way to reply to this purely hypothetical question is to pose another: *Would the experimenter be prepared to perform his experiment on an orphaned human infant, if that were the only way to save many lives?* (I say "orphan" to avoid the complication of parental feelings, although in doing so I am being overfair to the experimenter, since the nonhuman subjects of experiments are not orphans.) If the experimenter is not prepared to use an orphaned human infant, then his readiness to use nonhumans is simple discrimination, since adult apes, cats, mice and other mammals are more aware of what is happening to them, more self-directing and, so far as we can tell, at least as sensitive to pain, as any human infant. There seems to be no relevant characteristic that human infants possess that adult mammals do not have to the same or a higher degree. (Someone might try to argue that what makes it wrong to experiment on a human infant is that the infant will, in time and if left alone, develop into more than the nonhuman, but one would then, to be consistent, have to oppose abortion, since the fetus has the same potential as the infant—indeed, even contraception and abstinence might be wrong on this ground, since the egg and sperm, considered jointly, also have the same potential. In any case, this argument still gives us no reason for selecting a nonhuman, rather than a human with severe and irreversible brain damage, as the subject for our experiments.)

The experimenter, then, shows a bias in favor of his own species whenever he carries out an experiment on a nonhuman for a purpose that he would not think justified him in using a human being at an equal or lower level of sentience, awareness, ability to be self-directing, etc. No one familiar with the kind of results yielded by most experiments on animals can have the slightest doubt that if this bias were eliminated the number of experiments performed would be a minute fraction of the number performed today.

Experimenting on animals, and eating their flesh, are perhaps the two major forms of speciesism in our society. By comparison, the third and last form of speciesism is so minor as to be insignificant, but it is perhaps of some special interest to those for whom this article was written. I am referring to speciesism in contemporary philosophy.

Philosophy ought to question the basic assumptions of the age. Thinking through, critically and carefully, what most people take for granted is, I believe, the chief task of philosophy, and it is this task that makes philosophy a worthwhile activity. Regrettably, philosophy does not always live up to its historic role. Philosophers are human beings and they are subject to all the preconceptions of the society to which they belong. Sometimes they succeed in breaking free of the prevailing ideology: more often they become its most sophisticated defenders. So, in this case, philosophy as practiced in the universities today does not challenge anyone's preconceptions about our relations with other species. By their writings, those philosophers who tackle problems that touch upon the issue reveal that they make the same unquestioned assumptions as most other humans, and what they say tends to confirm the reader in his or her comfortable speciesist habits.

I could illustrate this claim by referring to the writings of philosophers in various fields—for instance, the attempts that have been made by those interested in rights to draw the boundary of the sphere of rights so that it runs parallel to the biological boundaries of the species *homo sapiens,* including infants and even mental defectives, but excluding those other beings of equal or greater capacity who are so useful to us at mealtimes and in our laboratories. I think it would be a more appropriate conclusion to this article, however, if I concentrated on the problem with which we have been centrally concerned, the problem of equality.

It is significant that the problem of *equality,* in moral and political philosophy, is invariably formulated in terms of human equality. The effect of this is that the question of the equality of other animals does not confront the philosopher, or student, as an issue itself—and this is already an indication of the failure of philosophy to challenge accepted beliefs. Still, philosophers have found it difficult to discuss the issue of human equality without raising, in a paragraph or two, the question of the status of other animals. The reason for this, which should be apparent from what I have said already, is that if humans are to be regarded as equal to one another, we need some sense of "equal" that does not require any actual, descriptive equality of capacities, talents or other qualities. If equality is to be related to any actual characteristics of humans, these characteristics must be some lowest common denominator, pitched so low that no human lacks them—but then the philosopher comes up against the catch that any such set of characteristics which covers *all* humans will not be possessed *only by humans.* In other words, it turns out that in the only sense in which we can truly say, as an assertion of fact, that all humans are equal, at least some members of other species are also equal—equal, that is, to each other and to humans. If, on the other hand, we regard the statement "All humans are equal" in some non-factual way, perhaps as a prescription, then, as I have already argued, it is even more difficult to exclude non-humans from the sphere of equality.

This result is not what the egalitarian philosopher originally intended to assert. Instead of accepting the radical outcome to which their own reasonings naturally point, however, most philosophers try to reconcile their beliefs in human equality and animal inequality by arguments that can only be described as devious.

As a first example, I take William Frankena's well-known article "The Concept of Social Justice." Frankena opposes the idea of basing justice on merit, because he sees that this could lead to highly inegalitarian results. Instead he proposes the principle that

. . . all men are to be treated as equals, not because they are equal, in any respect, but *simply because they are human*. They are human because they have *emotions* and *desires*, and are able to *think*, and hence are capable of enjoying a good life in a sense in which other animals are not.[7]

But what is this capacity to enjoy the good life which all humans have, but no other animals? Other animals have emotions and desires, and appear to be capable of enjoying a good life. We may doubt that they can think—although the behavior of some apes, dolphins and even dogs, suggests that some of them can—but *what is the relevance of thinking?* Frankena goes on to admit that by "the good life" he means "not so much the morally good life as the happy or satisfactory life," so thought would appear to be unnecessary for enjoying the good life; in fact to emphasize the need for thought would make difficulties for the egalitarian since only some people are capable of leading intellectually satisfying lives, or morally good lives. This makes it difficult to see what Frankena's principle of equality has to do with simply being *human*. Surely every sentient being is capable of leading a life that is happier or less miserable than some alternative life, and hence has a claim to be taken into account. In this respect the distinction between humans and nonhumans is not a sharp division, but rather a continuum along which we move gradually, and with overlaps between the species, from simple capacities for enjoyment and satisfaction, or pain and suffering, to more complex ones.

Faced with a situation in which they see a need for some basis for the moral gulf that is commonly thought to separate humans and animals, but finding no concrete difference that will do the job without undermining the equality of humans, philosophers tend to waffle. They resort to high-sounding phrases like "the intrinsic dignity of the human individual";[8] they talk of the "intrinsic worth of all men" as if men (humans?) had some worth that other beings did not,[9] or they say that humans, and only humans, are "ends in themselves," while "everything other than a person can only have value for a person."[10]

This idea of a distinctive human dignity and worth has a long history; it can be traced back directly to the Renaissance humanists, for instance to Pico della Mirandola's *Oration on the Dignity of Man*. Pico and other humanists based their estimate of human dignity on the idea that man possessed the central, pivotal position in the "Great Chain of Being" that led from the lowliest forms of matter to God himself; this view of the universe, in turn, goes back to both classical and Judeo-Christian doctrines. Contemporary philosophers have cast off these metaphysical and religious shackles and freely invoke the dignity of mankind without needing to justify the idea at all. Why should we not attribute "intrinsic dignity" or "intrinsic worth" to ourselves? Fellow-humans are unlikely to reject the accolades we so generously bestow on them, and those to whom we deny the honor are unable to object. Indeed, when one thinks only of humans, it can be very liberal, very progressive, to talk of the dignity of all human beings. In so doing, we implicitly condemn slavery, racism, and other violations of human rights. We admit that we ourselves are in some fundamental sense on a par with the poorest, most ignorant members of our own species. It is only when we think of humans as no more than a small subgroup of all the beings that inhabit our planet that we may realize that in elevating our own species we are at the same time lowering the relative status of all other species.

The truth is that the appeal to the intrinsic dignity of human beings appears to solve the egalitarian's problems only as long as it goes unchallenged. Once we ask *why* it should be that all humans—including infants, mental defectives, psychopaths, Hitler, Stalin and the rest—have some kind of dignity or worth that no elephant, pig, or chimpanzee can ever achieve, we see that this question is as difficult to answer as our original request for some relevant fact that justi-fies the inequality of humans and other animals. In fact, these two questions are really one: talk of intrinsic dignity or moral worth only takes the problem back one step, because any satisfactory defence of the claim that all and only humans have intrinsic dignity would need to refer to some relevant capacities or characteristics that all and only humans possess. Philosophers fre-quently introduce ideas of dignity, respect and worth at the point at which other reasons appear to be lacking, but this is hardly good enough. Fine phrases are the last resource of those who have run out of arguments.

In case there are those who still think it may be possible to find some relevant characteristic that distinguishes all humans from all members of other species, I shall refer again, before I con-clude, to the existence of some humans who quite clearly are below the level of awareness, self-consciousness, intelligence, and sentience, of many nonhumans. I am thinking of humans with severe and irreparable brain damage, and also of infant humans. To avoid the compli-cation of the relevance of a being's potential, however, I shall henceforth concentrate on per-manently retarded humans.

Philosophers who set out to find a character-istic that will distinguish humans from other animals rarely take the course of abandoning these groups of humans by lumping them in with the other animals. It is easy to see why they do not. To take this line without re-thinking our attitudes to other animals would entail that we have the right to perform painful experiments on retarded humans for trivial reasons; similarly it would follow that we had the right to rear and kill these humans for food. To most philoso-phers these consequences are as unacceptable as the view that we should stop treating nonhu-mans in this way.

Of course, when discussing the problem of equality it is possible to ignore the problem of mental defectives, or brush it aside as if some-how insignificant.[11] This is the easiest way out.

What else remains? My final example of species-ism in contemporary philosophy has been se-lected to show what happens when a writer is prepared to face the question of human equality and animal inequality without ignoring the ex-istence of mental defectives, and without resort-ing to obscurantist mumbo-jumbo. Stanley Benn's clear and honest article "Egalitarianism and Equal Consideration of Interests"[12] fits this description.

Benn, after noting the usual "evident human inequalities" argues, correctly I think, for equal-ity of consideration as the only possible basis for egalitarianism. Yet Benn, like other writers, is thinking only of "equal consideration of human interests." Benn is quite open in his defence of this restriction of equal consideration:

> . . . not to possess human shape *is* a disqualifying condition. However faithful or intelligent a dog may be, it would be a monstrous sentimentality to attribute to him interests that could be weighed in an equal balance with those of human beings . . . if, for instance, one had to decide between feeding a hungry baby or a hungry dog, anyone who chose the dog would generally be reckoned morally defective, unable to recognize a fundamental inequality of claims.
>
> This is what distinguishes our attitude to animals from our attitude to imbeciles. It would be odd to say that we ought to respect equally the dignity or personality of the imbecile and of the rational man . . . but there is nothing odd about saying that we should respect their interests equally, that is, that we should give to the inter-ests of each the same serious consideration as claims to considerations necessary for some stan-dard of well-being that we can recognize and endorse.

Benn's statement of the basis of the consider-ation we should have for imbeciles seems to me correct, but why should there be any fundamen-tal inequality of claims between a dog and a human imbecile? Benn sees that if equal consid-eration depended on rationality, no reason could be given against using imbeciles for research purposes, as we now use dogs and guinea pigs. This will not do: "But of course we do distinguish imbeciles from animals in this regard," he says. That the common distinction is justifiable is something Benn does not question; his problem is how it is to be justified. The answer he gives is this:

> . . . we respect the interests of men and give them priority over dogs not *insofar* as they are rational, but because rationality is the human norm. We say it is *unfair* to exploit the deficiencies of the imbecile who falls short of the norm, just as it would be unfair, and not just ordinarily dishonest, to steal from a blind man. If we do not think in this way about dogs, it is because we do not see the irrationality of the dog as a deficiency or a handicap, but as normal for the species. The characteristics, therefore, that distinguish the normal man from the normal dog make it intelligible for us to talk of other men having interests and capacities, and therefore claims, of precisely the same kind as we make on our own behalf. But although these characteristics may provide the point of the distinction between men and other species, they are *not* in fact the qualifying conditions for membership, or the distinguishing criteria of the class of morally considerable persons; *and this is precisely because a man does not become a member of a different species, with its own standards of normality, by reason of not possessing these characteristics.*

The final sentence of this passage gives the argument away. An imbecile, Benn concedes, may have no characteristics superior to those of a dog; nevertheless this does not make the imbecile a member of "a different species" as the dog is. *Therefore* it would be "unfair" to use the imbecile for medical research as we use the dog. But why? That the imbecile is not rational is just the way things have worked out, and the same is true of the dog—neither is any more responsible for their mental level. If it is unfair to take advantage of an isolated defect, why is it fair to take advan-

tage of a more general limitation? I find it hard to see anything in this argument except a defence of preferring the interests of members of our own species because they are members of our own species. To those who think there might be more to it, I suggest the following mental exercise. Assume that it has been proven that there is a difference in the average, or normal, intelligence quotient for two different races, say whites and blacks. Then substitute the term "white" for every occurrence of "men" and "black" for every occurrence of "dog" in the passage quoted; and substitute "high I.Q." for "rationality" and when Benn talks of "imbeciles" replace this term by "dumb whites"—that is, whites who fall well below the normal white I.Q. score. Finally, change "species" to "race." Now re-read the passage. It has become a defence of a rigid, no-exceptions division between whites and blacks, based on I.Q. scores, *not withstanding an admitted overlap* between whites and blacks in this respect. The revised passage is, of course, outrageous, and this is not only because we have made fictitious assumptions in our substitutions. The point is that in the original passage Benn was defending a rigid division in the amount of consideration due to members of different species, despite admitted cases of overlap. If the original did not, at first reading, strike us as being as outrageous as the revised version does, this is largely because although we are not racists ourselves, most of us are speciesists. Like the other articles, Benn's stands as a warning of the ease with which the best minds can fall victim to a prevailing ideology.

Notes

1. *The Methods of Ethics* (7th Ed.), p. 382.

2. For example, R. M. Hare, *Freedom and Reason* (Oxford, 1963) and J. Rawls, *A Theory of Justice* (Harvard, 1972); for a brief account of the essential agreement on this issue between these and other positions, see R. M. Hare, "Rules of War and Moral Reasoning," *Philosophy and Public Affairs*, vol. 1, no. 2 (1972).

3. *Introduction to the Principles of Morals and Legislation,* ch. XVII.

4. I owe the term "speciesism" to Richard Ryder.

5. In order to produce 1 lb. of protein in the form of beef or veal, we must feed 21 lbs. of protein to the animal. Other forms of livestock are slightly less inefficient, but the average ratio in the U.S. is still 1:8. It has been estimated that the amount of protein lost to humans in this way is equivalent to 90% of the annual world protein deficit. For a brief account, see Frances Moore Lappé, *Diet for a Small Planet* (Friends of The Earth/Ballantine, New York 1971) pp. 4–11.

6. Ruth Harrison, *Animal Machines* (Stuart, London, 1964). For an account of farming conditions, see my *Animal Liberation* (New York Review Company, 1975).

7. In R. Brandt (ed.) *Social Justice* (Prentice-Hall, Englewood Cliffs, 1962), p. 19.

8. W. Frankena (See ref. p. 384.)

9. H. A. Bedau, "Egalitarianism and the Idea of Equality" in *Nomos IX: Equality,* ed. J. R. Pennock and J. W. Chapman, New York, 1967.

10. G. Vlastos, "Justice and Equality" in Brandt, *Social Justice,* p. 48.

11. For example, Bernard Williams, "The Idea of Equality," in *Philosophy, Politics and Society* (second series), ed. P. Laslett and W. Runciman (Blackwell, Oxford, 1962), p. 118; J. Rawls, *A Theory of Justice,* pp. 509–10.

12. *Nomos IX: Equality;* the passages quoted are on p. 62ff.

Study Questions

1. According to Singer, what is the relationship between civil rights movements and the animal rights movement?
2. What is "speciesism"? Why is it bad? Do you agree?
3. Are all humans equal, according to Singer? In what way are all sentient beings equal?
4. How does Singer apply the notion of equal consideration of interests?
5. Is Singer a utilitarian or a deontologist? Explain. Do you agree with his arguments?

CHAPTER 49

A Utilitarian Critique of Animal Rights

R. G. FREY

R. G. Frey was educated at Oxford University, where he was a fellow student of Peter Singer. He is professor of philosophy at Bowling Green State University and the author of several books and articles on moral and political philosophy, including *Interests and Rights: The Case Against Animals* (1980) and *Rights, Killing and Suffering* (1983), from which this selection is taken. Frey accepts the utilitarian basis of Singer's animal liberation position but argues that Singer is mistaken in trying to build his program on utilitarianism. Utilitarianism calls for an amelioration of suffering but not its elimination—otherwise we would have to kill all sentient beings who had even any amount of pain in their lives. Rather than eliminate factory farms altogether and create great economic suffering, we should improve the conditions of large-scale commercial farming. Amelioration of suffering is the proper utilitarian response to the plight of animals. "Reform not Revolution" might be the utilitarian motto.

The Argument and the Concerned Individual

IF THE PAIN food animals undergo and the period over which they undergo it were insignificant, then I suspect many people would not be unduly worried by factory farming, with the result that they might well either see no need for the argument from pain and suffering, or see it as a manifestation of an undue sensitivity. Either way, the chances of the argument serving as the vehicle of widespread dietary change would recede.

The above, however, is certainly not the picture of factory farming which Singer paints, which, whether one considers *Animal Liberation,* and *Practical Ethics,* or (with James Mason) *Animal Factories,*[1] is in the blackest terms.

As we saw in the last chapter, he thinks, and would have us think, of factory farming in terms of animals who 'are so crowded together and restricted in their movements that their lives seem to be more of a burden than a benefit to them'[2] and who 'do not have pleasant lives'.[3] His view is that these animals lead miserable lives, that, in short, the pain inflicted upon them is substantial and its duration prolonged.

The argument itself points the direction in which the meat-eater will try to move: since what is held to be wrong with the particular farming practices objected to is that they are productive of pain, the meat-eater will, among other things, try to make improvements in and to find alternatives to these practices. It is by no means obvious that such improvements and alternatives are not to be had, so that the only

Abridged from Rights, Killing and Suffering *(Oxford: Basil Blackwell, 1983). Reprinted by permission of R. G. Frey; notes edited.*

remaining course is to abolish intensive farming. Nothing whatever in, say, *Animal Liberation* rules out such improvements and alternatives; thus, any conclusion to the effect that the only way to mitigate, reduce, or eliminate the pains of food animals is to abolish factory farming is simply not licensed by that book.

If we do think of factory farming as Singer would have us, then . . . vast numbers of intensively farmed food animals, such as cattle, cows, sheep, a great many hogs, some pigs, elude the argument from pain and suffering. For vast numbers of commercially farmed animals lead lives which are not, on balance, miserable, nor are those methods of rearing which are held to produce misery in the cases of laying hens and veal calves used on all food animals. Singer concedes the point: he remarks that, for example, 'as long as sheep and cattle graze outdoors . . . arguments directed against factory farming do not imply that we should cease eating meat altogether'.[4]

Two things follow. First, even if the argument from pain and suffering were successful, it would demand only that we abstain from the flesh of those creatures leading miserable lives; and even if we did so, large-scale, technology-intensive, commercial farming would by no means disappear, since there are numerous food animals so farmed who do not lead miserable lives.

Second, the *amelioration argument* becomes applicable. The more animals that can be brought to lead pleasant lives, the more animals that escape the argument from pain and suffering and so may be eaten. A concerned individual, therefore, can perfectly consistently strive, not for the abolition of factory farming, but for improvements and alternative methods on factory farms, in order that the animals no longer lead, on balance, miserable lives. With this the case, factory farming could continue, consistently with the application of the argument to it.

In short, if the argument demands that we abstain from the flesh of creatures whose lives are a burden to them, then a perfectly consis-

tent response from the concerned individual, besides pointing to the huge numbers of commercially farmed as well as traditionally farmed animals which escape the argument, is to do his best to reduce the misery incurred on factory farms. Thus, when Singer has us think of factory farms in terms of the quality of life being lived upon them (and remarks such as 'our society tolerates methods of meat production that confine sentient animals in cramped, unsuitable conditions for the entire duration of their lives'[5] leave little doubt that, at least for those animals covered by his argument, he regards the quality of their lives as very low), the task of the concerned individual is to improve the quality of the lives being lived on those farms. It is just not true, however, that the only way to do this, the only tactic available, is to abolish *large-scale, commercial farming*.

One can always insist, of course, that the quality of life of the commercially farmed animals in question (remember, vast numbers of such animals are not in question) will never rise high enough; but this sort of issue cannot be decided *a priori*. Precisely how high a quality of life must be reached before animals may be said to be leading pleasant lives is, as we have seen, a contentious and complex issue; but we may at least use as a benchmark the situation at present. As improvements in and alternatives to the particular farming practices objected to arise, we can reasonably regard the pain associated with these practices as diminishing, if the improvements and alternatives are of the sort our concerned individual is seeking.

We have here, then, two parties, the Singer vegetarian and the concerned individual, both of whom are concerned to reduce the pain and suffering involved in factory farming. The Singer vegetarian's way is to adopt vegetarianism; the concerned individual's way is, among other things, to seek improvements in and alternatives to those practices held to be the source of the pain and suffering in question.

Suffering: Miserable Life and Single Experience Views

Singer's remarks on suffering in farming are not always of the sort depicted in the previous section. In both *Animal Liberation* and *Practical Ethics*, he occasionally writes as if any amount of suffering whatever sufficed, in terms of his argument, to condemn some method of rearing animals for food. For instance, he remarks that his 'case against using animals for food is at its strongest when animals are made to lead miserable lives . . .',[6] with the implication that his argument applies even when food animals suffer on a few or even a single occasion. Again, of traditional livestock farming, he maintains that it involves suffering, even if one has on occasion to go to such things as the breaking up of herds in order to find it, and he remarks in *Animal Liberation,* of these and other aspects of traditional farming, that 'it is difficult to imagine how animals could be raised for food without suffering in any of these ways'.[7]

Passages such as these suggest that Singer believes his argument condemns any method of rearing animals for food which causes them any suffering, however transient, however low-level, indeed, which causes them even a single, isolated painful experience. When he speaks of the permissibility of eating only 'the flesh of animals reared and killed without suffering',[8] therefore, he might be taken to mean by 'without suffering', not suffering of an amount and duration short of that required to make a life miserable, but any suffering whatever, so that the permissibility claim extends only to animals who have not had a single painful experience, a single trace of suffering in being bred and killed for food. But if this is what he means, how can he allow, as we have seen that he does, that sheep and cattle (these he cites as examples only,[9] so there may well, even in his eyes, be others) escape his argument? For it seems extremely unlikely that sheep and cattle are reared for food without a single painful experience. So either he is inconsistent to allow these exceptions, because he is operating with something like the single experience view of suffering, or he consistently allows them, but only because he is operating with something like the miserable life view of suffering.

These two views of suffering plainly do not come to the same thing. In order to lead, on balance, a pleasant life, pain, even significant pain, need not be absent from that life; indeed, it can recur on a daily basis, provided it falls short of that quantity over that duration required to tip the balance in the direction of a miserable life. Certainly, isolated, painful experiences or, for that matter, painful interludes, cannot, without further argument, be said to produce a miserable life.

Singer's whole position is affected by this ambiguity, if not inconsistency, over suffering. For instance, one of the most important points he wants to make concerns the possibility of rearing animals painlessly:

> Whatever the theoretical possibilities of rearing animals without suffering may be, the fact is that the meat available from butchers and supermarkets comes from animals who did suffer while being reared. So we must ask ourselves, not: is it *ever* right to eat meat? but: is it right to eat *this* meat?[10]

In *Practical Ethics*, he says that the question is not 'whether animal flesh *could* be produced without suffering, but whether the flesh we are considering buying *was* produced without suffering'.[11] But he has already allowed that vegetarianism is not demanded of us with respect to sheep and beef cattle, precisely because they do not lead miserable lives; so how can he say of all meats that it is a fact 'that the meat available from butchers and supermarkets comes from animals who did suffer while being reared'? Again, there is a question of consistency. The problem can be favourably resolved, of course, if

Singer shifts from the miserable life view of suffering to something like the single experience view; for he can be reasonably certain that the meat on display in supermarkets, including that from sheep and beef cattle, has come from animals who have had at least one painful experience, in being reared for food.

Without this shift, Singer has difficulty in discouraging you from buying the meat in question. If you are standing before the meats from sheep and beef cattle in your supermarket, if you have read Singer's book, and if you put to yourself the question of whether the meats before you have come from animals who have suffered in the course of being reared for food, then, on the miserable life view of suffering, you may cite Singer's own works to justify your purchase of the meats. You have every reason to believe that sheep and beef cattle do not lead miserable lives and so escape his argument; you have no reason whatever to believe, of course, that commercially and traditionally farmed food animals of any sort have not suffered at least once at human hands.

We have here, then, two views of suffering and, accordingly, two views on the argument from pain and suffering of what counts as a morally unacceptable method of rearing animals for food. On one, a method is unacceptable if it so affects an animal's quality of life as to make it miserable. This is why Singer so often stresses confinement in cramped conditions: this has the effect, which isolated painful experiences or interludes do not, of converting a life from a benefit to a burden. This view of suffering is compatible, however, with farm animals experiencing pain. On the second view, a method of rearing is unacceptable if it produces any pain or suffering whatever, whether or not the animal's general quality of life is affected thereby.

This division over unacceptable methods has several obvious implications here. First, to see one's task as reducing suffering in commercial farming is on one view of suffering, at least in many cases, not really to the point. Since the reduction of suffering is nevertheless compatible with the presence of suffering, only if the method of reduction eliminates all suffering in rearing may reduction, on something like the single experience view, really be to the point. On the *miserable life view*, however, any reduction in suffering is *prima facie* to the point, since that view is concerned with the quality of life of animals. That is, though it is tempting to think one method of rearing more acceptable than another if it involves considerably less suffering, this is only true on the miserable life view, at least if the method which causes less suffering causes any suffering; for reduction in suffering is very likely to affect animals' quality of life. This is true of any attempt to reduce suffering in farming, whether it succeeds partially or wholly, since, extraordinary circumstances aside, any decrease in suffering represents an increase or a contributory factor to an increase in quality of life.

Second, a meat-eater will not respond to both views of suffering in the same way; in the case of the miserable life view, his response will be much more varied. Broadly speaking, there are the methods of rearing themselves and the animals, and the meat-eater will, for example, seek ever gradual reduction in suffering through, for example, ever better improvements in and alternatives to (very) painful methods and the development of new pain-preventing and pain-killing drugs. He will seek development on these fronts simultaneously. In the case of something like the single experience view, however, since it is unlikely that any improvements in or alternatives to present methods would not involve even a single painful experience, a single trace of suffering, there may seem little point in seeking continuous evolution in rearing methods, beyond, say, those initial measures which substantially improve on the methods under attack. Accordingly, the meat-eater will be forced to rely primarily on pain-preventing and pain-killing drugs, an area in which he will seek continuous technological advances.

There is also the further possibility of genetic engineering to consider, to which both John Rodman and Michael Martin have drawn attention. So far as something like the single experience view is concerned, genetic engineering would have to take the form of the development of food animals which lacked the ability to feel pain. Precisely how feasible that is, I do not know; but given the incredible advances in genetic engineering during the past 30 years, it would be rash to dismiss the idea out of hand. On the miserable life view, however, nothing so dramatic is required; here, the development of animals who felt pain less intensively or who felt it only in some minimal sense or who felt it only above a certain threshold would, especially given evolution in rearing methods and pain-preventing and pain-killing drugs, suffice to ensure the animals did not have miserable lives.

Finally, though the single experience view may strike some readers as reflecting an undue sensitivity, I shall not pursue this claim; rather, I want to draw attention to a rather curious upshot of the view. If the only acceptable method of rearing animals for food is one free of even a single painful experience or trace of suffering, then it is hard to see why the same should not be said of *pets*. It is extremely unlikely, however, that any method of rearing and keeping pets could be entirely without pain and suffering; so if we must give up farming animals because there are no morally acceptable ways of doing so, then it would appear that we must give up rearing and keeping pets on the same ground. But if the only acceptable method of rearing animals, whether for food or companionship, is one free of all pain and suffering, then it is hard to see why the same should not be said of our own children. It is extremely unlikely, however, that any method of rearing children could be entirely without pain or suffering; so if we must give up farming animals because there are no morally acceptable methods of doing so, then it would appear that we must give up having children on the same ground.

On the other hand, if it is acceptable to rear children by painful methods, why is it unacceptable to rear food animals by painful methods? Nothing is gained by saying that the pain we inflict upon children is in order to benefit them (this, I think, is questionable anyway, a good portion of the time), whereas the pain we inflict upon food animals is in order to benefit ourselves, i.e., in order to eat them; for, so far, it has not been shown that it is wrong to benefit ourselves in this way, that the end of eating meat is immoral. Indeed, it was the infliction of pain that was to have shown this. Nor is anything gained by saying that, in the case of children, we at least seek, or, probably more accurately, ought to seek to rear them by methods as painless as we can devise, since the concerned individual I have been describing is quite prepared to consent to this in the case of animals. Nor will it do to say that the level of pain and suffering in food animals cannot be brought to a level commensurate with their leading pleasant lives; not only is one not entitled to legislate in this way on what is not a conceptual matter but it is also not at all obvious, if the concerned individual pursues evolution in rearing methods, drugs, and genetic engineering, that this claim is true.

It is tempting to say that the suffering of children is necessary whereas that of food animals is unnecessary, but it is not at all clear that this is the case. If there is no method of rearing children which is free of all suffering, and if there is no method of rearing animals for food or as pets which is free of all suffering, then the suffering in each case is necessary. If there were a way to rear children or to turn them into responsible, upright citizens without suffering, then it would be incumbent upon us to adopt it; and if there were a way of turning animals into food without suffering, it would be equally incumbent upon us to take it. Certainly, my concerned individual concurs in this; so, on this score, if the suffering in the one case is necessary, then so is it in the other. If we shift the terms of the argument to a different level, so that suffering is necessary *only if* it is inflicted in order for us to live, then the suffering in both cases is unnecessary. Just as I can live without meat, so I can live without children; they are as superfluous to my existence, to my carrying on living, as cars, houses, rose bushes, and pets. In this sense, then, if the only way to avoid unnecessary suffering in pets and food animals is to give them up entirely and cease breeding them, then it seems that we should give up having children for the same reason.

Now I am not suggesting that one cannot draw any differences among these cases; that would be silly. On something like the single experience view of suffering, however, the criterion of acceptability in rearing methods is pitched so high that we appear barred from rearing any feeling creature, including our own children. Readers may well believe, therefore, that we must cast our sights lower. To do so, however, is to settle for a criterion of acceptability which permits some suffering. Precisely how much will be a matter of dispute; but a strong contender for the criterion, in both man and beast, will be the miserable life view. This in turn makes the varied course advocated by the concerned individual into an option on all fours with Singer's option of vegetarianism.

The Concerned Individual's Tactic as a Response to the Argument

The concerned individual's tactic is a direct response to Singer's argument: it addresses itself precisely to what the argument from pain and suffering objects to in factory farming. Indeed, it arises directly out of the terms of that argument. This fact enables us to appreciate several further points about the two tactics before us.

First, someone who took *Animal Liberation* and Singer's argument seriously might maintain that what Singer has shown is not that it is wrong to eat meat but that it is wrong to rear and kill animals by (very) painful methods; and

this same reader might very well go on to conclude, not that we must all become vegetarians, but rather that we must (a) strive to improve conditions on factory farms, to eradicate some of the devices and practices upon them, and to replace these devices and practices with more humane ones, (b) divert resources into the development of new and relatively painless methods of breeding, feeding, and killing animals, of new pain-preventing and pain-killing drugs, of new types of tranquillizers and sedatives, etc. and (c) seek further appropriate breakthroughs in genetic engineering. After all, as we have seen, if we could be practically certain that the meat before us did not come from an animal bred and/or killed by (very) painful methods, and if we ate the meat, then Singer's argument would provide no ground for complaint against us. Accordingly, why not seek to obtain that practical certainty? The problem would then be how to go about this, and the concerned individual's tactic arises as an option.

Once we see that the concerned individual's tactic arises out of the terms of Singer's argument, we are in a position to appreciate that, even if we take that argument in its own terms and take it seriously, vegetarianism is not the obvious conclusion to draw from it. The course advocated by the concerned individual could equally well be the conclusion drawn. One needs some further reason for picking the one tactic as opposed to the other.

Second, as the meat-eater's option flourishes, Singer's case for vegetarianism is progressively undercut. That case loses its applicability, as the amount and intensity of pain produced on factory farms diminish. In other words, his case for vegetarianism hinges upon the actual state of evolution in rearing methods, drugs, and genetic engineering: each development in these areas which reduces pain in farming undercuts Singer's position still further.

If it is true that pain in farming has been drastically reduced or eliminated, however, why should the erosion of his position bother Singer? Whether or not it bothers Singer, it certainly is going to bother countless other vegetarians. For the concerned individual's tactic envisages the continuation of meat-eating and, with (some) changed methods, intensive farming; and the whole point is that, under the conditions set out, the argument from pain and suffering is compatible with, and places no further barrier in the way of, these things.

Third, the meat-eater's option must be faced by all readers of *Animal Liberation* who feel the force of the argument from pain and suffering; *per se,* there is nothing about Singer's position which enables them to avoid a choice between the two tactics I have described. A concerned reader of *Animal Liberation* may well feel impelled by what he reads there about factory farming to take up the cudgels and seek among people at large for a commitment to evolution in rearing methods, drugs, and genetic engineering. Could he not thereby be said to be following the book's lesson, that what is seriously wrong is not eating meat but raising and killing animals by painful methods? Certainly, this individual, who seeks the elimination of (very) painful devices and practices on factory farms and their replacement with more humane ones, who seeks technological advances on all fronts likely to be relevant to the diminution of pain in farming, and who actively tries to stir people up to commit themselves to these ends, is responding directly to Singer's message.

Accordingly, anyone convinced by Singer's argument, anyone convinced that we must reduce, if not eliminate, pain in farming faces a choice between the concerned individual's tactic and vegetarianism as the way to go about this. Neither tactic is *per se* more favoured than the other.

Attempts to Prejudice the Choice Between Tactics

Finally, before turning to Singer's reasons for choosing vegetarianism as one's tactic for combating the pains of food animals, I want to consider two ways in which one might try at the outset to prejudice this choice in tactics between Singer and the concerned individual.

A Life Proper to Their Species

One way of trying to compromise the concerned individual's tactic involves a quite specific use of a very broad sense of pain or suffering. It might be suggested, that is, that to deprive animals of the sort of life proper to their species is a form of pain or suffering in some broad sense, even if the means involved in carrying out this deprivation are, as the result of the concerned individual's option flourishing, so far as new rearing methods and new advances in technology are concerned, free of all pain or suffering in the narrow sense. Thus, even if the concerned individual's tactic was entirely successful in its aims, so long as some intensive methods of rearing were held to deprive some food animals of the sort of life proper to their species, it might be suggested that these animals would continue to have pain or suffering inflicted upon them.

Singer's argument from pain and suffering takes these terms, in the light of the above distinction, in the narrow sense; and I myself do not find much value in inflating their extension, in the way the broad sense envisages.

So far as the concerned individual's tactic is concerned, one must not focus upon his concern with technology to the exclusion of his concern with improvements in and alternatives to some present rearing methods. Take confinement in cruelly narrow spaces, which is by far the most commonly cited reason not only for food animals' miserable lives but also, so it is claimed, for their not leading lives proper to their species: this is a cardinal instance where the concerned individual will seek improvements and alternatives. Already there is some movement in the right direction. For example, in perhaps the most widely cited case of abuse, veal calves, Quantock Veal, which dominates the British veal market, has introduced a new method of rearing these calves.[12] They are not kept alone but in groups of 30; they are not kept in narrow stalls with slatted bottoms but in straw-filled pens in which they can move around freely; they are not kept in darkness but in light; they are not fed an iron-deficient diet but can obtain iron-laced milk from automatic feeders at any time. In this particular case, too, Quantock Veal maintains that this method of rearing veal calves, particularly given the availability of the European Community's dairy surplus, is cheaper than the objectionable method. Plainly, a development of this sort is likely to have a profound, positive effect on the quality of veal calves' lives; as well, it moves to meet the claim that, under present conditions, veal calves are not allowed to lead lives proper to their species.

Or consider the other, major case of abuse commonly cited, laying hens: one development in this area has been the Aviary method. It does not confine hens in cages but allows them to roam freely in poultry sheds, as a result of which they can scratch, flap about, and exercise; they lay in nest boxes or shelves above the ground. So far as I know, debeaking forms no part of the method. This development is not the end of evolution in rearing laying hens, but it seems a beginning.

I give these two examples as instances of the sorts of developments the concerned individual will favour, but I do not pretend either that they are the end of the process of evolution or that they are representative of recent developments as a whole in intensive farming. Rather, they are but two sorts of developments for which the concerned individual must lobby and work, examples of the kinds of evolution in rearing methods for which he must press.

It may be objected, however, that while the concerned individual is pressing for such developments and for advances in technology, food animals are still suffering. But so they are on the other tactic, vegetarianism.

If you face up to the choice of tactics I have been delineating, and you opt for vegetarianism, you would be wrong to think the suffering of food animals is going to come to a halt. In fact, of course, you are going to be left waiting for a sufficient number of others to make a similar choice, in order to give your act any efficacy whatever on the rearing of food animals. And, clearly, you are in for a long wait: even as the number of vegetarians in the United States has grown, the amount of meat consumed there has reached even more colossal heights. It was estimated in December, 1979, that meat consumption in the United States would amount to 214.4 pounds per person during 1980.[13] For a more homely example, a single hamburger establishment in Oxford reported in mid-1981 that it had, since it had opened only six or seven years previously, sold more than 5½ million hamburgers. That is a single establishment, in a single, relatively small city, with a host of fast-food and other restaurants. In facing up to the decision before you, you know beyond doubt that, if you decide in favour of vegetarianism, food animals are going to continue to suffer. On this score, you have no real basis for choosing one tactic over the other.

In sum, evolution in rearing methods seems likely to meet the objection that some methods do not permit some food animals to lead lives proper to their species, if only because improvements in and alternatives to these methods can be sought specifically on this basis. And this moves to meet another objection: it might be charged that the concerned individual's tactic is uncharitable to food animals because it only tries to relieve and not abolish their pains; but this is not true. While the concerned individual does want to relieve animal pain, his response to that pain is varied and includes, through his stress on evolution in rearing methods, the search for improvements in and alternatives to precisely those rearing methods held to be the primary source of the pain in question.

I am also unhappy with this first attempt to prejudice the choice between tactics on another count as well. This has to do with the expression 'the sort of life proper to their species'.

The contemporary *penchant* for studying animals in the wild, in order to find out what they are really like, and, therefore, what sort of life is proper to their respective species, cannot be indulged here, since virtually none of our food animals are found in the wild. Beef, ham, pork, chicken, lamb, mutton, and veal all come from animals who are completely our own productions, bred by us in ways we select to ends we desire. Indeed, the gene pools of these creatures of ours have been manipulated by us to a point today where we can in a great many respects produce the type and strain of creature we want, and the amount of research presently going on in this area is enormous. My point is this: it is a *mistake* to use expressions like '*the sort of life proper to their species*' as if this sort of life were itself immune to technological advance; for by manipulating the gene pools of food animals, by varying our drugs and breeding practices, and by having funded research for progressive advances in all these areas, we already breed these animals to a sort of life which to their bred species—there is no other—is proper.

For example, chickens have been bred with weak leg and wing muscles and with shorter necks, both to reduce their mobility and so to help fatten them and to reduce the sheer amount of each chicken which cannot be turned into food. Even a variation in the size of their bones can now be bred into them. In a word, the descendants of these bred chickens have had bred out of them many of the traits which food producers have wanted eliminated, and they are characterized by reduced mobility, a larger appetite, increased lethargy, significantly increased (or decreased) size, etc. We have manipulated them to this end, and we are carrying on research in this area, funded by major food interests, government organizations, international bodies, and universities, at an accelerated pace. Thus, one very recent development has been a featherless chicken, for use in warm climates. In the southern United States, for example, plumed birds succumb to the heat at a sufficient rate to be a significant cost to farmers, and the featherless bird has in part been developed to meet this problem. (Developments to meet specific problems are increasingly commonplace. For example, cows have a slightly longer gestation period than women, which has meant that they can have only one calf a year; farmers have long wanted more. A procedure has now been developed, which involves the use of multiple ovulation hormones, artificial insemination, and the non-surgical implantation of fertilized eggs in other cows, to solve this problem.)

What sort of life is proper to these chickens? One cannot appeal to chickens in the wild or 'non-developed' chickens for an answer, since there are none; chickens are, to repeat, developments or productions of our own, produced in order to satisfy the fast-food chains and the demands of our Sunday lunches and school picnics. But if one asks what sort of life is proper to 'developed' chickens, we get the above answer. Or are we to turn back the clock and say that the sort of life proper to chickens is the sort they enjoyed when, say, they were first introduced into the United States, long before the first of the developmental farms and any thought of mass-producing them arose? Unless we artificially select some time as that time which reveals to us what chickens are really like, to ask 'What is it in the nature of chickens to be like?' is to ask a question the answer to which must be framed in the light of 'developed' chickens and of technological change.

Now the manipulation of animal gene pools to the extent that we have long since affected the very species of animal in question may well be repugnant to many, and I can easily imagine it being condemned as tampering with nature (and, through nature, with our kith and kin) or with God's handiwork. But I do not really see how it can be condemned on the grounds of inflicting pain and suffering, unless the extension of these terms is simply bloated, not merely beyond anything Singer envisages, but beyond any reasonable degree. There does not seem to be much difference, in fact, between the animal and human cases in this regard: much of the genetic research being conducted with respect to human beings, including experiments involving determination of sex and number of children, test-tube breeding, cloning, and eliminating an extra Y chromosome in males, is widely condemned; but no one condemns it on the ground of inflicting pain and suffering. . . .

Valuing Suffering but Not Life

A second way of trying to compromise the concerned individual's tactic is, in a quite specific way, to try to reduce it to absurdity. The concerned individual seeks to relieve, minimize, and eliminate the pains of food animals but continues to eat meat; it is tempting to portray him, therefore, as valuing animal suffering but not valuing animal life, and then, on the basis of this portrayal, to force him to draw the unpalatable conclusion that, since every animal is going to suffer at some time in its life, he ought now to exterminate all animals painlessly.

I do not myself think well of this argument, which I believe Michael Martin has shown how to answer; but, I contend, if it works against anyone, it works against Singer.

The difficulty with the argument, apart from the very obvious fact that the concerned individual is in no way whatever committed to giving animal life a value of zero, is that, in typically simplistic fashion, it makes it appear that minimizing animal suffering is the only factor applicable to the situation. This is obviously false. For example, to destroy all animals now would result in financial collapse of the meat markets, in financial ruin for food producers and those in related and support industries, in massive unemployment in these industries as well as among farmers, in financial loss to rail and road haulage firms, in a substantial loss in television, newspaper, and magazine advertising revenues, with consequent effect upon the media's viability and profitability, and so on. Here, in quite mercenary

terms, is one good reason why the concerned individual will not exterminate all animals. It is the effects upon human beings and their interests, financial and otherwise, which are here held to outweigh minimizing animal suffering through total extermination or are held at least to be applicable to the situation. Other factors come to mind with equal facility. To kill all animals now would mean the collapse of all experimentation upon animals for human benefit, would depopulate our zoos, which so many children and adults enjoy visiting, and would deprive countless lonely people of their companions. Here, it is human well-being and enjoyment which are held to outweigh minimizing animal suffering through total extermination, or are held at least to be applicable to the situation.

I must stress again, however, that the concerned individual is not compelled to give animal life *no value whatever;* all he has to do is to give human interests, human well-being, and human enjoyment the same or a higher value than minimizing animal suffering through complete extermination.

I do not, then, think much of this argument. But what is little recognized, is that, if the argument applies to anyone, it applies to Singer. His case for vegetarianism, as we have seen, turns exclusively upon minimizing animal pain and suffering, and not in the least upon the value of animal life, which, for the purposes of his case, he is prepared to allow to be anything you like, including zero. Again, he openly endorses the view that a genuine concern for the pains of animals demands that we become vegetarians, without in the least endorsing a view about the value of animal life demanding that we become vegetarians. Pain alone is the basis of his case, and its diminution, minimization, and elimination is his goal. Surely, if anyone must now envisage the complete extermination of animals, because of a concern with the minimization of their suffering, if anyone is forced to conclude that all animals should now be painlessly eliminated, it is Singer?

I am not concerned here to go into possible ways in which Singer might resist this conclusion, except to emphasize that, if they begin even partially to include or make reference to those already sketched, he will be using human interests, well-being, and enjoyment to justify restraint in slaughtering animals, a surprising result in his case.

Notes

1. Peter Singer and James Mason, *Animal Factories*, New York, Crown Publishers Inc., 1980.

2. Peter Singer, 'Killing humans and killing animals', p. 149.

3. Peter Singer, *Practical Ethics*, p. 105.

4. Ibid., p. 56.

5. Ibid., p. 55.

6. Ibid.

7. Peter Singer, *Animal Liberation*, p. 165.

8. Ibid.

9. 'These arguments do not take us all the way to a vegetarian diet, since some animals, for instance sheep and beef cattle, still graze freely outdoors' (Peter Singer, *Practical Ethics*, p. 56).

10. Peter Singer, *Animal Liberation*, p. 165 (italics in original).

11. Peter Singer, *Practical Ethics*, pp. 56–7 (italics in original).

12. See Hugh Clayton, 'Veal farmers aim to erase the stigma of cruelty', *The Times*, 8 May 1980; Ena Kendall, '"Welfare" for veal calves', *Observer*, 4 May 1980.

13. See Sue Shellenbarger, 'Pork Gains on Beef as Meat Choice in U.S.', *International Herald Tribune*, December 23, 1979.

Study Questions

1. How does Frey respond to Singer's utilitarian argument on our duties to animals?
2. What does Frey think should be done with regard to animal factories?
3. Should we all become vegetarians? Why or why not?

CHAPTER 50

The Radical Egalitarian Case for Animal Rights

TOM REGAN

Professor of philosophy at North Carolina State University and a leading animal rights advocate in the United States, Tom Regan is the author of several articles and books on moral philosophy, including *The Case for Animal Rights* (1983).

Regan disagrees with Singer's utilitarian program for animal liberation, for he rejects utilitarianism as lacking a notion of intrinsic worth. Regan's position is that animals and humans all have equal intrinsic value on which their right to life and concern are based. Regan is revolutionary. He calls for not reform but the total abolition of the use of animals in science, the total dissolution of the commercial animal agriculture system, and the total elimination of commercial and sport hunting and trapping. "The fundamental wrong is the system that allows us to view animals as *our resources* . . . Lab animals are not our tasters; we are not their kings."

I REGARD MYSELF as an advocate of animal rights—as a part of the animal rights movement. That movement, as I conceive it, is committed to a number of goals, including:

1. the total abolition of the use of animals in science
2. the total dissolution of commercial animal agriculture
3. and the total elimination of commercial and sport hunting and trapping.

There are, I know, people who profess to believe in animal rights who do not avow these goals. Factory farming they say, is wrong—violates animals' rights—but traditional animal agriculture is all right. Toxicity tests of cosmetics on animals violates their rights; but not important medical research—cancer research, for example. The clubbing of baby seals is abhorrent; but not the harvesting of adult seals. I used to think I understood this reasoning. Not any more. You don't change unjust institutions by tidying them up.

What's wrong—what's fundamentally wrong—with the way animals are treated isn't the details that vary from case to case. It's the whole system. The forlornness of the veal calf is pathetic—heart wrenching; the pulsing pain of the chimp with electrodes planted deep in her brain is repulsive; the slow, torturous death of the raccoon caught in the leg hold trap, agonizing. But what is fundamentally wrong isn't the pain, isn't the suffering, isn't the deprivation. These compound what's wrong. Sometimes—often—they make it much worse. But they are not the fundamental wrong.

The *fundamental wrong is the system that allows us to view animals as our resources*, here for us—to be eaten, or surgically manipulated, or put in our cross hairs for sport or money.

From In Defense of Animals, *edited by Peter Singer (Oxford: Basil Blackwell, 1985). Reprinted by permission.*

Once we accept this view of animals—as our resources—the rest is as predictable as it is regrettable. Why worry about their loneliness, their pain, their death? Since animals exist for us, here to benefit us in one way or another, what harms them really doesn't matter—or matters only if it starts to bother us, makes us feel a trifle uneasy when we eat our veal scampi, for example. So, yes, let us get veal calves out of solitary confinement, give them more space, a little straw, a few companions. But let us keep our veal scampi.

But a little straw, more space, and a few companions don't eliminate—don't even touch—the fundamental wrong, the wrong that attaches to our viewing and treating these animals as our resources. A veal calf killed to be eaten after living in close confinement is viewed and treated in this way: but so, too, is another who is raised (as they say) "more humanely." To right the fundamental wrong of our treatment of farm animals requires more than making rearing methods "more human"—requires something quite different—requires the *total dissolution of commercial animal agriculture.*

How do we do this—whether we do this, or as in the case of animals in science, whether and how we abolish their use—these are to a large extent political questions. People must change their beliefs before they change their habits. Enough people, especially those elected to public office, must believe in change—must want it—before we will have laws that protect the rights of animals. This process of change is very complicated, very demanding, very exhausting, calling for the efforts of many hands—in education, publicity, political organization and activity, down to the licking of envelopes and stamps. As a trained and practicing philosopher the sort of contribution I can make is limited, but, I like to think, important. The currency of philosophy is ideas—their meaning and rational foundation—not the nuts and bolts of the legislative process say, or the mechanics of community organization. That's what I have been exploring

over the past ten years or so in my essays and talks and, more recently, in my book, *The Case for Animal Rights.*[1] I believe the major conclusions I reach in that book are true because they are supported by the weight of the *best arguments.* I believe the idea of animal rights has reason, not just emotion, on its side.

In the space I have at my disposal here I can only sketch, in the barest outlines, some of the main features of the book. Its main themes—and we should not be surprised by this—involve asking and answering deep foundational moral questions, questions about what morality is, how it should be understood, what is the best moral theory all considered. I hope I can convey something of the shape I think this theory is. The attempt to do this will be—to use a word a friendly critic once used to describe my work—cerebral. In fact I was told by this person that my work is "too cerebral." But this is misleading. My feelings about how animals sometimes are treated are just as deep and just as strong as those of my more volatile compatriots. Philosophers do—to use the jargon of the day—have a right side to their brains. If it's the left side we contribute or mainly should—that's because what talents we have reside there.

How to proceed? We begin by asking how the moral status of animals has been understood by thinkers who deny that animals have rights. Then we test the mettle of their ideas by seeing how well they stand up under the heat of fair criticism. If we start our thinking in this way we soon find that some people believe that we have no duties directly to animals—that we owe nothing *to them*—that we can do nothing that *wrongs them.* Rather, we can do wrong acts that involve animals, and so we have duties regarding them, though none to them. Such views may be called indirect duty views. By way of illustration:

Suppose your neighbor kicks your dog. Then your neighbor has done something wrong. But not to your dog. The wrong that has been done is a wrong to you. After all, it is wrong to upset people, and your neighbor's kicking your dog upsets you. So you are the one who is wronged, not your dog. Or again: by kicking your dog your neighbor damages your property. And since it is wrong to damage another person's property, your neighbor has done something wrong—to you, of course, not to your dog. Your neighbor no more wrongs your dog than your car would be wronged if the windshield were smashed. Your neighbor's duties involving your dog are indirect duties to you. More generally, all of our duties regarding animals are indirect duties to one another—to humanity.

How could someone try to justify such a view? One could say that your dog doesn't feel anything and so isn't hurt by your neighbor's kick, doesn't care about the pain since none is felt, is as unaware of anything as your windshield. Someone could say this but no rational person will since, among other considerations, such a view will commit one who holds it to the position that no human being feels pain either—that human beings also don't care about what happens to them. A second possibility is that though both humans and your dog are hurt when kicked, it is only human pain that matters. But, again, no rational person can believe this. Pain is pain wheresoever it occurs. If your neighbor's causing you pain is wrong because of the pain that is caused, we cannot rationally ignore or dismiss the moral relevance of the pain your dog feels.

Philosophers who hold indirect duty views—and many still do—have come to understand that they must avoid the two defects just noted—avoid, that is, both the view that animals don't feel anything as well as the idea that only human pain can be morally relevant. Among such thinkers the sort of view now favored is one or another form of what is called *contractarianism.*

Here, very crudely, is the root idea: morality consists of a set of rules that individuals voluntarily agree to abide by—as we do when we sign a contract (hence the name: contractarianism). Those who understand and accept the terms of the contract are covered directly—have rights created by, and recognized and protected in, the contract. And these contractors can also have protection spelled out for others who, though they lack the ability to understand morality and so cannot sign the contract themselves, are loved or cherished by those who can. Thus young children, for example, are unable to sign and lack rights. But they are protected by the contract nonetheless because of the sentimental interests of others, most notably their parents. So we have, then, duties involving these children, duties regarding them, but no duties to them. Our duties in their case are indirect duties to other human beings, usually their parents.

As for animals, since they cannot understand the contract, they obviously cannot sign; and since they cannot sign; they have no rights. Like children, however, some animals are the objects of the sentimental interest of others. You, for example, love your dog . . . or cat. So these animals—those enough people care about: companion animals, whales, baby seals, the American bald eagle—these animals, though they lack rights themselves, will be protected because of the sentimental interests of people. I have, then, according to contractarianism, no duty directly to your dog or any other animal, not even the duty not to cause them pain or suffering; my duty not to hurt them is a duty I have to those people who care about what happens to them. As for other animals, where no or little sentimental interest is present—farm animals, for example, or laboratory rats—what duties we have grow weaker and weaker, perhaps to the vanishing point. The pain and death they endure, though real, are not wrong if no one cares about them.

Contractarianism could be a hard view to refute when it comes to the moral status of animals if it was an adequate theoretical approach to the moral status of human beings. It is not adequate in this latter respect, however, which makes the question of its adequacy in the former—regarding animals—utterly moot. For consider: morality, according to the (crude) contractarian position before us, consists of rules people agree to abide by. What people? Well, enough to make a difference—enough, that is, so that collectively they have the power to enforce the rules that are drawn up in the contract. That is very well and good for the signatories—but not so good for anyone who is not asked to sign. And there is nothing in contractarianism of the sort we are discussing that guarantees or requires that everyone will have a chance to participate equitably in framing the rules of morality. The result is that this approach to ethics could sanction the most blatant forms of social, economic, moral, and political injustice, ranging from a repressive caste system to systematic racial or sexual discrimination. Might, on this theory, does make right. Let those who are the victims of injustice suffer as they will. It matters not so long as no one else—no contractor, or too few of them—cares about it. Such a theory takes one's moral breath away . . . as if, for example, there is nothing wrong with apartheid in South Africa if too few white South Africans are upset by it. A theory with so little to recommend it at the level of the ethics of our treatment of our fellow humans cannot have anything more to recommend it when it comes to the ethics of how we treat our fellow animals.

The version of contractarianism just examined is, as I have noted, a crude variety, and in fairness to those of a contractarian persuasion it must be noted that much more refined, subtle, and ingenious varieties are possible. For example, John Rawls, in his *A Theory of Justice,* sets forth a version of contractarianism that forces the contractors to ignore the accidental features of being a human being—for example, whether one is white or black, male or female, a genius or of modest intellect. Only by ignoring such features, Rawls believes, can we insure that the principles of justice contractors would agree upon are not based on bias or prejudice. Despite the improvement a view such as Rawls's shows over the cruder forms of contractarianism, it remains de-

ficient: it systematically denies that we have direct duties to those human beings who do not have a sense of justice—young children, for instance, and many mentally retarded humans. And yet it seems reasonably certain that, were we to torture a young child or a retarded elder, we would be doing something that wrongs them, not something that is wrong if (and only if) other humans with a sense of justice are upset. And since this is true in the case of these humans, we cannot rationally deny the same in the case of animals.

Indirect duty views, then, including the best among them, fail to command our rational assent. Whatever ethical theory we rationally should accept, therefore, it must at least recognize that we have some duties directly to animals, just as we have some duties directly to each other. The next two theories I'll sketch attempt to meet this requirement.

The first I call the *cruelty-kindness* view. Simply stated, this view says that we have a direct duty to be kind to animals and a direct duty not to be cruel to them. Despite the familiar, reassuring ring of these ideas, I do not believe this view offers an adequate theory. To make this clearer, consider kindness. A kind person acts from a certain kind of motive—compassion or concern, for example. And that is a virtue. But there is no guarantee that a kind act is a right act. If I am a generous racist, for example, I will be inclined to act kindly toward members of my own race, favoring their interests above others. My kindness would be real and, so far as it goes, good. But I trust it is too obvious to require comment that my kind acts may not be above moral reproach—may, in fact, be positively wrong because rooted in injustice. So kindness, notwithstanding its status as a virtue to be encouraged, simply will not cancel the weight of a theory of right action.

Cruelty fares no better. People or their acts are cruel if they display either a lack of sympathy for or, worse, the presence of enjoyment in, seeing another suffer. Cruelty in all its guises *is* a bad thing—*is* a tragic human failing. But just as a person's being motivated by kindness does not guarantee that they do what is right, so the absence of cruelty does not assure that they avoid doing what is wrong. Many people who perform abortions, for example, are not cruel, sadistic people. But that fact about their character and motivation does not settle the terribly difficult question about the morality of abortion. The case is no different when we examine the ethics of our treatment of animals. So, yes, let us be for kindness and against cruelty. But let us not suppose that being for the one and against the other answers questions about moral right and wrong.

Some people think the theory we are looking for is *utilitarianism.* A utilitarian accepts two moral principles. The first is a principle of *equality: everyone's interests count, and similar interests must be counted as having similar weight or importance.* White or black, male or female, American or Iranian, human or animal: everyone's pain or frustration matter and matter equally with the like pain or frustration of anyone else. The second principle a utilitarian accepts is the principle of *utility: do that act that will bring about the best balance of satisfaction over frustration for everyone affected by the outcome.*

As a utilitarian, then, here is how I am to approach the task of deciding what I morally ought to do: I must ask who will be affected if I choose to do one thing rather than another, how much each individual will be affected, and where the best results are most likely to lie— which option, in other words, is most likely to bring about the best results, the best balance of satisfaction over frustration. That option, whatever it may be, is the one I ought to choose. That is where my moral duty lies.

The great appeal of utilitarianism rests with its uncompromising *egalitarianism:* everyone's interests count and count equally with the like interests of everyone else. The kind of odious discrimination some forms of contractarianism can justify—discrimination based on race or sex, for example—seems disallowed in principle by

utilitarianism, as is speciesism—systematic discrimination based on species membership.

The sort of equality we find in utilitarianism, however, is not the sort an advocate of animal or human rights should have in mind. Utilitarianism has no room for the *equal moral rights of different individuals because it has no room for their equal inherent value or worth.* What has value for the utilitarian is the satisfaction of an individual's interests, not the individual whose interests they are. A universe in which you satisfy your desire for water, food, and warmth, is, other things being equal, better than a universe in which these desires are frustrated. And the same is true in the case of an animal with similar desires. But neither you nor the animal have any value in your own right. *Only your feelings do.*

Here is an analogy to help make the philosophical point clearer: a cup contains different liquids—sometimes sweet, sometimes bitter, sometimes a mix of the two. What has value are the liquids: the sweeter the better, the bitter the worse. The cup—the container—has no value. It's what goes into it, not what they go into, that has value. For the utilitarian, you and I are like the cup; we have no value as individuals and thus no equal value. What has value is what goes into us, what we serve as receptacles for; our feelings of satisfaction have positive value, our feelings of frustration have negative value.

Serious problems arise for utilitarianism when we remind ourselves that it enjoins us to bring about the best consequences. What does this mean? It doesn't mean the best consequences for me alone, or for my family or friends, or any other person taken individually. No, what we must do is, roughly, as follows: we must add up—somehow!—the separate satisfactions and frustrations of everyone likely to be affected by our choice, the satisfactions in one column, the frustrations in the other. We must total each column for each of the options before us. That is what it means to say the theory is aggregative. And then we must choose that option which is most likely to bring about the best balance of totaled satisfactions over totaled frustrations. Whatever act would lead to this outcome is the one we morally ought to perform—is where our moral duty lies. And that act quite clearly might not be the same one that would bring about the best results for me personally, or my family or friends, or a lab animal. The best aggregated consequences for everyone concerned are not necessarily the best for each individual.

That utilitarianism is an aggregative theory— that different individual's satisfactions or frustrations are added, or summed, or totaled—is the key objection to this theory. My Aunt Bea is old, inactive, a cranky, sour person, though not physically ill. She prefers to go on living. She is also rather rich. I could make a fortune if I could get my hands on her money, money she intends to give me in any event, after she dies, but which she refuses to give me now. In order to avoid a huge tax bite, I plan to donate a handsome sum of my profits to a local children's hospital. Many, many children will benefit from my generosity, and much joy will be brought to their parents, relatives, and friends. If I don't get the money rather soon, all these ambitions will come to naught. The once-in-a-life-time-opportunity to make a real killing will be gone. Why, then, not really kill my Aunt Bea? Oh, of course I *might* get caught. But I'm no fool and, besides, her doctor can be counted on to cooperate (he has an eye for the same investment and I happen to know a good deal about his shady past). The deed can be done . . . professionally, shall we say. There is *very* little chance of getting caught. And as for my conscience being guilt ridden, I am a resourceful sort of fellow and will take more than sufficient comfort—as I lie on the beach at Acapulco—in contemplating the joy and health I have brought to so many others.

Suppose Aunt Bea is killed and the rest of the story comes out as told. Would I have done anything wrong? Anything immoral? One would have thought that I had. But not according to utilitarianism. Since what I did brought about the best balance of totaled satisfaction over frus-

tration for all those affected by the outcome, what I did was not wrong. Indeed, in killing Aunt Bea the physician and I did what duty required.

This same kind of argument can be repeated in all sorts of cases, illustrating time after time, how the utilitarian's position leads to results that impartial people find morally callous. It *is* wrong to kill my Aunt Bea in the name of bringing about the best results for others. A good end does not justify an evil means. Any adequate moral theory will have to explain why this is so. Utilitarianism fails in this respect and so cannot be the theory we seek.

What to do? Where to begin anew? The place to begin, I think, is with the utilitarian's view of the value of the individual—or, rather, lack of value. In its place suppose we consider that you and I, for example, do have value as individuals—what we'll call *inherent value*. To say we have such value is to say that we are something more than, something different from, mere receptacles. Moreover, to insure that we do not pave the way for such injustices as slavery or sexual discrimination, we must believe that all who have inherent value have it equally, regardless of their sex, race, religion, birthplace, and so on. Similarly to be discarded as irrelevant are one's talents or skills, intelligence and wealth, personality or pathology, whether one is loved and admired—or despised and loathed. The genius and the retarded child, the prince and the pauper, the brain surgeon and the fruit vendor, Mother Theresa and the most unscrupulous used car salesman—all have inherent value, all possess it *equally,* and *all have an equal right to be treated with respect,* to be treated in ways that do not reduce them to the status of things, as if they exist as resources for others. My value as an individual is independent of my usefulness to you. Yours is not dependent on your usefulness to me. For either of us to treat the other in ways that fail to show respect for the other's independent value is to act immorally—is to violate the individual's rights.

Some of the rational virtues of this view—what I call the rights view—should be evident. Unlike (crude) contractarianism, for example, the rights view *in principle* denies the moral tolerability of any and all forms of racial, sexual, or social discrimination; and unlike utilitarianism, this view *in principle* denies that we can justify good results by using evil means that violate an individual's rights—denies, for example, that it could be moral to kill my Aunt Bea to harvest beneficial consequences for others. That would be to sanction the disrespectful treatment of the individual in the name of the social good, something the rights view will not—categorically will not—ever allow.

The rights view—or so I believe—is rationally the most satisfactory moral theory. It surpasses all other theories in the degree to which it illuminates and explains the foundation of our duties to one another—the domain of human morality. On this score, it has the best reasons, the best arguments, on its side. Of course, if it were possible to show that only human beings are included within its scope, then a person like myself, who believes in animal rights, would be obliged to look elsewhere than to the rights view.

But attempts to limit its scope to humans only can be shown to be rationally defective. Animals, it is true, lack many of the abilities humans possess. They can't read, do higher mathematics, build a bookcase, or make *baba ghanoush*. Neither can many human beings, however, and yet we don't say—and shouldn't say—that they (these humans) therefore have less inherent value, less of a right to be treated with respect, than do others. It is the *similarities* between those human beings who most clearly, most noncontroversially have such value—the people reading this, for example—it is our similarities, not our differences, that matter most. And the really crucial, the basic similarity is simply this: *we are each of us the experiencing subject of a life, each of us a conscious creature having an individual welfare that has importance to us whatever our usefulness to others.* We want and prefer things;

believe and feel things; recall and expect things. And all these dimensions of our life, including our pleasure and pain, our enjoyment and suffering, our satisfaction and frustration, our continued existence or our untimely death—all make a difference to the quality of our life as lived, as experienced by us as individuals. And the same is true of those animals who concern us (those who are eaten and trapped, for example), they, too, must be viewed as the experiencing subjects of a life with inherent value of their own.

There are some who resist the idea that animals have inherent value. "Only humans have such value," they profess. How might this narrow view be defended? Shall we say that only humans have the requisite intelligence, or autonomy, or reason? But there are many, many humans who will fail to meet these standards and yet who are reasonably viewed as having value above and beyond their usefulness to others. Shall we claim that only humans belong to the right species—the species *Homo sapiens*? But this is blatant speciesism. Will it be said, then, that all—and only—humans have immortal souls? Then our opponents more than have their work cut out for them. I am myself not ill-disposed to there being immortal souls. Personally, I profoundly hope I have one. But I would not want to rest my position on a controversial ethical issue on the even more controversial question about who or what has an immortal soul. That is to dig one's hole deeper, not climb out. Rationally, it is better to resolve moral issues without making more controversial assumptions than are needed. The question of who has inherent value is such a question, one that is more rationally resolved without the introduction of the idea of immortal souls than by its use.

Well, perhaps some will say that animals have some inherent value, only *less* than we do. Once again, however, attempts to defend this view can be shown to lack rational justification. What could be the basis of our having more inherent value than animals? Will it be their lack of reason, or autonomy, or intellect? Only if we are willing to make the same judgement in the case of humans who are similarly deficient. But it is not true that such humans—the retarded child, for example, or the mentally deranged—have less inherent value than you or I. Neither, then, can we rationally sustain the view that animals like them in being the experiencing subjects of a life have less inherent value. *All who have inherent value have it equally, whether they be human animals or not.*

Inherent value, then, belongs equally to those who are the experiencing subjects of a life. Whether it belongs to others—to rocks and rivers, trees and glaciers, for example—we do not know. And may never know. But neither do we need to know, if we are to make the case for animal rights. We do not need to know how many people, for example, are eligible to vote in the next presidential election before we can know whether I am. Similarly, we do not need to know *how many* individuals have inherent value before we can know that some do. When it comes to the case for animal rights, then what we need to know is whether the animals who, in our culture are routinely eaten, hunted, and used in our laboratories, for example, are like us in being subjects of a life. And we *do* know this. We do *know* that many—literally, billions and billions—of these animals are the subjects of a life in the sense explained and so have inherent value if we do. And since, in order to have the best theory of our duties to one another, we must recognize our equal inherent value, as individuals, *reason*—not sentiment, not emotion—*reason compels us to recognize the equal inherent value of these animals.* And, with this, their equal right to be treated with respect.

That, *very* roughly, is the shape and feel of the case for animal rights. Most of the details of the supporting argument are missing. They are to be found in the book I alluded to earlier. Here, the details go begging and I must in closing, limit myself to four final points.

The first is how the theory that underlies the case for animal rights shows that the animal rights movement is a part of, not antagonistic to, the human rights movement. The theory that rationally grounds the rights of animals also grounds the rights of humans. Thus are those involved in the animal rights movement partners in the struggle to secure respect for human rights—the rights of women, for example, or minorities and workers. The animal rights movement is cut from the same moral cloth as these.

Second, having set out the broad outlines of the rights view, I can now say why its *implications for farming and science,* for example, are both clear and uncompromising. In the case of using animals in science, the rights view is categorically abolitionist. *Lab animals are not our tasters; we are not their kings.* Because these animals are treated—routinely, systematically—as if their value is reducible to their usefulness to others, they are routinely systematically treated with a lack of respect, and thus are their rights routinely, systematically violated. This is just as true when they are used in trivial, duplicative, unnecessary or unwise research as it is when they are used in studies that hold out real promise of human benefits. We can't justify harming or killing a human being (my Aunt Bea, for example) just for these sorts of reasons. Neither can we do so even in the case of so lowly a creature as a laboratory rat. It is not just refinement or reduction that are called for, not just larger, cleaner cages, not just more generous use of anesthetic or the elimination of multiple surgery, not just tidying up the system. It is replacement—completely. The best we can do when it comes to using animals in science is—not to use them. That is where our duty lies, according to the rights view.

As for commercial animal agriculture, the rights view takes a similar abolitionist position. The fundamental moral wrong here is not that animals are kept in stressful close confinement, or in isolation, or that they have their pain and suffering, their needs and preferences ignored or discounted. *All* these *are* wrong, of course, but they are not the fundamental wrong. They are symptoms and effects of the deeper, systematic wrong that allows these animals to be viewed and treated as lacking independent value, as resources for us—as, indeed, a renewable resource. Giving farm animals more space, more natural environments, more companions does not right the fundamental wrong, any more than giving lab animals more anaesthesia or bigger, cleaner cages would right the fundamental wrong in their case. Nothing less than the total dissolution of commercial animal agriculture will do this, just as, for similar reasons I won't develop at length here, morality requires nothing less than the total elimination of commercial and sport hunting and trapping. The rights view's implications, then, as I have said, are clear—and are uncompromising.

My last two points are about philosophy—my profession. It is most obviously, no substitute for political action. The words I have written here and in other places by themselves don't change a thing. It is what we do with the thoughts the words express—our acts, our deeds—that change things. All that philosophy can do, and all I have attempted, is to offer a vision of what our deeds could aim at. And the why. But not the how.

Finally, I am reminded of my thoughtful critic, the one I mentioned earlier, who chastised me for being "too cerebral." Well, cerebral I have been: indirect duty views, utilitarianism, contractarianism—hardly the stuff deep passions are made of. I am also reminded, however, of the image another friend once set before me—the image of the ballerina as expressive of disciplined passion. Long hours of sweat and toil, of loneliness and practice, of doubt and fatigue; that is the discipline of her craft. But the passion is there, too: the fierce drive to excel, to speak through her body, to do it right, to pierce our minds. That is the image of philosophy I would leave with you; not "too cerebral," but *disciplined passion*. Of the discipline, enough has been seen. As for the passion:

There are times, and these are not infrequent, when tears come to my eyes when I see, or read, or hear of the wretched plight of animals in the hands of humans. Their pain, their suffering, their loneliness, their innocence, their death. Anger. Rage. Pity. Sorrow. Disgust. The whole creation groans under the weight of the evil we humans visit upon these mute, powerless creatures. It *is* our heart, not just our head, that calls for an end, that demands of us that we overcome, for them, the habits and forces behind their systematic oppression. All great movements, it is written, go through three stages: ridicule, discussion, adoption. It is the realization of this third stage—adoption—that demands both our passion and our discipline, our heart and our head. *The fate of animals is in our hands. God grant we are equal to the task.*

Note

1. Tom Regan. *The Case For Animal Rights* (Berkeley: University of California Press, 1983).

Study Questions

1. How is Regan's position on animal rights different from Singer's? Explain.
2. What are Regan's reasons for granting animals equal moral rights?
3. Does Regan allow for experimentation on animals? If we have to test a dangerous AIDS vaccine, on whom should we test it?

CHAPTER 51

The Case for Animal Experimentation

ROBERT WHITE

Robert White is a physician. He does not argue for the superior value of human beings but takes it for granted. He offers several examples where experiments on animals have resulted in valuable knowledge that has enabled medical science to cure disease and enhance the quality of our lives. He contends that if we accepted the egalitarian views of People for the Ethical Treatment of Animals (PETA), we would not have these benefits today.

WE WEPT AND WATCHED, my wife and I, as a little girl fought for her life. She was tiny, frail, helpless, and so very vulnerable. Motionless except as her chest rose and fell spasmodically, there lay Lauren, our first grandchild, born so prematurely that each breath was a desperate and failing effort. We wept, our hearts torn by the growing realization that Lauren might not live. The next day she died. The best care that medicine could offer was not enough. The research on baby lambs and kittens that has given life to many premature infants such as Lauren was still in the future and would come too late for her.

In time, two grandsons, Jonathan and Bryan, were born. Premature babies, they also had to struggle for life. Our pain of uncertainty and of waiting was all to be endured twice again. But the little boys lived. The knowledge gained through research on lambs and kittens gave them life, a gift that Lauren could not have.

The memories of despair and grief at the death of one grandchild and of relief and hope and joy at the life of two others, all of these memories came back to me as I sat at my desk preparing to write this essay in defense of the moral and scientific necessity for the use of animals in medical research. And as I thought of the numerous advances in medical care that would have been impossible without experiments on cats and sheep and baby lambs, on dogs and pigs and monkeys and mice, on cows and horses and even armadillos, as I thought of all these advances in medical care that have given health and life to countless people, including my grandsons, my mind was flooded by a host of memories.

First was the memory of an esteemed colleague whose recovery from a near-fatal heart attack was made possible by the use of a newly discovered enzyme that dissolved the clot that fouled his arteries. Later he was restored to nearly perfect health by a coronary arteriogram and a percutaneous transluminal coronary angioplasty. He owes his life to scores of dogs on whom the studies were done to perfect the use of streptokinase, the enzyme that was used to dissolve the clotted blood from his coronary arteries. And he also owes his life to yet other dogs on whom the techniques of coronary arteriography and angioplasty were developed and perfected.

Reprinted from Robert White, "Beastly Questions," Hastings Center Report (March–April 1989) by permission. Copyright © The Hastings Center.

Another colleague whom I recently saw at a medical meeting came next to mind. He had developed disabling arthritis of one hip, but now was able to walk again, thanks to the surgical replacement of his crippled joint. He now walks with a limp, but he walks—only because of dogs that were operated on in the course of research that developed and perfected the artificial hip.

One memory evoked another and then another and then another. I recalled patients who were devastated by poliomyelitis in the terrible epidemic of the 1940s, an epidemic in which one of my closest friends and colleagues contracted the disease and nearly died. He survived miraculously after being confined for many days in a respirator, or, as it was called in those days, an iron lung.

And then came memories from the 1950s when I helped give Salk vaccine to the children in a small town in New England. The little ones howled when I approached them with the syringe and needle. A few years later such children were immunized without screams of fear and pain because by then vaccination against poliomyelitis involved nothing more than sucking on a little cube of sugar containing a few drops of vaccine. In his very moving history of the development of the oral vaccine against poliomyelitis, Albert Sabin gave a graphic description of the thirty years of research that were needed to develop his highly effective vaccine. He made clear that this outstanding contribution to the welfare of mankind would not have been possible without experiments on "many thousands of monkeys and hundreds of chimpanzees."[1] Dr. Sabin's vaccine, since its introduction in 1960, has provided nearly complete protection against poliomyelitis to hundreds of millions of people all over the world. The monkeys and chimps to which he referred have saved thousands of lives and spared hundreds of thousands of children a lifetime marred by paralyzed limbs. Poliomyelitis has been very nearly eradicated throughout the industrialized world and could be eradicated in developing nations if those countries had the resources to do so.

These memories were soon followed by recollection of my experience as a consultant on the burn wards here at my medical school and of the scores of severely burned children and adults whose survival often depended on care perfected through the study of burns experimentally inflicted on pigs and sheep and dogs in the research laboratory. In addition, some of those patients who survived did so because the skin of pigs was used as a temporary graft to cover the raw, oozing areas of their seared flesh.

Then came more recent recollections of my work as a consultant in the care of patients with the acquired immune deficiency syndrome, better known as AIDS. They die slowly and pathetically, these patients with AIDS, and we physicians stand by helplessly as they die because as yet we do not know enough about the virus that causes this dread disease. Thousands are dying from that virus now, and tens of thousands will die in this epidemic in the coming few years unless current research leads to an effective vaccine. This research must include the study of monkeys that are deliberately infected with the AIDS virus. Will the opponents of experimentation on animals prevent present-day researchers from eradicating the AIDS virus, as Dr. Sabin and others conquered the virus of poliomyelitis?

And finally, I thought of another friend and colleague whose belly was ripped by machine gun fire as he parachuted into Europe during the second world war. Without plasma and blood transfusions, this young medical officer would have died before he could be flown to a hospital in England. If those who oppose the use of animals in medical research had prevailed some fifty years ago, there would have been no research on hemorrhagic shock in dogs. This research cost the life of many dogs that were bled into a state of severe and, at times, fatal shock. But the knowledge gained through the sacrifice of these animals gave medicine the means to save this soldier when he nearly bled to death as he dangled helplessly in his parachute in the French sky in 1944. And there is no counting the number of others, soldiers and civilians, who owe their lives to these experiments on dogs.

And so my memories came, one after the other, but they all led to the same question: "How can any rational, compassionate, and thoughtful person oppose the use of animals in medical research?" Have those who oppose such research watched one grandchild die because of lack of medical knowledge and then, a few years later, watched two other grandchildren be saved by medical procedures that could not have been developed without research on animals? Would they have a young medical officer bleed to death somewhere in war-torn France rather than allow the experiments on dogs that were essential to the development of effective treatment of shock due to massive loss of blood? Are they so blindly opposed to the use of animals in medical research that they would prevent Dr. Sabin's experiments on his "thousands of monkeys and hundreds of chimpanzees" that were necessary to perfect the vaccine that conquered poliomyelitis? Will they tell the thousands of patients who today suffer from AIDS to give up hope because monkeys should not be used in the laboratory in our fight against this plague? Are those who oppose my view on the use of animals in medical research willing to tell my grandsons that it would have been preferable to let them and thousands of other children die rather than allow research on animals? I hope not.

But the fact is, there are people who would let my grandsons die rather than allow any animal to be used in medical research. These are not people who press only for the humane treatment of animals in the laboratory, a cause that no reasonable person can oppose. These are antivivisectionists who will, if they have their

way, put a stop to all experimentation on animals no matter the cost to the advancement of health care. The number and the political influence of people in this movement have grown alarmingly in recent years. They have lobbied successfully for a law in Massachusetts to forbid the use of pound animals in biomedical research. And now they are pressing Congress to impose similar restrictions nationwide. If such federal legislation is passed, it will seriously hamper all medical research in this country and will make the cost of some research prohibitively high, as it already has done in Massachusetts.[2]

Those who oppose the use of pound animals in biomedical studies make little or no mention of the fact that only two percent of those animals are used in scientific experiments, while the other ten to fifteen million meet a meaningless and useless death at the pound each year.

And the comments of some of the leaders in the antivivisectionist movement suggest that they are motivated more by personal needs to win a power struggle against the leaders of the biomedical community than by humanitarian concerns for either people or animals. For example, John McArdle, a nationally prominent antivivisectionist, has stated that he believes medical researchers have been placed by the public on a pedestal and he comments: "we're whacking away at the base of that pedestal, and it is going to fall."[3] He also has made the rather macabre suggestion that medical researchers should perform their experiments on brain-dead humans rather than animals. He stated, "It may take people awhile to get used to the idea, but once they do, the savings in animal lives will be substantial."

Another leading antivivisectionist is Ingrid Newkirk, the codirector of PETA, or People for the Ethical Treatment of Animals. She has said that scientists who experiment on animals have been "lying and misleading the public" about the value of research on animals.[4] She stated that the objective of PETA is to attack "the whole grubby system of biomedical research, because if you jeopardize an animal one iota [in doing research] . . . you're doing something immoral. Even painless research is fascism . . ." And, she added, "Animal liberationists do not separate out the human animal, so there is no rational basis for saying that a human being has special rights. A rat is a pig is a dog is a boy."

Jonathan and Bryan, my grandsons, disagree.

Notes

1. Albert B. Sabin, "Oral Poliovirus Vaccine: History of Its Development and Prospects for Eradication of Poliomyelitis," *Journal of the American Medical Association* 194, no. 8 (1965):872–76.

2. Katie McCabe, "Who Will Live, Who Will Die," *The Washingtonian* 21, no. 11 (1986):112–18.

3. Ibid.

4. Ibid.

Study Questions

1. Discuss the merits of White's argument that animal experiments have produced enormous knowledge and, hence, lifesaving benefits for humans. What assumptions underlie White's arguments?

2. How would Singer and Regan respond to White's claim that animal research is justified because it provides benefits for humans?

CHAPTER 52

The Case Against Animal Experimentation

TOM REGAN

In this selection from Tom Regan's (see Chapter 50 for a biographical sketch) book, *The Case for Animal Rights*, he applies his theory of animal rights to animal experimentation. He considers both toxicity tests for commercial products and experimentation in scientific research and argues that in both cases it is immoral to coerce animals into these experiments. These experiments violate the animal's rights to be treated as inherently valuable. In some cases human beings should experiment on other human beings in order to obtain the knowledge they need. Regan would allow research on mammalian embryos, since they are not yet persons.

HARMFUL TOXICITY TESTS of products on animals *are* wrong, . . . according to the rights view, not because they are an unreliable means for assessing what is toxic for humans (though the limitations of these tests, relative to establishing what is safe for humans, are real enough); nor are they wrong only when, because the results are predictable before the tests are done, certain tests are unnecessary (though this is true also); fundamentally, these tests are wrong because they violate the rights of laboratory animals. Since the only humans who might claim, however implausibly, that they would be made worse-off if these tests were not done (namely, those associated with the manufacture of new products) are the very ones who voluntarily waive their right not to be made worse-off as a result of their voluntary participation in a relevant business venture, and since no consumer would be made worse-off than any of the test animals if these tests were stopped and consumers were "deprived" of new products, appeal to the worse-off principle shows that these tests are morally unjustified. These harmful tests violate the basic moral right of these animals not to be harmed. Morally, they ought to cease.

The rights view is not anticonsumer or anti-worker protection. It is not opposed in principle to efforts to minimize the health risks individuals run in the work- and marketplace. Consumer and worker safety is a laudatory aim, and, human nature being what it is, perhaps it is not unreasonable for society to impose regulations on manufacturers whose products are intended for the public's use, in the hope of protecting the public against unscrupulous businesses out to make a quick buck at the public's expense. What the rights view opposes is practices that violate the basic rights of individuals in the name of "the public interest." Toxicity tests of new products that harm animals fall into this category. Anyone who objected to the rights view on the grounds that it is "morally indefensible" to release untested products into the market would miss the central point. What *is* morally indefensible is to rely on tests that violate anyone's rights. The options, then, are not *either* to continue to use these tests *or* to release untested

Reprinted from The Case for Animal Rights *(Berkeley: University of California Press, 1983) by permission.*

products. A third option is *not to allow products on the market if they were pretested for toxicity on animals*. That is the option those who would dispute the rights view in the way currently under review fail to recognize.

The rights view's denunciation of standard toxicity tests on animals is not antibusiness. It does not deny any manufacturer the liberty to introduce any new product into the marketplace, to compete with the others already there, and to sink or swim in the waters of free enterprise. All that the rights view denies is that the toxicity of any new product may be pretested on animals in ways harmful to them. *Nonanimal alternatives* are not ruled out by the rights view. On the contrary, their development should be encouraged, both on the grounds of the public interest and because of the legitimate legal interests of the manufacturers. Commercial firms should begin to devote their not inconsiderable financial and scientific resources toward the development of such tests. If, in reply, we are told that it is government regulatory agencies, such as the Food and Drug Administration, that require these tests, and that the manufacturers are only doing what the law requires, then the rights view's principal reply is that *these regulatory agencies do not require that any new product be produced*. To take refuge in what these agencies require neither provides a moral justification for introducing new products nor for testing their toxicity on animals. Moreover, in denouncing the present practice of testing the toxicity of new products on animals, the rights view does not bid cosmetic manufacturers, for example, to remove all their present products from the shelves. The wrong that has been done in the past cannot be undone. The vital point is not to let it continue in the future. Manufacturers can hardly complain that this is antibusiness or against the spirit of the free enterprise system. Let those companies competing in the marketplace compete with the products they already have or, even more in keeping with this economic philosophy, let them outdo one another by developing nonanimal alternatives and, as also befits this philosophy, let them labor to have the scientific validity of these tests recognized by the appropriate regulatory agencies. That sort of competition would be a paradigm of the free enterprise system at its finest.

In reply it will be claimed that no valid nonanimal alternatives exist. This is false. In the case of cosmetics, for example, the pioneering work of Beauty Without Cruelty demonstrates beyond any reasonable doubt that it is possible to manufacture and market attractive, reliable products whose toxicity for humans has not been pretested on animals. Moreover, in areas where no nonanimal tests presently exist, there is no reason why they cannot be explored, and to claim in advance that there *are none* to be found is to be guilty of being just as antiscientific as some of those who criticize animal toxicity tests. None are so blind as those who will not look. Whether found or not, whether looked for or not, the rights view's position is uncompromising: *Harmful toxicity tests of new products violate the rights of laboratory animals and ought to be stopped*. The least we, as consumers, can do to help achieve this goal is henceforth to refuse to buy any new product, including so-called new, improved varieties of old ones, when they hit the market, unless we know that they have not been pretested for their toxicity on animals. That is a modest deprivation anyone who respects the rights of these animals ought to be willing to endure.

Toxicity Tests of New Drugs

Someone might accept the preceding critique of toxicity tests on animals in the case of new products and claim that the case of doing such tests on *new therapeutic drugs* differs in morally relevant respects. No human being will be harmed in a way that is *prima facie* comparable to the harm caused test animals in an LD50 test, for example, by being deprived of a new brake fluid or paint. Some humans are harmed, however, right now, as a result of a variety of pathological conditions, and many more will be harmed if we fail to investigate the causes, treatments, and cures of these conditions. Indeed, some will today lose their lives as a result of these maladies, and many more will lose theirs in the future if we fail to investigate their causes and cures. Now, one thing we must do, it may be claimed, is reduce the risk that the treatment prescribed for a given malady will make patients worse-off than they otherwise would have been, and this will require establishing the toxic properties of each new drug before, not after, humans take them. Thus arises the need to test the toxicity of each new drug on test animals. If we do not test the toxicity of all new drugs on animals, humans who use these drugs will run a much greater risk of being made worse-off as a result of using them than they would if these drugs were pretested on animals. In the nature of the case, we cannot say which drugs are toxic for humans *in advance* of conducting tests on animals (if we could, there would be no need to do the test in the first place). Indeed, we cannot even eliminate all risks *after* the drug has been extensively pretested on animals (thalidomide is a tragic example). The best we can do is minimize the risks humans who use drugs face, as best we can, and that requires testing for their toxicity on animals.

The rights view rejects this defense of these tests. *Risks are not morally transferable to those who do not voluntarily choose to take them in the way this defense assumes.* If I hang-glide, then I run certain risks, including the possibility of serious head injury, and I shall certainly, if I am prudent, want to minimize my risks by wearing a protective helmet. You, who do not hang-glide, have no duty to agree to serve in tests that establish the safety of various helmet designs so that hang-gliders might reduce their risks, and hang-gliders, or those who serve the interests of these enthusiasts, would violate your rights if

they coerced or forced you to take part in such tests. *How much* you would be harmed is not decisive. What matters is that you would be *put at risk of harm, against your will,* in the name of reducing the risks that others voluntarily undertake and so can voluntarily decide *not* to undertake by the simple expedient of choosing not to run them in the first place (in this case, by choosing not to hang-glide). That tests on you would make it possible for those who hang-glide to lessen the risk of being made worse-off goes no way toward justifying placing you at risk of harm. As hang-gliders are the ones who stand to benefit from participation in this sport, they are the ones who must run the risks involved in participating. They may do all that they can to reduce the risks they run, but only so long as they do not coerce others to find out what these risks are or how to reduce them.

It would be a mistake to suppose that what is true in the case of high-risk activity is not true in the case of low-risk activity. Whenever I plug in my toaster, take an elevator, drink water from my faucet or from a clear mountain stream, I take some risks, though not of the magnitude of those who, say, sky-dive or canoe in turbid waters. But even in the case of my voluntarily taking minor risks, others have no duty to volunteer to establish or minimize my risks for me, and anyone who would be made to do this, against her will, would have her rights unjustifiably overridden. For example, the risks I run when I drive my car could be minimized by the design and manufacture of the most effective seat belts and the most crash-proof automobile. But it does not follow that anyone else has a duty to take part in crash tests in the name of minimizing my risks, and anyone who was coerced to do so, whether injured or not, would have every reason to claim that her rights had been violated or, if the test subject is incapable of making the claim, others would have every reason to make this claim on the subject's behalf. "No harm done" is no defense in circumstances such as these.

To minimize the risks humans who use new drugs would run by testing them on animals is morally no different. Anyone who elects to take a drug voluntarily chooses to run certain risks, and the risks we choose to run or, as in the case of moral patients for whom we choose, the risks we elect to allow them to run are not morally transferable to others. Coercively to harm others or to put others, whether human or animal, at risk of harm in order to identify or minimize the risks of those who voluntarily choose to run them, is to violate the rights of the humans or animals in question. It is not *how much* the test subjects are harmed (though the greater the harm, the worse the offense). What matters is that they are coercively used to establish or minimize risks for others. To place these animals at risk of harm so that others who voluntarily choose to run certain risks, and who thus can voluntarily choose not to run them, may minimize the risks they run, is to fail to treat the test animals with that respect they are due as possessors of inherent value. As is true of toxicity tests on new products, similar tests of new drugs on animals involve treating them as *even less* than receptacles, as if their value were reducible to their possible utility relative to the interests of others—in this case, relative to the interests humans who voluntarily take drugs have in minimizing their risks. Laboratory animals, to borrow an apt phrase from the Harvard philosopher Robert Nozick, "are distinct individuals who are not resources for others." To utilize them so that we might establish or minimize our risks, especially when it is within our power to decide not to take these risks in the first place, *is* to treat them as if they were "resources for others," most notably for us, and to defend these tests on the grounds that animals sometimes are not harmed is as morally lame as defending fox hunting on the grounds that the fox sometimes gets away.

The rights view is not in principle opposed to efforts to minimize the risks involved in taking new drugs. Toxicity tests are acceptable, so long as they violate no one's rights. To use human volunteers, persons who do not suffer from a particular malady but who give their informed consent as a test subject, is, though possible, not generally to be encouraged. To tie the progress of pharmacology and related sciences to the availability of healthy, consenting human subjects itself runs significant risks, including the risk that some may use deceptive or coercive means to secure participation. Moreover, few, if any, volunteers from the affluent classes are likely to step forward; the ranks of volunteers would likely be comprised of the poor, the uneducated, and those human moral patients whose relatives lack sufficient "sentimental interests" to protect them. There is a serious danger that the least powerful will be exploited. More preferable by far is the development of toxicity tests that harm no one—that is, tests that harm neither moral agents nor patients, whether humans or animals. Even at this date promising alternatives are being developed. To validate them scientifically is no small challenge, but it is the challenge that must be met if we continue to desire or require that new drugs be tested for their toxicity prior to being made available on the market. To test them on healthy human volunteers is dangerous at best; to test them coercively on healthy animals and human moral patients is wrong. The moral alternative that remains is: find valid alternatives.

A number of objections can be anticipated. One claims that there are risks and then there are risks. If we stopped testing new drugs for their toxicity, think of the risks people would run if they took them! Who could say what disastrous consequences would result? The rights view agrees. People would run greater risks if drugs were not pretested. But (a) the rights view does not oppose all pretesting (only those tests that coercively utilize some so that others may reduce those risks they may choose to run or choose not to run), and (b) those who had the choice to use an untested drug, assuming it was available, could *themselves* choose not to run the risks associated with taking it by deciding not to take it. Indeed, prudence would dictate acting in this way, except in the direst circumstances.

Of course, if untested drugs were allowed on the market and if people acted prudently, sales of new (untested) drugs would fall off, and we can anticipate that those involved in the pharmaceutical industry, people who, in addition to their chosen vocation of serving the health needs of the public, also have an economic interest in the stability and growth of this industry, might look with disfavor on the implications of the rights view. Four brief replies must suffice in this regard. First, whatever financial losses these companies might face if they were not permitted to continue to do toxicity tests on animals carry no moral weight, since the question of overriding basic moral rights is at issue. That these companies might lose money if the rights of animals are respected is one of the risks they run. Second, there is mounting evidence that these companies could save, rather than lose, money, if nonanimal tests were used. Animals are an expensive proposition. They must be bred or purchased, fed and watered, their living quarters must be routinely cleaned, their environment controlled (otherwise one runs the scientific risk of an uncontrolled variable), and so forth. . . .Third, anyone who defends present toxicological practice *merely* by claiming that these tests are required by the involved regulatory agencies (e.g., the Food and Drug Administration) would miss the essential moral point: though these agencies have yet to recognize nonanimal tests as meeting their regulations, these agencies themselves do not require that any pharmaceutical firm manufacture any new drug. That is a moral decision each company makes on its own and for which each must bear responsibility. Fourth, appeals to what the laws require can have no moral weight if we have good reason to believe that the laws in question are unjust. And we have good reasons in the present case. Laboratory animals are not a "resource" whose moral status in the world is to serve human interests. They are themselves the

subjects-of-a-life that fares better or worse for them as individuals, logically independently of any utility they may or may not have relative to the interests of others. They share with us a distinctive kind of value—inherent value—and whatever we do to them must be respectful of this value as a matter of strict justice. . . .

One can also anticipate charges that the rights view is antiscientific and antihumanity. This is rhetoric. The rights view is not antihuman. We, as humans, have an equal *prima facie* right not to be harmed, a right that the rights view seeks to illuminate and defend; but we do not have any right coercively to harm others, or to put them at risk of harm, so that we might minimize the risks we run as a result of our own voluntary decisions. That violates their rights, and that is one thing no one has a right to do. Nor is the rights view antiscientific. It places the *scientific* challenge before pharmacologists and related scientists: find scientifically valid ways that serve the public interest without violating individual rights. The overarching goal of pharmacology should be to reduce the risks of those who use drugs without harming those who don't. Those who claim that this cannot be done, in advance of making a concerted effort to do it, are the ones who are truly antiscientific.

Perhaps the most common response to the call for elimination of animals in toxicity testing is the benefits argument:

1. Human beings and animals have benefited from toxicity tests on animals.
2. Therefore, these tests are justified.

Like all arguments with missing premises, everything turns on what that premise is. If it read, "These tests do not violate the rights of animals," then we would be on our way to receiving an interesting defense of toxicity testing. Unfortunately for those who countenance these tests, however, and even more unfortunately for the animals used in them, that premise is not true. These tests do violate the rights of the test animals, for the reasons given. The benefits these tests have for others are irrelevant, according to the rights view, since the tests violate the rights of the individual animals. . . .

Scientific Research

One can imagine someone accepting the arguments advanced against toxicity tests on animals but putting his foot down when it comes to scientific research. To deny science use of animals in research is, it might be said, to bring scientific and allied medical progress to a halt, and that is reason enough to oppose it. The claim that progress would be "brought to a halt" is an exaggeration certainly. It is not an exaggeration to claim that, given its present dominant tendency, the rights view requires massive redirection of scientific research. The dominant tendency involves routinely harming animals. It should come as no surprise that the rights view has principled objections to its continuation.

A recent statement of the case for unrestricted use of animals in neurobiological research contrasts sharply with the rights view and will serve as an introduction to the critical assessment of using animals in basic research. The situation, as characterized by C. R. Gallistel, a psychologist at the University of Pennsylvania, is as follows. "Behavioral neurobiology tries to establish the manner in which the nervous system mediates behavioral phenomena. It does so by studying the behavioral consequences of one or more of the following procedures: (a) destruction of a part of the nervous system, (b) stimulation of a part, (c) administration of drugs that alter neural functioning. These three techniques are as old as the discipline. A recent addition is (d) the recording of electrical activity. All four cause the animal at least temporary distress. In the past they have frequently caused intense pain, and they occasionally do so now. Also, they often impair an animal's proper functioning,

sometimes transiently, sometimes permanently." The animals subjected to these procedures are, in a word, harmed. When it comes to advancing our knowledge in neurobiology, however, "there is no way to establish the relation between the nervous system and behavior without some experimental surgery" where by "experimental surgery" Gallistel evidently means to include the four procedures just outlined. The issue, then, in Gallistel's mind, is not whether to allow such surgery or not; it is whether any restrictions should be placed on the use made of animals. Gallistel thinks not.

In defense of unrestricted use of animals in research, Gallistel claims that "most experiments conducted by neurobiologists, *like scientific experiments generally,* may be seen in retrospect to have been a waste of time, in the sense that they did not prove or yield any new insight." But, claims Gallistel, "there is no way of discriminating in advance the waste-of-time experiments from the illuminating ones with anything approaching certainty." The logical upshot, so Gallistel believes, is that "restricting research on living animals is certain to restrict the progress in our understanding of the nervous system and behavior. Therefore," he concludes, "one should advocate such restrictions only if one believes that the moral value of this scientific knowledge and of the many human and humane benefits that flow from it cannot outweigh the suffering of a rat," something that, writing autobiographically, Gallistel finds "an affront to my ethical sensibility."

Even those unpersuaded by the rights view ought to challenge Gallistel's argument at every point. Is it true, as he claims, "that there is *no* way to establish the relation between the nervous system and behavior without some experimental surgery"? Can we learn nothing whatever about this connection from, say, clinical observation of those who have been injured? Again, is it true that *we can never say in advance* that a given proposal has been drawn up by an incompetent researcher who doesn't know what he is looking for and wouldn't recognize it if he found it? What could be the grounds for peer review of research proposals if Gallistel's views were accepted? Why not draw straws instead? Those stirrings in the scientific community, away from unrestricted use of animals toward the refinement of one's protocol (thereby eliminating so-called unnecessary experiments) and reduction in the number of animals used, will find no support from the no-holds-barred approach Gallistel advocates. Since there is, in his view, no way to separate the scientific wheat from the chaff in advance of experimenting, why worry about refinement? Why worry about reduction?

These matters aside, the rights view rejects Gallistel's approach at a more fundamental level. On the rights view, we cannot justify harming a single rat *merely* by aggregating "the many human and humane benefits" that flow from doing it, since, as stated, this is to assume that the rat has value only as a receptacle, which, on the rights view, is not true. Moreover, the benefits argument that Gallistel deploys is deficient. Not even a single rat is to be treated as if that animal's value were reducible to his *possible utility* relative to the interests of others, which is what we would be doing if we intentionally harmed the rat on the grounds that this *just might* "prove" something, *just might* "yield" a "new insight," *just might* produce "benefits" for others.

It bears emphasizing that the rights view's critique of the use of animals in research is unlike some that find favor in the literature on this matter. Some object on methodological grounds, arguing that the results of such research offer very little hope of benefits for humanity because of the by-now well-established difficulty of extrapolating results from animals tests to the species *Homo sapiens;* others challenge the necessity of a variety of experiments, cases where animals have been cut, blinded, deformed, mutilated, shocked into "learned helplessness," and so on, all in the name of research. Neither of these critical approaches, though each has clear validity as far as it goes, gets to the moral heart of the matter. It

is not that the methodology is suspect (though it is), nor that a great deal of research is, Gallistel's opinion to the contrary notwithstanding, known to be a waste of time before it is undertaken. The point to note is that both these challenges *invite the continuation of research on animals,* the latter because it would rule out only that research known to be a waste of time before it is conducted, and the former because it gives researchers a blank check to continue animal experiments in the hope of overcoming the deficiencies in the present methodology. If we are seriously to challenge the use of animals in research, we must challenge the *practice* itself, not only individual instances of it or merely the liabilities in its present methodology.

The rights view issues such a challenge. Routine use of animals in research assumes that their value is reducible to their possible utility relative to the interests of others. The rights view rejects this view of animals and their value, as it rejects the justice of institutions that treat them as renewable resources. They, like us, have a value of their own, logically independently of their utility for others and of their being the object of anyone else's interests. . . .

. . . Let us suppose that the lifeboat contains four normal adults and a dog. Provisions are plentiful this time and there is more than enough room. Only now suppose the humans have a degenerative brain disease, while the dog is healthy. Also on board, so it happens, is a new medicine that just might be the long awaited cure of the disease the humans have. The medicine has not been tested. However, it is known to contain some potentially fatal compounds. The means exist to give the degenerative disease to the dog. In these dire circumstances, would it be all right to do this and then to administer the medicine to the animal to assess its curative properties?

Quite possibly most people would give an affirmative reply, at least initially—but not those who subscribe to the rights view. Animals are not to be treated as if their value were reducible *merely* to their possible utility relative to human interests, which is what the survivors would be doing if they made the healthy animal (who, after all, stands to gain nothing and lose everything) run their risks in their stead. . . .

. . . To make the danger of generalizing on such cases clearer, imagine that the lifeboat contains four exceptional and one average human. Suppose the four are preeminent scientists, each on the verge of making discoveries that portend enormous health benefits for humanity. The fifth man delivers Twinkies to retail stores in Brooklyn. The four scientists have the degenerative brain disease. The Twinkies deliveryman does not. Would it be permissible to give the disease to him and then test for the drug's efficacy by administering it to him first? No doubt many people would be inclined to reply affirmatively (though not, again, those who subscribe to the rights view). Even among those who think the deliveryman should serve as the proverbial guinea pig in these exceptional circumstances, however, none with the slightest egalitarian tendencies would be willing to generalize on the basis of this unusual case and favor a policy or practice of doing research on average humans so that humans who are very bright or who make large social contributions might benefit. Such a practice leaves the bad taste of perfectionism in our mouths. The rights view categorically rejects perfectionism as a basis for assessing the justice of practices involving humans, whether in science or elsewhere. And so should we all. But just as perfectionism is not an equitable basis for assessing the justice of practices involving humans, so it is an unacceptable basis for assessing the justice of practices involving animals. And it is implicit allegiance to perfectionism that would tempt one to sanction the harmful use of animals in research, their "lesser" value being "sacrificed" for the "greater" value of humanity. Grounded in the recognition of the equal inherent value of all those who have inherent value, the rights view denies that a distinction between lesser and greater should be

made where the perfectionist defense of the use of animals in research requires it. Thus does it deplore the continuation of this practice.

The rights view does not oppose using what is learned from conscientious efforts to treat a sick animal (or human) to facilitate and improve the treatment tendered other animals (or humans). In *this* respect, the rights view raises no objection to the "many human and humane benefits" that flow from medical science and the research with which it is allied. What the rights view opposes are practices that cause intentional harm to laboratory animals (for example, by means of burns, shock, amputation, poisoning, surgery, starvation, and sensory deprivation) preparatory to "looking for something that just might yield some human or humane benefit." Whatever benefits happen to accrue from such a practice are irrelevant to assessing its tragic injustice. Lab animals are not our tasters; we are not their kings.

The tired charge of being antiscientific is likely to fill the air once more. It is a moral smokescreen. The rights view is not against research on animals, if this research does not harm these animals or put them at risk of harm. It is apt to remark, however, that this objective will not be accomplished merely by ensuring that test animals are anaesthetized, or given postoperative drugs to ease their suffering, or kept in clean cages with ample food and water, and so forth. For it is not only the pain and suffering that matters—though they certainly matter—but it is the *harm* done to the animals, including the diminished welfare opportunities they endure as a result of the deprivations caused by the surgery, *and* their untimely death. It is unclear whether a *benign* use of animals in research is possible or, if possible, whether scientists could be persuaded to practice it. That being so, and given the serious risks run by relying on a steady supply of human volunteers, research should take the direction away from the use of any moral agent or patient. If nonanimal alternatives are available, they should be used; if they are not available, they should be sought. That is the moral challenge to research, given the rights view, and it is those scientists who protest that this "can't be done," in advance of the scientific commitment to try—not those who call for the exploration—who exhibit a lack of commitment to, and belief in, the scientific enterprise—who are, that is, antiscientific at the deepest level. Like Galileo's contemporaries, who would not look through the telescope because they had already convinced themselves of what they would see and thus saw no need to look, those scientists who have convinced themselves that there can't be viable scientific alternatives to the use of whole animals in research (or toxicity tests, etc.) are captives of mental habits that true science abhors.

The rights view, then, is far from being antiscientific. On the contrary, as is true in the case of toxicity tests, so also in the case of research: it calls upon scientists *to do science* as they redirect the traditional practice of their several disciplines away from reliance on "animal models" toward the development and use of nonanimal alternatives. All that the rights view prohibits is science that violates individual rights. If that means that there are some things we cannot learn, then so be it. There are also some things we cannot learn by using humans, if we respect their rights. The rights view merely requires moral consistency in this regard. . . .

Animals in Science, Utilitarianism, and Animal Rights

The fundamental differences between utilitarianism and the rights view are never more apparent than in the case of the use of animals in science. For the utilitarian, whether the harm done to animals in pursuit of scientific ends is justified depends on the balance of the aggregated consequences for all those affected by the outcome. If the consequences that result from

harming animals would produce the best aggregate balance of good over evil, then harmful experimentation is obligatory. If the resulting consequences would be at least as good as what are otherwise obtainable, then harmful experimentation is permissible. Only if harmful experimentation would produce less than the best consequences would it be wrong. For a utilitarian to oppose or support harmful experimentation on animals, therefore, requires that he have the relevant facts—who will be benefited or harmed, how much, and so on. *Everyone's* interests, including the interests of those who do the tests or conduct the research, their employers, the dependents of these persons, the retailers and wholesalers of cages, animal breeders, and others, must be taken into account and counted equitably. For utilitarians, such *side effects count*. The animals used in the test have no privileged moral status. Their interests must be taken into account, to be sure, but not any more than anybody else's interests.

As is "almost always" the case, utilitarians simply fail to give us what is needed—the relevant facts, facts that we must have, given their theory, to determine whether use of animals in science is or is not justified. Moreover, for a utilitarian to claim or imply that there must be something wrong with a given experiment, if the experimenter would not be willing to use a less intelligent, less aware human being but would be willing to use a more intelligent, more aware animal, simply lacks a utilitarian basis. For all we know, and for all the utilitarian has thus far told us, the consequences of using such an animal, all considered, might be better than those that would result from using the human being. It is not *who* is used, given utilitarian theory, that matters; it is *the consequences* that do.

The rights view takes a very different stand. No one, whether human or animal, is ever to be treated as if she were a mere receptacle, or as if her value were reducible to her possible utility for others. We are, that is, never to harm the individual merely on the grounds that this will or just might produce "the best" aggregate consequences. To do so is to violate the rights of the individual. That is why the harm done to animals in pursuit of scientific purposes is wrong. The benefits derived are real enough; but some gains are ill-gotten, and all gains are ill-gotten when secured unjustly.

So it is that the rights view issues its challenge to those who do science: advance knowledge, work for the general welfare, but not by allowing practices that violate the rights of the individual. These are, one might say, the terms of the new contract between science and society, a contract that, however belatedly, now contains the signature of those who speak for the rights of animals. *Those who accept the rights view, and who sign for animals, will not be satisfied with anything less than the total abolition of the harm-ful use of animals in science—in education, in toxicity testing, in basic research.* But the rights view plays no favorites. No scientific practice that violates human rights, whether the humans be moral agents or moral patients, is acceptable. And the same applies to those humans who, for reasons analogous to those advanced in . . . regard to nonhumans, should be given the benefit of the doubt about having rights because of the weight of our ignorance—the newly born and the soon-to-be born. Those who accept the rights view are committed to denying any and all access to these "resources" on the part of those who do science. And we do this not because we oppose cruelty (though we do), nor because we favor kindness (though we do), but because justice requires nothing less.

Study Questions

1. What is Regan's view of harmful toxicity testing on animals? What are our moral options?
2. What are Regan's reasons for opposing experimentation on animals for human benefit? Do you agree with Regan's position? You may have to go back to his earlier essay "The Radical Egalitarian Case for Animal Rights" (Chapter 50) and review his arguments.
3. What should we do in order to obtain important scientific knowledge that will benefit humans?
4. How does Regan meet the objections to his position?
5. How strong are Regan's arguments?

CHAPTER 53

Difficulties with the Strong Animal Rights Position

MARY ANNE WARREN

Mary Anne Warren (see Chapter 33 for a biographical sketch) reconstructs Regan's argument for animal rights and criticizes it for depending on the obscure notion of inherent value. She then argues that all rational human beings are equally part of the moral community since we can reason with each other about our behavior, whereas we cannot so reason with an animal. She puts forth a "weak animal rights theory" asserting that we ought not to be cruel to animals or kill them without good reason.

TOM REGAN HAS PRODUCED what is perhaps the definitive defense of the view that the basic moral rights of at least some non-human animals are in no way inferior to our own. In *The Case for Animal Rights,* he argues that all normal mammals over a year of age have the same basic moral rights.[1] Non-human mammals have essentially the same right not to be harmed or killed as we do. I shall call this "the strong animal rights position," although it is weaker than the claims made by some animal liberationists in that it ascribes rights to only some sentient animals.[2]

I will argue that Regan's case for the strong animal rights position is unpersuasive and that this position entails consequences which a reasonable person cannot accept. I do not deny that some non-human animals have moral rights; indeed, I would extend the scope of the rights claim to include all sentient animals, that is, all those capable of having experiences, including experiences of pleasure or satisfaction and pain, suffering, or frustration.[3] However, I do not think that the moral rights of most non-human animals are identical in strength to those

of persons.[4] The rights of most non-human animals may be overridden in circumstances which would not justify overriding the rights of persons. There are, for instance, compelling realities which sometimes require that we kill animals for reasons which could not justify the killing of persons. I will call this view "the weak animal rights" position, even though it ascribes rights to a wider range of animals than does the strong animal rights position.

I will begin by summarizing Regan's case for the strong animal rights position and noting two problems with it. Next, I will explore some consequences of the strong animal rights position which I think are unacceptable. Finally, I will outline the case for the weak animal rights position.

Regan's Case

Regan's argument moves through three stages. First, he argues that normal, mature mammals are not only sentient but have other mental

Reprinted from Between the Species *2: 4 (fall 1987) by permission.*

capacities as well. These include the capacities for emotion, memory, belief, desire, the use of general concepts, intentional action, a sense of the future, and some degree of self-awareness. Creatures with such capacities are said to be subjects-of-a-life. They are not only alive in the biological sense but have a psychological identity over time and an existence which can go better or worse for them. Thus, they can be harmed or benefited. These are plausible claims, and well defended. One of the strongest parts of the book is the rebuttal of philosophers, such as R. G. Frey, who object to the application of such mentalistic terms to creatures that do not use a human-style language.[5] The second and third stages of the argument are more problematic.

In the second stage, Regan argues that subjects-of-a-life have inherent value. His concept of inherent value grows out of his opposition to utilitarianism. Utilitarian moral theory, he says, treats individuals as "mere receptacles" for morally significant value, in that harm to one individual may be justified by the production of a greater net benefit to other individuals. In opposition to this, he holds that subjects-of-a-life have a value independent of both the value they may place upon their lives or experiences and the value others may place upon them.

Inherent value, Regan argues, does not come in degrees. To hold that some individuals have more inherent value than others is to adopt a "perfectionist" theory, i.e., one which assigns different moral worth to individuals according to how well they are thought to exemplify some virtue(s), such as intelligence or moral autonomy. Perfectionist theories have been used, at least since the time of Aristotle, to rationalize such injustices as slavery and male domination, as well as the unrestrained exploitation of animals. Regan argues that if we reject these injustices, then we must also reject perfectionism and conclude that all subjects-of-a-life have equal inherent value. Moral agents have no more inherent value than moral patients, i.e., subjects-of-a-life who are not morally responsible for their actions.

In the third phase of the argument, Regan uses the thesis of equal inherent value to derive strong moral rights for all subjects-of-a-life. This thesis underlies the Respect Principle, which forbids us to treat beings who have inherent value as mere receptacles, i.e., mere means to the production of the greatest overall good. This principle, in turn, underlies the Harm Principle, which says that we have a direct *prima facie* duty not to harm beings who have inherent value. Together, these principles give rise to moral rights. Rights are defined as valid claims, claims to certain goods and against certain beings, i.e., moral agents. Moral rights generate duties not only to refrain from inflicting harm upon beings with inherent value but also to come to their aid when they are threatened by other moral agents. Rights are not absolute but may be overridden in certain circumstances. Just what these circumstances are we will consider later. But first, let's look at some difficulties in the theory as thus far presented.

The Mystery of Inherent Value

Inherent value is a key concept in Regan's theory. It is the bridge between the plausible claim that all normal, mature mammals—human or otherwise—are subjects-of-a-life and the more debatable claim that they all have basic moral rights of the same strength. But it is a highly obscure concept, and its obscurity makes it ill-suited to play this crucial role.

Inherent value is defined almost entirely in negative terms. It is not dependent upon the value which either the inherently valuable individual or anyone else may place upon that individual's life or experiences. It is not (necessarily) a function of sentience or any other mental capacity, because, Regan says, some entities which are not sentient (e.g., trees, rivers, or rocks) may, nevertheless, have inherent value (p. 246). It cannot attach to anything other than an individual; species, eco-systems, and the like cannot have inherent value.

These are some of the things which inherent value is not. But what is it? Unfortunately, we are not told. Inherent value appears as a mysterious non-natural property which we must take on faith. Regan says that it is a *postulate* that subjects-of-a-life have inherent value, a postulate justified by the fact that it avoids certain absurdities which he thinks follow from a purely utilitarian theory (p. 247). But why is the postulate that *subjects-of-a-life* have inherent value? If the inherent value of a being is completely independent of the value that it or anyone else places upon its experiences, then why does the fact that it has certain sorts of experiences constitute evidence that it has inherent value? If the reason is that subjects-of-a-life have an existence which can go better or worse for them, then why isn't the appropriate conclusion that all sentient beings have inherent value, since they would all seem to meet that condition? Sentient but mentally unsophisticated beings may have a less extensive range of possible satisfactions and frustrations, but why should it follow that they have—or may have—no inherent value at all?

In the absence of a positive account of inherent value, it is also difficult to grasp the connection between being inherently valuable and having moral rights. Intuitively, it seems that value is one thing, and rights are another. It does not seem incoherent to say that some things (e.g., mountains, rivers, redwood trees) are inherently valuable and yet are not the sorts of things which can have moral rights. Nor does it seem incoherent to ascribe inherent value to some things which are not individuals, e.g., plant or animal species, though it may well be incoherent to ascribe moral rights to such things.

In short, the concept of inherent value seems to create at least as many problems as it solves. If inherent value is based on some natural property, then why not try to identify that property and explain its moral significance, without appealing to inherent value? And if it is not based on any natural property, then why should we believe in it? That it may enable us to avoid some of the problems faced by the utilitarian is not a sufficient reason, if it creates other problems which are just as serious.

Is There a Sharp Line?

Perhaps the most serious problems are those that arise when we try to apply the strong animal rights position to animals other than normal, mature mammals. Regan's theory requires us to divide all living things into two categories: those which have the same inherent value and the same basic moral rights that we do, and those which have no inherent value and presumably no moral rights. But wherever we try to draw the line, such a sharp division is implausible.

It would surely be arbitrary to draw such a sharp line between normal, mature mammals and all other living things. Some birds (e.g., crows, magpies, parrots, mynahs) appear to be just as mentally sophisticated as most mammals and thus are equally strong candidates for inclusion under the subject-of-a-life criterion. Regan is not in fact advocating that we draw the line here. His claim is only that normal mature mammals are clear cases, while other cases are less clear. Yet, on his theory, there must be such a sharp line *somewhere,* since there are no degrees of inherent value. But why should we believe that there is a sharp line between creatures that are subjects-of-a-life and creatures that are not? Isn't it more likely that "subjecthood" comes in degrees, that some creatures have only a little self-awareness, and only a little capacity to anticipate the future, while some have a little more, and some a good deal more?

Should we, for instance, regard fish, amphibians, and reptiles as subjects-of-a-life? A simple yes-or-no answer seems inadequate. On the one hand, some of their behavior is difficult to explain without the assumption that they have sensations, beliefs, desires, emotions, and memories; on the other hand, they do not seem to exhibit very much self-awareness or very much conscious anticipation of future events. Do they have enough mental sophistication to count as subjects-of-a-life? Exactly how much is enough?

It is still more unclear what we should say about insects, spiders, octopi, and other invertebrate animals which have brains and sensory organs but whose minds (if they have minds) are even more alien to us than those of fish or reptiles. Such creatures are probably sentient. Some people doubt that they can feel pain, since they lack certain neurological structures which are crucial to the processing of pain impulses in vertebrate animals. But this argument is inconclusive, since their nervous systems might process pain in ways different from ours. When injured, they sometimes act as if they are in pain. On evolutionary grounds, it seems unlikely that highly mobile creatures with complex sensory systems would not have developed a capacity for pain (and pleasure), since such a capacity has obvious survival value. It must, however, be admitted that we do not *know* whether spiders can feel pain (or something very like it), let alone whether they have emotions, memories, beliefs, desires, self-awareness, or a sense of the future.

Even more mysterious are the mental capacities (if any) of mobile microfauna. The brisk and efficient way that paramecia move about in their incessant search for food *might* indicate some kind of sentience, in spite of their lack of eyes, ears, brains, and other organs associated with sentience in more complex organisms. It is conceivable—though not very probable—that they, too, are subjects-of-a-life.

The existence of a few unclear cases need not pose a serious problem for a moral theory, but in this case, the unclear cases constitute most of those with which an adequate theory of animal rights would need to deal. The subject-of-a-life criterion can provide us with little or no moral guidance in our interactions with the vast majority of animals. That might be acceptable if it could be supplemented with additional principles which would provide such guidance. However, the radical dualism of the theory precludes supplementing it in this way. We are forced to say that either a spider has the same right to life as you and I do, or it has no right to life whatever—and that only the gods know which of these alternatives is true.

Regan's suggestion for dealing with such unclear cases is to apply the "benefit of the doubt" principle. That is, when dealing with beings that may or may not be subjects-of-a-life, we should act as if they are.[6] But if we try to apply this principle to the entire range of doubtful cases, we will find ourselves with moral obligations which we cannot possibly fulfill. In many climates, it is virtually impossible to live without swatting mosquitoes and exterminating cockroaches, and not all of us can afford to hire someone to sweep the path before we walk, in order to make sure that we do not step on ants. Thus, we are still faced with the daunting task of drawing a sharp line somewhere on the continuum of life forms—this time, a line demarcating the limits of the benefit of the doubt principle.

The weak animal rights theory provides a more plausible way of dealing with this range of cases, in that it allows the rights of animals of different kinds to vary in strength. . . .

Why are Animal Rights Weaker than Human Rights?

How can we justify regarding the rights of persons as generally stronger than those of sentient beings which are not persons? There are a plethora of bad justifications, based on religious premises or false or unprovable claims about the differences between human and non-human nature. But there is one difference which has a clear moral relevance: people are at least sometimes capable of being moved to action or inaction by the force of reasoned argument. Rationality rests upon other mental capacities, notably those which Regan cites as criteria for being a subject-of-a-life. We share these capacities with many other animals. But it is not just because we are subjects-of-a-life that we are both able and morally compelled to recognize one another as beings with equal basic moral rights. It is also because we are able to "listen to reason" in order to settle our conflicts and cooperate in shared projects. This capacity, unlike the others, may require something like a human language.

Why is rationality morally relevant? It does not make us "better" than other animals or more "perfect." It does not even automatically make us more intelligent. (Bad reasoning reduces our effective intelligence rather than increasing it.) But it is morally relevant insofar as it provides greater possibilities for cooperation and for the non-violent resolution of problems. It also makes us more dangerous than non-rational beings can ever be. Because we are potentially more dangerous and less predictable than wolves, we need an articulated system of morality to regulate our conduct. Any human morality, to be workable in the long run, must recognize the equal moral status of all persons, whether through the postulate of equal basic moral rights or in some other way. The recognition of the moral equality of other persons is the price we must each pay for their recognition of our moral equality. Without this mutual recognition of moral equality, human society can exist only in a state of chronic and bitter conflict. The war between the sexes will persist so long as there is sexism and male domination; racial conflict will never be eliminated so long as there are racist laws and practices. But, to the extent that we achieve a mutual recognition of equality, we can hope to live together, perhaps as peacefully as wolves, achieving (in part) through explicit moral principles what they do not seem to need explicit moral principles to achieve.

Why not extend this recognition of moral equality to other creatures, even though they cannot do the same for us? The answer is that we cannot. Because we cannot reason with most non-human animals, we cannot always solve the problems which they may cause without harming them—although we are always obligated to try. We cannot negotiate a treaty with the feral cats and foxes, requiring them to stop preying on endangered native species in return for suitable concessions on our part.

> If rats invade our houses . . . we cannot reason with them, hoping to persuade them of the injustice they do us. We can only attempt to get rid of them.[7]

Aristotle was not wrong in claiming that the capacity to alter one's behavior on the basis of reasoned argument is relevant to the full moral status which he accorded to free men. Of course, he was wrong in his other premise, that women and slaves by their nature cannot reason well enough to function as autonomous moral agents. Had that premise been true, so would his conclusion that women and slaves are not quite the moral equals of free men. In the case of most non-human animals, the corresponding premise is true. If, on the other hand, there are animals with whom we can (learn to) reason, then we are obligated to do this and to regard them as our moral equals.

Thus, to distinguish between the rights of persons and those of most other animals on the grounds that only people can alter their behavior on the basis of reasoned argument does not commit us to a perfectionist theory of the sort Aristotle endorsed. There is no excuse for refusing to recognize the moral equality of some people on the grounds that we don't regard them as quite as rational as we are, since it is perfectly clear that most people can reason well enough to determine how to act so as to respect the basic rights of others (if they choose to), and that is enough for moral equality.

But what about people who are clearly not rational? It is often argued that sophisticated mental capacities such as rationality cannot be essential for the possession of equal basic moral rights, since nearly everyone agrees that human infants and mentally incompetent persons have such rights, even though they may lack those sophisticated mental capacities. But this argument is inconclusive, because there are powerful practical and emotional reasons for protecting non-rational human beings, reasons which are absent in the case of most non-human animals. Infancy and mental incompetence are human conditions which all of us either have experienced or are likely to experience at some time. We also protect babies and mentally incompetent people because we care for them. We don't normally care for animals in the same way, and when we do—e.g., in the case of much-loved pets—we may regard them as having special rights by virtue of their relationship to us. We protect them not only for their sake but also for our own, lest we be hurt by harm done to them. Regan holds that such "side-effects" are irrelevant to moral rights, and perhaps they are. But in ordinary usage, there is no sharp line between moral rights and those moral protections which are not rights. The extension of strong moral protections to infants and the mentally impaired in no way proves that non-human animals have the same basic moral rights as people.

Why Speak of "Animal Rights" at All?

If, as I have argued, reality precludes our treating all animals as our moral equals, then why should we still ascribe rights to them? Everyone agrees that animals are entitled to some protection against human abuse, but why speak of animal *rights* if we are not prepared to accept most animals as our moral equals? The weak animal rights position may seem an unstable compromise between the bold claim that animals have the same basic moral rights that we

do and the more common view that animals have no rights at all.

It is probably impossible to either prove or disprove the thesis that animals have moral rights by producing an analysis of the concept of a moral right and checking to see if some or all animals satisfy the conditions for having rights. The concept of a moral right is complex, and it is not clear which of its strands are essential. Paradigm rights holders, i.e., mature and mentally competent persons, are *both* rational and morally autonomous beings and sentient subjects-of-a-life. Opponents of animal rights claim that rationality and moral autonomy are essential for the possession of rights, while defenders of animal rights claim that they are not. The ordinary concept of a moral right is probably not precise enough to enable us to determine who is right on purely definitional grounds.

If logical analysis will not answer the question of whether animals have moral rights, practical considerations may, nevertheless, incline us to say that they do. The most plausible alternative to the view that animals have moral rights is that, while they do not have *rights,* we are, nevertheless, obligated not to be cruel to them. Regan argues persuasively that the injunction to avoid being cruel to animals is inadequate to express our obligations towards animals, because it focuses on the mental states of those who cause animal suffering, rather than on the harm done to the animals themselves (p. 158). Cruelty is inflicting pain or suffering and either taking pleasure in that pain or suffering or being more or less indifferent to it. Thus, to express the demand for the decent treatment of animals in terms of the rejection of cruelty is to invite the too easy response that those who subject animals to suffering are not being cruel because they regret the suffering they cause but sincerely believe that what they do is justified. The injunction to avoid cruelty is also inadequate in that it does not preclude the killing of animals—for any reason, however trivial—so long as it is done relatively painlessly.

The inadequacy of the anti-cruelty view provides one practical reason for speaking of animal rights. Another practical reason is that this is an age in which nearly all significant moral claims tend to be expressed in terms of rights. Thus, the denial that animals have rights, however carefully qualified, is likely to be taken to mean that we may do whatever we like to them, provided that we do not violate any human rights. In such a context, speaking of the rights of animals may be the only way to persuade many people to take seriously protests against the abuse of animals.

Why not extend this line of argument and speak of the rights of trees, mountains, oceans, or anything else which we may wish to see protected from destruction? Some environmentalists have not hesitated to speak in this way, and, given the importance of protecting such elements of the natural world, they cannot be blamed for using this rhetorical device. But, I would argue that moral rights can meaningfully be ascribed only to entities which have some capacity for sentience. This is because moral rights are protections designed to protect rights holders from harms or to provide them with benefits which matter *to them*. Only beings capable of sentience can be harmed or benefited in ways which matter to them, for only such beings can like or dislike what happens to them or prefer some conditions to others. Thus, sentient animals, unlike mountains, rivers, or species, are at least logically possible candidates for moral rights. This fact, together with the need to end current abuses of animals—e.g., in scientific research . . .—provides a plausible case for speaking of animal rights.

Conclusion

I have argued that Regan's case for ascribing strong moral rights to all normal, mature mammals is unpersuasive because (1) it rests upon the obscure concept of inherent value, which is defined only in negative terms, and (2) it seems to preclude any plausible answer to questions about the moral status of the vast majority of sentient animals. . . .

The weak animal rights theory asserts that (1) any creature whose natural mode of life includes the pursuit of certain satisfactions has the right not to be forced to exist without the opportunity to pursue those satisfactions; (2) that any creature which is capable of pain, suffering, or frustration has the right that such experiences not be deliberately inflicted upon it without some compelling reason; and (3) that no sentient being should be killed without good reason. However, moral rights are not an all-or-nothing affair. The strength of the reasons required to override the rights of a non-human organism varies, depending upon—among other things—the probability that it is sentient and (if it is clearly sentient) its probable degree of mental sophistication. . . .

Notes

1. Tom Regan, *The Case for Animal Rights* (Berkeley: University of California Press, 1983). All page references are to this edition.

2. For instance, Peter Singer, although he does not like to speak of rights, includes all sentient beings under the protection of his basic utilitarian principle of equal respect for like interests. (*Animal Liberation* [New York: Avon Books, 1975], p. 3.)

3. The capacity for sentience, like all of the mental capacities mentioned in what follows, is a disposition. Dispositions do not disappear whenever they are not currently manifested. Thus, sleeping or temporarily unconscious persons or non-human animals are still sentient in the relevant sense (i.e., still capable of sentience), so long as they still have the neurological mechanisms necessary for the occurrence of experiences.

4. It is possible, perhaps probable that some non-human animals—such as cetaceans and anthropoid apes—should be regarded as persons. If so, then the weak animal rights position holds that these animals have the same basic moral rights as human persons.

5. See R. G. Frey, *Interests and Rights: The Case Against Animals* (Oxford: Oxford University Press, 1980).

6. See, for instance, p. 319, where Regan appeals to the benefit of the doubt principle when dealing with infanticide and late-term abortion.

7. Bonnie Steinbock, "Speciesism and the Idea of Equality," *Philosophy 53* (1978):253.

Study Questions

1. Examine Warren's critique of Regan's position. What is her main criticism? How strong is her criticism?
2. What is the basis for granting human beings moral rights that we do not grant animals? Do you agree with her arguments?
3. What is the weak animal rights position? What is Warren's argument for it?

CHAPTER 54

The Case Against Animal Rights

CARL COHEN

Carl Cohen is a professor of law at the University of Michigan. He addresses the morality of animal experimentation and argues that while human beings have a duty to treat animals humanely, animals cannot have rights. The idea of rights does not apply to animals since "rights" is a concept appropriate only to members of the moral community and animals cannot make moral decisions. Humans are of far greater value than animals, and the result of not using animals for medical experimentation would be greater human suffering.

USING ANIMALS as research subjects in medical investigations is widely condemned on two grounds: first, because it wrongly violates the *rights* of animals, and second, because it wrongly imposes on sentient creatures much avoidable *suffering*. Neither of these arguments is sound. The first relies on a mistaken understanding of rights; the second relies on a mistaken calculation of consequences. Both deserve definitive dismissal.

Why Animals Have No Rights

A right, properly understood, is a claim, or potential claim, that one party may exercise against another. The target against whom such a claim may be registered can be a single person, a group, a community, or (perhaps) all humankind. The content of rights claims also varies greatly: repayment of loans, nondiscrimination by employers, noninterference by the state, and so on. To comprehend any genuine right fully, therefore, we must know *who* holds the right, *against whom* it is held, and *to what* it is a right.

Alternative sources of rights add complexity. Some rights are grounded in constitution and law (e.g., the right of an accused to trial by jury); some rights are moral but give no legal claims (e.g., my right to your keeping the promise you gave me); and some rights (e.g., against theft or assault) are rooted both in morals and in law.

The differing targets, contents, and sources of rights, and their inevitable conflict, together weave a tangled web. Notwithstanding all such complications, this much is clear about rights in general: they are in every case claims, or potential claims, within a community of moral agents. Rights arise, and can be intelligibly defended, only among beings who actually do, or can, make moral claims against one another. Whatever else rights may be, therefore, they are necessarily human; their possessors are persons, human beings.

The attributes of human beings from which this moral capability arises have been described variously by philosophers, both ancient and modern: the inner consciousness of a free will (Saint Augustine); the grasp, by human reason, of the binding character of moral law (Saint

Reprinted from the New England Journal of Medicine *(1986) by permission.*

Thomas Aquinas); the self-conscious participation of human beings in an objective ethical order (G. W. F. Hegel); human membership in an organic moral community (F. H. Bradley); the development of the human self through the consciousness of other moral selves (G. H. Mead); and the underivative, intuitive cognition of the rightness of an action (H. A. Prichard). Most influential has been Immanuel Kant's emphasis on the universal human possession of a uniquely moral will and the autonomy its use entails. Humans confront choices that are purely moral; humans—but certainly not dogs or mice—lay down moral laws, for others and for themselves. Human beings are self-legislative, morally *autonomous.*

Animals (that is, nonhuman animals, the ordinary sense of that word) lack this capacity for free moral judgment. They are not beings of a kind capable of exercising or responding to moral claims. Animals therefore have no rights, and they can have none. This is the core of the argument about the alleged rights of animals. The holders of rights must have the capacity to comprehend rules of duty, governing all including themselves. In applying such rules, the holders of rights must recognize possible conflicts between what is in their own interest and what is just. Only in a community of beings capable of self-restricting moral judgments can the concept of a right be correctly invoked.

Humans have such moral capacities. They are in this sense self-legislative, are members of communities governed by moral rules, and do possess rights. Animals do not have such moral capacities. They are not morally self-legislative, cannot possibly be members of a truly moral community, and therefore cannot possess rights. In conducting research on animal subjects, therefore, we do not violate their rights, because they have none to violate. . . .

Genuinely moral acts have an internal as well as an external dimension. Thus, in law, an act can be criminal only when the guilty deed, the *actus reus,* is done with a guilty mind, *mens rea.* No animal can ever commit a crime; bringing animals to criminal trial is the mark of primitive ignorance. The claims of moral rights are similarly inapplicable to them. Does a lion have a right to eat a baby zebra? Does a baby zebra have a right not to be eaten? Such questions, mistakenly invoking the concept of right where it does not belong, do not make good sense. Those who condemn biomedical research because it violates "animal rights" commit the same blunder.

In Defense of Speciesism

Abandoning reliance on animal rights, some critics resort instead to animal sentience—their feelings of pain and distress. We ought to desist from the imposition of pain insofar as we can. Since all or nearly all experimentation on animals does impose pain and could be readily forgone, say these critics, it should be stopped. The ends sought may be worthy, but those ends do not justify imposing agonies on humans, and by animals the agonies are felt no less. The laboratory use of animals (these critics conclude) must therefore be ended—or at least very sharply curtailed.

Argument of this variety is essentially utilitarian, often expressly so; it is based on the calculation of the net product, in pains and pleasures, resulting from experiments on animals. Jeremy Bentham, comparing horses and dogs with other sentient creatures, is thus commonly quoted: "The question is not, Can they reason? nor Can they talk? but, Can they suffer?"

Biomedical Research Must Still Proceed

Animals certainly can suffer and surely ought not to be made to suffer needlessly. But in inferring, from these uncontroversial premises, that biomedical research causing animal distress is largely (or wholly) wrong, the critic commits two serious errors.

The first error is the assumption, often explicitly defended, that all sentient animals have equal moral standing. Between a dog and a human being, according to this view, there is no moral difference; hence the pains suffered by dogs must be weighed no differently from the pains suffered by humans. To deny such equality, according to this critic, is to give unjust preference to one species over another; it is "speciesism." The most influential statement of this moral equality of species was made by Peter Singer:

> The racist violates the principle of equality by giving greater weight to the interests of members of his own race when there is a clash between their interests and the interests of those of another race. The sexist violates the principle of equality by favoring the interests of his own sex. Similarly the speciesist allows the interests of his own species to override the greater interests of members of other species. The pattern is identical in each case.

This argument is worse than unsound; it is atrocious. It draws an offensive moral conclusion from a deliberately devised verbal parallelism that is utterly specious. Racism has no rational ground whatever. Differing degrees of respect or concern for humans for no other reason than that they are members of different races is an injustice totally without foundation in the nature of the races themselves. Racists, even if acting on the basis of mistaken factual beliefs, do grave moral wrong precisely because there is no morally relevant distinction among the races. The supposition of such differences has led to outright horror. The same is true of the sexes, neither sex being entitled by right to greater respect or concern than the other. No dispute here.

Between species of animate life, however—between (for example) humans on the one hand and cats or rats on the other—the morally relevant differences are enormous, and almost universally appreciated. Humans engage in moral reflection; humans are morally autonomous; humans are members of moral communities, recognizing just claims against their own interest. Human beings do have rights; theirs is a moral status very different from that of cats or rats.

Speciesism Is Necessary

I am a speciesist. Speciesism is not merely plausible; it is essential for right conduct, because those who will not make the morally relevant distinctions among species are almost certain, in consequence, to misapprehend their true obligations. The analogy between speciesism and racism is insidious. Every sensitive moral judgment requires that the differing natures of the beings to whom obligations are owed be considered. If all forms of animate life—or vertebrate animal life—must be treated equally, and if therefore in evaluating a research program the pains of a rodent count equally with the pains of a human, we are forced to conclude (1) that neither humans nor rodents possess rights, or (2) that rodents possess all the rights that humans possess. Both alternatives are absurd. Yet one or the other must be swallowed if the moral equality of all species is to be defended. . . .

Those who claim to base their objection to the use of animals in biomedical research on their reckoning of the net pleasures and pains produced make a second error, equally grave. Even if it were true—as it is surely not—that the pains of all animate beings must be counted equally, a cogent utilitarian calculation requires that we weigh all the consequences of the use, and of the nonuse, of animals in laboratory research. Critics relying (however mistakenly) on animal rights may claim to ignore the beneficial results of such research, rights being trump cards to which interest and advantage must give way. But an argument that is explicitly framed in terms of interest and benefit for all over the long run must attend also to the disadvantageous consequences of not using animals in research, and to all the achievements attained and attainable only through their use. The sum of the benefits of their use is utterly beyond quantification. The elimination of horrible disease, the increase of longevity, the avoidance of great pain, the saving of lives, and the improvement of the quality of lives (for humans and for animals) achieved through research using animals is so incalculably great that the argument of these critics, systematically pursued, establishes not their conclusion but its reverse: to refrain from using animals in biomedical research is, on utilitarian ground, morally wrong.

When balancing the pleasures and pains resulting from the use of animals in research, we must not fail to place on the scales the terrible pains that would have resulted, would be suffered now, and would long continue had animals not been used. Every disease eliminated, every vaccine developed, every method of pain relief devised, every surgical procedure invented, every prosthetic device implanted—indeed, virtually every modern medical therapy is due, in part or in whole, to experimentation using animals. Nor may we ignore, in the balancing process, the predictable gains in human (and animal) well-being that are probably achievable in the future but that will not be achieved if the decision is made now to desist from such research or to curtail it. . . .

Finally, inconsistency between the profession and the practice of many who oppose research using animals deserves comment. This frankly *ad hominem* observation aims chiefly to show that a coherent position rejecting the use of animals in medical research imposes costs so high as to be intolerable even to the critics themselves.

One cannot coherently object to the killing of animals in biomedical investigations while continuing to eat them. Anesthetics and thoughtful animal husbandry render the level of actual animal distress in the laboratory generally lower than that in the abattoir. So long as death and discomfort do not substantially differ in the two contexts, the consistent objector must not only refrain from all eating of animals but also protest as vehemently against others eating them as against others experimenting on them. No less vigorously must the critic object to the wearing of animal hides in coats and shoes, to employment in any industrial enterprise that uses animal parts, and to any commercial development that will cause death or distress to animals. . . .

Scrupulous vegetarianism, in matters of food, clothing, shelter, commerce, and recreation, and in all other spheres, is the only fully coherent position the critic may adopt. At great human cost, the lives of fish and crustaceans must also be protected, with equal vigor, if speciesism has been forsworn. A very few consistent critics adopt this position. It is the *reductio ad absurdum* of the rejection of moral distinctions between animals and human beings.

Study Questions

1. What is Cohen's position on animal rights? What are his arguments?
2. How does Cohen defend speciesism?
3. Do you agree with Cohen that absurd consequences would follow from our embracing a strong position on animal rights?

CHAPTER 55

Vegetarianism and "The Other Weight Problem"

JAMES RACHELS

James Rachels (see Chapter 25 for biographical sketch) argues for a moral duty to be vegetarian. Meat eating is immoral because it wastes valuable protein that could be used to feed hungry people and because it causes enormous suffering to animals.

It is now common for newspapers and magazines to carry the ultimate indictment of glutted Americans: ads for weight salons or reducing schemes next to news accounts of starvation in Africa, Latin America, or elsewhere. The pictures of big-bellied children nursing on emptied breasts tell of the other "weight problem."[1]

THERE ARE MORAL PROBLEMS about what we eat, and about what we do with the food we control. In this essay I shall discuss some of these problems. One of my conclusions will be that it is morally wrong for us to eat meat. Many readers will find this implausible and even faintly ridiculous, as I once did. After all, meat eating is a normal, well-established part of our daily routines; people have always eaten meat; and many find it difficult even to conceive of what an alternate diet would be like. So it is not easy to take seriously the possibility that it might be wrong. Moreover, vegetarianism is commonly associated with Eastern religions whose tenets we do not accept, and with extravagant, unfounded claims about health. A quick perusal of vegetarian literature might confirm the impression that it is all a crackpot business: tracts have titles like "Victory Through Vegetables" and promise that if one will only keep to a meatless diet one will have perfect health and be filled with wisdom. Of course we can ignore this kind of nonsense. However, there are other arguments for vegetarianism that must be taken seriously. One such argument, which has recently enjoyed wide support, has to do with the world food shortage. I will take up that argument after a few preliminaries.

I

According to the United Nations Food and Agriculture Organization, about 15,000 people die of malnutrition every day—10,000 of them are children. Millions more do not die but lead miserable lives constantly on the verge of starvation. Hunger is concentrated in poor, underdeveloped countries, out of sight of the 70 million Americans who are overweight from eating too much.

Of course, there is some malnutrition in the United States—a conservative estimate is that 40 million Americans are poor enough to qualify for assistance under the Federal Food Stamp

Reprinted from World Hunger and Moral Obligation, *edited by William Aiken and Hugh LaFollette (Engelwood Cliffs, N.J.: Prentice Hall, 1977) by permission.*

Program, although fewer than half that number are actually helped. But it is easy to misinterpret this statistic: while many of these Americans don't get *enough* to eat, neither are they starving. They do not suffer the extreme deprivation that reduces one's life to nothing more than a continual desperate search for food. Moreover, even the milder degree of malnutrition is an embarrassing anomaly; we are not a poor country, especially not in food. We have an abundance of rich farmland which we use with astonishing efficiency. (Although in some important ways our use of land is very inefficient. I will come to that in a moment.) The "Food-grain Yield" of American farms is about 3,050 pounds per acre. For comparison, we may note that only Japan does significantly better, with a yield of 4,500 pounds per acre; but in Japan 87 workers per 100 acres are needed to obtain this yield, while in the United States only *one* worker per 100 acres is required![2] If some Americans do not get enough to eat, it is not because we lack the food.

It does not require a very sophisticated argument to show that, if we have an overabundance of food while others are starving, we should not waste our surplus but make it available to those who need it. Studies indicate that the average American family throws out with the garbage about 10 percent of the food it buys.[3] Of course, it would be impractical for us to try to package up our leftover beans and potatoes at the end of each meal and send them off to the poor. But it would not be impractical for us to buy somewhat less, and contribute the leftover money to agencies that would then purchase the food we did not buy and deliver it to those in need.

The argument may be put this way: First, suppose you are about to throw out a quantity of food which you are unable to use, when someone offers to take it down the street to a child who is starving. Clearly, it would be immoral for you to refuse this offer and insist that the food go into the garbage. Second, suppose it is proposed that you *not buy* the extra food, in-stead give the money to provide for the child. Would it be any less immoral of you to refuse, and to continue to buy unneeded food to be discarded? The only important difference between the two cases is that by giving money, and not leftover food, better nourishment can be provided to the child more efficiently. Aside from some slight inconvenience—you would have to shop a bit more carefully—the change makes no difference to *your* interests at all. You end up with the same combination of food and money in each case. So, if it would be immoral to refuse to give the extra food to the child and insist on throwing it into the garbage, it is also immoral for us to buy and waste food when we could buy less and give the extra money for famine relief.

II

It is sometimes objected that famine-relief efforts are futile because the problems of overpopulation and underdevelopment in some parts of the world are insoluble. "Feed the starving millions," it is said, "and they will survive only to produce more starving millions. When the population in those poor, overcrowded countries has doubled, and then tripled, *then* there will be famine on a scale we have hardly dreamed of. What is needed in those countries is population control and the establishment of sound agricultural systems. But, unfortunately, given the religious, political, and educational situations in those countries, and the general cultural malaise produced by generations of ignorance and grinding poverty, these objectives are impossible to attain. So we have to face the fact that transfusions of food today, no matter how massive, only postpone the inevitable starvation and probably even make it worse."

It must be conceded that, *if* the situation really were this hopeless, then we would have no obligation to provide relief for those who are starving. We are not obligated to take steps that would do no good. What is wrong with this argument is that it paints too gloomy a picture of the possibilities. We have no conclusive evidence that the situation is hopeless. On the contrary, there is good reason to think that the problems can be solved. In China starvation is no longer a serious problem. That huge population is now adequately fed, whereas thirty years ago hunger was common. Apparently, Chinese agriculture is now established on a sound basis. Of course, this has been accomplished by a social regimentation and a denial of individual freedom that many of us find objectionable, and, in any case, Chinese-style regimentation cannot be expected in other countries. But this does not mean that there is no hope for other countries. In countries such as India, birth control programs can help. Contrary to what is popularly believed, such programs are not foredoomed to failure. During India's third "Five Year Plan" (1961–66) the birth rate in Bombay was reduced to only 27 per 1,000 population, only a bit higher than the U.S. rate of 23 per 1,000.[4] This was the best result in the country, but there were other hopeful signs as well: for example, during the same period the birth rate in a rural district of West Bengal dropped from 43 to 36 per 1,000. Experts do not regard India's population problem as hopeless.

It is a disservice to the world's poor to represent the hunger problem as worse than it is; for, if the situation is made to appear hopeless, then people are liable to do nothing. Nick Eberstadt, of the Harvard Center for Population Studies, remarks that:

Bangladesh is a case in point. The cameramen who photograph those living corpses for your evening consumption work hard to evoke a nation of unrecognizable monsters by the roadside. Unless you have been there, you would find it hard to imagine that the people of Bangladesh are friendly and energetic, and perhaps 95% of them get enough to get by. Or that Bangladesh has the richest cropland in the world, and that a well-guided aid program could help turn it from a famine center into one of the world's great breadbaskets. To most people in America the situation must look hopeless and our involvement, therefore, pointless. If the situation is so bad, why shouldn't we cut off our food and foreign aid to Bangladesh, and use it to save people who aren't going to die anyway?[5]

So, even if it is true that shipments of food *alone* will not solve the problems of famine, this does not mean that the problems cannot be solved. Short-term famine-relief efforts, together with longer-range population control programs and assistance to improve local agriculture, could greatly reduce, if not altogether eliminate, the tragedy of starvation.

III

I have already mentioned the waste of food thrown out with the garbage. That waste, as great as it is, is small in comparison to a different sort of waste which I want to describe now.

But first let me tell a little story. In this story, someone discovers a way of processing food so as to give it a radically new texture and taste. The processed food is no more nutritious than it was unprocessed, but people like the way it tastes, and it becomes very popular—so popular, in fact, that a great industry grows up and almost everyone comes to dine on it several times a week. There is only one catch: the conversion process is extremely wasteful. Seven-eighths of the food is destroyed by the process; so that in order to produce one pound of the processed food, eight pounds of unprocessed food are needed. This means that the new kind of food is relatively expensive and only people in the richer countries can afford to eat much of it. It also means that the process raises moral questions: Can it be right for some people to waste seven-eighths of their food resources, while millions of others are suffering from lack of food? If the waste of 10 percent of one's food is objectionable, the waste of 87.5 percent is more so.

In fact, we do use a process that is just this wasteful. The process works like this: First, we use our farmland to grow an enormous quantity of grain—many times the amount that we could consume, if we consumed it as grain or grain products. But we do not consume it in this form. Instead, we feed it to animals, and then we eat the animals. The process is staggeringly inefficient: we have to feed the animals eight pounds of protein in the form of grain to get back one pound in the form of meat, for a wastage of 87.5 percent. (This is the inefficient use of farmland that I referred to earlier; farmland that could be producing eight pounds of "unprocessed" food produces only one pound "processed.")

Fully one-half of all the harvested agricultural land in the United States is planted with feed-crops. We feed 78 percent of all our grain to animals. This is the highest percentage of any country in the world; the Soviet Union, for example, uses only 28 percent of its grain in this way. The "conversion ratio" for beef cattle and veal calves is an astonishing *21 to 1*—that is, we feed these animals 21 pounds of protein in the form of grain to get back 1 pound in the form of meat. Other animals process protein more efficiently, so that the average conversion ratio is "only" 8 to 1. To see what this means for a single year, we may note that in 1968 we fed 20 million tons of protein to livestock (excluding dairy cattle), in return for which we got 2 million tons of protein in meat, for a net loss of 18 million tons. This loss, in the United States alone, was equal to 90 percent of the world's estimated protein deficit.[6]

If we did not waste grain in this manner, there would clearly be enough to feed everyone in the world quite comfortably. In 1972–1973, when the world food "shortage" was supposedly becoming acute, 632 pounds of grain was produced annually for every person on earth (500 pounds is enough for adequate nourishment). This figure is actually *rising*, in spite of population growth; the comparable figure for 1960 was under 600.[7]

What reason is there to waste this incredible amount of food? Why raise and eat animals, instead of eating a portion of the grain ourselves and using the rest to relieve hunger? The meat we eat is no more nourishing than the grain the animals are fed. The only reason for preferring to eat meat is our enjoyment of its taste; but this is hardly a sufficient reason for wasting food that is desperately needed by people who are starving. It is as if one were to say to a hungry child: "I have eight times the food I need, but I can't let you have any of it, because I am going to use it all to make myself something really tasty."

This, then, is the argument for vegetarianism that I referred to at the beginning of this essay. If, in light of the world food situation, it is wrong for us to waste enormous quantities of food, then it is wrong for us to convert grain protein into meat protein as we do. And if we were to stop doing this, then most of us would have to become vegetarians of at least a qualified sort. I say "of a qualified sort" for two reasons. First, we could still eat fish. Since we do not raise fish by feeding them food that could be consumed by humans, there is no argument against eating fish comparable to this one against eating livestock. Second, there could still be a small amount of beef, pork, etc., produced without the use of feeds suitable for human consumption, and this argument would not rule out producing and eating that meat—but this would be such a small amount that it would not be available to most of us.

This argument against meat eating will be already familiar to many readers; it has been used in numerous books and in magazine and newspaper articles.[8] I am not certain, however, that it is an absolutely conclusive argument. For one thing it may be that a mere *reduction* in the amount of meat we produce would release enough grain to feed the world's hungry. We are now wasting so much food in this way that it may not be necessary for us to stop wasting all of it, but only some of it; so we may be able to go on consuming a fair amount of meat without depriving anyone of food. If so, the argument from wasting food would not support vegetarianism, but only a simple decrease in our meat consumption, which is something entirely different. There is, however, another argument for vegetarianism which I think is conclusive. Unlike the argument from food wastage, this argument does not appeal to the interests of humans as grounds for opposition to meat eating. Instead, it appeals directly to the interests of the animals themselves. I now turn to that argument.

IV

The wrongness of cruelty to animals is often explained in terms of its effects on human beings. The idea seems to be that the animals' interests are not *themselves* morally important or worthy of protection, but, since cruelty to animals often has bad consequences for *humans,* it is wrong to make animals suffer. In legal writing, for example, cruelty to animals is included among the "victimless crimes," and the problem of justifying legal prohibitions is seen as comparable to justifying the prohibition of other behavior, such as homosexuality or the distribution of pornography, where no one (no human) is obviously hurt. Thus, Louis Schwartz says that, in prohibiting the torturing of animals:

> It is not the mistreated dog who is the ultimate object of concern . . . Our concern is for the feelings of other human beings, a large proportion of whom, although accustomed to the slaughter of animals for food, readily identify themselves with a tortured dog or horse and respond with great sensitivity to its sufferings.[9]

Philosophers also adopt this attitude. Kant, for example, held that we have no direct duties to nonhuman animals. "The Categorical Imperative," the ultimate principle of morality, applies only to our dealings with humans:

> The practical imperative, therefore, is the following: Act so that you treat humanity, whether in your own person or in that of another, always as an end and never as a means only.[10]

And of other animals, Kant says:

> But so far as animals are concerned, we have no direct duties. Animals are not self-conscious, and are there merely as means to an end. That end is man.[11]

He adds that we should not be cruel to animals only because "He who is cruel to animals becomes hard also in his dealings with men."[12]

Surely this is unacceptable. Cruelty to animals ought to be opposed, not only because of the ancillary effects on humans, but because of the direct effects on the animals themselves. Animals that are tortured *suffer*, just as tortured humans suffer, and *that* is the primary reason why it is wrong. We object to torturing humans on a number of grounds, but the main one is that the victims suffer so. Insofar as nonhuman animals also suffer, we have the *same* reason to oppose torturing them, and it is indefensible to take the one suffering but not the other as grounds for objection.

Although cruelty to animals is wrong, it does not follow that we are never justified in inflicting pain on an animal. Sometimes we are justified in doing this, just as we are sometimes justified in inflicting pain on humans. It does follow, however, that there must be a *good reason* for causing the suffering, and if the suffering is great, the justifying reason must be correspondingly powerful. As an example, consider the treatment of the civet cat, a highly intelligent and sociable animal. Civet cats are trapped and placed in small cages inside darkened sheds, where the temperature is kept up to 110°F by fires.[13] They are confined in this way until they finally die. What justifies this extraordinary mistreatment? These animals have the misfortune to produce a substance that is useful in the manufacture of perfume. Musk, which is scraped from their genitals once a day for as long as they can survive, makes the scent of perfume last a bit longer after each application. (The heat increases their "production" of musk.) Here Kant's rule—"Animals are merely means to an end; that end is man"—is applied with a vengeance. To promote one of the most trivial interests we have, thousands of animals are tormented for their whole lives.

It is usually easy to persuade people that this use of animals is not justified, and that we have a moral duty not to support such cruelties by consuming their products. The argument is simple: Causing suffering is not justified unless there is a good reason; the production of perfume made with musk causes considerable suffering; our enjoyment of this product is not a good enough reason to justify causing that suffering; therefore, the use of animals in this way is wrong. At least my experience has been that, once people learn the facts about musk production, they come to regard using such products as morally objectionable. They are surprised to discover, however, that an exactly analogous argument can be given in connection with the use of animals as food. Animals that are raised and slaughtered for food also suffer, and our enjoyment of the way they taste is not a sufficient justification for mistreating them.

Most people radically underestimate the amount of suffering that is caused to animals who are raised and slaughtered for food.[14] They think, in a vague way, that slaughterhouses are cruel, and perhaps even that methods of slaughter ought to be made more humane. But after all, the visit to the slaughterhouse is a relatively brief episode in the animal's life; and beyond that, people imagine that the animals are treated well enough. Nothing could be further from the truth. Today the production of meat is Big Business, and the helpless animals are treated more as machines in a factory than as living creatures.

Veal calves for example, spend their lives in pens too small to allow them to turn around or even to lie down comfortably—exercise toughens the muscles, which reduces the "quality" of the meat, and besides, allowing the animals adequate living space would be prohibitively expensive. In these pens the calves cannot perform such basic actions as grooming themselves, which they naturally desire to do, because there is not room for them to twist their heads around. It is clear that the calves miss their mothers, and like human infants they want something to suck: they can be seen trying vainly to suck the sides of their stalls. In order to keep their meat pale and tasty, they are fed a liquid diet deficient in both iron and roughage. Naturally they develop cravings for these things, because they need them. The calf's craving for iron is so strong that, if it is allowed to turn around, it will lick at its own urine, although calves normally find this repugnant. The tiny stall, which prevents the animal from turning, solves this "problem." The craving for roughage is especially strong since without it the animal cannot form a cud to chew. It cannot be given any straw for bedding, since the animal would be driven to eat it, and that would spoil the meat. For these animals the slaughterhouse is not an unpleasant end to an otherwise contented life. As terrifying as the process of slaughter is, for them it may actually be regarded as a merciful release.

Similar stories can be told about the treatment of other animals on which we dine. In order to "produce" animals by the millions, it is necessary to keep them crowded together in small spaces. Chickens are commonly kept eight or ten to a space smaller than a newspaper page. Unable to walk around or even stretch their wings—much less build a nest—the birds become vicious and attack one another. The problem is sometimes exacerbated because the birds are so crowded that, unable to move, their feet literally grow around the wire floors of the cages, anchoring them to the spot. An "anchored" bird cannot escape attack no matter how desperate it becomes. Mutilation of the animals is an efficient solution. To minimize the damage they can do to one another, the birds' beaks are cut off. The mutilation is painful, but probably not as painful as other sorts of mutilations that are routinely practiced. Cows are castrated, not to prevent the unnatural "vices" to which overcrowded chickens are prone, but because castrated cows put on more weight, and there is less danger of meat being "tainted" by male hormones.

> In Britain an anesthetic must be used, unless the animal is very young, but in America anesthetics are not in general use. The procedure is to pin the animal down, take a knife and slit the scrotum, exposing the testicles. You then grab each testicle in turn and pull on it, breaking the cord that attaches it; on older animals it may be necessary to cut the cord.[15]

It must be emphasized that the treatment I am describing—and I have hardly scratched the surface here—is not out of the ordinary. It is typical of the way that animals raised for food are treated, now that meat production is Big Business. As Peter Singer puts it, these are the sorts of things that happened to your dinner when it was still an animal.

What accounts for such cruelties? As for the meat producers, there is no reason to think they are unusually cruel men. They simply accept the common attitude expressed by Kant: "Animals are merely means to an end; that end is man." The cruel practices are adopted not because they are cruel but because they are efficient, given that one's only concern is to produce meat (and eggs) for humans as cheaply as possible. But clearly this use of animals is immoral if anything is. Since we can nourish ourselves very well without eating them, our only reason for doing all this to the animals is our enjoyment of the way they taste. And this will not even come close to justifying the cruelty.

V

Does this mean that we should stop eating meat? Such a conclusion will be hard for many people to accept. It is tempting to say: "What is objectionable is not eating the animals, but only making them suffer. Perhaps we ought to protest the way they are treated, and even work for better treatment of them. But it doesn't follow that we must stop eating them." This sounds plausible until you realize that it would be impossible to treat the animals decently and still produce meat in sufficient quantities to make it a normal part of our diets. As I have already remarked, cruel methods are used in the meat-production industry because such methods are economical; they enable the producers to market a product that people can afford. Humanely produced chicken, beef, and pork would be so expensive that only the very rich could afford them. (Some of the cruelties could be eliminated without too much expense—the cows could be given an anesthetic before castration, for example, even though this alone would mean a slight increase in the cost of beef. But others, such as overcrowding, could not be eliminated without really prohibitive cost.) So to work for better treatment for the animals would be to work for a situation in which most of us would have to adopt a vegetarian diet.

Still, there remains the interesting theoretical question: If meat could be produced humanely, without mistreating the animals prior to killing them painlessly, would there be anything wrong with it? The question is only of theoretical interest because the actual choice we face in the supermarket is whether to buy the remains of animals that are not treated humanely. Still, the question has some interest, and I want to make two comments about it.

First, it is a vexing issue whether animals have a "right to life" that is violated when we kill them for trivial purposes; but we should not simply assume until proven otherwise that they don't have such a right.[16] We assume that humans have a right to life—it would be wrong to murder a normal, healthy human even if it were done painlessly—and it is hard to think of any plausible rationale for granting this right to humans that does not also apply to other animals. Other animals live in communities, as do humans; they communicate with one another, and have ongoing social relationships; killing them disrupts lives that are perhaps not as complex, emotionally and intellectually, as our own, but that are nevertheless quite complicated. They suffer, and are capable of happiness as well as fear and distress, as we are. So what could be the rational basis for saying that we have a right to life, but that they don't? Or even more pointedly, what could be the rational basis for saying that a severely retarded human, who is inferior in every important respect to an intelligent animal, has a right to life but that the animal doesn't? Philosophers often treat such questions as "puzzles," assuming that there must be answers even if we are not clever enough to find them. I am suggesting that, on the contrary, there may not be any acceptable answers to these questions. If it seems, intuitively, that there *must* be some difference between us and the other animals which confers on us, but not them, a right to life, perhaps this intuition is mistaken. At the very least, the difficulty of answering such questions should make us hesitant about asserting that it is all right to kill animals, as long as we don't make them suffer, unless we are also willing to take seriously the possibility that it is all right to kill people, so long as we don't make them suffer.

Second, it is important to see the slaughter of animals for food as part of a larger pattern that characterizes our whole relationship with the nonhuman world. Animals are wrenched from their natural homes to be made objects of our entertainment in zoos, circuses, and rodeos. They are used in laboratories not only for experiments that are themselves morally questionable,[17] but also in testing everything from shampoo to chemical weapons. They are killed so that their heads can be used as wall decorations, or their skins as ornamental clothing or rugs. Indeed, simply killing them for the fun of it is thought to be "sport."[18] This pattern of cruel exploitation flows naturally from the Kantian attitude that animals are nothing more than things to be used for our purposes. It is this whole attitude that must be opposed, and not merely its manifestation in our willingness to hurt the animals we eat. Once one rejects this attitude, and no longer regards the animals as disposable at one's whim, one ceases to think it all right to kill them, even painlessly, just for a snack.

But now let me return to the more immediate practical issue. The meat at the supermarket was not produced by humane methods. The animals whose flesh this meat once was were abused in ways similar to the ones I have described. Millions of other animals are being treated in these ways now, and their flesh will soon appear in the markets. Should one support such practices by purchasing and consuming its products?

It is discouraging to realize that no animals will actually be helped simply by one person ceasing to eat meat. One consumer's behavior, by itself, cannot have a noticeable impact on an industry as vast as the meat business. However, it is important to see one's behavior in a wider context. There are already millions of vegetarians, and because they don't eat meat there *is* less cruelty than there otherwise would be. The question is whether one ought to side with that group, or with the carnivores whose practices cause the suffering. Compare the position of someone thinking about whether to buy slaves in the year 1820. He might reason as follows: "The whole practice of slavery is immoral, but I cannot help any of the poor slaves by keeping clear of it. If I don't buy these slaves, someone else will. One person's decision just can't by itself have any impact on such a vast business. So I may as well use slaves like everyone else." The first thing we notice is that this fellow was too pessimistic about the possibilities of a successful movement; but beyond that, there is something else wrong with his reasoning. If one really thinks that a social practice is immoral, that *in itself* is sufficient grounds for a refusal to participate. In 1848 Thoreau remarked that even if someone did not want to devote himself to the abolition movement, and actively oppose slavery, ". . . it is his duty, at least, to wash his hands of it, and, if he gives it no thought longer, not to give it practically his support."[19] In the case of slavery, this seems clear. If it seems less clear in the case of the cruel exploitation of non-human animals, perhaps it is because the Kantian attitude is so deeply entrenched in us.

VI

I have considered two arguments for vegetarianism: one appealing to the interests that humans have in conserving food resources, and the other appealing directly to the interests of the animals themselves. The latter, I think, is the more compelling argument, and in an important sense it is a deeper argument. Once its force is felt, any opposition to meat eating that is based only on considerations of food wastage will seem shallow in the same way that opposition to slavery is shallow if it is based only on economic considerations. Yet the second argument does in a way reinforce the first one. In this case at least, the interests of humans and nonhumans coincide. By doing what we ought to do anyway—ceasing to exploit helpless animals—we would at the same time increase the food available for hungry people.

Notes

1. Coleman McCarthy, "Would we sacrifice to aid the starving?" *Miami Herald*, 28 July 1974, page 2F.

2. These figures are based on studies conducted in 1969–1971. They are from James, Grant, "A New Development Strategy," *Foreign Policy*, 12 (1973).

3. One such study is reported in *Time*, 26 January 1976, p. 8.

4. B. L. Raina, "India," in Bernard Berelson, ed., *Family Planning and Population Programs: A Review of World Developments* (Chicago: University of Chicago Press, 1966), pp. 111–22.

5. Nick Eberstadt, "Myths of the Food Crisis," *The New York Review of Books*, 19 February 1976, p. 32. Eberstadt's article contains a good survey of the problems involved in assessing the world food situation—how bad it is, or isn't. He concludes that the situation is bad, but not at all hopeless. See also various articles in Philip H. Abelson, ed., *Food: Politics, Economics, Nutrition and Research* (Washington, D.C.: American Association for the Advancement of Science, 1975).

6. The figures in this paragraph are from Frances Moore Lappé, *Diet for a Small Planet* (New York: Ballantine Books, Inc., 1971), part I. This book is an excellent primer on protein.

7. Eberstadt, "Myths of the Food Crisis," p. 34.

8. For example, in Lappé's *Diet for a Small Planet,* and in several of the articles anthologized in Catherine Lerza and Michael Jacobson, eds., *Food for People Not for Profit: A Sourcebook on the Food Crisis* (New York: Ballantine Books, Inc., 1975).

9. Louis B. Schwartz, "Morals Offenses and the Model Penal Code," *Columbia Law Review,* 63 (1963); reprinted in Joel Feinberg and Hyman Gross, eds., *Philosophy of Law* (Encino, Calif. Dickenson Publishing Company, Inc., 1975), p. 156.

10. Immanuel Kant, *Foundations of the Metaphysics of Morals,* trans. Lewis White Beck (Indianapolis: The Bobbs-Merrill Co., Inc., 1959), p. 47.

11. Immanuel Kant, *Lectures on Ethics,* trans. Louis Infield (New York: Harper Torchbooks, 1963), p. 239.

12. Ibid., p. 240.

13. Muriel the Lady Dowding, "Furs and Cosmetics: Too High a Price?" in Stanley and Roslind Godlovitch and John Harris, eds., *Animals, Men and Morals* (New York: Taplinger Publishing Co., Inc., 1972), p. 36.

14. By far the best account of these cruelties is to be found in Chapter 3 of Peter Singer's *Animal Liberation* (New York: New York Review Books, 1975). I have drawn on Singer's work for the factual material in the following two paragraphs. *Animal Liberation*

should be consulted for a thorough treatment of matters to which I can refer here only sketchily.

15. Singer, *Animal Liberation*, p. 152.

16. It is controversial among philosophers whether animals can have any rights at all. See various essays collected in Part IV of Tom Regan and Peter Singer, eds., *Animal Rights and Human Obligations* (Englewood Cliffs, N.J.: Prentice-Hall, 1976). My own defense of animal rights is given in "Do Animals Have a Right to Liberty?" pp. 205–223, and in "A Reply to VanDeVeer," pp. 230–32.

17. See Singer, *Animal Liberation*, Chap. 2.

18. It is sometimes said, in defense of "non-slob" hunting: "Killing for pleasure is wrong, but killing for food is all right." This won't do, since for those of us who are able to nourish ourselves without killing animals, killing them for food *is* a form of killing for pleasure, namely, the pleasures of the palate.

19. Henry David Thoreau, *Civil Disobedience* (1848).

Study Questions

1. What is the relationship between the dietary habits of Americans and world hunger?
2. What are Rachels's arguments for vegetarianism?
3. Do you agree with Rachels that we should become vegetarians? You might want to go back and examine Frey's opposing arguments (Chapter 49).

For Further Reading

Frey, R. G. *Rights, Killing and Suffering*. Oxford: Basil Blackwell, 1983.

Rachels, James. *Created from Animals: The Moral Implications of Darwinism*. Oxford: Oxford University Press, 1990.

Regan, Tom. *The Case for Animal Rights*. Berkeley: University of California, 1983. The most comprehensive philosophical treatise in favor of animal rights.

Regan, Tom, and Peter Singer, eds. *Animal Rights and Human Obligations*. Englewood Cliffs, N.J.: Prentice Hall, 1976.

Rohr, Janelle, ed. *Animal Rights: Opposing Viewpoints*. San Diego: Greenhaven Press, 1989.

Robbins, John. *Diet for a New America: How Your Food Choices Affect Your Health, Happiness, and the Future of Life on Earth*. Walpole, N.H.: Stillpoint, 1987. A strong case for vegetarianism.

Peter Singer. *Animal Liberation*, 2d ed. New York: New York Review of Books, 1990.

VandeVeer, D., and C. Pierce, eds. *People, Penguins, and Plastic Trees*. Belmont, Calif.: Wadsworth, 1990.

Part XI

War

Introduction

Most people agree that moral rules apply to conflicts within a society, but not every-one agrees that these rules apply to conflicts between societies. Conventions exist within a society that generate expectations of how others should behave. In great abuses the law steps in to curb antisocial behavior. But international law with a mechanism for enforcement does not exist at present. Between nations we are closer to what Hobbes called a "state of nature" where the only thing that saves us from attack is the fact that it is too costly for the invader to risk aggressive action. A cold war exists even when there is no physical violence.

When war becomes a possibility or when one nation attacks another, three op-tions are available to the attacked nation: It may refuse to fight back; it may fight back with all its resources (total war); it may fight back but exercise restraint. Each option may be further qualified. For example, the nation that refuses to defend itself through violence may nevertheless engage in passive resistance.

The first option is pacifism, a commitment to nonviolence even if it means not defending oneself or others from aggression. Douglas Lackey has identified four types of pacifists: (1) Those who believe that killing other people (or animals) is immoral (e.g., Albert Schweitzer); (2) those who believe that all violence is immoral (universal pacifists, such as Tolstoy and Gandhi); (3) those who believe that personal violence is wrong but political violence may be justified (such as St. Augustine, who believed that it was immoral to defend oneself but endorsed wars against heretics); and (4) those who believe that war is always wrong but who accept personal self-defense, antiwar pacifists.[1]

In our readings, Jan Narveson examines several pacifist arguments and concludes that pacifism either reduces to personal taste or is incoherent. If we have any rights at all, we have the right to defend ourselves. Cheyney Ryan finds fault with Narveson's analysis and draws out the essence of pacifism as the idea that we ought not to be able easily to create the necessary distance between ourselves and others to make killing possible.

For those who reject pacifism and accept going to war as a necessary evil, the issues become (1) when is going to war morally justified and (2) how should war be fought? Assuming that mere might does not make right, moral people want to be justified in resorting to violence. Three classical theories of morality—utilitarianism, contractualism, and deontologism—prescribe three different answers to these questions. Utilitarian theories, which seek to maximize goodness ("the greatest good for the greatest number"), enjoin a cost-benefit analysis to determine the likely outcomes of diverse strategies. When nations are in conflict, war becomes one option that may be considered as a means of conflict resolution. The only question to be asked is, How likely is it that war will bring about a better total outcome than any alternative policy? If after careful analysis, war is judged likely to bring about the greatest total benefit, then war is justified.

Realpolitik (power politics) prevails. No civilian-combatant distinction exists. If you can accomplish more by killing civilians, you are justified in so doing, though this may set off a bad precedent in killing civilians—so be careful! The decision to drop the atom bomb on Hiroshima was justified from a utilitarian perspective. Reflect upon the words of President Truman:

> Having found the bomb, we have to use it. We have used it against those who attacked us without warning at Pearl Harbor, against those who have starved and beaten and executed American prisoners of war, against those who have abandoned all pretense of obeying international laws of warfare. We have used it in order to shorten the agony of war, in order to save the lives of thousands and thousands of young Americans.[2]

Assuming that more good will be done by sacrificing the enemy lives to American lives, the argument has utilitarian traits. Save lives by killing others.

Of course, Truman's reasoning could also be construed as enlightened self-interest, a view held by contractualist types of ethics. According to the contractualist, war is justified for a country whenever that country's self-interest is to go to war. Egoist enlightened self-interest is the leitmotif of contractualism, which leads nations into treaties. Once bound to treaties, the nations may support one another in battle. Where no contract exists, no moral obligation exists; and where a contract exists, the obligation must be surrounded with sanctions. Otherwise, the treaty is void, for, as Hobbes noted, "Covenants without the sword are but words, and of no strength to secure man at all." Generally, if it is in a country's self-interest to make a treaty, which includes the promise to defend another country, that treaty should be adhered to, for you will probably need that country's aid in the future, and backing out of a treaty is a poor advertisement to others. So if our government has a treaty with Saudi Arabia, Kuwait, or Israel, we should honor it and defend those countries when they are attacked or threatened. Interestingly enough, the United States had no treaty with Kuwait when it went to that country's aid.

As was the case with utilitarian theory, contractual theory recognizes no special rule distinguishing civilians from combatants. All are fair game.

The third major theory is a version of deontological ethics and is called just-war theory. Developed by the Roman Catholic theologians Augustine (354–430),

Thomas Aquinas (1225–1274), and Francisco Suarez (1548–1617), just-war theorists hold that war, although an evil, can be justified if certain conditions are met. As deontologists, they reject simple cost-benefit calculations and the whole notion of total war—all's fair in love and war. They distinguish between moral grounds for going to war (*jus ad bellum*) and right conduct while engaged in war (*jus in bello*). *Jus ad bellum*, the right to go to war, could be justified by the following circumstances. The war must be:

1. **Declared by a legitimate authority.** This would rule out revolutionary wars and rebel uprisings.
2. **Declared for a just cause.** In World War II, the declaration of war by the Allies on the Japanese and Germans, who were seen as bent on destroying Western democracy, is often cited as the paradigm case of such a just declaration of war. The 1991 war against Iraq was allegedly about the integrity of Kuwait as well as the danger to Saudi Arabia, Syria, and especially Israel. It was also about the control of oil in the Mideast.
3. **Declared as a last resort.** Belligerency may only commence after a reasonable determination has been made that war is the only way to accomplish good ends. In the 1991 war against Iraq, people argued that serious effort at negotiation had failed and that sanctions were not working, so war was the only alternative.
4. **Declared with the intention of bringing peace and in holding respect (and even love) for the enemy.** The opposition must be respected as human beings even as we attack them.

Note that just-war theory permits preemptive strikes if the leaders are certain of intended aggression, as in Israel's Six-Day War against Egypt in 1967.

Regarding carrying on the war (*jus in bello*) two further conditions are given:

5. **Proportionality.** The war must be carried out in moderation, exacting no more casualties than are necessary for accomplishing the good end. No more force than necessary to achieve the just goal may be exercised. Pillage, rape, and torture are forbidden. There is no justification for cruel treatment of innocents, prisoners, and the wounded. Nuclear war would violate the principle of proportionality.
6. **Discrimination.** Contrary to utilitarian and contractualist theories, the just-war theory makes a distinction between combatants and noncombatants—those deemed innocent in the fray. It is impermissible to attack nonmilitary targets and noncombatants. Civilian bombing is outlawed by international law. The massacre of civilians at My Lai was seen as the nadir of despicable behavior by American forces in the Vietnam War.

Robert Phillips has given a contemporary defense of the just-war theory. Our first reading is his defense of conditions 5 and 6.

While few would question conditions 2, 3, and 4, since they seem self-evidently necessary to doing any lesser evil, utilitarians would urge us to reject the sixth condition, discrimination. If by bombing a city in which 10,000 civilian lives were lost we could save 15,000 soldiers, we should bomb the city. Whatever does the least total evil should be done, regardless of the individual rules.

The distinction between innocents (noncombatants) and combatants is especially problematic. What if the civilians are used as protective shields for the combatants? Do you refrain from killing the enemy who is threatening you on the basis of not intending to kill the shield? Robert Phillips argues that you should not kill shields in our first reading.

Whatever your conclusion on which moral theory deals with war best, the threat of nuclear war puts the very concept of a just war in serious doubt. Consider the facts. The atomic bomb that fell on Hiroshima on August 6, 1945, killing 60,000 people, had an explosive force of 12,000 tons of TNT. The nuclear warhead on an American Minuteman missile has an explosive force of 1.2 million tons of TNT, 100 times the force of the bomb that fell on Hiroshima. A larger, 10-megaton hydrogen bomb has the explosive force 800 times that of the Hiroshima bomb. The United States and the former Soviet Union together have about 50,000 nuclear warheads. France, Great Britain, China, India, Israel, and Pakistan all have nuclear weapons— for a total of more than 60,000 nuclear warheads!

The destruction in a full-scale nuclear war would be so devastating that the living might well envy the dead, for they would have little to look forward to. Strontium 90 (which resembles calcium in its chemical composition, and so gets into milk products and then into humans through milk) eventually causes bone cancer. Most animals, especially large ones like cattle, and most trees would die; lakes and rivers would be poisoned by radiation; and the affected soil would lose its nutrients and, consequently, its ability to produce food. "In sum, a full-scale nuclear attack on the United States would devastate the natural environment on a scale unknown since early geological times, when, in response to natural catastrophes . . . sudden mass extinctions of species and whole ecosystems occurred all over the earth."[3] What would survive? Mainly grass and small insects. The United States would become a republic of insects and grass.

A nuclear war violates the principles of a just war. It violates principles 4 (aiming at bringing about peace in which the enemy is respected), 5 (proportionality), and 6 (discrimination between combatants and noncombatants). This is why U.S. Roman Catholic bishops have declared that using nuclear weapons is inherently immoral (see our fourth reading).

Utilitarians (e.g., Douglas Lackey in our sixth reading) and contractualists also generally condemn nuclear war. The short-term and long-term destruction of such a war would be so terrible that it defies the power of words to describe. However, these theories might justify selective use of nuclear weapons, as theorists from both of these camps justify the use of the atomic bomb on Hiroshima and Nagasaki in order to bring Japan to surrender and thus save hundreds of thousands of lives (though Lackey disputes this in his essay). For utilitarians, the principle of the lesser evil applied. Do whatever will minimize evil! For contractualists, the bombing was an instrument of enlightened self-interest.

But both utilitarians and contractualists agree that we must prevent a nuclear war. In the shadow of a nuclear holocaust, the deontological, utilitarian, and contractualist tend to converge, as do abolitionist and realist positions. Such an act of madness violates just-war principles, it violates the principle of utility, and it is not in anyone's interest.

Yet some utilitarians, such as Charles Krauthammer (in our fifth reading), argue that paradoxically the best way to avoid a nuclear catastrophe, given that some nations have nuclear weapons, is not unilateral disarmament but a strong policy of nuclear armament in the form of deterrence. The threat of nuclear war provides a powerful incentive for all nations to refrain from attacking each other.

Finally, William James's classic essay "The Moral Equivalent of War" argues that we need to find alternatives to release aggressive tension.

Notes

1. Douglas Lackey, *The Ethics of War and Peace* (Englewood Cliffs, N.J.: Prentice Hall, 1989), p. 7f.

2. Address to the nation by President Harry S Truman, August 9, 1945, quoted in Robert W. Tucker, *The Just War* (Westport, Conn.: Greenwood Press, 1978), p. 21f.

3. Jonathan Schell, *The Fate of the Earth* (New York: Knopf, 1982), p. 68.

CHAPTER 56

Just War Theory

ROBERT PHILLIPS

Professor of philosophy at the University of Connecticut at Hartford, Robert Phillips is the author of *War and Justice* (1984) from which this selection is taken.

Phillips defends two principles of just-war theory, those of proportionality (no more force is permitted than is necessary to the end sought) and discrimination between combatants and noncombatants. Much of his argument depends on the distinction between *intending* to kill someone and *foreseeing* that someone will die as a result of your action. Utilitarians and others often reject this distinction.

I OUTLINE BELOW, in point form, the doctrine of the just war. . . .

Bellum Justum [Just War]

Jus ad Bellum [Justice in going to war]

I. Last resort.

II. Declared by legitimate authority.

III. Morally justifiable:

   A. Defense against aggression.

   B. Correction of an injustice that has gone uncorrected by legitimate authority "in another place."

   C. Reestablishment of a social order which will distribute justice.

   D. Undertaken with the intention of bringing about peace.

Jus in Bello [Justice in waging war]

I. Proportionality: The quantity of force employed or threatened must always be morally proportionate to the end being sought in war.

II. Discrimination: Force must never be applied in such a way as to make noncombatants and innocent persons the intentional objects of attack. The only appropriate targets in war are combatants.

   A. The Principle of Double Effect: In a situation where the use of force can be foreseen to have actual or probable multiple effects, some of which are evil, culpability does not attach to the agent if the following conditions are met:

     1. The action must carry the intention to produce morally good consequences.

     2. The evil effects are not *intended* as ends in themselves or as means to other ends, good or evil.

     3. The permission of collateral evil must be justified by considerations of proportionate moral weight. . . .

Reprinted from War and Justice *(Norman: University of Oklahoma Press, 1984) by permission.*

The "other half" of *bellum justum* is *jus in bello*, or the doctrine of just behavior in combat. . . .

I. *Proportionality*

The principle of proportionality holds that in cases where the use of force is justified it cannot be employed in absolutely any measure. Obviously, if the aim of war is the correction of injustice, then the level of force must not be such as to create new and greater injustices. This principle is sometimes confused with the doctrine of "minimal force," which holds that the least amount of force consistent with effecting the desired ends ought to be our goal. While minimal force should always be used, we also have to consider the *degree* of violence, for some military tasks might very well require a minimum of force which would be disproportionate. That is, our calculations must include not only a forecast of necessary minimal means but also of consequences.

This distinction is of crucial importance because it directs our attention to the means of waging war and thus to the moral questions provoked by certain types of weaponry. In effect, proportionality is not to be calculated relative to a weapons system taken as a "given" but, rather, in terms of a calculus which will include the weapons themselves. So, for example, it may not be morally acceptable to say the following sort of thing: Given the fact of nuclear weapons deployed for massive retaliation, what casualty level is acceptable within the possibilities of these devices? Now this is precisely what some military thinkers have attempted to do . . . , but my contention here is that this move renders the whole conception of proportionality vacuous by making its significance dependent upon whatever weapons happen to exist at a given time. It is, of course, extremely difficult to counter in any meaningful way the onrush of weapons technology. The operative principle of the technocrat is: "If *x* is possible, then *x* ought to be";

but the alternative to not doing this is making morality completely subordinate to whatever technological development happens to be occurring at the moment.

I hasten to add that the motivation of those who argue that proportionality is relative to conditions is not simply self-serving. If one knows that certain sorts of weapons will be used which one also knows will cause casualties that are disproportionate on any objective basis, it is obviously morally preferable to attempt to obtain whatever proportionality is possible relative to the system—even in the case of massive retaliation with nuclear weapons. The danger here is that we will fall into the habit of doing no more than this. I suggest that modern history reveals just this pattern of thinking by just-war theorists. A weapon is invented and employed, and suddenly it is a fait accompli. Morality then tags along with a "justification" based ultimately on the principle that even if the means are disproportionate in themselves it is better to try to limit their use than to permit unrestrained employment. This is a principle with which one cannot disagree, but it must not be our guiding principle in thinking about means. Rather, we must evolve some conception of proportion which will allow us to include weapons and modes of warfare *as such* in our prohibitions. It is not, of course, the province of *bellum justum* to provide a criterion of nonrelative proportionality but only to establish that the principles of justice do in fact require such a standard.

II. *Discrimination*

What is true for proportionality is *a fortiori* true for the principle of discrimination. The notion that force ought to be morally justified only if it can be employed in a discriminate manner lies at the heart of *jus in bello*. The principle of double effect is, in turn, at the heart of discrimination.

(A) Put as simply as possible, by emphasizing intention as the defining feature of moral actions, the supporters of *bellum justum* attempt to mark a difference between killing in war and murder in two different cases. First, the killing of enemy combatants in a justified war may be morally acceptable under some circumstances. Second, the killing of noncombatants incidental to the prosecution of a necessary military operation in a justified war may also be morally acceptable under some circumstances. . . .

The principle of double effect is a refinement of a more general set of considerations having to do with the discriminating use of force. If the use of force by legitimate authority is to be justified, then obviously it cannot be administered in any quantity nor can it be directed at any and every target. This is "obvious" because we are assuming that if anything can be said to be evil it is direct acts of violence upon other people. If there is to be a distinction between killing in war and murder, there must also be a prior conception of relevant differences in potential targets. The most widely discussed aspect of double effect has been noncombatant immunity, and one of the key issues raised here is how to make such immunity compatible with the foreknowledge which we will normally possess of the certain death of noncombatants incidental to military operations.

Double effect is derived from a quite general criterion of moral judgment enunciated succinctly but clearly by Aquinas: "now moral acts take their species according to what is intended and not according to what is beside the intention, since this is accidental" (*Summa* 2.2. q. 64, art. 7).

Aquinas, I take it, is arguing not that the consequences of actions are morally irrelevant but, rather, that when one raises questions about the morality of a particular action (as opposed to its utility, its beauty, and so on) one is inevitably making reference to the agent's intentions. "Accidental" is used here not exclusively to mean the unforeseen but to include the foreseen but undesired consequences of the action. "Accidental" may be understood as "collateral."

Following this line, we may summarize the principle in the following way: In a situation where the use of force can be seen to have actual or probable multiple effects, some of which are evil, culpability does not attach to the agent if the following conditions are met: (1) the action is intended to produce morally good consequences; (2) the evil effects are not intended as ends in themselves or as means to other ends, good or evil; and (3) the permission of collateral evil must be justified by considerations of proportionate moral weight.

How do these considerations apply to the combat situation? There are at least two senses in which it is sometimes claimed that there is no relevant distinction between killing in war and murder. First is the view that all killing is murder, that it is always wrong deliberately to take another human life. This would mean that in the combat situation it would be wrong to kill both combatants *and* noncombatants and, indeed, that there is really no moral difference between these classes. This is clearly a version of pacifism. . . . This view holds that under no circumstances may the death of another human being be directly willed; killing is wrong even if one's own life is placed in grave risk and even if the other person is the aggressor.

According to the second view, the killing of noncombatants is murder, while the death of an aggressor combatant in wartime is morally acceptable. Thus if a war could be fought entirely between combatants, it would be, in principle, possible to avoid committing murder. It is further argued, however, that in an actual combat situation where there is foreknowledge that operations will cause the death of noncombatants, there is no relevant difference between killing and murder. This view has generated two rather strikingly different conclusions with respect to what a moral agent ought to do faced with the possibility of combat.

On the one hand, since modern weaponry is by its very nature indiscriminate, and since foreknowledge of the death of noncombatants cancels whatever good intentions we may offer by way of exculpation, we end up as pacifists by default. While admitting the theoretical possibility of a just war, the indiscriminate use of force which must necessarily be a feature of contemporary warfare makes us pacifists, as it were, "war by war."

On the other hand, starting from the same premises, it has sometimes been argued that since there are no relevant differences between killing and murder with respect to noncombatants, war may be fought without any restraint at all. That is, if a war is justified then the absence of criteria for distinguishing between killing and murder is a permission to employ any means whatever to bring about victory. This argument is frequently found embedded in a larger utilitarian framework which, in extreme cases, would permit the killing of noncombatants as a means of securing peace. This seems to have been the line taken by Sir Arthur Harris over the British terror bombing of German cities in the Second World War. When reproached with the indiscriminate character of carpet bombing Harris replied, "It is war itself which is evil," thus implying the pointlessness of attempting to make distinctions (at least for the purposes of bombing) between combatants and noncombatants.

These then are the two main lines of criticism directed against the moral significance of the principle of double effect and, consequently, of the distinction between killing in war and murder.

Let us turn first to the question: How can we escape the charge that killing an enemy combatant is murder? If force is ever to be morally justified, its employment must be against a target other than a person as such. One must not be directly seeking the death of another human being either as such or as a means to some further end. Therefore, the intention or purpose of the act of force must be toward *restraint* of the aggressor. This is the beginning of an answer to the pacifist. For he and the defender of *bellum justum* are surely in agreement, and correctly so, that the death of another human being ought never to be directly willed if the target is the man himself in his humanity or the man who represents the values of the enemy in a particular historical situation (this prohibition must imply the intrinsic value of other persons). Yet, if force may be justified, then what is the target? The answer must be that the proper target of the discriminate use of force is not the man himself but the combatant *in* the man.

It may be objected that it is a logical impossibility to separate out the totality of actions plus the underlying rationale for such behavior which together constitute the combatant in the man. That is, to speak of a particular man or of "man" in general apart from particular behavior patterns is to speak of a nonentity. Hence, the combatant in the man is not a possible target. Furthermore, it may be urged that even if some such distinction is possible, to kill one is to kill the other. A soldier going into combat with the intention of restraining or incapacitating combatants must know before he ever lifts a weapon that combat will result in the death of a great many persons.

A utilitarian might put the objection in the following way: Jones and Smith both go into combat armed with machine guns. Jones, a supporter of the traditional view, carries with him the intention to incapacitate or restrain the aggressor, whereas Smith intends merely to kill as many of the enemy as he can in order to avoid being killed himself. On meeting the enemy they both open fire, and they both kill one enemy each. What difference does "intention" make from the moral point of view? In both cases an act of extreme violence, the unleashing of a stream of bullets, has resulted in the death of a person. A corpse lies before both Smith and Jones—this is the brute, ultimate fact which no amount of "intentional" redescription can alter. Thus, there is only *one* action here, the killing (possibly murder) of a human being.

In trying to answer this there are two things that have to be said about intention. The first has to do with the way in which awareness of an agent's intentions is crucial in understanding the meaning of an action and consequently in knowing how correctly to describe it. If one were to universalize the utilitarian's position on the irrelevance of intention, the results would be quite disastrous for any attempt to understand human action. Setting the moral question entirely aside, we would be unable to make intelligible whole classes of human behavior if we supposed that such behavior could even be described as human action without making intention central. That is, there are cases where two quite different actions are identical with respect to result, observable behavior, and foreknowledge of the result; and the *only* way to distinguish the two is by reference to intention. As an example, take the case of self-killing. If we follow the critic's suggestion and consider as relevant only foreknowledge of result, behavior patterns, and end result (a corpse), then suicide would be effectively defined as *any* action which the agent knew would bring about his own death. This is clearly absurd, for it would not permit us to distinguish between an officer who shoots himself in order to avoid a court-martial and an officer of the same regiment who courageously fights a rear-guard action in such a way that he knows he will not survive. In both cases there is foreknowledge of one's own death, there are objective behavior patterns leading to that result, and there is the result itself. They differ importantly only with respect to intention. Intention is what makes them different actions. To put the point in a general way, failure to take account of intention means that we are unable to make the difference between doing x in order that y shall result and doing x knowing that y will result.[1]

Smith and Jones both have foreknowledge of the impending death of the enemy, they both take identical action, and the result is the same—the enemy soldier is dead. And yet there are two different actions here: Jones does x knowing that y will result; Smith does x in order that y shall result. Well, the critic might reply, there certainly is a difference in intention here, and, thus a description of what is happening will have to make reference to all the facts. Granted, if we want to understand thoroughly what is going on here, then we must take account not only of what the agent knows and foreknows, of behavior and results, but also of what the agent supposes himself to be doing; and that will involve us in including the element of intention in our explanation of his behavior. Having granted this, one has not shown that intention makes any *moral* difference.

The critic is correct. What has been established so far is that intention is a criterion for distinguishing *different* human actions. The importance of this is that in order to show that different moral verdicts are to be applied to Smith and Jones, we first have to show that there were two separate actions involved. The *moral* difference between their actions is, of course, a different matter. What is the difference? Let us recall the objection: The critic will say that it is sophistry to suppose any moral significance in directing force toward the restraint or incapacitation of the combatant while at the same time using means which we know will result in his death. The end result is the same and will be foreknown to be the same, whether or not we "directly" attack the man.

The crucial difference between Smith and Jones is that the latter is logically committed to behaving differently toward those enemy soldiers who have removed themselves from the role of combatant than is his companion Smith. The belief that force must be directed against the combatant and not against the man is the only presupposition which could provide a moral basis for taking prisoners. Smith would have no reason to observe this distinction. He might, on a whim or for immediate prudential reasons, decide to spare the life of the enemy, but he is not logically committed by his beliefs to doing so. The almost universal belief that a man who voluntarily restrains himself or who is restrained by being wounded ought to be immune from attack is only intelligible on the basis of the distinction between the man and the combatant in the man. The moral principle that prisoners ought to be taken and well treated will itself be justified by showing that it is impossible, except in some wholly imprudent fashion, to universalize the killing of those who have surrendered. That is, no rational being could consistently will the killing of all prisoners and include himself in his own prescription. Thus while Jones will have foreknowledge of the death of the aggressor (an admitted evil) the thrust of his actions will be against the combatant and not the man, and the moral payoff of this is that only he is logically committed to observe the moral principle concerning prisoner immunity. To summarize: To those who argue that there is no relevant difference between killing in war and murder in the case of one combatant killing another, we may reply that it is possible, given a well-thought-out doctrine for the justification of the use of force, to direct forceful actions in such a way that while the death of the enemy may be foreknown it is not willed. The purpose of combats as expressed in the actions of individual soldiers is the incapacitation or restraint of an enemy combatant from doing what he is doing as a soldier in a particular historical situation; it is not the killing of a man. This is the essence of the distinction between killing in war and murder in the case of combatants, and the moral relevance of the premise is exhibited in the obligation to acknowledge prisoner immunity, an obligation not incumbent upon someone who fails to observe the central distinction between the man and the combatant in the man.[2] . . .

So far we have been discussing double effect exclusively in connection with the killing of enemy combatants in an attempt to deal with the criticism that all killing in war is murder. We must now tackle the "other half" of that criticism, namely, that the killing of noncombatants

in war is murder. This is obviously a more difficult problem to come to grips with than the question of combatant deaths. For in the latter case the enemy soldier is armed and is personally directing acts of force against others. Although, as we have argued, in directing an act of force against an enemy combatant there should be no intention to kill the person, yet in the case of the aggressor there is an important sense in which he may be said to bring his own death upon himself, particularly in those cases where surrender is possible. A soldier fighting in a just cause may be forced to use weapons which will result in the death of the aggressor, but the aggressor will have participated directly in this outcome. A combatant may change his status by reverting to a noncombatant role; but if he refuses to do so, then much of the responsibility for what happens rests with him.

The problem of noncombatant immunity is frequently thought to center upon the difficulty of distinguishing a separate class of noncombatants, particularly in modern warfare. This is, I think, a large mistake, and it arises in part from an excessively literal reading of war solidarity propaganda. In fact, it is relatively easy to distinguish, in any historical war, whole classes of people who cannot, save in the inflamed world of the propagandist, be said to be combatants in any sense which would make them the object of attack. There will, as with every interesting distinction, be borderline cases. The criterion will be something like this: Generally speaking, classes of people engaged in occupations which they would perform whether or not a war were taking place, or services rendered to combatants both in war and out, are considered immune. This would exempt, for example, farmers and teachers (since education and food are necessities in and out of war) but not merchant sailors transporting war materiel or railway drivers in charge of munitions trains. In other words, the soldiers who are now eating and studying would have to do these things even if they were not soldiers, so that classes of people supplying those sorts of goods and services may be said to be immune from attack, whereas those who are engaged in the production and supply of goods used only in war are not immune. And, of course, certain classes of people may be said to be permanently noncombatant—young children, the mentally defective, and those who are in various ways physically incapacitated. Again, some "hard" or limiting cases will arise, particularly in guerrilla war, but they are less numerous than is sometimes supposed.

The *real* difficulty is not in delineating classes of individuals who merit immunity but in deciding what constitutes a direct attack upon them, for it is plausible to suppose that the deaths of noncombatants can be excused only if their deaths can be construed as collateral or beside the intention of the perpetrators. . . .

Two conclusions can be reached from all of this. To begin with, in a justified war combatants are the objects of attack by other combatants. In this context the use of force is directed toward incapacitation and not toward killing. Combatant deaths may be foreseen, but this is compatible with the intention to incapacitate. Second, noncombatant immunity is presupposed and will be stated in absolute terms. Noncombatant deaths may be foreseen but may also be regarded as collateral damage if they occur in the context of a justified war. . . . The critic's error in both cases is to run together intention and foreknowledge or expectation.

Notes

1. This is a modification of an example in A. McIntyre, "The Idea of a Social Science," in *Against the Self-Images of the Age* (London: Duckworth, 1971), pp. 211–229.

2. There are many excellent discussions of the problem of prisoner immunity. The best is in P. Ramsey, *The Just War.*

Study Questions

1. Discuss Phillips's description of just war theory. What are the major points? How applicable are these principles to modern warfare?
2. Examine the distinction between intending and foreseeing as it is set forth by Phillips. Is this a valid moral distinction?

CHAPTER 57

A Critique of Pacifism

JAN NARVESON

Jan Narveson is professor of philosophy at the University of Waterloo in Ontario, Canada, and the author of several articles and a book, *Morality and Utility*, on moral philosophy.

Narveson analyzes several doctrines that have gone under the name of "pacifism" and finds some of them aesthetic or trivial rather than of deep, moral significance. The interesting version says that everyone ought not to resist violence with force. He argues that this version is incoherent, because it not only acknowledges our right not to be attacked but also says that we may not defend that right. A right that no one is allowed to defend violates the very notion of a right.

SEVERAL DIFFERENT DOCTRINES have been called "pacifism," and it is impossible to say anything cogent about it without saying which of them one has in mind. I must begin by making it clear, then, that I am limiting the discussion of pacifism to a rather narrow band of doctrines, further distinctions among which will be brought out below. By "pacifism," I do *not* mean the theory that violence is evil. With appropriate restrictions, this is a view that every person with any pretensions to morality doubtless holds. Nobody thinks that we have a right to inflict pain wantonly on other people. The pacifist goes a very long step further. *His* belief is not only that violence is evil but also that it is morally wrong to use force to resist, punish, or prevent violence. This further step makes pacifism a radical moral doctrine. What I shall try to establish below is that it is in fact, more than merely radical—it is actually incoherent because it is self-contradictory in its fundamental intent. I shall also suggest that several moral attitudes and psychological views which have tended to be associated with pacifism as I have defined it

do not have any necessary connection with that doctrine. Most proponents of pacifism, I shall argue, have tended to confuse these different things, and that confusion is probably what accounts for such popularity as pacifism has had.

It is next in order to point out that the pacifistic attitude is a matter of degree, and this in two respects. In the first place, there is the question: How much violence should not be resisted, and what degree of force is one not entitled to use in resisting, punishing, or preventing it? Answers to this question will make a lot of difference. For example, everyone would agree that there are limits to the kind and degree of force with which a particular degree of violence is to be met: we do not have a right to kill someone for rapping us on the ribs, for example, and yet there is no tendency toward pacifism in this. We might go further and maintain, for example, that capital punishment, even for the crime of murder, is unjustified without doing so on pacifist grounds. Again, the pacifist should say just what sort of a reaction constitutes a forcible or violent one. If somebody attacks me with his fists and I pin his

Reprinted from Ethics, *Vol. 75. Copyright 1965 by the University of Chicago Press, by permission.*

arms to his body with wrestling holds which restrict him but cause him no pain, is that all right in the pacifist's book? And again, many non-pacifists could consistently maintain that we should avoid, to the extent that it is possible, inflicting a like pain on those who attempt to inflict pain on us. It is unnecessary to be a pacifist merely in order to deny the moral soundness of the principle, "an eye for an eye and a tooth for a tooth." We need a clarification, then, from the pacifist as to just how far he is and is not willing to go. But this need should already make us pause, for surely the pacifist cannot draw these lines in a merely arbitrary manner. It is his reasons for drawing the ones he does that count, and these are what I propose to discuss below.

The second matter of degree in respect of which the pacifist must specify his doctrine concerns the question: Who ought not to resist violence with force? For example, there are pacifists who would only claim that they themselves ought not to. Others would say that only pacifists ought not to, or that all persons of a certain type, where the type is not specified in terms of belief or non-belief in pacifism, ought not to resist violence with force. And finally, there are those who hold that everyone ought not to do so. We shall see that considerations about this second variable doom some forms of pacifism to contradiction.

My general program will be to show that (1) only the doctrine that everyone ought not to resist violence with force is of philosophical interest among those doctrines known as "pacifism"; (2) that doctrine, if advanced as a moral doctrine, is logically untenable; and (3) the reasons for the popularity of pacifism rest on failure to see exactly what the doctrine is. The things which pacifism wishes to accomplish, insofar as they are worth accomplishing, can be managed on the basis of quite ordinary and conservative moral principles.

Let us begin by being precise about the kind of moral force the principle of pacifism is intended to have. One good way to do this is to consider what it is intended to deny. What would non-pacifists, which I suppose includes most people, say of a man who followed Christ's suggestion and when unaccountably slapped, simply turned the other cheek? They might say that such a man is either a fool or a saint. Or they might say, "It's all very well for him to do that, but it's not for me"; or they might simply shrug their shoulders and say, "Well, it takes all kinds, doesn't it?" But they would *not* say that a man who did that ought to be punished in some way; they would not even say that he had done anything wrong. In fact, as I have mentioned, they would more likely than not find something admirable about it. The point, then, is this: The non-pacifist does *not* say that it is your *duty* to resist violence with force. The non-pacifist is merely saying that there's nothing wrong with doing so, that one has every right to do so if he is so inclined. Whether we wish to add that a person would be foolish or silly to do so is quite another question, one on which the non-pacifist does not *need* to take any particular position.

Consequently, a genuine pacifist cannot merely say that we may, if we wish, prefer not to resist violence with force. Nor can he merely say that there is something admirable or saintly about not doing so, for, as pointed out above, the non-pacifist could perfectly well agree with that. He must say, instead, that, for whatever class of people he thinks it applies to, there is something positively wrong about meeting violence with force. He must say that, insofar as the people to whom his principle applies resort to force, they are committing a breach of moral duty—a very serious thing to say. Just how serious, we shall ere long see.

Next, we must understand what the implications of holding pacifism as a moral principle are, and the first such implication requiring our attention concerns the matter of the size of the class of people to which it is supposed to apply. It will be of interest to discuss two of the four possibilities previously listed, I think. The first is that in which the pacifist says that only pacifists have the duty of pacifism. Let us see what this amounts to.

If we say that the principle of pacifism is the principle that all and only pacifists have a duty of not opposing violence with force, we get into a very odd situation. For suppose we ask ourselves, "Very well, which people are the pacifists then?" The answer will have to be "All those people who believe that pacifists have the duty not to meet violence with force." But surely one could believe that a certain class of people, whom we shall call "pacifists," have the duty not to meet violence with force without believing that one ought not, oneself, to meet violence with force. That is to say, the "principle" that pacifists ought to avoid meeting violence with force, is circular: It presupposes that one already knows who the pacifists are. Yet this is precisely what that statement of the principle is supposed to answer! We are supposed to be able to say that anybody who believes that principle is a pacifist; yet, as we have seen, a person could very well believe that a certain class of people called "pacifists" ought not to meet violence with force without believing that he himself ought not to meet violence with force. Thus everyone could be a "pacifist" in the sense of believing that statement and yet no one believes that he *himself* (or anyone in particular) ought to avoid meeting violence with force. Consequently, pacifism cannot be specified in that way. A pacifist must be a person who believes either that he himself (at least) ought not to meet force with force or that some larger class of persons, perhaps everyone, ought not to meet force with force. He would then be believing something definite, and we are then in a position to ask why.

Incidentally, it is worth mentioning that when people say things such as "Only pacifists have the duty of pacifism," "Only Catholics have the duties of Catholicism," and, in general, "Only *X*-ists have the duties of *X*-ism" they probably are falling into a trap which catches a good many people. It is, namely, the mistake of supposing that what it *is* to have a certain duty is to *believe* that you have a certain duty. The untenability of this is parallel to the untenability of the previously mentioned attempt to say what pacifism is. For, if having a duty is believing that you have a certain duty, the question arises, "*What* does such a person believe?" The answer that must be given if we follow this analysis would then be, "He believes that he believes that he has a certain duty"; and so on, *ad infinitum*.

On the other hand, one might believe that having a duty does not consist in believing that one has and yet believe that only those people really have the duty who believe that they have it. But in that case, we would, being conscientious, perhaps want to ask the question, "Well, *ought* I to believe that I have that duty, or oughtn't I?" If you say that the answer is "Yes," the reason cannot be that you already do believe it, for you are asking whether you *should*. On the other hand, the answer "No" or "It doesn't make any difference—it's up to you," implies that there is really no reason for doing the thing in question at all. In short, asking whether I ought to believe that I have a duty to do *x*, is equivalent to asking whether I should *do x*. A person might very well believe that he ought to do *x* but be wrong. It might be the case that he really ought *not* to do *x*; in that case the fact that he believes he ought to do *x*, far from being a reason why he ought to do it, is a reason for us to point out his error. It also, of course, presupposes that he has some reason other than his belief for thinking it is his duty to do *x*.

Having cleared this red herring out of the way, we must consider the view of those who believe that they themselves have a duty of pacifism and ask ourselves the question: What general kind of reason must a person have for supposing a certain type of act to be *his* duty, in a moral sense? Now, one answer he might give is that pacifism as such is a duty, that is, that meeting violence with force is, as such, wrong. In that case, however, what he thinks is not merely that *he* has this duty, but that *everyone* has this duty.

Now he might object, "Well, but no; I don't mean that everyone has it. For instance, if a man is defending, not himself, but *other* people, such as his wife and children, then he has a right to meet violence with force." Now this, of course, would be a very important qualification to his principle and one of a kind which we will be discussing in a moment. Meanwhile, however, we may point out that he evidently still thinks that, if it weren't for certain more important duties, everyone would have a duty to avoid meeting violence with force. In other words, he then believes that, other things being equal, one ought not to meet violence with force. He believes, to put it yet another way, that if one does meet violence with force, one must have a special excuse or justification of a moral kind; then he may want to give some account of just which excuses and justifications would do. Nevertheless, he is now holding a general principle.

Suppose, however, he holds that no one *else* has this duty of pacifism, that only he himself ought not to meet force with force, although it is quite all right for others to do so. Now if this is what our man feels, we may continue to call him a "pacifist," in a somewhat attenuated sense, but he is then no longer holding pacifism as a *moral* principle or, indeed, as a principle at all.[1] For now his disinclination for violence is essentially just a matter of taste. I like pistachio ice cream, but I wouldn't dream of saying that other people have a duty to eat it; similarly, this man just doesn't *like* to meet force, although he wouldn't dream of insisting that others act as he does. And this is a secondary sense of "pacifism," first, because pacifism has always been advocated on moral grounds and, second, because non-pacifists can easily have this same feeling. A person might very well feel squeamish, for example, about using force, even in self-defense, or he might not be able to bring himself to use it even if he wants to. But none of these has anything to do with asserting pacifism to be a duty. Moreover, a mere attitude could hardly license a man to refuse military service if it were required

of him, or to join ban-the-bomb crusades, and so forth. (I fear, however, that such attitudes have sometimes caused people to do those things.)

And, in turn, it is similarly impossible to claim that your support of pacifism is a moral one if your position is that a certain selection of people, but no one else, ought not to meet force with force, even though you are unprepared to offer any reason whatever for this selection. Suppose, for example, that you hold that only the Arapahoes, or only the Chinese, or only people more than six feet high have this "duty." If such were the case, and no reasons offered at all, we could only conclude that you had a very peculiar attitude toward the Arapahoes, or whatever, but we would hardly want to say that you had a moral principle. Your "principle" amounts to saying that these particular individuals happen to have the duty of pacifism just because they are the individuals they are, and this, as Bentham would say, is the "negation of all principle." Of course, if you meant that somehow the property of being over six feet tall *makes* it your duty not to use violence, then you have a principle, all right, but a very queer one indeed unless you can give some further reasons. Again, it would not be possible to distinguish this from a sheer attitude.

Pacifism, then, must be the principle that the use of force to meet force is wrong *as such,* that is, that nobody may do so unless he has a special justification.

There is another way in which one might advocate a sort of "pacifism," however, which we must also dispose of before getting to the main point. One might argue that pacifism is desirable as a tactic: that, as a matter of fact, some good end, such as the reduction of violence itself, is to be achieved by "turning the other cheek." For example, if it were the case that turning the other cheek caused the offender to break down and repent, then that would be a very good reason for behaving "pacifistically." If unilateral disarmament causes the other side to disarm, then certainly unilateral disarmament would be a desirable policy. But note that its desirability, if this is the argument, is due to the fact that peace is desirable, a moral position which anybody can take, pacifist or no, plus the purely contingent fact that this policy causes the other side to disarm, that is, it brings about peace.

And of course, that's the catch. If one attempts to support pacifism, because of its probable effects, then one's position depends on what the effects are. Determining what they are is a purely empirical matter, and, consequently, one could not possibly be a pacifist as a matter of pure principle if his reasons for supporting pacifism are merely tactical. One must, in this case, submit one's opinions to the governance of fact.

It is not part of my intention to discuss matters of fact, as such, but it is worthwhile to point out that the general history of the human race certainly offers no support for the supposition that turning the other cheek always produces good effects on the aggressor. Some aggressors, such as the Nazis, were apparently just "egged on" by the "pacifist" attitude of their victims. Some of the S.S. men apparently became curious to see just how much torture the victim would put up with before he began to resist. Furthermore, there is the possibility that, while pacifism might work against some people (one might cite the British, against whom pacifism in India was apparently rather successful—but the British are comparatively nice people), it might fail against others (e.g., the Nazis).

A further point about holding pacifism to be desirable as a tactic is that this could not easily support the position that pacifism is a *duty*. The question whether we have no *right* to fight back can hardly be settled by noting that not to fight back might cause the aggressor to stop fighting. To prove that a policy is a desirable one because it works is not to prove that it is *obligatory* to follow it. We surely need considerations a good deal less tenuous than this to prove such a momentous contention as that we have no *right* to resist.

It appears, then, that to hold the pacifist position as a genuine, full-blooded moral principle is to hold that nobody has a right to fight back when attacked, that fighting back is inherently evil, as such. It means that we are all mistaken in supposing that we have a right of self-protection. And, of course, this is an extreme and extraordinary position in any case. It appears to mean, for instance, that we have no right to punish criminals, that all of our machinery of criminal justice is, in fact, unjust. Robbers, murderers, rapists, and miscellaneous delinquents ought, on this theory, to be let loose.

Now, the pacifist's first move, upon hearing this, will be to claim that he has been misrepresented. He might say that it is only one's *self* that one has no right to defend, and that one may legitimately fight in order to defend other people. This qualification cannot be made by those pacifists who qualify as conscientious objectors, of course, for the latter are refusing to defend their fellow citizens and not merely themselves. But this is comparatively trivial when we contemplate the next objection to this amended version of the theory. Let us now ask ourselves what it is about attacks on *other* people which could possibly justify *us* in defending them, while we are not justified in defending ourselves? It cannot be the mere fact that they are other people than ourselves, for, of course, everyone is a different person from everyone else, and if such a consideration could ever of itself justify anything at all it could also justify anything whatever. That mere difference of person, as such, is of no moral importance, is a presupposition of anything that can possibly pretend to be a moral theory.

Instead of such idle nonsense, then, the pacifist would have to mention some specific characteristic which every *other* person has which we lack and which justifies us in defending them. But this, alas, is impossible, for, while there may be some interesting difference between *me* on the one hand and everyone else on the other, the pacifist is not merely addressing himself to me. On the contrary, as we have seen, he has to address himself to everyone. He is claiming that each person has no right to defend himself, although he does have a right to defend other people. And, therefore, what is needed is a characteristic which distinguishes *each* person from everyone else, and not just *me* from everyone else—which is plainly self-contradictory.

Again, then, the pacifist must retreat in order to avoid talking nonsense. His next move might be to say that we have a right to defend all those who are not able to defend themselves. Big, grown-up men who are able to defend themselves ought not to do so, but they ought to defend mere helpless children who are unable to defend themselves.

This last, very queer theory could give rise to some amusing logical gymnastics. For instance, what about groups of people? If a group of people who cannot defend themselves singly can defend themselves together, then when it has grown to that size ought it to stop defending itself? If so, then every time a person *can* defend someone else, he would form with the person being defended a "defensive unit" which was able to defend itself, and thus would by this very presence debar himself from making the defense. At this rate, no one will ever get defended, it seems: The defenseless people by definition cannot defend themselves, while those who can defend them would enable the group consisting of the defenders and the defended to defend themselves, and hence they would be obliged not to do so.

Such reflections, however, are merely curious shadows of a much more fundamental and serious logical problem. This arises when we begin to ask: But why should even defenseless people be defended? If resisting violence is inherently evil, then how can it suddenly become permissible when we use it on behalf of other people? The fact that they are defenseless cannot possibly account for this, for it follows from the theory in question, that everyone ought to put himself in the position of people who are defenseless by refusing to defend himself. This type of pacifist, in short, is using the very charac-

teristic (namely, being in a state of not defending oneself) which he wishes to encourage in others as a reason for denying it in the case of those who already have it (namely, the defenseless). This is surely inconsistent.

To attempt to be consistent, at least, the pacifist is forced to accept the characterization of him at which we tentatively arrived. He must say that no one ought ever to be defended against attack. The right of self-defense can be denied coherently only if the right of defense, in general, is denied. This in itself is an important conclusion.

It must be borne in mind, by the way, that I have not said anything to take exception to the man who simply does not wish to defend himself. So long as he does not attempt to make his pacifism into a principle, one cannot accuse him of any inconsistency, however much one might wish to say that he is foolish or eccentric. It is solely with moral principles that I am concerned here.

We now come to the last and most fundamental problem of all. If we ask ourselves what the point of pacifism is, what gets it going, so to speak, the answer is, of course, obvious enough: opposition to violence. The pacifist is generally thought of as the man who is so much opposed to violence that he will not even use it to defend himself or anyone else. And it is precisely this characterization which I wish to show is morally inconsistent.

To begin with, we may note something which at first glance may seem merely to be a matter of fact, albeit one which should worry the pacifist, in our latest characterization of him. I refer to the commonplace observation that, generally speaking, we measure a man's degree of opposition to something by the amount of effort he is willing to put forth against it. A man could hardly be said to be dead set against something if he is not willing to lift a finger to keep it from going on. A person who claims to be completely opposed to something yet does nothing to prevent it would ordinarily be said to be a hypocrite.

As facts, however, we cannot make too much of these. The pacifist could claim to be willing to go to any length, short of violence, to prevent violence. He might, for instance, stand out in the cold all day long handing out leaflets (as I have known some to do), and this would surely argue for the sincerity of his beliefs.

But would it really?

Let us ask ourselves, one final time, what we are claiming when we claim that violence is morally wrong and unjust. We are, in the first place, claiming that a person *has no right* to indulge in it, as such (meaning that he has no right to indulge in it, *unless* he has an overriding justification). But what do we mean when we say that he has no right to indulge in it? Violence, of the type we are considering, is a two-termed affair: one does violence *to* somebody, one cannot simply "do violence." It might be oneself, of course, but we are not primarily interested in those cases, for what makes it wrong to commit violence is that it harms the people to whom it is done. To say that it is wrong is to say that those to whom it is done have a right *not* to have it done to them. (This must again be qualified by pointing out that this is so only if they have done nothing to merit having that right abridged.)

Yet what could that right to their own security, which people have, possibly consist in if not a right at least to be protected from whatever violence might be offered them? But lest the reader think that this is a gratuitous assumption, note carefully the reason why having a right involves having a right to be defended from breaches of that right. It is because the prevention of infractions of that right is precisely what one has a right to when one has a right at all. A right just *is* a status justifying preventive action. To say that you have a right to X but that no one has any justification whatever for preventing people from depriving you of it, is self-contradictory. If you claim a right to X, then to describe some action as an act of depriving you of X, is logically to imply that its absence is one of the things that you have a right to.

Thus far it does not follow logically that we have a right to use force in our own or anyone's defense. What does follow logically is that one has a right to whatever may be necessary to prevent infringements of his right. One might at first suppose that the universe *could* be so constructed that it is never necessary to use force to prevent people who are bent on getting something from getting it.

Yet even this is not so, for when we speak of "force" in the sense in which pacifism is concerned with it, we do not mean merely physical "force." To call an action a use of force is not merely to make a reference to the laws of mechanics. On the contrary, it is to describe whatever is being done as being a means to the vinfliction on somebody of something (ordinarily physical) which he does not want done to him; and the same is true for "force" in the sense in which it applies to war, assault and battery, and the like.

The proper contrary of "force" in this connection is "rational persuasion." Naturally, one way there *might* be of getting somebody not to do something he has no right to do is to convince him he ought not to do it or that it is not in his interest to do it. But it is inconsistent, I suggest, to argue that rational persuasion is the only morally permissible method of preventing violence. A pragmatic reason for this is easy enough to point to: Violent people are too busy being violent to be reasonable. We cannot engage in rational persuasion unless the enemy is willing to sit down and talk; but what if he isn't? One cannot contend that every human being can be persuaded to sit down and talk before he strikes, for this is not something we can determine just by reasoning; it is a question of observation. But these points are not strictly relevant anyway, for our question is not the empirical question of whether there is some handy way which can always be used to get a person to sit down and discuss moral philosophy when he is about to murder you. Our question is: *If* force is the only way to prevent violence in a given case, is its use justified *in that case?* This is a purely moral question which we can discuss without any special reference to matters of fact. And, moreover, it is precisely this question which we should have to discuss with the would-be violator. The point is that if a person can be rationally persuaded that he ought not to engage in violence, then precisely what he would be rationally persuaded of if we were to succeed would be the proposition that the use of force is justifiable to prevent him from doing so. For note that if we were to argue that only rational persuasion is permissible as a means of preventing him, we would have to face the question: Do we mean *attempted* rational persuasion, or *successful* rational persuasion, that is, rational persuasion which really does succeed in preventing him from acting? Attempted rational persuasion might fail (if only because the opponent is unreasonable), and then what? To argue that we have a right to use rational persuasion which also succeeds (i.e., we have a right to its success as well as to its use) is to imply that we have a right to prevent him from performing the act. But this, in turn, means that, if attempts at rational persuasion fail, we have a right to the use of force. Thus what we have a right to, if we ever have a *right* to anything, is not merely the use of rational persuasion to keep people from depriving you of the thing to which you have the right. We do indeed have a right to that, but we also have a right to anything else that might be necessary (other things being equal) to prevent the deprivation from occurring. And it is a logical truth, not merely a contingent one, that what *might* be necessary is *force.* (If merely saying something could miraculously deprive someone of the ability to carry through a course of action, then those speech-acts would be called a type of force, if a very mysterious one. And we could properly begin to oppose their use for precisely the same reasons as we now oppose violence.)

What this all adds up to, then, is that *if* we have any rights at all, we have a right to use force to prevent the deprivation of the thing to which we are said to have a right. But the pacifist, of *all* people, is the one most concerned to insist that we do have some rights, namely, the right not to have violence done to us. This is logically implied in asserting it to be a duty on everyone's part to avoid violence. And this is why the pacifist's position is self-contradictory. In saying that violence is wrong, one is at the same time saying that people have a right to its prevention, by force if necessary. Whether and to what extent it may be necessary is a question of fact, but, since it is a question of fact only, the moral right to use force on some possible occasions is established.[2]

We now have an answer to the question. How much force does a given threat of violence justify for preventive purposes? The answer, in a word, is "Enough." That the answer is this simple may at first sight seem implausible. One might suppose that some elaborate equation between the aggressive and the preventive force is needed: the punishment be proportionate to the crime. But this is a misunderstanding. In the first place, prevention and punishment are not the same, even if punishment is thought to be directed mainly toward prevention. The punishment of a particular crime logically cannot prevent *that* instance of the crime, since it presupposes that it has already been performed; and punishment need not involve the use of any violence at all, although law-enforcement officers in some places have a nasty tendency to assume the contrary. But preventive force is another matter. If a man threatens to kill me, it is desirable, of course, for me to try to prevent this by the use of the least amount of force sufficient to do the job. But I am justified even in killing him *if* necessary. This much, I suppose, is obvious to most people. But suppose his threat is much smaller: suppose that he is merely pestering me, which is a very mild form of aggression indeed. Would I be justified in killing him to prevent this, under any circumstances whatever?

Suppose that I call the police and they take out a warrant against him, and suppose that when the police come, he puts up a struggle. He pulls a knife or a gun, let us say, and the police shoot him in the ensuing battle. Has my right to the prevention of his annoying me extended to killing him? Well, not exactly, since the immediate threat in response to which he is killed is a threat to the lives of the policemen. Yet my annoyer may never have contemplated real violence. It is an unfortunate case of unpremeditated escalation. But this is precisely what makes the contention that one is justified in using enough force to do the job, whatever amount that may be, to prevent action which violates a right less alarming than at first sight it seems. For it is difficult to envisage a reason why extreme force is needed to prevent mild threats from realization except by way of escalation, and escalation automatically justifies increased use of preventive force.

The existence of laws, police, courts, and more or less civilized modes of behavior on the part of most of the populace naturally affects the answer to the question of how much force is necessary. One of the purposes of a legal system of justice is surely to make the use of force by individuals very much less necessary than it would otherwise be. If we try to think back to a "state of nature" situation, we shall have less difficulty envisaging the need for large amounts of force to prevent small threats of violence. Here Hobbes's contention that in such a state every man has a right to the life of every other becomes understandable. He was, I suggest, relying on the same principle as I have argued for here: that one has a right to use as much force as necessary to defend one's rights, which include the right of safety of person.

And needless to say, my arguments here do not give us any reason to modify the obviously vital principle that if force should be necessary, then one must use the least amount of it compatible with maintaining the rights of those being protected. There is, for example, no excuse for sending armed troops against unarmed students to contain protest marches and demonstrations.

I have said that the duty to avoid violence is only a duty, other things being equal. We might arrive at the same conclusion as we have above by asking the question: Which "other things" might count as being *un*equal? The answer to this is that whatever else they may be, the purpose of preventing violence from being done is necessarily one of these justifying conditions. That the use of force is never justified to prevent initial violence being done to one logically implies that there is nothing wrong with initial violence. We cannot characterize it as being wrong if preventive violence is not simultaneously being characterized as justifiable.

We often think of pacifists as being gentle and idealistic souls, which in its way is true enough. What I have been concerned to show is that they are also confused. If they attempt to formulate their position using our standard concepts of rights, their position involves a contradiction: Violence is wrong, *and* it is wrong to resist it. But the right to resist is precisely what having a right of person is, if it is anything at all.

Could the position be reformulated with a less "commital" concept of rights? I do not think so. It has been suggested[3] that the pacifist need not talk in terms of this "kind" of rights. He can affirm, according to this suggestion, simply that neither the aggressors nor the defenders "have" rights to what they do, that to affirm their not having them is simply to be against the use of force, without this entailing the readiness to use force if necessary to protect the said rights. But this will not do I believe. For I have not maintained that having a right, or believing that one has a right, entails a *readiness* to defend that right. One has a perfect right not to resist violence to oneself if one is so inclined. But our question has been whether self-defense is justifiable, and not whether one's belief that violence is wrong entails a willingness or readiness to use it. My contention has been that such a belief does entail the justifiability of using it. If one came upon a community in which no sort of violence was ever resisted and it was claimed in that community that the non-resistance was a matter of conscience, we should have to conclude, I think, not that this was a community of saints, but rather that this community lacked the concept of justice—or perhaps that their nervous systems were oddly different from ours.

The true test of the pacifist comes, of course, when he is called upon to assist in the protection of the *safety of other persons* and not just of himself. For while he is, as I have said, surely entitled to be pacific about *his own person* if he is so inclined, he is not entitled to be so about the safety of others. It is here that the test of principles comes out. People have a tendency to brand conscientious objectors as cowards or traitors, but this is not quite fair. They are acting as if they were cowards or traitors, but claiming to do so on principle. It is not surprising if a community should fail to understand such "principles," for the test of adherence to a principle is willingness to act on it, and the appropriate action, if one believes a certain thing to be grossly wrong, is to take steps to prevent or resist it. Thus people who assess conscientious objection as cowardice or worse are taking an understandable step: from an intuitive feeling that the pacifist does not really believe what he is saying they infer that his actions (or inaction) must be due to cowardice. What I am suggesting is that this is not correct: The actions are due, not to cowardice, but to confusion.

Notes

1. Compare, for example, K. Baier, *The Moral Point of View* (Ithaca: Cornell University Press, 1958), p. 191.

2. This basic argument may be compared with a view of Kant's, to be found in the *Rechtslehre*, translated under the title *Metaphysical Elements of Justice* by J. Ladd, Library of Liberal Arts, pp. 35–36 (Introduction, D).

3. I owe this suggestion to my colleague, Leslie Armour.

Study Questions

1. Do you agree with Narveson's interpretation of pacifism?
2. Has Narveson shown that pacifism is incoherent "because it is self-contradictory in its fundamental intent"? How would a pacifist reply to Narveson?
3. Do we have a moral right to defend ourselves, our loved ones, and our country?

CHAPTER 58

A Defense of Pacifism

CHEYNEY RYAN

Cheyney Ryan teaches philosophy at the University of Oregon. In this essay Ryan defends a version of pacifism against attacks like Narveson's. Cheyney removes the idea from rights talk and puts it in the arena of virtue ethics. Pacifism seeks to inculcate the kind of respect for persons that makes it difficult to create the necessary distance between ourselves and other human beings so that killing is possible. He shows a tension between not distancing ourselves from others and yet respecting ourselves so that we are obliged to defend ourselves.

PACIFISM HAS BEEN CONSTRUED by some as the view that all violence or coercion is wrong. This seems to be too broad, though undoubtedly some pacifists have held to this position. I shall focus here on the pacifist's opposition to killing, which stands at the heart of his opposition to war in any form.

In recent years, prompted largely by an article of Jan Narveson's, there has been a good deal of clucking about the "inconsistency" and "incoherence" of the pacifist position. Narveson's argument, in a nutshell, is that, if the pacifist grants people the right not to be subjected to violence, or the right not to be killed, *then by logic he must accord them the right to engage in any actions (hence, those involving killing) to protect that right.* This argument fails for a number of reasons,[1] but the most interesting one involves the protective status of rights. *Possession of a right generally entitles one to take some actions in defense of that right, but clearly there are limits to the actions one may take.* To get back the washcloth which you have stolen from me, I cannot bludgeon you to death; even if this were the *only* way I had of securing my right to the washcloth, I could not do it. What the pacifist and the nonpacifist disagree about, then, are the limits to which one may go in defending one's right to life, or any other right. The "logic of rights" alone will not settle this disagreement, and such logic certainly does not render the pacifist's restrictions incoherent. That position might be incoherent, in Narveson's sense, if the pacifist allowed *no* actions in defense of the right to life, but this is not his position. The pacifist's position does seem to violate a fairly intuitive principle of proportionality, that in defense of one's rights one may take actions whose severity is equal to, though not greater than, the threat against one. This rules out the bludgeoning case but allows killing so as not to be killed. The pacifist can respond, though, that this principle becomes rather suspect as we move to more extreme actions. It is not *obviously* permissible to torture another so as not to be tortured or to rain nuclear holocaust on another country to prevent such a fate for oneself. Thus when the pacifist rejects the *proportionality* principle in cases of killing, insisting that such cases are themselves most extreme, the principle he

---

thereby rejects hardly has the status of a self-evident truth.

I have touched on this issue not merely to point out the shallowness of some recent arguments against pacifism but because I believe that any argument pro or con which hinges on the issue of rights is likely to get us nowhere. . . .

George Orwell tells how early one morning [during the Spanish Civil War] he ventured out with another man to snipe at the fascists from the trenches outside their encampment. After having little success for several hours, they were suddenly alerted to the sound of Republican airplanes overhead. Orwell writes,

> At this moment a man, presumably carrying a message to an officer, jumped out of the trench and ran along the top of the parapet in full view. He was half-dressed and holding up his trousers with both hands as he ran. I refrained from shooting at him. It is true that I am a poor shot and unlikely to hit a running man at a hundred yards. Still, I did not shoot partly because of that detail about the trousers. I had come here to shoot "Fascists"; but a man who is holding up his trousers isn't a "Fascist" he is *visibly a fellow creature*, similar to yourself, and you don't feel like shooting him.[2]

Orwell was not a pacifist, but the problem he finds in this particular act of killing is akin to the problem which the pacifist finds in *all* acts of killing. That problem, the example suggests, takes the following form.

The problem with shooting the half-clothed man does not arise from the rights involved, nor is it dispensed with by showing that, yes indeed, you are justified (by your rights) in killing him. But this does not mean, as some have suggested to me, that the problem is therefore not a *moral* problem at all ("sheer sentimentality" was an objection raised by one philosopher ex-marine). Surely if Orwell had gleefully blasted away here, if he had not at least felt the tug of the other's "fellow-creaturehood," then this would have reflected badly, if not on his action, then on *him*,

as a human being. The problem, in the Orwell case, is that the man's dishabille made inescapable the fact that he was a "fellow creature," and in so doing it stripped away the labels and denied the distance so necessary to murderous actions (it is not for nothing that armies give us stereotypes in thinking about the enemy). The problem, I am tempted to say, involves not so much the justification as the *possibility* of killing in such circumstances ("How could you *bring* yourself to do it?" is a natural response to one who felt no problem in such situations). And therein lies the clue to the pacifist impulse.

The pacifist's problem is that he cannot create, or does not wish to create, the necessary distance between himself and another to make the act of killing possible. Moreover, the fact that others obviously can create that distance is taken by the pacifist to reflect badly on them; they move about in the world insensitive to the half-clothed status which all humans, qua fellow creatures, share. This latter point is important to showing that the pacifist's position is indeed a moral position, and not just a personal idiosyncrasy. What should now be evident is the sense in which that moral position is motivated by a picture of the personal relationship and outlook one should maintain toward others, regardless of the actions they might take toward you. It is fitting in this regard that the debate over self-defense should come down to the personal relationship, the "negative bond" between Aggressor and Defender. For even if this negative bond renders killing in self-defense permissible, the pacifist will insist that the deeper bonds of fellow creaturehood should render it impossible. That such an outlook will be branded by others as sheer sentimentality comes to the pacifist as no surprise.

I am aware that this characterization of the pacifist's outlook may strike many as obscure, but the difficulties in characterizing that outlook themselves reflect, I think, how truly fundamental the disagreement between the pacifist and the nonpacifist really is. That disagreement far transcends the familiar problems of justice and equity; it is no surprise that the familiar terms should fail us. As to the accuracy of this characterization, I would offer as indirect support the following example of the aesthetic of fascism, which I take to be at polar ends from that of pacifism, and so illustrative in contrast of the pacifist outlook: "War is beautiful because it establishes man's dominion over the subjugated machinery by means of gas masks, terrifying megaphones, flame throwers, and small tanks. War is beautiful because it initiates the dreamt-of metalization of the human body. War is beautiful because it enriches the flowering meadow with the fiery orchids of machine guns."[3] What the fascist rejoices in the pacifist rejects, in toto—the "metalization of the human body," the insensitivity to fellow creaturehood which the pacifist sees as the presupposition of killing.

This account of the pacifist's position suggests some obvious avenues of criticism of the more traditional sort. One could naturally ask whether killing necessarily presupposes objectification and distance, as the pacifist feels it does. It seems to me though that the differences between the pacifist and the nonpacifist are substantial enough that neither side is likely to produce a simple "refutation" along such lines which the other conceivably could, or logically need, accept. If any criticism of pacifism is to be forthcoming which can make any real claim to the pacifist's attention, it will be one which questions the consistency of his conclusions with what I have described as his motivating impulse. Let me suggest how such a criticism might go.

If the pacifist's intent is to acknowledge through his attitudes and actions the other person's status as a fellow creature, the problem is that violence, and even killing, are at times a means of acknowledging this as well, a way of bridging the distance between oneself and another person, a way of acknowledging one's *own* status as a person. This is one of the underlying themes of Hegel's account of conflict in the master-slave dialectic, and the important truth it

contains should not be lost in its seeming glorification of conflict. That the refusal to allow others to treat one as an object is an important step to defining one's own integrity is a point well understood by revolutionary theorists such as Fannon. It is a point apparently lost to pacifists like Gandhi, who suggested that the Jews in the Warsaw Ghetto would have made the superior moral statement by committing collective suicide, since their resistance proved futile anyway. What strikes us as positively bizarre in the pacifist's suggestion, for example, that we *not* defend our loved ones when attacked is not the fact that someone's rights might be abused by our refusal to so act. Our real concern is what the refusal to intervene would express about our relationships and ourselves, for one of the ways we acknowledge the importance of a relationship is through our willingness to take such actions, and that is why the problem in such cases is how we can bring ourselves *not* to intervene (how is passivity possible).

The willingness to commit violence is linked to our love and estimation for others, just as the capacity for jealousy is an integral part of affection. The pacifist may respond that this is just a sociological or psychological fact about how our community links violence and care, a questionable connection that expresses thousands of years of macho culture. But this connection is no *more* questionable than that which views acts of violence against an aggressor as expressing hatred, or indifference, or objectification. If the pacifist's problem is that he cannot consistently live out his initial impulse—the posture he wishes to assume toward others requires that he commit violence and that he not commit violence—does this reflect badly on his position? Well, if you find his goals attractive it may well reflect badly on the position—or *fix*—we are all in. Unraveling the pacifist's logic may lead us to see that our world of violence and killing is one in which regarding some as people requires we regard others as things and that this is not a fact that can be excused or absolved through the techniques of moral philosophy. If the pacifist's error arises from the desire to smooth this all over by hewing to one side of the dilemma, he is no worse than his opponent, whose "refutation" of pacifism serves to dismiss those very intractable problems of violence of which pacifism is the anxious expression. As long as this tragic element in violence persists, pacifism will remain with us as a response; we should not applaud its demise, for it may well mark that the dilemmas of violence have simply been forgotten.

Impatience will now ask: so do we kill or don't we? It should be clear that I do not have the sort of answer to this question that a philosopher, at least, might expect. One can attend to the problems involved in either choice, but the greatest problem is that the choice does not flow naturally from a desire to acknowledge in others and in ourselves their importance and weaknesses and worth.

Notes

1. Narveson claims that the right to X entitles you to whatever is necessary to protect that right. It would follow that there can be no real problem about civil disobedience, since logic alone tells us that if the state infringes on our rights we can take whatever measures are required to protect them, including defying the state. But surely the problem is more complicated than this. Hence it is reasonable to reject the claim about the "logic" of rights which leads to such a facile conclusion.

2. George Orwell, "Looking Back on the Spanish Civil War," in *A Collection of Essays by George Orwell* (New York: Doubleday & Co., 1954), p. 199.

3. The quote is from Marinetti, a founder of Futurism, cited in Walter Benjamin's essay, "The Work of Art in the Age of Mechanical Reproduction," *Illuminations* (New York: Schocken Books, 1969), p. 241.

Study Questions

1. How does Ryan characterize pacifism?
2. How does Ryan respond to Narveson's charge that pacifism is incoherent?
3. What is Ryan's argument for pacifism?

CHAPTER 59

Against the Use of Nuclear Weapons

THE U.S. CATHOLIC BISHOPS

The U.S. Catholic bishops issued a pastoral letter in 1982, *The Challenge of Peace: God's Promise and Our Response,* in which they condemned the use of nuclear weapons against population centers, called for a "no first use" policy, and accepted deterrence only as a step toward progressive disarmament.

AS BISHOPS IN THE UNITED STATES, assessing the concrete circumstances of our society, we have made a number of observations and recommendations in the process of applying moral principles to specific policy choices.

On the Use of Nuclear Weapons

1. Counter Population Use

Under no circumstances may nuclear weapons or other instruments of mass slaughter be used for the purpose of destroying population centers or other predominantely civilian targets. Retaliatory action which would indiscriminately and disproportionately take many wholly innocent lives, lives of people who are in no way responsible for reckless actions of their government, must also be condemned.

2. The Initiation of Nuclear War

We do not perceive any situation in which the deliberate initiation of nuclear war, on however restricted a scale, can be morally justified. Non-nuclear attacks by another state must be resisted by other than nuclear means. Therefore, a serious moral obligation exists to develop non-nuclear defensive strategies as rapidly as possible. In this letter we urge NATO to move rapidly toward the adoption of a "no first use" policy, but we recognize this will take time to implement and will require the development of an adequate alternative defense posture.

3. Limited Nuclear War

Our examination of the various arguments on this question makes us highly skeptical about the real meaning of "limited." One of the criteria of the just-war teaching is that there must be a reasonable hope of success in bringing about justice and peace. We must ask whether such a reasonable hope can exist once nuclear weapons have been exchanged. The burden of proof remains on those who assert that meaningful limitation is possible. In our view the first imperative is to prevent any use of nuclear weapons and we hope that leaders will resist the notion that nuclear conflict can be limited, contained or won in any traditional sense.

On Deterrence

In concert with the evaluation provided by Pope John Paul II, we have arrived at a strictly conditional moral acceptance of deterrence. In this letter we have outlined criteria and recommendations which indicate the meaning of conditional acceptance of deterrence policy. We cannot consider such a policy adequate as a long-term basis for peace.

Moral Principles and Policy Choices

Targeting doctrine raises significant moral questions because it is a significant determinant of what would occur if nuclear weapons were ever to be used. Although we acknowledge the need for deterrence, not all forms of deterrence are morally acceptable. There are moral limits to deterrence policy as well as to policy regarding use. Specifically, it is not morally acceptable to intend to kill the innocent as part of a strategy of deterring nuclear war. The question of whether U.S. policy involves an intention to strike civilian centers (directly targeting civilian populations) has been one of our factual concerns.

This complex question has always produced a variety of responses, official and unofficial in character. The NCCB Committee has received a series of statements of clarification of policy from U.S. government officials. Essentially these statements declare that it is not U.S. strategic policy to target the Soviet civilian population as such or to use nuclear weapons deliberately for the purpose of destroying population centers. These statements respond, in principle at least, to one moral criterion for assessing deterrence policy: the immunity of non-combatants from direct attack either by conventional or nuclear weapons.

These statements do not address or resolve another very troublesome moral problem, namely, that an attack on military targets or militarily significant industrial targets could involve

"indirect" (i.e., unintended) but massive civilian casualties. We are advised, for example, that the United States strategic nuclear targeting plan (SIOP—Single Integrated Operational Plan) has identified 60 "military" targets within the city of Moscow alone, and that 40,000 "military" targets for nuclear weapons have been identified in the whole of the Soviet Union.[1] It is important to recognize that Soviet policy is subject to the same moral judgment; attacks on several "industrial targets" or politically significant targets in the United States could produce massive civilian casualties. The number of civilians who would necessarily be killed by such strikes is horrendous. This problem is unavoidable because of the way modern military facilities and production centers are so thoroughly interspersed with civilian living and working areas. It is aggravated if one side deliberately positions military targets in the midst of a civilian population. In our consultations, administration officials readily admitted that, while they hoped any nuclear exchange could be kept limited, they were prepared to retaliate in a massive way if necessary. They also agreed that once any substantial numbers of weapons were used, the civilian casualty levels would quickly become truly catastrophic, and that even with attacks limited to "military" targets, the number of deaths in a substantial exchange would be almost indistinguishable from what might occur if civilian centers had been deliberately and directly struck. These possibilities pose a different moral question and are to be judged by a different moral criterion: the principle of proportionality.

While any judgment of proportionality is always open to differing evaluations, there are actions which can be decisively judged to be disproportionate. A narrow adherence exclusively to the principle of noncombatant immunity as a criterion for policy is an inadequate moral posture for it ignores some evil and unacceptable consequences. Hence, we cannot be satisfied that the assertion of an intention not to strike civilians directly, or even the most honest effort to implement that intention, by itself constitutes a "moral policy" for the use of nuclear weapons.

The location of industrial or militarily significant economic targets within heavily populated areas or in those areas affected by radioactive fallout could well involve such massive civilian casualties that, in our judgment, such a strike would be deemed morally disproportionate, even though not intentionally indiscriminate.

The problem is not simply one of producing highly accurate weapons that might minimize civilian casualties in any single explosion, but one of increasing the likelihood of escalation at a level where many, even "discriminating," weapons would cumulatively kill very large numbers of civilians. Those civilian deaths would occur both immediately and from the long-term effects of social and economic devastation.

A second issue of concern to us is the relationship of deterrence doctrine to war-fighting strategies. We are aware of the argument that war-fighting capabilities enhance the credibility of the deterrent, particularly the strategy of extended deterrence. But the development of such capabilities raises other strategic and moral questions. The relationship of war-fighting capabilities and targeting doctrine exemplifies the difficult choices in this area of policy. Targeting civilian populations would violate the principle of discrimination—one of the central moral principles of a Christian ethic of war. But "counterforce targeting," while preferable from the perspective of protecting civilians, is often joined with a declaratory policy which conveys the notion that nuclear war is subject to precise rational and moral limits. We have already expressed our severe doubts about such a concept. Furthermore, a purely counterforce strategy may seem to threaten the viability of other nations' retaliatory forces, making deterrence unstable in a crisis and war more likely.

While we welcome any effort to protect civilian populations, we do not want to legitimize or encourage moves which extend deterrence beyond the specific objective of preventing the use of nuclear weapons or other actions which could lead directly to a nuclear exchange.

These considerations of concrete elements of nuclear deterrence policy, made in light of John Paul II's evaluation, but applying it through our own prudential judgments, lead us to a strictly conditioned moral acceptance of nuclear deterrence. We cannot consider it adequate as a long-term basis for peace.

This strictly conditioned judgment yields *criteria* for morally assessing the elements of deterrence strategy. Clearly, these criteria demonstrate that we cannot approve of every weapons system, strategic doctrine, or policy initiative advanced in the name of strengthening deterrence. On the contrary, these criteria require continual public scrutiny of what our government proposes to do with the deterrent.

On the basis of these criteria we wish now to make some specific evaluations:

1. If nuclear deterrence exists only to prevent the *use* of nuclear weapons by others, then proposals to go beyond this to planning for prolonged periods of repeated nuclear strikes and counterstrikes, or "prevailing" in nuclear war, are not acceptable. They encourage notions that nuclear war can be engaged in with tolerable human and moral consequences. Rather, we must continually say "no" to the idea of nuclear war.

2. If nuclear deterrence is our goal, "sufficiency" to deter is an adequate strategy; the quest for nuclear superiority must be rejected.

3. Nuclear deterrence should be used as a step on the way toward progressive disarmament. Each proposed addition to our strategic system or change in strategic doctrine must be assessed precisely in light of whether it will render steps toward "progressive disarmament" more or less likely.

Moreover, these criteria provide us with the means to make some judgments and recommendations about the present direction of U.S.

strategic policy. Progress toward a world freed of dependence upon nuclear deterrence must be carefully carried out. But it must not be delayed. There is an urgent moral and political responsibility to use the "peace of a sort" we have as a framework to move toward authentic peace through nuclear arms control, reductions, and disarmament. Of primary importance in this process is the need to prevent the development and deployment of destabilizing weapons systems on either side; a second requirement is to insure that the more sophisticated command and control systems do not become mere hair triggers for automatic launch on warning; a third is the need to prevent the proliferation of nuclear weapons in the international system.

In light of these general judgments *we oppose* some specific proposals in respect to our present deterrence posture:

1. The addition of weapons which are likely to be vulnerable to attack, yet also possess a "prompt hard-target kill" capability that threatens to make the other side's retaliatory forces vulnerable. Such weapons may seem to be useful primarily in a first strike;[2] we resist such weapons for this reason and we oppose Soviet deployment of such weapons which generate fear of a first strike against U.S. forces.

2. The willingness to foster strategic planning which seeks a nuclear war-fighting capability that goes beyond the limited function of deterrence outlined in this letter.

3. Proposals which have the effect of lowering the nuclear threshold and blurring the difference between nuclear and conventional weapons.

In support of the concept of "sufficiency" as an adequate deterrent, and in light of the present size and composition of both the U.S. and Soviet strategic arsenals, *we recommend*:

1. Support for immediate, bilateral, verifiable agreements to halt the testing, production, and deployment of new nuclear weapons systems.[3]

2. Support for negotiated bilateral deep cuts in the arsenals of both superpowers, particularly those weapons systems which have destabilizing characteristics; U.S. proposals like those for START (Strategic Arms Reduction Talks) and INF (Intermediate-range Nuclear Forces) negotiations in Geneva are said to be designed to achieve deep cuts; our hope is that they will be pursued in a manner which will realize these goals.

3. Support for early and successful conclusion of negotiations of a comprehensive test ban treaty.

4. Removal by all parties of short-range nuclear weapons which multiply dangers disproportionate to their deterrent value.

5. Removal by all parties of nuclear weapons from areas where they are likely to be overrun in the early stages of war, thus forcing rapid and uncontrollable decisions on their use.

6. Strengthening of command and control over nuclear weapons to prevent inadvertent and unauthorized use.

These judgments are meant to exemplify how a lack of unequivocal condemnation of deterrence is meant only to be an attempt to acknowledge the role attributed to deterrence, but not to support its extension beyond the limited purpose discussed above. Some have urged us to condemn all aspects of nuclear deterrence. This urging has been based on a variety of reasons, but has emphasized particularly the high and terrible risks that either deliberate use or accidental detonation of nuclear weapons could quickly escalate to something utterly disproportionate to any acceptable moral purpose. That determination requires highly technical judgments about hypothetical events. Although reasons exist which move some to condemn reliance on nuclear weapons for deterrence, we have not reached this conclusion for the reasons outlined in this letter.

Nevertheless, there must be no misunderstanding of our profound skepticism about the moral acceptability of any use of nuclear weapons. It is obvious that the use of any weapons which violate the principle of discrimination merits unequivocal condemnation. We are told that some weapons are designed for purely "counterforce" use against military forces and targets. The moral issue, however, is not resolved by the design of weapons or the planned intention for use; there are also consequences which must be assessed. It would be a perverted political policy or moral casuistry which tried to justify using a weapon which "indirectly" or "unintentionally" killed a million innocent people because they happened to live near a "militarily significant target."

Even the "indirect effects" of initiating nuclear war are sufficient to make it an unjustifiable moral risk in any form. It is not sufficient, for example, to contend that "our" side has plans for "limited" or "discriminate" use. Modern warfare is not readily contained by good intentions or technological designs. The psychological climate of the world is such that mention of the term "nuclear" generates uneasiness. Many contend that the use of one tactical nuclear weapon could produce panic, with completely unpredictable consequences. It is precisely this mix of political, psychological, and technological uncertainty which has moved us in this letter to reinforce with moral prohibitions and prescriptions the prevailing political barrier against resort to nuclear weapons. Our support for enhanced command and control facilities, for major reductions in strategic and tactical nuclear forces, and for a "no first use" policy (as set forth in this letter) is meant to be seen as a complement to our desire to draw a moral line against nuclear war.

Any claim by any government that it is pursuing a morally acceptable policy of deterrence must be scrutinized with the greatest care. We are prepared and eager to participate in our country in the ongoing public debate on moral grounds.

The need to rethink the deterrence policy of our nation, to make the revisions necessary to reduce the possibility of nuclear war, and to move toward a more stable system of national and international security will demand a substantial intellectual, political, and moral effort. It also will require, we believe, the willingness to open ourselves to the providential care, power and word of God, which call us to recognize our common humanity and the bonds of mutual responsibility which exist in the international community in spite of political differences and nuclear arsenals.

Indeed, we do acknowledge that there are many strong voices within our own episcopal ranks and within the wider Catholic community in the United States which challenge the strategy of deterrence as an adequate response to the arms race today. They highlight the historical evidence that deterrence has not, in fact, set in motion substantial processes of disarmament.

Moreover, these voices rightly raise the concern that even the conditional acceptance of nuclear deterrence as laid out in a letter such as this might be inappropriately used by some to reinforce the policy of arms buildup. In its stead, they call us to raise a prophetic challenge to the community of faith—a challenge which goes beyond nuclear deterrence, toward more resolute steps to actual bilateral disarmament and peacemaking. We recognize the intellectual ground on which the argument is built and the religious sensibility which gives it its strong force.

The dangers of the nuclear age and the enormous difficulties we face in moving toward a more adequate system of global security, stability and justice require steps beyond our present conceptions of security and defense policy.

Notes

1. Zuckerman, *Nuclear Illusion and Reality*. New York: (1982); D. Ball, "U.S. Strategic Forces," *International Security*, vol. 7 (1982–1983), pp. 31–60.

2. Several experts in strategic theory would place both the MX missile and the Pershing II missiles in this category.

3. In each of the successive drafts of this letter we have tried to state a central moral imperative: that the arms race should be stopped and disarmament begun. The implementation of this imperative is open to a wide variety of approaches. Hence we have chosen our own language in this paragraph, not wanting either to be identified with one specific political initiative or to have our words used against specific political measures.

Study Question

1. Describe the position of the Catholic bishops on the use of nuclear weapons. Is there a discrepancy between their condemnation of the use of nuclear weapons and their acceptance of deterrence?

CHAPTER 60

On Nuclear Morality

CHARLES KRAUTHAMMER

Charles Krauthammer defends the defense strategy of nuclear deterrence against attacks by the U.S. Roman Catholic bishops and others who call for unilateral nuclear disarmament. He accuses the bishops' statement of incoherence since it says we may have a policy of deterrence but may not have a countervalue strategy (aim at civilian targets) or a counterforce strategy (aim at military targets), which amounts to not having a deterrent policy at all but only a nuclear-bluff policy. He argues that those who advocate unilateral nuclear disarmament are actually destabilizing a workable balance of power and making war more likely. Nuclear deterrence is the least evil policy available to us at this time.

THE CONTEMPORARY ANTI-NUCLEAR case takes two forms. There is, first, the prudential argument that the nuclear balance is inherently unstable and unsustainable over time, doomed to breakdown and to taking us with it. The animating sentiment here is fear, a fear that the anti-nuclear campaign of the 1980's has fanned with great skill. One of its major innovations has been its insistence on a technique of graphic depiction, a kind of nuclear neorealism, as a way of mobilizing mass support for its aims. Thus the Hiroshima slide show and the concentrically circular maps showing where and precisely when one will die in every home town. But there are limitations to this approach. The law of diminishing returns applies even to repeated presentations of the apocalypse. Ground Zero Day can be celebrated, as it were, once or perhaps twice, but it soon begins to lose its effectiveness. The numbing effect of detail, as well as the simple inability of any movement to sustain indefinitely a sense of crisis and imminent calamity, has led to the current decline in popularity of the pragmatic anti-nuclear case.

Consequently there has been a subtle shift in emphasis to a second line of attack, from a concern about what nuclear weapons might do to our bodies to a concern about what they are doing to our souls. Medical lectures on "the last epidemic" have been replaced by a sharper, and more elevated, debate about the ethics of possessing, building, and threatening to use nuclear weapons. (The most recent and highly publicized document on the subject is the pastoral letter of the U.S. bishops on war and peace.)

The moral anti-nuclear argument is based on the view that deterrence, the central strategic doctrine of the nuclear age, is ethically impermissible. Yet two auxiliary issues, one a requirement of deterrence, the other an extension of it, have received the most public attention and become the focus for much of the fervor of the anti-nuclear crusade. The requirement is nuclear modernization, which is opposed under the banner of "the freeze"; the extension is the American nuclear umbrella (the threat of nuclear retaliation against an attack, conventional or nuclear, on America's NATO allies),

Reprinted from "On Nuclear Morality," Commentary (October 1983) by permission.

which is opposed under the slogan of "no-first-use." In examining the different strands of the anti-nuclear argument, it is useful to start with the more fundamental challenge to deterrence itself.

The doctrine of deterrence holds that a nuclear aggressor will not act if faced with a threat of retaliation in kind. It rests, therefore, on the willingness to use these weapons in response to attack. The moral critique of deterrence holds that the actual use of nuclear weapons, even in retaliation, is never justified. As the bishops put it, simply, one is morally obliged to "say no to nuclear war."

But things are not so simple. There are different kinds of retaliation, and different arguments (often advanced by different proponents) for the inadmissibility of each.

The popularly accepted notion of deterrence (often mistakenly assumed to be the only kind) is "countervalue" retaliation, an attack on industrial and population centers aimed at destroying the society of the aggressor. The threat to launch such retaliation is the basis of the doctrine of Mutual Assured Destruction, also known as MAD, massive retaliation, or the balance of terror. It is a balance constructed of paradox: weapons built never to be used, purely defensive weapons, like the ABM, more threatening to peace than offensive weapons; weapons aimed at people lessening the risk of war, weapons aimed at weapons increasing it. In Churchill's summary, "Safety will be the sturdy child of terror, and survival the twin brother of annihilation."

The bishops—and others, including non-pacifists like Albert Wohlstetter, who advocate deterrence based on a "counterforce" strategy of striking military targets—are neither assured nor amused by such paradoxes: they are appalled by them. For them MAD is unequivocally bad. Deliberate attacks on "soft targets" grossly violate the just-war doctrine of discrimination. They are inadmissible under any circumstance, because they make no distinction between combatants and noncombatants. Indeed, they are primarily aimed at innocent bystanders.

The bishops, however, reject not just a countervalue strategy, but also a counterforce strategy. Since military targets are often interspersed with civilian population centers, such an attack would kill millions of innocents, and thus violate the principle of proportionality, by which the suffering inflicted in a war must not outweigh the possible gains of conducting such a war. "It would be a perverted political policy or moral casuistry," write the bishops, "which tried to justify using a weapon which 'indirectly' or 'unintentionally' killed a million innocent people because they happened to live near a 'militarily significant target.'" The bishops also reject, in a second sense, the idea that a counterforce war would be limited. They share the widespread conviction that limited nuclear war is a fiction, that counterforce attacks must inevitably degenerate into countervalue warfare, and thus bring us full circle back to the moral objections to MAD and all-out nuclear war.

That does not leave very much. If a countervalue strategy is rejected for violating the principle of discrimination, and a counterforce strategy is rejected for violating the principle of proportionality (and also for leading back to total war), one runs out of ways of targeting nuclear weapons. That suits the bishops: they make a point of insisting that their doctrine is "no-use-ever." The logic, and quite transparent objective, of such a position is to reject deterrence in toto. However, the bishops suffer from one constraint. Vatican policy seems to contradict this position. Pope John Paul II has declared that "in current conditions 'deterrence' based on balance, certainly not as an end in itself but as a step on the way toward a progressive disarmament, may still be judged morally acceptable." What to do? The bishops settle for the unhappy compromise of not opposing deterrence itself, but simply what it takes to make deterrence work. Accordingly, they do not in principle oppose the possession of nuclear weapons when its sole intention is to deter an adversary from using his; they only oppose any plan, intent, or strategy to use these weapons in the act of retaliation. You may keep the weapons, but you may not use them. In sum, the only moral nuclear policy is nuclear bluff.

It is a sorry compromise, neither coherent nor convincing. It is not coherent, because it requires the bishops to support a policy—deterrence—which their entire argument is designed to undermine. And it is not convincing because the kind of deterrence they approve is no deterrence at all. Deterrence is not inherent in the weapons. It results from a combination of possession and the will to use them. If one side renounces, for moral or other reasons, the intent of ever actually using nuclear weapons, deterrence ceases to exist.

Pacifists unencumbered by papal pronouncements are able more openly to oppose deterrence. To take only the most celebrated recent example, in *The Fate of the Earth* Jonathan Schell makes the case the bishops would like to make, and stripped of any theological trappings. In its secular version it goes like this: biological existence is the ultimate value; all other values are conditional upon it; there can be neither liberty nor democracy nor any other value in defense of which Western nuclear weapons are deployed, if mankind itself is destroyed; and after nuclear war the earth will be "a republic of insects and grass." Therefore nothing can justify using nuclear weapons. Deterrence is more than a hoax, it is a crime.

Schell's argument enjoys a coherence that the bishops' case lacks, but it is still unsatisfying. Judged on its own terms—of finding a policy that best serves the ultimate and overriding value of biological survival—it fails.

For one thing, it willfully ignores history. Deterrence has a track record. For the entire postwar period it has maintained the peace between the two superpowers, preventing not only nuclear war, but conventional war as well. Un-

der the logic of deterrence, proxy and brushfire wars are permitted, but not wars between the major powers. As a result, Europe, the central confrontation line between the two superpowers, has enjoyed its longest period of uninterrupted peace in a century. And the United States and the Soviet Union, the two most powerful nations in history, locked in an ideological antagonism and a global struggle as profound as any in history, have not exchanged so much as smallarms fire for a generation.

This is not to say that deterrence cannot in principle break down. It is to say that when a system that has kept the peace for a generation is to be rejected, one is morally obliged to come up with a better alternative. It makes no sense to reject deterrence simply because it may not be infallible; it only makes sense to reject it if it proves more dangerous than the alternatives. And a more plausible alternative has yet to be offered. Schell's recommended substitute is a call for a new world order in which all violence, nuclear and conventional, is renounced. Yet his 231-page brief against deterrence neglects to go into the details of exactly how this proposal is to be implemented. Of the job of remaking politics and man, he says, "I have left to others those awesome, urgent tasks."

There is one logical alternative to deterrence, and it does not require remaking man or politics, though neither Schell nor the bishops are quite willing to embrace it: unilateral disarmament. (The bishops' position that one may possess but never use nuclear weapons, however, is unilateralist in all but name.) It has a track record, too. The only nuclear war ever fought was as one-sided as it was short. It ended when the non-nuclear power suffered the destruction of two cities (and then surrendered unconditionally). Unilateralism has similar consequences in other contexts, like bacteriological warfare. In Southeast Asia today yellow rain falls on helpless tribesmen. The same Vietnamese forces in the same place a decade before never used these weapons against a far more formidable American enemy. The reason is obvious. The primitive Hmong, technologically disarmed, cannot retaliate; the Americans could. Similarly for our experience with chemical weapons in World War II, which were not used by either side even after the breakdown of peace, because both sides were capable of retaliation.

Far from being a guarantor of survival, unilateralism is a threat to it. Thus, whether one's ethical system calls its overriding value the sanctity of life or mere biological survival, unilateralism fails within its own terms, and with it the moral critique of deterrence. The breakdown of deterrence would lead to a catastrophic increase in the probability of precisely the inadmissible outcome its critics seek to avoid. The bishops unwittingly concede that point in a subsidiary argument against counterforce when they speak of such a strategy "making deterrence unstable in a crisis and war more likely."

The critics argue that no ends can justify such disproportionate and nondiscriminatory means as the use of nuclear weapons. That would be true if the ends of such a war were territory, or domination, or victory. But they are not. The sole end is to prevent a war from coming into existence in the first place. That the threat of retaliation is the best available this-world guarantee against such a war is a paradox the bishops and other pacifists are unwilling to face. As Michael Novak writes: "The appropriate moral principle is not the relation of means to ends but the choice of a moral act which prevents greater evil. Clearly, it is a more moral choice and occasions lesser evil to hold a deterrent intention than it is to allow nuclear attack."[1] Or recklessly to increase the danger of such an attack.

Nevertheless, debate does not end with the acceptance of the necessity, and thus the morality, of deterrence. Not everything is then permitted. There is a major argument between proponents of countervalue and counterforce deterrence. The former claim that counterforce threats lower the nuclear threshold and make nuclear war more likely because it becomes "more thinkable." The latter argue that to retaliate against defenseless populations is not only disproportionate and nondiscriminatory, but dangerous as well, since the threat is not credible and thus actually lowers the nuclear threshold. (Note that the countervalue vs. counterforce debate is over the relative merits of different kinds of retaliation, and not, as is sometimes pretended, between a "party of deterrence" and a "war-fighting party." The latter distinction is empty: all deterrence rests on the threat of nuclear retaliation, i.e., "war-fighting": and all retaliatory [i.e., non-lunatic] war-fighting strategies from McNamara to today are designed to prevent attack in the first place i.e., for deterrence. The distinction between these two "parties" has to do with candor, not strategy: the "war-fighters" are willing to spell out the retaliatory steps that the "deterrers" rely on to prevent war, but which they prefer not to discuss in public.)

Nevertheless, whichever side of the intramural debate among deterrence advocates one takes, it seems to me that deterrence wins the debate with its opponents simply because it is a better means of achieving the ultimate moral aim of both sides—survival.

There is another argument in favor of deterrence, though in my view it carries less weight. It appeals not to survival but to other values. It holds that (1) there are values more important than survival, and (2) nuclear weapons are necessary to protect them. The second proposition is, of course, true. The West is the guarantor of such fragile historical achievements as democracy and political liberty; a whole constellation of ideals and values ultimately rests on its ability to deter those who reject these values and have a history of destroying them wherever they dominate. Unilaterally to reject deterrence is to surrender these values in the name of survival.

The rub comes with the first proposition. Are there values more important than survival? Sidney Hook was surely right when he once said that when a person makes survival the highest value, he has declared that there is nothing he will not betray. But for a civilization self-sacrifice makes no sense since there are not survivors to give meaning to the sacrificial act. In that case, survival may be worth betrayal. If this highly abstract choice were indeed the only one, it would be hard to meet Schell's point that since all values hinge on biological survival, to forfeit that is to forfeit everything. It is thus simply not enough to say (rightly) that nuclear weapons, given the world as it is today, keep us free; one must couple that statement with another, equally true: they keep us safe. A nuclear policy—like unilateralism—that forces us to choose between being dead or red (while increasing the chances of both) is a moral calamity. A nuclear policy—like deterrence—that protects us from both perils is the only morally compelling alternative.

Although the attack on deterrence itself is the most fundamental assault on American nuclear doctrine, the case is difficult and complicated. It has, therefore, not seized the public imagination the way two auxiliary issues have. These other issues deal not with the basic assumptions of deterrence but with the weapons and some of the tactics that underpin it. These two campaigns have been conducted under the slogan of the "freeze" and "no-first-use."

The moral attack on the weapons themselves takes two curiously contradictory approaches. The first, a mainstay of freeze proponents, is that beyond existing levels new weapons are simply redundant, that we are wasting billions of dollars on useless weapons that will do no more than make the rubble bounce, to borrow another memorable Churchillian formulation. The moral crime, it is alleged, is that these monies are being taken away from human needs, like housing and health care and aid to poorer countries. This theme runs through much of the moral literature on armaments. It is featured, for example, in the Brandt North–South report

which calculates that for every bomber one could instead build so many pharmacies in the Third World. The bishops also protest "the economic distortion of priorities—billions readily spent for destructive instruments while pitched battles are waged daily in our legislatures over much smaller amounts for the homeless, the hungry, and the helpless here and abroad."

It is extraordinary that an argument so weak can enjoy such widespread currency. Compared to other types of weapons, strategic nuclear weapons are remarkably cheap. In the U.S. they account for less than 10 percent of the military budget, and about one-half of 1 percent of the gross national product. The reasons are clear. Strategic nuclear weapons are not labor-intensive. Once in place, they need a minimal amount of maintenance, and fulfill their function simply by existing. Indeed, the argument turns against the anti-nuclearists. A shift away from strategic to conventional weapons would be extremely expensive. That is precisely why the West decided in the 1950's and 1960's to rely so heavily on nuclear weapons and to permit the current conventional imbalance in Europe. Rather than match the Soviet bloc tank for tank, plane for plane, the West decided to go nuclear, because this offered, in John Foster Dulles's immortal phrase, "more bang for the buck." The decision to buy cheap nuclear defense permitted the West vastly to expand social spending. A decision to move away from nuclear to conventional defense would require a willingness to divert enormous resources away from social to defense spending. Thus, if social priorities are to enter the moral calculus, as the nuclear critics demand, it is the anti-nuclear case that is undercut.

On the other hand, freeze advocates often argue that these weapons are not useless but dangerous, destabilizing, and likely to precipitate a nuclear war. The more weapons we build, the closer we come to nuclear war. The assumption is that high weapons levels *in themselves* increase the likelihood of war. That reverses cause and effect. Weapons are a result of tensions between nations, not their primary cause. It is true that distrust can be a dangerous by-product of an uncontrolled arms race. And yet arms-control agreements like SALT can reduce the risk of war by building mutual confidence and trust, while at the same time permitting *higher* weapons levels. Historically, nuclear tension simply does not correlate well with weapons levels. The worst nuclear crisis took place in October 1962, when the level of nuclear arms was much lower·than it is today. And nuclear tensions were probably at their lowest during the heyday of détente, in the mid-70's; at that time U.S.–Soviet relations were at their peak, while each side had by then vastly increased its capacity for multiple overkill.

There is an understandable built-in prejudice against new weapons. Even those willing grudgingly to grant the need for minimal deterrence recoil from building and deploying new weapons of mass destruction. "Enough is enough," they say. What is ignored in this critique is that deterrence has requirements, and one is survivability (the ability of one's weapons to sustain a first strike and still deliver a second strike). And survivability, in an era of technological innovation, requires modernization, often to counteract non-nuclear advances like those in anti-submarine or anti-aircraft warfare (advances, incidentally, which a freeze would do nothing to curb). Thus, the proposed new American bomber, whether it be the B-1 or the Stealth, will be better able to elude destruction on the ground and Soviet defenses in the air. It will not be any more destructive—or immoral—than the B-52. Similarly for the Trident subs, which are quieter and (because they have longer-range missiles) can hide in larger areas of the ocean than Poseidons. In short, mainstream non-unilateralist freeze proponents are caught in the position of accepting the fundamental morality of deterrence but rejecting the addition of any new weapon for preserving it.

The penchant for providing ends without means also characterizes the final flank attack on

deterrence: the rejection of the doctrine of "extended deterrence," the threat to use nuclear weapons, if necessary, in response to an attack (even a conventional attack) by the Soviet Union on NATO. That policy, which derives ultimately from Western unwillingness to match Soviet conventional strength in Europe, has long troubled many Americans. But since the alternatives are massive conventional rearmament or abandonment of our European allies, it has had to serve through half-a-dozen administrations as the guarantor of the Western alliance.

The campaign waged against this policy has been spearheaded by four former high administration officials, all with interesting histories. Robert McNamara and McGeorge Bundy are the authors of "flexible response" (a euphemism for limited nuclear war); George Kennan, of "containment"; and Gerard Smith, of SALT I. In an influential 1982 article in *Foreign Affairs,* they joined forces to call for adoption of a "no-first-use" policy on nuclear weapons.

This position has found an echo in many quarters, including, not surprisingly, the bishops' pastoral letter. It, too, doubts the possibility of a limited nuclear war remaining limited, and resolutely opposes ever crossing the line separating conventional from nuclear war. Therefore any nuclear retaliation against any conventional attack is rejected in principle.

Leave aside the consideration that the impossibility of limited nuclear war is both historically unproven and by no means logically necessary. Assume that limited nuclear war is indeed a fiction. We are still faced with the central problem of the no-first-use approach: its intent is to prevent any war from becoming nuclear, but its unintended consequence is to make that eventuality more likely. For thirty years war between the superpowers has been deterred at its origin. The prospect that even the slightest conventional conflict might escalate into a nuclear war has been so daunting that neither has been permitted to happen. Current policy sets the "firebreak" at the line dividing war from peace; a no-first-use policy moves it to the line dividing conventional war from nuclear war. No-first-use advocates are prepared to risk an increased chance of conventional war (now less dangerous and more "thinkable") in return for a decreased chance of any such war going nuclear. But a no-first-use pledge is unenforceable. Who will guarantee that the loser in any war will stick to such a pledge? A conventional European war would create the greatest risk ever of nuclear war. Any policy, however pious its intent, that makes conventional war more thinkable makes nuclear war more likely.

And that is the fundamental flaw in both this argument and the general attack on deterrence. It examines current policy in the light of some ideal, and finds it wanting. It ignores the fact that rejecting these policies forces the adoption of more dangerous alternatives, and makes more likely the calamities we are trying to avoid. In the end these arguments defeat themselves.

Nuclear weapons are useful only to the extent that they are never used. But they are more likely to fulfill their purpose, and never be used, if one's adversary believes that one indeed has the will to use them in retaliation for attack. That will to use them is what the moralists find unacceptable. But it is precisely on that will that the structure of deterrence rests. And it is on the structure of deterrence that rest not only "secondary" values of Western civilization but also the primary value of survival in the nuclear age.

Notes

1. "Moral Clarity in the Nuclear Age," *National Review,* April 1, 1983.

Study Questions

1. What is the difference between *countervalue* and *counterforce?* What role does it play in nuclear strategy?
2. How does Krauthammer defend the doctrine of deterrence against those who advocate unilateral nuclear disarmament?

CHAPTER 61

Missiles and Morals

DOUGLAS LACKEY

Douglas Lackey is professor of philosophy at the City University of New York Graduate Center and the author of several books on war, including *Moral Principles and Nuclear Weapons* (1984) and *The Ethics of War and Peace* (1989).

   In the following essay Lackey first describes three strategies regarding nuclear armament: the superiority strategy, the equivalence strategy (deterrence), and the nuclear disarmament strategy. He then compares these strategies on four different counts. He argues that the nuclear disarmament strategy is morally and prudentially the best of the three.

Three Strategies

Though there are many strategies for nuclear armament, three have been at the center of the strategic debate at least since the late 1950s:

   S: Maintain second-strike capacity; seek first-strike capacity; threaten first and second strikes ("Superiority").

   E: Maintain second-strike capacity; do not seek first-strike capacity; threaten second strikes only ("Equivalence").

   ND: Do not seek to maintain second-strike capacity ("Nuclear Disarmament").

In the statement of these strategies the terminology is standard: Nation A is presumed to have *first-strike capacity* against B if A can launch a nuclear attack on B without fear of suffering unacceptable damage from B's subsequent counterstrike; nation A is said to have *second-strike capacity* against B if A is capable of inflicting unacceptable damage on B after having suffered a nuclear first strike by B.

   Strategy S has been the favored strategy of hard-line anticommunists ever since the early 1950s. In its original form, as we find it in John Foster Dulles, the Superiority Strategy called for threats of American first strikes against Russian cities in retaliation for what American policy defined as Soviet acts of aggression. In its present form, as it is developed by Paul Nitze, Colin Gray, and others, the Superiority Strategy calls for threats, or implied threats, of American first strikes against Soviet military forces combined with large-scale increases in American strategic arms.[1]

   The Superiority Strategy, however, is not the exclusive property of doctrinaire anticommunists or hard-line "forward" strategists. Since aiming one's missiles before they are launched, that is, a desire to launch a first strike, all retargeting of American missiles from Soviet cities to Soviet missiles, up to and including President

---

Carter's Directive 59 in the summer of 1980, imply partial endorsement of Strategy S. Such "counterforce" as opposed to "countervalue" targetings are entailed by Strategy S even if they do not in fact bring first-strike capacity; Strategy S as defined implies that the United States will *seek* first-strike capacity, not that it will in fact obtain it. Strategy S advocates steps which will produce first-strike capacity unless new counter-measures are developed by the Soviet Union to cancel them out.

Strategy E, the "equivalence" strategy, enshrines the Wohlstetter–McNamara doctrine of Mutual Assured Destruction, and includes both massive retaliations against massive strikes and flexible responses against lesser strikes.[2] The possibility and permanence of Strategy E seemed assured by SALT I in 1972, since negotiated restrictions on the deployment of antiballistic missiles seemed to guarantee permanent second-strike capacity to both sides. Unfortunately, SALT I did not limit the development and deployment of MIRVs (multiple independently targeted reentry vehicles), and the deployment of MIRVs through the 1970s has led to cries on both sides that mutual second-strike capacity is dissolving and mutual first-strike capacity is emerging.

Notice that although Strategy E permits bilateral arms control, it actually prohibits substantial reductions in nuclear arms. The delicate balance of mutual second-strike capacity becomes increasingly unstable as arms levels are lowered, and sooner or later, mutual disarmament brings a loss of second-strike capacity on one side and the emergence of first-strike capacity on the other, contrary to E.

Strategy ND calls for a unilateral halt in the development of American nuclear weapons and delivery systems, even if such a halt eventuates in Soviet first strike capacity. Strategy ND is a policy of *nuclear* disarmament; it does *not* call for the abandonment of conventional weapons, and should not be equated with pacifism or con-fused with general and complete disarmament. In fact, increases in conventional weapons levels are compatible with Strategy ND.

Expected Value

Perhaps the most natural of all responses to the problem of uncertainty is to discount the weight of consequences by whatever chance there is that they will not occur. To compute the "expected value" of a policy, then, we should consider each possible outcome of the policy, multiply the utility of that outcome by the probability that it will occur, and take the sum of all these products. In the area of nuclear strategy we cannot supply precise numbers for the probabilities of the outcomes, nor can we attempt to supply precise figures for the corresponding utilities. Nevertheless, we *do* have much more information about these subjects than an ordering of probabilities, and what imprecision there is in our information can be respected by stating the information in the form of approximations. For example, we can classify the probability of outcomes as "negligible," "small but substantial," "fifty-fifty," "very likely," and "almost certain," and we can classify outcomes as "extremely bad," "bad," "neutral," and so forth. In considering the products of utilities and outcomes, we can neglect all outcomes of negligible probability, and all outcomes of small but substantial probability *except* those classified as extremely good or extremely bad. In many cases, use of such estimates will yield surprisingly definite results.

Now, what are the "outcomes" the probabilities of which we ought to consider? Given the traditionally assumed goals of deterrence, we should certainly consider the effects of each policy on the probability of nuclear war, the probability of Soviet nonnuclear aggression, and the probability of Soviet nuclear blackmail. Considering the probability of nuclear war, it is essential to distinguish the probability of a one-sided nuclear strike from the probability of all-out nuclear war. Among other outcomes, we will consider only the effects of nuclear strategies on military spending, since the impact of policies on spending can be determined with little controversy. Since we have four outcomes and three policies to consider, the probabilities can be represented on a three by four grid (see Table 1). Each probability assessment will be defended in turn.

Value of the Superiority Strategy

(a) Strategists disagree about the probability of Soviet or American first strike under the Superiority Strategy. All students of the subject rate it as having at least a small but substantial probability. I believe that it is more reasonable to rate the probability as fifty-fifty within a time frame of about fifty years, since (1) every real or presumed step towards first strike capacity by either side raises the chance of a preemptive first strike by the side falling behind; (2) the concentration on technological development prompted by the Superiority Strategy raises that chance of a tech-

nological breakthrough that might destabilize the balance of power; (3) the increasing technological complexity of weapons required by the Superiority Strategy raises the chance of a first strike as a result of accident or mistake; (4) the constant changes of weaponry required by the Superiority Strategy create pressure for proliferation, either because obsolete weapons are constantly disposed of on the international arms market or because wealthy developing countries, dazzled by new weapons, make buys to keep up with appearances.

(b) Under Superiority, the chance of an American second strike—given a Soviet first strike—is practically the same as the chance of a Soviet first strike. Though it is always possible that the President or his survivor will not respond to a Soviet first strike, the military and technological systems installed under the Superiority Strategy are geared for belligerence. Accordingly the chance of an American failure to respond is negligible.

(c) Even in the face of the Superiority Strategy, the chance of Soviet nonnuclear aggression (an invasion of West Germany or Iran, for example) must be rated as small but not negligible. The prospect of an American first strike in response to a Soviet conventional attack may not

Table 1

	One-sided Strike*	All-out Nuclear War	Soviet Agression	Very High Military Spending
Superiority	Fifty-fifty [a]	Fifty-fifty [b]	Small [c]	Certain [d]
Equivalence	Small [e]	Small [f]	Small [g]	Fifty-fifty [h]
Nuclear Disarmament	Small [i]	Zero [j]	Small [k]	Small [l]

*A "one-sided strike" is a first strike that may or may not be answered by a second strike. A comparison of the probability of one-sided strikes and two-sided strikes in a given row indicates that a first strike will lead to an all-out nuclear war.

be taken seriously by the Soviets, especially if Soviet military personnel think that they can deter any American first strike with the prospect of a massive Soviet second strike.

(d) The sums of money required to sustain the Superiority Strategy are staggering. The Reagan administration's rejection of SALT and its apparent acceptance of the Superiority Strategy will produce an increase in the fraction of the American gross national product devoted to defense from five to six and one-half percent: an increase of over $150 billion per year over the Carter projections, which were largely keyed to the Equivalence Strategy.

Value of the Equivalence Strategy

(e) Most students of strategy agree that the chance of an American or Soviet first strike under the Equivalence Strategy is small but substantial. The peculiar pressures for a first strike listed under the Superiority Strategy are absent, but there is still the chance of a first strike through accident, mistake, human folly, or a suicidal leadership.

(f) Since the chance of a first strike is less under Equivalence than under Superiority, there is less chance of an all-out nuclear war under Equivalence than under Superiority. The chance of a first strike under Equivalence is small, and the chance of all-out war following a first strike is smaller still. Since the primary aim of the Equivalence Strategy is not to "defeat" the Soviet Union or to develop a first-strike capacity, but to deter a Soviet first strike, it may be obvious to the President or his survivor that once a Soviet first strike is actually launched, there is no point whatsoever in proceeding with an American second strike. If the chance that the President will fail to respond is substantial, the chance of an all out war under Equivalence is considerably less than the chance of a first strike under Equivalence. On the other hand, the credibility of the American deterrent to a first strike depends on the perception by Soviet planners that an American second strike is inevitable once a Soviet first strike is launched, and the President and his defense strategists may decide that the only convincing way to create this perception is to make the American second strike a *semiautomatic* response. Thus it might be difficult to stop an American second strike even if the President wished to forgo it. On balance, it seems reasonable to rate the chance of the second strike as greater than one-half the chance that the Soviet first strike will be launched. This would make the chance small but still substantial.

(g) Over the years two arguments have been proposed to show that Superiority provides a more effective deterrent against Soviet aggression than does Equivalence.

(1) The Superiority Strategy requires constant technological innovation and technological innovation is an area in which the United States possesses a relative advantage. If the United States presses forward with strategic weapons development, the Soviet Union will be so exhausted from the strain of keeping up with the United States that it will have little money or energy left over for nonnuclear aggression. In the end, the strain such competition will exert on the Soviet economy might produce food riots like those in Poland in 1970, and might even bring down the Soviet socioeconomic system.

But since "the strain of keeping up" did not stop the Soviets from invading Hungary, Czechoslovakia, and Afghanistan, the level of expenditure needed to produce truly effective strain is unknown. Furthermore, the assumption of *relative* economic stress is undemonstrated: at least one economist who has seriously studied the subject has argued on various grounds that a unit of military spending by the United States disrupts the American economy far more than the equivalent military spending by the Soviet Union.[3]

(2) It is occasionally argued that the Soviets will take the possibility of an American second

strike more seriously under the Superiority Strategy than under the Equivalence Strategy, since the Superiority Strategy gives the United States something closer to first-strike capacity and therefore something less to fear from a Soviet second strike.

But in the game of nuclear strategy one cannot "almost" have first-strike capacity; either one has it or one doesn't. There is no reason to think that the Superiority Strategy will ever yield first-strike capacity, since the Soviet Union will feel forced to match the United States step for step. The Soviets know that the President will never be confident enough in American striking capacity to risk the survival of the United States on a nuclear response to Soviet nonnuclear aggression. Consequently, there is no reason to think that Superiority provides a better deterrent against Soviet aggression than does Equivalence. The chance of serious nonnuclear Soviet aggression under Equivalence is small.

(h) In the presence of serious efforts at arms control, expenditures will remain very high. The chance of very high expenditures under Equivalence would best be put at about fifty-fifty.

Value of the Nuclear Disarmament Strategy

(i) Most strategists are agreed that the chance of a Soviet first strike under the Equivalence Strategy is small. I believe that the chance of a Soviet first strike is small even under the strategy of Nuclear Disarmament.

(1) Since under Nuclear Disarmament at most one side retains nuclear arms, the chance of nuclear war occurring by accident is reduced at least by one-half, relative to the Equivalence Strategy. Since only half the technology is deployed, there is only half the chance of a mechanical malfunction leading to war.

(2) Since at most one side remains armed, there is considerably less chance under Nuclear

Disarmament that a nuclear war will occur by mistake. The principal mistake that might cause a nuclear war is the mistake of erroneously thinking that the other side is about to launch a nuclear attack. Such mistakes create enormous pressure for the launching of preemptive strikes, in order to get one's weapons in the air before they are destroyed on the ground. There is no chance that this mistake can occur under Nuclear Disarmament. The side that remains armed (if any) need not fear that the other side will launch a nuclear attack. The side that chooses to disarm cannot be tempted to launch a preemptive strike no matter what it believes the other side is doing, since it has no weapons with which to launch the strike.

(3) Even the opponents of Nuclear Disarmament describe the main peril of nuclear disarmament as nuclear blackmail by the Soviet Union. Opponents of disarmament apparently feel that after nuclear disarmament, nuclear threats are far more probable than nuclear disasters.

(4) Though nuclear weapons are not inherently more destructive than other sorts of weapons, conceived or actual (the napalm raids on Tokyo in March 1945 caused more deaths than Hiroshima or Nagasaki), nuclear weapons are universally *perceived* as different in kind from nonnuclear weapons. The diplomatic losses a nation would incur upon using even tactical nuclear weapons would be immense.

(5) A large scale nuclear attack by the Soviet Union against the United States might contaminate the American and Canadian Great Plains, a major source of Soviet grain imports. The Soviets could still turn to Argentina, but the price of grain after the attack would skyrocket, and no combination of Argentinean, Australian, or other grain sources could possibly compensate for American or Canadian losses.

(6) The Soviets will find it difficult to find actual military situations in which it will be practical to use atomic weapons against the United States, or against anyone else. Nuclear weapons proved superfluous in the Soviet invasions of

Hungary and Czechoslovakia, and they do not seem to be practicable in Afghanistan, where the human costs of the Soviet attempt to regain control are high. If the Soviets did not use nuclear weapons against China between 1960 and 1964 in order to prevent the development of Chinese nuclear capacity, it is hardly likely that they could use them against a nonnuclear United States. Of course it is always *possible* that the Soviet Union might launch a nuclear attack against a nonnuclear United States, perhaps as an escalatory step in a conventional conflict, but it is also *possible* that the Soviet Union will launch a nuclear attack on the United States *right now*, despite the present situation of Equivalence. The point is that there is no such thing as a guarantee against nuclear attack, but the probability of an actual attack is small under either strategy.

(j) The chance of all-out nuclear war under the Equivalence Strategy is slight, but the chance of all-out nuclear war under Nuclear Disarmament is zero. There cannot be a two-sided nuclear war if only one side possesses nuclear arms.

(k) In considering the threat of Soviet nonnuclear aggression under Nuclear Disarmament, we must consider Soviet nuclear threats—usually called "nuclear blackmail"—as well as possible uses of conventional arms by the Soviets.

(1) Suppose that the United States unilaterally gives up second-strike capacity. What are the odds that the Soviet Union would attempt to influence American behavior through nuclear threats? Obviously, one's views about the chances for successful nuclear blackmail depends on one's views about the chances of a Soviet first strike against a nonnuclear United States. If the chances of a Soviet first strike are slight, then the chances of successful blackmail will also be slight. We have already argued on a variety of grounds that chances of a Soviet first strike under ND are small. I would suggest that the ability of the Soviet Union to manipulate a nonnuclear United States would be the same as

the ability of United States to manipulate the Soviet Union from 1945 to 1949, when strategic conditions were reversed. Anyone who reflects on events from 1945 to 1949 will conclude that nuclear threats have little effect on nations capable of acting with resolve.

There is always the chance that the Soviet Union will carry out its nuclear threats, but there is always the chance that the Soviet Union will carry out its threats even if the United States retains nuclear weapons. There is no device that provides a guarantee against nuclear blackmail. Consequently it cannot be argued that Equivalence provides a guarantee against blackmail that Nuclear Disarmament does not.

The foregoing dismissal of nuclear blackmail violates conventional strategic wisdom, which is concerned with nuclear blackmail almost to obsession. Numerous authors, for example, cite the swift fall of Japan after Hiroshima as evidence of the strategic usefulness of nuclear weapons and nuclear threats. The case of Japan is worth considering. Contrary to the canonical view certified by Secretary Stimson in his famous (and self-serving) *Harper's* article in 1947,[4] I believe that the bombings of Hiroshima and Nagasaki had almost no effect on events leading to the surrender of Japan. If so, the force of the Japanese precedent, which still influences strategic thought, is greatly attenuated.

Obviously the bombings of Hiroshima and Nagasaki had no effect on the popular desire for peace in Japan, since the Japanese public did not know of the atomic bombings until the war was over. What is more surprising is that the bombings do not seem to have influenced either the Emperor or the military command in making the decision to sue for peace. The Emperor, as is now well known, had decided for peace as early as January 1945, and if he was set on peace in January, he did not need the bombings of August to make up his mind. The military, on the other hand, do not seem to have desired peace even after the bombs were dropped; the record shows that the military (a) correctly surmised that the United States had a small supply of these bombs, (b) debated improved antiaircraft measures to prevent any further bombs from being delivered, and (c) correctly inferred that bombs of this type could not be used to support a ground invasion, which they felt they could repulse with sufficient success to secure a conditional surrender. What tipped the political scales so that the Emperor could find his way to peace was not the bombing of Nagasaki on 9 August, but the Russian declaration of war on 8 August. Unaware of Stalin's commitment at Yalta to enter the war against Japan, the Japanese had hoped through the spring and summer of 1945 that the Soviets would mediate a negotiated settlement between the United States and Japan rather than send the Red Army into a new theater of war. When the Russians invaded Manchuria on 9 August, Premier Suzuki, according to reports, cried, "The game is over," and when the Emperor demanded surrender from the Council of Elders on 10 August, he never mentioned atomic bombs as the occasion of his demand for peace.[5] Little can be inferred from such evidence about the effectiveness of nuclear threats.

(2) The strategy of Nuclear Disarmament does not forbid uses of conventional arms in response to acts of aggression. Since there is no reason to believe that adoption of the strategy of Nuclear Disarmament by the United States will make acts of Soviet aggression any more palatable than they are at present, in all probability the American government under ND will appropriate funds for conventional arms sufficient to provide a deterrent to Soviet aggression roughly comparable to the deterrent provided by nuclear arms under S and E. This argument assumes that the deterrent effects of the American strategic nuclear arsenal (whatever they are) can be obtained with a developed arsenal of modern conventional weapons. A review of the difficulties involved in the use of strategic nuclear weapons in concrete situations may convince the reader that conventional weapons can match the deterrent effect of nuclear weapons. Indeed, the whole development of "flexible response" system during the McNamara era testifies to the widespread recognition that strategic nuclear weapons provide little leverage to nations who would seek to control the flow of world events.

(1) Since it is impossible to predict how much money must be spent on conventional forces in order to supply a deterrent equal to the present (nuclear) deterrent against Soviet nonnuclear aggression, it is possible that levels of military spending under ND will be greater than level[s] under E. But it is also possible that the levels of spending will be much less. The technical equipment needed to maintain E is fantastically expensive, but the labor costs of training and improving conventional forces can also be staggering. All things considered, it is still likely that spending will be less under ND than under E, especially if the draft is revived.

Comparison of Superiority and Equivalence

The chance of a Soviet first strike is greater under Superiority than under Equivalence, and the chance of all-out nuclear war is greater under Superiority than under Equivalence. The ability of Equivalence to deter Soviet nonnuclear aggression is equal to the ability of Superiority to deter such aggression, and the Equivalence Strategy costs less. Thus Equivalence is preferable to Superiority from both the prudential and the moral point of view.

Comparison of Equivalence and Nuclear Disarmament

We have argued that Nuclear Disarmament and Equivalence are equal in their ability to deter Soviet nonnuclear aggression. In the category of military spending Nuclear Disarmament is preferable to Equivalence. In the category of "all-out war" ND is clearly superior to E, and in the category of "first strikes," ND seems to be about equal to E. Thus we have what seems to be a decisive prudential and moral argument in favor of Nuclear Disarmament: in every category, ND is either equal to or superior to E.

Notes

1. On "massive retaliation" see John Foster Dulles, Dept. of State Bulletin 30, 791, 25 Jan. 1954. For Superiority policy in the 1960s see, for example, Barry Goldwater, *Why Not Victory?* (New York: McGraw-Hill, 1962), p. 162:

> We must stop lying to ourselves and our friends about disarmament. We must stop advancing the cause of the Soviet Union by playing along with Communist inspired deception.

"Disarmament," for Goldwater, includes arms control, since he warns against the danger of "disarmament, or arms control, as the 87th Congress cutely puts it" (p. 99). For a recent interpretation of Superiority, see Colin Gray and Keith Payne, "Victory Is Possible," *Foreign Policy* 39 (Summer 1980): 14–27, and Colin Gray, "Nuclear Strategy: The Case for a Theory of Victory," *International Security* 4 (Summer 1979): 54–87.

2. Crudely speaking, Wohlstetter sold the strategy in the 1950s and McNamara bought it in the 1960s.

See especially Albert Wohlstetter, "The Delicate Balance of Terror," *Foreign Affairs* (January 1959); and Robert McNamara, *The Essence of Security* (London: Hodder and Stoughton, 1968).

3. See Seymour Melman, *Our Depleted Society* (New York: Holt, Rinehart & Winston, 1965), and *Pentagon Capitalism* (New York: McGraw-Hill, 1970).

4. Stimson's "The Decision to Use the Atomic Bomb" appeared in the February 1947 *Harper's Magazine*, pp. 97–107. Typical of Stimson's *post hoc ergo propter hoc* is:

> We believed that our attacks struck cities which must certainly be important to the Japanese military leaders, both Army and Navy, and we waited for a result. We waited one day.

5. For the Emperor's active attempts to obtain peace, see Herbert Feis, *The Atomic Bomb and the End of World War II* (Princeton: Princeton University Press, 1966), p. 66. For the military response to the atomic bombings, see Hanson Baldwin, *Great Mistakes of the War* (New York: Collins-Knowlton-Wing, 1950), pp. 87–107. For Suzuki's remark that "The game is over," see W. Craig, *The Fall of Japan* (New York: Dial, 1967), p. 107. One interesting suggestion about the special effectiveness of the atomic bomb against Japan is found in a remark made by General Marshall to David Lilienthal in 1947, "We didn't realize its value to give the Japanese such a shock that they could surrender without loss of face" (quoted in Feis, *The Atomic Bomb*, p. 6). Marshall's remark is prima facie reasonable, but I can find nothing in the documents on the Japanese side that supports it.

Study Questions

1. Describe the three strategies on nuclear armament.
2. What are the criteria for assessing the various strategies regarding nuclear armament? Do you agree with Lackey's assessment?
3. Compare Krauthammer's and Lackey's arguments and positions. Which position seems more compelling?

CHAPTER 62

The Moral Equivalent of War

WILLIAM JAMES

Philosopher and psychologist, brother of the writer Henry James, and leading proponent of pragmatism, William James (1842–1910) taught at Harvard University and was the author of several books, including *Principles of Psychology* (1890), *The Will to Believe* (1897), and *The Varieties of Religious Experience* (1902).

In his essay on war James first laments the tragic history of humankind, marked by war and destruction. But he sees in militarism something worth preserving: ideals such as courage, contempt for softness, obedience to command, endurance, and honor. Unless we can transpose these virtues into a peaceful context, we will not take the yearning for war from humanity. James calls for a peace army to combat nature, into which every male is conscripted. Had he lived in our day, perhaps he would have said every young man and woman should be inducted into the service of humanity at large: in environmental work, teaching the illiterate, and service in such organizations as the Peace Corps.

THE WAR AGAINST WAR is going to be no holiday excursion or camping party. The military feelings are too deeply grounded to abdicate their place among our ideals until better substitutes are offered than the glory and shame that come to nations as well as to individuals from the ups and downs of politics and the vicissitudes of trade. There is something highly paradoxical in the modern man's relation to war. Ask all our millions, north and south, whether they would vote now (were such a thing possible) to have our war for the Union expunged from history, and the record of a peaceful transition to the present time substituted for that of its marches and battles, and probably hardly a handful of eccentrics would say yes. Those ancestors, those efforts, those memories and legends, are the most ideal part of what we now own together, a sacred spiritual possession worth more than all the blood poured out. Yet ask those same people whether they would be willing in cold blood to start another civil war now to gain another similar possession, and not one man or woman would vote for the proposition. In modern eyes, precious though wars may be, they must not be waged solely for the sake of the ideal harvest. Only when forced upon one, only when an enemy's injustice leaves us no alternative, is a war now thought permissible.

It was not thus in ancient times. The earlier men were hunting men, and to hunt a neighboring tribe, kill the males, loot the village and possess the females, was the most profitable, as well as the most exciting, way of living. Thus were

This essay was printed in 1910 as a tract, and 30,000 copies were distributed. It can be found in The Writings of William James, *edited by John McDermott (New York: Random House, 1967).*

the more martial tribes selected, and in chiefs and peoples a pure pugnacity and love of glory came to mingle with the more fundamental appetite for plunder.

Modern war is so expensive that we feel trade to be a better avenue to plunder; but modern man inherits all the innate pugnacity and all the love of glory of his ancestors. Showing war's irrationality and horror is of no effect upon him. The horrors make the fascination. War is the *strong* life; it is life *in extremis;* war-taxes are the only ones men never hesitate to pay, as the budgets of all nations show us.

History is a bath of blood. The *Iliad* is one long recital of how Diomedes and Ajax, Sarpedon and Hector *killed.* No detail of the wounds they made is spared us, and the Greek mind fed upon the story. Greek history is a panorama of jingoism and imperialism—war for war's sake, all the citizens being warriors. It is horrible reading, because of the irrationality of it all—save for the purpose of making "history"—and the history is that of the utter ruin of a civilization in intellectual respects perhaps the highest the earth has ever seen.

Those wars were purely piratical. Pride, gold, women, slaves, excitement, were their only motives. In the Peloponnesian war, for example, the Athenians ask the inhabitants of Melos (the island where the "Venus of Milo" was found), hitherto neutral, to own their lordship. The envoys meet, and hold a debate which Thucydides gives in full, and which, for sweet reasonableness of form, would have satisfied Matthew Arnold. "The powerful exact what they can," said the Athenians, "and the weak grant what they must." When the Meleans say that sooner than be slaves they will appeal to the gods, the Athenians reply: "Of the gods we believe and of men we know that, by a law of their nature, wherever they can rule they will. This law was not made by us, and we are not the first to have acted upon it; we did but inherit it, and we know that you and all mankind, if you were as strong as we are, would do as we do. So much for the gods;

we have told you why we expect to stand as high in their good opinion as you." Well, the Meleans still refused, and their town was taken. "The Athenians," Thucydides quietly says "thereupon put to death all who were of military age and made slaves of the women and children. They then colonized the island, sending thither five hundred settlers of their own."

Alexander's career was piracy pure and simple, nothing but an orgy of power and plunder, made romantic by the character of the hero. There was no rational principle in it, and the moment he died his generals and governors attacked one another. The cruelty of those times is incredible. When Rome finally conquered Greece, Paulus Aemilius was told by the Roman Senate to reward his soldiers for their toil by "giving" them the old kingdom of Epirus. They sacked seventy cities and carried off a hundred and fifty thousand inhabitants as slaves. How many they killed I know not; but in Etolia they killed all the senators, five hundred and fifty in number. Brutus was "the noblest Roman of them all," but to reanimate his soldiers on the eve of Philippi he similarly promises to give them the cities of Sparta and Thessalonica to ravage, if they win the fight.

Such was the gory nurse that trained societies to cohesiveness. We inherit the warlike type; and for most of the capacities of heroism that the human race is full of we have to thank this cruel history. Dead men tell no tales, and if there were any tribes of other type than this they have left no survivors. Our ancestors have bred pugnacity into our bone and marrow, and thousands of years of peace won't breed it out of us. The popular imagination fairly fattens on the thought of wars. Let public opinion once reach a certain fighting pitch, and no ruler can withstand it. In the Boer War both governments began with bluff but couldn't stay there, the military tension was too much for them. In 1898 our people had read the word "war" in letters three inches high for three months in every newspaper. The pliant politician McKinley was swept away by their eagerness, and our squalid war with Spain became a necessity.

At the present day, civilized opinion is a curious mental mixture. The military instincts and ideals are as strong as ever, but are confronted by reflective criticisms which sorely curb their ancient freedom. Innumerable writers are showing up the bestial side of military service. Pure loot and mastery seem no longer morally avowable motives, and pretexts must be found for attributing them solely to the enemy. England and we, our army and navy authorities repeat without ceasing, arm solely for "peace," Germany and Japan it is who are bent on loot and glory. "Peace" in military mouths today is a synonym for "war expected." The word has become a pure provocative, and no government wishing peace sincerely should allow it ever to be printed in a newspaper. Every up-to-date dictionary should say that "peace" and "war" mean the same thing, now *in posse,* now *in actu.* It may even reasonably be said that the intensely sharp competitive *preparation* for war by the nations *is the real war,* permanent, unceasing; and that the battles are only a sort of public verification of the mastery gained during the "peace" interval.

It is plain that on this subject civilized man has developed a sort of double personality. If we take European nations, no legitimate interest of any one of them would seem to justify the tremendous destructions which a war to compass it would necessarily entail. It would seem as though common sense and reason ought to find a way to reach agreement in every conflict of honest interests. I myself think it our bounden duty to believe in such international rationality as possible. But, as things stand, I see how desperately hard it is to bring the peace-party and the war-party together, and I believe that the difficulty is due to certain deficiencies in the program of pacifism which set the militarist imagination strongly, and to a certain extent justifiably, against it. In the whole discussion both sides are on imaginative and sentimental ground. It is but one utopia against another,

and everything one says must be abstract and hypothetical. Subject to this criticism and caution, I will try to characterize in abstract strokes the opposite imaginative forces, and point out what to my own very fallible mind seems the best utopian hypothesis, the most promising line of conciliation.

In my remarks, pacificist though I am, I will refuse to speak of the bestial side of the war *regime* (already done justice to by many writers) and consider only the higher aspects of militaristic sentiment. Patriotism no one thinks discreditable; nor does any one deny that war is the romance of history. But inordinate ambitions are the soul of every patriotism, and the possibility of violent death the soul of all romance. The military patriotic and romantic-minded everywhere, and especially the professional military class, refuse to admit for a moment that war may be a transitory phenomenon in social evolution. The notion of a sheep's paradise like that revolts, they say, our higher imagination. Where then would be the steeps of life? If war had ever stopped, we should have to re-invent it, on this view, to redeem life from flat degeneration.

Reflective apologists for war at the present day all take it religiously. It is a sort of sacrament. Its profits are to the vanquished as well as to the victor; and quite apart from any question of profit, it is an absolute good, we are told, for it is human nature at its highest dynamic. Its "horrors" are a cheap price to pay for rescue from the only alternative supposed, of a world of clerks and teachers, of coeducation and zoophily, of "consumer's leagues" and "associated charities," of industrialism unlimited, and feminism unabashed. No scorn, no hardness, no valor any more! Fie upon such a cattleyard of a planet!

So far as the central essence of this feeling goes, no healthy minded person, it seems to me, can help to some degree partaking of it. Militarism is the great preserver of our ideals of hardihood, and human life with no use for hardihood would be contemptible. Without risks or prizes for the darer, history would be insipid indeed; and there is a type of military character which every one feels that the race should never cease to breed, for every one is sensitive to its superiority. The duty is incumbent on mankind, of keeping military characters in stock—of keeping them, if not for use, then as ends in themselves and as pure pieces of perfection,—so that Roosevelt's weaklings and mollycoddles may not end by making everything else disappear from the face of nature.

This natural sort of feeling forms, I think, the innermost soul of army-writings. Without any exception known to me, militarist authors take a highly mystical view of their subject, and regard war as a biological or sociological necessity, uncontrolled by ordinary psychological checks and motives. When the time of development is ripe the war must come, reason or no reason, for the justifications pleaded are invariably fictitious. War is, in short, a permanent human *obligation.* General Homer Lea, in his recent book "The Valor of Ignorance," plants himself squarely on this ground. Readiness for war is for him the essence of nationality, and ability in it the supreme measure of the health of nations.

Nations, General Lea says, are never stationary—they must necessarily expand or shrink, according to their vitality or decrepitude. Japan now is culminating; and by the fatal law in question it is impossible that her statesmen should not long since have entered, with extraordinary foresight, upon a vast policy of conquest—the game in which the first moves were her wars with China and Russia and her treaty with England, and of which the final objective is the capture of the Philippines, the Hawaiian Islands, Alaska, and the whole of our Coast west of the Sierra Passes. This will give Japan what her ineluctable vocation as a state absolutely forces her to claim, the possession of the entire Pacific Ocean; and to oppose these deep designs we Americans have, according to our author, nothing but our conceit, our ignorance, our commercialism, our corruption, and our feminism. General Lea makes a minute technical comparison of the military strength which we at present could oppose to the strength of Japan, and concludes that the islands, Alaska, Oregon, and Southern California, would fall almost without resistance, that San Francisco must surrender in a fortnight to a Japanese investment, that in three or four months the war would be over, and our republic, unable to regain what it had heedlessly neglected to protect sufficiently, would then "disintegrate," until perhaps some Caesar should arise to weld us again into a nation.

A dismal forecast indeed! Yet not unplausible, if the mentality of Japan's statesmen be of the Caesarian type of which history shows so many examples, and which is all that General Lea seems able to imagine. But there is no reason to think that women can no longer be the mothers of Napoleonic or Alexandrian characters; and if these come in Japan and find their opportunity, just such surprises as "The Valor of Ignorance" paints may lurk in ambush for us. Ignorant as we still are of the innermost recesses of Japanese mentality, we may be foolhardy to disregard such possibilities.

Other militarists are more complex and more moral in their considerations. The "Philosophie des Krieges," by S. R. Steinmetz is a good example. War, according to this author, is an ordeal instituted by God, who weighs the nation in its balance. It is the essential form of the State, and the only function in which peoples can employ all their powers at once and convergently. No victory is possible save as the resultant of a totality of virtues, no defeat for which some vice or weakness is not responsible. Fidelity, cohesiveness, tenacity, heroism, conscience, education, inventiveness, economy, wealth, physical health and vigor—there isn't a moral or intellectual point of superiority that doesn't tell, when God holds his assizes and hurls the peoples upon one another. *Die Weltgeschichte ist das Weltgericht;*[1] and Dr. Steinmetz does not believe that in the long run chance and luck play any part in apportioning the issues.

The virtues that prevail, it must be noted, are virtues anyhow, superiorities that count in peaceful as well as in military competition; but the strain on them, being infinitely intenser in the latter case, makes war infinitely more searching as a trial. No ordeal is comparable to its winnowings. Its dread hammer is the welder of men into cohesive states, and nowhere but in such states can human nature adequately develop its capacity. The only alternative is "degeneration."

Dr. Steinmetz is a conscientious thinker, and his book, short as it is, takes much into account. Its upshot can, it seems to me, be summed up in Simon Patten's word, that mankind was nursed in pain and fear, and that the transition to a "pleasure-economy" may be fatal to a being wielding no powers of defense against its disintegrative influences. If we speak of the *fear of emancipation from the fear-regime,* we put the whole situation into a single phrase; fear regarding ourselves now taking the place of the ancient fear of the enemy.

Turn the fear over as I will in my mind, it all seems to lead back to two unwillingnesses of the imagination, one aesthetic, and the other moral; unwillingness, first to envisage a future in which army-life, with its many elements of charm, shall be forever impossible, and in which the destinies of peoples shall nevermore be decided quickly, thrillingly and tragically, by force, but only gradually and insipidly by "evolution"; and, secondly, unwillingness to see the supreme theatre of human strenuousness closed, and the splendid military aptitudes of men doomed to keep always in a state of latency and never show themselves in action. These insistent unwillingnesses, no less than other aesthetic and ethical insistencies, have, it seems to me, to be listened to and respected. One cannot meet them effectively by mere counter-insistency on war's expensiveness and horror. The horror makes the thrill; and when the question is of getting the extremest and supremest out of human nature, talk of expense sounds ignominious. The weakness of so much merely negative criticism is evident—pacificism makes no converts from the military party. The military party denies neither the bestiality nor the horror, nor the expense; it only says that these things tell but half the story. It only says that war is *worth* them; that, taking human nature as a whole, its wars are its best protection against its weaker and more cowardly self, and that mankind cannot *afford* to adopt a peace-economy.

Pacificists ought to enter more deeply into the aesthetical and ethical point of view of their opponents. Do that first in any controversy, says J. J. Chapman, *then move the point,* and your opponent will follow. So long as anti-militarists propose no substitute for war's disciplinary function, no *moral equivalent* of war, analogous, as one might say, to the mechanical equivalent of heat, so long they fail to realize the full inwardness of the situation. And as a rule they do fail. The duties, penalties, and sanctions pictured in the utopias they paint are all too weak and tame to touch the military-minded. Tolstoi's pacificism is the only exception to this rule, for it is profoundly pessimistic as regards all this world's values, and makes the fear of the Lord furnish the moral spur provided elsewhere by the fear of the enemy. But our socialistic peace-advocates all believe absolutely in this world's values; and instead of the fear of the Lord and the fear of the enemy, the only fear they reckon with is the fear of poverty if one be lazy. This weakness pervades all the socialistic literature with which I am acquainted. Even in Lowes Dickinson's exquisite dialogue,[2] high wages and short hours are the only forces invoked for overcoming man's distaste for repulsive kinds of labor. Meanwhile men at large still live as they always have lived, under a pain-and-fear economy—for those of us who live in an ease-economy are but an island in the stormy ocean—and the whole atmosphere of present-day utopian literature tastes mawkish and dishwatery to people who still keep a sense for life's more bitter flavors. It suggests, in truth, ubiquitous inferiority.

Inferiority is always with us, and merciless scorn of it is the keynote of the military temper. "Dogs, would you live forever?" shouted Frederick the Great. "Yes," say our utopians, "let us live forever, and raise our level gradually." The best thing about our "inferiors" to-day is that they are as tough as nails, and physically and morally almost as insensitive. Utopianism would see them soft and squeamish, while militarism would keep their callousness, but transfigure it into a meritorious characteristic, needed by "the service," and redeemed by that from the suspicion of inferiority. All the qualities of a man acquire dignity when he knows that the service of the collectivity that owns him needs them. If proud of the collectivity, his own pride rises in proportion. No collectivity is like an army for nourishing such pride; but it has to be confessed that the only sentiment which the image of pacific cosmopolitan industrialism is capable of arousing in countless worthy breasts is shame at the idea of belonging to *such* a collectivity. It is obvious that the United States of America as they exist to-day impress a mind like General Lea's as so much human blubber. Where is the sharpness and precipitousness, the contempt for life, whether one's own, or another's? Where is the savage "yes" and "no," the unconditional duty? Where is the conscription? Where is the blood-tax? Where is anything that one feels honored by belonging to?

Having said thus much in preparation, I will now confess my own utopia. I devoutly believe in the reign of peace and in the gradual advent of some sort of a socialistic equilibrium. The fatalistic view of the war-function is to me nonsense, for I know that war-making is due to definite motives and subject to prudential checks and reasonable criticisms, just like any other form of enterprise. And when whole nations are the armies, and the science of destruction vies in intellectual refinement with the sciences of production, I see that war becomes absurd and impossible from its own monstrosity. Extravagant ambitions will have to be replaced by reasonable

claims, and nations must make common cause against them. I see no reason why all this should not apply to yellow as well as to white countries, and I look forward to a future when acts of war shall be formally outlawed as between civilized peoples.

All these beliefs of mine put me squarely into the anti-militarist party. But I do not believe that peace either ought to be or will be permanent on this globe, unless the states pacifically organized preserve some of the old elements of army-discipline. A permanently successful peace-economy cannot be a simple pleasure-economy. In the more or less socialistic future towards which mankind seems drifting, we must still subject ourselves collectively to those severities which answer to our real position upon this only partly hospitable globe. We must make new energies and hardihoods continue the manliness to which the military mind so faithfully clings. Martial virtues must be the enduring cement; intrepidity, contempt of softness, surrender of private interest, obedience to command, must still remain the rock upon which states are built—unless, indeed, we wish for dangerous reactions against commonwealths fit only for contempt, and liable to invite attack whenever a center of crystallization for military-minded enterprise gets formed anywhere in their neighborhood.

The war-party is assuredly right in affirming and reaffirming that the martial virtues, although originally gained by the race through war, are absolute and permanent human goods. Patriotic pride and ambition in their military form are, after all, only specifications of a more general competitive passion. They are its first form, but that is no reason for supposing them to be its last form. Men now are proud of belonging to a conquering nation, and without a murmur they lay down their persons and their wealth, if by so doing they may fend off subjection. But who can be sure that *other aspects of one country* may not, with time and education and suggestion enough, come to be regarded with similarly effective feelings of pride and shame? Why should men not some day feel that it is worth a blood-tax to belong to a collectivity superior in *any* ideal respect? Why should they not blush with indignant shame if the community that owns them is vile in any way whatsoever? Individuals, daily more numerous, now feel this civic passion. It is only a question of blowing on the spark till the whole population gets incandescent, and on the ruins of the old morals of military honor, a stable system of morals of civic honor builds itself up. What the whole community comes to believe in grasps the individual as in a vise. The war-function has grasped us so far; but constructive interests may some day seem no less imperative, and impose on the individual a hardly lighter burden.

Let me illustrate my idea more concretely. There is nothing to make one indignant in the mere fact that life is hard, that men should toil and suffer pain. The planetary conditions once for all are such, and we can stand it. But that so many men, by mere accidents of birth and opportunity, should have a life of *nothing else* but toil and pain and hardness and inferiority imposed upon them, should have *no* vacation, while others natively no more deserving never get any taste of this campaigning life at all,—*this* is capable of arousing indignation in reflective minds. It may end by seeming shameful to all of us that some of us have nothing but campaigning, and others nothing but unmanly ease. If now—and this is my idea—there were, instead of military conscription a conscription of the whole youthful population to form for a certain number of years a part of the army enlisted against *Nature,* the injustice would tend to be evened out, and numerous other goods to the commonwealth would follow. The military ideals of hardihood and discipline would be wrought into the growing fiber of the people; no one would remain blind as the luxurious classes now are blind, to man's relations to the globe he lives on, and to the permanently sour and hard foundations of his higher life. To coal and iron mines, to freight trains, to fishing fleets in December, to dish-washing, clothes-washing, and window-washing, to road-building and tunnel-making, to foundries and stoke-holes, and to the frames of sky-scrapers, would our gilded youths be drafted off, according to their choice, to get the childishness knocked out of them, and to come back into society with healthier sympathies and soberer ideas. They would have paid their blood-tax, done their own part in the immemorial human warfare against nature; they would tread the earth more proudly, the women would value them more highly, they would be better fathers and teachers of the following generation.

Such a conscription, with the state of public opinion that would have required it, and the many moral fruits it would bear, would preserve in the midst of a pacific civilization the manly virtues which the military party is so afraid of seeing disappear in peace. We should get toughness without callousness, authority with as little criminal cruelty as possible, and painful work done cheerily because the duty is temporary, and threatens not, as now, to degrade the whole remainder of one's life. I spoke of the "moral equivalent" of war. So far, war has been the only force that can discipline a whole community, and until an equivalent discipline is organized, I believe that war must have its way. But I have no serious doubt that the ordinary prides and shames of social man, once developed to a certain intensity, are capable of organizing such a moral equivalent as I have sketched, or some other just as effective for preserving manliness of type. It is but a question of time, of skillful propagandism, and of opinion-making men seizing historic opportunities.

The martial type of character can be bred without war. Strenuous honor and disinterestedness abound elsewhere. Priests and medical men are in a fashion educated to it, and we should all feel some degree of it imperative if we were conscious of our work as an obligatory service to the state. We should be *owned,* as soldiers are by the army, and our pride would rise accordingly. We could be poor, then, without humiliation, as army officers now are. The only thing needed henceforward is to inflame the civic temper as past history has inflamed the military temper. H. G. Wells, as usual, sees the center of the situation. "In many ways," he says,

> Military organization is the most peaceful of activities. When the contemporary man steps from the street, of clamorous insincere advertisement, push, adulteration, underselling and intermittent employment into the barrack-yard, he steps on to a higher social plane, into an atmosphere of service and cooperation and of infinitely more honorable emulations. Here at least men are not flung out of employment to degenerate because there is no immediate work for them to do. They are fed and drilled and trained for better services. Here at least a man is supposed to win promotion by self-forgetfulness and not by self-seeking. And beside the feeble and irregular endowment of research by commercialism, its little short-sighted snatches at profit by innovation and scientific economy, see how remarkable is the steady and rapid development of method and appliances in naval and military affairs! Nothing is more striking than to compare the progress of civil conveniences which has been left almost entirely to the trader, to the progress in military apparatus during the last few decades. The house-appliances of to-day, for example, are little better than they were fifty years ago. A house of to-day is still almost as ill-ventilated, badly heated by wasteful fires, clumsily arranged and furnished as the house of 1858. Houses a couple of hundred years old are still satisfactory places of residence, so little have our standards risen. But the rifle or

battleship of fifty years ago was beyond all comparison inferior to those we possess,—in power, in speed, in convenience alike. No one has a use now for such superannuated things.[3]

Wells adds that he thinks that the conceptions of order and discipline, the tradition of service and devotion, of physical fitness, unstinted exertion, and universal responsibility, which universal military duty is now teaching European nations, will remain a permanent acquisition, when the last ammunition has been used in the fireworks that celebrate the final peace. I believe as he does. It would be simply preposterous if the only force that could work ideals of honor and standards of efficiency into English or American natures should be the fear of being killed by the Germans or the Japanese. Great indeed is Fear; but it is not, as our military enthusiasts believe and try to make us believe, the only stimulus known for awakening the higher ranges of men's spiritual energy. The amount of alteration in public opinion which my utopia postulates is vastly less than the difference between the mentality of those black warriors who pursued Stanley's party on the Congo with their cannibal war-cry of "Meat! Meat!" and that of the "general-staff" of any civilized nation. History has seen the latter interval bridged over: the former one can be bridged over much more easily.

Notes

1. Schiller, "The history of the world is the judgment of the world."—ED.]
2. "Justice and Liberty," New York, 1909.
3. "First and Last Things," 1908, p. 215.

Study Questions

1. Do you agree with James that the history of the human race has been a bloodbath? Do you agree that this is a great evil, or do you see some good in it?
2. What does James mean by "the moral equivalent of war"? Examine and discuss his position.

For Further Reading

Christopher, Paul. *The Ethics of War and Peace*. Englewood Cliffs, N.J.: Prentice Hall, 1994.

Cohen, Marshall, Thomas Nagel, and Thomas Scanlon, eds. *War and Moral Responsibility*. Princeton, N.J.: Princeton University Press, 1974.

Fotion, Nicholas, and Gerald Elfstrom. *Military Ethics*. Boston: Routledge & Kegan Paul, 1986.

Lackey, Douglas. *The Ethics of War and Peace*. Englewood Cliffs, N.J.: Prentice Hall, 1989.

———. *Moral Principles and Nuclear Weapons*. Totowa, N.J.: Rowman and Allenheld, 1984.

Schell, Jonathan. *Fate of the Earth*. New York: Knopf, 1982.

Sterba, James, ed. *The Ethics of War and Nuclear Deterrence*. Belmont, Calif.: Wadsworth, 1985.

Stoessinger, John G. *Why Nations Go to War,* 4th ed. New York: St. Martin's Press, 1985.

Walzer, Michael. *Just and Unjust Wars*. London: Penguin Books, 1977.

Wasserstrom, Richard, ed. *War and Morality*. Belmont, Calif.: Wadsworth, 1970.

Part XII

World Hunger

Hunger is a child with shrivelled limbs and a swollen belly.
It is the grief of parents, or a person gone blind for lack of vitamin A.

(ARTHUR SIMON, *Bread for the World*)

The victim of starvation burns up his own body fats, muscles and tissues for fuel. His
body quite literally consumes itself and deteriorates rapidly. The kidneys, liver and
endocrine system often cease to function properly. A shortage of carbohydrates, which
play a vital role in brain chemistry, affects the mind. Lassitude and confusion set in,
so that starvation victims often seem unaware of their plight. The body's defenses
drop; disease kills most famine victims before they have time to starve to death. An
individual begins to starve when he has lost about a third of his normal body weight.
Once this loss exceeds 40% death is almost inevitable.

(*TIME* MAGAZINE, November 11, 1974)

Ten thousand people starve to death every day, another 2 billion (out of a global
population of 5 billion) are malnourished, and 460 million are permanently hungry.
Almost half of these are children. More than one third of the world goes to bed
hungry each night. In the past twenty-five years, devastating famines have occurred
in Bangladesh (1974), Ethiopia (1972–1974, 1984), Cambodia (1978), Chad and
Sudan (1985), and in many of the other forty-three countries making up the Sub-
Saharan region of Africa, throughout the 1970s and 1980s. Since the 1960s conditions have deteriorated in many parts of the world.[1]

On the other hand, another third of the world lives in affluence. Imagine ten
children eating at a table. The three healthiest eat the best food and throw much of
it away or give it to their pets. Two other children get just enough to get by on. The
other five do not get enough food. Three of them who are weak manage to stave off
hunger pangs by eating bread and rice, but the other two are unable to do even that

and die of hunger-related diseases, pneumonia, and dysentery. Such is the plight of the children of the world.

In the United States enough food is thrown into the garbage each day to feed an entire nation, more money is spent on pet food than aid to the world's starving, and many people are grossly overweight.

Problems of global scarcity, poverty, hunger, and famine are among the most urgent facing us. What is our duty to the hungry in our country and in other lands? What obligations do we have toward the poor at home and abroad? What rights do the starving have? To what extent should hunger relief be tied to population control? These are some of the questions discussed in the readings in this part of the book.

We begin with Garrett Hardin's famous article, "Lifeboat Ethics: The Case Against Helping the Poor," in which Hardin argues that affluent societies, like lifeboats, ought to ensure their survival by preserving a safety factor of resources. To give away their resources to needy nations or admitting needy immigrants is like taking on additional passengers who threaten to capsize the lifeboat. We help neither them nor ourselves. Aiming at perfect distributive justice ends up a perfect catastrophe. Furthermore, we have a duty to our children and grandchildren that will be compromised if we endeavor to help the poor.

In our second reading, William Murdoch and Allan Oaten take strong issue with Hardin's assessment. They argue that Hardin's arguments rest on misleading metaphors—*lifeboat, commons,* and *ratchet*—and a fuller analysis will reveal that the situation is far more hopeful than Hardin claims. We are responsible for the plight of the poor and must take steps to alleviate their suffering.

In our third reading, Peter Singer sets forth two principles, a strong and a moderate one, which show that we have a duty to give substantial aid to those who are starving. The strong principle is "If it is in our power to prevent something bad from happening, without thereby sacrificing anything of *comparable* moral importance, we ought, morally, to do it" (emphasis added). The weak principle is "If it is in our power to prevent something very bad from happening, without thereby sacrificing anything *morally significant,* we ought, morally, to do it" (emphasis added). Singer believes that the strong principle is correct, but he is content to argue for the weaker one, which if adhered to would result in vast changes in our lifestyles. Singer intends his principles to be applicable to a wide spectrum of moral theories, but they have been interpreted as being founded on a utilitarian perspective.

In our fourth selection, "Reason and Morality in a World of Limited Food," Richard Watson argues from a deontological perspective that in a world of scarcity the principle of equity demands that we share our food equally even if it leads to universal malnourishment or the extinction of the human race. For a discussion of Watson's article, I refer you to the companion volume to this reader (Chapter 10, World Hunger).

In the final article John Arthur argues that Singer's utilitarian principles fail to take into consideration the rights of the affluent. What is "morally significant" can vary from person to person. He sets forth an alternative theory wherein the principle of benevolence sometimes requires the affluent to come to the aid of the poor.

Note

1. Statistics in this chapter come from the U.N. Food and Agriculture Organization. Some of the discussion is based on Arthur Simon's *Bread for the World* (New York: Paulist Press, 1975).

CHAPTER 63

Lifeboat Ethics: The Case Against Helping the Poor

GARRETT HARDIN

Garrett Hardin is professor emeritus of biology at the University of California at Santa Barbara and one of the leading environmental scientists of our age. He is the author of several books, including *Population, Evolution and Birth Control* (1969), *The Limits of Altruism: An Ecologist's View of Survival* (1972), and *Promethean Ethics: Living with Death, Competition and Triage* (1980).

Hardin argues that the proper metaphor that characterizes our global ecological situation is not "spaceship" but "lifeboat." The spaceship metaphor is misleading since the earth has no captain to steer it through its present and future problems. Rather, each rich nation is like a lifeboat in an ocean in which the poor of the world are swimming and in danger of drowning. Hardin argues that affluent societies, like people in lifeboats, ought to ensure their own survival by preserving a safety factor of resources. Giving away their resources to needy nations or admitting needy immigrants is like taking on additional passengers who would threaten to cause the lifeboat to capsize. Under these conditions it is our moral duty to refrain from aiding the poor.

ENVIRONMENTALISTS USE the metaphor of the earth as a "spaceship" in trying to persuade countries, industries and people to stop wasting and polluting our natural resources. Since we all share life on this planet, they argue, no single person or institution has the right to destroy, waste, or use more than a fair share of its resources.

But does everyone on earth have an equal right to an equal share of its resources? The spaceship metaphor can be dangerous when used by misguided idealists to justify suicidal policies for sharing our resources through uncontrolled immigration and foreign aid. In their enthusiastic but unrealistic generosity, they confuse the ethics of a spaceship with those of a lifeboat.

A true spaceship would have to be under the control of a captain, since no ship could possibly survive if its course were determined by committee. Spaceship Earth certainly has no captain; the United Nations is merely a toothless tiger, with little power to enforce any policy upon its bickering members.

If we divide the world crudely into rich nations and poor nations, two thirds of them are desperately poor, and only one third comparatively rich, with the United States the wealthiest of all. Metaphorically each rich nation can be seen as a lifeboat full of comparatively rich

 Reprinted from "Living on a Lifeboat," Bioscience *24 (1974) by permission.*

people. In the ocean outside each lifeboat swim the poor of the world, who would like to get in, or at least to share some of the wealth. What should the lifeboat passengers do?

First, we must recognize the limited capacity of any lifeboat. For example, a nation's land has a limited capacity to support a population and as the current energy crisis has shown us, in some ways we have already exceeded the carrying capacity of our land.

Adrift in a Moral Sea

So here we sit, say fifty people in our lifeboat. To be generous, let us assume it has room for ten more, making a total capacity of sixty. Suppose the fifty of us in the lifeboat see 100 others swimming in the water outside, begging for admission to our boat or for handouts. We have several options: we may be tempted to try to live by the Christian ideal of being "our brother's keeper," or by the Marxist ideal of "to each according to his needs." Since the needs of all in the water are the same, and since they can all be seen as "our brothers," we could take them all into our boat, making a total of 150 in a boat designed for sixty. The boat swamps, everyone drowns. Complete justice, complete catastrophe.

Since the boat has an unused excess capacity of ten more passengers, we could admit just ten more to it. But which ten do we let in? How do we choose? Do we pick the best ten, the neediest ten, "first come, first served"? And what do we say to the ninety we exclude? If we do let an extra ten into our lifeboat, we will have lost our "safety factor," an engineering principle of critical importance. For example, if we don't leave room for excess capacity as a safety factor in our country's agriculture, a new plant disease or a bad change in the weather could have disastrous consequences.

Suppose we decide to preserve our small safety factor and admit no more to the lifeboat.

Our survival is then possible, although we shall have to be constantly on guard against boarding parties.

While this last solution clearly offers the only means of our survival, it is morally abhorrent to many people. Some say they feel guilty about their good luck. My reply is simple: "Get out and yield your place to others." This may solve the problem of the guilt-ridden person's conscience, but it does not change the ethics of the lifeboat. The needy person to whom the guilt-ridden person yields his place will not himself feel guilty about his good luck. If he did, he would not climb aboard. The net result of conscience-stricken people giving up their unjustly held seats is the elimination of that sort of conscience from the lifeboat.

This is the basic metaphor within which we must work out our solutions. Let us now enrich the image, step by step, with substantive additions from the real world, a world that must solve real and pressing problems of overpopulation and hunger.

The harsh ethics of the lifeboat become even harsher when we consider the reproductive differences between the rich nations and the poor nations. The people inside the lifeboats are doubling in numbers every eighty-seven years; those swimming around outside are doubling, on the average, every thirty-five years, more than twice as fast as the rich. And since the world's resources are dwindling, the difference in prosperity between the rich and the poor can only increase.

As of 1973, the U.S. had a population of 210 million people, who were increasing by 0.8 percent per year. Outside our lifeboat, let us imagine another 210 million people, (say the combined populations of Colombia, Ecuador, Venezuela, Morocco, Pakistan, Thailand and the Philippines) who are increasing at a rate of 3.3 percent per year. Put differently, the doubling time for this aggregate population is twenty-one years, compared to eighty-seven years for the U.S.

Multiplying the Rich and the Poor

Now suppose the U.S. agreed to pool its resources with those seven countries, with everyone receiving an equal share. Initially the ratio of Americans to non-Americans in this model would be one-to-one. But consider what the ratio would be after eighty-seven years, by which time the Americans would have doubled to a population of 420 million. By then, doubling every twenty-one years, the other group would have swollen to 354 billion. Each American would have to share the available resources with more than eight people.

But, one could argue, this discussion assumes that current population trends will continue, and they may not. Quite so. Most likely the rate of population increase will decline much faster in the U.S. than it will in the other countries, and there does not seem to be much we can do about it. In sharing with "each according to his needs," we must recognize that needs are determined by population size, which is determined by the rate of reproduction, which at present is regarded as a sovereign right of every nation, poor or not. This being so, the philanthropic load created by the sharing ethic of the spaceship can only increase.

The Tragedy of the Commons

The fundamental error of spaceship ethics, and the sharing it requires, is that it leads to what I call "the tragedy of the commons." Under a system of private property, the men who own property recognize their responsibility to care for it, for if they don't they will eventually suffer. A farmer, for instance, will allow no more cattle in a pasture than its carrying capacity justifies. If he overloads it, erosion sets in, weeds take over, and he loses the use of the pasture.

If a pasture becomes a commons open to all, the right of each to use it may not be matched by a corresponding responsibility to protect it. Asking everyone to use it with discretion will hardly do, for the considerate herdsman who refrains from overloading the commons suffers more than a selfish one who says his needs are greater. If everyone would restrain himself, all would be well; but it takes only one less than everyone to ruin a system of voluntary restraint. In a crowded world of less than perfect human beings, mutual ruin is inevitable if there are no controls. This is the tragedy of the commons.

One of the major tasks of education today should be the creation of such an acute awareness of the dangers of the commons that people will recognize its many varieties. For example, the air and water have become polluted because they are treated as commons. Further growth in the population or per capita conversion of natural resources into pollutants will only make the problem worse. The same holds true for the fish of the oceans. Fishing fleets have nearly disappeared in many parts of the world, technological improvements in the art of fishing are hastening the day of complete ruin. Only the replacement of the system of the commons with a responsible system of control will save the land, air, water and oceanic fisheries.

The World Food Bank

In recent years there has been a push to create a new commons called a World Food Bank, an international depository of food reserves to which nations would contribute according to their abilities and from which they would draw according to their needs. This humanitarian proposal has received support from many liberal international groups, and from such prominent citizens as Margaret Mead, U.N. Secretary General Kurt Waldheim, and Senators Edward Kennedy and George McGovern.

A world food bank appeals powerfully to our humanitarian impulses. But before we rush ahead with such a plan, let us recognize where the greatest political push comes from, lest we be disillusioned later. Our experience with the "Food for Peace program," or Public Law 480, gives us the answer. This program moved billions of dollars worth of U.S. surplus grain to food-short, population-long countries during the past two decades. But when P.L. 480 first became law, a headline in the business magazine *Forbes* revealed the real power behind it: "Feeding the World's Hungry Millions: How It Will Mean Billions for U.S. Business."

And indeed it did. In the years 1960 to 1970, U.S. taxpayers spent a total of $7.9 billion on the Food for Peace program. Between 1948 and 1970, they also paid an additional $50 billion for other economic-aid programs, some of which went for food and food-producing machinery and technology. Though all U.S. taxpayers were forced to contribute to the cost of P.L. 480, certain special interest groups gained handsomely under the program. Farmers did not have to contribute the grain; the Government, or rather the taxpayers, bought it from them at full market prices. The increased demand raised prices of farm products generally. The manufacturers of farm machinery, fertilizers and pesticides benefited by the farmers' extra efforts to grow more food. Grain elevators profited from storing the surplus until it could be shipped. Railroads made money hauling it to ports, and shipping lines profited from carrying it overseas. The implementation of P.L. 480 required the creation of a vast Government bureaucracy, which then acquired its own vested interest in continuing the program regardless of its merits.

Extracting Dollars

Those who proposed and defended the Food for Peace program in public rarely mentioned its importance to any of these special interests. The public emphasis was always on its humanitarian effects. The combination of silent selfish interests and highly vocal humanitarian apologists made a powerful and successful lobby for extracting money from taxpayers. We can expect the same lobby to push now for the creation of a World Food Bank.

However great the potential benefit to selfish interests, it should not be a decisive argument against a truly humanitarian program. We must ask if such a program would actually do more good than harm, not only momentarily but also in the long run. Those who propose the food bank usually refer to a current "emergency" or "crisis" in terms of world food supply. But what is an emergency? Although they may be infrequent and sudden, everyone knows that emergencies will occur from time to time. A well-run family, company, organization or country prepares for the likelihood of accidents and emergencies. It expects them, it budgets for them, it saves for them.

Learning the Hard Way

What happens if some organizations or countries budget for accidents and others do not? If each country is solely responsible for its own well-being, poorly managed ones will suffer. But they can learn from experience. They may mend their ways, and learn to budget for infrequent but certain emergencies. For example, the weather varies from year to year, and periodic crop failures are certain. A wise and competent government saves out of the production of the good years in anticipation of bad years to come. Joseph taught this policy to Pharaoh in Egypt more than 2,000 years ago. Yet the great majority of the governments in the world today do not follow such a policy. They lack either the wisdom or the competence, or both. Should those nations that do manage to put something aside be forced to come to the rescue each time an emergency occurs among the poor nations?

"But it isn't their fault!" some kindhearted liberals argue. "How can we blame the poor people who are caught in an emergency? Why must they suffer for the sins of their governments?" The concept of blame is simply not relevant here. The real question is, what are the operational consequences of establishing a world food bank? If it is open to every country every time a need develops, slovenly rulers will not be motivated to take Joseph's advice. Someone will always come to their aid. Some countries will deposit food in the world food bank, and others will withdraw it. There will be almost no overlap. As a result of such solutions to food shortage emergencies, the poor countries will not learn to mend their ways, and will suffer progressively greater emergencies as their populations grow.

The Ratchet Effect

An "international food bank" is really, then, not a true bank but a disguised oneway transfer device for moving wealth from rich countries to poor. In the absence of such a bank, in a world inhabited by individually responsible sovereign nations, the population of each nation would repeatedly go through a cycle of the sort shown in Figure 1. P_2 is greater than P_1, either in absolute numbers or because a deterioration of the food supply has removed the safety factor and and produced a dangerously low ratio of resources to population. P_2 may be said to represent a state of overpopulation which becomes obvious upon the appearance of an "accident," e.g., a crop failure. If the "emergency" is not met by outside help, the population drops back to the "normal" level—the "carrying capacity" of the environment—or even below. In the absence of population control by a sovereign, sooner or later the population grows to P_2 again and the cycle repeats. The long-term population curve is an irregularly fluctuating one, equilibrating more or less about the carrying capacity.

A demographic cycle of this sort obviously involves great suffering in the restrictive phase, but such a cycle is normal to any independent country with inadequate population control. The third century theologian Tertullian expressed what must have been the recognition of many wise men when he wrote: "The scourges of pestilence, famine, wars, and earthquakes have come to be regarded as a blessing to overcrowded nations, since they serve to prune away the luxuriant growth of the human race."

Only under a strong and farsighted sovereign—which theoretically could be the people themselves, democratically organized—can a population equilibrate at some set point below the carrying capacity, thus avoiding the pains normally caused by periodic and unavoidable disasters. For this happy state to be achieved it is necessary that those in power be able to contemplate with equanimity the "waste" of surplus food in times of bountiful harvests. It is essential that those in power resist the temptation to convert extra food into extra babies. On the public relations level it is necessary that the phrase "surplus food" be replaced by "safety factor."

Figure 1

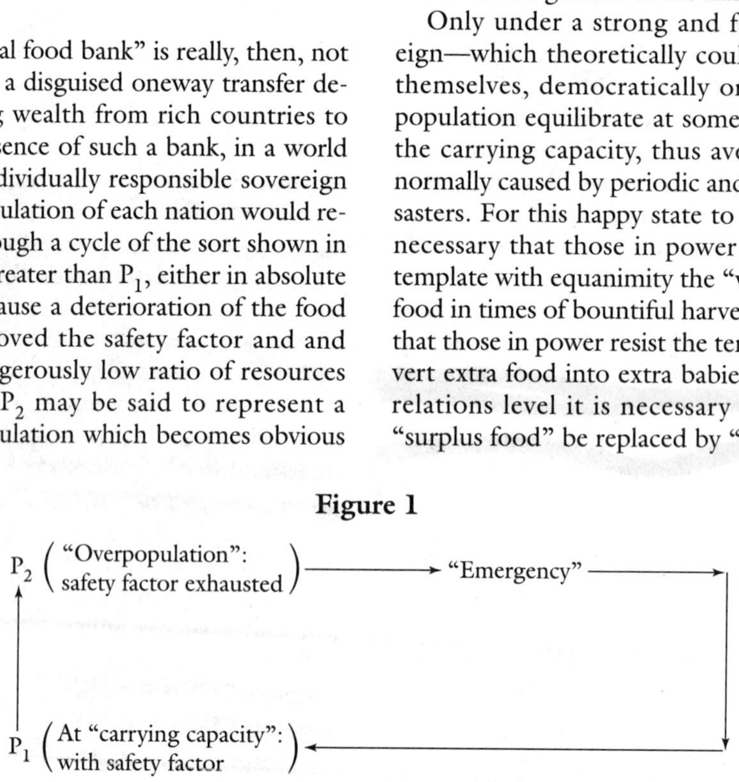

But wise sovereigns seem not to exist in the poor world today. The most anguishing problems are created by poor countries that are governed by rulers insufficiently wise and powerful. If such countries can draw on a world food bank in times of "emergency," the population *cycle* of Figure 1 will be replaced by the population *escalator* of Figure 2. The input of food from a food bank acts as the pawl of a rachet, preventing the population from retracing its steps to a lower level. Reproduction pushes the population upward, inputs from the world bank prevent its moving downward. Population size escalates, as does the absolute magnitude of "accidents" and "emergencies." The process is brought to an end only by the total collapse of the whole system, producing a catastrophe of scarcely imaginable proportions.

Such are the implications of the well-meant sharing of food in a world of irresponsible reproduction. . . .

Population Control the Crude Way

On the average, poor countries undergo a 2.5 percent increase in population each year; rich countries, about 0.8 percent. Only rich countries have anything in the way of food reserves

set aside, and even they do not have as much as they should. Poor countries have none. If poor countries received no food from the outside, the rate of their population growth would be periodically checked by crop failures and famines. But if they can always draw on a world food bank in time of need, their population can continue to grow unchecked, and so will their "need" for aid. In the short run, a world food bank may diminish that need, but in the long run it actually increases the need without limit.

Without some system of worldwide food sharing, the proportion of people in the rich and poor nations might eventually stabilize. The overpopulated poor countries would decrease in numbers, while the rich countries that had room for more people would increase. But with a well-meaning system of sharing, such as a world food bank, the growth differential between the rich and the poor countries will not only persist, it will increase. Because of the higher rate of population growth in the poor countries of the world, 88 percent of today's children are born poor, and only 12 percent rich. Year by year the ratio becomes worse, as the fast-reproducing poor outnumber the slow-reproducing rich.

A world food bank is thus a commons in disguise. People will have more motivation to draw from it than to add to any common store. The less provident and less able will multiply at the

Figure 2

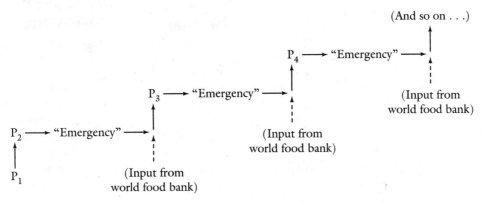

expense of the abler and more provident, bringing eventual ruin upon all who share in the commons. Besides, any system of "sharing" that amounts to foreign aid from the rich nations to the poor nations will carry the taint of charity, which will contribute little to the world peace so devoutly desired by those who support the idea of a world food bank.

As past U.S. foreign-aid programs have amply and depressingly demonstrated, international charity frequently inspires mistrust and antagonism rather than gratitude on the part of the recipient nation.

Chinese Fish and Miracle Rice

The modern approach to foreign aid stresses the export of technology and advice, rather than money and food. As an ancient Chinese proverb goes: "'Give a man a fish and he will eat for a day; teach him how to fish and he will eat for the rest of his days." Acting on this advice, the Rockefeller and Ford Foundations have financed a number of programs for improving agriculture in the hungry nations. Known as the "Green Revolution," these programs have led to the development of "miracle rice" and "miracle wheat," new strains that offer bigger harvests and greater resistance to crop damage. Norman Borlaug, the Nobel Prize winning agronomist who, supported by the Rockefeller Foundation, developed "miracle wheat," is one of the most prominent advocates of a world food bank.

Whether or not the Green Revolution can increase food production as much as its champions claim is a debatable but possibly irrelevant point. Those who support this well-intended humanitarian effort should first consider some of the fundamentals of human ecology. Ironically, one man who did was the late Alan Gregg, a vice president of the Rockefeller Foundation. Two decades ago he expressed strong doubts about the wisdom of such attempts to increase food

production. He likened the growth and spread of humanity over the surface of the earth to the spread of cancer in the human body, remarking that "cancerous growths demand food; but, as far as I know, they have never been cured by getting it."

Overloading the Environment

Every human born constitutes a draft on all aspects of the environment: food, air, water, forests, beaches, wildlife, scenery and solitude. Food can, perhaps, be significantly increased to meet a growing demand. But what about clean beaches, unspoiled forests, and solitude? If we satisfy a growing population's need for food, we necessarily decrease its per capita supply of the other resources needed by men.

India, for example, now has a population of 600 million, which increases by 15 million each year. This population already puts a huge load on a relatively impoverished environment. The country's forests are now only a small fraction of what they were three centuries ago, and floods and erosion continually destroy the insufficient farmland that remains. Every one of the 15 million new lives added to India's population puts an additional burden on the environment, and increases the economic and social costs of crowding. However humanitarian our intent, every Indian life saved through medical or nutritional assistance from abroad diminishes the quality of life for those who remain, and for subsequent generations. If rich countries make it possible, through foreign aid, for 600 million Indians to swell to 1.2 billion in a mere twenty-eight years, as their current growth rate threatens, will future generations of Indians thank us for hastening the destruction of their environment? Will our good intentions be sufficient excuse for the consequences of our actions?

My final example of a commons in action is one for which the public has the least desire for rational discussion—immigration. Anyone who publicly questions the wisdom of current U.S. immigration policy is promptly charged with bigotry, prejudice, ethnocentrism, chauvinism, isolationism or selfishness. Rather than encounter such accusations, one would rather talk about other matters, leaving immigration policy to wallow in the crosscurrents of special interests that take no account of the good of the whole, or the interests of posterity.

Perhaps we still feel guilty about things we said in the past. Two generations ago the popular press frequently referred to Dagos, Wops, Polacks, Chinks and Krauts, in articles about how America was being "overrun" by foreigners of supposedly inferior genetic stock. But because the implied inferiority of foreigners was used then as justification for keeping them out, people now assume that restrictive policies could only be based on such misguided notions. There are other grounds.

A Nation of Immigrants

Just consider the numbers involved. Our Government acknowledges a net inflow of 400,000 immigrants a year. While we have no hard data on the extent of illegal entries, educated guesses put the figure at about 600,000 a year. Since the natural increase (excess of births over deaths) of the resident population now runs about 1.7 million per year, the yearly gain from immigration amounts to at least 19 percent of the total annual increase, and may be as much as 37 percent if we include the estimate for illegal immigrants. Considering the growing use of birth-control devices, the potential effect of educational campaigns by such organizations as Planned Parenthood Federation of America and Zero Population Growth, and the influence of inflation and the housing shortage, the fertility rate of American women may decline so much that immigration could account for all the yearly increase in

population. Should we not at least ask if that is what we want?

For the sake of those who worry about whether the "quality" of the average immigrant compares favorably with the quality of the average resident, let us assume that immigrants and nativeborn citizens are of exactly equal quality, however one defines that term. We will focus here only on quantity; and since our conclusions will depend on nothing else, all charges of bigotry and chauvinism become irrelevant.

Immigration vs. Food Supply

World food banks *move food to the people,* hastening the exhaustion of the environment of the poor countries. Unrestricted immigration, on the other hand, *moves people to the food,* thus speeding up the destruction of the environment of the rich countries. We can easily understand why poor people should want to make this latter transfer, but why should rich hosts encourage it?

As in the case of foreign-aid programs, immigration receives support from selfish interests and humanitarian impulses. The primary selfish interest in unimpeded immigration is the desire of employers for cheap labor, particularly in industries and trades that offer degrading work. In the past, one wave of foreigners after another was brought into the U.S. to work at wretched jobs for wretched wages. In recent years the Cubans, Puerto Ricans and Mexicans have had this dubious honor. The interests of the employers of cheap labor mesh well with the guilty silence of the country's liberal intelligentsia. White Anglo-Saxon Protestants are particularly reluctant to call for a closing of the doors to immigration for fear of being called bigots.

But not all countries have such reluctant leadership. Most educated Hawaiians, for example, are keenly aware of the limits of their environment, particularly in terms of population growth. There is only so much room on the islands, and the islanders know it. To Hawaiians, immigrants from the other forty-nine states present as great a threat as those from other nations. At a recent meeting of Hawaiian government officials in Honolulu, I had the ironic delight of hearing a speaker, who like most of his audience was of Japanese ancestry, ask how the country might practically and constitutionally close its doors to further immigration. One member of the audience countered: "How can we shut the doors now? We have many friends and relatives in Japan that we'd like to bring here some day so that they can enjoy Hawaii too." The Japanese-American speaker smiled sympathetically and answered: "Yes, but we have children now, and someday we'll have grandchildren too. We can bring more people here from Japan only by giving away some of the land that we hope to pass on to our grandchildren some day. What right do we have to do that?"

At this point, I can hear U.S. liberals asking: "How can you justify slamming the door once you're inside? You say that immigrants should be kept out. But aren't we all immigrants, or the descendents of immigrants? If we insist on staying, must we not admit all others?" Our craving for intellectual order leads us to seek and prefer symmetrical rules and morals: a single rule for me and everybody else; the same rule yesterday, today, and tomorrow. Justice, we feel, should not change with time and place.

We Americans of non-Indian ancestry can look upon ourselves as the descendants of thieves who are guilty morally, if not legally, of stealing this land from its Indian owners. Should we then give back the land to the now living American descendants of those Indians? However morally or logically sound this proposal may be, I, for one, am unwilling to live by it and I know no one else who is. Besides, the logical consequence would be absurd. Suppose that, intoxicated with a sense of pure justice, we should decide to turn our land over to the Indians.

Since all our wealth has also been derived from the land, wouldn't we be morally obliged to give that back to the Indians too?

Pure Justice vs. Reality

Clearly, the concept of pure justice produces an infinite regression to absurdity. Centuries ago, wise men invented statutes of limitations to justify the rejection of such pure justice, in the interest of preventing continual disorder. The law zealously defends property rights, but only relatively recent property rights. Drawing a line after an arbitrary time has elapsed may be unjust, but the alternatives are worse.

We are all the descendants of thieves, and the world's resources are inequitably distributed. But we must begin the journey to tomorrow from the point where we are today. We cannot remake the past. We cannot safely divide the wealth equitably among all peoples so long as people reproduce at different rates. To do so would guarantee that our grandchildren, and everyone else's grandchildren, would have only a ruined world to inhabit.

To be generous with one's own possessions is quite different from being generous with those of posterity. We should call this point to the attention of those who, from a commendable love of justice and equality, would institute a system of the commons, either in the form of a world food bank, or of unrestricted immigration. We must convince them if we wish to save at least some parts of the world from environmental ruin.

Without a true world government to control reproduction and the use of available resources, the sharing ethic of the spaceship is impossible. For the foreseeable future, our survival demands that we govern our actions by the ethics of a lifeboat, harsh though they may be. Posterity will be satisfied with nothing less.

Study Questions

1. What is Hardin's case against helping poor, needy countries? What is the significance of the lifeboat metaphor?
2. What is the relationship of population policies to world hunger?
3. Explain the "ratchet effect." Do you agree with Hardin that in bringing aid to countries who do not control their population we act immorally?

CHAPTER 64

Population and Food: Metaphors and the Reality

WILLIAM W. MURDOCH AND ALLAN OATEN

William W. Murdoch is professor of biological science at the University of California at Santa Barbara and is the author of *Environment: Resources, Pollution and Society* (2d ed., 1975). Allan Oaten is also a biologist who has taught at the University of California at Santa Barbara and who specializes in mathematical biology and statistics.

Murdoch and Oaten begin by attacking Hardin's metaphors of lifeboat, commons, and ratchet as misleading. They then argue that other factors are needed to understand the population and hunger problem, including parental confidence in the future, low infant-mortality rates, literacy, health care, income and employment, and an adequate diet. They claim that once the socioeconomic conditions are attended to, population size will take care of itself. Nonmilitary foreign aid to third world countries is both just and necessary if we are to prevent global disaster.

Misleading Metaphors

[Hardin's] "lifeboat" article actually has two messages. The first is that our immigration policy is too generous. This will not concern us here. The second, and more important, is that by helping poor nations we will bring disaster to rich and poor alike:

> Metaphorically, each rich nation amounts to a lifeboat full of comparatively rich people. The poor of the world are in other, much more crowded lifeboats. Continuously, so to speak, the poor fall out of their lifeboats and swim for a while in the water outside, hoping to be admitted to a rich lifeboat, or in some other way to benefit from the "goodies" on board. What should the passengers on a rich lifeboat do? This is the central problem of "the ethics of a lifeboat."
> (Hardin, 1974, p. 561)

Among these so-called "goodies" are food supplies and technical aid such as that which led to the Green Revolution. Hardin argues that we should withhold such resources from poor nations on the grounds that they help to maintain high rates of population increase, thereby making the problem worse. He foresees the continued supplying and increasing production of food as a process that will be "brought to an end only by the total collapse of the whole system, producing a catastrophe of scarcely imaginable proportions" (p. 564).

Turning to one particular mechanism for distributing these resources, Hardin claims that a world food bank is a commons—people have more motivation to draw from it than to add to it; it will have a ratchet or escalator effect on population because inputs from it will prevent population declines in over-populated countries.

Reprinted from "Population and Food: Metaphors and the Reality," Bioscience 25 (1975) by *permission.*

Thus "wealth can be steadily moved in one direction only, from the slowly-breeding rich to the rapidly-breeding poor, the process finally coming to a halt only when all countries are equally and miserably poor" (p. 565). Thus our help will not only bring ultimate disaster to poor countries, but it will also be suicidal for us.

As for the "benign demographic transition" to low birth rates, which some aid supporters have predicted, Hardin states flatly that the weight of evidence is against this possibility.

Finally, Hardin claims that the plight of poor nations is partly their own fault: "wise sovereigns seem not to exist in the poor world today. The most anguishing problems are created by poor countries that are governed by rulers insufficiently wise and powerful." Establishing a world food bank will exacerbate this problem: "slovenly rulers" will escape the consequences of their incompetence—"Others will bail them out whenever they are in trouble"; "Far more difficult than the transfer of wealth from one country to another is the transfer of wisdom between sovereign powers or between generations" (p. 563).

What arguments does Hardin present in support of these opinions? Many involve metaphors: lifeboat, commons, and ratchet or escalator. These metaphors are crucial to his thesis, and it is, therefore, important for us to examine them critically.

The lifeboat is the major metaphor. It seems attractively simple, but it is in fact simplistic and obscures important issues. As soon as we try to use it to compare various policies, we find that most relevant details of the actual situation are either missing or distorted in the lifeboat metaphor. Let us list some of these details.

Most important, perhaps, Hardin's lifeboats barely interact. The rich lifeboats may drop some handouts over the side and perhaps repel a boarding party now and then, but generally they live their own lives. In the real world, nations interact a great deal, in ways that affect food supply and population size and growth, and the ef-

fect of rich nations on poor nations has been strong and not always benevolent.

First, by colonization and actual wars of commerce, and through the international marketplace, rich nations have arranged an exchange of goods that has maintained and even increased the economic imbalance between rich and poor nations. Until recently we have taken or otherwise obtained cheap raw material from poor nations and sold them expensive manufactured goods that they cannot make themselves. In the United States, the structure of tariffs and internal subsidies discriminates selectively against poor nations. In poor countries, the concentration on cash crops rather than on food crops, a legacy of colonial times, is now actively encouraged by western multinational corporations (Barraclough 1975). Indeed, it is claimed that in famine-stricken Sahelian Africa, multinational agribusiness has recently taken land out of food production for cash crops (Transnational Institute 1974). Although we often self-righteously take the "blame" for lowering the death rates of poor nations during the 1940s and 1950s, we are less inclined to accept responsibility for the effects of actions that help maintain poverty and hunger. Yet poverty directly contributes to the high birth rates that Hardin views with such alarm.

Second, U.S. foreign policy, including foreign aid programs, has favored "pro-Western" regimes, many of which govern in the interests of a wealthy elite and some of which are savagely repressive. Thus, it has often subsidized a gross maldistribution of income and has supported political leaders who have opposed most of the social changes that can lead to reduced birth rates. In this light, Hardin's pronouncements on the alleged wisdom gap between poor leaders and our own, and the difficulty of filling it, appear as a grim joke: our response to leaders with the power and wisdom Hardin yearns for has often been to try to replace them or their policies as soon as possible. Selective giving and withholding of both military and nonmilitary aid has been an important ingredient of our efforts to maintain political leaders we like and to remove those we do not. Brown (1974b), after noting that the withholding of U.S. food aid in 1973 contributed to the downfall of the Allende government in Chile, comments that "although Americans decry the use of petroleum as a political weapon, calling it 'political blackmail,' the United States has been using food aid for political purposes for twenty years—and describing this as 'enlightened diplomacy.'"

Both the quantity and the nature of the supplies on a lifeboat are fixed. In the real world, the quantity has strict limits, but these are far from having been reached (University of California Food Task Force 1974). Nor are we forced to devote fixed proportions of our efforts and energy to automobile travel, pet food, packaging, advertising, corn-fed beef, "defense" and other diversions, many of which cost far more than foreign aid does. The fact is that enough food is now produced to feed the world's population adequately. That people are malnourished is due to distribution and to economics, not to agricultural limits (United Nations Economic and Social Council 1974).

Hardin's lifeboats are divided merely into rich and poor, and it is difficult to talk about birth rates on either. In the real world, however, there are striking differences among the birth rates of the poor countries and even among the birth rates of different parts of single countries. These differences appear to be related to social conditions (also absent from lifeboats) and may guide us to effective aid policies.

Hardin's lifeboat metaphor not only conceals facts, but misleads about the effects of his proposals. The rich lifeboat can raise the ladder and sail away. But in real life, the problem will not necessarily go away just because it is ignored. In the real world, there are armies, raw materials in poor nations, and even outraged domestic dissidents prepared to sacrifice their own and others' lives to oppose policies they regard as immoral.

No doubt there are other objections. But even this list shows the lifeboat metaphor to be dangerously inappropriate for serious policy making because it obscures far more than it reveals. Lifeboats and "lifeboat ethics" may be useful topics for those who are shipwrecked; we believe they are worthless—indeed detrimental—in discussions of food-population questions.

The ratchet metaphor is equally flawed. It, too, ignores complex interactions between birth rates and social conditions (including diets), implying as it does that more food will simply mean more babies. Also, it obscures the fact that the decrease in death rates has been caused at least as much by developments such as DDT, improved sanitation, and medical advances, as by increased food supplies, so that cutting out food aid will not necessarily lead to population declines.

The lifeboat article is strangely inadequate in other ways. For example, it shows an astonishing disregard for recent literature. The claim that we can expect no "benign demographic transition" is based on a review written more than a decade ago (Davis 1963). Yet, events and attitudes are changing rapidly in poor countries: for the first time in history, most poor people live in countries with birth control programs; with few exceptions, poor nations are somewhere on the demographic transition to lower birth rates (Demeny 1974); the population-food squeeze is now widely recognized, and governments of poor nations are aware of the relationship. Again, there is a considerable amount of evidence that birth rates can fall rapidly in poor countries given the proper social conditions (as we will discuss later); consequently, crude projections of current population growth rates are quite inadequate for policy making.

The Tragedy of the Commons

Throughout the lifeboat article, Hardin bolsters his assertions by reference to the "commons" (Hardin 1968). The thesis of the commons, therefore, needs critical evaluation.

Suppose several privately owned flocks, comprising 100 sheep altogether, are grazing on a public commons. They bring in an annual income of $1.00 per sheep. Fred, a herdsman, owns only one sheep. He decides to add another. But 101 is too many: the commons is overgrazed and produces less food. The sheep lose quality and income drops to 90¢ per sheep. Total income is now $90.90 instead of $100.00. Adding the sheep has brought an overall loss. But Fred has gained: *his* income is $1.80 instead of $1.00. The gain from the additional sheep, which is his alone, outweighs the loss from overgrazing, which he shares. Thus he promotes his interest at the expense of the community.

This is the problem of the commons, which seems on the way to becoming an archetype. Hardin, in particular, is not inclined to underrate its importance: "One of the major tasks of education today is to create such an awareness of the dangers of the commons that people will be able to recognize its many varieties, however disguised" (Hardin 1974, p. 562) and "All this is terribly obvious once we are acutely aware of the pervasiveness and danger of the commons. But many people still lack this awareness . . ." (p. 565).

The "commons" affords a handy way of classifying problems: the lifeboat article reveals that sharing, a generous immigration policy, world food banks, air, water, the fish populations of the ocean, and the western range lands are, or produce, a commons. It is also handy to be able to dispose of policies one does not like and "only a particular instance of a class of policies that are in error because they lead to the tragedy of the commons" (p. 561).

But no metaphor, even one as useful as this, should be treated with such awe. Such shorthand can be useful, but it can also mislead by discouraging and obscuring important detail. To dismiss a proposal by suggesting that "all you need to know about this proposal is that it institutes a commons and is, therefore, bad" is to as-

sert that the proposed commons is worse than the original problem. This might be so if the problem of the commons were, indeed, a tragedy—that is, if it were insoluble. But it is not.

Hardin favors private ownership as the solution (either through private property or the selling of pollution rights). But, of course, there are solutions other than private ownership; and private ownership itself is no guarantee of carefully husbanded resources.

One alternative to private ownership of the commons is communal ownership of the sheep—or, in general, of the mechanisms and industries that exploit the resource—combined with communal planning for management. (Note, again, how the metaphor favors one solution: perhaps the "tragedy" lay not in the commons but in the sheep. "The Tragedy of the Privately Owned Sheep" lacks zing, unfortunately.) Public ownership of a commons has been tried in Peru to the benefit of the previously privately owned anchoveta fishery (Gulland 1975). The communally owned agriculture of China does not seem to have suffered any greater over-exploitation than that of other Asian nations.

Another alternative is cooperation combined with regulation. For example, Gulland (1975) has shown that Antarctic whale stocks (perhaps the epitome of a commons since they are internationally exploited and no one owns them) are now being properly managed, and stocks are increasing. This has been achieved through cooperation in the International Whaling Commission, which has by agreement set limits to the catch of each nation.

In passing, Hardin's private ownership argument is not generally applicable to nonrenewable resources. Given discount rates, technology substitutes, and no more than an average regard for posterity, privately owned nonrenewable resources, like oil, coal and minerals, are mined at rates that produce maximum profits, rather than at those rates that preserve them for future generations. . . .

Birth Rates: An Alternative View

Is the food-population spiral inevitable? A more optimistic, if less comfortable, hypothesis, presented by Rich (1973) and Brown (1974a), is increasingly tenable: contrary to the "ratchet" projection, population growth rates are affected by many complex conditions beside food supply. In particular, a set of socioeconomic conditions can be identified that motivate parents to have fewer children; under these conditions, birth rates can fall quite rapidly, sometimes even before birth control technology is available. Thus, population growth can be controlled more effectively by intelligent human intervention that sets up the appropriate conditions than by doing nothing and trusting to "natural population cycles."

These conditions are: parental confidence about the future, an improved status of women, and literacy. They require low infant mortality rates, widely available rudimentary health care, increased income and employment, and an adequate diet above subsistence levels. Expenditure on schools (especially elementary schools), appropriate health services (especially rural paramedical services), and agricultural reform (especially aid to small farmers) will be needed, and foreign aid can help here. It is essential that these improvements be spread across the population; aid can help here, too, by concentrating on the poor nations' poorest people, encouraging necessary institutional and social reforms, and making it easier for poor nations to use their own resources and initiative to help themselves. It is *not* necessary that per capita GNP be very high, certainly not as high as that of the rich countries during their gradual demographic transition. In other words, low birth rates in poor countries are achievable long before the conditions exist that were present in the rich countries in the late 19th and early 20th centuries.

Twenty or thirty years is not long to discover and assess the factors affecting birth rates, but a body of evidence is now accumulating in favor of this hypothesis. Rich (1973) and Brown (1974a) show that at least 10 developing countries have managed to reduce their birth rates by an average of more than one birth per 1,000 population per year for periods of 5 to 16 years. A reduction of one birth per 1,000 per year would bring birth rates in poor countries to a rough replacement level of about 16/1,000 by the turn of the century, though age distribution effects would prevent a smooth population decline. We have listed these countries in Table 1, together with three other nations, including China, that are poor and yet have brought their birth rates down to 30 or less, presumably from rates of over 40 a decade or so ago.

These data show that rapid reduction in birth rates is possible in the developing world. No doubt it can be argued that each of these cases is in some way special. Hong Kong and Singapore are relatively rich; they, Barbados, and Mauritius are also tiny. China is able to exert great social pressure on its citizens; but China is particularly significant. It is enormous; its per capita GNP is almost as low as India's; and it started out in 1949 with a terrible health system. Also, Egypt, Chile, Taiwan, Cuba, South Korea, and Sri Lanka are quite large, and they are poor or very poor (Table 1). In fact, these examples represent an enormous range of religion, political systems, and geography and suggest that such rates of decline in the birth rate can be achieved whenever the appropriate conditions are met. "The common factor in these countries is that the *majority* of the population has shared in the economic and social benefits of significant national progress. . . . [M]aking health, education and jobs more broadly available to lower income groups in poor countries contribute[s] significantly toward the motivation for smaller families that is the prerequisite of major reduction in birth rates" (Rich 1973).

The converse is also true. In Latin America, Cuba (annual per capita income $530), Chile ($720), Uruguay ($820), and Argentina ($1,160) have moderate to truly equitable dis-

Table 1   Declining birth rates and per capita income in selected developing countries. (These are crude birth rates, uncorrected for age distribution.)

| Country | Time Span | Births/1,000/year | | $ per capita per year 1973 |
		Avg. annual decline in crude birth rate	Crude birth rate 1972	
Barbados	1960–69	1.5	22	570
Taiwan	1955–71	1.2	24	390
Tunisia	1966–71	1.8	35	250
Mauritius	1961–71	1.5	25	240
Hong Kong	1960–72	1.4	19	970
Singapore	1955–72	1.2	23	920
Costa Rica	1963–72	1.5	32	560
South Korea	1960–70	1.2	29	250
Egypt	1966–70	1.7	37	210
Chile	1963–70	1.2	25	720
China			30	160
Cuba			27	530
Sri Lanka			30	110

tribution of goods and services and relatively low birth rates (27, 26, 23, and 22, respectively). In contrast, Brazil ($420), Mexico ($670), and Venezuela ($980) have very unequal distribution of goods and services and high birth rates (38, 42, and 41, respectively). Fertility rates in poor and relatively poor nations seem unlikely to fall as long as the bulk of the population does not share in increased benefits. . . .

. . . As a disillusioning quarter-century of aid giving has shown, the obstacles of getting aid to those segments of the population most in need of it are enormous. Aid has typically benefitted a small rich segment of society, partly because of the way aid programs have been designed but also because of human and institutional factors in the poor nations themselves (Owens and Shaw 1972). With some notable exceptions, the distribution of income and services in poor nations is extremely skewed—much more uneven than in rich countries. Indeed, much of the population is essentially outside the economic system. Breaking this pattern will be extremely

difficult. It will require not only aid that is designed specifically to benefit the rural poor, but also important institutional changes such as decentralization of decision making and the development of greater autonomy and stronger links to regional and national markets for local groups and industries such as cooperative farms.

Thus, two things are being asked of rich nations and of the United States in particular: to increase nonmilitary foreign aid, including food aid, and to give it in ways, and to governments, that will deliver it to the poorest people and will improve their access to national economic institutions. These are not easy tasks, particularly the second, and there is no guarantee that birth rates will come down quickly in all countries. Still, many poor countries have, in varying degrees, begun the process of reform, and recent evidence suggests that aid and reform together can do much to solve the twin problems of high birth rates and economic underdevelopment. The tasks are far from impossible. Based on the evidence, the policies dictated by a sense of decency are also the most realistic and rational.

References

Barraclough, G. "The Great World Crisis: I." *The N.Y. Review Books* 21 (1975): 20–29.

Brown, L. R. *In the Human Interest.* New York: W. W. Norton & Co., Inc., 1974a.

———. *By Bread Alone.* New York: Praeger, 1974b.

Davis, K. "Population." *Scientific American* 209, no. 3 (1963): 62–71.

Demeny, P. "The Populations of the Underdeveloped Countries." *Scientific American* 231, no. 3 (1974): 149–159.

Gulland, J. "The Harvest of the Sea." In *Environment: Resources, Pollution and Society,* ed. W. W. Murdoch. 2d ed. Sunderland, Mass: Sinauer Associates, 1975. 167–189.

Hardin, G. "The Tragedy of the Commons." *Science* 162 (1968): 1243–1248.

———. "Living on a Lifeboat." *BioScience* 24, no. 10 (1974): 561–568.

Owens, E., and R. Shaw. *Development Reconsidered.* Lexington, Mass.: D.C. Heath & Co., 1972.

Rich, W. *Smaller Families Through Social and Economic Progress.* Overseas Development Council. Washington, D.C. 1973. Monograph #7.

Teitelbaum, M. S. "Relevance of Demographic Transition Theory for Developing Countries." *Science* 188 (1975): 420–425.

Transnational Institute, *World Hunger: Causes and Remedies.* Institute for Policy Studies. Washington, D.C., 1974.

United Nations Economic and Social Council. *Assessment of Present Food Situation and Dimensions and Causes of Hunger and Malnutrition in the World.* E/Conf. 65/Prep/6, 8 May 1974.

University of California Food Task Force, Division of Agricultural Sciences. *A Hungry World: the Challenge to Agriculture.* 1974.

Study Questions

1. What are the criticisms leveled against Hardin's arguments?
2. What is Murdoch and Oaten's view on the question of population growth? What is the gradual demographic transition theory? Is their view plausible?
3. Compare Hardin's arguments with Murdoch and Oaten's response. Where does the evidence lie?

CHAPTER 65

Famine, Affluence, and Morality

PETER SINGER

Peter Singer (see Chapter 48 for a biographical sketch) argues that we have a duty to provide aid to famine victims and others who are suffering from hunger and poverty. He proposes two principles, a strong and a moderate one, which show that we have a duty to give substantial aid to those who are starving. The strong principle is, "if it is in our power to prevent something bad from happening, without thereby sacrificing anything of *comparable* moral importance, we ought, morally, to do it" (emphasis added). The weak principle is, "if it is in our power to prevent something very bad from happening, without thereby sacrificing anything *morally significant*, we ought, morally, to do it" (emphasis added).

As I write this, in November, 1971, people are dying in East Bengal from lack of food, shelter, and medical care. The suffering and death that are occurring there now are not inevitable, not unavoidable in any fatalistic sense of the term. Constant poverty, a cyclone, and a civil war have turned at least nine million people into destitute refugees; nevertheless, it is not beyond the capacity of the richer nations to give enough assistance to reduce any further suffering to very small proportions. The decisions and actions of human beings can prevent this kind of suffering. Unfortunately, human beings have not made the necessary decisions. At the individual level, people have, with very few exceptions, not responded to the situation in any significant way. Generally speaking, people have not given large sums to relief funds; they have not written to their parliamentary representatives demanding increased government assistance; they have not demonstrated in the streets, held symbolic fasts, or done anything else di-

rected toward providing the refugees with the means to satisfy their essential needs. At the government level, no government has given the sort of massive aid that would enable the refugees to survive for more than a few days. Britain, for instance, has given rather more than most countries. It has, to date, given £14,750,000. For comparative purposes, Britain's share of the nonrecoverable development costs of the Anglo–French Concorde project is already in excess of £275,000,000, and on present estimates will reach £440,000,000. The implication is that the British government values a supersonic transport more than thirty times as highly as it values the lives of the nine million refugees. Australia is another country which, on a per capita basis, is well up in the "aid to Bengal" table. Australia's aid, however, amounts to less than one-twelfth of the cost of Sydney's new opera house. The total amount given, from all sources, now stands at about £65,000,000. The estimated cost of keeping the refugees alive for one

"Famine, Affluence, and Morality," by Peter Singer, Philosophy and Public Affairs *1:3 (1972), pp. 229–243. Reprinted by permission of Princeton University Press.*

year is £464,000,000. Most of the refugees have now been in the camps for more than six months. The World Bank has said that India needs a minimum of £300,000,000 in assistance from other countries before the end of the year. It seems obvious that assistance on this scale will not be forthcoming. India will be forced to choose between letting the refugees starve or diverting funds from her own development program, which will mean that more of her own people will starve in the future.[1]

These are the essential facts about the present situation in Bengal. So far as it concerns us here, there is nothing unique about this situation except its magnitude. The Bengal emergency is just the latest and most acute of a series of major emergencies in various parts of the world, arising both from natural and from man-made causes. There are also many parts of the world in which people die from malnutrition and lack of food independent of any special emergency. I take Bengal as my example only because it is the present concern, and because the size of the problem has ensured that it has been given adequate publicity. Neither individuals nor governments can claim to be unaware of what is happening there.

What are the moral implications of a situation like this? In what follows, I shall argue that the way people in relatively affluent countries react to a situation like that in Bengal cannot be justified; indeed, the whole way we look at moral issues—our moral conceptual scheme—needs to be altered, and with it, the way of life that has come to be taken for granted in our society.

In arguing for this conclusion I will not, of course, claim to be morally neutral. I shall, however, try to argue for the moral position that I take, so that anyone who accepts certain assumptions, to be made explicit, will, I hope, accept my conclusion.

I begin with the assumption that suffering and death from lack of food, shelter, and medical care are bad. I think most people will agree about this, although one may reach the same view by different routes. I shall not argue for this view. People can hold all sorts of eccentric positions, and perhaps from some of them it would not follow that death by starvation is in itself bad. It is difficult, perhaps impossible, to refute such positions, and so for brevity I will henceforth take this assumption as accepted. Those who disagree need read no further.

My next point is this: if it is in our power to prevent something bad from happening, without thereby sacrificing anything of comparable moral importance, we ought, morally, to do it. By "without sacrificing anything of comparable moral importance" I mean without causing anything else comparably bad to happen, or doing something that is wrong in itself, or failing to promote some moral good, comparable in significance to the bad thing that we can prevent. This principle seems almost as uncontroversial as the last one. It requires us only to prevent what is bad, and not to promote what is good, and it requires this of us only when we can do it without sacrificing anything that is, from the moral point of view, comparably important. I could even, as far as the application of my argument to the Bengal emergency is concerned, qualify the point so as to make it: if it is in our power to prevent something very bad from happening, without thereby sacrificing anything morally significant, we ought, morally, to do it. An application of this principle would be as follows: if I am walking past a shallow pond and see a child drowning in it, I ought to wade in and pull the child out. This will mean getting my clothes muddy, but this is insignificant, while the death of the child would presumably be a very bad thing.

The uncontroversial appearance of the principle just stated is deceptive. If it were acted upon, even in its qualified form, our lives, our society, and our world would be fundamentally changed. For the principle takes, firstly, no account of proximity or distance. It makes no moral difference whether the person I can help is a neighbor's child ten yards from me or a Bengali whose name I shall never know, ten thousand miles away. Secondly, the principle makes no distinction between cases in which I am the only person who could possibly do anything and cases in which I am just one among millions in the same position.

I do not think I need to say much in defense of the refusal to take proximity and distance into account. The fact that a person is physically near to us, so that we have personal contact with him, may make it more likely that we *shall* assist him, but this does not show that we *ought* to help him rather than another who happens to be further away. If we accept any principle of impartiality, universalizability, equality, or whatever, we cannot discriminate against someone merely because he is far away from us (or we are far away from him). Admittedly, it is possible that we are in a better position to judge what needs to be done to help a person near to us than one far away, and perhaps also to provide the assistance we judge to be necessary. If this were the case, it would be a reason for helping those near to us first. This may once have been a justification for being more concerned with the poor in one's town than with famine victims in India. Unfortunately for those who like to keep their moral responsibilities limited, instant communication and swift transportation have changed the situation. From the moral point of view, the development of the world into a "global village" has made an important, though still unrecognized, difference to our moral situation. Expert observers and supervisors, sent out by famine relief organizations or permanently stationed in famine-prone areas, can direct our aid to a refugee in Bengal almost as effectively as we could get it to someone in our own block. There would seem, therefore, to be no possible justification for discriminating on geographical grounds.

There may be a greater need to defend the second implication of my principle—that the fact that there are millions of other people in the same position, in respect to the Bengali refugees, as I am, does not make the situation significantly different from a situation in which I am the only person who can prevent something very bad from occurring. Again, of course, I admit that there is a psychological difference between the cases; one feels less guilty about doing nothing if one can point to others, similarly placed, who have also done nothing. Yet this can make no real difference to our moral obligations.[2] Should I consider that I am less obliged to pull the drowning child out of the pond if on looking around I see other people, no further away than I am, who have also noticed the child but are doing nothing? One has only to ask this question to see the absurdity of the view that numbers lessen obligation. It is a view that is an ideal excuse for inactivity; unfortunately most of the major evils—poverty, overpopulation, pollution—are problems in which everyone is almost equally involved.

The view that numbers do make a difference can be made plausible if stated in this way: if everyone in circumstances like mine gave £5 to the Bengal Relief Fund, there would be enough to provide food, shelter, and medical care for the refugees; there is no reason why I should give more than anyone else in the same circumstances as I am; therefore I have no obligation to give more than £5. Each premise in this argument is true, and the argument looks sound. It may convince us, unless we notice that it is based on a hypothetical premise, although the conclusion is not stated hypothetically. The argument would be sound if the conclusion were: if everyone in circumstances like mine were to give £5, I would have no obligation to give more than £5. If the conclusion were so stated, however, it would be obvious that the argument has no bearing on a situation in which it is not the case that everyone else gives £5. This, of course, is the actual situation. It is more or less certain that not everyone in circumstances like mine will give £5. So there will not be enough to provide the needed food, shelter, and medical care. Therefore by giving more than £5 I will prevent more suffering than I would if I gave just £5.

It might be thought that this argument has an absurd consequence. Since the situation appears to be that very few people are likely to give substantial amounts, it follows that I and everyone else in similar circumstances ought to give as much as possible, that is, at least up to the point at which by giving more one would begin to cause serious suffering for oneself and one's dependents—perhaps even beyond this point to the point of marginal utility, at which by giving more one would cause oneself and one's dependents as much suffering as one would prevent in Bengal. If everyone does this, however, there will be more than can be used for the benefit of the refugees, and some of the sacrifice will have been unnecessary. Thus, if everyone does what he ought to do, the result will not be as good as it would be if everyone did a little less than he ought to do, or if only some do all that they ought to do.

The paradox here arises only if we assume that the actions in question—sending money to the relief funds—are performed more or less simultaneously, and are also unexpected. For if it is to be expected that everyone is going to contribute something, then clearly each is not obliged to give as much as he would have been obliged to had others not been giving too. And if everyone is not acting more or less simultaneously, then those giving later will know how much more is needed, and will have no obligation to give more than is necessary to reach this amount. To say this is not to deny the principle that people in the same circumstances have the same obligations, but to point out that the fact that others have given, or may be expected to give, is a relevant circumstance: those giving after it has become known that many others are giving and those giving before are not in the same circumstances. So the seemingly absurd consequence of the principle I have put forward can occur only if people are in error about the actual circumstances—that is, if they think they

are giving when others are not, but in fact they are giving when others are. The result of everyone doing what he really ought to do cannot be worse than the result of everyone doing less than he ought to do, although the result of everyone doing what he reasonably believes he ought to do could be.

If my argument so far has been sound, neither our distance from a preventable evil nor the number of other people who, in respect to that evil, are in the same situation as we are, lessens our obligation to mitigate or prevent that evil. I shall therefore take as established the principle I asserted earlier. As I have already said, I need to assert it only in its qualified form: if it is in our power to prevent something very bad from happening, without thereby sacrificing anything else morally significant, we ought, morally, to do it.

The outcome of this argument is that our traditional moral categories are upset. The traditional distinction between duty and charity cannot be drawn, or at least, not in the place we normally draw it. Giving money to the Bengal Relief Fund is regarded as an act of charity in our society. The bodies which collect money are known as "charities." These organizations see themselves in this way—if you send them a check, you will be thanked for your "generosity." Because giving money is regarded as an act of charity, it is not thought that there is anything wrong with not giving. The charitable man may be praised, but the man who is not charitable is not condemned. People do not feel in any way ashamed or guilty about spending money on new clothes or a new car instead of giving it to famine relief. (Indeed, the alternative does not occur to them.) This way of looking at the matter cannot be justified. When we buy new clothes not to keep ourselves warm but to look "well-dressed" we are not providing for any important need. We would not be sacrificing anything significant if we were to continue to wear our old clothes, and give the money to famine relief. By doing so, we would be preventing another person from starving. It follows from what I have said earlier that we ought to give money away, rather than spend it on clothes which we do not need to keep us warm. To do so is not charitable, or generous. Nor is it the kind of act which philosophers and theologians have called "supererogatory"—an act which it would be good to do, but not wrong not to do. On the contrary, we ought to give the money away, and it is wrong not to do so.

I am not maintaining that there are no acts which are charitable, or that there are no acts which it would be good to do but not wrong not to do. It may be possible to redraw the distinction between duty and charity in some other place. All I am arguing here is that the present way of drawing the distinction, which makes it an act of charity for a man living at the level of affluence which most people in the "developed nations" enjoy to give money to save someone else from starvation, cannot be supported. It is beyond the scope of my argument to consider whether the distinction should be redrawn or abolished altogether. There would be many other possible ways of drawing the distinction— for instance, one might decide that it is good to make other people as happy as possible, but not wrong not to do so.

Despite the limited nature of the revision in our moral conceptual scheme which I am proposing, the revision would, given the extent of both affluence and famine in the world today, have radical implications. These implications may lead to further objections, distinct from those I have already considered. I shall discuss two of these.

One objection to the position I have taken might be simply that it is too drastic a revision of our moral scheme. People do not ordinarily judge in the way I have suggested they should. Most people reserve their moral condemnation for those who violate some moral norm, such as the norm against taking another person's property. They do not condemn those who indulge in luxury instead of giving to famine relief. But given that I did not set out to present a morally

neutral description of the way people make moral judgments, the way people do in fact judge has nothing to do with the validity of my conclusion. My conclusion follows from the principle which I advanced earlier, and unless that principle is rejected, or the arguments shown to be unsound, I think the conclusion must stand, however strange it appears.

It might, nevertheless, be interesting to consider why our society, and most other societies, do judge differently from the way I have suggested they should. In a well-known article, J.O. Urmson suggests that the imperatives of duty, which tell us what we must do, as distinct from what it would be good to do but not wrong not to do, function so as to prohibit behavior that is intolerable if men are to live together in society.[3] This may explain the origin and continued existence of the present division between acts of duty and acts of charity. Moral attitudes are shaped by the needs of society, and no doubt society needs people who will observe the rules that make social existence tolerable. From the point of view of a particular society, it is essential to prevent violations of norms against killing, stealing, and so on. It is quite inessential, however, to help people outside one's own society.

If this is an explanation of our common distinction between duty and supererogation, however, it is not a justification of it. The moral point of view requires us to look beyond the interests of our own society. Previously, as I have already mentioned, this may hardly have been feasible, but it is quite feasible now. From the moral point of view, the prevention of the starvation of millions of people outside our society must be considered at least as pressing as the upholding of property norms within our society.

It has been argued by some writers, among them Sidgwick and Urmson, that we need to have a basic moral code which is not too far beyond the capacities of the ordinary man, for otherwise there will be a general breakdown of compliance with the moral code. Crudely stated, this argument suggests that if we tell people that they ought to refrain from murder and give everything they do not really need to famine relief, they will do neither, whereas if we tell them that they ought to refrain from murder and that it is good to give to famine relief but not wrong not to do so, they will at least refrain from murder. The issue here is: Where should we draw the line between conduct that is required and conduct that is good although not required, so as to get the best possible result? This would seem to be an empirical question, although a very difficult one. One objection to the Sidgwick–Urmson line of argument is that it takes insufficient account of the effect that moral standards can have on the decisions we make. Given a society in which a wealthy man who gives 5 percent of his income to famine relief is regarded as most generous, it is not surprising that a proposal that we all ought to give away half our incomes will be thought to be absurdly unrealistic. In a society which held that no man should have more than enough while others have less than they need, such a proposal might seem narrow-minded. What it is possible for a man to do and what he is likely to do are both, I think, very greatly influenced by what people around him are doing and expecting him to do. In any case, the possibility that by spreading the idea that we ought to be doing very much more than we are to relieve famine we shall bring about a general breakdown of moral behavior seems remote. If the stakes are an end to widespread starvation, it is worth the risk. Finally, it should be emphasized that these considerations are relevant only to the issue of what we should require from others, and not to what we ourselves ought to do.

The second objection to my attack on the present distinction between duty and charity is one which has from time to time been made against utilitarianism. It follows from some forms of utilitarian theory that we all ought, morally, to be working full time to increase the balance of happiness over misery. The position I have taken here would not lead to this conclusion in all circumstances, for if there were no bad occurrences that we could prevent without sacrificing something of comparable moral importance, my argument would have no application. Given the present conditions in many parts of the world, however, it does follow from my argument that we ought, morally, to be working full time to relieve great suffering of the sort that occurs as a result of famine or other disasters. Of course, mitigating circumstances can be adduced—for instance, that if we wear ourselves out through overwork, we shall be less effective than we would otherwise have been. Nevertheless, when all considerations of this sort have been taken into account, the conclusion remains: we ought to be preventing as much suffering as we can without sacrificing something else of comparable moral importance. This conclusion is one which we may be reluctant to face. I cannot see, though, why it should be regarded as a criticism of the position for which I have argued, rather than a criticism of our ordinary standards of behavior. Since most people are self-interested to some degree, very few of us are likely to do everything that we ought to do. It would, however, hardly be honest to take this as evidence that it is not the case that we ought to do it.

It may still be thought that my conclusions are so wildly out of line with what everyone else thinks and has always thought that there must be something wrong with the argument somewhere. In order to show that my conclusions, while certainly contrary to contemporary Western moral standards, would not have seemed so extraordinary at other times and in other places, I would like to quote a passage from a writer not normally thought of as a way-out radical, Thomas Aquinas.

Now, according to the natural order instituted by divine providence, material goods are provided for the satisfaction of human needs. Therefore the division and appropriation of property, which proceeds from human law, must not hinder the satisfaction of man's necessity from such goods.

Equally, whatever a man has in superabundance is owed, of natural right, to the poor for their sustenance. So Ambrosius says, and it is also to be found in the *Decretum Gratiani:* "The bread which you withhold belongs to the hungry; the clothing you shut away, to the naked; and the money you bury in the earth is the redemption and freedom of the penniless."[4]

I now want to consider a number of points, more practical than philosophical, which are relevant to the application of the moral conclusion we have reached. These points challenge not the idea that we ought to be doing all we can to prevent starvation, but the idea that giving away a great deal of money is the best means to this end.

It is sometimes said that overseas aid should be a government responsibility, and that therefore one ought not to give to privately run charities. Giving privately, it is said, allows the government and the noncontributing members of society to escape their responsibilities.

This argument seems to assume that the more people there are who give to privately organized famine relief funds, the less likely it is that the government will take over full responsibility for such aid. This assumption is unsupported, and does not strike me as at all plausible. The opposite view—that if no one gives voluntarily, a government will assume that its citizens are uninterested in famine relief and would not wish to be forced into giving aid—seems more plausible. In any case, unless there were a definite probability that by refusing to give one would be helping to bring about massive government assistance, people who do refuse to make voluntary contributions are refusing to prevent a certain amount of suffering without being able to point to any tangible beneficial consequence of their refusal. So the onus of showing how their refusal will bring about government action is on those who refuse to give.

I do not, of course, want to dispute the contention that governments of affluent nations should be giving many times the amount of genuine, no-strings-attached aid that they are giving now. I agree, too, that giving privately is not enough, and that we ought to be campaigning actively for entirely new standards for both public and private contributions to famine relief. Indeed, I would sympathize with someone who thought that campaigning was more important than giving oneself, although I doubt whether preaching what one does not practice would be very effective. Unfortunately, for many people the idea that "it's the government's responsibility" is a reason for not giving which does not appear to entail any political action either.

Another, more serious reason for not giving to famine relief funds is that until there is effective population control, relieving famine merely postpones starvation. If we save the Bengal refugees now, others, perhaps the children of these refugees, will face starvation in a few years' time. In support of this, one may cite the now well-known facts about the population explosion and the relatively limited scope for expanded production.

This point, like the previous one, is an argument against relieving suffering that is happening now, because of a belief about what might happen in the future; it is unlike the previous point in that very good evidence can be adduced in support of this belief about the future. I will not go into the evidence here. I accept that the earth cannot support indefinitely a population rising at the present rate. This certainly poses a problem for anyone who thinks it important to prevent famine. Again, however, one could accept the argument without drawing the conclusion that it absolves one from any obligation to do anything to prevent famine. The conclusion that should be drawn is that the best means of preventing famine, in the long run, is population control. It would then follow from the position reached earlier that one ought to be doing all one can to promote population control (unless one held that all forms of population control were wrong in themselves, or would have significantly bad consequences). Since there are organizations working specifically for population control, one would then support them rather than more orthodox methods of preventing famine.

A third point raised by the conclusion reached earlier relates to the question of just how much we all ought to be giving away. One possibility, which has already been mentioned, is that we ought to give until we reach the level of marginal utility—that is, the level at which, by giving more, I would cause as much suffering to myself or my dependents as I would relieve by my gift. This would mean, of course, that one would reduce oneself to very near the material circumstances of a Bengali refugee. It will be recalled that earlier I put forward both a strong and a moderate version of the principle of preventing bad occurrences. The strong version, which required us to prevent bad things from happening unless in doing so we would be sacrificing something of comparable moral significance, does seem to require reducing ourselves to the level of marginal utility. I should also say that the strong version seems to me to be the correct one. I proposed the more moderate version—that we should prevent bad occurrences unless, to do so, we had to sacrifice something morally significant—only in order to show that even on this surely undeniable principle a great change in our way of life is required. On the more moderate principle, it may not follow that we ought to reduce ourselves to the level of marginal utility, for one might hold that to reduce oneself and one's family to this level is to cause something significantly bad to happen. Whether this is so I shall not discuss, since, as I have said, I can see no good reason for holding the moderate version of the principle rather than the strong version. Even if we accepted the principle only in its moderate form, however, it should be clear that we would have to give away enough to ensure that the consumer society, dependent as it is on people

spending on trivia rather than giving to famine relief, would slow down and perhaps disappear entirely. There are several reasons why this would be desirable in itself. The value and necessity of economic growth are now being questioned not only by conservationists, but by economists as well.[5] There is no doubt, too, that the consumer society has had a distorting effect on the goals and purposes of its members. Yet looking at the matter purely from the point of view of overseas aid, there must be a limit to the extent to which we should deliberately slow down our economy; for it might be the case that if we gave away, say, 40 percent of our Gross National Product, we would slow down the economy so much that in absolute terms we would be giving less than if we gave 25 percent of the much larger GNP that we would have if we limited our contribution to this smaller percentage.

I mention this only as an indication of the sort of factor that one would have to take into account in working out an ideal. Since Western societies generally consider one percent of the GNP an acceptable level for overseas aid, the matter is entirely academic. Nor does it affect the question of how much an individual should give in a society in which very few are giving substantial amounts.

It is sometimes said, though less often now than it used to be, that philosophers have no special role to play in public affairs, since most public issues depend primarily on an assessment of facts. On questions of fact, it is said, philosophers as such have no special expertise, and so it has been possible to engage in philosophy without committing oneself to any position on major public issues. No doubt there are some issues of social policy and foreign policy about which it can truly be said that a really expert assessment of the facts is required before taking sides or acting, but the issue of famine is surely not one of these. The facts about the existence of suffering are beyond dispute. Nor, I think, is it disputed that we can do something about it, either through orthodox methods of famine relief or through population control or both. This is therefore an issue on which philosophers are competent to take a position. The issue is one which faces everyone who has more money than he needs to support himself and his dependents, or who is in a position to take some sort of political action. These categories must include practically every teacher and student of philosophy in the universities of the Western world. If philosophy is to deal with matters that are relevant to both teachers and students, this is an issue that philosophers should discuss.

Discussion, though, is not enough. What is the point of relating philosophy to public (and personal) affairs if we do not take our conclusions seriously? In this instance, taking our conclusion seriously means acting upon it. The philosopher will not find it any easier than anyone else to alter his attitudes and way of life to the extent that, if I am right, is involved in doing everything that we ought to be doing. At the very least, though, one can make a start. The philosopher who does so will have to sacrifice some of the benefits of the consumer society, but he can find compensation in the satisfaction of a way of life in which theory and practice, if not yet in harmony, are at least coming together.

Notes

1. There was also a third possibility: that India would go to war to enable the refugees to return to their lands. Since I wrote this paper, India has taken this way out. The situation is no longer that described above, but this does not affect my argument, as the next paragraph indicates.

2. In view of the special sense philosophers often give to the term, I should say that I use "obligation" simply as the abstract noun derived from "ought," so that "I have an obligation to" means no more, and no less, than "I ought to." This usage is in accordance with the definition of "ought" given by the *Shorter Oxford English Dictionary:* "the general verb to express duty or obligation." I do not think any issue of substance hangs on the way the term is used; sentences in which I use "obligation" could all be rewritten, although somewhat clumsily, as sentences in which a clause containing "ought" replaces the term "obligation."

3. J. O. Urmson, "Saints and Heroes," in *Essays in Moral Philosophy,* ed. Abraham I. Melden (Seattle: University of Washington Press, 1958), p. 214. For a related but significantly different view see also Henry Sidgwick, *The Methods of Ethics,* 7th edn. (London: Dover Press, 1907), pp. 220–21, 492–93.

4. *Summa Theologica,* II–II, Question 66, Article 7, in *Aquinas, Selected Political Writings,* ed. A. P. d'Entreves, trans. J. G. Dawson (Oxford: Basil Blackwell, 1948), p. 171.

5. See, for instance, John Kenneth Galbraith, *The New Industrial State* (Boston: Houghton Mifflin, 1967); and E. J. Mishan, *The Costs of Economic Growth* (New York: Praeger, 1967).

Study Questions

1. Examine Singer's strong principle: "If it is in our power to prevent something bad from happening, without thereby sacrificing anything of comparable moral importance, we ought, morally, to do it." Do you agree with it? Explain.
2. What is Singer's weak principle? How does it differ from the strong principle? Do you agree with Singer about our obligations to sacrifice in order to help those in distant lands? What would happen if we took Singer's principles seriously?

CHAPTER 66

Reason and Morality in a World of Limited Food

RICHARD WATSON

Richard Watson is a professor of philosophy at Washington University in St. Louis and the coauthor with Patty Jo Watson, of *Man and Nature, an Anthropological Essay in Human Ecology*.

Watson argues from a deontological perspective that in a world of scarcity the principle of equity demands that we share our food equally even if it leads to universal malnourishment or the extinction of the human race.

A FEW YEARS AGO, President Johnson said:

There are 200 million of us and 3 billion of them and they want what we've got, but we're not going to give it to them.

In this essay I examine the conflict between reasonable and moral behavior in a world of limited food. It appears to be unreasonable—and conceivably immoral—to share all food equally when this would result in everyone's being malnourished. Arguments for the morality of unequal distribution are presented from the standpoint of the individual, the nation, and the human species. These arguments fail because, although it is unreasonable to share limited food when sharing threatens survival, the moral principle of equity ranks sharing above survival. I accept the principle of equity, and conclude by challenging the ideological basis that makes sharing unreasonable.

The contrast of the moral with the reasonable depends on distinguishing people from things. Moral considerations pertain to behavior of individuals that affects other people by acting on them directly or by acting on things in which they have an interest. The moral context is broad, for people have interests in almost everything, and almost any behavior may affect someone.

If reasonable and moral behavior were coextensive, then there would be no morality. Thus, there is no contrast at the extremes that bound the moral milieu, reason and morality being the same at one pole, and morality not existing at the other. These extremes meet in evolutionary naturalism: If it is moral to treat people as animals surviving, then reason augmenting instinct is the best criterion for behavior, and a separate discipline of morality is extraneous. Only between the extremes can reason and morality conflict.

Between the extremes, some moralists use 'rational' to indicate conclusions that tend toward moral behavior, and 'practical' for conclusions that excusably do not. The use of these terms often constitutes special pleading, either to gain sympathy for a position that is not strictly reasonable but is "rational" (because it is "right"), or that is not strictly moral but is "practical" (because it "should" be done). These hedges hide the sharp distinction between

Reprinted from World Hunger and Moral Obligation, *edited by William Aiken and Hugh LaFollette (Englewood Cliffs, N.J.: Prentice Hall, 1977).*

people and things in the context of reason and morality. The rational and the practical are obviously reasonable in a way that they are not obviously either moral or immoral. Reasonable behavior is either moral, immoral, or amoral. When reason and morality conflict, there can be confusion, but no compromise.

Attacks on morality by reason disguised in practical dress are so common as to go almost without notice. The practical ousts morality as a determinant of behavior, particularly in industrialized nations. Many argue that the practical imperatives of survival preclude moral behavior even by those who want to be moral. If only it were practical to be moral, then all would gladly be so.

It is difficult to be moral in a world of limited food because the supreme moral principle is that of equity. The principle of equity is based on the belief that all human beings are moral equals with equal rights to the necessities of life. Differential treatment of human beings thus should be based only on their freely chosen actions and not on accidents of their birth and environment. Specific to this discussion, everyone has a right to an equal share of available food.

However, we find ourselves in a world about which many food and population experts assert the following:

1. One-third of the world's people (the West) consume two-thirds of the world's resources.

2. Two-thirds of the world's people (the Third World) are malnourished.

3. Equal distribution of the world's resources would result in everyone's being malnourished.

There is ample evidence that these statements are true, but for this discussion it is enough that many people in the West—particularly those who occupy positions of responsibility and power—understand and accept them.

These moral and factual beliefs drive one to this practical conclusion: Although morally we should share all food equally, and we in the West eat more than we need, equal sharing would be futile (unreasonable), for then no one would be well nourished. Thus, any food sharing is necessarily symbolic, for no practical action would alleviate the plight of the malnourished.

For example, practical action—moral as far as it goes—might be to reduce food consumption until every Westerner is just well-nourished. But if the surplus were distributed equally to the other two-thirds of the world's people, they would still be malnourished. Thus, an easy excuse for not sharing at all is that it would neither solve the nourishment problem nor change the moral situation. Two-thirds would still be malnourished, and one-third would still be consuming more than equal shares of the world's food, to which everyone has equal rights.

Another argument for unequal distribution is as follows: All people are moral equals. Because everyone has a right to be well-nourished, it would be immoral to take so much food from someone who has enough as to leave him without enough. Anyone who takes the food would be acting immorally, even if the taker is starving. This argument can go two ways. One could simply say that it would be immoral to deprive oneself of what one has. But if one wanted to discredit morality itself, one could claim that morality in this instance is self-contradictory. For if I behave morally by distributing food equally, I behave immorally by depriving someone (myself) of enough food to remain well-nourished. And noticing that if all food were shared equally, everyone would be malnourished instead of just some, one might argue that it cannot be moral to deprive one person of his right to enough food so that two people have less than enough. Proper moral action must be to maintain the inequity, so at least one person can enjoy his rights.

Nevertheless, according to the highest principles of traditional Western morality, available food should be distributed equally even if everyone then will be malnourished. This is belabored by everyone who compares the earth to a lifeboat, a desert island, or a spaceship. In these situations, the strong are expected to take even a smaller share than the weak. There is no need for us to go overboard, however. We shall soon be as weak as anyone else if we just do our moral duty and distribute the food equally.

Given this, the well-nourished minority might try to buttress its position morally by attempting to solve the nourishment problem for everyone, either by producing enough food for everyone, or by humanely reducing the world's population to a size at which equal distribution of food would nourish everyone adequately. The difficulty with this is that national survival for the food-favored industrial nations requires maintenance of political and economic systems that depend on unequal distribution of limited goods.[1] In the present world context, it would be unreasonable (disastrous) for an industrialized nation to attempt to provide food for everybody. Who would pay for it? And after all, well-nourished citizens are obviously important to the survival of the nation. As for humanely reducing the world's population, there are no practical means for doing it. Thus, the practical expediencies of national survival preclude actions that might justify temporary unequal distribution with the claim that it is essential for solving the nourishment problem. Equal distribution is impossible without total (impractical) economic and political revolution.

These arguments are morally spurious. That food sufficient for well-nourished survival is the equal right of every human individual or nation is a specification of the higher principle that everyone has equal right to the necessities of life. The moral stress of the principle of equity is primarily on equal sharing, and only secondarily on what is being shared. The higher moral principle is of human *equity per se*. Consequently, the moral action is to distribute all food equally, *whatever the consequences*. This is the hard line apparently drawn by such moralists as Immanuel Kant and Noam Chomsky—but then, morality is hard. The conclusion may be unreasonable

(impractical and irrational in conventional terms), but it is obviously moral. Nor should anyone purport surprise; it has always been understood that the claims of morality—if taken seriously—supersede those of conflicting reason.

One may even have to sacrifice one's life or one's nation to be moral in situations where practical behavior would preserve it. For example, if a prisoner of war undergoing torture is to be a (perhaps dead) patriot even when reason tells him that collaboration will hurt no one, he remains silent. Similarly, if one is to be moral, one distributes available food in equal shares (even if everyone then dies). That an action is necessary to save one's life is no excuse for behaving unpatriotically or immorally if one wishes to be a patriot or moral. No principle of morality absolves one of behaving immorally simply to save one's life or nation. There is a strict analogy here between adhering to moral principles for the sake of being moral, and adhering to Christian principles for the sake of being Christian. The moral world contains pits and lions, but one looks always to the highest light. The ultimate test always harks to the highest principle—recant or die—and it is pathetic to profess morality if one quits when the going gets rough.

I have put aside many questions of detail—such as the mechanical problems of distributing food—because detail does not alter the stark conclusion. If every human life is equal in value, then the equal distribution of the necessities of life is an extremely high, if not the highest, moral duty. It is at least high enough to override the excuse that by doing it one would lose one's own life. But many people cannot accept the view that one must distribute equally even if the nation collapses or all people die.

If everyone dies, then there will be no realm of morality. Practically speaking, sheer survival comes first. One can adhere to the principle of equity only if one exists. So it is rational to suppose that the principle of survival is morally higher than the principle of equity. And though one might not be able to argue for unequal distribution of food to save a nation—for nations can come and go—one might well argue that unequal distribution is necessary for the survival of the human species. That is, some large group—say one-third of present world population—should be at least well-nourished for human survival.

However, from an individual standpoint, the human species—like the nation—is of no moral relevance. From a naturalistic standpoint, survival comes first; from a moralistic standpoint—as indicated above—survival may have to be sacrificed. In the milieu of morality, it is immaterial whether or not the human species survives as a result of individual moral behavior.

A possible way to resolve this conflict between reason and morality is to challenge the view that morality pertains only to the behavior of individual human beings. One way to do this is to break down the distinction between people and things. It would have to be established that such abstract things as "the people," "the nation," and "the human species" in themselves have moral status. Then they would have a right to survival just as human beings have a right to life: We should be concerned about the survival of these things not merely because human beings have an interest in them, but because it would be immoral *per se* to destroy them.

In the West, corporation law provides the theoretical basis for treating things as people.[2] Corporate entities such as the State, the Church, and trading companies have long enjoyed special status in Western society. The rights of corporate entities are precisely defined by a legal fiction, the concept of the corporate person. Christopher D. Stone says that corporate persons enjoy as many legal rights as, and sometimes more than, do individual human persons.[3] Thus, while most of us are not tempted to confuse ordinary things like stones and houses with people, almost everyone concurs with a legal system that treats corporate entities as people. The great familiarity and usefulness of this system supports the delusion that corporate entities have rights in common with, and are the moral equals of, individual human beings.

On these grounds, some argue that because of the size, importance, and power of corporate entities, institutional rights have priority over the rights of individuals. Of course, to the extent that society is defined by the economy or the State, people are dependent on and subordinate to these institutions. Practically speaking, institutional needs come first; people's needs are satisfied perhaps coextensively with, but secondarily to, satisfying institutional needs. It is argued that to put individual human needs first would be both illogical and impractical, for people and their needs are defined only in the social context. Institutions come first because they are prerequisite to the very existence of people.

A difficulty with the above argument as a support for any given institution is that it provides merely for the priority of *some* institutions over human individuals, not, say, for the priority of the United States or the West. But it does appear to provide an argument for the priority of the human species.

Given that the human species has rights as a fictional person on the analogy of corporate rights, it would seem to be rational to place the right of survival of the species above that of individuals. Unless the species survives, no individual will survive, and thus an individual's right to life is subordinate to the species' right to survival. If species survival depends on the unequal distribution of food to maintain a healthy breeding stock, then it is morally right for some people to have plenty while others starve. Only if there is enough food to nourish everyone well does it follow that food should be shared equally.

This might be true if corporate entities actually do have moral status and moral rights. But obviously, the legal status of corporate entities as fictional persons does not make them moral equals or superiors of actual human persons. Legislators might profess astonishment that anyone would think that a corporate person is a *person* as people are, let alone a moral person. However, because the legal rights of corporate entities are based on individual rights, and because corporate entities are treated so much like persons, the transition is often made.

Few theorists today would argue that the state or the human species is a personal agent.[4] But all this means is that idealism is dead in theory. Unfortunately, its influence lives, so it is worth giving an argument to show that corporate entities are not real persons.

Corporate entities are not persons as you and I are in the explicit sense that we are self-conscious agents and they are not. Corporate entities are not *agents* at all, let alone moral agents. This is a good reason for not treating corporate entities even as fictional persons. The distinction between people and other things, to generalize, is that people are self-conscious agents, whereas things are not.

The possession of rights essentially depends on an entity's being self-conscious, i.e., on its actually being a person. If it is self-conscious, then it has a right to life. Self-consciousness is a necessary, but not sufficient, condition for an entity's being a moral equal of human beings; moral equality depends on the entity's also being a responsible moral agent as most human beings are. A moral agent must have the capacity to be responsible, i.e., the capacity to choose and to act freely with respect to consequences that the agent does or can recognize and accept as its own choice and doing. Only a being who knows himself as a person, and who can effect choices and accept consequences, is a responsible moral agent.

On these grounds, moral equality rests on the actuality of moral agency based on reciprocal rights and responsibilities. One is responsible to something only if it can be responsible in return. Thus, we have responsibilities to other people, and they have reciprocal rights. We have no responsibilities to things as such, and they have no rights. If we care for things, it is because people have interests in them, not because things in themselves impose responsibilities on us.

That is, as stated early in this essay, morality essentially has to do with relations among people, among persons. It is nonsense to talk of things that cannot be moral agents as having responsibilities; consequently, it is nonsense to talk of whatever is not actually a person as having rights. It is deceptive even to talk of legal rights of a corporate entity. Those rights (and reciprocal responsibilities) actually pertain to individual human beings who have an interest in the corporate entity. The State or the human species have no rights at all, let alone rights superior to those of individuals.

The basic reason given for preserving a nation or the human species is that otherwise the milieu of morality would not exist. This is false so far as specific nations are concerned, but it is true that the existence of individuals depends on the existence of the species. However, although moral behavior is required of each individual, no principle requires that the realm of morality itself be preserved. Thus, we are reduced to the position that people's interest in preserving the human species is based primarily on the interest of each in individual survival. Having shown above that the principle of equity is morally superior to the principle of survival, we can conclude again that food should be shared equally even if this means the extinction of the human race.

Is there no way to produce enough food to nourish everyone well? Besides cutting down to the minimum, people in the West might quit feeding such nonhuman animals as cats and dogs. However, some people (e.g., Peter Singer) argue that mere sentience—the capacity to suffer pain—means that an animal is the moral equal of human beings.[5] I argue that because nonhuman animals are not moral agents, they do not share the rights of self-conscious responsible persons. And considering the profligacy of nature, it is rational to argue that if nonhuman animals have any rights at all, they include not the right to life, but merely the right to fight for life. In fact, if people in the West did not feed grain to cattle, sheep, and hogs, a considerable amount of food would be freed for human consumption. Even then, there might not be enough to nourish everyone well.

Let me remark that Stone and Singer attempt to break down the distinction between people on the one hand, and certain things (corporate entities) and nonhuman animals on the other, out of moral concern. However, there is another, profoundly antihumanitarian movement also attempting to break down the distinction. All over the world, heirs of Gobineau, Goebbels, and Hitler practice genocide and otherwise treat people as nonhuman animals and things in the name of the State. I am afraid that the consequences of treating entities such as corporations and nonhuman animals—that are not moral agents—as persons with rights will not be that we will treat national parks and chickens the way we treat people, but that we will have provided support for those who would treat people the way we now treat nonhuman animals and things.

The benefits of modern society depend in no small part on the institution of corporation law. Even if the majority of these benefits are to the good—of which I am by no means sure—the legal fiction of corporate personhood still elevates corporate needs above the needs of people. In the present context, reverence for corporate entities leads to the spurious argument that the present world imbalance of food and resources is morally justified in the name of the higher rights of sovereign nations, or even of the human species, the survival of which is said to be more important than the right of any individual to life.

This conclusion is morally absurd. This is not, however, the fault of morality. We *should* share all food equally, at least until everyone is well-nourished. Besides food, *all* the necessities of life should be shared, at least until everyone is adequately supplied with a humane minimum. The hard conclusion remains that we should share all

food equally even if this means that everyone starves and the human species becomes extinct. But, of course, the human race would survive even equal sharing, for after enough people died, the remainder could be well-nourished on the food that remained. But this grisly prospect does not show that anything is wrong with the principle of equity. Instead, it shows that something is profoundly wrong with the social institutions in which sharing the necessities of life equally is "impractical" and "irrational."

In another ideological frame, moral behavior might also be practical and rational. As remarked above, equal sharing can be accomplished only through total economic and political revolution. Obviously, this is what is needed.

Notes

1. See Richard Watson, "The Limits of World Order," *Alternatives: A Journal of World Policy* (1975), 487–513.

2. See Christopher D. Stone, *Should Trees Have Standing? Toward Legal Rights for Natural Objects* (Los Altos, Calif.: William Kaufmann, 1974). Stone proposes that to protect such things as national parks, we should give them legal personhood as we do corporations.

3. Ibid., p. 47: "It is more and more the individual human being, with his consciousness, that is the legal fiction." Also: "The legal system does the best it can to maintain the illusion of the reality of the individual human being." (footnote 125) Many public figures have discovered that they have a higher legal status if they incorporate themselves than they do as individual persons.

4. Stone (ibid., p. 47) does say that "institutions . . . have wills, minds, purposes, and inertias that are in very important ways their own, i.e., that can transcend and survive changes in the consciousnesses of the individual humans who supposedly comprise them, and whom they supposedly serve," but I do not think Stone actually believes that corporate entities are persons like you and me.

5. See Peter Singer, *Animal Liberation* (New York: The New York Review of Books/Random House, 1975).

Study Questions

1. What is Watson's principle of equity, and how does it function with regard to world hunger?
2. What is the relationship between morality and rationality? Is it always rational to be moral, according to Watson? What is your view?

CHAPTER 67

Famine Relief and the Ideal Moral Code

JOHN ARTHUR

John Arthur is a professor of philosophy at the State University of New York at Binghamton. He responds to Peter Singer's argument (Chapter 65) that we have a duty to make personal sacrifices to prevent something bad from happening unless that sacrifice will result in comparable evil. Arthur develops the notion of an ideal moral code, which, he argues, would include entitlement as well as desert to our earnings. Arthur also criticizes Watson's equity principle (Chapter 66): Because all human life is equal, we should distribute resources equally even if it results in the death of everyone.

WHAT DO THOSE OF US who are relatively affluent owe, from a moral standpoint, to those who are hungry and sick and who may die without assistance? In a provocative and important article "Famine, Affluence, and Morality" [Chapter 65], Peter Singer defends what he terms an "uncontroversial" moral principle, that we ought to prevent evil whenever we can do so without sacrificing something of comparable moral significance. In doing so, he argues, there is a duty to provide aid whenever others are in greater need and will suffer without our help. Other philosophers [Richard Watson], relying on the principle that all human life is of equal value, have reached similar conclusions. My first concern, then, is to assess such arguments on their own terms, asking whether these arguments do, in fact, establish a duty to give aid. I will argue, in response, that our moral "intuitions" include not only the commitments they emphasize but also entitlements, which suggest that people who deserve or have rights to their earnings may be allowed to keep them.

But the fact that our social moral code includes entitlements is not a complete answer, for it is possible that contemporary moral attitudes are mistaken and our accepted code is defective. So, in the final sections I ask whether a moral reformer might reasonably claim that an "ideal" moral code would reject entitlements, arguing that in fact it would not.

A Duty to Prevent Evil?

What do we intuitively believe, on the basis of our accepted moral views, about helping people in desperate need? Some have argued that the ideal of treating people equally requires that we do much more to aid other than is usually supposed. Richard Watson [see previous reading], for example, emphasizes what he calls the "principle of equity." Since "all human life is of equal value," and since differences in treatment should be "based on freely chosen actions and not accidents of birth or environment," he thinks that we have "equal rights to the necessities of life." To distribute food unequally assumes that some lives are worth more than others, an assumption that, he says, we do not accept. Watson believes, in fact that we put such importance on the "equity principle" that it should not be violated even if unequal distribution is the only way for anybody to survive. (Leaving aside for the moment whether or not he is correct about our code, it seems to me that if it really did require us to commit mass suicide rather than allow inequality in wealth, we would want to abandon it for a more suitable set of moral rules. But more on that later.)

Begin with the premise: Is Watson correct that all life is of equal value? Did Adolph Hitler and Martin Luther King, for example, lead equally valuable lives? Clearly one did far more good, the other far more harm; who would deny that while King fought for people's rights, Hitler violated them on a massive scale? Nor are moral virtues like courage, kindness, and trustworthiness equally distributed among people. So there are many important senses in which people are not, in fact, morally equal: Some lives are more valuable than others, and some people are just, generous, and courageous, whereas others are unjust, cheap, and cowardly.

Yet, all the same, the ideal of equality is often thought to be a cornerstone of morality and justice. But what does it mean to say all people are "equal"? It seems to me that we might have in mind one of two things. First is an idea that Thomas Jefferson expressed in the Declaration of Independence. "All men are created equal" meant, for him, that no man is the moral inferior of another, that, in other words, there are certain rights that all men share equally, including life and liberty. We are entitled in many areas to pursue our own lives without interference from others, just as a person is not the natural slave of another. But, as Jefferson also knew, equality in that sense does not require

equal distribution of the necessities of life, only that we not interfere with one another, allowing instead every person the liberty to pursue his own affairs, so long as he does not violate the rights of others.

Some people, however, have something different in mind when they speak of human equality. To develop this second idea, we turn to Singer's argument in "Famine, Affluence, and Morality." In that essay, Singer argues that two general moral principles are widely accepted and then that those principles imply an obligation to eliminate starvation.

The first of the two principles he thinks we accept is simply that "suffering and death from lack of food, shelter, and medical care are bad." Some may be inclined to think that the mere existence of such an evil in itself places an obligation on others, but that is, of course, the problem that Singer addresses. I take it that he is not begging the question in this obvious way and will *argue* from the existence of evil to the obligation of others to eliminate it. But how, exactly, does he establish this? The second principle, he thinks, shows the connection, but it is here that I wish to raise some questions. This second principle, which I call the "greater moral evil principle," states that:

> If it is in our power to prevent something bad from happening, without thereby sacrificing anything of comparable moral importance, we ought, morally, to do it.

In other words, people are entitled to keep their earnings only if there is no way for them to prevent a greater evil by giving them away. Providing others with food, clothing, and housing is generally of more importance than buying luxuries, so the greater moral evil principle now requires substantial redistribution of wealth.

Certainly few of us live by that principle, although, as Singer emphasizes, that hardly means that we are justified in behaving as we do. We often fail to live up to our own standards. Why does Singer think our shared morality requires that we follow the greater moral evil principle? What argument does he give for it?

He begins with an analogy. Suppose you came across a child drowning in a shallow pond. Certainly we feel it would be wrong for you not to help. Even if saving a child meant you would dirty your clothes, we would emphasize that those clothes are not of comparable significance to the child's life. The greater moral evil principle thus seems a natural way of capturing why we think it would be wrong not to help.

But the argument for the greater moral evil principle is not limited to Singer's claim that it explains our feelings about the drowning child or that it appears "uncontroversial." Moral equality also enters the picture, in the following way. In addition to the Jeffersonian idea that we share certain rights equally, most of us are also attracted to another conception of equality, namely, that like amounts of suffering (or happiness) are of equal significance, no matter who is experiencing them. I cannot reasonably say that, while my pain is no more severe than yours, I am somehow special and that it's therefore more important, objectively speaking, that mine be alleviated. Impartiality requires us to admit the opposite—that no one has a unique status that warrants such special consideration.

But if we fail to give money to famine relief and instead purchase a new car when the old one will do, or buy fancy clothes for a friend when his or her old ones are perfectly good, are we not assuming that the relatively minor enjoyment we or our friends may get is as important as another person's life? And that, it seems, is a form of prejudice; we are acting as if people were not equal in the sense that their interests deserve equal consideration. We are giving special consideration to ourselves or to our group, rather as a racist does. Equal consideration of interests thus leads naturally to the greater moral evil principle.

Entitlements

Equal consideration seems to require that we prevent harm to others if in doing so we do not sacrifice anything of comparable moral importance. But there is also another side to the coin, which Singer ignores. This idea can be expressed rather awkwardly by the notion of entitlements, by which I have in mind the thought that having either a right or justly deserving something can also be important as we think about our obligations to others. A few examples will show what I mean.

One way we can help others is by giving away body parts. While your life may be shortened by the loss of a kidney or less enjoyable if lived with only one eye, those cases are probably not comparable to the loss experienced by a person who will die without a kidney transplant or who is totally blind. Or perhaps, using Judith Thomson's analogy, somebody needs to remain hooked up to you for an extended period of time while awaiting a transplant. It seems clear, however, that our code does not *require* such heroism; you are entitled to your second eye and kidney and to control who uses your body, and that entitlement blocks the inference from the fact that you could prevent harm to the conclusion that you ought to let others have or use your body.

We express these ideas in terms of rights; it's your body, you have a right to it, and that weighs against whatever duty you have to help. To give up your right to your kidney for a stranger is more than is required; it's heroic—unless, of course, you have freely agreed to let the person use your body, which brings us to the next point.

There are two types of rights, negative and positive. Negative rights are rights against interference by others. The right to life, for example, is a right not to be killed by others; the right against assault is a right not to suffer physical harm from others. The right to one's body, the right to property, the right to privacy, and the right to exercise religious freedom are also negative, requiring only that people leave others alone and not interfere. Positive rights, however, are rights, to receive some benefit. By contracting to pay wages, employers acquire the duty to pay the employees who work for them; if the employer backs out of the deal, the employees' positive right to receive a paycheck is violated.

Negative rights also differ from positive rights in that the former are natural or human, in the sense that they depend on what you are, not what you've done. All persons, we assume, have the right to life. If lower animals lack negative moral rights to life or liberty, it is because there is a relevant difference between them and us. But the positive rights you may have are not natural in that sense; they arise because others have promised, agreed, or contracted to do something, just as you may have an obligation to let them use your property or even your body if you have so agreed. The right not to be killed does not depend on anything you or anybody else has done, but the right to be paid a wage makes sense only on the basis of prior agreements.

None of that is to say that rights, whether negative or positive, are beyond controversy. Rights come in a variety of shapes and sizes, and people often disagree about both their shape and their size. And while some rights are part of our generally shared moral code and widely accepted, others are controversial and hotly disputed.

Normally, then, a duty to help a stranger in need is based not on a *right* the person has but, instead, on the general duty all people have to aid those in need (as Singer's drowning child illustrates). A genuine right to be aided requires something more, such as a contract or promise to accept responsibility for the child. Consider, for example a babysitter who agrees to watch out for someone else's children but instead allows a child to drown. We would think that under the circumstances the parent whose child has drowned would in fact be doubly wronged.

First, like everybody else, the person who agreed to watch the child should not have cruelly or thoughtlessly let it drown. But it's also the case that here, unlike Singer's example, we can also say there are rights at stake; promises were made that imposed special obligations on the babysitter. Other bystanders also act wrongly by cruelly ignoring the child, but the babysitter violates rights as well.

I am not suggesting that rights are all we need to take into account. Moral rights are one—but only one—factor to be weighed; we also have other obligations that should be considered. This view, like the greater moral evil principle, is an oversimplification. In reality, our moral code expects us to help people in need *as well as* to respect negative and positive rights. But it also seems clear that, besides being asked by our moral code to respect the rights of others, we are entitled, at least sometimes, to invoke our own rights as justification for what we do. It is not as if we promised to help, or are in any way responsible for the person's situation. Our social moral code teaches that although passing by a drowning child whom we can easily save is wrong, we need not ignore our own rights and give away our savings to help distant strangers solely on the basis of the greater moral evil principle.

A second form of entitlement involves just deserts: the idea that sometimes people deserve to keep what they have acquired. To see its role in our moral code, imagine an industrious farmer who manages through hard work to produce a surplus of food for the winter while a lazy neighbor spends the summer relaxing. Must our industrious farmer give the surplus away because without it that neighbor, who refused to work, will suffer? Under certain circumstances we might say because of the greater moral evil principle the farmer should help, but not necessarily. What this shows is that once again we have more than one factor to weigh. Besides, the evil that could be prevented, we (and the hard-working farmer, too) should also consider the fact that one person earned the food, through hard work.

And while it might be the case that just desert is outweighed by the greater need of a neighbor, being outweighed is in any case not the same as weighing nothing!

Sometimes just desert can be negative in the sense of unwanted, as well as something regarded as a good. The fact that the Nazi war criminals did what they did means they deserve punishment: We have a good reason to send them to jail, on the basis of just desert. Other considerations, for example, the fact that nobody will be deterred or that the criminal is old and harmless, may weigh against punishment, and we may even decide not to pursue the case for that reason. But, again, that does not mean that deserving to be punished is irrelevant, just that we've decided for other reasons to ignore desert in this case. But again I repeat: A principle's being outweighed is not the same as its having no importance.

Our social moral code thus honors both the greater moral evil principle and entitlements. The former emphasizes equality, claiming that from an objective point of view all comparable suffering, whomever its victim, is equally significant. It encourages us to take an impartial look at all the various effects of our actions and is therefore forward-looking. When we consider entitlements, however, our attention is directed to the past. Whether we have rights to money, property, or even our body depends on how we came to possess them. If money was stolen, for example, then the thief has no right to it. Or perhaps a person has promised to trade something; this would again (under normal circumstances) mean loss of entitlement. Like rights, just desert is also backward-looking, emphasizing past effort or past transgressions that now warrant responses such as reward, gratitude, or punishment.

I am suggesting, then, that, expressing both equality and entitlements, our social moral code pulls in different directions. How, then, are we to determine when one principle is more important? Unless we are moral relativists, the mere fact that equality and entitlements are both part of our moral code does not in itself justify a person's reliance on them, any more than the fact that our moral code once condemned racial mixing while condoning sexual discrimination and slavery should convince us that those principles are justified. We all assume (I trust) that the more enlightened moral code—the one we now subscribe to—is better in part just because it condemns discrimination and slavery. Because we know that the rules that define acceptable behavior are continually changing, and sometimes changing for the better, we must allow for the replacement of inferior principles with more reasonable guidelines.

Viewed in that light, the issue posed by Singer's argument is really whether we should reform our current social moral code and reject entitlements, at least insofar as they conflict with the greater moral evil principle. What could justify our practice of evaluating actions by looking backward to rights and just desert instead of only to their consequences? To pursue these questions, we need to look more closely at how we might justify the moral rules and principles that constitute a society's moral code; we will then be able to ask whether, although entitlements are part of our current code, we would improve that code—bring it closer to an ideal code—if they were not included.

The Concept of a Social Moral Code

So I suggest that we first say something more about the nature and purpose of social moral codes in general; then we will turn to entitlements. We can begin with the obvious: A moral code is a system of principles, rules, and other standards that guide people's conduct. As such, it has characteristics in common with other systems of rules and standards, such as the rules of organizations. Social clubs, sports leagues, corporations, bureaucracies, professional associations, even *The* Organization all have standards that govern the behavior of members.

Such rules function in various ways, imposing different sanctions depending on the nature of the organization. Violation of a university's code of conduct leads to one sort of punishment, while different types of sanctions are typically imposed by a social club or by the American Bar Association.

Some standards of conduct are not limited to members of a specific organization but instead apply more broadly, and it is to those that we now turn. Law, for example, is a social practice rather than an organization. So are etiquette and customs. All these codes apply broadly, not just to members of an organization who have chosen to join. It will be most helpful in our thinking about the nature of a moral code to compare it with these other social practices, along a variety of dimensions.

As we noted with organizations, here too the form sanctions take vary among the different types of codes. While in our legal system transgressions are punished by fines, jail, or even execution, informal sanctions of praise, criticism, and ostracism encourage conformity to the standards of morality and etiquette. Besides the type of sanctions, a second difference among these codes is that while violation of a moral principle is always a serious affair, this need not be so for legal rules or the norms of etiquette and custom. Many of us think it unimportant whether a fork is on the left side of a plate or the right, or whether an outmoded and widely ignored Sunday closing law is violated. But violation of a moral principle is not ignored or thought trivial; indeed, the fact that a moral principle has lost its importance is often indicated by its "demotion" to mere custom.

A third contrast, in addition to differences in sanctions and in importance, is that, unlike morality, custom, and etiquette, legal systems include, besides criminal and civil rules, other "constitutional" rules governing how those laws are to be created, modified, and eliminated. Under the U.S. Constitution, for instance, if Congress acts to change the tax laws, then as of the date stated in the statute the rules are changed. Moral rules, etiquette, and customs also change, of course, but they do so without benefit of any agreed procedure identifying who or how the changes occur or when they take effect.

So far, then, we've noted that different codes and standards of behavior can vary widely, along a number of dimensions, Some apply narrowly, only to members of a specific organization, while others extend broadly. And while all codes include rules or other standards to guide conduct, the sanctions that are imposed by different codes differ widely, as do the ways rules for change and the importance assigned to violations of the different codes.

The final point I want to make about rules generally, before looking specifically at morality, is that all standards serve a purpose, although what that purpose is will again vary with the organization or practice in question. Rules that govern games, for example, are often changed, either informally among players or by a governing organization like the National Football League. This is done in order to more effectively achieve the goals of the game, although the goals often vary and are sometimes open to dispute. Sometimes, for example, rules may be changed to improve safety (e.g., car design in auto racing) or even to make the sport more exciting but less safe. Other times rules might be changed to accommodate younger players, such as abolishing the walk in kids' baseball. Similar points can be made about organizations, as, for example, when a corporation changes its standards for how many hours people work or a university changes the deadline for dropping a class.

Like the rules that govern games and organizations, legal and moral rules and principles also change in ways that serve their purposes either better or worse. But here enters one final, important point—because there can be deep dis-agreement about the purposes of such practices, there can also be disagreement about the rules themselves, including when there should be ex-ceptions, what exactly they require, and the cir-cumstances under which they can be ignored. Such a dispute about rules can rest on deeper, sometimes hidden disagreements about the pur-poses of the organization, just as differences be-tween fundamentalists and liberals over religious rules and principles can also uncover disagree-ments about the purposes of religious practices.

Turning to morality, first consider a tradi-tional rule such as the one prohibiting homo-sexual behavior. Assuming people could agree that the rule serves no useful purpose but in-stead only increases the burden of guilt, shame, and social rejection borne by a significant por-tion of society, then it seems that people would have good reason to alter their rules about sexual conduct and no longer condemn homo-sexuality. But people who see morality as serving another purpose, for instance, encouraging be-havior that is compatible with God's will or with "natural" law, might oppose such a change. Or suppose, less controversially, that rules against killing and lying help us to accomplish what we want from a moral code. In that case, we have good reason to include those rules in our "ideal" moral code.

My suggestion, then, is that there is a con-nection between what we ought to do and how well a code serves its purposes. If a rule serves well the goals of a moral code, then we have rea-son to obey it. But if, on the other hand, a rule is useless, or if it frustrates the purposes of mo-rality, we have reason neither to support it, teach it, nor to follow it (assuming, as I said, we agree what the purpose of a social moral code is).

This suggests, then, the following conception of a right action: Any action is right if and only if it conforms with an ideal moral code for the so-ciety in which we are living. We will say more about this shortly, but most basically we must consider what, exactly, an *ideal* moral code is. In order to answer that, we must first ask ourselves the purpose that we hope to accomplish by cre-ating, reaching, and enforcing a moral code for society.

The Ideal Social Moral Code

One possibility, already suggested, is that morality's purpose depends on God—that mo-rality serves to encourage people to act in ac-cord with God's will. But I want to suggest, and very briefly defend, another view, namely, that the ideal moral code is the one that, when recognized and taught by members of society, would have the best consequences. By best consequences, I mean that it would most effec-tively promote the collective well-being of those living under it. (It's worth noting right off, however, that a religious person need not reject this out of hand but instead might reason that the general well-being is also what God would wish for creation.)

In pursuing this idea, it is helpful to return to the comparison between legal and moral stan-dards. Clearly, both morality and law serve to *discourage* some of the same types of behavior—killing, robbing, and beating—while they both also *encourage* other acts, such as repaying debts, keeping important agreements, and pro-viding for one's children. The reason for rules that discourage acts like killing and beating seems clear enough, for imagine the disastrous consequences for human life absent such moral and legal rules. This idea is further substantiated when we think about how children are taught that it is wrong to hit a baby brother or sister. Parents typically explain such rules in terms of their purpose, emphasizing that it hurts and can harm others when we hit them. At root, then, it seems at least plausible to suppose that these rules of morality and law function to keep people from causing unjustified harm to each other. A world in which people were allowed to kill and assault each other without fear of legal or moral sanctions would be far more miserable than a world in which such behavior is discouraged. Concern for general welfare explains how we learn moral standards as children and why we support them as adults.

In addition to justifying rules that prevent harmful behavior, the other rules I mentioned that encourage different types of behavior can also be justified by their social consequences. Our own well-being, as well as that of our friends, family, and, indeed, society as a whole, depends on people's generally keeping promises and fulfilling agreements. Without laws and moral rules to encourage such behavior, the institutions of promising and contracting would likely be unsustainable, and with their passing would be lost all the useful consequences that flow from our ability to bind ourselves and others by promising and contracting.

Moral rules thus promote our own welfare by discouraging acts of violence and creating and by maintaining social conventions like promising and paying debts. They also perform the same service for our family, friends, and, indeed, all of us. A life wholly without legal and moral codes would be in danger of deteriorating into what Thomas Hobbes long ago feared: a state of nature in which life is solitary, poor, nasty, brutish, and short.

Many may find these thoughts fairly uncontroversial, thinking it obvious that moral codes are justified by their good consequences. But what more might be said to those who remain skeptical? One suggestion, from David Hume, emphasizes the importance of sentiment and feeling in human actions. It is, said Hume, only on the basis of feelings and sentiment that people can be moved to act at all, so that the key to understanding morality is that human nature is marked not only by self-interest but also by a sentimental attachment to the well-being of others. We take pleasure, Hume thinks, in the

thought that others are happy, as well as in our own happiness. This can be seen, he reasoned, from the fact that we

> frequently bestow praise on virtuous actions, performed in very distant ages and remote countries; where the utmost subtlety of imagination would not discover any appearance of self-interest, or find any connexion with our present happiness and security with events so widely separated from us.

Hume might have added that there is evidence that sympathy and concern for others' well-being are a natural part of our biological heritage, as well as an outgrowth of common sense. Some biologists, for example, think that many animals, particularly higher ones, take an interest in the welfare of other members of their species because such altruistic attitudes enable the species to survive better. Others emphasize the inevitability of acquiring such sentiments through learning, arguing that feelings of benevolence originate naturally, via classical conditioning. We first develop negative associations with our own pain behavior (we associate screaming and writhing with our own pain), and this negative attitude is then generalized to the pain behavior of anybody.

But whatever the reason behind sympathy, Hume concludes from this that we must renounce any moral theory

> which accounts for every moral sentiment by the principle of self-love. We must adopt a more public affection, and allow, that the interests of society are not, even on their own account, indifferent to us.

Moral approval and condemnation, Hume is claiming, rest finally on sentiments rather than reason, but such sentiments extend beyond our own happiness to encompass the whole of humanity. Given such universal, sympathetic feelings for the well-being of others, he concludes, it is natural to understand a social moral code in terms of its utility or consequences on everybody's well-being.

But suppose that not everybody shares these sympathetic attitudes toward others. It might seem that such a person would therefore have reason to reject the idea that the ideal moral code is the one with the best overall consequences. Instead, such an egoist might say that the truly best code would be the one that maximizes *his own* welfare, even if others are not benefited at all. Caring for nobody else, he might regard as "ideal" a code that gives him absolute power over the lives and property of others, for example. How, then, should such a person be responded to by somebody who, like me, thinks that the ideal code is the one that would have the best consequences for everybody and not just one individual?

One possibility, of course, is to acknowledge that such a person has a mistaken view of morality precisely because the ideal code would benefit not only one person but to admit that such a person cannot be reasoned with, let alone refuted. But while that may seem right, it would of course leave the egoist unpersuaded and without any reason to behave in accord with the ideal moral code. Yet why should we care if we cannot convince such a person that the ideal code would be one that has the best consequences for everybody? Some people may remain unmoved by moral considerations, but maybe that should not concern those of us who are.

But, that said, it's instructive that we still do, in fact, have available a response to our imaginary egoist, one based on the social nature of a social moral code. Suppose we were to ask the rational egoist concerned only to promote his own well-being to consider whether it really would be rational for him to publicly support the moral code benefiting only himself. How, we might ask, would he expect others to react to the idea that society should recognize and teach a code that serves only his interest? The answer seems clear: Any egoists who spent time supporting such a code, defending it in public, and trying to have it adopted by others would not in fact be acting rationally. For that reason, even the egoist who cares only about his own well-being would be driven toward a conception of the ideal moral code (understood, for him, in the egoistic way as the one it is in his self-interest to recognize and encourage others to adopt) that is not only acceptable from the perspective of a single person but that could be supported by others as well. But that means, in turn, that even our egoist's conception of the ideal moral code begins to look more like the one that other people with more normal, sympathetic feelings would find ideal, namely, the one that would have the best consequences for everybody. A social moral code must be one that can function in the world, which means it must be able to win general public support.

This line of thought, emphasizing the practical side of the ideal moral code, brings us finally to the issue with which we began: Would an ideal moral code (which I will now assume is the one that would have the best consequences generally, not just for one person) include principles that respect rights and just deserts, or would it, as Singer suggested, reject them completely in favor of the greater moral evil principle? The answer, I will argue, rests on the fact that an ideal moral code must not only be one that can hope to win public support but must be practical and workable in other important ways as well. The ideal code is one that works for people as they are, or at least can be encouraged to become.

Are Rights Part of the Ideal Code?

What we want to know is whether rights (and also just desert) would be included in the ideal code, understood as the one that, in the real world, would have the best consequences. Initially, it may seem they would not, since it appears that the best consequences could be realized by substituting the greater moral evil principle for entitlements, requiring people to prevent something bad whenever the cost to them is less significant than the benefit to another. This is true because, unlike entitlements, the greater moral evil principle more clearly and directly expresses the consequentialism I have been defending.

But would such a single moral principle, recognized by society as its ideal, really have the best consequences? I suggest that the ideal code would not in fact ignore rights, for two reasons, each based on the fact that the ideal moral code must rest on realistic, accurate assumptions about human beings and our life in this world.

The first takes us back to the discussion of self-love and altruism. Although I did suggest, following Hume, that we ought not ignore people's altruistic side, it is also important that a social moral code not assume people are more altruistic than they are. Rules that would work only for angels are not the ideal ones for a society of human beings. While we do care about others' well-being, especially those we love, we also care very deeply about ourselves. It would therefore be quite difficult to get people to accept a code that requires that they give away their savings or duplicate organs to a stranger simply because doing so would avoid even more evil, as would be required by the greater moral evil rule if not balanced by entitlements. Many people simply wouldn't do as that rule required; they care too deeply about their own lives and welfare, as well as the welfare of loved ones.

Indeed, were the moral code to attempt to require such saintliness despite these problems, three results would likely follow. First, because many would not live up to the rules, despite having been taught they should, feelings of guilt would increase. Second, such a code would encourage conflict between those who met what they thought of as their moral obligations and those who did not. Such a situation is in contrast, of course, to one in which people who give

generously and selflessly are thought of as heroes who have gone beyond what is morally required; in that event, unlike instances in which people don't live up to society's demands of them, the normal response is to praise them for exceeding the moral minimum. And, third, a realistic code that doesn't demand more than people can be expected to do might actually result in more giving than a code that ignores rights in favor of the greater moral evil rule. Think about how parents try to influence how their children spend their money. Perhaps the children will buy less candy if they are allowed to do so occasionally but are also praised for spending on other things than they would if the purchase of candy were prohibited. We cannot assume that making what is now a charitable act into a requirement will always encourage such behavior. In summary, impractical rules would not only create guilt and social conflict, neither of which is compatible with the ideal code, but would also tend to encourage the opposite of the desired result. By giving people the right to keep their property yet praising those who do not exercise the right but help others instead, we have struck a good balance.

My second point is that an ideal moral code must not assume that people are more objective, informed, and unbiased than they are. People often tend, we know, to rationalize when their interests are at stake—a fact that has many implications for the sorts of principles we would include in an ideal, welfare maximizing code. For example, we might at first be tempted to discourage slavish conformity to counterproductive rules, teaching people to break promises whenever doing so would have the best consequences. But again practicality enters: An ideal code would not be blind to people's tendency to give special weight to their own welfare or to their inability always to be objective in tracing the effects of different actions even when they want to be. So, while an ideal code would not teach that promises must never be broken no matter what the consequences, we also would not want to encourage breaking promises whenever people convince themselves that doing so would produce less evil.

Similar considerations apply to property. Imagine a situation in which a person contemplates preventing an evil to herself or himself by taking something from a large store where it won't be missed. Such theft could easily be rationalized by the greater moral evil principle on grounds that stealing prevents something bad from happening (to the person who decides to steal) without sacrificing anything of comparable moral significance (the store won't miss the goods). So, although a particular act of theft may sometimes be welfare maximizing, it does not follow that a *principle* like Singer's is part of an ideal code. To recognize and teach that theft is right whenever the robber is preventing greater evil, even to himself, would work only if people were far more objective, less liable to self-deception, and more knowledgeable about the long-term consequences than they are. So here again, including rights that block such conclusions in our moral code serves a useful role, discouraging the tendency to rationalize our behavior by underestimating the harm we may cause to others or exaggerating the benefits that may accrue to ourselves.

Is Just Desert Part of the Ideal Moral Code?

Similar practical considerations argue for including desert as well as rights in the ideal moral code. The case of the farmers, recall, was meant to illustrate that our current social moral code encourages the attitude that people who work hard deserve to be rewarded, just as people who behave badly deserve to be punished. Most of us feel that while it would be nice of the hard worker to help out a lazy neighbor, the worker also has reason—based on his past effort—to refuse. But, as I have stressed, it's still an open question whether an ideal code would allow such "selfishness."

But as with rights, here again we must be careful that our conception of an ideal code is realistic and practical and does not assume people are more altruistic, informed, or objective than they are. To see why this is relevant to the principle of just desert, we should first notice that for many people, at least, working and earning a living is not their favorite activity. People would often prefer to spend time doing something else, but they know they must work if they and their family hope to have a decent life. Indeed, if humans generally are to live well, then goods and services must be produced and made available for wide use, which means that (I argue) incentives to work are an important factor in motivating people.

One such incentive, of course, is income. A moral code can encourage hard work by allowing people to keep a large part of what they earn, by respecting both rights and the principle of just desert. "I worked hard for it, so I can keep it" is a familiar thought that expresses this attitude.

But suppose we eliminated the notion of deserving what we work for from our code and asked people to follow the greater moral evil rule instead. What might happen? There are three possibilities. First, they might continue to produce as before, only this time motivated by the desire, derived from their social moral code, to prevent whatever evil they could, as long as the cost to them of doing so was not greater evil. But this seems to me quite unrealistic: While people are not egoists, neither are they that saintly and altruistic.

Given that, one of two other outcomes could be expected. Perhaps people would stop working as hard, feeling that it is no longer worth the effort to help strangers rather than themselves or their family since they are morally required to give away all but what they can use without imposing a greater evil on anybody else. Suppose, to make it vivid, that the tax system enforces the greater moral evil rule, taking away all income that could be used to prevent a greater evil's befalling somebody else. The result would be less work done, less total production of useful commodities, and therefore a general reduction in people's well-being. The other possibility is that people would simply fail to live up to the standards of society's moral code (having replaced desert with the greater moral evil rule), leading to widespread feelings of guilt and resentment by those (few?) who did behave as the code commands. In either case, I am suggesting, replacing the principle of just desert with the greater moral evil principle would actually worsen the situation. Like rights, the principle of just desert is also part of an ideal code.

Conclusion

The first sections of this paper attempted to show that our moral code is a bit self-contradictory. It seems to pull us in opposite directions, sometimes toward helping people who are in need and other times toward the view that rights and desert justify keeping things we have even if greater evil could be avoided were we to give away our extra eye or our savings account. This apparent inconsistency led us to a further question: Is the emphasis on rights and desert really defensible, or should we try to resolve the tension in our own code by rejecting entitlements in favor of the greater moral evil rule? In the last sections I have considered this question, focusing on the idea that we should understand the ideal moral code as the one that, if acknowledged and taught, would have the overall best consequences. Having suggested why it might seem sensible to conceive the ideal code this way, as the one that would produce the best consequences, I concluded by showing that an ideal code would not reject entitlements in favor of the greater moral evil rule. Concern that our moral code encourage effort and not fail because it unrealistically assumes people are more altruis-

tic, informed, or objective than they are means that our rules giving people rights to their possessions and encouraging distribution according to desert are part of an ideal moral code. The ideal moral code would therefore not teach people to try to seek the best consequences in each individual case, insisting they give entitlements no weight whatsoever. But neither have I argued, nor do I believe, that an ideal moral code would allow people to overlook those in desperate need by making entitlements absolute, any more than it would ignore entitlements in favor of the greater moral evil rule discussed earlier.

But where would it draw the line? It's hard to know, of course, but the following seems to me to be a sensible stab at an answer. Concerns of the sort I have outlined argue strongly against expecting too much of people's selflessness or ability to make objective and informed decisions. A more modest proposal would require people to help strangers when there is no substantial cost to themselves, that is, when what they are sacrificing would not mean *significant* reduction in their own or their family's level of happiness. Since most people's savings accounts and nearly everybody's second kidney are not insignificant, entitlements would in those cases outweigh another's need. But if what is at stake is truly trivial, as dirtying one's clothes would normally be, then an ideal moral code would not allow rights to override the greater evil that can be prevented.

Another point is that, again mindful of the need to be realistic in what it expects of people, an ideal code might also distinguish between cases in which the evil is directly present to a person (as in the drowning child) and cases involving distant people. The reason, of course, is again practical: People are more likely to help people with whom they have direct contact and when they can see immediately the evil they will prevent than they are to help strangers. So while such a distinction may seem morally arbitrary, viewed from the perspective of an ideal moral code it seems to make good sense.

Despite our code's unclear and sometimes self-contradictory posture, it seems to me that these conclusions are not that different from our current moral attitudes; an ideal moral code thus might not be a great deal different from our own. We tend to fault selfish people who give little or nothing to charity and expect those with more to give more. Yet we do not ask people to make large sacrifices of their own or their family's well-being in order to aid distant strangers. Singer's arguments do remind us, however, that entitlements are not absolute and that we all have some duty to help. But the greater moral evil rule expresses only part of the story and is not needed to make that point.

Study Questions

1. How does Arthur respond to Watson's principle of equity that we must distribute resources equally in meeting basic needs even if it leads to the demise of all human life? Evaluate his argument.
2. Why does Arthur discuss the ideal moral code? What does it consist of? Do you agree with his assessment?
3. Why are entitlements important? How do they work in the moral code? What is their purpose?
4. How does the idea of desert fit into Arthur's response to Singer?
5. Compare Arthur's argument with Singer's. Evaluate the strength of their arguments. Then answer the question, what exactly is our obligation to help those who are starving in distant lands?

For Further Reading

Aiken, William, and Hugh LaFollette, eds., *World Hunger and Moral Obligation*. Englewood Cliffs, N.J.: Prentice Hall, 1977. The best collection of readings available, containing four of the readings in this book plus others of great importance.

Ehrlich, Paul. *The Population Bomb*. New York: Ballantine Books, 1971. An important work, warning of the dangers of the population explosion.

Lappé, Francis, and Joseph Collins. *Food First: Beyond the Myth of Scarcity*. New York: Ballantine Books, 1978. An attack on neo-Malthusians like Hardin in which the authors argue that we have abundant resources to solve the world's hunger problems.

O'Neill, Onora. *Faces of Hunger*. London: Allen & Unwin, 1986. A penetrating Kantian discussion of the principles and problems surrounding world hunger.

Simon, Arthur. *Bread for the World*. New York: Paulist Press, 1975. A poignant discussion of the problem of world hunger from a Christian perspective, with some thoughtful solutions.